PROCESSION

Books by John Gunther

PROCESSION

THE LOST CITY

A FRAGMENT OF AUTOBIOGRAPHY:
The Fun of Writing the Inside Books

INSIDE EUROPE TODAY

TAKEN AT THE FLOOD

INSIDE RUSSIA TODAY

INSIDE AFRICA

INSIDE U.S.A.

INSIDE LATIN AMERICA

INSIDE ASIA

INSIDE EUROPE

THE RIDDLE OF MACARTHUR

EISENHOWER

ROOSEVELT IN RETROSPECT

BEHIND THE CURTAIN

DEATH BE NOT PROUD

D DAY

THE TROUBLED MIDNIGHT

DAYS TO REMEMBER (*with Bernard Quint*)

MEET NORTH AFRICA (*with Sam and Beryl Epstein*)

MEET SOUTH AFRICA (*with Sam and Beryl Epstein*)

MEET THE CONGO

MEET SOVIET RUSSIA

ALEXANDER THE GREAT

JULIUS CAESAR

THE GOLDEN FLEECE

JOHN GUNTHER

PROCESSION

HARPER & ROW, PUBLISHERS

NEW YORK, EVANSTON, AND LONDON

FIRST EDITION

LIBRARY OF CONGRESS CATALOG CARD NUMBER: 65-16257

D-P

Dedicated with love

to

Nicholas Langdon Gunther

Contents

Author's Note   xiii

Part One: THREE DICTATORS

1. Hitler   3
2. Mussolini   20
3. Stalin   37

Part Two: THREE PORTRAITS IN MINIATURE

4. Captain Eden, Lord Privy Seal   57
5. The Bucharest Du Barry   63
6. Chancellor Dollfuss: Flyweight Champion of Europe   68

Part Three: THE TURBULENT THIRTIES

7. Trotsky at Elba   77
8. Masaryk the Magnificent   88
9. The Turkish Colossus   92
10. De Valera   98
11. Lavaluation   108
12. The Socialist Exquisite of the Ile St. Louis   115
13. The Incomparable Winston   122

Part Four: ACROSS ASIA

14. The Emperor of Japan   139
15. Generalissimo Chiang Kai-shek   155
16. The Mahatma   166
17. Have You Seen Jawaharlal?   187
18. Kings of the Middle East   204
19. First Citizen of the Jews   211

Part Five: SOUTH OF THE BORDER

20. Cárdenas Days and Years   221

Part Six: WAR IN SICILY

21. Montgomery and Alexander   229

Part Seven: A GALLERY OF AMERICANS

22. FDR: The Historical Perspective   239
23. Coast to Coast   255
    a. The Man from Missouri   256
    b. Earl Warren of California   261
    c. A Freshman from the Mountain Slopes   263
    d. Saltonstall of Massachusetts   267
24. The Not-So-Little Flower   272
25. The Case of Mr. Crump   283
26. Caesar of the Pacific   288
27. Ike   308

Part Eight: BEHIND THE CURTAIN

28. Tito of Yugoslavia   327

Part Nine: I HOLD THEE FAST, AFRICA

29. The Northern Tier   345
    a. Lord of the Atlas   345
    b. The Grand Vizier   354
    c. Bey of Tunis   354
    d. His Majesty King Idris I of Libya   357

30. Nasser   361
31. The King of Kings   374
32. Showboy   388
33. Mr. Tubman of Liberia   403
34. A Visit to Dr. Albert Schweitzer   417

Part Ten: INTO THE SIXTIES

35. Macmillan   439
36. The Old Man on the Rhine   453
37. The Person of de Gaulle   465
38. Mr. K.   475
39. Inside England 1964   489

     Index   501

For, the noblest deeds do not always shew men's virtues and vices, but oftentimes a light occasion, a word, or some sport makes men's natural dispositions and manners appear more plain, than the famous battles won, wherein are slain ten thousand men, or the great armies, or cities won by siege or assault.

—Plutarch

Author's Note

This book is a collection of some of the personality pieces I have written in the past thirty years or so. It covers a broad arc from Hitler to the present and deals with public characters all over the world. For a long time I have wanted to pull some of the chapters about people out of their old beds in the *Inside* books and elsewhere, and stand them up together in a single volume. This is it.

My effort has been to play fair with the reader. I have not amended any judgments. If I was wrong I was wrong. These profiles, essays, estimates, character sketches, brief biographies—call them what you will —appear exactly as I wrote them, with the qualification that I have amended a few verbal slips, corrected a handful of typographical errors, transposed or consolidated a few passages, and added a sentence or two here and there for purposes of identification or clarification. Also I have cut a good deal. Except for this the articles appear as they were originally published. There have been no changes in substance at all.

Preceding each chapter the reader will find a brief passage noting clearly when it was written and in some cases giving details of the background of the time. Then too I have added passages at the ends of chapters bringing the story up to date or indulging in a bit of reappraisal or personal explanation and reminiscence. These sections before and after the body of each chapter are printed in italics so that they may be easily differentiated from the basic text.

These chapters are not, incidentally, interviews. Even in the old days I seldom used the question-and-answer form, although I was as eager to meet and talk to political leaders as any of my colleagues. But when I came to deal with my subjects I sought earnestly to avoid the interview technique. I cannot imagine anything more dull than a book of interviews. What interested me was not news, but appraisal. What I sought was to grasp the flavor of a man, his texture, his impact, what he stood for, what he believed in, what made him what he was, and what color he gave to the fabric of his time.

There are some fifty characters in this book, but I could easily have made it much longer. About half of what might crudely be called my total bag is omitted. For reasons of space I have had to leave out almost as many people as I include. Perhaps I may gather some of these together someday in another book.

Again let me say that I have not touched up or tinted any judgments. The arrangement is roughly chronological and, to repeat, the date of the original writing or publication of each chapter is clearly given.

J. G.

New York, 1964

Part One

~~~~~~~~~

THREE DICTATORS

CHAPTER 1

〰〰〰〰

Hitler

This profile, drawn out of the text of the original edition of Inside
Europe *(1936), was written in 1935 and appeared first in* Harper's Magazine *in January, 1936. It created a certain amount of commotion
when it first appeared. Hitler's capacity for evil was not broadly understood. He had written down his program copiously, but few readers took*
Mein Kampf *with the seriousness it deserved. In any case my article
was one of the first extended estimates of the Führer as a man. It
shocked many people, and awakened others to painful realities. In those
days there were any number of persons of consequence in the United
States and Britain who thought that "we could still do business with
Hitler," and a good many others who thought that he was no more than
a bad Austrian joke.*

*The chapter presented here includes only a part of what I put down
about Hitler and Germany in* Inside Europe. *So now for the record I
might add a bare skeleton of details about his career up to the time I
wrote. After serving in the Bavarian army in World War I Hitler founded
the Nazi party in Munich in the early 1920's and sought to seize power
in 1923 by the "Beer Hall Putsch." This failed, and he went to jail for a
brief period. His movement rose fantastically and presently the Nazis
were the leading power in Germany. On January 30, 1933, President
von Hindenburg, in full senility, made Hitler chancellor and a few
months later he contrived to get himself voted into power as dictator of
the Reich.*

*I mention several times in the text that follows the Blood Purge of
June 30, 1934, and there should be a word of explanation about this
for readers who have forgotten it or for those too young to remember.
Hitler had to allay frictions between his own Storm Troopers and the*

*Reichswehr. Trouble was afoot. Hitler stamped it out by the neat ex-
pedient of having some two hundred men hounded down and executed
—including Captain Ernst Roehm, his closest friend, and General Kurt
von Schleicher, his predecessor as chancellor.*

*Writing in 1935, I mentioned that Hitler still wanted to be an artist.
It is not uninteresting in this connection that in 1939 he told Sir Nevile
Henderson, the British ambassador in Berlin, that his only ambition was
to retire to the Berchtesgaden hills and paint. At this very moment he
was putting his armies on the march and World War II followed within
a week. Hitler's sublimation of the artistic instinct certainly took a
sinister and dramatic form.*

~~~~~~

*The union of theorizer, organizer, and leader in one man is the rarest
phenomenon on earth; therein lies greatness.*

—ADOLF HITLER

ADOLF HITLER, irrational, contradictory, complex, is an unpredictable
character; therein lie his power and his menace. To millions of
honest Germans he is sublime, a figure of adoration; he fills them with
love, fear, and nationalist ecstasy. To many other Germans he is meager
and ridiculous—a charlatan, a lucky hysteric, and a lying demagogue.
What are the reasons for this paradox? What are the sources of his extraordinary power?

This paunchy, Charlie-Chaplin-mustached man, given to insomnia
and emotionalism, who is the head of the Nazi party, commander-in-
chief of the German army and navy, Leader of the German nation, creator, President, and chancellor of the Third Reich, was born in Austria
in 1889. He was not a German by birth. This was a highly important
point inflaming his early nationalism. He developed the implacable patriotism of the frontiersman, the exile. Only an Austrian could take
Germanism so seriously.

The inside story of Hitler includes many extraordinary and bizarre
episodes. Before discussing his birth and childhood and outlining his
career [in later chapters of *Inside Europe* which are not reprinted in the
present book], it may be well to present a broad detailed picture of his
character and his daily routine and his attitudes and habits, his personal characteristics and limitations.

Hitler the Human Being

His imagination is purely political. I have seen his early paintings,
those which he submitted to the Vienna art academy as a boy. They

are prosaic, utterly devoid of rhythm, color, feeling, or spiritual imagination. They are architect's sketches: painful and precise draftsmanship; nothing more. No wonder the Vienna professors told him to go to an architectural school and give up pure art as hopeless. Yet he still wants deeply to be an artist.

He went only to elementary school, and by no stretch of generosity could he be called a person of genuine culture. He is not nearly so cultivated, so sophisticatedly interested in intellectual affairs as is, say, Mussolini. He reads almost nothing. The Treaty of Versailles was probably the most concrete single influence on his life; but it is doubtful if he ever read it in full. He dislikes intellectuals. He has never been outside Germany since his youth in Austria (if you except his war experiences in Flanders) and he speaks no foreign language, except a few words of French.

To many who meet him, Hitler seems awkward and ill at ease. This is because visitors, even among his subordinates, obtrude personal realities which interfere with his incessant fantasies. He has no poise. He finds it difficult to make quick decisions: capacity for quick decisions derives from inner harmony, which he lacks. He is no "strong, silent man."

Foreigners, especially interviewers from British or American papers, may find him cordial and even candid but they seldom have opportunity to question him, to participate in a give-and-take discussion. Hitler rants. He orates. He is extremely emotional.[1] He seldom answers questions. He talks to you as if you were a public meeting, and nothing can stop the gush of words.

For a time it was said commonly that Hitler's best trait was loyalty. He would never, the sardonic joke put it, give up three things: the Jews, his friends, and Austria. Nobody would make that joke today, now that Captain Roehm is dead. Nor would anyone of knowledge and discernment have made it even before June 30, 1934, because the scroll of Hitler's disloyalties was written in giant words.

One after another he eliminated those who helped him to his career: Drexler, Feder, Gregor Strasser. It is true that he has been loyal to some colleagues—those who never disagreed with him, who gave him absolute obedience. This loyalty is not an unmixed virtue, considering the unsavoriness of such men as Streicher, the Nuremberg Jew baiter. Nothing can persuade Hitler to give up Streicher and some other comrades. Unsavoriness alone is not enough to provoke his Draconian ingratitude.

His physical courage is doubtful. When his men were fired on in the Munich *Putsch* of 1923, he flung himself to the street with such vio-

[1] He told one astonished group of interviewers that they could "crucify" him if he did not keep his promises.

lence that his shoulder was broken. Nazi explanations of this are two: (1) linked arm in arm with a man on his right who was shot and killed, he was jerked unwittingly to the pavement; (2) he behaved with the reflex action of the veteran front-line soldier, viz., sensibly fell flat when the bullets came.

Hitler has told an acquaintance his own story of the somewhat mysterious circumstances in which he won the Iron Cross. He was a dispatch bearer. He was carrying messages across a part of No-Man's Land which was believed to be clear of enemy troops, when he heard French voices. He was alone, armed only with a revolver; so with great presence of mind he shouted imaginary orders to an imaginary column of men. The Frenchmen tumbled out of a deserted dugout, seven in all, hands up, and Hitler alone delivered all seven to the German lines.[2]

Like that of all fanatics, his capacity for self-belief, his ability to delude himself, is enormous. Thus he is quite "sincere"—he really believes it—when in a preposterous interview with the *Daily Mail* he says that the Nazi revolution cost only twenty-six lives. He believes absolutely in what he says—at the moment.

But his lies have been notorious. Heiden[3] mentions some of the more recondite untruths, and others are known to every student. Hitler promised the authorities of Bavaria not to make a *Putsch;* and promptly made one. He promised to tolerate the Papen government; then fought it. He promised not to change the composition of his first cabinet; then changed it. He promised to kill himself if the Munich coup failed; it failed, and he is still alive.

The Man Without Habits

Hitler, at forty-six, is not in first-rate physical condition. He has gained about twelve pounds in the past few years, and his neck and midriff show it. His physical presence has always been indifferent; the sloppiness with which he salutes is, for instance, notorious. The forearm barely moves above the elbow. He had lung trouble as a boy, and was blinded by poison gas in the war.

In August, 1935, it was suddenly revealed that the Leader had suffered a minor operation some months before to remove a polyp on his vocal cords—penalty of years of tub thumping. The operation was successful. The next month Hitler shocked his adherents at Nuremberg by alluding, in emotional and circumlocutory terms, to the possibility of

[2] This story is not the official version, which is more grandiloquent. Some mystery attaches to the exact circumstances. Cf. *Heil,* a bright anonymous British book about Germany, p. 9.

[3] *History of National Socialism,* by Konrad Heiden, a book indispensable for the study of the new Germany.

his death. "I do not know when I shall finally close my eyes," he said, "but I do know that the party will continue and will rule. Leaders will come and Leaders will die, but Germany will live. . . . The army must preserve the power given to Germany and watch over it." The speech led to rumors (quite unconfirmed) that the growth in Hitler's throat was malignant, and that he had cancer.

He takes no exercise, and his only important relaxation—though lately he has begun to like battleship cruises in the Baltic or North Sea —is music. He is deeply musical. Wagner is one of the cardinal influences on his life; he is obsessed by Wagner. He goes to the opera as often as he can, and he was attending the Bayreuth Festival when, on July 25, 1934, Nazi putschists murdered Chancellor Dollfuss of Austria. Sessions of the Reichstag, which take place in the Kroll Opera House, sometimes end with whole performances of Wagner operas—to the boredom of non-musical deputies.

When fatigued at night in the old days, his friend and court jester Hanfstaengl was sometimes summoned to play him to sleep, occasionally with Schumann or Verdi, more often with Beethoven and Wagner, for Hitler needs music like dope. Hanfstaengl is a demoniac pianist. I have heard him thump the keys at the Kaiserhof with such resonance that the walls shook. When Hanfstaengl plays, he keeps time to his own music by puffing out his cheeks and bellowing like a trumpet. The effect is amazing. You cannot but believe that a trumpeter is hidden somewhere in the room.

Hitler cares nothing for books; nothing for clothes (he seldom wears anything but an ordinary brown-shirt uniform, or a double-breasted blue serge suit, with the inevitable raincoat and slouch hat); very little for friends; and nothing for food and drink. He neither smokes nor drinks, and he will not allow anyone to smoke near him. He is practically a vegetarian. At the banquet tendered him by Mussolini he would eat only a double portion of scrambled eggs. He drinks coffee occasionally, but not often. Once or twice a week he crosses from the Chancellery to the Kaiserhof Hotel (the G.H.Q. of the Nazi party before he came to power), and sits there and sips—chocolate.

This has led many people to speak of Hitler's "asceticism" but asceticism is not quite the proper word. He is limited in æsthetic interests, but he is no flagellant or anchorite. There is very little of the *austere* in Hitler. He eats little but vegetables—but these are prepared by an exquisitely competent chef. He lives "simply"—but his flat in Munich is the last word in modern sumptuousness.

He works, when in Berlin, in the palace of the Reichskanzler on the Wilhelmstrasse. He seldom uses the President's palace a hundred yards away on the same street, because when Hindenburg died he wanted to eliminate as much as possible the memory of presidential Germany. The building is new, furnished in modern glass and metal, and Hitler helped design it. Murals of the life of Wotan adorn the walls. An improvised balcony has been built over the street, from which, on public occasions, the Leader may review his men. Beneath the hall—according to reports—is a comfortable bomb-proof cellar.

Hitler dislikes Berlin. He leaves the capital at any opportunity, preferring Munich or Berchtesgaden, a village in southern Bavaria, where he has an alpine establishment, Haus Wachenfeld. Perched on the side of a mountain, this retreat, dear to his heart, is not far from the former Austrian frontier, a psychological fact of great significance. From his front porch he can almost see the homeland which repudiated him, and for which he yearns.

Friends

By a man's friends may ye know him. But Hitler has none.

For years his most intimate associate, beyond all doubt, was Captain Ernst Roehm, chief of staff of the SA (*Sturm Abteilung*—storm troops —Brown Shirts), who was executed in June 30, 1934. From one of the half dozen men in Germany indisputably most qualified to know, I have heard that Roehm was the *only* man in Germany, the single German out of 65,000,000 Germans, with whom Hitler was on *Du-Fuss* (thee and thou) terms. Now that Roehm is dead, there is no single German who calls Hitler "Adolf." Roehm was a notorious homosexual, but one should not deduce from this that Hitler is homosexual also.

The man who is probably closest to Hitler since Roehm's death is his chief bodyguard, Lieutenant Brückner. The only two men who can see him at any time, without previous appointment, are Herr von Ribbentrop, his adviser on foreign affairs, and Dr. Hjalmar Horace Greeley Schacht, the economics dictator. His chief permanent officials, like Dietrich, his press secretary, may see him daily, and so may Hess, the deputy leader of the party; but even Hess is not an *intimate* friend. Neither Goering nor Goebbels may see Hitler without appointment.

He is almost oblivious of ordinary personal contacts. A colleague of mine traveled with him, in the same airplane, day after day, for two months during the 1932 electoral campaigns. Hitler never talked to a soul, not even to his secretaries, in the long hours in the air; never stirred; never smiled. My friend remembers most vividly that, in order to sneak a cigarette when the plane stopped, he had to run out of sight of the *entourage*. He says that he saw Hitler a steady five or six hours a day during his trip, but that he is perfectly sure Hitler, meeting him by chance outside the airplane, would not have known his name or face.

He dams profession of emotion to the bursting point, then is apt to break out in crying fits. A torrent of feminine tears compensates for the months of uneasy struggle not to give himself away. For instance, when he spent a whole night trying to persuade a dissident leader, Otto Strasser, from leaving the party, he broke into tears three times. In the early days he often wept, when other methods to carry a point failed.[4]

Hitler does not enjoy too great exposure of this weakness, and he tends to keep all subordinates at a distance. They worship him: but they would never dare to be familiar. Hanfstaengl told me once that in all the years of their association he had never called Hitler anything except "Herr Hitler" or "Herr Reichskanzler" after the Leader reached power; and that Hitler had never called him by first name or his diminutive (Putzi), but always "Hanfstaengl" or "Dr. Hanfstaengl." There is an inhumanity about the inner circle of the Nazi party that is scarcely credible.

An old-time party member, today, would address Hitler as "Mein Führer"; others as "Herr Reichskanzler." When greeted with the Nazi salute and the words "Heil Hitler," Hitler himself replies with "Heil Hitler." Speechmaking, the Leader addresses his followers as "My" German people. In posters for the plebiscites he asks, "Dost thou, German man, and thou, German woman—etc." It is as if he feels closer to the German people in bulk than to any individual German, and this is indeed true. The German *people* are the chief emotional reality of his life.

Let us, now, examine Hitler's relation to the imperatives which dominate the lives of most men.

Attitude Toward Women

He is totally uninterested in women from any personal sexual point of view. He thinks of them as housewives and mothers or potential mothers, to provide sons for the battlefield—other people's sons.

"The life of our people must be freed from the asphyxiating perfume of modern eroticism," he says in *Mein Kampf*, his autobiography.[5] His personal life embodies this precept to the fullest. He is not a woman hater, but he avoids and evades women. His manners are those of the wary chevalier, given to hand kissing—and nothing else. Many women are attracted to him sexually, but they have had to give up the chase. Frau Goebbels formerly had evening parties to which she asked pretty and distinguished women to meet him, but she was never able to arrange a match. Occasional rumors of the engagement of the coy Leader to

---

[4] Compare with Stalin, for instance. Can one imagine Stalin bawling after a hard day, or summoning a comrade to play him music?

[5] Most of my quotations from *Mein Kampf* are from the English edition. (Hurst & Blackett, Ltd., 1933.)

various ladies are nonsense. It is quite possible that Hitler has never had anything to do with a woman in his life.

Nor, as is so widely believed, is he homosexual. Several German journalists spent much time and energy, when such an investigation was possible, checking every lodging that Hitler, in Munich days, had slept in; they interviewed beer-hall proprietors, coffee-house waiters, landladies, porters. No evidence was discovered that Hitler had been intimate with anybody of any sex at any time. His sexual energies, at the beginning of his career, were obviously sublimated into oratory. Most of those German writers and observers best equipped to know think that Hitler is a virgin.

Attitude Toward Money

Hitler has no use for money personally and therefore very little interest in it, except for political purposes. He has virtually no financial sophistication; his lack of knowledge of even the practical details of finance, as of economics, is profound.

Nowadays what would he need money for? The state furnishes him with servants, residences, motorcars. One of his last personal purchases was a new raincoat for the visit to Mussolini in June, 1934. Incidentally, members of his staff got into trouble over this, because on their advice he carried only civilian clothes; when he stepped from his airplane and saw Mussolini and all the Italians in uniform, he was ashamed of his mufti nakedness, and even suspected his advisers of purposely embarrassing him.

Hitler takes no salary from the state; rather he donates it to a fund which supports workmen who have suffered from labor accidents; but his private fortune could be considerable, if he chose to save. He announced late in 1935 that he—alone among statesmen—had no bank account or stocks or shares. Previous to this, it had been thought that he was part owner of Franz Eher & Co., Munich, the publishers of the chief Nazi organs, *Völkischer Beobachter, Angriff,* etc., one of the biggest publishing houses in Europe. Its director, Max Amman, was Hitler's top sergeant in the war, and later became his business manager.

If Hitler has no personal fortune, he must have turned all his earnings from his autobiography, *Mein Kampf,* to the party. This book is obligatory reading for Germans and, at a high price (RM 7.20 or about $3.00), it has sold 1,930,000 copies since its publication in 1925, now being in its 494th edition. If his royalty is 15 percent, a moderate estimate, Hitler's total proceeds from this source at the end of 1935 should have been about $800,000.

Nothing is more difficult in Europe than discovering the facts of the private fortunes of leading men. It is sacrosanct and thus forbidden

ground to questioners in all countries. . . . Does any dictator, Hitler
or Mussolini or Stalin, carry cash in his pocket, or make actual purchases in cash? It is unlikely.

Attitude Toward Religion

Hitler was born and brought up a Roman Catholic. But he lost faith
early and he attends no religious services of any kind. His Catholicism
means nothing to him; he is impervious even to the solace of confession.
On being formed his government almost immediately began a fierce
religious war against Catholics, Protestants, and Jews alike.

Why? Perhaps the reason was not religion fundamentally, but politics. To Hitler the overwhelming first business of the Nazi revolution
was the "unification," the *Gleichschaltung* (coordination) of Germany.
He had one driving passion, the removal from the Reich of any competition, of whatever kind. The Vatican, like Judaism, was a profoundly
international (thus non-German) organism. Therefore—out with it.

The basis of much of the madness of Hitlerism was his incredibly
severe and drastic desire to purge Germany of non-German elements,
to create a hundred percent Germany for one hundred percent Germans only. He disliked bankers and department stores—as Dorothy
Thompson pointed out—because they represented non-German, international, financial and commercial forces. He detested socialists and
communists because they were affiliated with world groups aiming to
internationalize labor. He loathed, above all, pacifists, because pacifists,
opposing war, were internationalists.

Catholicism he considered a particularly dangerous competitive force,
because it demands two allegiances of a man, and double allegiance was
something Hitler could not countenance. Thus the campaign against the
"black moles," as Nazis call priests. Protestantism was—theoretically
—a simpler matter to deal with, because the Lutheran Church presumably was German and nationalist. Hitler thought that by the simple
installation of an army chaplain, a ferocious Nazi named Mueller, as
Reichsbishop, he could "coordinate" the Evangelical Church in Germany, and turn it to his service. The idea of a united Protestant Church
appealed to his neat architect's mind. He was wrong. The church question has been an itching pot of trouble ever since.

It was quite natural, following the confused failure to Nazify Protestantism, that some of Hitler's followers should have turned to pagan-
ism. The Norse myths are a first-class nationalist substitute. Carried
to its logical extreme, Nazism in fact demands the creation of a new
and nationalist religion. Hitler indicated this in a speech at Nuremberg in September, 1935. "Christianity," he said, "succeeded for a time
in uniting the old Teutonic tribes, but the Reformation destroyed this

unity. Germany is now a united nation. National Socialism has succeeded where Christianity failed." And Heiden has quoted Hitler's remark, "We do not want any other God than Germany itself." This is a vital point. *Germany* is Hitler's religion.

One of Hitler's grudges against God is the fact that Jesus was a Jew. He can't forgive either Christians or Jews for this. And many Nazis *deny* that Jesus was Jewish. Another grudge is nationalist in origin. The basis of the Nazi revolution was the defeat of Germany in the war. Thus religion had to be Nazified because no God who permitted the French and other "inferior" races to win the war could be a satisfactory God for Germany.

Hitler's attempt to unify religion in Germany may lead to one danger. He himself may become a god. And divinity entails difficulties. Gods have to perform miracles.

Vividly in *Mein Kampf* Hitler tells the story of his first encounter with a Jew. He was a boy of seventeen, alone in Vienna, and he had never seen a Jew in his life. The Jew, a visitor from Poland or the Ukraine, in native costume, outraged the tender susceptibilities of the youthful Hitler.

"Can this creature be a Jew?" he asked himself. Then, bursting on him, came a second question: "Can he possibly be a *German?*"

This early experience had a profound influence on him, forming the emotional base of his perfervid anti-Semitism. He was provincially mortified that any such creature could be one with himself, a sharer in German nationality. Later he "rationalized" his fury on economic and political grounds. Jews, he said, took jobs away from "Germans"; Jews controlled the press of Berlin, the theater, the arts; there were too many Jewish lawyers, doctors, professors; the Jews were a "pestilence, worse than the Black Death."

No one can properly conceive the basic depth and breadth of Hitler's anti-Semitism who has not carefully read *Mein Kampf*. This book was written ten years ago. He has changed it as edition followed edition, in minor particulars, but in all editions his anti-Jewish prejudice remains implacable.

Long before he became chancellor, Hitler would not allow himself to speak to a Jew even on the telephone. A publicist as well known as Walter Lippmann, a statesman as eminent as Lord Reading, would not be received at the Brown House. An interesting point arises. Has Hitler, in maturity, actually ever been in the company of a Jew, ever once talked to one? Probably not.

"Am I My Brother's Keeper?"

Extreme precautions are, naturally, taken to guard Hitler against assassination. When he rides out in Berlin, he travels in a Mercedes-Benz

as big as a locomotive. Lieutenant Brückner, his chief aide, usually sits
beside him. Other bodyguards follow in another car, or in several cars.
The principal chauffeur is named Schaub, who was an early comrade.
SS men with rifles may stand on the running boards. If the occasion is
ceremonial and large crowds are present, the route is lined with SS men
(black shirts) alternately facing inward and outward.

There was no authentic evidence of any attempt on Hitler's life up
to the end of 1935. Rumors, however, dealt in several. On June 17, 1934,
a fortnight before the June 30 cleanup, shots are supposed to have been
fired at Hitler's car as he was returning from the burial of Goering's first
wife. In the autumn of 1934 an SS bodyguard was allegedly shot in the
finger in the Hotel Kaiserhof, by a bullet meant for Hitler.

Insurance rates on his life are quoted in London. A man with important business in Germany, which might be ruined by the terror and
revolution which would very likely follow Hitler's assassination, paid
$52.50 per month for each $1,000 of insurance against Hitler's death.[6]

Personal Sources of Power

Now we may proceed to summarize Hitler's positive qualities.

First, consider his single-mindedness, his intent fixity of purpose.
His tactics may change; his strategy may change; his *aim*, never. His
aim is to create a strong national Germany, with himself atop it. No
opportunistic device, no zigzag in polemics, is too great for him; but the
aim, the goal, never varies.

Associated with his single-mindedness is the quality of stamina. All
dictators have stamina; all need it. Despite Hitler's flabbiness and lack
of vigorous gesture, his physical endurance is considerable. I know
interviewers who have talked to him on the eve of an election, after he
has made several speeches a day, all over Germany, weeks on end; they
found him fresh and even calm. "When I have a mission to fulfill, I will
have the strength for it," he said.

Unlike most dictators, he has no great capacity for hard work, for
industry; he is not the sloghorse for punishment that, for instance,
Stalin is. He is not a good executive; his desk is usually high with
documents requiring his decision, which he neglects. He hates to make
up his mind. His orders are often vague and contradictory.

Yet he gets a good deal of work done. "Industry" in a dictator or
head of a state means, as a rule, ability to read and listen. The major
part of the work of Hitler or Mussolini is perusal of reports and attention to the advice of experts and subordinates. Half their working time
they are receiving information. Therefore it is necessary for a dictator
(a) to choose men intelligently—many of Hitler's best men he inherited

---

[6] Cf. *News Chronicle*, London, May 21, 1935. The charge for similar insurance
against Mussolini's assassination was $20 on $500 for three months.

from the old civil service, (b) to instill faith in himself in them. Hitler has succeeded in this double task amply. And when his men fail him, he murders them.

Hitler's political sense is highly developed and acute. His calculations are shrewd and penetrating to the smallest detail. For instance, his two major decisions on foreign policy, Germany's departure from the League of Nations and the introduction of conscription, were deliberately announced on Saturday afternoon, to ease the shock to opinion abroad. When he has something unpleasant to explain, the events of June 30 for instance, he usually speaks well after 8 P.M., so that foreign newspapers can carry only a hurried and perhaps garbled account of his words.

He made good practical use of his anti-Semitism. The Jewish terror was, indeed, an excellent campaign maneuver. The Nazis surged into power in March, 1933, with an immense series of electoral pledges. They promised to end unemployment, rescind the Versailles Treaty, regain the Polish corridor, assimilate Austria, abolish department stores, socialize industry, eliminate interest on capital, give the people land. These aims were more easily talked about than achieved. One thing the Nazis could do. One pledge they could redeem—beat the Jews.

Hitler bases most decisions on intuition. Twice, on supreme occasions, it served him well. In the spring of 1932 his most powerful supporters, chiefly Roehm, pressed him to make a *Putsch*. Hitler refused, *feeling* absolute certainty that he could come to power in a legal manner. Again, in the autumn of 1932, after the Nazis had lost heavily in the November elections, a strong section of the party, led by Gregor Strasser, urged him to admit defeat and enter a coalition government on disadvantageous terms. Hitler, with consummate perspicacity, refused. And within three months he reached power such as the maddest of his followers had not dreamed of.

Another source of Hitler's power is his impersonality. His vanity is extreme, but in an odd way it is not personal. He has no peacockery. Mussolini must have given autographed photographs to thousands of admirers since 1922. Those which Hitler has bestowed on friends may be counted on the fingers of two hands. His vanity is the more effective because it expresses itself in nonpersonal terms. He is the vessel, the instrument, of the will of the German people; or so he pretends. Thus his famous statement, after the June 30 murders, that for twenty-four hours he had been the supreme court of Germany.

Heiden says that Hitler's power is based on intellect, and his intellect on logic. This would seem a dubious interpretation because Hitler's mind is not ratiocinative in the least: he is a man of passion, of instinct, not of reason. His "intellect" is that of a chameleon who knows when to change his color; his "logic" that of a panther who is hungry, and thus seeks food. He himself has said proudly that he is a "Somnambulist"—strange giveaway!

His brain is small and vulgar, limited, narrow, and suspicious. But behind it is the lamp of passion, and this passion has such quality that it is immediately discernible and recognizable, like a diamond in the sand. The range of his interests is so slight that any sort of stimulus provokes the identical reflex: music, religion, economics mean nothing to him except exercise in German nationalism.

Anthony Eden, when he visited Berlin in the spring of 1935, and talked with Hitler seven hours, was quoted as saying that he showed "complete mastery" of foreign affairs. This is, of course, nonsense. Hitler does not know one-tenth as much about foreign affairs as, say, H. R. Knickerbocker, or Vernon Bartlett, or Hamilton Fish Armstrong, or Dorothy Thompson, or Mr. Eden himself. What Eden meant was that Hitler showed unflagging mastery of *his own view* of foreign affairs.

Demosthenes in Brown Shirt

Then there is oratory. This is probably the chief external explanation of Hitler's rise. He talked himself to power. The strange thing is that Hitler is a bad speaker. He screeches; his mannerisms are awkward; his voice breaks at every peroration; he never knows when to stop. Goebbels is a far more subtle and accomplished orator. Yet Hitler, whose magnetism across the table is almost nil, can arouse an audience, especially a big audience, to frenzy.

He knows, of course, all the tricks. At one period he was accustomed to mention at great length the things that "We Germans" (*wir*) had, or did not have, or wanted to do, or could not do. The word *wir* drove into the audience with the rhythmic savagery of a pneumatic drill. Then Hitler would pause dramatically. That, he would say, was the whole trouble. In Germany the word *wir* had no meaning; the country was disunited; there was no "we."

Recently Hitler told a French interviewer about an early oratorical trick and triumph, eighteen years ago in a Communist stronghold in Bavaria. He was savagely heckled. "At any moment they might have thrown me out of the window, especially when they produced a blind war invalid who began to speak against all the things that are sacred to me. Fortunately I had also been blind as the result of the war. So I said to these people, 'I know what this man feels. I was even more bewildered than he at one moment—but *I* have recovered my sight!' "

Hitler's first followers were converts in the literal sense of the term. They hit the sawdust trail. Hitler might have been Aimee Semple McPherson or Billy Sunday. Men listened to him once and were his for life—for instance, Goebbels, Brückner, Goering, Hess.

"Ruin Seize Thee, Ruthless King"

Hitler never flinched from the use of terror, and terror played a powerful role in the creation of the Nazi state. From the beginning he encouraged terror. The only purely joyous passage in *Mein Kampf* is the description of his first big mass meeting, in which the newly organized SA pummeled hecklers bloody. The function of the SA was roughhouse: first, roughhouse with the aim of preserving "order" at public meetings; second, roughhouse on the streets, to frighten, terrorize and murder Communists.

He gave jobs, big jobs, to confessed and admitted terrorists like Killinger and Heines. When a Communist was murdered at Potempa, in Silesia, in circumstances of peculiarly revolting brutality, Hitler announced publicly his spiritual unity with the murderers. When, in August, 1932, he thought that Hindenburg might appoint him chancellor, he asked for a three-day period during which the SA could run wild on the streets, and thus revenge themselves upon their enemies.

Führer Prinzip

Hitler's chief contribution to political theory was the *Führer Prinzip* (Leader Principle). This means, briefly, authority from the top down, obedience from the bottom up, the reversal of the democratic theory of government. It was, as Heiden points out, a remarkably successful invention, since almost anybody could join the movement, no matter with what various aims, and yet feel spiritual cohesion through the personality of the leader. The Nazi movement gave wonderful play to diverse instincts and desires.

Then again, Germans love to be ruled. "The most blissful state a German can experience is that of being bossed," a friend of mine put it in Berlin. And Edgar Ansel Mowrer has recorded the shouts of Nazi youngsters on the streets, "We spit at freedom." A German feels undressed unless he is in uniform. The *Führer Prinzip* not only exploited this feeling by transforming the passive character of German docility, German obedience, into an active virtue; it gave expression also to the bipolar nature of obedience: namely, that most men—even Germans— associate with a desire to be governed a hidden will to govern. The *Führer Prinzip* created hundreds, thousands, of sub-*Führers*, little Hitlers, down to the lowest storm-troop leader. It combined dignified submission with opportunity for leadership.

Mein Kampf, for all its impersonality, reveals over and over again Hitler's faith in "the man." After race and nation, personality is his main preoccupation. It is easy to see that the *Führer Prinzip* is simply a rationalization of his own ambition; the theory is announced on the

implicit understanding that the "man" is Hitler himself. "A majority,"
he says, "can never be a substitute for the Man."

Another Hitlerite doctrine is, of course, that of race. But Hitler did
not invent the concept of Aryanism; he took it over from Gobineau and
Houston Chamberlain. Most—if not all—neutral anthropologists think
that Hitler's "racist doctrine" is nonsense. They do not believe that
"pure" races exist.

Opposition

Hitlerism in its first stages was the process of "unifying" Germany. Yet
the Nazis struck at Protestants, Catholics, Jews; they mortally affronted
the working classes; they could not put any serious program of economic amelioration into effect without offending the industrialists; they
alienated, by brutality and terror, the republicans, democrats, Socialists, Communists.

Hitler has held two major plebiscites so far. One asked vindication
of Germany's departure from the League, and he received a 92.3 percent vote of confidence. The second sought acceptance of his combination of chancellorship and presidency after the death of Hindenburg;
the affirmative vote was 38,362,760 out of 43,529,710 ballots cast. Of
course neither was a fair vote in the Anglo-Saxon sense of the term. The
plebiscite in the Saar gave him 90 percent but it probably would have
been the same under any other chancellor. The last general election in
Danzig, where every effort was made to bring out the vote and which
was a better indication than the Saar of public feeling on a straight for-
or-against-Hitler issue, brought him 139,043 votes out of 234,956—good
enough, but not the two-thirds majority he hoped for.

The last reasonably fair German election, on March 5, 1933—even
though it took place under the shadow of the Reichstag fire—gave Hitler 37 percent. I believe in an election today he would better this considerably. Even so, the total Marxist (Communist-cum-Socialist) vote
in 1933 was 11,845,000. This number has probably receded, but just
the same there is still a large opposition submerged in Germany. What
has happened to these millions of hidden voters?

They are terrified. They are hounded by the police and by spies. They
vote Yes in plebiscites because they are frightened of their skins. Some
few of them have sought cover actually by joining the SA. Most simply
swallow their opinions, their feelings, their inward decency—and wait.
They are waiting for their Day. But are they an active political force? No.

The reason is that revolution is a profoundly difficult matter in a
police state like Germany, Russia, or Fascist Italy. It is almost an axiom
these days that no revolution can succeed until the equipment in arms
and ammunition of the revolutionaries is equal or superior to that of the

government. And this margin of superiority is transcendently difficult to achieve.

If the people riot, Hitler can simply shoot them down. He has the Reichswehr (regular army) to do this, not merely the SA and SS. The Reichswehr (the ranks are mostly peasant boys) might not shoot at a rising in the agrarian districts, but the farmers are the most tractable people in Hitler's Reich. An urban population would get short shrift. But, one may say, no man, not even Hitler, could shoot down tens of thousands of unarmed or roughly armed rebels. The answer to this is that it is not necessary to shoot down tens of thousands. A few hundreds will be enough.

What is more likely to happen than open rebellion is the slow pressure upward of mass discontent, grumbling, and passive resistance, sabotage caused by growing privation, until the morale of the government cracks, and the government, panicky, does foolish things. Discontent may corrosively simmer to the top, disorganizing the headship of state, causing new rivalries between sub-leaders, creating fissures between, say, Ribbentrop on the left and Goering on the right, so deep and so unbridgeable that Hitler is powerless to compose the conflict. But there are no signs that this is happening yet.

*   *   *

As long as Hindenburg lived, there was some possibility, although it was remote, that he might dismiss Hitler from the chancellorship. With his death [in 1934] this possibility passed. Hitler was now Head of State. He could only dismiss himself. His undeviating path had reached its natural end. Only God could remove him now. And God, he claimed, was on his side.

〰〰〰〰〰〰〰〰〰〰〰〰〰〰〰〰〰〰〰〰〰〰〰〰〰〰〰〰

God wasn't. Hitler, a snarling maniac, beaten to a pulp after having spread himself over more countries than any man since Napoleon, killed himself ignominiously in Berlin on April 30, 1945. With him died Eva Braun, his mistress whom he had married at the very end. When I wrote the preceding text I said that Hitler had never had relations with a woman. Perhaps I was wrong.

For most of a glittering decade Hitler passed from triumph to triumph. He upset the established order by sending troops into the demilitarized Rhineland in 1936, made the Anschluss *with Austria (March, 1938), took the Sudetenland from Czechoslovakia as a result of the Munich surrender (September, 1938), seized the remainder of Czechoslovakia (1939), and invaded Poland in September, 1939. Hitler conquered and* occupied Poland, Denmark, Norway, France, and the Balkans. Violating the Russo-German Pact (August 23, 1934), he invaded Russia in June, 1941, and soon invested enormous areas of the Russian heartland. Hitler stood from the Arctic Circle in Norway and the crests of the Pyrenees to the gates of Moscow and the Aegean. Nothing like it has been seen since Napoleon.

Hitler made two mistakes. He underestimated Russia. And he underestimated Britain. Napoleon made these same two mistakes.

The war Hitler provoked was the bloodiest, most unnecessary, and most disrupting war in history. He changed irremediably the pattern of the world, and was responsible for the killing of six million Jews.

Rereading this chapter now after almost thirty years, I feel that I did not emphasize sufficiently Hitler's sheer detestableness, nor did I give enough stress to foreign policy. I make it abundantly clear in other passages in Inside Europe (not reprinted in the present book) that I thought that Hitler's policies would make war inevitable, and that the day of reckoning would certainly come for him, but at the time of writing in 1935 I occupied myself mostly with domestic aspects of Hitler's regime. German rearmament had scarcely begun in 1935, and the Führer was largely preoccupied with internal problems and the consolidation of domestic power.

What I wrote in 1935 caused the Hitler government acute annoyance. Inside Europe was formally prohibited in the Reich, and later I was put on a select small list of journalists and public figures who, if ever caught, were to be hanged.

CHAPTER 2

Mussolini

This, like the Hitler profile, was a chapter in Inside Europe *(1936), and was first published in* Harper's Magazine *in February, 1936. It jolted many readers, as the Hitler article did. Mussolini has, it would seem, become more dated than either Hitler or Stalin. He left nothing. His career was not nutritious. But he was a remarkably copious as well as flamboyant character. At the moment there appears to be a revival of interest about him. After all, the Duce ruled Italy single-handed for twenty-two solid years, and during the late 1920's and early 1930's he was by far the best known as well as most challenging political personality in Europe. What I tried to do was catch his essence at the height of his power and fame in 1935.*

> *I shall make my own life a masterpiece.*
> —BENITO MUSSOLINI

> *I am desperately Italian. I believe in the function of Latinity.*
> —BENITO MUSSOLINI

BENITO MUSSOLINI, tempestuous and ornate, a blacksmith's son, the creator of modern Italy and the author of the Abyssinian War, was born July 29, 1883, at Dovia di Predappio, a village in the Romagna. His career is that of the most formidable combination of turncoat, ruffian, and man of genius in modern history.

The obvious motivations, except poverty, are lacking. His father, a revolutionary socialist, was the anarchist of the village square, yes; but no tragedy occurred in Mussolini's life to compare with the execution of Lenin's elder brother, or Pilsudski's. His mother, a schoolteacher, was an exceptional woman, like the mothers of most great men, but her influence on Mussolini was, it seems, slight; adoration of her never made him, like Hitler, a prisoner of infantile fixations. Kamal Ataturk's mother was mistreated by the Greeks, and years later the Turkish dictator drove the Greeks into the sea; in Mussolini's life there is no such dramatic and direct impulse to redemption.

Nor can one easily discover any extraordinary personal accidents without which the Duce might have lived and died a blacksmith's boy in Forli. It is quite possible, as Bertrand Russell has pointed out, that the revolution in Russia might never have occurred had not a German general permitted Lenin to travel across Germany in a sealed train. It is quite probable that Soviet Russia would never have had a Five-Year plan had not Trotsky succumbed to a fit of pique and refused to attend Lenin's funeral. The Dollfuss dictatorship in Austria was made possible because a Socialist deputy went to the bathroom during a crucial parliamentary vote.

Such personal accidents, which play a large part in history, are not prominent in Mussolini's life. He made his own luck. His career has been a growth, steady and luxuriant, like that of some monstrous weed.

The chief personal influence on Mussolini as a young man was probably that of a Russian exile in Switzerland, Madame Angelica Balabanov. She took care of him in his early revolutionary days, mended his health, gave him food of both the body and the spirit. Mussolini, a bricklayer, apparently met Lenin through Balabanov. Years later Lenin rebuked the Italian Socialists for having "lost" Mussolini, their best man.

Every man is an arena, a pool, of forces. Those in Mussolini's early life were mostly literary and intellectual. Voraciously intelligent, he read Marx, Hegel, Machiavelli, La Salle, Nietzsche, Pareto, Sorel. He absorbed them like a blotter. From Nietzsche he learned to hate the mob, from Marx to love it. He records that in his early days he kept a medallion of Marx in his pocket.

Bombastes Furioso

The son of Alessandro Mussolini (who named him after Benito Juárez, the Mexican revolutionist who ordered the execution of the Emperor Maximilian) and of Rosa Maltoni, he grew up in the most crushing poverty. He never tasted coffee until he was twenty. He slept on a bundle of hay instead of a mattress, and the bedroom in his birthplace, which has been made a museum, preserves this symbol of extreme indigence. Mussolini often returns to his native village, and has built a model farm in the vicinity. Unlike Hitler, he takes some interest in the lives of his surviving relatives.

Though his father was a blacksmith, the family for generations had tilled the soil. Speaking to an assembly of peasants in October, 1935, he said: "The sort of people who like to rummage among old papers thought they would please me by discovering that my ancestors were of noble birth. So I said to them, 'Stop it.' All my grandfathers, all my great-grandfathers were tillers of the soil, and to remove all doubts of it I stuck a tablet on the wall of the old farm which says that generations of Mussolinis before me have always tilled the soil with their own hands."

Mussolini, at his mother's insistence, went to a religious school (like Stalin and Kamal Ataturk), though his father was an extreme anti-clerical. Then he taught school himself, at a wage of 56 lire (then $10.25) per month, until he fled to Switzerland—note well—to avoid military service. This was when he was nineteen. He earned a living as a mason and a laborer in a chocolate factory; he was hungry often, and Balabanov describes how on one occasion he snatched food from two Englishwomen picnicking in a park. At night he studied socialism. Becoming an agitator, he got into trouble with the police, and was jailed and expelled from one Swiss canton after another. Altogether, in Italy as well as Switzerland, Mussolini was arrested eleven times.

He hated jail; he despised the moral obloquy and physical discomforts of confinement. Once he was fingerprinted by the Geneva police; he has loathed Switzerland ever since, and it is not fanciful to assume that his dislike of the League of Nations was partly conditioned by this early Genevan insult. Certainly Mussolini's prison experiences caused his present pronounced claustrophobia. Once he refused to enter the Blue Grotto in Capri. And it is obvious that his famous predilection for enormous rooms, like his office in the Palazzo Venezia, which is sixty feet by forty by forty, is overcompensation for early confinement in small prison cells.

Mussolini returned to Italy in 1904 at the age of twenty-one and spent ten years as a red-hot Socialist.

He earned a living the while by teaching school and by incessant journalism. Not as great a pamphleteer as Shaw or Trotsky, he is nevertheless one of the best journalists alive. An early venture into creative writing, a novel called *The Cardinal's Mistress*, was not successful; it was, however (I quote Francis Hackett), "hard, violent, cynical, proud, strong, and troubled." He also wrote a biography of John Huss. At Forli in 1909 he founded his own paper, *La Lotta di Classi* (*The Class Struggle*), and it made him known among Socialists and revolutionaries all over Italy. In 1912 he became editor of the *Avanti*, the official Socialist daily, and he trebled its circulation in three months. In 1914 he was one of the organizers of "Red Week," an attempt at Socialist uprising in the Romagna.

The immense catastrophe of the Great War amputated his Socialist career. The orthodox Socialists wanted Italian neutrality; Mussolini stood for intervention on the side of the allies. "To know why he became a warrior," says Dr. Finer in his penetrating and exhaustive *Mussolini's Italy*, "it is hardly necessary to do more than observe his physique." On political nationalist grounds and purely personally through love of adventure, Mussolini wanted war. He gave up the editorship of *Avanti* and was expelled from the Socialist party. When his former comrades howled him down, he shouted, with rare psychological discernment, "You hate me because you still love me." A few months later, he founded the newspaper he still directs, *Popolo d'Italia*. French money—since France was eager to drag Italy into the war—helped him.

Mussolini, so recently an antimilitarist, sounded a violent call to arms. "We must distinguish between war and war," he said, "as we distinguish between crime and crime, between blood and blood. . . . We are not, and we do not wish to be, mummies, everlastingly immovable." (Finer, p. 101). He did not, however, go to the front himself until December, 1916, and he had only thirty-eight days in the trenches when he was wounded through the stupidity of an officer who ordered him to fire one more shell from a trench mortar, though Corporal Mussolini pointed out that the gun was red hot. It exploded; four privates were killed and Mussolini's backside was splintered with forty wounds.

After the war, on March 23, 1919, Mussolini formed the first *Fasci di Combattimento*, mostly from men who had joined him early in the war demanding intervention. He was still a socialist, though not a member of the party; his first program asked an 85 percent tax on war profits. He disliked and distrusted the *bourgeoisie* and capitalist aristocracy. "Fascio" is simply the Italian word for group or bundle; to Mussolini it conveniently symbolized the "Fasces" of Imperial Rome. The original Fascists were augmented by local correspondents of the *Popolo d'Italia* in Lombardy, who organized the movement. It was not a party at first, but a militia. Its chief strength was among ex-soldiers, especially the *arditi*, front-line volunteers. "We, the survivors, who have returned," Mussolini wrote, "demand the right of governing Italy."

The movement developed speedily. Its roots were those which grew analogously in Germany and produced Hitler later: unemployment among the ex-soldiers, the weakness of democratic cabinets, parliamentary corruption, powerful nationalist feeling, restlessness on the left coupled with dissatisfaction at orthodox international socialism. As Mussolini became stronger, the army backed him, exactly as the Reichswehr backed Hitler. The politicians, watching him warily, tried to buy his movement; Giolitti was the Italian Papen. The industrialists, precisely as in Germany, prepared to give his machine support.

Labor troubles shook Italy in 1920 and 1921. The workmen rose against intolerable wages and living conditions. Mussolini appears to have first supported the "Occupation of the Factories," when six hundred thousand workers in the industrial north attempted to take over the means of production. The Occupation was a failure, partly because Socialist leadership was weak. This made it easier for Mussolini to appeal to the mob. But the legend that he "saved" Italy from Bolshevism was nonsense. Even Italians do not believe this any more.

In 1921 and 1922 Mussolini steadily extended his influence, and by a weapon which later dictators were to imitate—violence. He became a sort of gang chieftain. (He was still an active journalist, however; he covered the Cannes Conference in 1922 and sought interviews with Briand and Lloyd George. This trip taught him, he records, his first lesson in the mysteries of foreign exchange, when he discovered to his shame that an Italian lira was not worth as much as a French franc.) Mussolini's gangs slugged their way to power in half a dozen districts. Balbo in Ferrara, Grandi in Bologna, Farinacci in Cremona, attacked the "reds." Virtual civil war, of a minor guerrilla type, terrorized Italy. Mussolini still claimed, theoretically, to be a socialist, but to gain power he had to have an enemy; thus he fought the working classes, under the pretense that he was "liberating" them.

The full reaction—and more violence—came after the March on Rome, in October, 1922, which made him prime minister. He had become big enough to bluff the government into submission. He did not demand full power until he was quite certain that the army would not oppose him and when he was sure that the King would make him prime minister. The March on Rome was not, of course, a March on Rome at all; the Fascists took possession of a number of cities, with the army, "neutral," standing aside. Mussolini traveled to Rome by sleeping car, and the fifty thousand Fascists who had assembled in Rome quietly dispersed the next day.

After 1922 Mussolini's history is familiar. He formed a coalition government, then, like Hitler ten years later, kicked the non-Fascists out. His only severe crisis till the Abyssinian War in 1935 was the Matteotti affair. Most critics nowadays do not think that the Duce directly ordered the assassination of Matteotti, the Socialist leader, but his moral responsibility is indisputable. What happened, good informants think, is not only that Mussolini threatened Matteotti in the chamber, but angrily denounced him in private, spurting irritably at mention of his name. One can easily imagine him exploding to his underlings, "That Matteotti—!" (Similarly, by a chance remark, Henry II caused the murder of Thomas à Becket.) The underlings, taking the hint, and thinking to gain favor with the Duce, went ahead on their own initiative and kidnaped and murdered the young Socialist. Such a sequence of events is convenient for a dictator; if the business turns out "well," the result is simple gain, if it turns out badly, viz., makes a scandal, the dictator can disclaim complicity. Mussolini, however, was bold enough to admit his responsibility; and he had to concede that the murderers were Fascists of "high station." Indeed some of his closest associates were involved. In a famous speech to the chamber he blustered his way out as follows:

But after all, gentlemen, what butterflies are we looking for under the arch of Titus? Well, I declare here before this assembly, before all the Italian people, that I assume, I alone, the political, moral, historical responsibility for everything that has happened. If sentences, more or less maimed, are enough to hang a man, out with the noose! If Fascism has only been castor oil or a club, and not a proud passion of the best Italian youth, the blame is on me!

This, be it noted, is almost the same technique that Hitler followed after the June 30 murders. He too assumed all responsibility; and in Italy and Germany both this removed the burden of bad conscience from large quarters of the nation. The Matteotti affair, however, shook the Duce deeply. But on the whole it was of great value to him, because following it he was able to isolate and thus the more conveniently destroy the opposition.[1]

"And Changes Fill the Cup of Alteration"

It is interesting in the light of the Abyssinian campaign to think back to the Italo-Turkish war of 1911-1912 and recollect that Mussolini vigorously opposed it. This war, also fought in Africa, seemed to Mussolini, then a socialist, an imperialist crime. He organized an anti-war strike in Forli, and spent five months in prison as a result. He wrote that the newspaper articles evoked by the Lybian war were "manifestations, typical, qualified, and cynical, of nationalist delirium tremens."

In one editorial in the *Avanti* he wrote a passage which read strangely at the time of the Abyssinian War in 1935:

We are in the presence of a nationalist, clerical, conservative Italy which proposes to make of the sword its law, of the army the nation's school. We foresaw this moral perversion; it does not surprise us. But those who think that preponderance of militarism is a sign of strength are wrong. Strong nations do not have to descend to the sort of insane carnival in which the Italians are indulging to-day; strong nations have a sense of proportion. Nationalist, militarist Italy shows that it lacks this sense. *So it happens that a miserable war of conquest is celebrated as a Roman triumph.*

Dr. Finer has unearthed a precious quotation of similar vintage. "Imagine an Italy," wrote Mussolini indignantly in 1912, "in which

---

[1] The actual assassins of Matteotti got very light sentences. One was an American gangster from St. Louis.

thirty-six millions should all think the same, as though their brains were made in an identical mold, and you would have a madhouse, or rather, a kingdom of utter boredom or imbecility."

Man Mussolini

Most people meeting Mussolini are surprised at his shortness of stature He is, like Napoleon, only five feet six. His shoulders are powerful and his hands finely formed and almost delicate. His smile is gritty. Usually he wears the uniform of a corporal in the Fascist Militia.[2] He works in the Palazzo Venezia, in the center of Rome, and lives about ten minutes away by car, in the Villa Torlonia, a comfortable house with a luxuriant garden near the Porta Pia. A Roman aristocrat, Prince Torlonia, offered the villa to Mussolini because he couldn't afford its upkeep; now he would like to have it back, but Mussolini has fallen in love with the place, especially the garden.

For some years his wife, Donna Rachele Guidi, was a virtual exile in Milan, but now she lives in the Villa Torlonia. Donna Rachele, whose origins are obscure, was, according to one story, a waitress in a Forli pub, according to another the servant of Mussolini's father after he retired from blacksmithing, according to a third the daughter of his father's first wife by a different marriage and thus the Duce's stepsister. She has borne Mussolini five children.

Indeed Mussolini is the only contemporary dictator conspicuously fecund; he is also the only dictator with a very strong regard for family life. Like Napoleon (and Hindenburg) he trusts members of his immediate family, and not many other people. For years his only real friend was his brother Arnaldo, who succeeded him as editor of the *Popolo d'Italia:* Mussolini telephoned him from Rome to Milan almost every evening. Arnaldo's sudden death was a serious blow to the Duce. His daughter Edda, who is his living image, is the only person who dares to twit or heckle him; he adores her. Her husband, Count Galeazzo Ciano, became Mussolini's press director, and then the leader of the *Disperata* squadron of bombing and pursuit planes in Ethiopia. Mussolini's two elder sons, Vittorio, then nineteen, and Bruno, seventeen, also went to the war as aviators. As if to give the two younger children, Romano and Anna Maria, a touch of the air, Mussolini himself piloted the plane which gave them their first experience off the ground.

At fifty-two Mussolini is in powerfully good health, partly as a result of attention to a severe regime. Shortly after he became prime minister he was desperately ill with a stomach ailment; he eats very little nowadays but milk and fruit. He told a recent American interviewer, pointing to a basket of fruit on the table, "That is the secret of my continued

[2] Note the Napoleonic significance.

health—fruit, fruit, fruit. In the morning I have a cup of coffee and fruit; at noon I have soup or broth and fruit, and at night I have fruit. I never touch meat, but sometimes I have a little fish." He loves exercise, and takes a lot of it: riding in the Torlonia gardens, fencing, swimming, hiking. He neither drinks nor smokes. He was fond of women in his younger days, but for the last few years he has paid little attention to them.

Mussolini is built like a steel spring. (Stalin is a rock of sleepy granite by comparison, and Hitler a blob of ectoplasm.) Mussolini's ascetic frugality is that of a strong man who scorns indulgence because he has tasted it often and knows that it may weaken him; Hitler's, that of a weak man fearful of temptation. Stalin, on the other hand, is as normal in appetites as a buffalo.

The Duce has no social life. When, as foreign minister, it is incumbent on him to entertain, he greets his guests not at the Palazzo Venezia or the Villa Torlonia but in a hotel he hires for the occasion. No friend of the rich, he despises the decadent and profligate Roman aristocracy. He gave up the theater, of which he was very fond, because he could not spare the time; he sometimes has private movie shows at home. In his autobiography, written in 1928, he says that in his first six years of power he never once passed the threshold of an aristocrat's salon or even of a coffee house.

As a rule, Mussolini works very hard for five or six hours a day—except when a crisis makes more time necessary—and spends the rest of the day in reading, meditation, or exercise. He is neat, precise, orderly; as Ludwig[3] records, he hates the *à peu près*. His work is systematized to the ultimate detail; he is a perfect executive, considering the floriferousness of other aspects of his character; he never leaves the Palazzo Venezia till the day's work is done.

He cares very little for money, though his large family makes him less impervious to financial considerations than other dictators. His official salary is 8,000 lire per month (about $660), but he has a drawing account, "small, unspecified, and variable," at the treasury. For his autobiography he received $25,000 in America; he gave some of this to the Rome poor. For a long period his chief source of income was $1,500 per week from the Hearst press; early in 1935, however, he gave up writing regular articles because international politics were so delicate that he could not express himself frankly.

The Duce is the only modern dictator who has come to terms with religion. In 1929 the Lateran Treaty adjusted the relations of church and state in Italy. Shortly thereafter Mussolini and the then Pope, strong characters both, clashed over the education of Fascist youth; in 1932

[3] Cf. *Talks with Mussolini*, by Emil Ludwig, a fascinating record.

the Duce went to the Vatican, knelt in prayer, and, it is believed, took holy communion. He was an avowed atheist, like his father, in youth; latterly he has become very religious. He prays daily. His wedding gift to Edda was a golden rosary; his youngest child, Anna Maria, was his first to be given a religious name.

The most accessible of Europe's statesmen, Mussolini sees an enormous number of people. His first visitor every day is the chief of police (Alexander of Yugoslavia likewise saw a security official the first thing every morning). The Duce, pervasively curious, interested in human nature, and an accomplished brain tapper, like Franklin Roosevelt, enjoys his visitors. Finer quotes him as saying that he has given over sixty thousand audiences; he has interested himself in 1,887,112 individual "affairs of citizens."

Mussolini listens to people—but he seldom takes advice. He alone makes decisions. When he wishes, he can make himself as inaccessible as a Tibetan Lama. During the Geneva crises in 1935, when he was in a roaring temper, no one could get near him. Baron Aloisi and others made reports; he listened or not, as he chose. Mussolini is proud of having thousands of acquaintances, and—with Arnaldo dead—no friends; he told Ludwig that he trusted "no one." This remark was expurgated from the Italian translation of Ludwig's book, since many Italians have served the Duce well and think that they deserve his trust.

A very good journalist himself, he likes newspapermen. But he is very much a *prima donna*, and needs careful handling. He is never "charming"; he is contemptuous of all but the most skillful flattery; he may be brutal, gruff, cheerful, or stentorian, depending on his mood, which he seldom bothers to gloss over or conceal. He pays intelligent interlocutors the compliment of interviewing them; sometimes he asks many more questions than he answers. Boldness is the best avenue to his favor. I remember seeing Francis Hackett after his interview for the *Survey Graphic*, a little breathless because he had dared to ask a supremely audacious question: "Where, Your Excellency, would you have been in *your* career, if you had applied to yourself the Fascist virtues of discipline, loyalty and obedience?"[4]

Interviews, Mussolini knows, are the best of all possible forms of propaganda; thus, he is so lavish with them. Most newspapermen—and their editors—cannot resist the flattery of conversation with a dictator or head of a state; once they have been received by a Mussolini or Hitler, they feel a sense of obligation which warps their objectivity. It is very difficult for the average correspondent to write unfavorably about a busy and important man who has just donated him a friendly hour of conversation.

[4] Rather weakly Mussolini replied that "the war" had changed things.

A British interviewer saw Mussolini recently and, rare phenomenon, Mussolini laughed at one of his remarks. Preparing a draft of the interview, the correspondent wrote, "The Duce's laughter encouraged me to make one criticism of the Fascist regime, that it permitted very little expression of humor." Reading the draft for approval before publication (as he does with most interviews), Mussolini sternly elided the reference to the fact that he had laughed. Dictators never laugh!

Two newspapermen were the source of the only recorded instance of public embarrassment of the Duce. He was in Locarno to initial the security pact of 1925. (Incidentally, from that day until he visited Germany in 1936, he never stepped off Italian soil; before that, he had as prime minister been abroad only twice; he attended the Lausanne conference in 1922, and in 1923 fleetingly visited London.) His regime had just taken over the great liberal newspapers of Italy; the corps of international correspondents resented this, and boycotted his press conference. Annoyed, pouting, Mussolini found himself surrounded in the hotel lobby by the journalists who had slighted him. He addressed George Slocombe of the London *Daily Herald,* a conspicuous red-bearded figure, whom he had met covering the conference of Cannes. "Ha!" exclaimed Mussolini surlily. "How are your Communist friends getting on?" Slocombe replied with perfect good temper, "I am not a Communist, *Monsieur le Président,* but a Socialist." "Ha!" Mussolini snorted again. "Then I am mistaken." Whereupon a Dutch correspondent, George Nypels, piped out, "And it is not the first time."

Mussolini reads all the time; no modern statesman except perhaps Masaryk is so well acquainted with current literature. He keeps a systematic notebook of his reading. Like most people who like to read, he likes to write, and he writes extremely well. He compressed in the dozen pages of his pamphlet on Fascism what it analogously took Hitler six hundred pages to express in *Mein Kampf.* He is easily the best educated as well as the most sophisticated of the dictators—he is the only modern ruler who can genuinely be termed an intellectual—and he taught himself both French and German, which he speaks expertly. In about 1925 he began to learn English, so that he might read the political editorials in the London *Times.* He chose an English newspaperwoman, Miss Gibson, as his teacher.

The things that Mussolini hates most are Hitler, aristocrats, money, cats, and old age. He detests old people, especially old women. He dislikes references to the fact that he is a grandfather; and when, on July 29, 1933, he reached the age of fifty, the Italian press was not allowed to mention it. The things that Mussolini loves most are the city of Rome (he has assiduously fostered the "cult of Rome"), his daughter Edda, peasants, books, airplanes, and speed.

He is apt to straddle a motorcycle, and like the late Colonel Lawrence hurl himself across country at night. He learned to pilot an airplane shortly after the war, and recounts in his autobiography a number of crashes and forced landings, from which he escaped miraculously, and which intensely exhilarated him.

"The Race by Vigor, Not by Vaunts, Is Won"

From the complex strands of Mussolini's character one may draw bright and brittle threads indicating the sources of his power.

He has, first of all, spine and starch, in a country sometimes lacking both.

For all his bombast and braggadocio, his intelligence is cold, analytical, deductive, and intensely realistic.

His flaming egoism, his *sacro egoismo,* is cherished by Italians. His vanity is, as is obvious, extreme; for instance he stabilized the lira at nineteen to the dollar, far too high a rate, mostly to better the figure chosen by the French. He was called a paranoiac as far back as 1910.

Overwhelmingly he is a man of action. The single episode that amazed him most about the 30th of June in Germany was that Hitler consumed five hours *talking* to a man (Roehm) who was potentially a traitor.

His intuition, personal and political, is sensitive. He says: "I cannot change myself. I am like the beasts. I smell the weather before it changes. If I submit to my instincts, I never err."

He is an orator of the pen. He *wrote* his way to power.

Like all dictators, he is implacable. No Hitler, no Stalin, no Mussolini has ever forgiven an enemy.

He is no hypocrite. He never made any secret of his ambition, which, he said frankly, was to seize power and stay in power as long as possible. On the other hand, he insists that he is no mere "profiteer in patriotism." *Duty* to Italy is his passion. "Is it lust for power that possesses me?" he once said. "No, I believe, in all conscience, no Italian thinks this. Not even my worst adversary. It is duty. A precise duty towards the revolution and towards Italy."

His histrionic ability is extreme. No modern politician except possibly Trotsky is so good an actor.

Above all, he possesses a passionate physical magnetism. His vitality expresses itself in every gesture; when he salutes, for instance, he shoots out his arm with such intensity you think the hand may fall off. This vitality is readily absorbed by others. When he arrives before troops ready for review, his presence has almost the effect of an electric shock.

Among the more negative qualities in Mussolini the following might be mentioned:

He is intensely touchy. A journalist well known to him, whom he admired, visited Italy in August, 1935, and wrote a quite objective story saying that the Abyssinian campaign was not universally popular. Mussolini saw it (he reads most of his press cuttings) and canceled an appointment for an interview, a few hours before it was to take place. Again, a minor instance, he caused the Italian number of *Fortune,* which was very fair to him, to be suppressed in Italy, largely it is believed because of one remark, quoting him (in his early days) as follows: "What do I do first when I wake up? Jump straight out of bed! No matter how beautiful the head beside me on the pillow."

He is superstitious. Early in his career he had accepted, among the thousands of gifts which poured in on him, an Egyptian mummy. Then Lord Carnarvon, excavator of the Tomb of Tutankhamen, died. Mussolini ordered the mummy to be removed. He woke up the staff of the Palazzo Chigi (where he then worked) to have it instantly taken away, his fright of it having descended on him late at night.

He is not strikingly original. Many of his ideas are derivative. Ideologically Fascism is the distorted creation of Marx, Nietzsche, and Sorel. Mussolini did not invent the Fascist salute, which was a suggestion of d'Annunzio's; he did not devise the symbol of the Black Shirt, which he copied from the uniform of the *arditi.*

Mussolini, who is quite aware of the complexities of his character, read with interest a serial discussion of it in a Fascist newspaper. Then he telegraphed the local prefect: "Be so good as to send for the editor and ask him to close his series of articles with the following statement! 'Inasmuch as Mussolini himself says that he does not know exactly what he is, it is somewhat difficult for others to find out.'"

Violence

There are those who have to be crushed by truth before they can understand it.
—MUSSOLINI

Not believing in force is the same as not believing in gravitation.
—TROTSKY

Mussolini's first published work, written when he was twenty-one under the strong influence of Nietzsche, was an essay on the philosophy of force. The concept of force has always fascinated him. Yet, as he says, violence should be "surgical," not "sporting"; defining the terror in Italy as "national prophylactics," he wrote that certain "individuals should be removed from circulation as the doctor removes an infected person from circulation." At one point in his career, early in 1921, he resigned—extremely temporarily—the leadership of the Fascist movement, in protest at violence which he considered excessive by *squadristi* bands. He did not, however, abolish the *squadristi* till 1927, when their work with castor oil and clubs was safely done.

There have been five or six attempts to assassinate Mussolini; he is a profound fatalist, but not so much so that severe precautions to guard him are not taken. The story is that only one man in Rome, the chief of police, can or cannot tell Mussolini what to do; the Duce obeys him in regard to routes he takes. There are some streets in Rome he never travels on. On the other hand, he travels daily from home to office without special guard.

Hitler, the story goes, keeps a small revolver in his desk drawer. Suicide would be understandable with Hitler if his regime collapsed. Not so the Duce. Mussolini, a compact gorilla, will not perish by such facile means.

What Fascism Is

When Mussolini took power he had no program except to retain his job. He admits this candidly. But he quickly found a program, which derived from a desire to replace the class struggle, which—certainly— he had done more than most men to intensify, by some sort of class collaboration. This was the origin of Fascism in practice. The contrast to Hitler is striking. Hitler came to power with a very definite program, and soon lost it; Mussolini, devoid of program, quickly invented one.

The outlines of Fascist economy are known to everyone. Private property, private profits are preserved, but under strict state control. The entire productive capacity of the country, theoretically represented by employers and employees both, is organized into a series of twenty-two "corporations," from which deputies to the lower chamber of parliament are chosen. Representation [is on the] basis of occupation instead of geography; a deputy will represent, say, the hotel business instead of the province of Turin.

The scheme was put forward cautiously, and expanded very slowly; in 1935 it was still an embryo structure. The state, being supreme, regulates economy for its exclusive benefit. Fascism may be, spiritually, "an attempt to make Romans out of Italians," but physically it made Italy a prison. "Fascism is a series of ideas turned into a person," according to Gentile; and the peculiar person and character of Mussolini determined the repressive shape it took.

Mussolini told an English publicist late in 1935 that he would find no orthodox capitalism surviving in Fascist Italy. And in a famous speech to the National Council of Corporations he announced that the world economic crisis of 1931-34 had bored so deeply into the capitalist system that it had become an organic crisis of the system itself. "Today," he said, "I declare to you that the capitalist method of production is finished."

On the other hand, the disadvantages to labor under Fascism are infinitely more severe. Liberty, in a Fascist system, ceases; the question for the individual is whether the merits of the regime compensate for its loss. Workers have lost their right to bargain; their trade unions have been dissolved; they are the weaker party *vis-à-vis* the employers in the syndicates; they are still subject to the crises of capitalist economy; their wages may be (and have been) mercilessly deflated by decree; above all, they have lost the right to strike. The capitalist, on the other hand, even if he has suffered inconvenience, maintains his fundamental privilege, that of earning private profits. Fascism as Mussolini introduced it was not, probably, a deliberate artifice for propping up the capitalist structure, but it had that effect.

Mussolini, in his essay on Fascism in the *Enciclopedia Italiana,* begins by saying how a series of "aphorisms, anticipations and aspirations" were welded by time into "an ordered expression of doctrine." He sketches the history of Fascism by describing the things it combated: (1) Pacifism, (2) Marxian Socialism, (3) Liberal Democracy. He attacks the materialist conception of history: "Fascism, now and always, believes in holiness and heroism." And as to democracy: "Fascism denies that the majority, by the simple fact that it is a majority, can direct human society; it denies that numbers alone can govern by means of a periodical consultation, and it affirms the immutable, beneficial, and fruitful inequality of mankind."

His best passage is devoted to Fascism as the totalitarian expression of the state:

No doctrine has ever been born completely new, completely defined, and owing nothing to the past. . . . The foundation of Fascism is its conception of the state, its character, its duty, and its aim. Fascism conceives of the state as an absolute, in comparison with which all individuals or groups are relative, only to be conceived of in their relation to the state. . . . The state, as conceived of and as created by Fascism, is a spiritual and moral fact in itself, since political, juridical, and economic organization of the nation is a concrete thing; and such an organization must be in its origins and development a manifestation of the spirit. . . .

The Fascist state is unique, and an original creation. It is not reactionary, but revolutionary, in that it anticipates the solution of the universal political problems which elsewhere have to be settled in the political field by the rivalry of parties, the excessive power of the parliamentary régime and the irresponsibility of political assemblies; while it meets the problems of the economic field by a system of syndicalism which is continually increasing in importance, as much in the sphere of labor as of industry; and in the moral field enforces order, discipline, and obedience to that which is the determined moral code of the country.

And he ends the essay by an urgent appeal to imperialism: "For Fascism, the growth of empire, that is to say the expansion of the nation, is an essential manifestation of vitality."

The Job and the Future

If I advance, follow me; if I retreat, kill me; if I die, avenge me.
—MUSSOLINI

There is no revolution that can change the nature of man.
—MUSSOLINI

Mussolini is three things: the *Duce* (leader) of the Fascist party, the *Capo del Governo,* or prime minister, and the head of the Grand Fascist Council, the highest organ of government in Italy. The three posts, quite distinct, merge in his person. As *Capo del Governo,* he is theoretically responsible to the King; as Duce of the party, he appoints the Grand Fascist Council and presides over it. The Grand Fascist Council controls parliament. Hitler, in Germany, has united party and state; he is *Reichsführer.* Not so Mussolini, though the effect is the same. In the U.S.S.R., Stalin, in contrast to Mussolini, is—in theory—appointed by and is responsible to the other members of the central committee of the Communist party, whereas in Italy the members of the Grand Fascist Council are Mussolini's underlings. Stalin, however, like Mussolini, keeps party and state theoretically separate.

The Duce is the only dictator who, so far as is known, has made arrangements for his succession. The Grand Fascist Council numbers about twenty-five men; its membership, except for ex-officio and life members, shifts continually and is secret, and it meets in secret. (The secretary of the party and certain other dignitaries are members so long as they hold their party or cabinet jobs; the three surviving quadrumvirs of the March on Rome—Balbo, De Bono, and De Vecchi—are life members.) If Mussolini dies, the Grand Council has the duty of submitting a list of men from which the King will choose a successor. Three names are, at present, understood to be on the list, selected in advance—of course—by Mussolini.

Mussolini told Ludwig that there will never be a second Duce; he meant obviously that there will never be a second Duce like himself. The men around him are, indeed, small fish. There is no Goering in Italy, no Kaganovitch. Whenever a subordinate like Grandi or Balbo becomes too prominent, Mussolini, who doesn't like the luxury of No. 2 men, contrives to get rid of him. De Bono was removed from Abyssinia as soon as he had captured Adowa and Makale.

The Duce *is* the Fascist system; if he dies, can it survive him? The temptation is to answer in the negative. As to affairs at present, Mussolini might get a big vote of confidence if he gave the people liberty, *plus* his system; but instead he gave them suppression, privation, and the obscenity of war.

"Jesters Do Oft Prove Prophets"

"There is a widespread belief," wrote the *Manchester Guardian* recently, "that dictators are iron-souled and thick-skinned; the truth is that they are the most sensitive creatures in the world. . . . It is the leaders of the democracies who are tough and wiry. They can stand criticism, and either bear it in good part or put up with it. Not so the dictator; an unfriendly remark or even good-humored banter is so intolerable that the very sinews of the state are felt to shake dangerously in response to the jangled nerves of the dictator."

Jokes in the U.S.S.R. mostly deal with the rigors of the Five-Year Plan; German jokes are based most often on the terror; jokes in Italy perhaps significantly—aside from those international jokes which are applied indiscriminately to all the dictators—deal mostly with corruption. Mussolini himself is above any whisper of financial irregularity, but if the current of suppressed laughter in Italy is any indication, the rank-and-file Fascists think poorly of the integrity of the petty bosses and sub-leaders. The party, of course, controls all the best jobs; on this fact the wits flourish.

Most Italian jokes hinge on the word *mangiare,* which means two things, "to eat" and "to graft."

Little Romano Mussolini, for instance, says to the Duce at the dinner table, "Father, what must I do to become a great man like yourself?" Mussolini answers, *"Mangi e taci"* (Eat and be quiet).

The most Fascist of animals is the elephant; because it first makes the Fascist salute—and then eats. The Fascist insignia have been placed on all locomotives—because they "eat up" the tracks. Mount Vesuvius was recently given an honorary degree, because it opened its mouth—to eat. A traveler stops a policeman, "Where can I eat well in this town?" Reply: "At the party headquarters."

Another type of story goes like this. At a congress of veteran Fascists someone called out, "To whom does Italy belong?" Chorus: *"A NOI!"* (to us). "To whom belongs victory?" Chorus: *"A NOI!"* "To whom the Duce?" Chorus: *"A NOI!"* Then a voice interrupts: "To whom belongs work?" (*A chi il lavoro?*) The chorus stops in embarrassment, then begins to sing the Fascist anthem, *"Giovinezza."*

No street has ever been named for Mussolini. This is because the word *via* means not only street, but "away."

~~~~~~

Clearly I was taken in a bit by Mussolini. Well, so were a great many other people, including practically the entire British and American "establishments" of the period. (Of course the word "establishment" was unknown in this connection in 1936.) Even Mr. Churchill admired the Duce on occasion. So did Bernard Shaw. Those who saw through him or refused to take him at face value were dismissed as radicals, eccentrics, or "intellectuals." Mussolini was the man who cleared the beggars off the streets, and "made the trains run on time," achievements which were thought to excuse Fascism. I may say, incidentally, that it pleases me to discover that there is no mention in my own text of these two clichés. Even then I had enough savvy to know that running trains on time or chasing beggars did not justify a total suppression of civil liberties and that there were plenty of countries in the world where trains, believe it or not, managed to run on time without having to suffer a Mussolini.

It was not the excesses and outrages of Fascism at home which brought the Duce into disfavor among reactionary and privileged classes abroad. Mussolini began to slip in general esteem when he began to make an international nuisance of himself and obtrude on rival national interests, although plenty of conservatives continued to admire him extravagantly. But his invasion of Abyssinia, now called Ethiopia, in 1935, was a hard pill for almost anybody to swallow. The Fascist intervention in Spain and the formation of the Rome-Berlin Axis the next year alienated half the world. Came World War II and Mussolini stabbed France in the back, after which nobody could pretend that he was respectable.

What ruined Mussolini was Hitler. Hitler sucked him into the abyss. Everybody knows that his regime collapsed (July, 1943) after the allied invasion of Sicily. In the end (1945) he died like a jackal, shot by Italian partisans and hung by his heels in a public square in Milan, together with his mistress. Such grand opera! I was right when I said that he would not perish by facile means.

CHAPTER 3

~~~~~~~~

Stalin

I never met Stalin or talked to him, but I saw him once. He was dead. He had been dead for three years. He lay in Lenin's mausoleum alongside the Kremlin wall, embalmed for all posterity to see. Lying there like a paraffin model, he was smaller than I had imagined him to be. The Soviet specialists in mummification, who made his body, like that of Lenin, permanent, did their work well, and millions of Russian and other visitors paid homage to his terrifyingly lifelike corpse or visited it in simple curiosity.

Stalin died in March, 1953. Khrushchev posthumously kicked him in the guts and his body was hoisted out of the Kremlin tomb in 1961 and removed to some burial place less grandiose and not on public display. This was at the peak of the process known as de-Stalinization. An attempt was made to erase Stalin from his previous positions in folkways, history, and hagiology. Even the names of hero cities like Stalingrad were changed. But it can never be forgotten that Stalin ruled Russia with a thumb of steel for almost thirty years.

This article appeared first in Harper's Magazine (December, 1935) and then, like the sketches of Hitler and Mussolini, became part of Inside Europe, various editions of which appeared between 1936 and 1941.

~~~~~~

No revolution can be made with silk gloves.
—JOSEF STALIN

STALIN is probably the most powerful single human being in the world. Even dialectical materialism demands personality to assert itself, as the case of Stalin proves. He is different from other dictators because he is not only the undisputed leader of a national state but of a movement, the Communist Internationale, which has roots in almost all countries. Also he differs from Hitler and Mussolini in that he is of the second generation of dictators, having taken over authority from a predecessor, Lenin.

He was not appointed by Lenin to the job. Indeed, quite the contrary. Stalin was the man whom Lenin did *not* want to be his successor. Lenin was quite explicit on this point. Listen:

> Comrade Stalin is too rude. . . . I propose to the comrades to find a way of removing him from that position [secretary-general of the party] and appointing another man who in all respects differs from Stalin only in superiority— namely, more patient, more loyal, more polite, and more attentive to comrades, less capricious, etc. . . .

This was in 1924. Today, eleven years later, Stalin is extolled by his subordinates in terms much more extravagant than those which Lenin himself evoked. In the Soviet press you may find him fulsomely called "Great," "Beloved," "Bold," "Wise," "Inspirer," "Genius." Half a dozen cities have been named for him, like Stalingrad, Stalinbad, Stalinogorsk, Stalinsk. In speeches he has been addressed by ordinarily uneffusive folk as "Our Best Collective Farmer Worker," "Our Shockworker, Our Best of Best," and "Our Darling, Our Guiding Star." Celebrations have concluded with the words, "Long Live Our Dear Leader, Our Warmly Beloved Stalin, Our Comrade, Our Friend."

Sources of Power

First, one may mention his durability and physique. He suffers from a dilated heart, but otherwise his physical strength and endurance are enormous. He is no high-strung neurotic or somnambulist like Hitler, nor is his command of physical power closely associated with emotion, as is the case with other dictators. Stalin is about as emotional as a slab of basalt. If he has nerves, they are veins in rock.

Then, consider his patience, his tenacity. His perseverance, as Walter Duranty says, is "inhuman." He is a slow builder of bricks, so slow that often his followers are impatient, because they do not see the outline of the finished structure he is building. His line is undeviating; he takes only "the long view."

Again, his shrewdness—cunning or craft is perhaps a better word to express this quality—is obvious. He is, of course, an Oriental; moreover he admits it. "Welcome," he said to the first interviewer, a Japanese, whom he ever received, "I too am an Asiatic." Years ago he sought to suppress Lenin's testament denigrating him. He had not quite the power to do this. But presently the U.S.S.R. was flooded with 500,000 copies of a photograph showing Stalin and Lenin sitting on a bench together, conversing with earnest friendliness. Stalin's double campaign, first to rid himself of the Left opposition of Trotsky, Zinoviev, and Kamenev, second the Right opposition of Bukharin, Rykov, and Tomsky, was a triumph not only of extreme ruthlessness, but of great imaginative shrewdness and subtlety.

When candor suits his purpose, no man can be more candid. He has the courage to admit his errors, something few other dictators dare do. In his article "Dizzy from Success" he was quite frank to admit that the collectivization of the peasants had progressed too quickly. He wrote in *Leninism*:

> The main thing in this matter is to have the courage to admit one's errors and to have the strength to correct them in the shortest possible time. The fear of admitting one's errors after the recent intoxication by successes, the fear of self-criticism, unwillingness to correct one's errors rapidly and decisively— that is the main difficulty.

This book, *Leninism*, is one of the frankest—if long-winded—expositions of political philosophy ever written. In its 825 pages you may find record of things good, bad, and indifferent in the Soviet Union in illimitable profusion. Stalin emphasizes the good, naturally, but he does not conceal the bad. The book has sold over two million copies in the Soviet Union.[1]

Again, there is his sense of detail, which is very great. His wary eye penetrates to the smallest elements in the national life, and in general he tends to detail in a way neither Hitler nor Mussolini would dream of doing. Hitler, for instance, refuses to read any of his mail, even the most glowing samples. Stalin reads everything, down to the last paragraph in *Pravda*. His day begins with the perusal of local reports, carefully sifted from all parts of the Soviet Union. W. H. Chamberlin (cf. *Russia's Iron Age*, p. 187), certainly no friendly critic, notes that Stalin, by personal intervention, remedied injustices in spheres very far removed from his normal business.

In the summer of 1933 Stalin wanted to see the building of Magnitogorsk, the industrial city created in Siberia during the Five-Year Plan, dramatized and made colorful in the newspapers. He remembered a bright feature reporter on *Izvestia* named Garry and asked what had become of him. He was found in a concentration camp! Stalin had him released, and sent him to write about Magnitogorsk.

During the February, 1934, congress of the Communist party Stalin was listening to a speech by his first assistant, Kaganovitch. He was

---

[1] The complete works of Lenin, incidentally, in twenty-seven volumes, have sold four million *sets* in the U.S.S.R. since publication.

talking about certain textbooks which had been unsatisfactory. Stalin interrupted, "Not those textbooks, but the loose-leaf textbooks."

Still again, one must mention his ability to handle men. He is a good political tactician, a party boss and organizer *par excellence*. Friends told me in Moscow in 1935 that Stalin possessed great magnetism, that you felt his antennae as soon as he entered a room. His personal as well as political intuition is considerable. Plenty of Communists would deny that he had any sense of human relationship—to put it mildly!— but he chooses men with great perspicacity.

He is no orator. His speeches are simple and businesslike but very long. His writing, when he tackles the dreary wastes of Marxist dialectics, particularly when he voices the ideological differences with the opposition, is dull and tedious; he sounds like an applicant for a Ph.D. in a minor university. When, as in his recent address to graduates of the Red Army college, he avoids philosophical issues, he is much more successful—direct, simple, full of a sense of the concrete. Generally, he likes the question-and-answer method of exposition. His speeches are like catechisms. And in style he aims to hit the broad level of the masses.

His intelligence is wary, cautious, thorough, rather than acute or brilliant. Yet witness his talk with H. G. Wells, wherein he more than held his own with that glib and eloquent interlocutor. And witness his remarkable interview in 1927 with an American workmen's delegation when he answered questions for four solid hours, questions of great diversity and difficulty. He talked strictly extemporaneously, but with perfect organization of material, of a kind only possible to a man completely sure of himself. The verbatim report, about 11,800 words, comprises one of the most comprehensive and discerning statements of Soviet aims ever made; it was a *tour de force* quite beyond the capacity of any but an exceptionally intelligent man.

When the delegation, thoroughly exhausted, had concluded its queries, Stalin asked if *he* might ask questions about America—and he did so for two hours more. His questions were penetrating and showed considerable knowledge of American conditions; Stalin, single-handed, answered the delegation's questions much better than they replied to him. During this six solid hours of talk, the telephone did not ring once; no secretary was allowed to interrupt—another indication of Stalin's habit of utter concentration on the job in hand.

Again, there is the very important factor of ruthlessness. He is extravagantly ruthless. It is stupid or silly to deny this. The Russian Terror was a wholesale punitive assault on a class. Soviet Russia differed from other dictatorships in that it assumed from the beginning the necessity of destruction of class enemies. Stalin did not, at the moment

of crisis, flinch from obliterating several million peasants by literally
starving them to death. All governments, in the last analysis, rule by
force. In Soviet Russia force is applied directly, and with social aims
in view which are intended—by the Communists—to benefit not only
165,000,000 Russians, but the whole human race. The end justifies the
means, in the Soviet view. Stalin is perfectly frank about this. Lady
Astor asked him, "How long are you going to go on killing people?"
Stalin replied, "As long as it is necessary."

A Soviet worthy, absent from the U.S.S.R., was asked his opinion
of Stalin. He replied, "The man is just a little too bloody for me." Rare
burst of indiscretion!

Still another source of power is his early career. Almost alone,
Stalin[2] had the guts to stay and work inside Russia after the collapse
of the revolution of 1905. The other revolutionaries scattered into exile,
and lived, like Lenin, in libraries or coffee houses [abroad] till 1917. Stalin
remained within Russia the whole time. He did the dirty work; he was
"the hall sweeper." Thus he built up an immense acquaintance with
submerged revolutionaries, and was able to transform an underground
organization into his own party structure when he needed it.

Then there is the party and his control of it. The Communist party
is no longer divided on questions of principle, as it was during the
Trotsky episode; no discernible opposition remains; Stalin is absolutely
its boss, its master. Discipline in the party is overwhelmingly severe;
and Stalin controls discipline. Party and state are one, and Stalin, as
Louis Fischer puts it, "controls every wheel and screw of the party
machine."

Note well that Stalin created the importance of the post of party
secretary, not vice versa. Several men were secretaries of the party before
Stalin. One was Bogdanoff, now a nonentity; one was Krestinsky, later
an official in the foreign ministry. Stalin alone saw the advantages to
be accrued from control of the party mechanism; thus, as he packed each
office with his men, friends from underground days, his power grew.

He is not a dictator of the first generation, I have noted, but the
successor to Lenin. His tactics have always been to use Lenin as a stick
to beat opponents with. In his long struggle with Trotsky, Stalin pretended never to put himself forward for his own sake, but only as the
"instrument of Lenin"; he persistently accused Trotsky of "false Leninism," the most heinous sin in Russia, thus doubly confounding him.
No man ever quoted Scripture to better purpose than Stalin quoted
Lenin. Mussolini and Hitler can plead only themselves for justification;
Stalin always had the mighty shadow of Lenin for support.

This leads to another point. The basic strength of the Soviets is that

[2] Cf. *Duranty Reports Russia*, p. 234.

all the outside world is the enemy. Thus the Soviet state, thrown back on itself, is close-knit and self-sufficient. It has its cohesive ideology, the Marx-Lenin dogma, without possibility of deviation. Stalin, representing himself as the authentic voice of dogma, is the mouthpiece not merely of the masses in Russia, but of Russians *vis-à-vis* the hostile world.

Job

Stalin holds no government post, except that since 1934 he has been one of the thirty-seven members of the Presidium of the All-Union Central Executive Committee. This is the keystone of what might be called the Soviet parliament. The cabinet (council of people's commissars) is responsible to it—theoretically. But Stalin is not a cabinet member, not a commissar.

He is no longer "secretary general" of the Communist party, incidentally—as is generally assumed—but is merely one of five theoretically equal party "secretaries," the others being Kaganovitch, Zhdanov, Ezhov, and Andreyev. He is, it goes without saying, one of the nine members of the Politburo, the highest party organ, which controls everything in Russia.

The Central Committee of the party, from which the secretaries and members of the Politburo are drawn, could—in principle—dismiss Stalin. He is theoretically subject to majority decisions of the Central Committee. In practice his dismissal is out of the question, since election of the committee members is absolutely in his hands.

Party and state in Soviet Russia are, I have said, one; but Stalin maintains rigid theoretical separation between party and governmental functions. Lenin was not only head of the party but chairman of the council of people's commissars—prime minister. Stalin has rejected this coalescence. He prefers to remain in the background—the party boss.

Boy of Tiflis

His real name is Yosif (Josef) Visarionovitch Dzhugashvili, and he was born in the town of Gora, near Tiflis, Georgia, in 1879. The legend is that Lenin gave him his nickname, Stalin, which is the Russian word for "steel," as tribute to his iron durability. In reality some anonymous comrade suggested it as an "underground" name way back in 1910 or 1911, long before Lenin knew him well.

Stalin was the son of a cobbler who had been a peasant. The family was miserably poor, probably as poor as Mussolini's, but Josef nevertheless got an education. For four years, from the ages of fifteen to nineteen, he attended the Orthodox Theological Seminary in Tiflis, training, of all things, for the priesthood.

His father, like Hitler's, of blunt imagination, wanted him to follow the parental vocation. But Stalin's mother—apparently, like Hitler's, an exceptional woman—refused to have him become a cobbler. She insisted that Josef go to school. It is commonly thought that Stalin was expelled from the seminary for Marxist activities. This may not be so. One story is that his mother withdrew him after four years because privation had hurt his health.

H. R. Knickerbocker has interviewed this old Georgian mother of Stalin's, Ekaterina Dzhugashvili, who speaks hardly a word of Russian. She said that "Soso," as she called him, had been quite "a good boy" and she seemed quite bewildered at his immense success. Stalin fetched her to Moscow some years ago. She spent an unhappy month in the Kremlin, puzzled, so the story went, at her boy's prominence, because she could not discover what it was he "did" to earn a living! Then she retreated to the Tiflis hills, morose, content.

Georgians are not Russians. Even today Stalin speaks Russian with a hint of Georgian accent. The Georgian language not only differs from Russian as much, say, as English differs from Portuguese; even the alphabets are dissimilar. The Georgians are a southern race of complex Caucasian blood; they are mountaineers, with the primitive defensive instincts of the frontiersman; tenacity, temper, are ingrained in their physiognomy; like Armenians, they have their own proud national history; they have purple-black hair, and eyes black as midnight.

Stalin's motivation to revolution came first from poverty, second from his experiences in the seminary. He detested authority as it was voiced by the cunning, dogmatic priests, who combined parochial intolerance with the backwardness of the provincial Orthodox church. The years in the seminary were crucially important in the formative period of Stalin's life. He left the seminary, met Marxist friends—and his long revolutionary career began.

Those submerged nineteen years, from 1898 to 1917, were years of incessant, overwhelming labor, always to the same end—revolution; of patient, tenacious establishment of an organization; of pain, cruelty, persecution, arrest. Both Hitler and Mussolini have seen the inside of jails. But Stalin was much more real a jailbird. Five times he was caught by the Tsar's police, five times exiled. Four times, a veritable Houdini, he escaped; the 1917 revolution liberated him from the fifth imprisonment, when he was incarcerated above the Arctic Circle.

Stalin was an actual terrorist, personally. The party needed money and undertook a policy of "expropriations," raids on banks which were simon-pure robberies, nothing more, nothing less. As member of the Tiflis party committee he was partly responsible for an outrage in 1907 wherein some twenty persons were killed: his men bombed a shipment of currency, and got away with $75,000. The bloodshed was criticized by Stalin's superiors, and on Lenin's insistence he was expelled from the party for a short period.

He found time—between jail sentences and exile—for much activity of less tumultuous nature. At Baku, on the Caspian Sea, he edited a Bolshevik paper, *Vremia,* in the Georgian language. He went to Stockholm, Cracow, and Prague, to attend party congresses. He had managed to write a book, *Socialism and the National Question,* as early as 1912. He was leader at this time of the Bolshevik section of the social democratic party in the Duma, and an editor of *Pravda,* the party newspaper; then in 1913 he was arrested and sent to his last exile.

All this was preparation. In 1917 real life began. The revolution, overnight, transformed his function—and that of thousands of others—from conspiracy to organization, from insurrections to administration. He was a member of the Politburo from the moment of its creation, on October 10, 1917; other members, besides Lenin, were Trotsky, Zinoviev, Kamenev, Sokolnikov, Bubnov. Also he held two cabinet portfolios when the government was organized: commissar for workers and peasants inspection, and commissar for nationalities.

He was not so active as Trotsky during the civil war period, though he was a member of the revolutionary military committee, and saw service both in the Ukraine and in Petrograd against Yudenitch. In 1921 Lenin, little dreaming what use Stalin would make of it, gave him the secretary-generalship of the party. His main work was then in the sphere of nationalities. As a non-Russian, he was peculiarly fitted for this task. Soviet Russia was a *mélange* of at least one hundred quite separate races and nationalities, and the job was to combine them into a stable unity while conceding some measure of provincial autonomy, at least in spirit. Stalin, under Lenin, invented the idea of the U.S.S.R.—the convenient device by which "independent" and "autonomous" republics became the Soviet "Union," surrendering central authority to Moscow, but retaining local administrative privileges.

Stalin was jealous of Trotsky from the beginning, and they came into conflict early. Duranty records that Stalin, mending a breach in the front, shot a group of officers for inefficiency, and that Trotsky, as supreme War Lord, telegraphed in protest. Stalin scrawled across the telegram, "Pay no attention," and left it to molder in the archives.

Another anecdote of this period shows him in different mood. He was reviewing troops near Petrograd. A sullen soldier refused to salute. Stalin questioned him and the man pointed first to his own feet, wrapped in coarse burlap, soaked in snow and dirt, then at Stalin's substantial boots. Without a word Stalin took his boots off, tossed them to the soldier, insisted on donning the soldier's wet and stinking rags—and continued to wear them till Lenin himself made him resume normal footgear.

Stalin, says Duranty, was picked by Lenin as one of his successors because he knew the Georgian could *endure*. The proverb in those days said, "Lenin trusts Stalin; Stalin trusts no one." Some authorities assert that Lenin and Stalin broke about four months before Lenin's death, because Lenin distrusted his ambition, and thought that Stalin was already intriguing to supersede him. Certainly we have seen that Lenin, in his testament, showed his disapproval of some aspects of Stalin's character. "This cook," he wrote, "will make too hot a stew."

The Georgian began to act the moment that Lenin died. He and Zinoviev carried Lenin's coffin. This was in 1924. It took Stalin just five years to perfect his organization, unmercifully weed out heretical opponents—whom he attacked by accusing them of a deviation from the sacred "party line," which he alone was competent to interpret—and establish himself as undisputed dictator of the U.S.S.R.

The Struggle with Trotsky

Stalin denies (cf. *Leninism*, I, p. 377) that his differences with Trotsky were personal. Nevertheless, personal differences occurred. The two leaders cordially disliked each other. They came from different worlds, and not even the bridge of Marx could link them. Stalin called Trotsky an aristocrat and an actor. And Trotsky *was* an aristocrat, in all save the social sense, i.e., he had brains, he had courage, and he had style. Trotsky called Stalin a boor, treacherous, barbarous, and corrupt.

It is an odd fact that such a *bourgeois* and "trivial" conception as personal hatred, based on the irrationality of passion, should have been an important factor in the history of the Russian revolution. But it was so—though, of course, the personal considerations were buttressed by other factors. Trotsky detested Stalin so heartily that he studiously insulted him in public; for instance, in committee meetings he would ostentatiously pick up a newspaper and begin to read to himself whenever Stalin made a speech.

The difference in their characters was, of course, profound. Stalin, a passionate politician, above all a creature of committees; Trotsky, a lone wolf, a violent individualist, who for twenty years could not bear to shackle himself with allegiance to either the Bolshevisk or Menshevik divisions in the party. Stalin, patient as an icon; Trotsky, vivacious as a satyr. Stalin, immobile, silent, cautious; Trotsky, a lively, frank, and inveterate conversationalist. Stalin, a bomb thrower, literally; Trotsky, horrified by sporadic violence. Stalin, a hardheaded practical wire puller, unyieldingly jealous of his career; Trotsky, lover of the abstract, impulsive, vain. Stalin, a supreme organizer; Trotsky, a bad politician, incapable of compromise, very hard to work with. Observe their smiles. Stalin smiles like a tiger who has just swallowed the canary. Trotsky smiles brightly and spontaneously like a child. Observe their escapes from Siberia. Stalin went about it somberly, efficiently, with methodical coldness; Trotsky—puff!—has disappeared into clear air; he escapes like Ariel.

Above and beyond their personal conflict was divergence in political views of extreme importance. The passion of each came to embody cardinally opposed theories of the operation of the Soviet Union. Trotsky's "Left Opposition" arose out of the doctrine of "permanent revolution." He did not believe, as Stalin did, that socialism could succeed in a single state. He believed that the Marxist regime could maintain itself in Russia only if permanent, progressive revolution took place outside.

The Trotskyists were horrified at the way things went after Lenin's death. They thought that the socialization of the U.S.S.R. was going on far too slowly. They feared that Lenin's tactical and temporary concession to capitalist forces, the N.E.P. (New Economic Policy) would continue indefinitely; they thought that communism in Russia itself, with such meager spoils of victory, would perish without help from proletarian revolutions in the external world.

Stalin took the opposite view. He said, in effect, "You comrades outside cool your heels for a couple of decades, then we'll get around to you." Trotsky said, "Join your Russian comrades in revolution and free yourself from your chains at once." Stalin said, "Russia first. When we get our state in order, then comes your turn." Trotsky said. "The world comes first." Russia, as Stalin saw it, was settling down to the prosaic ardors of married life. But Trotsky, an incorrigible romantic, wanted permanent revolution as a perpetual honeymoon.

Stalin broke Trotsky and his friends by the same method he subsequently employed to break the "Right Opposition" (which thought that the socialization of Russia was going at too *rapid* a pace). He (1) controlled the party machine, (2) his interpretation of Leninism made all his opponents heretics, and therefore punishable.

Stalin's detestation of Trotsky led him to exaggerated meanness in revenge. Yet his extirpation of Trotsky's name from the official records and schoolbooks, so that unborn generations may hardly know his name, is not as complete as one is led to believe. In his *October Revolution,* which is purchasable anywhere in Russia, Stalin pays tribute, albeit grudgingly, to his enemy. "Let us admit this, it is impossible to deny that Comrade Trotsky fought well at the time of October" (p. 72).

Stalin hated Trotsky partly, in the complicated way of human beings, because he, Stalin, owed him so much: he stole part of his program. Trotsky advocated super-industrialization in the manner of the Five-

Year Plan as far back as 1921, and he wanted to expel the kulaks (rich farmers) in 1925, a task which Stalin did not set himself till almost five years later. But that was the trouble. Trotsky, impulsive, demanded these things prematurely, at the wrong time; Stalin had the strength to wait.

And Trotsky never seemed to realize that when Stalin said he could build socialism in a single country, the country was *Russia*, which is not a country at all—but a continent. Nor did it occur to Trotsky apparently that far and away the best single advertisement for world communism, in the future, would be a Russia which was successful, stable, safe.

The Iron Will of Stalin

Of course there was a famine. None can deny this any longer. It occurred in the spring of 1933, in the great grain-producing areas of the U.S.S.R., the North Caucasus and Ukraine. Communists, after preliminary hesitancy, now admit the fact of the famine, though in circumlocutory jargon. For instance, Miss Anna Louise Strong writes (*New Republic*, August 7, 1935), "There was a serious grain shortage in the 1932 harvest due chiefly to inefficiencies of the organizational period of the new large-scale mechanized farming among peasants unaccustomed to machines." This is quite a mouthful—a mouthful that the peasants didn't get.

The chief point about the famine is not—it might be said—that several million people died. Chamberlin puts the mortality as high as five or six million. The point is that the Soviet government was engaged in a tremendous, epochal struggle to socialize the land, for what they claimed to be the eventual good of the peasants; the peasants, however, resisted and—terribly enough—suffered. To balk the government, they refused to harvest grain. Therefore they did not have enough to eat. And died.

The real story of the famine is briefly this. The Five-Year Plan included "collectivization" of the peasantry. Russia, overwhelmingly an agrarian country, contained in 1927 almost 25,000,000 peasant holdings; Stalin's plan was to unite them into socialized collective farms. The peasants would turn over implements and livestock to a farm manager, and work in common on comparatively large rather than very small holdings, assisted by tractors furnished by the state. This was the idea. On it, the future of socialism in the U.S.S.R. depended.

What happened was that the peasants, bitterly indignant, staged two major resistances to the immense forcible process of collectivization. First, they slaughtered their livestock, rather than turn it over to the collectives. It was an extraordinary and tragic event—though not so

tragic as the human starvation later. There was no organization among
the peasants, no communication; yet in hundreds of villages, separated
by hundreds of miles, a *simultaneous* destruction of animals began.
Rather than turn over their precious pigs, sheep, cattle, to the collective
authorities, the peasants murdered them.

The cost was terrible. Stalin—four years late—admitted it. The agrarian economy of the Soviet Union suffered a blow from which it cannot
fully recover till about 1940; it will take till then to replenish the slaughtered stock. For, once the killing began, it progressed till about 50 *percent* of the animals in the Soviet Union were killed. Official figures
admit that the number of horses in the country diminished from 33,-
500,000 in 1928 to 19,600,000 in 1932; the number of cattle from
70,500,000 to 40,700,000; sheep and goats from 146,700,000 to 52,-
100,000; pigs from 25,900,000 to 11,600,000.[3]

The peasants, stunned by this catastrophe, sank into temporary
stupor. The government—when the worst of the damage was done—
retreated hastily. Probably Stalin had not realized the formidable extent
of the slaughter until it was too late. . . . The tempo of collectivization
had been far too rapid. The plan called for full collectivization only after
ten years, but within two years, in 1930, 65 percent of all the farms
had been collectivized. So the pace was toned down.

Even so, in 1932, the peasants, stiffening into a final vain protest,
rebelled again. As if by underground agreement, another psychic epidemic spread through the rich fields of the Caucasus and Ukraine. The
farmers, those still outside the collectives, were paid miserable prices;
either they could buy no manufactured goods at all, or goods only of
indifferent quality. They hit on a plan. They had sowed the crop, which
was abundant; but they decided not to harvest all of it. They harvested
exactly what they calculated they would themselves need during the winter, and left the rest to rot. "What was the use of slaving to produce a
handsome crop, if the state simply seized it all?"

This was, of course, mutiny. It was not only defiance of Stalin; it
was a threat to starve him into submission. The Soviet government
needed grain to distribute to the industrial regions, the great cities; it
needed grain for export, to pay for the machinery it had to import for
the Five-Year Plan.

Even the farmers already in the collectives let their grain rot. There
were few Communist overseers, few trained and loyal farm managers.
Word got to Moscow that the harvest, which should have been handsome, was largely lost. Stalin saw that this was a major crisis. If the
peasants were permitted to get away with this, the revolution was beaten.

[3] Premier Molotov's speech at the 1934 party congress. (Cf. *Socialism Victorious*,
p. 394.)

"Obsolete classes don't voluntarily disappear," he told Wells.) He had to act. And he acted.

Government grain collectors descended on the farms, tall with weeds, and seized that small share of the crop that the peasants had saved *for their own use!* One by one, they visited every holding, and took every lick of grain due the government in taxes. If a man's normal crop was, say, sixty bushels, the tax might be twenty bushels. But the farmer had only harvested, say, twenty-five bushels. So when the government took twenty, the farmer and his family had only five—instead of twenty-five —to live on the whole winter and spring.

Russian economy is still extremely primitive. The question of grain, of bread, is a matter of life and death. When there was no grain left, the people began to die. The government might have diverted some grain from the cities—though that was a pinched, hungry year everywhere— to feed the peasants. But the government did not do so. Stalin decided that the peasants must pay the penalty for their rebellion. They had re- fused, blindly, stupidly, to provide grain; very well, let them starve. And they starved.

Meantime, the kulaks had been liquidated by a more direct process. These were peasants of more than average industry or ability or wealth: the capitalist farmers, "class enemies on the agrarian front." In 1928 there were 750,000 people officially classed as kulaks in the Soviet Union. Today there are none. They were rooted out like trees, packed into prison trains, dispatched to labor camps in far parts of the country, put to forced labor on building railways, digging canals.

The famine broke the back of peasant resistance in the U.S.S.R. Since the famine collectivization has proceeded slowly but steadily. From 1930 to 1935 another 25 percent of the land was socialized. All but a small fraction of the best arable land in Russia is now organized into about 250,000 farms. The peasants tried to revolt. The revolt might have brought the Soviet Union down. But it collapsed on the iron will of Stalin. The peasants killed their animals, then they killed themselves.

Private Life

Stalin lives, as is well known, in the Kremlin when he is in Moscow. The Kremlin is not a building, but a compound, a walled fortress, con- taining forty or fifty buildings, churches, barracks, gardens. Stalin lives in three rooms. He does not, however, as is generally believed, *work* in the Kremlin. The legend that Stalin, a virtual prisoner, stays always within Kremlin walls is without much foundation. For a long time he worked daily outside the Kremlin, in the building of the central com- mittee of the party, on Staraya Ploshad, in the busiest part of Moscow.

Also he spends much time in the country, at his *datcha*, or country villa. This is about an hour from Moscow, in the region of Usova Arkangelskaya, near the Moskva River. The house belonged to a former millionaire, a gold miner and merchant, who had a persecution complex and therefore surrounded the ten-acre estate with a heavy wall. Stalin has a good, healthy persecution complex himself. He has not torn down the wall.

The region of the *datcha* is, indeed, heavily guarded, and so is the Moscow road leading to it. Stalin usually drives there in an entourage of three cars, Packards, going very fast; he sits as a rule with the chauffeur, and the position of his car in the procession is changed daily. Picknickers and sightseers in the vicinity are told to move on.

Yet Stalin is not, on the whole, so drastically guarded as Hitler or Mussolini. He exposes himself a good deal more than they do. He has several times been seen returning to the Kremlin from the opera on foot, walking with friends through the crowded square. And at least twice a year, on May 1 and November 7, the two great Soviet holidays, Stalin stands on the tomb of Lenin and literally several million people pass him at a range of about thirty yards.

Stalin's usual routine is to work hard for about a week or longer, then go to the *datcha* for two or three days to rest. He has few relaxations, but he likes opera and ballet, and attends the Bolshoi Theater often; sometimes a movie catches his fancy, and he saw *Chapayev*, a film of the civil wars, four times. He reads a great deal, and plays chess occasionally. He smokes incessantly, and always a pipe; the gossip in Moscow is that he likes Edgeworth tobacco, but is a little hesitant to smoke publicly this non-Soviet product. He is fond of alcohol, especially brandy, and holds his liquor well.

His attitude to sex is quite normal and healthy. He has married twice. He is supposed now to be living with the sister of Kaganovitch, his first assistant. He is rather naïve, apparently. One evening, dropping in to see his friend Karl Radek, he noted on the table a volume by a German named Fuchs, called *Sitten Geschichte* (*History of Morals*), a pseudo-scientific picture book. Stalin turned the pages idly, and saw one of the more fantastic illustrations. He turned to his friend: "Tell me, Radek: do people really do this sort of thing?"

Records of his first wife are lost in the mists of pre-revolutionary days. She died of pneumonia in 1917. In those days love was more or less an instrument of the class war; the old Bolsheviks paid little attention to the forms of marriage. By this first wife, Stalin had a son, now about twenty-five. He has not turned out well. He did badly at technical school—the rumor has it that he spent most of his time playing billiards with a classmate, the son of Menzhinsky, late head of the G.P.U.—and Stalin, annoyed, packed him off to work in a factory in Tiflis.

In 1919 Stalin dropped in to see an old revolutionary friend in Leningrad, Sergei Alliluiev (the name means Hallelujah), a locksmith. He met his daughter, the seventeen-year-old Nadyezhda (Nadya), and married her. By her he had two children, a boy, Vassily, now fourteen, and a girl, Svetlana, twelve. Mrs. Stalin entered the promakademia, or school for industrial arts, in 1929, studying the manufacture of artificial silk. There was no publicity attached to this; she worked like anyone else, and even battled her way into the ordinary streetcars, instead of using a Kremlin Packard. Her ambition was to become head of the rayon trust.

On November 8, 1932, in seemingly mysterious circumstances, Nadyezhda Alliluiev Stalin died suddenly. She had been seen, apparently in normal health, at the Opera only a few days before. The news of her death was announced without elaboration, and she was buried (not, curiously enough, cremated) in the churchyard of the Convent of New Virgins.

Reports were quick to spread that she tasted all food prepared for Stalin and had been poisoned. But the facts seem to be that she had been having acute intestinal pains for several days, and had neglected them. She did not wish to trouble her husband with what she thought was a minor ailment. Probably she was somewhat afraid of him. . . . She sought to hide her pain, to keep up the tough spirit of the Bolsheviks. The ailment was appendicitis, and by the time she admitted she was ill it was too late, and she died of peritonitis.

Stalin's relation to his younger children is quite paternal, but he has taken pains to see that in school they are treated exactly as other children. He has never visited the school, which is one of three model schools in Russia; it is called School No. 25, and is on Pimenovsky Street, just off Tverskaya. The boy had seven fairs, five goods, on his last report card; no very goods or excellents. His best subject was literature.

Money, Attitudes, Friends

Stalin's salary is about 1,000 rubles per month, or about $200. He is completely uninterested in money. Like all the Soviet leaders he is a poor man; no financial scandal has ever touched any of them. Salaries of Communists are adjusted by category, this system having replaced the former rule whereby no man in the party could earn more than 225 rubles per month. There is no upward limit; the average is 600. No Communist may accept a salary for more than one post, no matter how many he holds; and no member of the party is allowed in theory at least to retain royalties from books.

On the other hand, Stalin could, like the Tsars, eat off gold plate if he so wished. There is no wealth in all of Russia that he could not have, if he wanted it. He lives modestly, but his *datcha* is the Soviet equivalent of the country home of an American millionaire. He has servants, motorcars, books.

His attitude toward conventional religion is purely negative. His religion, like that of all the dictators, is his work; communism is enough faith for him. Stalin has said, "The party cannot be neutral toward religion, because religion is something opposite to science." Nevertheless, it is noteworthy that he permitted his wife an almost orthodox religious burial. He is the only dictator who may be said thoroughly to have read the Bible; he did so, of course, in his seminary days.

He has few friends. Voroshilov and Kaganovitch are the two closest. He is on thee-and-thou footing with old colleagues in the party, but it is hard to address him intimately because there is no ordinary diminutive for Yosif, his Christian name. People who know him well call him "Yosif Visarionovitch"; others simply say *Tovarish* (Comrade) Stalin. He has no title.

He seldom sees outsiders. William C. Bullitt, the American ambassador, dined with him once. Until Bullitt arrived in Moscow, Stalin had never received a foreign diplomat; even Lord Chilston, the British ambassador, had not met him until Anthony Eden's visit in the spring of 1933. Retiring, uncommunicative, in twenty years he has seen only seven journalists—two Germans, two Japanese, three Americans—for formal interviews.

He "received" Bullitt in typical and indirect fashion. Voroshilov had arranged a dinner party, and Stalin simply dropped in. He was cheery and cordial, toasted everybody around the table, talked with great intelligence and knowledge of America, and relaxed, smoking his pipe, while the commissars sat at piano, singing songs almost like brothers in a fraternity.

Lately Stalin has given evidence that he may come out of his shell. He visited the new subway unannounced; he spoke over the radio recently for the first time; he has even kissed babies—final concession to popularity—in the Culture Park. When he received Eden, Laval, and Beneš in the spring and summer of 1935, he jointly signed the *communiqués* with Molotov, which was unprecedented.

Also, Stalin has taken a new tack lately, as the champion of men as men—even nonparty men—provided they follow *his* line. In May, 1935, he denounced the "heartless bureaucracy" and said that "first of all we must learn to value *people*, to value cadres, to value every worker capable of benefiting our common cause. It is time to realize that of all the valuable capital the world possesses, the most valuable and decisive is people."

But this concession to humanity came very late, after terrible struggles, terrible sacrifices. If Stalin can relax now and search for human values, well and good. But his historical mission was quite different. Stalin is the man who took over the Russian revolution and made it work. Human values disappeared. He is the creator of the "Iron Age," the director of the Five-Year Plan, the man who, by ruthlessly industrializing Russia, made the beginnings of socialism possible in a single state.

~~~~~~

When I wrote this estimate of Stalin in 1935 his great years had scarcely begun. He had been in indisputable power in the Soviet Union for a decade, but his years after 1935 were much more important to Russia and the world than those before. Rereading my text I note that I say that "the basic strength of the Soviets is that all the outside world is the enemy." I meant bourgeois world of course. This concept still plays a role in Soviet policy that is sometimes neglected, and is a clue to much. I also say that Russian agriculture under Stalin endured a blow from which "it could not fully recover until about 1940." It hasn't fully recovered yet.

I see that, in a period when many liberal writers were softheaded about Stalin, I give considerable emphasis to his brutality. Perhaps I handled him too gently in some respects, but at least I did not minimize his ruthlessness or neglect to tell the story of the famine and the mass murder of the kulaks. After I wrote my chapter came the period of real blight and terror—the era of the great purges, murderous treason trials, and unmitigated black oppression and rule by fright. No one knew it at the time, but in one brief period (1936-1938) when the terror reached its grisly peak, fifty-five of the seventy-one members of the Central Committee of the party disappeared, and no fewer than six out of fourteen members of the Politburo—the supreme ruling body of the party—were shot.

Everybody knows the story of World War II—how Stalin was double-crossed by Hitler, how the Russians almost lost Leningrad and Moscow, how they defended Stalingrad, and how they finally turned the tables and chased the Nazi invaders out of Russia. More than this, the victorious Red Army swept through the Balkans, reached Belgrade, Vienna, and Berlin, and met the advancing Americans on the Elbe. After the war Stalin conferred with President Roosevelt and Mr. Churchill at Yalta to work out details for the peace to come after victory against Japan. The arrangements made at Yalta represented probably the greatest triumph in Stalin's life, although Roosevelt and Churchill did not mean this to be so. What Stalin got, as events turned out, was a virtually free hand in Eastern Europe which enabled him to build up the Communist regimes which now rule East Germany, Poland, Hungary, and the other European satellites.

It is the fashion to criticize Stalin these days and minimize his achievements, but in some respects these bordered on the colossal. As I say in the text above, he was the man who took over the Russian Revolution and made it work. He made Russia a success. He put through the Five-Year Plans, made industrialization possible, vastly increased Soviet military and technological strength, and, with a mighty concentration of will and an utterly ruthless imposition of his will on the body of the largest nation on earth, made it the second most powerful country in the world. It is also necessary to point out that Stalin was probably responsible for more human misery and more deaths than any man in history, with the possible exception of Adolf Hitler and Genghis Khan.

Part Two

~~~~~~

THREE PORTRAITS IN
MINIATURE

CHAPTER 4

≈≈≈≈≈

Captain Eden, Lord Privy Seal

This article was written for Vanity Fair, *a magazine now unfortunately extinct, and it appeared there in June, 1935.*

≈≈≈≈≈≈≈≈≈≈≈≈≈≈≈≈≈≈≈≈≈≈≈≈≈≈≈≈≈≈≈

No ONE UNDERSTANDS the British, not even the British themselves. The country is a thicket of stylistic difficulties. It is funny, yes, when some French or German newspaper calls Sir John Simon, the Foreign Secretary, "Sir Simon." The ritual of English names and titles is bewildering. It is incomprehensible, even to many British, let alone a continental visitor, that the King's son, the Duke of Kent, only became a peer on the occasion of his recent marriage, that a peeress like Lady Astor sits in the House of Commons, and that Mr. Anthony Eden, the lord privy seal, is—a commoner.

The Rt. Hon. Capt. Anthony Eden, M.P., P.C., aged thirty-seven, the best-looking and best-dressed diplomat in Europe, is Not-So-Simple-Simon's assistant in the realm of foreign affairs. As lord privy seal Eden is a sort of minister without portfolio. Be it noted, however—another idiosyncratic confusion—that he is not yet in the cabinet, although traditionally the lord privy seal is a high-ranking cabinet member.

Not so long ago Eden completed a tour of Berlin, Moscow, Warsaw, and Prague, an emissary-at-large for the British government, and did the job brilliantly, though illness stopped him at the end. "Thank goodness," I heard it said in London, "that we sent Simon to Berlin, Eden to Moscow." Because the frigid and unpopular Simon was just the person to throw cold water on Hitler, whereas Eden, with his plausibility and charm, was just the person to shake hands, after all these years, with Stalin.

Robert Anthony Eden was born in June, 1897, the second son of a "county" baronet. He went to Eton and Christ Church, Oxford, thus charting a course of perfect orthodoxy. The war came, and, at the ripe old age of eighteen, he joined up, emerging as a captain and wearing the Military Cross. He and Hitler discovered in Berlin that they had faced each other on the same segment of battlefront. Returning to Oxford, Eden began to show his talent for the unusual; he took first-class honors in as dubious and unorthdox a subject as Oriental languages. "Unexpected fellow!" a friend of his exclaimed when I asked what the languages were. "Known Anthony ten years, never knew till this minute he had done any Oriental languages at all."

In 1923 Eden married the eighteen-year-old daughter of Sir Gervase Beckett, and promptly encountered a typical enough politico-personal "county" confusion. He had decided to enter politics, and was adopted as a Conservative candidate in the constituency of Warwick. Only a genealogist could get the details straight, but the labor candidate opposing him was a lady, the Countess of Warwick, who was both his sister's mother-in-law and his wife's stepmother's sister. Incidentally, just to show the occasionally strange ramifications of county families, Eden's brother-in-law, the husband of his wife's sister, is London correspondent of the *Berliner Tageblatt*, an amiable German.

Eden entered Parliament, having vanquished the lady who was so complicatedly related to him, and his rise thereafter was phenomenal.

He made an exploratory trip to Canada, New Zealand, and Australia, in 1925, writing a series of articles for the *Yorkshire Post* which later were assembled in an excellent little book, *Places in the Sun*. His journalism showed brains and common sense, plenty of hard statistical digging and a graceful style. Settling down in the House, Eden specialized in foreign affairs. He gained attention quickly. The prime minister, then Stanley Baldwin, himself wrote a foreword for his book, and in 1926 he became parliamentary private secretary to Sir Austen Chamberlain, the foreign secretary. This was partly because of Baldwin's friendship, partly because the Conservative backbenchers were demanding jobs for their young men.

In 1931, he was named parliamentary under-secretary to the Foreign Office, in which position he was virtually disarmament minister, or minister to the League, because he began going to Geneva regularly, and came to be trusted with most of the tiresome and difficult disarmament negotiations. Whenever a big coup was ready, Simon, who had become foreign secretary, flew to Geneva to superintend it and the reap the kudos. Eden stayed and did the work. He became immensely popular at Geneva; he liked the League and believed in it. Finally, in 1934, when London-plus-Geneva was too much work for one man, the duties of the foreign office were more or less divided, and Eden became lord privy seal.

It doesn't matter a tinker's dam that Anthony Eden's trousers are the best-pressed in all Mayfair. What really matters is that this young man is possessed of two great qualities, charm and real intelligence. One might think, from his background, that he was the perfect type of dumb British man-about-politics. Good family; war service; handsome wife; two sturdy boys; comfortable private means; impeccable clothes; conventional good looks—everything would seem to point to an entirely standardized character.

The discriminating among outsiders first grasped his quality when, in 1929, he spoke in defense of the Anglo-French naval compromise. He followed Chamberlain, who was vacuous in the extreme, and talked to an almost empty House; but the speech, delivered extemporaneously, was one of the most subtle and trenchant expositions of a difficult subject that the Commons had ever heard from so young a member. People began to note his charm when, last year, he reported on a mission of investigation in Berlin. Winston Churchill rose to heckle him with congratulatory but skeptical wit. First, Eden crossed his long legs and looked at the ceiling. Second, he tried to conceal a modest yawn. Third, as Churchill's banter continued, he blushed like a baby; his cheeks turned flaming red; he boiled in embarrassment at being praised.

Plenty of young men have Eden's background; a good many have his tact and charm; a few may be as intelligent. What else accounts for his precocious and meteoric rise? For one thing, he has an infinite capacity to make people like him. He is one of those perfectly balanced men, honest and disinterested, whom it is almost impossible to dislike. Among journalists at Geneva he was called "Lord Eyelash," but he is the most popular Englishman who ever came to the League. In the Foreign Office, which adores him, no one ever thinks of calling him anything but Anthony.

Two events recently revived the moribund League of Nations to considerable prestige and power. One was the decision to send an international army to the Saar for supervision of the plebiscite [January, 1934]. The other was the settlement of the Hungaro-Yugoslav dispute which threatened Europe with an ugly crisis in December. The architect, in each case, was Eden. He terrified the British cabinet by insisting that British troops be sent to the Saar, against the vociferous protests of the isolationist press; and he was right, because this step, far from being unpopular, turned out to be a cardinal achievement of the National Government. He wheedled, coddled, cozened the Hungarians and Yugoslavs into agreement on an almost insoluble issue, a task something like putting Goering and Trotsky together and making them kiss.

In March, 1935, Eden set out on his flying tour to Moscow. He was the first British minister to enter Russia since the revolution in 1917. The job called for the maximum of tact, resilience, and negotiating power. The Soviets have been deeply suspicious of British policy, and the British conservatives, whom Eden represents, thought Stalin and his friends were poison. Eden and Stalin began a conversation both cordial and pointed, and Stalin asked Eden if he thought the danger of war in 1935 was as great as it had been before 1914. Eden said No. Stalin thought Yes. They began to argue. At the end, they signed a joint communiqué of great historical importance, pointing out that there is no conflict of interest between their respective countries, and recognizing that the "integrity and prosperity" of each are to the advantage of the other.

Eden returned to Warsaw and there met that complicated and inscrutable old villain, Pilsudski of Poland. Their talk was brief, because Pilsudski is too old for sustained mental effort. He patted Eden on the back, called him a nice young fellow, congratulated him on his precocity, and told him to come back someday.

Journeying further, Eden saw Dr. Beneš, the pertinacious Czechoslovak foreign minister, in Prague. They saw eye to eye on the necessity of collective security in Europe. Returning to London by air, Eden and his entourage encountered a violent storm over Germany, and the lord privy seal was violently ill. When the plane stopped at Cologne, he was unable to rise from his seat for about five minutes. Then he pulled himself together, left the plane to get a breath of air, and insisted on going on. The pilot refused. When Eden arrived in London the next day, he was sent to bed for a month, suffering from heart strain, but the illness is not expected to be permanent or serious.

The trouble with Eden is his job, especially if he becomes foreign minister. The British are confronted with the same dilemma as in 1914, and seem to be facing it with similar equivocation. Eden may have a policy, but Britain is bigger than he is, and British policy is always to walk the fence, play both ends against the middle. Haldane went to Berlin in 1912 on just such a mission as Simon's; Hitler has proclaimed air parity with Britain just as the Kaiser sought to assert naval parity. Fearful of joining France and Soviet Russia in an outright alliance against Germany, the British are temporizing and compromising, just as they did in 1914. The danger is that Hitler, like Bethmann-Hollweg, may be deceived into believing that the British *could* afford to remain neutral in the event of war.

At thirty-seven, Eden is lord privy seal, and the most popular and promising politician in England. The quickness of his rise has its dangers. Britain has a certain quaint tendency to venerate senility in politics, as in literature, and there is a tradition that no man becomes foreign minister until he has filled other cabinet posts and is sixty at least. Eden may spend twenty years getting old enough to be respectable. On the other hand, the present National Government is breaking up, and will reconstruct itself after the Jubilee, perhaps in June.

If another job is found for the glacial Simon, Eden is a certain candidate for foreign secretary, despite his tender years. He is the coming man. And the prophets have it that he is almost sure to become prime minister someday in the future, if his luck, his health, and the British Isles themselves hold out.

~~~~~~

It took exactly twenty years for this prophecy to be fulfilled. Mr. Eden (now Lord Avon) became prime minister in April, 1955, in succession to Winston Churchill. His tenure at 10 Downing Street was brief and tragic. Both illness and his catastrophic miscalculation over Suez cut him down. The Suez crisis came to a climax in October, 1956. Colonel Nasser, the Egyptian leader, had nationalized the Suez Canal and the indignant British, French, and Israelis embarked on military action to take it back. The invasion had to be called off in midstream because of the fierce emotions aroused in the United States and the United Nations; public opinion would not countenance such a flagrant adventure. Eden bore the brunt of disapprobation in England, and his carreer was wrecked.

Two things symbolized Mr. Eden and provided his basic sources of power during the thirties, when I wrote this piece—he stood for peace but he would not appease. His idealism was what counted. He became foreign minister in 1935 if only because his prestige was such that no government of the day, no matter how slipshod, could afford not to include him. In 1938 he had the courage to resign as foreign minister in protest at Neville Chamberlain's vacillation toward the dictators, but he was summoned back to office—as dominions secretary—when World War II broke out in 1939, and he returned to the foreign office the next year.

I met Eden first at a small stag dinner given by the late Captain Victor Cazalet, M.P., at the Hotel Dorchester, London, on September 13, 1939. Harold Nicolson, Alfred Duff Cooper, and several American journalists were the other guests. Eden's air was at once devil-may-care, languid, rollicking, and shy. I remember my surprise at one small detail. The cocktail he asked for was something called a White Lady, a drink I had never seen before nor seen since. He looked tired, but his eyes danced. Though his manner carried a curiously vague and I-don't-want-to-be-bothered note his ideas were sound and solid with challenge. The war was scarcely ten days old, but what he talked about most was how to solve the German problem, the root problem of all Europe, after the war. There was no faintest doubt expressed about winning the war. And he said that the old League of Nations had failed chiefly because nobody would sacrifice sufficient sovereignty and that the new League, which must surely come into being if the world was to survive, had to have teeth in it and should be based on a federal concept.

During the war years and later I met Eden several times. I interviewed him during the Blitz. High office and the strain of events widened his shoulders. Once at a weekend party near Oxford I heard him tell anecdotes about "Uncle Joe"—Stalin—and this was an exhilarating experience. I saw him last in Barbados in the West Indies in February, 1964, where he was staying with his great friends Ronald and Marietta Tree. Eden (he had suffered grave illness) was frail but alert, graceful, incomparably distinguished, and passionately eager to be in the know of things. Another guest was the Hon. Errol W. Barrow, the premier of Barbados. Mr. Barrow, a Negro thirty years younger, had been an R.A.F. pilot during the war when Eden was foreign minister, and I had the feeling that Eden, out of the swim now, wanted just as much to be part of the new world represented by Mr. Barrow as Barrow had once wanted to be part of his world and the struggle to save Europe from Hitler.

I do not know how I managed it but I see rereading my Vanity Fair *sketch that I refrained from pointing out that a lord privy seal in England is not necessarily a lord, a privy, or a seal.*

CHAPTER 5

〰〰

The Bucharest Du Barry

This article about Madame Lupescu also appeared in Vanity Fair *(July, 1934). It was reprinted almost thirty years later in* Vanity Fair, *an anthology published by the Viking Press. At the time I wrote it Rumania was an extravagantly giddy country full of romantic hi-jinks, plots, and counterplots. But eventually this Graustark had to get down to harsh facts and figures.*

〰〰〰〰〰〰〰〰〰〰〰〰〰〰〰〰〰〰〰〰〰〰

THEY SAY IN BUCHAREST, those who know (and in Bucharest there are plenty who know), that old Papa Lupescu came to his daughter Magda some months ago, walking the hundred yards that separate his automobile accessories shop from the royal palace, and proceeded to lecture her smartly. There was scandal in Bucharest. The amorous court was being amorous again. King Carol had settled, as it were, down. But his younger brother Nicholas was acting up. Nicholas was about to commit marriage with a girl not exactly regal. "Daughter, daughter!" old Lupescu scolded, "What kind of a family are you getting mixed into!"

Indeed, the point might be made that Magda Lupescu, the King's Favorite, is the most respectable person in Rumania. She lives in a country monstrously corrupt and monstrously licentious, but her fidelity to King Carol, a scamp, is notorious. She sins in the flesh but shines in the spirit; she is loyal, she is discreet, and she has character. Being a King's Favorite is one of the most conspicuous of jobs, and inside Rumania she fills it unostentatiously. She is the most famous female in the kingdom, but probably not twenty people outside her immediate circle have ever seen her.

Magda Lupescu is a striking anachronism. Kings are dull folk these days. Royal mistresses, like court jesters, have practically been driven from the field by the cruel rationalizations of the twentieth century. Magda Lupescu is a last, but not forlorn, survivor. Yet, conservatively speaking, there must be about 100,000,000 women in the world today who cherish the secret, perilous wish to be mistress to a king.

Louise de La Vallière was the daughter of an officer; Magda Lupescu of a Jewish junk dealer. Nell Gwynn sold oranges in Drury Lane; Lupescu frequented that most inveterately Balkan of hotels, the Athena Palace of Bucharest. Lola Montez was born in Limerick, Ireland, went to Spain and India, and was the mistress of Mad King Ludwig of Bavaria; Lupescu's stage has been smaller, but she picked a king who isn't, for all his peccadillos, crazy. Her mileage is good. Montez lasted a year as King's Mistress; Du Barry five years; La Vallière seven years. Lupescu has been with Carol since 1924.

She met him, so the gossips say, by a pleasant bit of trickery. She knew that he was returning to Bucharest one fine evening after dinner in Sinaia, and she contrived to ambush him along the lonely mountain road. She planted herself there, tore off some of her clothes, let down her red hair, and staggered into the searchlights of his car. He lurched to a stop, "rescued" her, and carried her back to Bucharest and destiny.

Her flaming hair and vigorous good looks burst for the first time in the tabloids of the world a year later, when Carol "abdicated." It has been said that he gave up his crown for her, but this is not exactly true. Carol was the victim of a frame-up, and the comely person of Lupescu was no more than a lever in the hands of his enemies, the Bratianu brothers, who really ruled Rumania. They were out to "get" Carol, the unruly crown prince. They did. Carol was shipped out of the country to attend the funeral in London of Dowager Queen Alexandra, in 1925, and he took Lupescu with him. Reaching Milan on his return, he found messages from the Bratianus to come back to Rumania at once, without his mistress, or forfeit the crown. Carol had been victimized in other matters by the Bratianus and he lost his temper, telegraphing them to go to hell. The Bratianus persuaded King Ferdinand and Queen Marie, Carol's parents, to accept the renunciation at its face value; Carol was instantly disinherited, his royal honors removed, and the "abdication" accepted. Thus began the five years of his exile, during which Lupescu never once left his side.

They lived first at Neuilly, near Paris, and then on the Riviera. They did not have much money. Newspapermen have seen Lupescu on the back porch of a modest villa, doing the family washing. Her hold on Carol grew. She made him forget his first wife, Zizi Lambrino, and his second, Helene of Greece; she made him remember, when Ferdinand died and his son Michael took the throne, that he was still King of Rumania. When Carol flew back to Bucharest in June, 1930, and grabbed the crown from Michael's head, she followed him in a week or two—smuggled across the frontier in a black wig.

The situation was piquant. Queen Helene had divorced Carol in exile. He made her tentative offers of reconciliation, because he wanted a coronation, and he could not be crowned without a queen. Helene would accept only if Carol promised to give up Lupescu. This he resolutely refused to do. Irritated at Helene, he presently removed her from the country, and Lupescu became the queen in everything but name. Ever since, she has been the virtual ruler of Rumania.

Lupescu was installed in a comfortable villa on the outskirts of town. Officially, Carol could not be seen with her. So a sort of double court grew up; inside the regular circle Carol and Lupescu founded an inner camarilla. Carol spent less and less time in the official court. He could not bear to be separated from Lupescu. Soon the double domicile in Bucharest became a nuisance, and he came to prefer residence in Sinaia, the summer capital. In Bucharest he was hemmed in by whispers and whisperers; in Sinaia, a lovely mountain village a couple of hours from Bucharest, he created a sort of private Zenda all his own. Carol spends most of his time in Sinaia now. Sinaia became the headquarters of the Lupescu clique.

Lupescu is practically an ideal mistress. She has no desire to marry Carol. She could, if she wanted to, at the snap of a finger; but she knows full well that this might mean the end of the dynasty. She is not avaricious, and he has never given her more than normal gifts. She lets him play around—a bit—when he wants to. She has not burdened him with children (and Madame de Montespan, be it remembered, inflicted on Louis XIV no fewer than seven). She is a sensible adviser on politics. Her influence on him is enormous. Politics may, however, be her doom, and if she falls Carol may fall with her.

People say freely in Bucharest that Michael will again be king before Carol dies—that it would not be utterly surprising if Carol should skip, if things get too hot, again in Lupescu's company. It takes a lot of dreary work to be a king, even in Rumania. Ciro's and Chantilly were ever so much more fun. Lupescu may prefer ironing shirts to ironing out the incessant contradictions of Rumanian domestic politics. Not that she would need to do the washing nowadays. If Carol hasn't saved something from his pretty civil list, all Rumania's a fool.

But more likely than voluntary departure is the possibility—still remote—that Carol may be kicked out, and largely on Lupescu's account. In February, 1933, the battle against Lupescu reached its first climax. The Jesuit Transylvanian leader, Julius Maniu, was prime minister at the time, and he demanded the dismissal from office of two men high in the Sinaia camarilla. Carol proved stronger in this first fierce clash. The King's cronies were retained in their posts, and Maniu was dismissed.

During the next year a formidable revolutionary movement grew in Rumania, partly encouraged by Maniu's party. An organization known as the Iron Guard (or Knights of the Archangel Michael) mustered 200,000 fanatics pledged to the "cleansing of Rumania," the rebirth of its national life—and the extermination of the Jews. It was one of the sub-Hitler quicksilvers streaming across Europe. It sought to put Rumania into Fascist hands. An Iron Guardist assassinated the prime minister, Jon Duca, on December 30, 1933, and the country (which is unused to such masculine deeds) all but expired in panic.

The Iron Guard movement was so particularly dangerous for Carol because it had a concrete object for its anti-Semitism—Lupescu. The King's Mistress is Jewish. Lupescu came to incarnate the discontent of the rich, sprawling country. Rumania was smothering under its glut of grain. Salaries were unpaid. The budget was split wide open. The peasants were starving. For these ills Lupescu, a conspicuously shining target for calumny, came to be blamed. Violent outbursts against her began—because she is Jewish, because she is the heart of the camarilla, because she keeps the King out of Bucharest, because on account of her he cannot be crowned.

The Duca killing left Rumania shaken. Foreign office functionaries showed their fright with disconcerting candor. Carol's Sinaia palace was guarded by frozen-faced sentries every hundred yards. It was said that the Iron Guardists had prepared a death list of twenty or thirty people doomed to assassination—with Lupescu as Number One.

Enter, then, Monsieur Nicolas Titulescu, the smartest living Rumanian, the only Rumanian with real international prestige, and a character of peculiarly fabulous quality. He refused to enter the new government as its foreign minister until Carol promised some drastic housecleaning. For a week a titanic struggle took place behind the scenes between Lupescu, the King's Mistress, and Monsieur Titulescu, who is not interested in mistresses, royal or otherwise. Carol was torn between the woman he loved and the man whose services were indispensable. Titulescu demanded that he break up the Sinaia clique, and discharge not only the two men whom Maniu had tried to get rid of the year before, but even General Stangaciu, the chief of police, and young Poui Dimitrescu, Carol's own private secretary, and next to Lupescu the most powerful personage in all backstairs Rumania. Carol was confronted with the necessity of dismissing his cronies in order to get what he needed more—a government. Titulescu is a voluble and pertinacious man. He won. Carol's friends went. Titulescu consented to enter the government, and Rumania, such as it is, was saved.

Behind this struggle, the core of which was the person of Lupescu, much more than the petty warfare of Ins and Outs in Rumania was at stake. What was at stake was the position of Rumania in Europe. Traditionally a loyal member of the Little Entente and an ally of France, the Rumanians had begun to veer toward Germany. The Iron Guard was Fascist. The army was discontented with French policy. Carol himself is, after all, a Hohenzollern. Like all countries, Rumania is in the business of nationhood for what it brings her, and it seemed, at the turn of the year, that affiliation with Germany might bring her most, as Germany began to supersede France as *the* European power.

[But] even Titulescu did not dare ask the dismissal of Lupescu herself. He realizes that no one can ask Carol that and survive. So Lupescu stayed.

~~~~~~

Events gaudy in the extreme continued to afflict Rumania after this article was written. Carol established a royal dictatorship in 1938, when the country seemed on the point of blowing apart, but he was deposed in 1940, as I predicted that he might be. A Fascist dictator, representing the Iron Guard, seized power, and Rumania joined the Axis. Carol fled abroad, and eventually married Madame Lupescu in Brazil in 1947. She took the title Princess Elena. Carol's successor on the throne was his son Michael who, something unique in history, had also preceded him, as pointed out above. He did not last long.

I never met Lupescu. I had a long interview with Carol himself in the royal palace in Bucharest way back in May, 1931. Bucharest was still a city of sin, gaiety, and tinsel. Carol wore a white uniform and looked somewhat like a plum partially encased in dough. He was cooperative and informal. He said that what I wrote about him must be checked and approved by somebody, and, to cut through bureaucratic red tape, he would undertake this chore himself. So I sat down in an anteroom after our talk and wrote my dispatch longhand and then Carol looked it over. It was the first and only time I have ever been censored by a king.

Carol, after long years of exile, died in Portugal in 1953. The Princess Elena lives in Estoril, near Lisbon, and is still a poised, competent, and pleasant lady. Rumania itself became a Communist satrapy after the war, and the dynasty lost all importance.

CHAPTER 6

≋

Chancellor Dollfuss: Flyweight
Champion of Europe

*The attempt to kill Dollfuss mentioned at the beginning of this chapter,
which appeared originally in* Vanity Fair *in December, 1933, has long
since been forgotten, if only because it was followed later by one which
succeeded. At the time I wrote the struggle for power in Austria had just
become clarified. Dollfuss had begun his spirited fight to keep the Nazis
out of Austria but at the same time he took a course which brought
him into irreversible conflict with the Socialists. The situation became
hopelessly triangular, and Dollfuss's attempts to deal with it made him a
world figure.*

≋≋≋≋≋≋≋≋≋≋≋≋≋≋

NOT TO EVERY MAN in public life is it given to be four feet eleven
inches tall. These lucky ones find merit in the worm's eye view.
They don't have to hurdle obstacles; they squeeze through them. Lacking bulk, they learn shrewdness and tenacity. They are conspicuous
because of their very inconspicuousness—like Dr. Engelbert Dollfuss,
the midget chancellor, the milli-Metternich of Austria. The most popular dictator in Europe, as well as the youngest and smallest, his recent
miraculous escape from an assassin's bullets made him the world's
news-reel hero and evoked unprecedented expressions of sympathy, even
from the government of his severest, to put it mildly, critic, Hitler.

Dollfuss's luck at all times has been of phenomenal quality, but
on October third, [1933], at 2:15 P.M., occurred the luckiest thing that
has happened to him yet: he was shot. At 2:14, he was only a chan-

cellor. At 2:16, he became a martyr, and what is more, a living martyr. Only his good luck stood between his heart and two bullets fired at less than two meters away. But it was his intuitive political genius that led him to deliver a radio speech from his bedside and made him the world's pet convalescent. A literal deluge of telegrams, flowers, gifts poured in from every curve of the universe. The would-be assassin turned out to be a slightly vander-loony Nazi. How Hitler must have wanted to choke him for having made a hero out of his worst enemy!

Little Dollfuss is the only man on earth so far who has made a monkey out of Hitler. Running six million people, he has made Germany, with sixty million, eat dirt. Like David, he exasperates and infuriates the clumsy, powerful German Goliath. Like a wasp in an elephant's ear, he sings his penetrating little song, and produces paroxysms of impotent fury in the slow-moving northern giant.

Vienna, an easygoing city, rather bored by politics, proud of taking nothing seriously, least of all itself, is taking Dr. Dollfuss very seriously indeed, and his fight against the Nazis. Dollfuss has dramatized himself into the heart of the Austrian nation. Partly because of his policies. But also because of his size. You can be angry at a six-footer, but a prime minister less than five in his stocking feet is irresistible. Hitler is an ogre, Dollfuss a sort of mascot.

Already the legends about him pile up shoulder high. They combine the irreverence of Vienna, the affection, and the soft seductive wit. It is being echoed—softly from the housetops—that a new issue of postage stamps is impending, with portraits of Dollfuss, life size.

As tough as he is small, Dollfuss has been chancellor of Austria a year and a half. He was born in the hill country along the Danube in 1892. Thus he is the youngest prime minister in Europe as well as the smallest. His people are peasants. They have knotty hands like boulders. His mother works in the fields today, near the small farm where he was born.

Dollfuss came to Vienna as a boy and got a degree in law at the university. Practically all Viennese who can read or write are doctors, and so his degree does not, necessarily, mean very much. He went to Berlin to study economics. The war came and he enlisted as a private and came out a lieutenant, rather a feat in those days, in the Imperial Austrian army. (A corporalship was the best Adolf Hitler got in Germany.) Dollfuss liked the land and returned to it, at least in spirit. He became an agrarian expert and presently, at a very tender age, the director of the Lower Austrian Chamber of Agriculture.

He got the chancellorship late in May, 1932, after an elaborate and confusing cabinet crisis; no other politician, so shaky were Austria's finances, wanted the job; moreover no one else wanted to rule with a majority of exactly one, which was the best the government could muster in the chamber.

Dollfuss seemed just another stopgap chancellor, if abler and more amiable than most; an Austrian given, like all Austrians, inveterately to compromise; a nice young fellow whom the job would break. Then, in the north, came the enormous phenomenon of Hitlerism. And Dollfuss, like a marionette, was jerked upward into the spheres of history.

Hitlerism, be it understood, is not only a political movement but a religion. A top point in the Hitlerite dogma is *Anschluss, i.e.*, union of Austria with Germany. Both sentiment and politics contribute to the German thesis that Austria is not truly an independent nation but merely a limb truncated from the body of the Reich. And then the puny Dollfuss decided that Austria was not going to be swallowed whole.

He had to fight on two fronts, an external war and at the same time a civil war, so to speak. Externally there was an enormous incursion of north German propaganda to face, propaganda distributed by able agitators, backed by men, money, arms. Internally he had to confront the fact that his people were, after all, Germans and that among them was a very active pan-German spirit, stimulated toward fruition by the triumph of the Nazis. When Hitler reached the premiership in Berlin a mass meeting of twenty thousand Viennese rose to shout that he was their chancellor too, not Dollfuss. But Dollfuss began to fight back.

First of all, the dying parliament, with his shaky majority of one, was a nuisance. He went to the President and threatened to resign unless he was given semidictatorial powers: he won.

Next, he crippled the strong Socialist opposition by dissolving the private Socialist army, the Schutzbund. Austria, having been forbidden any but a nominal public army by the peace treaties, had built up two private ones. With the Schutzbund out of the way the arena was clear for the rival army, the Heimwehr, representative of the forces of clerical conservatism.

The Socialists, even with their army gone, made a pretty problem. Dollfuss announced that he was building a government strictly of the center, equally opposed to both National Socialist (Fascist) and Social Democrat (semi-Marxist) reaction. The Socialists do not like Dollfuss. But, unhappy devils, they have been maneuvered into a position literally between frying pan and fire. And so far at least they have endured mild broiling by Dollfuss in order to avoid complete incineration by the Nazis. Dollfuss, for good or ill, is their best—in fact only—defense against Hitler.

At first the Nazis were contemptuous of Dollfuss. The contempt changed to consternation and anger after May 1, 1933. On this date,

Dollfuss called out the army and in effect dared Hitler to do something.

Hitler, in Berlin, was furious. He sent Papen and Goering to Rome. Dollfuss hopped in a plane after them. Both the Germans and the little Austrian courted Mussolini feverishly, and Dollfuss won. All the cards, in this one episode, were in his favor, because Mussolini is no friend of *Anschluss;* he does not want strong Germans on the Brenner Pass and behind Trieste. He much prefers soft Austria as a buffer state.

Hitler then sent Dr. Frank, a Bavarian cabinet minister, to Austria, to explore this highly unexpected situation. Dollfuss, with amazing cheek, sent a policeman to the airport to welcome Frank with the statement that his visit was "not very desirable." Then, smart as a chicka-dee, he fixed it so that Frank and his companions were led through deserted side streets to the Nazi headquarters in Vienna, while—perhaps by lucky coincidence—the Heimwehr staged an enormous parade on the Ring.

Those thousands who saw Dollfuss take the Heimwehr salute got the surprise of their lives. There was the little man, coming up to his aide-de-camp's armpit, in the uniform, not of the chancellor of the Austrian republic, but of the old imperial army. Dollfuss deliberately revived the time-worn, tattered, faded insignia of the Hapsburgs. It gave the crowd an immense emotional throb. It made them believe again in Austria as Austria.

The cards were on the table now. It was obviously a fight to a finish. Austrians themselves shuddered at their pocket Napoleon's temerity. Dr. Frank began to grumble. With infinite politeness, Dollfuss threw him out of the country. The Nazis talked wildly of "invasion." This was exactly to Dollfuss's hand. He used a scare story of an impending *Putsch* on the Austro-Bavarian frontier as pretext for banning Brown Shirts in Austria. For a short time the frontier was closed.

The climax soon came. Nazi violence began to break out like eczema over Austria. Dollfuss retaliated with the final weapon: he outlawed the Nazi party. This was on June 19, 1933. The Germans retaliated. By imposing a thousand-mark fine on any German visiting Austria. By sending airplanes to drop anti-Dollfuss literature over Austrian territory. By beginning an anti-Dollfuss radio campaign.

The powers themselves then protested, France and Britain publicly, Mussolini privately. The Germans promised Mussolini they would stop. Mussolini told France and Britain that the Germans would stop. The Germans did not stop—quite. Mussolini's role of mediator-in-chief to Europe-at-large became just a tiny bit funny. A statesman can forgive anything except being made ridiculous, especially an Italian statesman. Mussolini hasn't forgotten that incident.

Moreover, in September, as good luck would have it, came the 250th anniversary of the freeing of Vienna from the Turks, combined with a great Catholic jubilee. Vienna swarmed with visitors and stirred with new vitality. Before a crowd of a hundred thousand on the race course in the Prater, Chancellor Dollfuss announced that his new movement, the *Vaterlaendische Front,* would embrace all parties.

An interpretive fight on this speech threatened to break up his cabinet. Dollfuss settled the fight by dissolving his cabinet and rebuilding it overnight. Vienna went to bed at ten one night in a republic, and woke up at ten next morning in a dictatorship. In the reorganized cabinet of eight members, Dollfuss took five portfolios, chancellory, foreign affairs, defense, public security, agriculture.

Immediately after this *coup-de-cabinet,* Dollfuss went to Geneva again, and speaking before a packed house that included the Nazi propagandist Goebbels, he got the biggest ovation the Assembly has ever given anybody since Briand blessed Locarno.

How long Dollfuss will last is, of course, problematical. He may get licked. His present clevernesses may seem very small a year from now. Ultimateley six million people may indeed have to succumb to the pressure of sixty million. And Dollfuss has to fight on many fronts. There is treason in his own party to watch; there are the powerful, obdurate Social Democrats who must be conciliated, if Austria is to survive decently; there are the international forces represented by France and Italy to control.

Dollfuss is the first Austrian statesman since the war to believe ruggedly in the independence of Austria. All other Austrian politicians were defeatists. They all—an amazing paradox—believed in the abolition of Austria! Dollfuss believes in Austria as Austria. Europe, be it said, has suffered deeply from the excesses of nationalism, and additional nationalism is not exactly what the world would seem to need; nevertheless, if Dollfuss can create an independent, stable, perpetually neutral Austria *à la* Switzerland, he will, as the French say, have deserved well of his own republic.

~~~~~~

I was the Vienna correspondent of the Chicago Daily News *in the early 1930's and I had ample opportunity to observe Dr. Dollfuss carefully and I knew him quite well. As is clear from the text above, I liked him. I admired his fight against the Nazis. He was refreshing and alive. He had courage as well as cunning and cut through the musty obscurantism of old Vienna. Yet in my day-to-day reporting I several times sounded warnings about him because I knew that he was indissolubly tied up with the clerical reactionaries in Austria and that this was bound to produce a conflict with the Social Democrats out of which the Nazis were sure to gain.*

In February, 1934, came a searing episode. Dollfuss, stimulated by Mussolini, took military action against the Socialist administration in Vienna and bombarded the great workers' tenements by field artillery in the streets. I saw this ugly little civil war at first hand. Of course the Socialists bore part of the blame, but this does not excuse what Dollfuss did.

Six months later, on July 25, 1934, Dollfuss himself was murdered by the Nazis. Plotters gained entrance to the Bundeskanzleramt, his office, by means of a daring stragagem, and ruthlessly shot him down. I was a witness to the externals of this tragedy, and wrote an article about it for Harper's Magazine called "Policy by Murder," which has, I think, been anthologized more widely than anything I have ever written. Also I have touched on these events, both the February civil war and the July assassination, in fictional terms in The Lost City, published in 1964.

Anschluss—*the actual taking-over of Austria by Hitler*—did not occur until 1938. Today Austria is a well-run neutral state governed by a coalition between conservatives and Social Democrats, the kind of administration Dollfuss should have had.

Part Three

THE TURBULENT THIRTIES

CHAPTER 7

〜〜〜〜〜

Trotsky at Elba

This essay was published in Harper's Magazine *in April, 1933, and has never reprinted before. I have cut it to an extent.*

〜〜〜〜〜〜〜〜〜〜〜〜〜〜〜〜〜〜〜〜〜〜〜〜〜〜〜〜〜〜〜〜

IS TROTSKY A DEAD HORSE? His recent trip from Prinkipo, his island exile in Turkey, to Copenhagen warmed Europe with the recollected fire of those earlier journeys of his which helped upset a world. He was the chief engineer of the greatest revolution in modern history. Today, in a world blighted by economic chaos, we hear a great deal of possible revolutions, social, technical, or political, and it is at least conceivable that Trotsky may someday make another. He is only fifty-three. Is Trotsky coming or going? What if Stalin should die? His wife did, in mysteriously sudden circumstances. Might Trotsky then return to Russia? Russia aside, what is the revolutionary importance of Trotsky to the world?

I saw Trotsky a few months ago in Prinkipo, before the Copenhagen trip. It was a little difficult to think of him as pre-eminently a revolutionary, so gay and gracious was his manner. But the world does not forget. Trotsky left Prinkipo for a few days, and the clock turned back twenty flaming years. Like a packet of dynamite, wrapped in asbestos, he was again shunted from country to country; gingerly he was forked across frontiers as if the very elements of his person might spontaneously explode. He returned to Turkey, and the countries he had traversed, including such fairly stable states as France and Italy, breathed again, as if astounded they were still standing. There is no other single person in the world in whom, rightly or wrongly, the bourgeois governments of mankind see so much latent danger.

[77]

This is because Trotsky is, among other things, a genius. I do not mean merely that his accomplishments are legendary. It is something to have been an obscure journalist who became a considerable military chieftain; something to have been one of the best writers on pure political theory alive who also was a dazzlingly successful practical tactician; something to have been a hunted exile who held for a few years joint control over one-seventh of the surface of the globe. But Trotsky is above and beyond his own works.

A fascinating story might be written someday about his childhood. He cannot himself explain precisely why he became a revolutionary, any more than Michelangelo could explain why he became an artist. His parents were well-to-do; he was not crushed or downtrodden as a child; no external tragedy motivated him as Lenin was tortured into action by the execution of his eldest brother; and there are hundreds of thousands of other boys in whose lives is stored some "load of social protest." But Trotsky was in jail, a revolutionist, by the time he was eighteen. And at twenty-five he had organized the 1905 revolution and was chairman of the St. Petersburg Soviet. His career, which it is absurd to foreshorten in a paragraph, cannot be explained by any rationalization of the historical process. He is a "sport," a genius, still as unpredictable and dangerous as a tremendous child.

Again, the Western world fears him because, of course, he stands for "permanent revolution." Lenin was the soul of the revolution, Trotsky the brain, Stalin, perhaps, the hands. The soul marches on; the hands have seized power; the brain meantime works. Russia, one might say, has settled down to the prosaic ardors of married life. Trotsky outside, an incorrigible romantic, continues to devote his career to permanent revolution as a sort of perpetual honeymoon.

There are a good many people who, admitting Trotsky to be a genius, have sought to dismiss him as a super busybody of the revolution, a man who wrote, if indeed superlatively well, simply because there was nothing else he could do, a capricious and visionary disciple of Marx who did more harm to Russia than good. Nothing could be farther removed from the facts. Trotsky may—and this is quite another point —have outlived his best and most essential usefulness to Russia; but his positive creation of world revolution as an aim and an ideal in the sphere of practical politics makes him a permanent contributor to history.

It was Trotsky too who devised the technique of the modern coup d'état. This was discussed recently by a young Italian intellectual, Curzio Malaparte. Trotsky invented "technicological revolution"; that is, he laughed at barricades and scorned street fighting. What he did was to shake the world by seizing unobtrusively, through a few picked men, the power stations, the water mains, the telephone exchanges, the electric-light plants, of Petrograd. The Winter Palace was stormed later, almost incidentally. The revolution had already been won, and without shedding an ounce of blood! There are many things in Trotsky's autobiography of surpassing interest; one of them is the revelation that the October victory, which still rumbles throughout the world, and which is as much a landmark as the American and French revolutions, passed off so quietly in Petrograd itself that there was no mention of it in the city's newspapers next day.

Everyone knows what the doctrine of "permanent revolution" is, but few pause to consider its implications. Trotsky does not believe, as does Stalin, that socialism can succeed in a single state. He believes that a Marxist society can maintain itself on a world scale only as a result of permanent, progressive revolution that does not put its biggest stake in any one country.

Mainly on this issue Trotsky's "Left Opposition" rose after the days of his power; Trotsky and his friends thought that the world revolution was being starved for the sake of limited success at home; Trotsky was beaten and he was expelled from Russia. Since that time all energies in Russia have been spent inside Russia, and the success or failure of the Five-Year Plan will, or will not, prove Stalin to be right. Meantime Stalin has temporarily forgotten all about world revolution. Trotsky has not. Trotsky is the man in the world who wants revolution everywhere, and wants its now.

The Stalin-Trotsky quarrel on this issue served, to a limited degree, to split international communism. We must try to explore some of the ramifications of this split. But first there is Trotsky himself to visit.

II

Prinkipo is an island that lies like a pansy on the water. The gradual purple shores slope upward to a center of reddish golden hill. It was a calm, bright morning. I crossed from Constantinople on a steamer filled with chattering excursionists. Over the telephone a Russian voice—it might have been Trotsky's—had told me that a secretary would meet me at the pier. I looked for someone in the agitated, quickly melting crowd. There was no one there. Vaguely, I had imagined Trotsky's secretary as rather a burly person, probably bearded, possibly in a Russian smock. After a few minutes a young man hurried up; he was slight and dapper, rather ingratiating, and he wore a dark formal coat, gray-striped trousers, a pale gray formal tie, and a new gray hat with a dash and a swirl to its brim.

I have before me now the notes we struggled with while sitting at a café table on the waterfront. They are pretty confusing. You should have seen us writing them. I had submitted some questions to Trotsky in writing; his answer, which the secretary bore, was in Russian. The secretary knew no English and only a little French. He was patient and tenacious. Every word had to be just so. Mr. Trotsky would not risk a bad translation. Mr. Trotsky was extremely careful with his rare interviews. When we had hammered out an English draft we walked slowly up the hill, to Trotsky's villa.

The room opens in a burst of sunlight. The villa, of red plaster, is hung with vines, and the garden is heavy with the scent of lilac and mimosa. It is also full of police dogs. That is, two police dogs, very large, stand at leash, next to a mustard-faced, sleepy Turkish soldier. This is the protection which the Turkish government feels it necessary to impose on its distinguished guest.

Trotsky is busy at a big desk. I am astounded at his face. This is the man-monster of the London *Daily Mail* and *Morning Post*. The skin of his face is as delicate and pink as a child's and his hands are glistening, shining, delicate and pink. This is the man who nationalized women and ate their babies. It is odd, but I suppose you do not easily get over the stupidity of thinking of "revolutionaries" as coarse-grained, dark, or rough; the thing that made an overwhelming first impression on me was Trotsky's lightness and cleanness. He was shining and almost transparent and looked as if he had just emerged from an extremely happy Turkish bath.

His spoken English is terrible, although he reads and understands it well enough. He says, "Now, you will please read me the interview, as you have made the translation. I am of-ten misquoted. I do not like it, being misquoted. If you will read it in English slow-ly, I will understand." His face breaks out smiling. "You will read it ve-ry, ve-ry slow-ly. You will pretend I am a lit-tle child."

He corrects the translation. Not "capital," but "capitalism." Not "circle," but "cycle." I am stupid and do not get properly a little joke: Kreuger played with matches, and it is a god of lightning which destroys him; Trotsky darts to a dictionary. The room is full of dictionaries. Also of newspapers. There were some unread New York *Timeses* in their sleek tubular wrappers. Trotsky gaily shows me some books hollowed out; here he keeps precious documents. He handles books, and words, as if he loves them, and one should not forget that he never thought of power in his early life; his ambition from childhood was to be a writer.

Precision, graciousness, vitality: you note these qualities. He explains that he would like to go to America, to study our Civil War; he is at the moment putting the final polish on his history of the Russian Revolution, and he finds the analogies between the Russian civil war, which he won, and certain campaigns in our own South very striking; he calls them *stupéfiant*. His health? Oh, fair, very fair. But he shrugs, and for an instant loses his vivacity—he looks tired.

Gracious, yes, and gay, but also busy. I am definitely a time waster. There is no gossip. We get on with reading the interview, very slowly, word for word in slow, congested English. I can hardly read my own translation, scribbled confusedly as it was on the sunny pier. Trotsky has three main points to make. They are these:

About the crisis, he does not think that it is the "last crisis" of capitalism. The history of capitalism is a series of fluctuations within general cycles. In the preceding epoch the general curve advanced. Now it descends. This does not preclude upward fluctuations hereafter within the orbit of a generally descending curve. These, indeed, are almost inevitable. But the present crisis is so severe that the next upward turn will probably be short-lived, to be followed by a downward paroxysm even more acute. "The whole extremely diseased process can be ended only by a change in the entire social system."

About disarmament Trotsky was very skeptical. The French and Japanese have a sort of deal, France supporting Japanese aggression in the Far East, Japan supporting the French thesis of "disarmament" at Geneva. Wars are not conducted by the arms which the belligerent countries possess on the eve of war, but by the arms they produce during the course of a war. The United States of America gave a pretty good illustration of this principle to the world, including Germany, in 1917-1918. Nowadays you can equip five million men in a few months, after starting naked at scratch. The result of a new war will be determined by the degree of technical power and resources at the command of a given state. Thus, the greater the industrial power of a country the greater its interest in "limitation" at a disarmament conference; it is the weaker states who correspondingly suffer more. The disarmament conference is dangerous; it lulls people to false security. If any force does exist on this planet to limit arms it is the will of the popular masses.

About Russia Trotsky did not want to talk for publication. He said that rumors of his possible return were not founded on any concrete fact and had been circulated doubtless owing to the general international disquietude. In the event of war or the danger of war, he and his faction would put themselves unreservedly at the disposition of the Soviet government. He recalled that during the civil war of 1919-1920, Stalin, Voroshilov, and some of the other present chiefs of the U.S.S.R. had been in opposition to the Lenin-Trotsky policy, but had nevertheless been drafted for work in the face of a common danger.

Trotsky was accused during the days of his struggle with Stalin of "aristocratism," although he led a radical left opposition. Stalin, amongst much else, detested Trotsky's pride [and Trotsky was certainly one of the proudest men of our times]. I thought, when saying good-by in Prinkipo, of his entrance into Turkey in 1929. Here he was, out of Russia after a miserable year of exile (but he was never so miserable that he lost his sense of humor: on the train carrying him to Turkestan he nicknamed the towel Menjinsky, after the chief of the G.P.U.); here he was, about to land at last in the one country that consented to give him asylum, Turkey. Was he grateful? Was he pleased? Did he sneak in, head bowed? Here is the letter he addressed to Mustafa Kamal Pasha:

Dear Sir:
At the gate of Constantinople, I have the honor to inform you that I have arrived at the Turkish frontier not of my own choice, and that I will cross this frontier only by submitting to force. I request you, Mr. President, to accept my appropriate sentiments.

L. Trotsky.[1]

I boarded the Constantinople boat. Prinkipo disappeared.

III

Now there are considerably more Communists outside of Russia than in. The Communist party, which considers itself a sort of committee acting for the workers and peasants as a whole, numbers in Russia scarcely two and a half millions, whereas in Germany alone the Communist poll at the last election was about five millions. Of course all these may not be actually members of the party. There are hundreds of thousands of Communists in Central Europe, in Scandinavia, in Spain, in France, in the Far East. Such a comparatively small country as Czecho-slovakia, population 13,000,000, has 800,000 Communist voters, enough to make Communism the second strongest party in the country. Berlin is the biggest Communist city in the world, next to Moscow. These millions of Communists, if they subscribe to Moscow doctrine—and most of them do—are, theoretically at least, affiliated with the Third International, or Comintern.

The existence of this organization is predicated on internationalism. It is the international agency to which official Communists of all countries adhere. It is presumably the vehicle of world revolution. Trotsky was its father, and is now its cast-off son.

The Third International is so called because it is the third. The First was formed by Marx himself to organize workers to his new theories; it split when Bakhunin and the anarchists seceded, and quietly expired in, of all places, New York in 1876. The Second International was organized subsequently by social democrats the world over to continue

[1] Trotsky, *My Life, an Attempt at an Autobiography.* New York, 1930.

the work of the first, and it still exists. Nowadays, however, it consists of moderate socialists, devoted, it has been cruelly said, to a policy of "preventing socialism in our time." Lenin and Trotsky were members of the Second International until the war.

In 1915 they seceded, and at a conference at Zimmerwald, Switzerland, set up a new, rival International, the present Third. Trotsky relates that there were members sufficient to fill only a couple of railway coaches. Their aim was to oppose the war, which some social democrats were supporting. Their manifesto stated that "the defeat of their own countries [in the war] should be the slogan of social democrats in all countries." This is still Trotsky's idea. The Third International was then formally organized in Petrograd in 1919, as exclusively a Communist organization, devoted to world revolution, of which the Russian revolution was supposed to be merely the first, preliminary step. And the Third International had a few heady, vigorous years.

But now it is all but dead. The Stalin policy, Russia First, has naturally killed it. Its headquarters were always Moscow, and on Moscow it depended for the majority of its funds; but Moscow began to starve it. The Kremlin gives it money, if any, in something of the grudging spirit with which the United States Congress, say, now supports the Hoover moratorium. The International has not even had a president since Zinoviev was kicked out in 1927. Theoretically, it is only marking time; let Russia finish half a dozen new five-year plans, and then it will be time to turn to world revolution.

Meantime, however, Russia's relations with almost all her neighbors are steadily improving. The Soviet government, which controls the Third International, has signed friendship treaties with Poland, with France, with its Baltic neighbors. One would certainly have thought that Moscow would have welcomed the Japanese adventure in Manchuria with diplomatic horror and private glee; here was a marvelous field for the development of international revolution! But, as I saw it put recently, "the Soviet government regards the Japanese adventure hardly less leniently than Sir John Simon." There is even talk of a Soviet-Japanese pact guaranteeing the independence of that parody of a state, Manchukuo.

Of course what Stalin wants, and needs, is peace. Let the governments of the world give him peace for another five years, another ten; then may Stalin repay them in his own way.

But this policy to Trotsky and to Trotskyist Communists is of the devil. It negates the very spirit of their doctrine, based on the necessity of a perpetual pyramid of revolutions by which Communist state after Communist state shall successively come into being to make a truly Socialist world.

And as the power of the Third International wanes, the power of Trotsky correspondingly grows. Since the Third International is falling down on the job, let someone else take it over. Communists inside Russia may be satisfied with the Stalin program, but the comrades outside are getting short shrift. This is the basis of Trotsky's power in Europe, and of Stalin's fear of him. Stalin is, at the moment, offering nothing to world communism. Trotsky is.

Trotsky, an extraordinarily magnetic person, could rally the five million Communist Germans to his side in a year or two if he lived in Germany, I have heard it said. Lunacharsky once said that "Trotsky walked about like an electric battery, and that each contact with him brought forth a discharge." He still has this quality, plus his amazing personal charm. Let Trotsky loose in a country, let him be seen, let him talk, and his natural genius will do the rest.

For this reason, of course, he is an exile in Prinkipo. No government, fearing the breath of his revolutionary vitality, will have him as a permanent resident. But Stalin and the official machinery of the Communist party are probably almost as responsible for Trotsky's difficulty in getting a visa as Whitehall or the Quai d'Orsay. The governments fear for their institutions; Stalin fears for the Third International. In Turkey Trotsky can do comparatively little damage—not only to capitalism but to orthodox communism. This is a rare irony. Stalin, by salting Trotsky away in Prinkipo, has become a full cooperator with Sir Austen Chamberlain, General von Schleicher, and Hamilton Fish, Jr., in throttling world revolution.

IV

The scene changes. We are in Madrid. Up a long flight of stairs in a comfortable-looking apartment building; the door opens cautiously, and we enter a small, bright room. On the table I see a couple of books by Dreiser and other American writers in Spanish translation, published by the gentleman who is our host and who now enters, Andreas Nin.

Nin is the Trotskyist leader in Spain, a brilliant and provocative figure. He knows Max Eastman. So do I, although very slightly. We talk about Eastman. He was in Spain the week before and was arrested by the Spanish police. Nin talks about Trotsky. He shows me letters and manifestoes from Prinkipo and elucidates the Spanish Trotsky movement.

A few evenings later I visit a Trotskyist meeting. It is held in a hall on the second floor of a shabby building in the center of the city. The ceiling is low, there is a quiet restlessness to the crowd, and the policeman who is appointed by the government to listen in shifts from one foot to the other at the door. Nin speaks. Others speak. A friend with me translates. The comrades, mostly workingmen in caps and scarves, with a few writers and intellectuals, tall dark young men, knot into little groups, talk heatedly, then unravel into the street. We walk to a coffee house with glances over our shoulders. We sit with legs folded under a small, dirty table, after the proprietor has peeked through the door to let us in. Talk. About Trotsky. About the revolution. About Trotsky again. It all seems very futile, and rather unreal. But not many years ago Lenin and Plekhanov, Zinoviev and Radek and Bukharin were hovering in close, taut groups at similar coffee-house tables, talking, talking, talking; and it was probably very amusing to the police of the Tsar.

The Trotsky movement has a definite organization, though primitive, and a rather rickety series of publications. In several countries a nucleus of Trotskyist agitators exist. They take orders from Prinkipo direct. They are poor, and Trotsky himself finances as much of the movement as he can; odd that the good prices he gets from the Curtis Publishing Company and Simon and Schuster may contribute some-day to promoting new revolution. There is a sort of communication between the various groups, through their publications and manifestoes but mostly through private letters. The various central committees are linked to an international headquarters in Berlin. In no country are the Trotskyists strong enough to challenge directly the Stalinist or-ganization, but in Greece and Czechoslovakia, Germany, and especially Spain, their power is growing.

In Spain I found out that the general opinion, both in bourgeois and radical circles, is that Nin and his small Trotskyist band greatly out-ranked in importance the larger official party. The official party has, indeed, had to struggle for its life, and its leader was recently called back to Moscow and arrested. Trotsky is much admired in Spain. Nowhere else in Western Europe have I seen so many of his books, so much of his literature publicly available. The Spaniard is an inveterate individualist; so, above all, is Trotsky; Spain has a romantic feeling that he is "one of ours."

Trotsky himself has predicted that Spain would be the first of the Western countries to go Communist, and I believe that he thinks, or perhaps hopes, that the present liberal democratic government, led by President Zamorra and his prime minister, Don Manuel Azaña, is a Kerensky interlude, to give way presently to fullbodied reaction to the left. I do not think this is likely, although it is a debatable point. For one thing, communism has no historic roots in Spain, and extreme radical sentiment in the country has been traditionally in the hands of the an-archo-syndicalist organization of Barcelona, which numbers almost a million men. It is true that moderate left governments usually are forced farther to the left. But it is also true that the chief enemy of Communist reaction is not, as a rule, the aristocracy or the bourgeoisie, but rather the middle-left groups; Communists detest social democrats much more deeply than capitalists and they despise the childish violence of anarchism; but social democracy and anarchism are both very strong in Spain.

v

I am a little bored with discussions of the "differences" between Trotsky and Stalin in so far as their policies diverge in matters of collectivization, the speed of the industrial program, the attack on the kulak, and so on. This is all beside the point. What counts is the peculiar romantic hatred each has for the other.

I like to recall an episode which Mrs. Trotsky recounts in connection with her husband's escape from Siberia in 1905. Trotsky had been shipped toward exile in an excessively remote quarter, Obdorsk. He escaped, miraculously, before he even reached his destination. Boldly he returned west. It had taken the Tsar's police a month to make the eastward trip; Trotsky got back, alone, in eleven days. Nearing civilization, he telegraphed his wife, asking her to meet him at a junction of the railway line near St. Peterbsurg. She met him, but only after difficulties; the telegram was garbled and the name of the junction omitted. Here was Trotsky then, secretly embracing all that was dear to him, life, opportunity for further work, freedom, his family. Here he was, miraculously free. What happened? His wife mentioned the garbling of the telegram. And she had to restrain him almost by force from registering, then and there, a formal complaint about this inefficiency to the authorities! Had he done so, would he not have been promptly rearrested? Almost surely. And this little story illustrates some of the elements in Trotsky's character which Stalin simply cannot understand, his impulsiveness, his recklessness, and his "impracticality."

Stalin probably hates Trotsky, among other reasons, because he has done him an injury, i.e., stolen his program. At least I have heard many Communists say that, having thrown Trotsky out, Stalin proceeded to steal both his land policy and his theory of super-industrialization. And Stalin probably intends to get around to the permanent revolution—in time.

It is a sort of double fight that goes on in international communism; Stalin to make Russia strong enough so that later external adventures will be possible; Trotsky to hold out, hope for Stalin's downfall in Russia, and meantime bend every bit of energy to unceasing perfection of his counter-Communist organization abroad.

It is a pity that insurmountable obstacles in the character of each prevented them from working together. If I were a Russian and a revolutionist, I should agree, I think, that Stalin has justified himself; he has done, one might say, "the right thing" by Russia. But, from the strict Leninist point of view, I should deeply deplore that Trotsky was not allowed to work with him, to add his indomitable vivacity to a common aim.

~~~~~~

Prinkipo never became the equivalent of Elba. Trotsky never returned to Russia. I was writing in far too romantic a vein, and his variety of international communism never took root significantly during his lifetime. He left Turkey in 1933, spent two frustrating years in France, and, searching for a country that would take him in, was accepted by Norway in 1935. Here too he was hounded by the Stalinist police and secret agents and the Kremlin forced the Norwegian government to expel him two years later. At last he moved to Mexico and in August, 1940, was murdered there. Moscow got him at last—with an axe.

Trotsky's importance is literary as well as political. His History of the Russian Revolution will, I imagine, be read for excitement and pleasure as well as for its historical aspects as long as books about the Soviet Union are read at all. His autobiography is as vivid a feat of writing as those of Rousseau or Casanova in different fields, he was a pamphleteer and polemicist of genius, and his intellectual force as a revolutionist is comparable to that of Robespierre.

Probably Trotsky has more political relevance today than at any time since this artcle was written thirty-one years ago. The Communist world is loosening up. Its monolithic solidarity has been shaken, with the result that Trotskyist murmurings have begun to be heard again, particularly in Italy. And look at China. Mao Tse-tung and Chou En-lai would certainly deny indignantly any allegation that they were Trotskyists, but the arcane and acriminious dialogue that has been taking place between Moscow and Peking since 1960 resembles to a marked degree the old bitter dialogues between Stalin and Trotsky. Much in Chinese Communist policy today shows Trotsky's influence. For instance the Peking leaders seem to be becoming more and more committed to the principle of active territorial expansion and progressive world revolution, as against the standpatters, relatively speaking, in the Kremlin.

Most Orthodox Communists today still think of Trotsky as a hyena. But Communist standards and evaluations have—to put it mildly— been known to change.

CHAPTER 8

〰〰〰〰

Masaryk the Magnificent

This is taken from the first edition of Inside Europe, *published in 1936. Czechoslovakia was then a free republic.*

〰〰〰〰〰〰〰〰〰〰〰〰〰〰〰〰〰〰〰〰〰〰〰〰〰〰〰〰〰

> *The master of Bohemia is the master of Europe.*
> —BISMARCK

> *We shall always be a small minority in the world, but, when a small nation accomplishes something with its limited means, what it achieves has an immense and exceptional value, like the widow's mite. . . . It is a deliberate and discerning love of a nation that appeals to me, not the indiscriminate love that assumes everything to be right because it bears a national label. . . . Love of one's own nation should not entail non-love of other nations. . . .*
> —MASARYK

MASARYK—what grandeur the name connotes! The son of a serf who created a nation; the blacksmith boy who grew to have "the finest intellect of the century"; the pacifist who organized an army that performed a feat unparalleled in military annals—the Czechoslovak legions who marched across Siberia to the Pacific; the philosopher who became a statesman in spite of himself; the living father of a state who is also its simplest citizen; an unchallengeably firm democrat who, in the *débâcle* of the modern world, still believes in rule by tolerance; the man who more than any other smashed the old Austro-Hungarian empire, so that Czechoslovakia, a free republic, rose from its ruins—the stablest, strongest, and most prosperous of the succession states.

In his autobiography Masaryk says that his life has been "shot through with paradox." He is, for instance, the son of a coachman—

[88]

and he lives today in the castle of the old Bohemian kings. His father was, moreover, a servant on an imperial estate, so that in throwing the Hapsburgs out of Czechoslovakia Masaryk also symbolically threw them from the front yard where he grew up in the most crushing poverty.

He was, for instance, both a locksmith's apprentice and a helper in a blacksmith's shop, because in early youth he disliked school. During the war he was a first-class practical conspirator, a specialist in decoys, codes, and stratagems. Yet the whole basis of his career was moral-intellectual. He was one of the most formidably learned men of his time, a philosopher and prophet of almost Judaic stature.

The greatest of living Czechoslovaks, the first act in his life to bring him prominence was an investigation which proved a set of documents hallowed and revered by the Czech and Slovak peoples to be forgeries. A Roman Catholic who turned Protestant, he gained early distinction by defending a Jew wrongfully accused of an obscure ritual murder. He exposed as fabrications of the Austrian foreign office the documents in the Friedjung case, which ruined what was then his official career; but this made him a hero of the oppressed Slavic peoples. Dominating his life have been two factors, faith in Czechoslovakia and the pursuit of truth.

It was not idly that Masaryk called his philosophy "Realism." Once he all but decided to return to Austria during the war so that he might be hanged—he knew that his martyrization would help the Czech national cause. There were several attempts on his life which he shrugged off—he was psychologically incapable of fear—but he took the precaution of drawing up his own obituary so that it would be the best possible propaganda for the liberation of his people.

He founded the most central of central European states in Pittsburgh, Pennsylvania, where he negotiated a Czech-Slovak unity pact, and in Washington, D.C., where he issued the Czechoslovakian declaration of independence. He was proclaimed President of Czechoslovakia after he had not set foot in it for four years, and when he was 3,500 miles away.

His autobiography is warm and rigid with insistence on the most complete intellectual, moral, and emotional probity. He records how a simple lie might have saved his life when he was in acute danger in Moscow—to gain cover in a hotel he would have had to say incorrectly that he was registered there; he refused although the bullets were splattering about him—and his life was saved anyway. Yet in his career he was a splendid opportunist.

In Washington, before attempting to make any appointment at the White House, Masaryk spent weeks in a detailed and penetrating study of Wilson's writings. The old professor was knee deep in books about and by Wilson. Then he drew up his manifesto on Czech aspirations for independence and presented it to Wilson. Half a dozen times in the document Masaryk had cleverly used citations from Wilson's own works as legal and political authority for the Czech claims.

Thomas Garrigue Masaryk was born on March 7, 1850, in the Moravian town of Hodonin. His mother, a cook, seems to have been a remarkable woman; Masaryk pays touching tribute to her strength, her ideals, her clamor to give her son an education. Apparently he had little sympathy with his father. He went to school in Vienna, became a professor at Prague, wrote exhaustively (of some psychological interest is the fact that his first book was on suicide), and entered politics. His wife was an American woman, Miss Charlotte Garrigue, whom he met in student days at Leipzig and whose name he added to his own. He writes of her: "She was beautiful to look at; she had a magnificent intellect, better than mine."[1]

Masaryk's real career did not begin until he was well over sixty. He records a testimonial dinner given him at the time, a sort of climax to his work as a distinguished scholar; he tells wryly of his inner feeling that he was being buried before he was dead. Then came the high years, between sixty-five and seventy, when he fled from Prague to organize the Czech movement abroad. His final work, nurture of the new Czechoslovak state, began at an age when the lives as well as careers of most men are long since over.

He is a very old man now, but still alert, and the range of his interests is extraordinary. His conversation is a bit diffuse; he is inclined to get lost in the flow of his own sentences. In one half-hour's talk I had with him he mentioned, aside from domestic politics, such things as birth control, Irish nationalism and the Catholic Church, Senator Borah, biology, modern American literature (of which he has an amazing knowledge), the Polish corridor, the amount of pocket money of American soldiers in France, the Hapsburgs, Dostoevsky (he is, at eighty-five, just finishing a book on Dostoevsky), the Yugoslav sculptor Mestrovic, and a new English novel he had just been reading and the title of which he couldn't for the life of him remember.

I had expected to meet a man excessively stern, even self-righteous. But Masaryk has a strong sense of humor. He cackled vigorously. His interest in human nature, immense, neglects no comic facet. He told Capek that academic psychology was of no help to him in learning about human nature—"only life and novels." For seventy years, he said, he has been reading novels every day. "Man is a damned complicated and puzzling machine. And each man different." During the whole period of the war, he has related, he slept [soundly] only half a dozen nights; presumably he read novels instead.

[1] Capek, *President Masaryk Tells His Story*, p. 121.

After seeing him I made a few rough notes as follows: "Warm, strong handshake; no glasses; old man's eyes, hard to tell the color of them, probably deep gray; still a fuzz of white hair on the scalp; all his own teeth, plus a bit of gold shining when he laughs; plenty of mustache, small beard; glazed, hard, shiny cheeks; prominent nose; a typical *peasant's* face; distinctly not patrician or 'intellectual'; a boulder, shrunken, hard-bitten, out of the soil."

Masaryk is old. But his work is done. He has built a nation. The story, in its perfection of sequence in cause and effect, is like a Greek tragedy —except that it ended happily. He will die soon. There is no man of our time who will leave a better memory, for others to remember.

〰〰〰〰〰〰〰〰〰〰〰〰〰〰〰〰〰〰〰〰〰〰〰〰

Thomas Garrigue Masaryk died in September, 1937, at the age of eighty-seven. As one man his country mourned him. Czechoslovakia itself had a briefer life as a free republic than its founder. It lasted only twenty-one years from 1918 to 1939, when it was swallowed up by Hitler. The allied armies led by General Patton liberated Czechoslovakia in 1945, but the Communists seized power by means of a coup d'état in February, 1948, and the country has been a Kremlin marionette ever since—probably the most subservient of all the satellites.

Readers who do not remember the late thirties may confuse the elder Masaryk with the younger. Jan Masaryk (1886-1948), the son of Thomas and the Czech foreign minister for some years, was a complex as well as attractive human being—moody, candid, turbulent, powerful, humorous, and a lover of all the virilities. I met him in London in the early 1930's when he was a Czechoslovak minister there, and knew him well. He liked parties and the mixing up of people and the good things of life. He was utterly dedicated to his country. He was severely criticized when he continued to hold office as foreign minister in Prague under a coalition government led by the Communists (1946) and after the Communist coup d'état, but he thought that he had no choice and that he could make Czechoslovakia a bridge between the worlds of East and West. He died in Prague soon after the complete takeover by the Communists in 1948 in circumstances that have never been satisfactorily explained. Either he was pushed out of a window or he jumped.

CHAPTER 9

〜〜〜〜〜

The Turkish Colossus

This too is a chapter out of the original Inside Europe (1936). *Ataturk died in November, 1938.*

〜〜〜〜〜〜〜〜〜〜〜〜〜〜〜〜〜〜〜〜〜〜〜〜〜〜〜〜〜〜〜〜

THE BLOND, blue-eyed combination of patriot and psychopath who is dictator of Turkey has changed his name seven times. First he was simply Mustafa, so called by his parents in Salonika. At school he was given the name Mustafa Kemal to distinguish him from other little Mustafas, and because a teacher admired his skill in mathematics; "Kemal" in Turkish means "perfection." After the Dardanelles campaign, [in World War I], he became Mustafa Kemal Pasha, "pasha" being a military title equivalent to general. After he crushed the Greeks in 1921 he assumed the name Ghazi Mustafa Kemal Pasha; "ghazi" means "destroyer of infidels," an odd sobriquet for Kemal, inasmuch as he was the greatest infidel in Turkish history. Then years later he became Ghazi Mustafa Kemal when he abolished military titles. In 1934 he ordered every Turk to assume a patronymic in the Western fashion and chose for himself "Ataturk," which means "Father of Turks." So he was simply Kemal Ataturk. Finally he modified this to the Turkish form of the Arabic, to become Kamal Ataturk.

His own is by no means the only name he changed. When I went to Constantinople recently after an absence of several years I was astounded at the metamorphosis in names placarded on the streets. Kamal westernized the Turkish alphabet—quite completely! Modern Turkish is strictly a phonetic tongue. These were some of the compulsory renderings of names which greeted me:

Kahve	instead of	Coffee
Tabldot	"	Table d'Hôte
Jorj	"	George
La Jones	"	La Jeunesse (a shop)
Star Su Sop	"	Star Shoe Shop
Vagonli-Kook	"	Wagon-Lit-Cook
Enstitu do Boté	"	Institut de Beauté
Or Duvr	"	Hors-d'Oeuvre
Waytaus	"	White House (a shop)

Kamal Ataturk, who strides the Turkish landscape like a colossus—significantly a bronze statue of him in a dinner jacket (with the trousers cuffed) commands the Golden Horn—is in the position of a man with no more worlds to conquer. His reforms have been so drastic and so comprehensive that in cultural and social fields at least there is very little left to do. He abolished the fez, turned the mosques into granaries, and Latinized the language. He ended polygamy, installed new legal codes, and experimented with a (paying) casino in the sultan's palace. He compulsorily disinfected all the buildings in Istanbul, adopted the Gregorian calendar and metric system, and took the first census in Turkish history. He cut political holidays down to three a year, demanded physical examination of those about to marry, and built a new capital, Ankara, in the Anatolian highlands, replacing proud Constantinople. He limited most business activity to Turkish nationals and Turkish firms, abolished books of magic, emancipated the women (more or less), tossed the priests into the discard, and superintended the writing of a new history of the world proving that Turkey is the source of all civilization.

Kamal Ataturk, a somewhat Bacchic character, the full record of whose personal life makes you blink, is the dictator type carried to its ultimate extreme, the embodiment of totalitarian rule by character. This man, in personality and accomplishments, resembles no one so much as Peter the Great, who also westernized his country at frightful cost. Kamal Ataturk is the roughneck of dictators. Beside him, Hitler is a milksop, Mussolini a perfumed dandy, and Goemboes [the prime minister of Hungary] a creature of the drawing room. At one of his own receptions Kamal, slightly exhilarated, publicly slapped the Egyptian minister when he observed the hapless diplomat wearing the forbidden fez.

No man has ever betrayed more masters, and always from motives of his own view of patriotism. In 1918, a staff officer, he was chosen to accompany Vahydu'd-Din, the Crown Prince, to Berlin, and there assist him in consultations with Hindenburg, Ludendorff, and the German high command. Three years later Kamal booted him, as Sultan Mehmed VI, out of Turkey.

After the Armistice Kamal was sent by the authorities as inspector-general of the eastern vilayets to investigate a nationalist insurrection in Kurdistan. He was ordered to find and quell these rebels. He found them all right. But instead of crushing the movement he took charge of it! Within two years he brought victory in all of Turkey to the very organization his superiors had sent him to suppress.

In 1926, following a not very professional attempt on his life, he hanged what amounted to the entire leadership of the opposition. Among those he allowed to be sentenced to death and executed were Colonel Arif, who had been his comrade-at-arms in the Greek campaign, and Djavid Bey, the best financial mind in Turkey. Kamal had a champagne party in his lonely farmhouse at Chankaya, near Ankara, to celebrate the occasion, and invited all the diplomats. Returning home at dawn, they saw the corpses hanging in the town square.

(In 1930 Kamal decided that totalitarian rule to the extremity which he carried it was a bore, and, uniquely among dictators, he proceeded to *create* an opposition, naming various men to be its leaders. Somewhat timidly, they accepted. Kamal wanted to see if Western democratic methods would work; he wanted an opposition bench to argue with in parliament. The system didn't work. The Turks, with the memory of 1926 in mind, didn't seem to understand. . . .)

His psychological history is of surpassing interest. Two things have dominated the secret springs of his life, his mother and illness. For his mother he had an unusual love-hate obsession. During the early years he was continually fetching her to live with him, then flinging off alone again. Finally he brought her to the Chankaya farmhouse and she died there. She was the only woman he was ever faithful to. It is possible that his merciless campaign against the Greeks was subconsciously motivated by his mother's experiences in a refugee camp in Salonika during the Balkan wars. Kamal popped across the Aegean (he had been fighting in Tripoli against the Italians) to see her, and found her a prisoner of the Greeks in indescribable circumstances of suffering.

In 1917 Kamal took time off from the war to visit Carlsbad for a cure. A famous Viennese professor, Dr. Zuckerkandl, looked him over and told him that if he did not stop drinking he would die in a year. The illness was troublesome. Kamal returned to the front (he had just been the most important Turkish officer in beating back the British at the Dardanelles) for service in Syria and to his well-known habits. His health remained, and has remained, about the same. The dear old Viennese professor, however, died two years after prophesying Kamal's collapse and demise.

A favorite theory is that Kamal's extraordinary bursts of reformist energy are due to chronic pain. The familiar and excruciating twinges return, and lo! the dictator abolishes the Turkish alphabet or decrees the formation of a dozen new investigating commissions; if true, this is an interesting example of what the psychiatrists call "displacement." Kamal punishes someone else for his own early sins, purifies a nation as a surrogate for purification of his own painful blood.

Kamal was born in 1881, the son (like Hitler) of a minor customs official. The father, Ali Risa, was nothing more than a petty and narrow bureaucrat, but the mother, named Zubeida, was, like the mothers of Pilsudski, Mussolini, and Masaryk, a woman far above the normal of her station. She wanted her son to get an education and become a priest— exactly like Stalin's mother, who sent the future dictator of all the Russias to a theological school in Tiflis. Kamal's mother, not an unimportant point, married again after her first husband's death, and young Mustafa bitterly hated his stepfather, an interloper in the home.

Ali Risa, Kamal's father, was apparently of Albanian origin. Zubeida, the mother, was the daughter of a Turkish peasant whose wife was Macedonian. Kamal is thus far from being purely Turkish. As great an authority as Toynbee (*Great Contemporaries*, p. 291) suggests that Jewish blood may have been in the family. Salonika has, of course, been a citadel of Jews since the Diaspora; many, called "Dönme," were converts to Islam. But Kamal's irrefragable blondness and his cold blue eyes would seem to preclude more than a hint of Jewish—or for that matter Turkish—ancestry.

Kamal's early life was that of a rebel and above all of a hater. He wrote revolutionary pamphlets and even poems. He was sentenced to jail in Constantinople, but his skill as an officer made him valuable, and he was released. Although a "Young Turk," his position was that of a suppressed oppositionist; he detested the Young Turk triumvirs, Talaat, Enver, and Djemal, a feeling which they reciprocated. But his reputation as a soldier was invincible, after service on the most remote, dangerous and hopeless fronts, and the way to his career was open.

That career is without parallel in modern times. Kamal engineered the Congresses of Erzerum and Sivas and organized the nationalist movement, leading it to victory. Other people have created nations. Kamal's job was harder. He took a nation that was centuries deep in rot, pulled it to its feet, wiped its face, reclothed it, transformed it, and made it work. In 1919 Turkey was so crushed and broken that it would have welcomed renunciation of sovereignty and a British mandate. In 1922 Turkey was the one enemy state so strong that it practically dictated its own peace terms.

In those three years Kamal (1) drove out the Sultan, (2) abolished the caliphate, (3) fought and won the war against the Greeks and drove them into the sea, (4) bluffed Great Britain to a standstill at Chanak, (5) negotiated, through Ismet Pasha, the Treaty of Lausanne, which ended the regime of capitulations (foreign judicial rights) in Turkey and established the new frontiers on a basis that the wildest Turkish nationalist could not have dreamed possible, (6) wrote a republican constitution and created a parliament in his new impregnable capital, Ankara, and (7) became Turkey's first—and only—President.

Kamal alone, it may be said, does not deserve credit for all this. The general program of westernization was planned by the Young Turks and he simply appropriated it. The Greeks were destroyed by the duplicity of Lloyd George and the treason of the allies, also by their own incapacity, not by Kamal's armies. Sultan and caliph were doomed in any case, and it is no tribute to Kamal that he kicked them out. The Treaty of Lausanne was won not by Ismet Pasha, but because of jealous squabbles between the Western powers. And so on.

Kamal lives these days in Chankaya, a complete recluse. His model farm is his avocation; a true megalomaniac, he designed the water reservoir in the shape of the Sea of Marmora. He married a woman named Latifé Hanum in 1923, but divorced her a few years later; now he lives alone. He is the most inaccessible public character in Europe. Unlike all other dictators, he keeps from the foreground; the Turkish papers do not mention his name half a dozen times a month. He has a group of soldier underlings and cronies with whom he plays poker. Rarely, he gambles at cards with foreign diplomats; he usually wins, then insists on returning his winnings. He still likes to drink.

The Turkish dictator differs from almost all others in that he had no socialist period in youth and even in maturity betrays not the faintest interest in socio-economic stresses. His only policy was Turkey for the Turks. He is certainly a revolutionary, but as far as economics is concerned he might be President of Switzerland. The theory that all nationalist dictators must bear to extreme right or extreme left breaks down on Kamal Ataturk, as it did on Pilsudski.

The two foreign powers that Kamal is most interested in are (except Great Britain, which he hates) the U.S.S.R. and Italy. In the bleak year 1932 he set a new peak in picturesque achievement by procuring loans from both these countries, which are states not given to the export of credit in the best of years. Kamal plays them, of course, against each other. Italy wants Turkish support in the eastern Mediterranean, and Turkey is bound always to be an important factor in Soviet foreign policy because the Dardanelles comprise Russia's only outlet to warm seas.

Clearly Ataturk was one of the most striking men of modern times, a wrecker who was also a creator, a man of the camp who became a formidable man of state. Practically everything that has happened in Turkey since his death follows the deep lines he carved. Contemporary Turkey remains his unique creation—its bad spots as well as good. One thing that might have surprised Kamal was that his country became a member of NATO and a vigorous ally of the United States after World War II.

Ataturk's successor was the soldier and diplomat Ismet Pasha, now known as Ismet Inonu, born in 1884 and for many years Kamal's chief of staff. He was prime minister almost uninterruptedly from 1924 to 1937, under Ataturk as President, and he succeeded to the presidency when his master died. There followed various ups and downs, but the wiry and extraordinarily recessed and cagy Inonu still runs Turkey today. This is one example among few available of a dictator naming his own successor, moreover a successor who stuck.

CHAPTER 10

≈≈≈≈≈

De Valera

I wrote this for The Strand Magazine, *London, where it appeared in July, 1936. Ireland was still the "Irish Free State," not a fully independent republic, when I met Mr. de Valera in that year. Later my article was incorporated into* Inside Europe.

≈≈≈≈≈≈≈≈≈≈≈≈≈≈≈≈≈≈≈≈≈≈≈≈≈≈≈≈≈≈≈≈≈≈≈≈

LIKE MANY MODERN CHIEFTAINS, Eamon de Valera was not born a citizen of the country he rules. Hitler, as we have seen, was an Austrian; Pilsudski was Lithuanian in origin, as well as Polish; Josef Stalin still speaks with his native Georgian accent; Kamal Ataturk was born in Salonika, Greece, and Dr. Kurt von Schuschnigg, the Austrian chancellor, in Riva, Italy.

This is a demonstration, among other things, of the way frontiers have danced about since the war. Salonika was still part of Turkey when Kamal Ataturk was an infant; Riva was part of Austria when Schuschnigg went to school. Eamon de Valera's birthplace is separated from his capital by three thousand miles of ocean. He was born, in 1882, in New York; his father was a Spanish immigrant from Cuba, his mother an Irishwoman lately an arrival in America. De Valera's American birth— and citizenship—saved his life.

Whereas Austrianism has been something of an incumbrance to Hitler, the fact that the Irish leader was American made him President of the Free State. For he was saved from execution after the Easter rebellion in 1916 purely because the British military tribunal had no wish to alienate American opinion by shooting an American citizen. Almost every other commandant in the rebellion was shot. Had he been born elsewhere than in America, the history of Ireland would have been very different. Perhaps—it is quite possible—there would have been no Free State at all.

Eamon de Valera is one of those rare statesmen, like Disraeli and Theodore Roosevelt, who are blessed by a universally known nickname. To everyone in Ireland de Valera is simply "Dev." This at once gives some indication of his quality. A nationally used nickname indicates intimacy and affection; it is a tribute worth thousands in votes; it is the ultimate in honors conferred upon a statesman by the lay public. Mere demagoguery cannot win a nickname, nor can mere success, no matter how great. Hitler has never been nicknamed, and neither was Woodrow Wilson. But Theodore Roosevelt became "Teddy" or "T.R." and Mr. Lloyd George became "L.G." No one in his own country has ever dared to nickname Mussolini or Kamal Ataturk. But everywhere in Ireland Eamon de Valera is just Dev.

Not many people, however, call him Dev to his face. His wife does, and those who are intimate enough to address him by his Christian name, if it were commonly used. Some of his mother's relatives in County Limerick, where he was raised, still call him Eddie. His friends and colleagues usually say Chief, or if adressing him in Irish, Uachtaran (President). He himself addresses most of his staff by their first names, in their Irish form. But "Dev" is what people call him when he is not in the room.

Like most men with a single-track mind, de Valera gets a lot of work done. He puts in a grueling day. Usually he arrives at his office in Government Buildings between 9:30 and 10. He receives, as a rule, the heads of all departments under his direct administration; he scrupulously pays attention to the smallest details. He returns home for luncheon and is in the office again shortly afterward. He works till six, goes home to tea, and frequently returns to the office again at night. Often, passing Government Buildings, one may see lights in the President's quarters till after midnight. He has bread and butter for supper. He has never, except for reasons of illness, taken a holiday.

He has the spare but rugged frame that fanatics need. He was a first-class rugger player in his youth, and is still an excellent horseman, very fond of riding. He likes to hike and climb. Almost every Sunday he may be seen walking across a pass in the hills about ten miles from Dublin. His car, empty except for the chauffeur and detectives, drives slowly along; Dev walks behind it, very rapidly, hatless, his hair on end. His clothes, even on this occasion, are usually black. Members of his family have a hard time keeping up with him, so rapid is his pace. Behind are other detectives—members of a group of eight chosen men—who are never far from his person.

He never touches a drop of any kind of alcohol in Ireland or England.

He believes drink—hard drink—to be the curse of his country. But, an odd point, he drinks wine or beer when he is on the Continent. He likes nothing better than to sit in a café in Zürich or Geneva sipping a glass of beer and watching people. He does not smoke. But until 1916 he was a heavy smoker. The story is told that he filled his pipe and was about to light it when, after the Easter rebellion, he was on his way to penal servitude. He stopped suddenly and said, "I will not let them deprive me of this pleasure in jail!" He threw away the pipe, and has never smoked since.

His hobbies, apart from exercise, are chess, listening to the radio, and, above all, mathematics. He was an omnivorous reader until his eye complaint grew serious. He especially read Shakespeare and the Gaelic writers. He speaks Irish fluently and correctly, but with a strong guttural accent. The intellectual pleasure that matters most to him is mathematics. One day going to Rome he asked the secretary what he thought of the quaternary theorem. "Nothing," the secretary replied, who knew only elementary mathematics. It was a boiling-hot day, and the rest of the staff dozed, but Dev spent twelve solid hours teaching the secretary the quaternary theorem. The secretary said that Dev's twelve-hour lecture was the most brilliant intellectual performance he had ever known. When in jail in 1918, incidentally, de Valera spent all his time mastering the Einstein theory.

His wife was a schoolteacher, Sinéad Ní Fhlannagáin (Jeannie O'Flanagan), whom he met at the Gaelic League when he was learning Irish. The legend is that de Valera was unable to enter the Civil Service because he failed in his examinations in Gaelic; the story may be apocryphal, and, anyway, Dev married his teacher. That was in 1910. They had seven children. One boy, Brian, was killed riding in Phoenix Park, Dublin, last February. The eldest boy, Vivian, has his Master of Science degree from the National University of Ireland and is now a demonstrator in University College, Dublin; he has also been gazetted as a lieutenant in the National Volunteers. The eldest girl is also a graduate of the National University. The younger children are still in secondary school or college.

Mrs. de Valera was a beautiful fair girl. Her golden hair is now turning gray. She is reserved in character, like her husband. The family has almost no social life, except the minimum necessary for official functions. When de Valera became President his wife said that she wished the government would give him an official wife to tend to the official entertaining. The de Valeras live in a simple house on Cross Avenue, Blackrock. They have only one servant, a maid. Before 1932 they had no servants at all, and lived in a much smaller house; Mrs. de Valera did all the work. They entertained guests in the dining room. Like all the Irish, Mrs. de Valera has a long memory. The younger children are clever and very popular in Blackrock. They have been invited to parties by families who were desperate political opponents of de Valera in the early days. Mrs. de Valera refuses the invitations on the ground that the children are "too busy."

President de Valera is extremely accessible as a statesman and he receives a great number of people. (He is very particular about newspaper interviews, however; everything must be checked and okayed by him.) He has many friends. One is his secretary, Kathleen O'Connell. She has been with the chief for almost twenty years, and knows his work and the method of his mind inside out. De Valera is very attractive to women, but pays no attention to them. They follow him about at functions; he is smiling but reserved, and, without ever being rude or pompous, manages to create a sense of distance between himself and them.

He has utterly no interest in money. He reduced his salary from £2,500 to £1,500 on taking office. He has no private means, no expensive hobbies, and no taste for luxury. He is very fond of music. His views on art are unknown; he does not appear to be much interested in graphic art. He is, of course, extremely religious, but his Catholicism is neither ostentatious nor bigoted; several of his friends are Protestant. Whenever possible, de Valera is a daily communicant at Mass. As one of his staff expressed it to me, "His whole life is a prayer."

His sense of humor is hardly robust; but it exists. It is on the ironic side. He rarely makes jokes, but he appreciates comic situations, and when he laughs, he laughs very heartily. Once he was arrested, at Ennis, in the middle of a speech. A year later he was released. He went forthwith to Ennis, and began to speak again with the words, "As I was saying when I was interrupted—"

His personal traits are clearly marked: rigid self-control; fanatic faith in his duty to Ireland; extreme seriousness of mind; complete unworldliness; a certain didacticism; stubborness and humanity. People say that he has lost his temper publicly only once in his life; it occurred during a debate on the Irish Press bonds. Similarly his friends can recall only rare and isolated cases where he gave way to emotion. Once in 1921, when the treaty had been ratified by seven votes, he got up and said, "During these last four years we have worked together like brothers . . ."; then his voice broke and he sat down and cloaked his face with his hands. He was intensely fond of his son Brian; but immediately after his tragic death he appeared at a party meeting quite calm. When he enters a public place—for instance, the stands at a football match—he does not smile or nod to the crowd. He walks straight ahead, very reserved, and seems to pretend that the crowd is not there.

Eamon de Valera discovered Ireland at the age of two. His father (in New York) died and he was dispatched to Ireland in the care of his

mother's brother. He lived in his grandmother's home near Bruree, in
County Limerick. His mother, who stayed in America, married again;
no one seems to know accurately how much contact there was between
mother and son during his early years. He went to the local school, living
meanwhile on a farm, and won a scholarship, owing to his skill at mathematics, in a religious school near Cork. For a time he thought of entering
a Jesuit college. Instead he went to Blackrock College, near Dublin,
where his own children were subsequently educated. He got his degree
at the Royal University, learned Irish, became a teacher, and opened
his career as a nationalist and a revolutionary.

In many European countries today many young men follow roughly
the same pattern. In Yugoslavia, in Bulgaria, in Turkey, in Syria and
Egypt and Palestine, I have met young de Valeras of various breeds.
They may also—who knows?—become fathers of countries. Not many
have the great intellectual equipment de Valera possessed, and very few
can be his equals in force of character; but the general type is the same.
Poverty in youth; the struggle for an education combined inextricably
with nationalism; deep religious faith in many cases; dedication of the
totality of life to a passionate desire for freedom. Many of the nationalisms represented by these young men seem feeble and petty. The
hatreds they engender—that of a young Syrian for the French, for
instance, or a Croat for the Serb government in Belgrade—seem de-
plorable. But they are living factors in the Europe of today.

De Valera, from the beginning, was an extremist of extremists. It
was inevitable that he should join Pearce, MacDonough, MacDermott,
and the others in the proclamation of the Irish Republic at Easter, 1916.
It was a mad adventure. It could not possibly succeed. It was sheer
suicide. So the levelheaded ones said at the time. They were wrong.
The rebellion was put down by force of arms, true, after a week's
fighting; all the leaders except de Valera, true, were sentenced to death
and shot. But the Easter rebellion was not a failure. It was a success.
So at least de Valera would look at it. For out of its fire and bloodshed
came—after tragic years—the Irish Free State, with himself on top of it.

De Valera was one of the "commandants" who were charged with the
actual military operations, and his handful of men were in occupation
of a place outside Dublin called Boland's Mills. This was a key spot,
because the British had to pass it to reach Dublin from the sea. De
Valera's men were the best trained, the best led, in the Irish army. The
British themselves conceded this. One of de Valera's tricks was to station
a very few men, with a couple of machine guns, in an outbuilding from
which the Irish flag was flying. This deceived the British into thinking
that it housed his main force. De Valera did not want to surrender when
the revolt—inside Dublin—was crushed, but he obeyed his superior offi-

cers. He came out of Boland's Mills to surrender, saying: "Shoot me if you like. Let my men alone."

He was sentenced to death by a military tribunal, but the sentence was commuted to life imprisonment when, as I have said above, it became known that the leader was an American. He spent only a year in Dartmoor, because in 1917 there was a general amnesty. Promptly— since most of the other republican leaders had been shot—he was elected president of Sinn Fein. He was also Sinn Fein M.P. for Clare. He never got a chance to sit at Westminster—of course he was an abstentionist and he would not have gone to London even if permitted—because early in 1918 he was again arrested, and this time sent to jail in Lincoln.

About his escape from Lincoln there are many legends. The true story appears to be this. He drew a grotesque picture on a postcard; it showed a drunken man fitting an enormous key into a lock. The card passed the censor, but its Irish recipient, dull-witted, put it away in a drawer, thinking that Dev was off his head. The picture, in reality, was an accurate drawing of the key to the prison yard. Later the friend got another similarly grotesque postcard, this time depicting a smaller key. The friend now saw what Dev meant. A key was made and smuggled in to de Valera. It did not fit. Then Dev managed to make a wax cast of a key from a bit of candle. This was smuggled out; later a key blank and file, concealed in a cake, were smuggled in. And one fine evening Dev walked out of jail.

There was a tremendous manhunt for him. De Valera got to Manchester and hid in the house of a priest. As he walked in, the priest had been reading in the Bible the words "Knock, and it shall be opened unto you." De Valera got to Liverpool, and made his way—with some difficulty—to Ireland. One story is that he disguised himself as an ordinary seaman, and was scrubbing the decks under the very feet of the detectives who searched every boat for him; another is that he was hidden by a friend in the potato stores, literally buried in potatoes till the search was over. Then he went to America, disguised as a stoker. His arrival in New York was a nine days' wonder. The police were still scouring England and Ireland for him. He spoke all over the United States, raised money for the Irish cause, and established himself as the undisputed spokesman of free Ireland.

He returned to Ireland to the tune of more narrow escapes and adventures. He landed first in Liverpool, aboard the *Celtic*. He bribed an officer of a tramp steamer to smuggle him into Ireland; the fee was £100. Whereupon the officer went ashore and got drunk. De Valera was hidden in his cabin. The officer did not return as the ship was due to sail. The captain, furious, came to his cabin to investigate. Thinking quickly de Valera pretended to be very drunk himself. After a tense few moments, the captain dismissed him as a harmless if exhilarated friend of his absent officer. And the ship sailed. Once in Ireland again— this was in 1919—history began.

It was history of a most disorderly, cruel, factional, and bloody kind. De Valera was elected President of the Dáil Eireann, comprising the Sinn Fein deputies from Southern Ireland. The de Valerists constituted themselves a national assembly, refused to take the oath to the King, and proclaimed their independence. Civil war began; the Black-and-Tans and Irish nationalists slaughtered one another. The war ended in a truce in July, 1921, and negotiations went on for five months until the Irish Treaty was signed. This gave Ireland dominion status, but separated the Free State from Ulster. The de Valerists split. De Valera, though the delegates who went to London were his plenipotentiaries, disowned them and refused to accept the treaty. He wanted more. He went into opposition; which meant that civil war started once again.

It ended with mutual exhaustion, and in the spring of 1923 a cease-fire order stopped the bloodshed. De Valera and his group of followers, now a minority, insisted that the treaty had been imposed on the Free State by Lloyd George's threat of war, and refused to sit in the Dáil so long as members took the oath to the King. In June, 1927, the government of W. T. Cosgrave passed a bill requiring that candidates for the Dáil must, if elected, promise to take their seats; this brought de Valera and his forty-three men into the Dáil. A new election increased their strength to fifty-seven. Finally, in 1932, he won a majority, by coalition with the Labour party, and displaced Mr. Cosgrave as President. He went to the country in 1933 and got a clear majority—but a slight one—and has been in power ever since.

When I saw de Valera [in 1936] it was with the understanding that I would not quote him directly on Irish affairs. It was not an interview; merely a brief chat. His office is a simple small room, with "President" printed in black on the frosted window. It resembled the kind of room which a modest executive of a modest business might use. No particular decoration; no covey of secretaries; no swank. Just a big desk next to a small window and a tall, gaunt man behind it.

De Valera looks less severe than his pictures. The long nose and the deep lines to the mouth are his most characteristic features. He seemed younger, I thought, than his fifty-four years. He was alert, interested, and extremely courteous. He speaks with a perceptible brogue; words like "that" or "this" come out with the "th's" thickened.

I explained that I had recently been appointed London correspondent of my newspaper and that this was my first visit to Ireland. I said that I was very happy, after many years on the Continent, to be exploring these new realms, and that life in the British Isles was most exciting. My use of the term "British Isles" was an unconscious little slip. Mr. de Valera did not allow it to go uncorrected. Quite soberly he smiled and said that if I had meant to include Ireland in the British Isles, he trusted that I did so only as a "geographical expression." I explained that my chief duty to my newspaper was to gain knowledge, background, education. "Very well," Mr. de Valera said. "Let your instruction begin at once." And he set out to explain the difference between Ireland and the "British Isles." Some moments later, having again necessity to describe my field of operations, I sought a phrase and said, after a slight pause, "a group of islands in the northern part of Europe." Mr. de Valera sat back and laughed heartily.

We talked a good deal about Austria and Central Europe, whence I had recently come. The President was exceptionally well informed on European conditions and affairs. For a time it seemed that he was interviewing me, not vice versa. He asked a great many questions, all of them acute. What would be the result of a plebiscite in Austria? Was there any possibility of Austrian union with Hungary? What was the attitude of Starhemberg to this and that? What was the character of Dr. Schuschnigg? And so on.

The President thought that the most disconcerting thing about Europe as a whole was the way people—good and intelligent people—had been forced by the pressure of events to think of war as an inevitability. Five years ago that was not true, he was inclined to think. War was something that people feared, and which they hoped would not come. But nowadays it seemed that people considered war as the normal thing to expect. He shook his head gravely, and said that if he had been born a German or a Frenchman he would have devoted his whole life to trying to make permanent peace between France and Germany.

Then Mr. De Valera turned to Ireland, and my "instruction" began. He was patient, explicit, and formidably, somberly reasonable. But in that gaunt face I saw the eyes of a fanatic. When I left him, deeply impressed by his terrific Irishness, I recalled the little story about his first talk with Lloyd George. "How did you get along with de Valera?" the Welshman was asked. "We have talked for two days," Lloyd George sighed, "and he has got up to Brian Boru."

Beyond the obvious things—tenacity, intelligence, and so on—it would seem that a main source of de Valera's power is his community with people. His position—especially since the abolition of the Senate—is virtually that of a dictator, but he is an unchallengeably firm democrat. He believes in the people; his people believe in him. He said recently that he did not think he would ever again have to take arms in his hands and fight for Ireland, but that he would gladly fight—and die—for democracy. His faith in the fundamental goodness and rightness of people is profound. In 1933, however, he was quick to smash the Blueshirt (Fascist) movement, because he was well aware that even the best of people may be misled, and that the first duty of democracy is to protect itself. Almost immediately on reaching power, it will be recalled, he submitted himself to an election which he did not, technically, have to hold. The instant his majority is lost, he will resign. In 1934 an organized campaign against local rates and taxes began. Some of his friends appealed for more vigorous action against saboteurs who were felling trees across roads and cutting telegraph wires. "No," de Valera said. "Leave them to the people. The people themselves will check them."

The faith of the average Free Stater in de Valera is little short of idolatrous. Way back in 1921, when it seemed that civil war was imminent again, de Valera organized his volunteers. During a test mobilization near Dublin a road mine was found to be defective. De Valera examined it, discovered what was wrong, and put it right. "He's a greater soldier than Napoleon," one of his men exclaimed. Now, however good a military amateur de Valera may be, this comparison is, of course, ridiculous. "But it is a great thing," the Irishman who told me this story commented, "that a leader should have followers who really think of comparing him to Napoleon."

Since reaching power de Valera has, as was inevitable, tweaked the British lion's tail. The Dáil has abolished the oath of allegiance to the King, greatly reduced the power and privileges of the governor-general, denied the right of appeal from the Irish Supreme Court to the Privy Council, and withheld the land annuities. These were payments of roughly £5,000,000 per year by Ireland to Britain on account of loans during the last century by which Irish tenant farmers purchased land. The British retaliated by a prohibitive tariff on Irish goods, chiefly the agricultural produce—cattle and milk and butter—which was the bulk of Ireland's export business. An economic war began, and still continues. As a result de Valera has had profoundly to change the texture of Irish economic life. He has cut down imports, built sugar factories, sown the land with wheat, and killed off his surplus cattle by trying to encourage leather and meat-meal industries; in a word, he has been forced by Britain to an experiment in self-sufficiency. The effort has been great, and the cost tremendous.

De Valera's whole life has been dominated by one idea and ideal: a united and independent Ireland. This he has not achieved. What he has achieved is the creation of a Free State which, as it was aptly expressed, is a compromise between republican aspirations and the blunt realities of British power. De Valera's feeling is, perhaps, that a generation is very short in the life of mankind, and that the creation of the Free State is a beginning that will develop to its proper end. He wants and needs only two things, one of his friends told me—peace and time.

De Valera got both. He pushed through a new constitution which transformed the Free State into an entity known as Eire in 1937, sovereign but still a member of the British Commonwealth. Naturally he became the first Taoiseach, or prime minister, of Eire, and he held this post until 1948. Meantime, when World War II came, he declared Eire's neutrality and stayed stubbornly out of the war to the end, which provoked thorny problems.

One curious episode came in 1945 when Hitler killed himself in the ruins of the Berlin Chancellery. Mr. de Valera made a personal call at the German Legation in Dublin to "express condolences for his death." The excuse was that he was merely following "the protocol required of a neutral state." The real reason was probably something else—he was still tweaking the British lion's tail.

Eire left the Commonwealth and, swimming alone, finally became the independent Republic of Ireland in 1949 and subsequently joined the United Nations. Dev became prime minister again from 1951 to 1954, after several years in opposition. The six Protestant counties in the north (Ulster) have, of course, remained loyal to Britain and are still a part of the United Kingdom. This is one thing Dev wanted that he didn't get— the incorporation of Ulster into the rest of Ireland.

In 1959 Mr. de Valera reached the natural summit of his career by being chosen President of the Republic, although eye trouble impeded his activity. At the moment of writing (1964) he still holds this post, aged eighty-two.

CHAPTER 11

~~~~~~

Lavaluation

In this chapter I have used material from both the original edition of Inside Europe *(1936) and its successors. French prime ministers changed so fast in those days that, for a period, I had to write a new chapter about each new premier for each successive edition.*

I saw Laval only once. I thought he was the most nervous man of high station in public life I had ever met.

~~~~~~

There are five or six men in the world on whom peace depends. Destiny has placed me among them.
— PIERRE LAVAL

PIERRE LAVAL, mayor of the tough Paris suburb Aubervilliers, senator for the department of the Seine, prime minister and foreign minister of France, was born in 1883 in the village of Châteldon, in the Auvergne. He is called *"Le Bougnat"*—slang for Auvergnese—figuratively "coal and wood man." The Auvergne is a deep fastness in south-central France, made of granite as old as the earth; the Auvergnese are the grimmest of French peasants, hard-working, shrewd, with primitive reflexes, close to the soil. All over France they are the coal and wood dealers. There is a strong Negroid cast of feature to many Auvergnese; Laval has thick lips and heavy, black, oily hair.

His father, who is supposed to be descended from the Moorish invaders of France, was the village butcher. Pierre did odd jobs as a child, went to school, read voraciously, and taught himself Greek. For two years, when he was about nineteen, he was schoolteacher in the village. Then he studied law, went to Paris, and entered politics. Nominally he is still a barrister at the Paris court of appeals. In his comparatively short period as an active lawyer he had few conspicuous cases; mostly he was an "inside" man on corporate work; he was an indifferent pleader. The great world of politics seized him—and here he pled well.

Laval's chief characteristic is his sense of the concrete, plus wiliness. He is, as the French say, *malin*—a word for which there is no precise translation; it means a sort of worthy unscrupulousness, slyness without evil. The joke goes that Laval was clever enough even to be born with a name which spells the same backward and forward, left to right or right to left. He rose from extreme poverty to wealth; yet he is one of the few French politicians untouched by financial scandal. He is supple as a cat. Like a cat, he never attempts anything he is not perfectly sure of; he calculates every jump to the inch. He gets out of things marvelously.

The great Aristide Briand, whose protégé he was, said of him, alluding to his slipperiness, "Alas, it is impossible to agree with everyone *and* M. Laval." Yet Laval is all things to all people. His manners in the lobbies of the chamber are the quintessence of tact. He is a *couloir* (corridor) politician, a fixer, *par excellence*. He is unassuming, unpretentious; among his friends are men in every party, journalists of every nation. He is on thee-and-thou terms, people say, with more men than any personage in France.

Not only is his capacity for friendship comprehensive; he treats one and all with an unvarying shrewd and watchful eye. Laval is too sly to trust anyone too fully. His character, in fact, embodies to a signal degree the national French trait of suspiciousness. The story is that he taps the telephone conversation even of M. Rochat, his *chef du cabinet*.

His career opened in 1914 when he was first selected deputy from Aubervilliers, where he chose to settle down. He has maintained the closest connection to this proletarian Paris suburb ever since. It is strongly Communist, but enough Communists vote for him to keep him perpetually mayor. He was up for re-election in 1935 while the government was negotiating the Moscow pact—so the Communists didn't fight him very hard. His constituency knows him universally as "Pierrot"; he gets along with everybody, and the poor people of the districts like his homely manners, his bad teeth.

He began political life as a violent Socialist, and until at least 1922 he was known as a man of the extreme left. Since then he has moved steadily right, until now he occupies a center position. He belongs to no political party, and describes himself as "independent." It is not quite

fair to say that socialism brought Laval to power and that he then
kicked it over, as did other notable French politicians. Laval was never
an orthodox party man. He was a lone wolf, on the make. The story goes
that after a split in the Socialist party in Tours in 1920, when he voted
with the majority that favored affiliation with the Third (Communist)
International, he took membership in both the Socialist and Communist
parties.[1]

He was a passionate pacifist at the beginning of his career, when
pacifism took real courage. His name was in the famous "Carnet B" of
the ministry of interior; he was called a "dangerous" antimilitarist. He
refused to volunteer in the French army, and on being drafted he served
as a common *poilu*—for a very brief time. His pacifism made him popular with the disaffected infantry in the black middle period of the war.
In 1916 he cried out in the chamber, "Except for [Tsarist] Russia, we
shouldn't be at war at all!" A year later, referring to the Socialist
peace congress in Sweden, he shouted, "Stockholm is the pole star of
our hopes."

He lost his deputy's seat in 1919, and remained in the political wilderness till 1924. Then his qualities as a negotiator boosted him suddenly
to cabinet rank. The *Cartel des Gauches* (left coalition) [not to be confused with the Popular Front, which came later] was undergoing
one of its frequent shuffles, and Laval acted as an intermediary between Paul Painlevé and Joseph Caillaux; as reward, he became minister
of public works. Caillaux lived in his house, Briand liked him, and
when Briand became prime minister, Laval was first appointed his general secretary—a valuable key post—and later minister of justice.

Then the left coalition crashed and during the regime of Raymond
Poincaré which followed Laval was very much out in the cold. He was
was far too leftish—still—for the harsh, legalist Poincaré. This taught
him a lesson, and he cultivated the friendship of a man distinctly not on
the left—André Tardieu. And when Tardieu formed a cabinet in 1930,
Laval was his minister of labor. Laval played with Briand and Tardieu
both. In January, 1931, he became prime minister—at Briand's
urgent intercession—and included Tardieu as minister of agriculture by
sacrificing left support. His first premiership lasted thirteen months
—a long time for France.

Laval, among other things, went to Berlin, the first French prime
minister to visit Germany since the war. All things to all men, it looked
as if he intended to be all things to all nations too. The Germans gave

---

[1] For a time, too, according to Robert Dell (cf. *Nation*, October 28, 1931), he
joined an abortive "Communist-Socialist" party, which, however, never spread beyond the working class districts of Paris and soon died.

him an imposing reception.[2] In June, 1931, he showed the world his
stubbornness by haggling for seventeen bitter days before France accepted the Hoover moratorium. In October he went to America—the
first French prime minister to do so—and talked to Hoover at Rapidan.
Meanwhile, the influence of Briand was waning. The Old Man of Peace
was sick and tired, but reports that Laval deliberately undercut him are
not true. The two men had great regard for each other, and Briand was
too ill to work; when in January, 1932, he resigned, Laval became
foreign minister as well as premier.

But the next month Laval himself went out of office. He had angered
the all-powerful Banque de France, because he insisted that France stick
to the British pound, and when the pound went off gold (partly as a result of Laval's long haggle over the Hoover moratorium), the Banque
de France lost $100,000,000 on paper. So he went. This taught him a
lesson; the next time he became prime minister he listened to the
Banque more carefully. He was "out" two and a half years. In October,
1934, he became foreign minister after the assassination of King
Alexander of Yugoslavia and Louis Barthou in Marseilles; in June, 1935,
he became prime minister again, when the financial oligarchy vanquished his friend Pierre-Etienne Flandin.

Personal

Laval is a bad speaker, and he never talks in the chamber unless it is
absolutely necessary. He keeps his left hand in his trousers pocket and
saws the air with his right hand. His oratorical delivery, say the sophisticated critics of the lobbies, lacks "elegance." But elegance is the last
quality this swarthy peasant's son would pretend to. And why worry
about public talk in the chamber when private whispers just outside are
more effective?

Laval is probably the only important man in French public life who
has never written a book, and the only one whose final ambition is not
to become a member of the Académie Française. He is not, like Léon
Blum or Edouard Herriot, passionately erudite. His intellect is that of an
engineer, not a scholar. He dislikes abstractions, and he has little use for
art, science, or pure literature. He is a lawyer, but he cares nothing for
legal forms.

The prime minister has other qualities as well as wariness, wiliness, and great political sense. For one thing, his stubborn adhesive-
ness, his tenacity, is notable. *"Tenez bon!"* ("Hold fast!") a man yelled in

---

[2] But the story is that Dr. Brüning, then chancellor, careful to risk no hostile
demonstration at the station, filled it with several thousand detectives and their
wives—disguised as the cheering populace.

a political meeting Laval was addressing. He replied, "I always do."

Laval has no vices—except perhaps that since his doctor told him he must cut down on cigarettes, he now smokes a mere eighty per day. He still wears the kind of white tie that he adopted back in 1914—because white ties don't fade and are washable.

And Laval, a typical Frenchman of the middle class—not a Parisian —is quick, shrewd, logical, practical, and lucid. Compare his intelligence to that of a German, for instance Alfred Rosenberg, Hitler's principal "philosophical adviser" on foreign affairs. Rosenberg is, as Dorothy Thompson once said, a man of great intelligence who is also a complete fool: like so many Germans, he is both brilliant and incredibly stupid; he is capable of erecting dialectical structures of extreme brilliance upon hypotheses which a child could knock apart. Laval is at the other extreme. He thinks not only with his head but with his finger tips.

Every German has a sense of national mission. Every Frenchman, like Laval, has a sense of individual destiny. Scratch a German, and you find a sheep; scratch a Frenchman, and you have an anarchist.

A famous *mot* is attributed to Clemenceau. "Briand," he said, "knows nothing, understands everything; Poincaré knows everything, understands nothing." Laval is in the middle ground. He knows a lot, but not everything; he understands even more than he knows, but he admits limits to his understanding. He loves to reconcile opposites. And he has one trait excessively rare among politicians: he is not vain.

Laval married a woman from the Auvergne, who, like the wives of most French politicians, takes no part in public life. The Lavals, in Paris, live in the little impasse Villa Saïd, next door to Anatole France's old house. He prefers the country to Paris, and often returns to Châteldon, his birthtown, where, the local boy who made good, he owns an imposing château. Even during cabinet crises he tries to get out of Paris for the weekend. He has two or three country estates, including a stock farm in Normandie at La Corbière.

"A countryman has no story," he told one interviewer. "I cannot tell you mine. I have come from the soil and I return to the soil. I don't let this property to anyone. I run it myself. I give my own orders to the peasants. I see myself if a cow is giving as much milk as I expect, if a sick calf is getting well. Often I telephone my workers from Paris, 'Is the buckwheat ready yet for harvest? How are the oats getting on?' I read very little. I walk a great deal. I like dogs and cows. No man is so intelligent as a dog. Nothing is so absurd and delightful as a cow."

His attractive daughter, José, was his companion in all his Europe trotting, until, in August, 1935, she married Count René de

hambrun, who is a second cousin to Franklin D. Roosevelt. The
hambruns, a distinguished French family, are also hereditary citizens
f the United States—by special act of congress—since they are
escendants of another Auvergnese, the Marquis de Lafayette. René de
hambrun's mother, Clara Longworth, was, of course, American by
irth.

* * *

Laval had, it seems, no taste for the prime minister's job in June,
935. He much preferred to stick to his chosen field of foreign affairs
vhere, indeed, his record was much brighter. He assumed the premier-
hip only with great reluctance, because he knew that he could not last,
vhereas as a foreign minister his tenure would be longer. It is his life's
imbition to be the great and permanent foreign minister of France, to
effect French security by long-range settlements with England, Italy,
and Germany.

Meantime he went to Rome, and concluded his famous arrangement
with Mussolini, which, it was announced, settled all outstanding difficulties between France and Italy. He gave Mussolini some worthless
sand in Libya; in return he got promises of joint Franco-Italian action
in Central Europe. But these celebrated conversations with Mussolini
gave him plenty of trouble later, because when the Abyssinian war
began, the Frenchman was torn between his promises to Mussolini—
who assumed that Laval had given him a free hand in Abyssinia—and
the burning necessity to keep on good terms with Britain within the
League of Nations fold.

So Laval went on, the story said, trying to save "both his faces."
Promptly after his Rome visit he helped to negotiate an Anglo-French
accord stipulating the unity of British and French aims in Western
Europe. Hitler's answer to this was the reintroduction of conscription.

When, later in 1935, the Abyssinian crisis split Europe wide open
like a rotten melon, Laval was in a difficult and delicate position. He
trimmed and haggled, trying to extricate himself. His understanding
with Italy had the approval of the French general staff, the most important force in the republic next to the Banque de France. He needed
Italy as a vital element in his defense against Germany. If he offended
Mussolini, with whom he was on cordial terms, he might drive the
inflamed Duce straight into the arms of Hitler. Then where would
French security be? Would Britain, across its narrow but comfortable
Channel, be as useful as a military ally?

Laval dodged and panted, trying to explain to Mussolini the difficulties of his position. Then the situation rapidly changed. The British,
fearful that Laval would pass over altogether to Mussolini's side,

pressed him closer and closer to agreeing to sanctions against Italy b
offering him virtually an Anglo-French alliance. Britain, said Sir Samue
Hoare, the foreign secretary, would resist unprovoked aggression any
where in Europe. This presumably meant that the British would defi
nitely stand by France in the event of attack by Germany. Britain was a
better ally than Italy by far—if Britain could be believed. So Lava
looked about him warily, put his left foot in the British camp, grimace
at Mussolini—and waited to see what would come next.

~~~~~~

*What came next was the Hoare-Laval plan, in December, 1935, t
settle the Ethiopian conflict by giving most of Ethiopia to Mussolini. Thi
caused so much outraged protest in France that it forced Laval out o
office, and forced Hoare to resign in England as well. So ended Laval'
days of "respectability" and he spent five years out of office.*

*He did not return to power until France fell in 1940, when he becam
foreign minister and successor-designate to Marshal Pétain under th
Vichy regime, no less. From 1942 till the end of the war he ran Franc
for the Nazis with dictatorial authority; it was he who turned ove
thousands of his own people to the Germans.*

*Laval was caught and arrested as soon as France was liberated, con
demned to death as a traitor, and shot in October, 1945. He tried—stil
a slippery person—to cheat the firing squad by taking poison, but in th
end died bravely, with the words "Aim at my heart. Vive la France!" o
his lips. The rank and file of patriotic French citizens were not im
pressed.*

*I said early in this chapter that Laval always "gets out of things
marvelously." He did not get out of being shot.*

CHAPTER 12

The Socialist Exquisite of the Ile St. Louis

This article about Léon Blum was written for the Strand Magazine, *London, and was later reprinted in the* Menorah Journal *(Winter, 1937). Then I used parts of it in a revision of* Inside Europe.

M. LÉON BLUM, the Socialist prime minister of France, has become a key figure in the world struggle between Fascism and democracy. This elegant and fastidious man of letters, surrounded by beautiful books and a few delicately chosen objets d'art, is the main counterweight in contemporary Europe to the black shirts, the mass propaganda, the crushing totalitarianism of Hitler and Mussolini. The man of thought stands in opposition to the man of action. Against the bruiser's fist is M. Blum's silver poniard of wit and intellect. Against the loudspeaker echoing the dictated will of a nation in bulk comes the thin but penetrating voice of M. Blum, the cultivated individualist. He has emerged from his ivory tower to confront Hitler and Mussolini, men of the market place.

Blum, leader of a mass movement, is not, however, a man of the masses. Therein lie both weaknesses and strength.

Nor was he, for many years, predominantly a man of politics. "Thank God!" exclaimed one of France's ambassadors, called to meet Blum for the first time. "The new prime minister is not a politician!"

When Anthony Eden saw Blum just before he became Président du Conseil, their conversation—about politics and the international situation

—languished. Then a change came. For an hour the veteran Socialist and the young British diplomat bubbled with reciprocal enthusiasm. They were discussing Proust.

After he had been in power a week, one of his chief political opponents, as if to condone Blum's momentary supremacy, sighed, "After all, Léon *is* an aristocrat and a gentleman."

When Blum came to London in July, 1936, for vitally important discussions with the Locarno powers, he finished his work, then disappeared—into the British Museum. With his friend Princess Elizabeth Bibesco, he was renewing his acquaintance with the timeless beauty of the Elgin marbles.

Blum is no demagogue. He is utterly devoid of personal ambition. He is no opportunist, no adventurer. He is old—almost sixty-five. Yet history called him to fulfill at least one important function, perhaps two. He is the first leader of a Popular Front government in an important bourgeois country since the war. It was historically inevitable that the parties of the left, sometime, somewhere, should unite. Blum performed their first successful fusion. And, in an age of violence and unreason, with Fascism spreading like an eczema beyond Germany and Italy, he represents something like a breath of the past—the spirit of scholarship, intellectual detachment, humanism.

Boulevardier into Socialist

Léon Blum was born on April 9, 1872, in Paris. Very few French politicians, it happens, are Paris born; Blum and his inveterate antagonist, André Tardieu, are exceptions. Blum's family came originally from Alsace. His father was a manufacturer of silk ribbon, with a well-known business which still exists on the Rue du Quatre Septembre. The business, once prosperous, has suffered since styles in millinery changed. Léon was one of five brothers; when the father died the business was given to them jointly. Léon, however, and his younger brother, René, who is art director of the Monte Carlo ballet, leave the other three in charge. The family is Jewish, and all the Blums have a strong family sense. Léon is not an orthodox communicant, but friends call him a "good" Jew. The five brothers meet piously on each anniversary of their father's death.

Léon's maternal grandmother was a remarkable woman, a *Frondeuse,* blind for many years, who nevertheless owned a bookstore on the Île de la Cité, had profound radical convictions, voiced them on fit occasions, and held political *salons* twice a week. Young Blum was devoted to her. Jules Renard, the dramatist, tells in his invaluable *Journal* how Blum attended her. "Graceful as Antigone, Léon serves her, tells her what to eat, prepares her food. Blind for thirty-six years, she looks in the direction of his voice. . . ." In 1901 Blum took her on a holiday through Italy, giving her sight with his lucid explanatory conversation.

Blum's mother emphasized the Jewish family tradition of unity, loyalty, and affection. The father was a merchant; she was an intellectual. She believed, almost too firmly, in justice, social and otherwise. At least the story is told that when she gave apples to her five sons, during their childhood, each got a different half of a different apple, so that full impartiality might be attained. Blum adores her memory, and speaks touchingly of her. He is, however, extremely stubborn about the privacy of his non-public life. Questions about his family or home life are, with charm, rebuffed.

From the earliest days Blum's charm, as well as his intelligence and erudition, was noted widely. For instance, here are two items from the Renard *Journal*:

Nov. 1, 1895. Léon Blum, a smooth-cheeked young man with the voice of a girl, who for two hours by the clock can recite Pascal, La Bruyère, Saint Evrémond . . .

1898 [the time of the Fashoda crisis]: Léon Blum explained precisely and eloquently the absurdity of an Anglo-French war. Charming, this beardless young man, who might be a trifler, but who instead comments luminously on the most difficult subjects . . .

Blum had a first-rate education in classics and the humanities. He went first to the Lycée Charlemagne, then the Lycée Henri IV (where he studied philosophy under Henri Bergson), and finally the Ecole Normale Supérieure. Edouard Herriot, the Radical leader, was his classmate there. Later he took degrees in both philosophy and law. He was, at this time—an odd contradiction—an experienced duelist. But challenges were few after he wounded one antagonist. A recent cinema history of Blum, tracing his career in photographs, shows him dueling —lithe, graceful, with wrists of steel.

His career progressed in concurrent phases. As a lawyer he became an *auditeur* in the Conseil d'Etat, the highest organ of the French civil service. It is a sort of supreme court of France which, though it cannot declare any law passed by the parliament illegal, may pass on injustices in the application of a law. Blum reached the high post of *Maître de Requêtes*, viz., solicitor-general, in charge of the state's cases. This was the top rank he could achieve in the civil service.

But meantime he was inveterately occupied with literature and journalism. He was a sort of literary man-about-town; Stéphane Mallarmé, Paul Valéry, André Gide, Tristan Bernard, Jules Renard, Jules Lemaître, the Guitrys, Alfred Capus, Anatole France were his friends. Passionately fond of the theater, he was dramatic critic first of the *Revue Blanche*, an *avant-garde* literary journal, then of the *Matin*, finally of *Comoedia,* the "official" theatrical newspaper. He wrote half a dozen books, one on marriage, one on Stendhal, one on Eckermann.

Across the life of this young lawyer-aesthete-philosopher was now flung the massive shadow of Karl Marx. Mallarmé left the boulevards for symbolism; Anatole France retreated into irony; Blum became a Socialist. Two persons and one terrible fact combined to transform him into what he has been ever since. The persons were Lucien Herr, the Socialist librarian of the Ecole Normale, and the great Jean Jaurès; the terrible fact was the Dreyfus case. Convinced by Herr's "incredible and truly unique force" (the words are Blum's) he became a Dreyfusard; through Herr he met Jaurès, the dynamic founder of modern French socialism. Blum was still a dandy, *précieux* to his slim finger tips; Jaurès was historically uncouth, famous for spitting into his handkerchief. The two were staunch companions through all the inferno of the Dreyfus affair. Blum discovered in himself a passion not only for the theater, but for social justice. Jaurès took him into the streets, showed him people. Delicately—at first—he fingered proletarian Paris. The enormous ebullience of Jaurès taught him much. And in 1906 Blum and Jaurès together founded a daily Socialist newspaper, *L'Humanité.*

So then politics. Blum wrote the leading article every day. Jaurès with the voice, Blum with the cutting pen: this was the partnership. Jaurès asked him to stand for the chamber; he refused. But his friends say that at that time he could, out of his head, give you the votes on any issue of every deputy, as an American baseball fan can give batting averages. Just before the outbreak of the war Jaurès was assassinated. A month later Blum did finally become a politician, to take up the Jaurès mantle: not, however, in the manner of a subordinate leader carrying on, but as a friend who wished to make a gesture in memory of his friend. Almost at once he was appointed *chef de cabinet* in the Ministry of Public Works. This was Blum's only actual experience of political administration before his premiership—twenty-two years later —in 1936.

After the war he became a deputy from the Seine, though comparatively few Socialists got in; it was a "khaki" election like the one in England at the same time. He was beaten in 1928, and re-elected—for Narbonne—in 1929. The same year he became president of the parliamentary group of the French Socialist party. Meantime *L'Humanité* had become the Communist organ; Blum founded a new paper, *Le Populaire.* To this, the official Socialist newspaper, he contributed a daily leading article, year in, year out. As Socialist leader, he steadily and stubbornly refused participation in the various Radical cabinets of the time. He would not accept power, he said, without responsibility; he would not

accept responsibility without power. Then in May, 1936, the Socialists—
for the first time—became the largest single party. Blum was offered the
premiership and accepted it.

* * *

Blum lives on the Île Saint-Louis, facing the Seine in the oldest and
loveliest part of Paris. The legend that he is very rich is without foundation. He has many books, and everything in the apartment is "a very
good choice," as the French would say; but the elegance is by no means
sumptuous. The Blums were interested in another apartment on the
Quai before they took their present home; it had once been occupied by
Paul Painlevé, a former premier. The landlord said, "I'd be happy to
rent it to you, but I don't like the swarm of journalists and politicians
who came to see Painlevé, and I suppose you too will be *Président du
Conseil* someday." Blum replied that it was altogether improbable that
he would ever become *Président du Conseil*, but he refused to sign a
clause in the lease saying so; and the negotiations were broken off.

Madame Blum is his second wife. His first wife, a sister of the composer Paul Dukas, died some years ago, after long illness. By her he
had one son, now employed in the Hispaño-Suiza factory. The second
marriage is childless. Madame Blum was a Mademoiselle Thérèse
Pereira, an important member of the Socialist party and a member of
a firm of decorators. The marriage has been extremely happy, and
Madame Blum accompanies her husband everywhere. At every political
meeting she is with him, and in the days preceding his premiership she
was practically his *chef de cabinet*. His secretary, nowadays, is—ap-
propriately enough—named Blumel.

Blum works at the Hôtel Matignon, on the rue de Varenne, the
history of which is curious. It is one of the most distinguished of the
hôtels particuliers of eighteenth-century Paris, a stately house behind a
high solid gate and graveled court, with wide gardens and flowering
trees. It was the Austro-Hungarian Embassy before the war. When
Pierre-Etienne Flandin was French prime minister in 1933, he discovered that unless the *Président du Conseil* also held a ministerial job,
he had no office, no place to work. So a bill was prepared making the
Hôtel Matignon the permanent headquarters of the prime minister, like
No. 10 Downing Street. There are living quarters available and Flandin
lived in it; Blum, however, prefers to live at home.

Blum's day is fairly busy, but he keeps his evenings to himself, clear
of official business so that he may read and study. He gets up at eight,
reads the newspapers himself, receives his closest associates after breakfast, and arrives at the Matignon at about 10:30. He always goes home
to lunch, like most Frenchmen. He returns to the Matignon, does his

job, and finishes the day at about 8:30 P.M. He never dines out. He is
not in really robust health, and he has to be sparing of his energy. Very
occasionally he goes to the theater; his most recent visit was to *Le 14
Juillet,* a patriotic pageant. He sleeps well. His bedside reading is Balzac
and Saint-Simon.

Blum's method of work is a combination of apparent slipshodness
and actual precision. He is an inveterate note-taker. He writes everything down, not only ideas as they come to him, but notes on other
people's conversation. An idea may arrive in a taxi, at a meal, during a
debate, in an airplane, during a conference. Out of the pocket comes a
notebook; the pencil flies. If the notebook is not available, Blum uses
any odd bit of paper that may be handy, even a newspaper. But everything must go down—in writing—and at once. These notes, which are
voluminous, are carefully checked, filed, and preserved. Many are
written at night just before he goes to bed.

Although he represents an agricultural and mainly winegrowing
constituency, Blum is almost—not quite—a teetotaler. He is a *con-
venable*—i.e., quite normal—eater, not a famous gourmet, like Herriot.
He smokes French cigarettes—*"grises Gitanes,"* denicotinized—which
are mild and cost fr. 3.50 for twenty; he needs a package or two per day.
He plays good bridge, but plays it seldom. He wears a big black Latin
Quarter hat. He loves conversation, and his friends are legion.

Charm, fastidiousness, intellectual detachment, and humanism are
not Blum's only qualities. There is, for instance, his supernal patience. I
have noted his long refusal to take office—until he could take it on his
own terms. His mind is salty, and he has great sense of phrase. Once
Poincaré remarked, to a group of friends, "I smell war." Blum said
simply, "Let him disinfect himself."

His intellectual honesty is complete. "The free man," he once told
Jules Renard, "is he who does not fear to go to the end of his thought."

His manners are good, and he gets along with people, though at a
certain distance; he was on thee-and-thou terms even with Laval. But
no one could accuse him of being a person of the corridors. His political
discernment is, however, shrewd. As long ago as 1933, quietly, almost
surreptitiously, he was feeling his way toward the Popular Front.

Until the summer of 1936, people invariably accused him of being
doctrinaire. He is not a good mob speaker, being far too rational and
precise. It is doubtful if he ever can become a popular hero, and he has
yet to prove himself as supple as Briand or as flintlike as Clemenceau.
He is not, most people think, a fighter. He has no shoulders: only
antennae. And most observers fear that he seriously lacks physical
stamina, which prime ministers notably need.

But at a time when most democratic politicians were objects of derisive laughter, when the general public in France was sick to death of the venality, the inefficiency, the opportunism, the vulgar heroics of most of the Paris politicians, Blum emerged with one supreme quality: namely, that he commanded *respect*. No one who knew him well could fail to admire the disinterested honesty of his career and mind. Blum stood for reason, and reason was on his side.

Just before becoming prime minister Blum and Msgr. Maglione, the papal nuncio, crossed in the anteroom of M. Serrault. Msgr. Maglione expressed the desire to make Blum's acquaintance. "Soon I am leaving France," he said (he was en route to Rome to become a cardinal), "and I cannot go without having shaken hands with Léon Blum." They talked for a minute or two. As Maglione took leave, Blum remarked, "I don't suppose I may dare to ask your benediction." The nuncio reflected, then replied, "I shall pray God to give you His."

~~~~~~

The Popular Front, which consisted of the Radical, Socialist, and Communist parties, lasted from June, 1936, to April, 1938. Blum's indispensable collaborator during this period, without whom he could have done little, was Edouard Daladier, the leader of the Radicals and—later—a principal author of the Munich sellout. The two major elements leading to creation of the Popular Front were, first, fear of Hitler on all sides, and, second, the turnabout in Soviet policy which (temporarily) permitted the French Communist party and other Communist parties outside Russia to cooperate with the bourgeois left.

Even though the Popular Front itself went to pieces, Blum's impact and accomplishments were substantial. Indeed he changed France more than any man in the twentieth century except de Gaulle. France has today one of the most advanced and comprehensive social welfare administrations in Europe, little as this is generally known, and the responsibility for this is largely Blum's. He introduced collective bargaining, established a forty-hour week, dissolved the Fascist legions which at that time marauded daily on the streets, coordinated the railways, nationalized the aviation and munitions industries, and, above all, curtailed some of the feudal privileges of the Deux Cent Families—the two hundred leading financial families—which had dominated French industry and much else in France for a generation.

Blum was arrested by the Vichy government in 1940, tried for "war guilt" in 1942, and held prisoner by the Germans until France was liberated. He became prime minister of a straight-out Socialist government for a brief period in 1946-1947, and died in 1950.

CHAPTER 13

~~~~~~

The Incomparable Winston

What follows grew out of an article written about Mr. Churchill for Reader's Digest in 1939 and then appeared in the last editions of Inside Europe. Churchill had just been called back to office following the outbreak of World War II and was serving as first lord of the Admiralty. He did not become prime minister until May, 1940, eight months later. The prophecy I made in my first paragraph turned out to be correct.

~~~~~~

There is not much collective security in a flock of sheep on the way to the butcher.

—WINSTON CHURCHILL

I HAVE MENTIONED Mr. Churchill often in these pages [of *Inside Europe*], and I shall mention him often again. This is inevitable, since he is the most vital, pungent, and potentially powerful figure in British public life today. Neville Chamberlain is prime minister. But warfare is a dynamic process, and just as Lloyd George replaced Asquith in 1916, so the ineluctable force of events may eventually push Churchill into Chamberlain's seat. When war came in 1939, the nation demanded that Churchill—who had been in the wilderness for ten years—be included in the government. And he became first lord of the Admiralty, the same position he had held in 1914.

Churchill's squat figure has Renaissance quality. He is omnivorous for experience; he has a swashbuckling love of life and experiment; he is basically an artist and at the same time a builder; he is incredibly versatile. Like the giants of seventeenth-century Italy he can turn his pliable and powerful fingers to almost anything. He has been a war correspondent, soldier, historian, sportsman, water-color painter, politician, lecturer, administrator, journalist, and bricklayer. His oratory has stimulated thousands; his politics have maddened, perplexed, or encouraged millions. He has scarcely been idle five minutes in his life. Two supreme attributes—energy and abstract *talent*—merge to make his character and career the restless dramatic success they have been.

He is an artist, yes—few men write better English prose—but also he is a man of action. Consider the following passage:

Once again I was on the hard, crisp desert, my horse at a trot. I had the impression of scattered Dervishes running to and fro in all directions. Straight before me a man threw himself on the ground. The reader must remember that I had been trained as a cavalry soldier to believe that if ever cavalry broke into a mass of infantry, the latter would be at their mercy. My first idea therefore was that the man was terrified. But simultaneously I saw the gleam of his curved sword as he drew it back for a ham-stringing cut. I had room and time enough to turn my pony out of his reach, and leaning over on the off side I fired two shots into him at about three yards. As I straightened myself in the saddle, I saw before me another figure with uplifted sword. I raised my pistol and fired. So close were we that the pistol itself actually struck him. Man and sword disappeared below and behind me. . . . I pulled my horse into a walk and looked around again.

No, this is not a paragraph from an old-time thriller by Henty or even part of the script of a Hollywood *Beau Geste*. It is by the Rt. Hon. Winston Leonard Spencer Churchill, M.P., P.C., His Britannic Majesty's first lord of the Admiralty. It describes the youthful author's experiences in the cavalry charge at Omdurman (in 1898), when Kitchener destroyed the forces of the Khalifa, and is taken from *A Roving Commission*, Churchill's fascinating autobiography of his early years. Proceed:

In one respect a cavalry charge is very like ordinary life. So long as you are all right, firmly in your saddle, your horse in hand, and well armed, lots of enemies will give you a wide berth. But as soon as you have lost a stirrup, have a rein cut, have dropped your weapon, are wounded, or your horse is wounded, then is the moment when from all quarters enemies rush upon you. . . . I pulled my horse up and looked about me. There was a mass of Dervishes about forty or fifty yards away on my left. . . . They seemed wild with excitement, dancing about on their feet, shaking their spears up and down. The whole scene seemed to flicker. . . . Where was my troop? Where were the other troops of the squadron? Within a hundred yards of me I could not see a single officer or man. . . . What a fool I was to loiter like this in the midst of the enemy! . . .

The other three troops of the squadron were reforming close by. Suddenly in the midst of the troop up sprang a Dervish. How he got there I do not know. He must have leaped out of some scrub or hole. All the troopers turned upon him thrusting with their lances; but he darted to and fro causing for the moment a frantic commotion. Wounded several times, he staggered towards me raising his spear. I shot him at less than a yard. He fell on the sand, and lay there dead. How easy to kill a man! But I did not worry about it. I found I had fired the whole magazine of my Mauser pistol, so I put in a new clip of ten cartridges before thinking of anything else.

Churchill's blood is not merely blue, but practically purple. He was born, on November 30, 1874, in Blenheim Castle, the son of Lord Randolph Churchill and grandson of the seventh Duke of Marlborough. His mother was, as everyone knows, American; Winston—though on many occasions he has seemed to dislike things American—is half-American by birth. His mother, an extraordinarily beautiful and magnetic woman, was the daughter of Leonard W. Jerome, a famous New Yorker of the sixties and seventies, a part owner of the New York *Times* and other newspapers and one of the fathers of American sport and horse racing.

So far as I know, no good biography of Winston Churchill exists. His own books—from *A Roving Commission* straight through the six massive volumes of *The World Crisis* and *The Aftermath*—are of course tantamount to a biography, though we have no detailed record from roughly 1902 to 1911. They are indispensable to the student, and marvelous reading besides. But I wish that some intelligent modern biographer with a gift for psychological insight and the patience to read a million words of documents would tackle the formidable job of writing a full critical biography of Winston. Treasure in limitless profusion awaits him.

The pattern of a man's career, to an extraordinary degree, is written in infancy and childhood. No man ever escapes himself, it seems; no man ever changes himself completely. At birth or before, characteristics are implanted which are like the metal divisions in *cloisonné*. Later, the color, the enamel, is filled in, and the surface texture acquires refinement. Every man is born with a mental and psychological as well as a physical skeleton. The bony structure of the mind, the character, is there along with ribs and jawbone.

Churchill's childhood is a forecast of his whole career. He lived dangerously from the earliest times. Who but Winston would have had concussion of the brain at four and a half, as a result of being thrown from a donkey? Who but Winston would recall with extreme vividness —as his very first memories, memories of events that took place before he was five—such things as a viceroy, "a great black crowd," processions of terrorists and revolutionaries, and "scarlet soldiers on horseback." At five, he sees a white stone tower in Dublin, and is told that

Oliver Cromwell blew it up. Winston writes[1] "I understood definitely that he [Cromwell] had blown up all sorts of things and was therefore a very great man." From the beginning, he loved conversation, audacity, experiment, and soldiers.

He adored his mother, one of the most brilliant women of the time; she was his "fairy princess, a radiant being possessed of limitless riches and power." With his father he was never close, though he admired him passionately. He records that he never had more than "three or four" really intimate conversations with him. His father died when Winston was twenty-one, wrecking the son's hopes that they would work and fight together in the House of Commons. Winston found his mother an "ardent ally" when Lord Randolph died. "She was still at forty young, beautiful, and fascinating. We worked together on even terms, more like brother and sister than mother and son.[2]

Young Churchill's scholastic records and achievements should be a considerable spiritual solace to those young men who, even nowadays, dislike school and do badly at it. He loathed—and to this day loathes—the classics; he found Latin a bore and Greek a useless luxury; he detested—and still detests—mathematics. He was the bottom boy in his class at Harrow, where he was acutely unhappy; he failed three times in the entrance examinations for Sandhurst (the officers training school) before passing finally after merciless cramming. His father once saw him, when he was a schoolboy, playing with his fifteen hundred toy soldiers, arrayed with the utmost flowery precision and exactitude. Lord Randolph asked him if he would like to go into the army. Winston said, "Yes." The boy thought that his father really appreciated his talent for military things. But, he records, Lord Randolph suggested military life because he didn't think he was clever enough for any other career.

(But during his school years Winston showed other qualities. He learned to like English prose. He learned to stay on horses. He learned to speak. It is of considerable interest that, even as a boy, he dictated essays, walking up and down the room, pacing, dictating, exactly as he paces and dictates now.)

At twenty-three Winston wrote a novel, called *Savrola*. It was published and still exists, but copies are very rare. Its theme was that of a liberal politician who, in an imaginary Balkan state, attacks and overthrows a conservative dictatorship—to be overthrown in turn by a socialist revolution! It is extraordinary that Winston, in 1897, was thinking in such terms. The climax of the book—another highly revealing psychological detail—is an attempt by a fleet of battleships to force "a

[1] *A Roving Commission*, page 2.
[2] *Ibid.*, page 62.

sort of Dardanelles" in order to win final victory over the opponent revolutionaries. Exactly eighteen years later Winston Churchill conceived the real Dardanelles campaign, and sent the British fleet to attack the real Dardanelles.

After Sandhurst young Churchill was commissioned in a fashionable cavalry regiment (much to the distress of his father, who had an infantry regiment picked out), and his life as a soldier began. At once—typically —he managed to get leave, and went to Cuba to inspect the rebellion which led to the Spanish American war. His sympathies were with the Cubans; he fought, however, with the Spaniards. On his twenty-first birthday—again typically!—he heard gunfire for the first time in his life. He returned to England, having won a decoration for bravery, and went to India with his regiment. Here he spent two exciting years. He played expert polo, fought in the Mamund Valley, learned to like whisky, wrote a book about the Malakand field force, contrived to get work as a newspaper correspondent at the same time that he was an officer— something quite unprecedented—and by the exercise of every possible artifice succeeded in joining the Tirah Expeditionary Force that went into action on the northwest frontier.

But at the same time, during those Indian years, Winston—no one ever dreamed of calling him anything but Winston—was learning, not merely to act, but something more important—to think. He became suddenly aware that he had had a very bad education indeed. So, while his fellow officers napped in the hot afternoons, he began to read. He thirsted for books and knowledge as a sponge thirsts for water. His mother sent him cargoes of books: for the first time in his life, he read serious books seriously—everything from Plato to Gibbon and back again. Having learned to read, he set himself to learn to write. He studied the art of the English sentence, and found that "paragraphs must fit on to one another like the automatic couplings of railway carriages." When subsequently he returned to England, he determined to go to school all over again, and sought to enter Oxford; but he was too old, and Oxford wouldn't take him.

Then came two experiences in Africa. He joined Kitchener's expedition down the Nile and fought at Omdurman. He wrote a book on this campaign, *The River War,* which is still its standard history, and then quit the army. But in 1899 he was back in Africa again, this time as a war correspondent for the London *Morning Post,* at a very large salary indeed for those days. He participated in the great adventure of the armored train (November 15, 1899), and was captured by the Boers. The man who captured him, by remarkable coincidence, happened to be a Boer officer named Botha, who in later years rose in South African politics exactly as did Churchill in British politics; the two, captor and prisoner, became the warmest friends. Churchill escaped from confinement at Pretoria by a combination of luck, ingenuity, daring, and intuition. Once more he returned to England. This time he found himself a national hero.

Already he had stood for parliament once, and had been defeated. He ran again. And in 1901—he was now twenty-seven years old—he became Conservative M.P. for Oldham. Churchill determined to settle down, and devote his whole life to politics. And he has devoted his whole life to politics ever since, except for interstices filled with bricklaying, the study of military science, half a dozen lecture tours, plenty of travel, painting, playing polo, and the writing of nineteen big books. When his political career began he needed something that had not bothered him before—money. He was by no means rich, as wealth goes in aristocratic England. But money had never been an urgent preoccupation. Now he wanted money. So in five months he proceeded to make $50,000 on a lecture tour!

Churchill's career as a politician after 1901 is so well-known that it scarcely needs repeating. He changed party three times. This is as if, say, Mr. Roosevelt had begun life as a Democrat, spent long years in office as a Republican, and then turned Democrat again—again to receive high office. Winston was a Conservative from 1899 to 1906. Then, disagreeing with his party on Free Trade, he crossed the floor of the house—amidst a blast of objurgation—and became a Liberal. It was as a Liberal that he participated in the 1914 war cabinet. In 1924 he became a Conservative again, and crossed the floor again. Winston's great reputation for "unreliability," the deep-seated antipathy with which both die-hard Tories and surviving pure Liberals held him for years, was not caused so much by his audacity, or even his reputation for "cleverness," but because he had so signally changed his party spots, deserted his party line.

Churchill's first cabinet post came early. He was president of the Board of Trade in 1908, when he was only thirty-four. He became home secretary in 1910, and first lord of the Admiralty in 1911, which post he held till 1915. Asquith chose him for the Admiralty because, in the growing international storm, his energy and fruitfulness were necessary to revitalize the fleet. Churchill developed battleships of the Queen Elizabeth class and had the fleet mobilized for instant action when war came. It is hopelessly unsatisfactory to attempt even to mention the drama, the excitement, the spectacular crowded activity, of Churchill's Great War years. One must read his own *World Crisis*. Even to summarize briefly such episodes as the Antwerp and the Dardanelles expeditions would take pages.

When the Dardanelles campaign failed he resigned from the government almost in disgrace—though the failure was not his fault—and went to France as an active infantry officer. Lloyd George brought him back in 1917 as minister of munitions. Then he served in turn as war minister, air minister, and secretary for the colonies. Again, these years, crammed and packed with events, bursting with decisive action, cannot be told here. They are in the history books. Churchill was a major force in settling the Irish question; humanely, he sought to lift the blockade of Germany; he promoted allied intervention in Russia; he "invented" the country of Transjordan. In 1924 he became chancellor of the exchequer —the boy who could not understand mathematics—under Baldwin, and held this post until 1929. He went out when Labour came in, and the ensuing National Government would not have him. For ten years he retired into the wilderness. But it was a wilderness which he tidied and cultivated neatly. He wrote his books, worked over his ideas, learned to relax—a little—and improved his mind.

During the ten years 1929-1939 [while he was out of office] Churchill —who was becoming grayer, stouter, solider—remained, of course, a Member of Parliament. He became the leader of a small dissident band of last-ditch imperialists who bitterly, for long years, fought Baldwin's quasi-liberal India bill. Then in about 1933, from his lonely and isolated corner seat, Churchill turned into the great Cassandra. He—almost alone among British politicians—sensed the peril to Britain in the rise of Hitler. For six years, day in, day out, he spoke, wrote, argued, exhorted, about Hitler's dangerousness, exploring especially every phase of German rearmament. Few paid him much attention. But gradually his hammering voice became heard. His two compilations of speeches and articles in the middle thirties, *Arms and the Covenant* and *Step by Step,* are outstanding examples of political realism and prescience.

Then when World War II came, in September 1939, Prime Minister Chamberlain accepted the inevitable, and Churchill re-entered the cabinet.

Today, at sixty-five, Churchill looks at least ten years younger than he is. And, of course, considering the tradition of venerableness in British politics—and considering his great vitality—sixty-five is mere babyhood. His cheeks are a clear child's pink, his sparse reddish hair is curly at the edges. He has extremely pale but very bright blue eyes. His manner, receiving someone, is at first deliberate. Those very bright eyes survey the visitor with a curious mixture of patience, reserved amusement, and curiosity. When Churchill begins to talk, with an odd clucking intonation, the words roll and bounce. He chooses words, even in conversation, as a lapidary sets gems. He loves rhetoric, and is a formidable phrasemaker. In a forty-minute talk I had with him, he used at least one word I had never heard aloud before, "marplot," and chose others with expert care. His talk is so good, so full of balance and antithesis, and so incredibly fluent, that one longs for a secret dictaphone to take it down.

But Mr. Churchill can listen too. And good listening is, in a way, the basis of good conversation. He asks more questions than he answers.

As to his inveterate habit of rhetoric—in writing as well as speech—consider the famous and perhaps too purple passage about Lenin from *The Aftermath*:[3]

Implacable vengeance, rising from a frozen pity in a tranquil, sensible, matter-of-fact, good-humored integument! His weapon logic; his mood opportunist. His sympathies cold and wide as the Arctic Ocean; his hatreds tight as the hangman's noose. His purpose to save the world: his method to blow it up . . . but a good husband; a gentle guest; happy, his biographers assure us, to wash up the dishes or dandle the baby; as mildly amused to stalk a capercailzie as to butcher an Emperor . . . Confronted with the need of killing any particular person he showed reluctance—even distress. But to blot out a million, to proscribe entire classes . . . —these were sublime abstractions. . . .

Lenin was the Grand Repudiator. He repudiated everything. He repudiated God, King, Country, morals, treaties, debts, rents, interest, the laws and customs of centuries, all contracts written or implied, the whole structure—such as it is—of human society. In the end he repudiated himself . . . He alone could have led Russia into the enchanted quagmire; he alone could have found the way back to the causeway. He saw; he turned; he perished. The strong illuminant that guided him was cut off at the moment when he had turned resolutely for home. The Russian people were left floundering in the bog. Their worst misfortune was his birth: their next worse—his death.

His wit and irony, rather heavy sometimes, are famous. Once he called Neville Chamberlain "that undertaker from Birmingham." Once he wrote a letter to the *Times* in answer to Lord Hugh Cecil, who had been denouncing Italy, France, Japan, Soviet Russia, and Germany with equal firmness. Winston wrote, "It must be very painful to a man of Lord Hugh Cecil's natural benevolence and human charity to find so many of God's children wandering simultaneously so far astray . . ." Then he points out that the French don't deserve as much censure as the others. He concludes, "In these circumstances I would venture to suggest to my noble friend, whose gifts and virtues I have all my life admired, that some further refinement is needed in the catholicity of his condemnations."[4]

In December, 1937, during a debate on non-intervention in Spain, Mr. Churchill had good fun with Mussolini. The British and French had recently managed to check activity by pirate (Italian) submarines in the

[3] Published by Charles Scribner's Sons, New York.
[4] London *Times*, May 12, 1936.

Mediterranean. The Italians then decided to join the piracy control. Mr. Churchill said, as reported by the *Times*:

In this connection he [Mr. Churchill] must pay his tribute to Signor Mussolini, who joined the common exertions of the Mediterranean powers— (laughter) and whose prestige and authority by the mere terror of his name quelled the wicked depradations of these pirates. (Loud laughter.) Since the days of Caesar himself there has been no more salutary clearance of pirates from the Mediterranean. (Laughter.)

One of the most delightful of Mr. Churchill's ironical sallies came many years ago, when he discovered—just as he himself was becoming a well known author—that an American novelist, the author of *Richard Carvel, Coniston,* and so on, also bore the name Winston Churchill. He wrote to his namesake as follows:

London,
June 7, 1899.

Mr. Winston Churchill presents his compliments to Mr. Winston Churchill, and begs to draw his attention to a matter which concerns them both. He has learnt from the Press notices that Mr. Winston Churchill proposes to bring out another novel, entitled *Richard Carvel.* . . . Mr. Winston Churchill is also the author of a novel now being published in serial form . . . He has no doubt that Mr. Winston Churchill will recognize from this letter—if indeed by no other means—that there is grave danger of his works being mistaken for those of Mr. Winston Churchill. He feels sure that Mr. Winston Churchill desires this as little as he does himself. In future to avoid mistakes as far as possible, Mr. Winston Churchill has decided to sign all published articles, stories, or other works, 'Winston Spencer Churchill,' and not 'Winston Churchill' as formerly. He trusts that this arrangement will commend itself to Mr. Winston Churchill, and he ventures to suggest . . . that both Mr. Winston Churchill and Mr. Winston Churchill should insert a short note in their respective publications explaining to the public which are the works of Mr. Winston Churchill and which those of Mr. Winston Churchill . . .[5]

Mr. Winston Churchill, the American, replied in kind, with equal grace and charm.

Sir Edward Marsh, who was for many years Churchill's private secretary, tells in his engaging memoirs, *A Number of People,* a good many Churchill anecdotes. Once Wedgwood Benn, a small man, rose in the Commons and spluttered with indignation at something Winston had said. Churchill replied, "My Right Honorable Friend should not develop more indignation than he can contain." Once he almost missed a train. Mrs. Churchill was alarmed. But Marsh simply remarked, "Winston is such a sportsman, he always gives the train a chance to get away." Once Marsh accompanied him on an election campaign in the Midlands. Winston walked out in the slums. " 'Fancy,' he said, 'living in one of

---

[5] *A Roving Commission,* pages 217-8.

these streets—never seeing anything beautiful—never eating anything savory—*never saying anything clever!'* ”

Churchill's attitudes are, indeed, sometimes juvenile. He has once or twice been somewhat ridiculous, for instance when he summoned artillery—way back in 1911—to blast some miserable anarchists out of a house in Whitechapel. For years it seemed that he stood always on the wrong side of great social issues. He was against the suffragists. He was against a liberal constitution for India. He was against every shade and aspect of even the very mild brand of socialism advocated by the British Labour party. During the General Strike, when he edited the official government newspaper, he behaved like a schoolboy. In 1919—as if the world were not sufficiently exhausted by war—he was the moving spirit behind the utterly useless and disastrous intervention of the allies in Russia.

Sometimes, when one inspects his leading political ideas, one feels that they are the ideas of an incredibly talented, willful, badly educated child. He seems planted in the nineteenth century, while the world has moved on. For years, he adored warfare. He blamed "democracy" for taking the fun, the style, the glamour out of war. He writes of the Mamund campaign, "Sir Bindon sent orders that we were to stay in the Mamund valley and lay it waste with fire and sword in vengeance. This accordingly we did." He is a convinced constitutionalist and democrat, but elections have at times bored him. He wrote in *A Roving Commission*: "I have fought up to the present fourteen contested elections, which take about a month of one's life apiece. It is melancholy, when one reflects upon our brief span, to think that no less than fourteen months of life have been passed in this wearing clatter."

Winston has an estate, Chartwell, in Kent, twenty miles from London where he likes to spend most of his time. He has built pools, gardens, brick walls, fences, and several small structures with his own hands. For years his favorite exercise was bricklaying; for a time he belonged to the bricklayers trade union, though his hatred of socialists was ferocious. He wears blue overalls, smokes his inevitable long dark cigar, hunches himself before the wall, mixes the mortar, slaps the bricks into place. For relaxation he paints. There have been several exhibitions of his work, for which he uses the name Charles Morin.

Churchill's health is good—though for years he suffered from a dislocated shoulder incurred in an accident in India—and his stamina is sufficient for his task. He records that by taking a short nap every afternoon, he can increase his working day by two hours. He is something of a sybarite in food and drink; he loves the good things of life. Lord Birkenhead once said of him, "It is simple to satisfy Winston; he demands only the best." The best things cost money, and thus he works so hard. His income as journalist and lecturer probably averages $100,000 per year. Of this he spends plenty.

He has a very warm family sense; years ago he married Miss Clementine Ogilvy Hozier, and their life has been very happy. She was—and is —an exceptionally beautiful and talented woman. They have one son and three daughters. The son, Randolph, has already had a stormy career in politics—he fought several by-elections unsuccessfully—and journalism. Until war broke out, he wrote the Londoners Diary in the *Evening Standard*; when war came, he joined up. One of the Churchill daughters, Sarah, an actress, married an American actor, Vic Oliver. Another married a rising young M.P., Duncan Sandys.

When one attempts to list Churchill's qualities and the sources of his power, the first item to come to mind is, perhaps, imagination. For instance, he was largely responsible for the evolution of the tank, which revolutionized modern warfare and helped enable the allies to break the deadlock in the west in 1918. Associated with his brilliantly fertile imagination is the quality of foresight. He was not only the first British politician to appraise correctly Hitler's power; he was the first to see that this made big-scale British rearmament inevitable, and from the earliest days he appealed for it.

Another source of power is his pertinacity. His powerful, stocky body with the very big head bears a not unreasonable resemblance to that of a bulldog. His escapades seeking permission to join Kitchener's force in Africa, when every obstacle—including Kitchener's own acute personal distaste—confronted him, when he was repeatedly checked and rebuffed, are an early case in point. Nothing could stop him in his almost comically stubborn and dogged determination to get what he wanted. As to his courage, it has never been questioned. Once, when a boy, he spent three months in bed, as a result of injuries suffered when he jumped thirty feet off a bridge, in order to avoid capture in a game of hide-and-seek.

His energy, too, is prodigious. On finishing his huge life of Marlborough, he plunged at once into a long history of the Anglo-Saxon peoples, though he was continuing his ordinary work in parliament and politics. He is willing to do any kind of spadework. For years, because he was afraid he did not speak fluently, he committed to memory every speech he delivered. Hard work—as well as a natural genius for language— contributed to his present almost excessively accomplished oratory.

Again, his political realism has always been acute. He could see fundamentals, even if they were distasteful. After the occupation of Prague, for instance, early in 1939, he would instantly have made a pact with Russia, on almost any terms, despite his hatred of the Bolsheviks. His first radio speech to the people of America, in October, 1939, was a masterpiece of political acumen, though he did inadvertently offend some

Americans in the South by his innocent enough peroration about the Civil War.

Finally, he is a supreme and sagacious individualist. He wrote once that he always had a tendency "to swim against the stream." Another point worth emphasizing—and unique—is that he is the only top-rank cabinet officer or leader on either side during the last war who survives to hold important office today.

~~~~~~

Just after the outbreak of World War II a friendly British information officer in London asked me if I would like to have a talk with Churchill, and on September 12, 1939, when the war was ten days old, I was summoned to Admiralty House for a "conversation." It lasted from 5:20 P.M. to 6:05. Mr. Churchill (not then Sir Winston) was courteous and his mood informal. He looked like an extraordinary kewpie made of iron and shiny pink leather. I noticed that his powerful body rose atop thin legs. There were three phones on a clear desk—white, black, and green. He said, "I'm sorry to have kept you waiting," with a deliberate, rather amused, patient expression, and then asked amiably about a colleague of mine, H. R. Knickerbocker, another American correspondent in London, whom he was fond of. Once or twice Mr. Churchill looked abstracted. He smoked a big cigar slowly from the extreme corner of his mouth and asked me to have a "highball." It was amusing to hear this Americanism. There appeared promptly a bottle of Johnny Walker.

After a few moments he rose to show me a large folding wooden frame behind his desk in the great Admiralty Room. He opened it and there I saw a chart. He explained that he had ordered this chart to be constructed in 1911, when he had become first lord of the Admiralty for the first time, so that he could see the position of every battleship, both British and German, at any moment. Returning to the Admiralty in 1939, the first thing he did was to see if that old chart was still there. It was, and no one had opened the frame to look at it for more than twenty years. I did not need to ask if he had resumed the habit of having it posted and inspecting it every day.

Perhaps, even though so many years have passed, it may be interesting to set down some details of Mr. Churchill's mood and talk. He mentioned the United States and seemed to have no illusions about early American entrance into the war. But he knew full well how vital American aid would be. He said that the war would be a long, grim business, and that "the German" was always a "tough creature to beat." Poland was at the moment being submerged, but the West was quiet. He thought that the Nazis were bound to strike elsewhere soon, possibly in Hungary and Yugoslavia, possibly in Switzerland or the Low Countries. I asked if it were not conceivable that Germany might fight merely a defensive war. Mr. Churchill grinned. "They might find it a bit dull."

I went on to ask two basic questions. First, how did this war in 1939 differ from that of 1914? Second, were the allies stronger this time than last? Mr. Churchill became eloquent. He said that World War I had been largely the business of governments, nationalisms, and politics on the conventional level, run in the main by the general staffs of each country. The present war was, however, in sharp contrast, a war of peoples, a conflict of ideologies, a war involving the strongest passions of all mankind, which would reach every man in every street. Yes, the allies were without question stronger vis-à-vis their antagonists than in 1914. He gave two reasons for this assertion, first that the British people, the democracies, were free people who fought of their own free will. They had not been dragooned into combat by a Gestapo, and "democratic" strength was what counted. Second, Germany was weaker today in fundamental resources. Hitler's Reich did not have any money stashed away abroad, whereas the Germany of the Kaiser did. Moreover, the British Empire was an incalculably rich reservoir, wealthy not merely in resources and tradition but "in humankind." The "living energy" of Britain, France, and their associates would establish victory.

It became Mr. Churchill's turn to question me, and this may have been the reason I had been called in to see him. It happened that I had just arrived in London from Moscow. There were not many observers in London then who had been in Moscow when the Russo-German Pact was signed a fortnight before and who could give a first-hand account of Russian moods and challenges. Mr. Churchill proceeded to pump me. Then occurred something memorable, at least to me. Mr. Churchill, brooding aloud on the Soviet Union and its mysterious characteristics, suddenly burst out with a phrase to the effect that Soviet policy was "a mystery in a mystery in a mystery," but that there was a key to it, namely, Russian national interest.

Leaving the Admiralty I could not get Mr. Churchill's phrase out of my head. I certainly could not quote it myself but it seemed to me a shame that it should disappear back into the recesses of Mr. Churchill's mind and be lost forever. It was not right, I thought, that this choice and illuminating statement should have been wasted in casual talk with me. I did not have to worry long. Mr. Churchill made his first broadcast to the British nation as a war minister on October 1, 1939. To my surprise and delight I heard him say, "Russia is a riddle wrapped in a mystery inside an enigma." Far from having forgotten his phrase, he had improved on it. To this day I do not know whether he had first thought of this bit of language during our talk and automatically filed it away for later use, or had invented it earlier and was trying it out on me.

My sketch of Sir Winston which forms this chapter was, I repeat, written in 1939. It reads like the summation of a life already plentifully as well as brilliantly lived. Yet Mr. Churchill, although sixty-five at the time, was at that moment at what, it turned out, was the beginning of his greatest years, not the end. Still to come were Hitler's attack on Norway in May, 1940, and Churchill's rise to the prime ministership; still to come were the German onslaught through the Low Countries and France, the Battle of Britain, and the great Churchill speeches which still make the spine tingle; still to come were the Hitlerite invasion of Russia, the spectacle of nine-tenths of Europe lying under "the dark curse of Hitler," who led, in Mr. Churchill's own words, "the foulest and most soul-destroying tyranny ever to stain the pages of history"; still to come were the turn of the tide, the Normandy landings, the historic meetings with Roosevelt, and the conferences of Casablanca, Teheran, and Yalta; still to come were episodes as various as the Iron Curtain speech in Fulton, Missouri, and Sir Winston's last appearance in the House of Commons in 1964.

I have quoted some Churchill epigrams in the text above. The following are among others I have treasured since my chapter was written. Sir Winston once answered a member of the House who had rebuked him for changing his mind with the words, "My views are a harmonious process which keeps them in relation to the current movement of events." Once he told off a fellow member, Lord Winterton, by saying, "Unless in the future his [Lord Winterton's] sagacity and knowledge of the House are found to be markedly more superior to what he has exhibited today, I must warn him that he will run a very grave risk of falling into senility before he is overtaken by old age."

Mr. Churchill called Ramsay MacDonald "a sheep in sheep's clothing," described Lord Attlee as a very nice modest little man "who had a good deal to be modest about," and said of another eminent colleague, "There but for the grace of God goes God."

Churchill visited Niagara Falls in 1943. He was asked by a reporter whether he had ever seen the falls before and he replied, "I was here for the first time in 1900." The reporter asked him if the falls had changed much. Churchill said, "The main principles remain."

There have been quips ticking him off as well. Lord Balfour once described his World Crisis as "Winston's autobiography disguised as a history of the universe."[6]

To conclude I would like to indicate once more Mr. Churchill's phenomenal multiplicity. My wife, Jane Perry Gunther, and I happened

[6] Sources for these items are variously *Time*, August 23, 1943; *USA*, June, 1962; *Life*, March 5, 1948, and Maurice Edelman in *The Listener*, August 6, 1964.

to be weekend guests at Chequers, the country house used by British prime ministers, in the summer of 1958. Mr. Churchill was, of course, no longer prime minister, but he had left his traces there. A fellow guest showed us an immense seventeenth-century painting, "The Lion and the Mouse" by Peter Paul Rubens, in the central hall—dim, rich in plumage, and magnificent. It portrays the well-known Aesop fable about the lion and the mouse. By gnawing at a knot in a rope, the lowly mouse frees the lordly but shackled lion. The mouse, we saw, was small in size on the huge canvas, but it shone conspicuously—a tiny luminous spot of silvery gray. But it had not always been that way. For a couple of centuries, in fact, the mouse had been becoming less visible as the painting became caked over with age. Then Mr. Churchill noticed on a weekend during the war that the mouse was scarcely visible at all. That night he procured a ladder, assembled his paints, and, in circumstances of the utmost secrecy, painted the mouse in. He dared to touch up Rubens! Well, Mr. Churchill touched up a great many things in his robust and victorious life, and the world is better for it.

Sir Winston Churchill, having suffered a stroke early in 1965, died in London on January 24, 1965, at the age of ninety. The whole free world joined in mourning the passing of its greatest citizen.

Part Four

~~~~~~~~

ACROSS ASIA

CHAPTER 14

~~~~~~

The Emperor of Japan

In 1937-1938 I took a long trip across Asia, out of which came Inside Asia; *various chapters appeared serially in* Reader's Digest, *the* Atlantic Monthly, *the* Saturday Evening Post, *the* Nation, *and a number of other magazines. During this period Japan was coiled to spring. It was fighting an ugly undeclared war in China and was preparing to assault the United States; Pearl Harbor was to come soon. This essay on the Emperor Hirohito appeared in* Harper's Magazine *in February, 1939. In those days little was known about him personally, and to try to find out was an interesting experience.*

~~~~~~

EVEN THE Emperor of Japan is a human being. He eats, sleeps, and has an individual life like the rest of us. He was born; he begat children; he will die. But his human characteristics, interesting as they may be, are overwhelmingly outweighed by the factor of divinity. The Emperor of Japan was "born": but not to a tradition shared by merely mortal men. The Emperor of Japan will "die": but his death, like his birth, will be no more than an episode in what the Japanese call a cosmic, eternal process. He is human, but also he is something of a god.

The Japanese Emperor, being divine, is more than the head of the state. He *is* the state. Sovereignty is believed by the orthodox to reside actually *in* the person of the Emperor, not in any organ of government. The Emperor and the people are one. All Japanese, not merely the Emperor, consider themselves to be of divine or semi-divine origin; the Emperor is the ruling deity, a kind of father, uniting the entire population in his august, impersonal, and radiant "being."

The godlike qualities of the Emperor of Japan are difficult concepts to describe. First, we plunge at once into mysticism. But no understanding of Japan is possible until the position of the throne is made reasonably clear, which is quite above and beyond that of any throne in the West, largely because of the religious factor. Second, we risk offending the Japanese, to whom the person of the Emperor is not a fit subject for description.

The veneration, the indubitable awe, with which loyal and patriotic Japanese—which means a very considerable proportion of the Japanese nation—hold the Emperor is a phenomenon unique in contemporary politics. To westerners it may be a baffling phenomenon. But most westerners, who inherit the tradition of Aristotle and Newton, who believe in the validity of scientific inquiry, in the free play of the free mind, in the rational investigation of experience, will find a very great deal that is baffling in the mysticism of Japan. By mysticism I do not mean self-delusion. I mean merely the instinct of a people to accept freely phenomena which cannot be accounted for by purely intellectual processes.

* * *

The bulk of the Japanese people have great reverence for their Emperor, but very few have ever seen him. This is because they are supposed to cast down their eyes when, in some ceremonial procession, he approaches. They are not, strictly speaking, permitted to *look* at him —though doubtless some bold spirits peek. The origin of this practice is the mythological belief that direct view of the Son of Heaven will cause blindness.

Portraits of the Emperor are comparatively rare. By common custom the face is covered with tissue or cellophane.

When the Emperor travels, even if it is for hundreds of miles across Japan, every window shade along the entire route must be drawn— which necessitates a good deal of work by the assiduous police.

No one must look *down* on the Emperor. The tower of the new police building in Tokyo has never been completed, partly because it was discovered that its windows might give a view of the imperial gardens. (On the other hand, modern exigencies have compelled modifications of this rule; for instance, when the Emperor opens the Diet, journalists in the gallery do look down on him.)

Recently, the Japanese police forbade a production of *Hamlet*, because its "dangerous thoughts are likely to cause disrespect for royalty."

Time magazine published a front-cover portrait of the Emperor in 1936. The editors were asked to appeal to their readers not to handle the magazine upside down, or to place any object on it. The cartoonist William Gropper once caricatured the Emperor in *Vanity Fair*—not very savagely. The Japanese Embassy in Washington immediately lodged an official protest. The Japanese issue of *Fortune,* an admirable job, was suppressed in Japan not so much for its contents, but because on the cover it printed the imperial chrysanthemum, a precious Japanese symbol. (Curiously, *Fortune* gave the chrysanthemum fifteen petals instead of the correct sixteen. Or perhaps this was a clever—but unsuccessful—dodge to avoid offense, by means of deliberate inaccuracy.)

When a member of the imperial family visits the Yamato Hotel in Mukden, he occupies the entire third floor, which is the most comfortable. The fourth floor is then cleared of other guests.

A distinguished foreign ambassador asked his Japanese secretary his opinion of the Emperor's appearance (which was quite good and normal) after both had attended an imperial garden party. The secretary refused to reply on the grounds that a reply would be blasphemy.

Once a traffic policeman misdirected the imperial procession during a village ceremony. He killed himself in shame. (It is not true, however, that the Emperor's chauffeur or locomotive driver must commit *hara kiri* if their conveyances are late.)

Doctors were not allowed to touch the bodies of the Emperor's father and grandfather, except with silk gloves. The legend is that even the court tailor had to measure the late Emperor's clothes from a respectful distance—which made a good fit somewhat difficult.

A well-known jurist and professor, Dr. Minobe, who had held the chair in government at Tokyo Imperial University for thirty years, lost his job and narrowly escaped assassination because it was discovered that in a book published twenty years before he had referred to the Throne as merely an "organ" of the state.

Details like these, which are chosen from among dozens available, are sufficient preliminary indication of both the brightness and the opacity of the aura that surrounds the Emperor. We must try to define this aura, to circumscribe it. The Emperor is the living symbol, the emblem, the personification, of Japanese destiny, which is in vital conflict with that of the United States, and which demands complete and impartial investigation.

Son of the Sun

His Imperial Majesty Hirohito, one hundred twenty-fourth emperor of Japan in an unbroken dynasty, was born on April 29, 1901, in Tokyo at 10:10 P.M. He was educated by tutors, in the Peers' School, and on a trip to Europe. He became regent in 1922, when his father was overcome by illness. In 1924 he married Princess Nagako Kuni, by whom he has six children. On Christmas Day, 1926, Hirohito ascended the throne, and in 1928 was formally enthroned.

First let us tackle the name. Japan has had only one dynasty in 2,599 years, according to Japanese mythologists and historians; thus no family or dynastic name is necessary. Literally Hirohito, the given name of the Emperor, which is written in two ideographs (symbols) in Japanese, means "humane" or "exalted." The second ideograph in the name, "hito" (exalted), appears in the names of most emperors. Only the first ideograph (in English each ideograph is two syllables) varies. No one else in Japan is likely to use the ideograph "hito" in his name; the law does not forbid it, but custom does. Rumor is that a peasant in a remote district once named his son "Hirohito"; when he discovered that this was the Emperor's name, he killed his family and committed *hara kiri*.

Immediately an Emperor begins his reign, he chooses another name. This is the name of the reign, while he lives; when he dies, by recent custom, *he* becomes known by this name. Thus the last Emperor, Hirohito's father, was named (at birth) Yoshihito; now he is called "Taisho," the name he adopted for his reign. The present Emperor calls his reign "Showa," which means—quaintly enough—"Radiant Peace." After his death his reign will be called the Showa period, and he himself will be known, not as Hirohito, but as Showa.

Japanese seldom refer to the Emperor by his name. To do so is to commit sacrilege. They seldom, in fact, even mention him, if they can avoid doing so; when they must, they refer simply to the Throne, or say *Tenno-Heika* (His Majesty the Emperor), or *Tenshi-Sama* (Son of Heaven). After an emperor dies the word "Tenno" (literally, emperor) is added to his name, like Meiji-Tenno. Of course, Japanese continue to venerate and indeed worship the Emperor, as they do all ancestors, after death as well as before.

The term "Mikado" is seldom used in Japan to identify the Emperor, except in classic literature. Literally "Mikado" means "gate" with an honorific prefix; hence "Gate of Heaven," which is analogous to terminology in our experience, like Sublime Porte. Japanese sometimes use "Mikado" as an indirect way of referring to the Emperor impersonally, as someone in London might say "the Court" to indicate George VI. But he is *never* called "the" Mikado, which is purely foreign usage.

Emperors seldom even write their own names; names were not, in fact, used on official proclamations until 1868. Now the Emperor signs some papers, but a seal is used as a rule, not a signature. When a law is promulgated in the official gazette, two characters meaning simply "Honorable Name" are printed to indicate the seal. Once or twice in bestowing decorations to foreigners the Emperor has signed his name in English.

There have been three emperors in the modern period, i.e., since the "Meiji Restoration" in 1868, when Japan re-entered the world with such a rush and push as the world has seldom seen before. The Emperor who was "restored," that is, liberated from control by the shoguns (dictators), was Mutsuhito, known now as Meiji. He was the present Emperor's grandfather, and one of the great men of Asia; he ruled from 1868 to 1912—forty-four tremendous years. His son, Yoshihito or Taisho, the present Emperor's father, was a lesser man. In fact he died unbalanced. It would be worth one's life to mention this openly in Japan.

But the family of Hirohito, the present Emperor, goes back considerably more than these two generations. Indeed, it goes back in uninterrupted succession for 2,599 years, all the way to 660 B.C. when the first Emperor Jimmu[1] founded the dynasty! It goes back even further than that, for Jimmu himself was a fifth-generation descendant of the Sun Goddess, the chief Japanese deity, who was herself a descendant of other deities. The legend is that the Sun Goddess sent Jimmu to Japan to found "her" dynasty of chosen people there; it is, of course, pure mythology, since written records of Japanese history do not exist before the fifth century A.D. But a Japanese historian would lose his job for saying this. The point to make is that the orthodox Japanese like to believe that the mythology, even if it is mythology, is true. For instance the actual *date* (February 11 by our reckoning) of Jimmu's accession is celebrated as one of the great Japanese national holidays.

The dynasty has never died out. It has survived almost 2,600 years. One reason is a fertility natural to the Japanese. Another is that adoption is the legal equivalent of actual kinship. Another is that, until recent times, a considerable number of Japanese emperors had concubines; monogamy was not established till 1889. At any rate there are today no less than fifteen different branches of the royal house. Women may not inherit the throne, but there is no danger that the males will give out. The remarkable thing is not so much that the imperial line survived naturally, but that it was never overthrown. During many centuries the emperors were shadows, utterly without temporal power, but no Japanese tyrant, shogun, or mayor-of-the-palace ever dared to suppress or change the dynasty.

Japanese emperors are not crowned. They simply accede to the succession. There is no crown. At once the new emperor issues his first imperial rescript. That of Hirohito, following traditional phraseology, began as follows:

Having succeeded, through the benign influence of Our Imperial Ancestors, to the Throne of a lineal succession unbroken for ages eternal, and having assumed the power to reign over and govern the Empire, We have now performed the solemnity of the accession to the Throne. It is Our resolve to observe the fundamental rules of the State, to cultivate the inherited virtues, and to maintain intact the glorious tradition set by Our Ancestors.

[1] One of Jimmu's female successors had the nice name "Jingo."

The equivalent of coronation is the great festival of enthronement (*Go-Tairei*) and the food festival (*Daijo-sai*), held in Kyoto, the old capital, after the accession. These are a combination of secular and religious rites—just as is a coronation in Westminster Abbey—but the religious element is more pronounced. First in circumstances of great ceremony the Emperor approaches a small, simple Shinto shrine and "informs the spirits of his ancestors that he has ascended the throne." Second, appearing in dull orange robes ("the earliest color of the rising sun"), he listens to the official communication from the prime minister announcing the accession. The scene is tremendous; nothing in Europe or even Asia can rival it. "The living world is informed of what previously had been announced to the world of spirits." Finally, quite alone, the Emperor celebrates a kind of harvest rite, by giving food to the gods, and communing in a lonely hut with his heavenly kin.

Three paramount symbols of kingship and divinity play their role in these rites, the mirror, the necklace, and the sword, which the Sun Goddess "gave" Jimmu as symbols of sovereignty. Of these the mirror is the most sacrosanct, because in it one sees the soul of the sun; even the Emperor is supposed never actually to look at it; in a black box, bound with white silk, it reposes hidden in the shrine at Ise. A replica of the mirror, however, is kept in that room of the Tokyo palace known as the Kashikodokoro, or Place of Awe. According to legend the mirror was the supreme instrument of welfare in the early days; its reflection caught the august and terrible eye of the sun, and thus blinded all adversaries.

The necklace or chaplet, composed of stones—rather like our wampum—is kept in Tokyo. The sword exists only in replica, since the original was "lost" in battle in feudal times. When a new emperor accedes to the throne, his first privilege is to accept custody of the sword replica, the mirror replica, and the necklace. All three, the supreme holinesses of Japan, go with him to Kyoto for the enthronement; but the *original* mirror never leaves the shrine at Ise, near Nagoya, which is the most hallowed place in Japan. It was put there—so the mythology goes—by an emperor in the year A.D. 3.

The shrine of Ise, that of the Sun Goddess herself, is visited by the Emperor on great occasions. He goes there ceremoniously to inform the Sun Goddess, to report to her, as it were, of imposing events. He went after his father's death; both before and after his trip to Europe; after his marriage, and so on. All cabinet ministers or other high officials must go to Ise, pray there, and *notify* the Sun Goddess of their appointment. This is their first duty. Some years ago a cabinet minister named Mori, visiting the shrine, inadvertently committed the sacrilege of lifting its curtain with his walking stick. He was assassinated, and his murderer exalted as a hero.

I quote from Hugh Byas in the Enthronement Edition of the *Japan
Advertiser*:

Not only is the Shrine of Ise a holy spot in the religious sense, but it is
the visible symbol of the nation's whole being. The Japanese attitude toward
it is one of *makoto*, a word which can not be accurately rendered into English. Patriotism, nationalism, Emperor worship, the attitude toward the
throne, are words or phrases used for *makoto*, but each of them is very in-
exact. Loyalty, filial piety, the emphasis on the family rather than on the
individual, are still other attempts to put *makoto* in English. *Makoto* embraces
all of these, but no one of them has the exact connotation to the Japanese
consciousness that it has to the American or European. Foreign thought
does not comprehend the reverence, loving loyalty, respectful *kinship* of the
Japanese toward his Emperor, and therefore toward the nation, and therefore
toward himself as a part of the nation.

Recently I stood near the entrance of the great Meiji shrine in Tokyo.
Few things can be more interesting than to watch Japanese prayer. It
was a rainy afternoon, but ladies in kimonos, old gentlemen in frock
coats, walked along the shiningly neat grass, up the combed gravel path,
and stood there briefly in the rain. It is all done outdoors. The devotee
approaches, bows, then sharply claps his hands. This is to summon the
spirit of the ancestor with whom he wishes to confer. A few moments
then of conversation with the ancestor—in a quick, urgent, audible
whisper. Then another bow, copper pennies tossed across the straw mat,
a final bow, and departure backward.

When I arrived in Japan I distinguished myself for naïveté by asking
what I thought was a simple question: "If the Emperor is himself a god,
to whom does *he* pray?"

He prays, of course, to his forebears. But inadvertently I had raised
a complex theological point. Is the Emperor himself actually a god? Of
course he is divine, but is he "a god"? Authorities vary. By some orthodox
Japanese he is considered definitely to be, in his own person, "an actual,
living Deity." Others say merely that he is to the Japanese mind "the
supreme Being in the Cosmos of Japan as God is in the universe to a
pantheistic philosopher."

Shinto, the national religion, is a difficult concept to define. Recently
a government commission spent three years trying to do so, and then
gave up. In essence it is simply worship of Japan—the nation itself. It
exists in two forms, secular and theological; all Japanese patriots are
believers in Shinto, but they may be Buddhists—or even Christians—at
the same time. Its distinguishing mark is a combination of ancestor
worship and patriotism; all Japanese have a common descent from the
Sun Goddess, and they venerate their ancestors; all may derivatively be
said to be members of the same great family, with the Emperor at its
head. There are eight *million* gods in the Japanese pantheon. Every

soldier killed in battle is enshrined, revered by his descendants, and be comes, if not an actual god, at least a definite figure in the general re ligious scheme of things.

In his beautiful and indispensable book, *Japan: A Short Cultural History*, Sir George Sansom says:

At the core of all Shinto Ceremonial is the idea of purity, and at the core of all Shinto belief is the idea of fertility. . . . In its earliest days the reli gion which, much later, came to be known as Shinto, the Way of the Gods, seems to have been a polytheism of a crude and exuberant type. . . . To say that primitive Japanese conceived of all natural objects as harbouring a spirit, or that their religion was an animistic nature worship, is to apply exact terms to things which are too vague and various for simple definition.

The chief point to make about Shinto is its comparatively recent revival as a political as well as a religious force. Like the temporal power of the Emperor himself, Shinto was in eclipse until the Meiji Restoration in 1868. Gradually the architects of the restoration discovered the ex tremely practical use of such religio-patriotic symbolism. The Emperor, as head of the nation, was also head of a vast single *family,* if Shinto doc trine was to be believed; thus—to put it crudely—Shinto could be made to serve an extremely pertinent political aim, namely, the conception of indissoluble unity of the people. Japanese worship of the Emperor has existed since the earliest times, but it is extraordinarily significant that this worship has been latterly much reinforced and re-emphasized. For instance, the Emperor Meiji was the first *recent* emperor to pray on his accession at the Ise shrine.

When you ask an intelligent, modern-minded Japanese, a research student in biology, for instance, or a political journalist who went abroad to school, if he believes the Emperor of Japan to be divine, he will prob ably reply—if the door is shut—that he does not. The official story of the Emperor's descent from the Sun Goddess is too preposterous to swallow. But most Japanese, even the minority with highly modern minds, believe it to be a good and valuable thing that the bulk of Japanese *should* believe in imperial sanctity. Thus even the skeptics encourage the mythology. And they serve their purpose best by behaving as if they believed in the mythology too.

Thus we reach a cardinal point. The divinity of the Emperor is a political weapon of great potency in the hands of those who rule Japan.

Personal Life of the Emperor

The Emperor lives today in the inner, hidden halls of the Kyujo or palace in the center of Tokyo, one of the most formidably picturesque buildings in the world. For centuries it was the fortress and castle of the shoguns; the imperial family took it over on being restored to temporal power in

1868. With great pictorial impact it symbolizes the complex phenomenon it houses. A broad outer moat (once there were three separate moats), with water of iridescent green, reflecting the gnarled pines alongside, bounds a tremendous granite wall. The bulwark of this irregularly circular wall, some miles in length, is interrupted by forty gates, and by a series of commanding towers. The wall is built of very large square gray boulders, set against a bank of earth without mortar or plaster, so that it is earthquake proof. Inside the wall are the green lawns, the gardens, the villas, the palace, and the various subsidiary paraphernalia of the imperial establishment. Entrance, except to specially invited guests, is forbidden.

In summer Hirohito and his family go as a rule to Hayama, a watering place near Kamakura, about thirty miles from Tokyo. Here the Emperor swims (he is an excellent swimmer) and otherwise relaxes. Often he collects specimens of marine biology for laboratory work. His beach is, of course, private, but in the adjacent area other male bathers must wear tops to their suits, which is not obligatory elsewhere in Japan. The imperial family has other villas scattered through eastern Japan—perhaps fifty in all. The Emperor seldom visits them.

His routine of work, his official occupations, are determined by ancient custom and are severely circumscribed. Twenty-one times each year there are ceremonies of worship to conduct. Once a year the Emperor attends services at the Yasukuni shrine, where the Japanese military dead are enshrined; once a year he attends the graduation exercises of the military and naval academies; he attends the opening of the Diet and similar ceremonies; he is consulted by the prime minister and the army chieftains. He receives newly accredited foreign ambassadors, and occasionally gives audiences to other distinguished foreigners.

The presentation of letters of credence by a new ambassador is an extremely formal ceremony. The new ambassador is received quite alone. None of his staff enters. He advances, bows three times, and reads his letter. The Emperor then reads his reply. After this there may be a few moments of conversation. The Emperor speaks through an interpreter, who must keep his eyes on the ground, and who *whispers*. The new ambassador then bows again three times, and departs backward.

When the Vice-President of the United States, Mr. Garner, visited Tokyo en route to the Philippines, he told friends in his jovial way that when he was received by the Emperor he was going to take an American dollar watch from his pocket, and say, "Your Majesty, here is *one* thing you folks can't imitate and undersell!" Horrified, the Americans in Japan told Mr. Garner that he must under no circumstances do this, since, if he did, the Emperor's aides in the room would consider that the Emperor had been insulted and would have to commit suicide. In any case Garner gave up the idea—after finding several Japanese watches that *were* imitation Ingersolls selling for thirty cents.

Twice a year the Emperor gives a large garden party—a cherry blossom party in April and a chrysanthemum party in November—to which some 7,000 guests are invited. The invitation contains no R.S.V.P.: it is a command. Guests assemble in formal afternoon dress, and the Emperor and Empress walk slowly through the garden from the imperial pavilion. Hats may be worn by gentlemen (of course they are doffed as the Emperor passes), but not overcoats, no matter how cold the weather. Until recently the old-style frock coat was *de rigueur*, because it covered more of a person than a cutaway, and hence was considered to be more modest. The garden parties have been canceled since 1937, when the China War, or, as the Japanese say, "incident," began.

Occasionally before the war the Emperor would give a dinner party, for instance if a visitor like a British royal prince were in Tokyo. At a big banquet, the Emperor sits alone on a small dais, higher than his guests. If the party is small, his chair is at the normal level. The Emperor knows a little English and French, but he converses in Japanese through an interpreter. Guests at an imperial party, by universal Japanese custom, must take food away with them. In the old days they were supposed to carry away fruit or rice, as a symbol of the Emperor's hospitality; now a small box of cake is given each guest. This should be carefully preserved. Food, any food, is precious in Japan; historically it is a hungry country, and the custom derives from this. Ministers and ambassadors, once a year, receive small teacups as gifts; you can tell how long any diplomat has been in Tokyo by the number of these cups carefully and conspicuously placed in his dining room.

The Emperor plays tennis and golf—persistent rumors describe a nine-hole golf course inside the palace wall, but few outsiders have ever seen it—but his chief hobby is marine biology. (His golf score, by the way, is a zealously guarded secret.) Visiting biologists of distinction saw him fairly regularly before the war, though the visits were never officially announced. Several rooms of the palace serve as a laboratory, and the Emperor is happiest when he is working with his microscope, inspecting minute growths and organisms, which he likes to collect himself. Photography is another hobby, as it is of almost all Japanese. He likes to ride occasionally, and his white stallion, *Shirayuki* (White Snow), is well known.

He is up at six as a rule, and retires early. He neither drinks nor smokes. His health is stated to be good, though he was frail as a boy. He is, as everyone knows, shortsighted. One curious item is that he is said never to wear any clothes twice, not even underwear. The used clothing is given to minor officials, provincial administrators, and the like, and is a precious gift. When he must leave the palace for some ceremony, he is driven in a maroon limousine, a color reserved for the imperial family; no other maroon automobiles are allowed in Japan. Extreme precautions are taken to guard him. Streets are shut off; every building on the route is rigidly inspected.

The Emperor had several tutors as a child, one of whom, General Nogi, who captured Port Arthur in the Russo-Japanese War, committed suicide with his wife as a mark of devotion when the Emperor Meiji died. A subsequent tutor was Admiral Togo, the greatest Japanese hero of the day. The Emperor, it is recorded, showed marked talent as a schoolboy; one of his early enthusiasms was Aesop, and before he was ten he was composing fables in the Aesop manner. At eleven he began keeping a diary, and has kept it methodically ever since. When, at thirteen or fourteen, he was asked what person in Japanese history impressed him most, he nominated the Emperor Kameyama, who prayed that his life be sacrificed to spare Japan from the Mongol invasion. Asked for his favorite poem, he quoted one which says: "The light of the sun and moon withholds no favors; they shine equally upon all."

In 1921, when heir apparent, he went abroad—something that no Japanese royal prince had done for 2,581 years. When his departure was announced, one hundred Tokyo boys offered to commit *hara kiri* jointly if he would give up the trip. He went. Presumably the boys are still alive. . . . Most of the existing anecdotes about the Emperor—there are not many—derive from this period of travel. Aboard a warship a pet monkey put a screw in his mouth. No one could make him disgorge it—until Hirohito had the bright idea of giving him a piece of sugar instead. In the London underground Hirohito, who is not allowed to touch money, had no ticket, and replied to the rebuke of the conductor with "exemplary sang-froid." And so on. In Gibraltar the Prince bet on the races. He won. "With rare presence of mind and exquisite tact," wrote a Japanese witness quoted by *Time*, "His Imperial Highness took the bundle of notes, handing it at once to Admiral Oguri so that it might be properly dealt with."

Cautiously—very cautiously—attempts were made in the late 1930's to "humanize" the Emperor. He has never spoken on the radio, and has never been photographed inspecting workers' dwellings or even greeting winners at athletic meets, but gradually—very gradually—he is being presented to the Japanese people as a human as well as a divine being. For instance, statements were recently issued by the Imperial Household, an unprecedented occurrence, mentioning the "arduousness" of His Majesty's inspection of troops, his "assiduous" work in politics, and describing in "warm, human, and intimate" terms his daily routine and regime.

Emperor as Poet

Every New Year's Day the poetry bureau of the Imperial Household announces the results of the annual poetry competition, and the winning poems are ceremoniously read aloud. All subjects of the Empire of Japan, without regard to rank or station, may submit a poem of the *tanka* variety, which means that it must consist of thirty-one syllables, on a given subject, every year. The Emperor and members of the imperial family always write poems in association with the competition, though they do not take prizes, being *hors concours*; the Emperor's poem is read first, and then the efforts of the ten prize winners. Normally about seven thousand poems are submitted. But last year thirty thousand poems came in, partly, it was thought, because of the number of soldiers in the field, who have the ear of His Majesty through the circumstances of this event, and by no other.

The Emperor's poem in 1936 was:

> As I
> was visiting
> the Shinto Point in Kii
> clouds were drifting far
> over the Sea.

In 1938 he wrote:

> Peaceful
> is the morning in the shrine garden;
> World conditions it is hoped
> will also be
> peaceful.

And like a subterranean hiss the word went through Japan, quite without other basis: the Emperor is unhappy because of the [China] war; the Emperor wants the soldiers to come home; he wants peace.

Richer Than Croesus?

From one point of view, even though traditionally he never handles money, the Emperor of Japan is beyond doubt the richest individual in the world. This is because he owns Japan. The entire country is his. The statement may seem astounding, but Japanese authorities bear it out. Consider, for instance, the words of a cabinet minister named Uyehara, author of *Political Development of Japan*: "From the Emperor everything emanates; in him everything subsists; there is nothing on the soil of Japan existent independent of him. He is the sole *owner* of the Empire."

This conception, even though acknowledged by Japanese law, is not strictly adhered to; much of the forest land of Japan is the actual property of the Imperial House, and is exploited as such; but agricultural land—though theoretically belonging to the Emperor—is in practice the property of individual landowners. In the old days the emperors allotted agricultural land to the feudal lords, who in turn let it to peasant occupants. These peasants still hold it. Japan is the country par excellence of small peasant landholders. There are few big farms, few big estates.

The actual civil list is not abnormally high—4,500,000 yen ($1,350,-000) per year. But of course the imperial family has its private investments. When Prince Ito went to Berlin to get Bismarck's advice about the Japanse Constitution, the old Prussian is supposed to have said that the monarch must be independently rich if the monarchy was to work on a constitutional pattern. The exact extent, variety, and amount of imperial investments are not authentically known. But good authorities agree that the House is the third or fourth biggest capital enterprise in the kingdom.

Imperial Family

Hirohito is almost unique among emperors; his marriage was a love match, so far as that is possible in Japanse imperial circles. A love match, moreover, in the teeth of a convention established thirteen centuries ago.

At a reception in Tokyo the youthful Crown Prince met Princess Nagako, eldest daughter of Prince Kuniyoshi Kuni. The young princess was certainly of excellent blood; her mother, for instance, was a member of the Satsuma clan, one of the two clans that made the Meiji restoration. But—the Princess Nagako was *not* directly a member of the great and distinguished Fujiwara family, which, by tradition thirteen hundred years old, was the sole family group in Japan from which empresses might be chosen. Nevertheless young Hirohito fell in love with her, and the marriage was arranged. There was very serious opposition among the orthordox; wounded feelings were salved, however, by the fact that the Princess Nagako, though not directly a member of one of five eligible lines of Fujiwaras, did have remote Fujiwara blood, which is indeed shared by most of the aristocracy of Japan.

The Empress is an exceptionally pretty woman. Between her betrothal and marriage she made a good many public appearances; for instance, at such functions as art exhibitions, teas at the Tokyo Woman's Club, and so on. In those days she usually wore native-style kimono;

since the enthronement she appears as a rule in western dress. But her public appearances nowadays are very rare. The Empress was born in 1903, and thus is two years younger than His Majesty. She is an accomplished musician, so people say. Following the Russo-Japanese border incident in 1938 she wrote a poem, and presented it with a box of candy to the families of each of the Japanese dead.

Six children have been born to the throne. The first three, one of whom died, were daughters. Vast pleasure surged through Japan with the birth of a boy, the Crown Prince Tsugu, on December 23, 1933. Since then another boy, Prince Yoshi, has been born. The eldest daughter, Princess Teru, now thirteen, is a student at the Peeresses' School, a long-legged youngster who is seen occasionally in middy uniform. Recently—enormous concession—she was permitted to take a streetcar ride alone. (But no one else was allowed in the streetcar!)

The Crown Prince has his own household. As ancient custom prescribed, he had to leave the palace of the Emperor and Empress at the age of three and move into his own establishment, which is in the grounds of another Tokyo royal residence, the Omiya "detached" palace. He visits his parents constantly, but does not live with them.

A very remarkable member of the imperial family is the Empress Dowager Sadako, widow of the Emperor Taisho and mother of Hirohito. It was she, by common consent, who supported her son when he insisted on marrying the lady of his choice; it was she who fought off the great court nobles, like Prince Yamagata, who bitterly opposed the marriage. The Empress Dowager, an accomplished old lady with keen political sense, is still a power, though she is no longer conspicuous publicly. She has received few foreigners since Taisho died.[2]

The Imperial Household maintains a large secretarial staff; in fact five thousand employees work in the palace, and eleven pages of the official handbook are necessary to name the chief officials. One group of functionaries is in charge of the imperial forests, another of the orchestra which plays old court music. There are 121 imperial mausoleums in Japan, all of which have keepers; the tomb of one emperor, incidentally, has never been found. Another odd point is that whereas Hirohito is one hundred twenty-fourth emperor, his father, Taisho, was officially the one hundred twenty-second. The explanation is that, in 1926, it was decided to include in the imperial line an obscure emperor of the fourteenth century who abdicated after a brief reign.

[2] The Empress Dowager was a member of the Kujo line and a proper Fujiwara. By Fujiwara tradition she, like other Kujo princesses, was taken from her parents at the age of seven *days*, and put in charge for five years of peasant farmers near Tokyo, who treated her exactly as one of their own children. She was carried on the back of the peasant foster mother, who worked in the rice fields.

"L'Etat, C'est Moi!"

By terms of the Japanese Constitution promulgated in 1889, the Emperor has legal powers far exceeding those of a normal "constitutional" monarch. He has (like most heads of states) supreme command of army and navy and is empowered to declare war and make peace; but also he may "determine the organization and peace standing of the army and navy," he may convoke or prorogue the parliament, he may initiate and veto legislation, and in time of crisis he may suspend the Constitution.

But the point is also severely established in Japan that the Emperor is outside politics. He may not, by the rule of unchallengeable precedent, participate actively in political affairs. When, for instance, a military coup d'état in February, 1936, threatened the existence of the state, many people thought that the Emperor should step in; had he faced the mutineers on his white horse, they might have instantly dispersed. But he did not do so. His advisers presumably prevailed upon him not to do so. Even at such a moment, it was inconceivable that he himself should do something.

Thus a paradox. Japan is ruled, not "by" the Emperor, but in the name of the Emperor. The Emperor is a man, as we have seen; he is a god, as we have seen; he is a symbol, as we have seen; he is an embodiment, a projection, of a conglomerate mass of theories and traditions and influences; but is *not* a ruler—much less a dictator—in the normal sense of the term.

As *Fortune* says, the object of political struggle in Japan is "control of the means of access to the Imperial Person." In blunter terms, "Since the year 536 the sole political question of any realistic significance in Japan has been the question 'Who is using the Emperor now?'" The Constitution would make it easy for any strong and ambitious Emperor to become a legal dictator; but it hasn't happened yet. The Emperor is the state; but other people run it in his name.

～～～～～～～～～～～～～～～～～～～～～～～～～～～～～～

At the time I wrote this I had never met the Emperor. I had talked in Tokyo with Prince Konoye, the prime minister of the day, and several other high men of state, but not the Emperor. When I returned to Japan in 1950, just before the Korean War, my wife and I were granted an audience with His Imperial Majesty and the Empress. This was made possible by the courtesy of General MacArthur. Japan was still under allied occupation. The occasion was formal and picturesque. I have described it fully in my book The Riddle of MacArthur. *At the beginning*

I was placed next to the Empress on one side of a pleasant room, and my wife was given a position next to the Emperor on the other. Interpreters stood by to assist us smoothly, and after twenty minutes a signal was given and my wife and I changed places; she then talked to the Empress while I moved over to the Emperor. The audience lasted fifty minutes in all. There was little, if any, opportunity for general conversation.

The Emperor shook hands with me with muscular energy, and kept his eyes cast down when he spoke. He wore western clothes, an old suit of grayish tweed; a garter kept slipping down one leg. Speaking with firmness and vigor he gave it as his opinion that the democratization of Japan would endure after the end of the occupation but that it would perhaps be of its own special type, different from the democracy that exists in England or America, that General MacArthur, whom he admired extravagantly, had done a magnificent, epochal job in Japan, and that the last war, which he wholeheartedly lamented, was a tragedy which he had done everything possible to prevent.

The Emperor has been much cut down in his imperial, constitutional, and religious significance since the end of World War II. The new Constitution, written by the occupation forces, specifically states that he shall no longer have any powers related to government. No longer is the sovereignty of the country believed by the orthodox to reside actually in the person of the Emperor, nor has he theoretical power any longer to suspend the Constitution, initiate and veto legislation, and determine the policies of army and navy. His financial position has been drastically curtailed, the palace staff has been reduced by half, and he himself now lives on a civil list like a normal constitutional monarch. Above all, his privileges and prerogatives have been reduced from the religious point of view. He has not only been constitutionalized, but his divinity has been removed. On January 1, 1946, an amazed Japanese nation read an Imperial Rescript signed by Hirohito himself (but of course written by SCAP, the MacArthur administration), not merely announcing that he was no longer divine, but in effect stating that he had never been divine, and denouncing the myth of his own divinity. Hirohito is not, however, even today, in 1964, to be dismissed as a mere puppet or symbol. Although he is bereft of most of his former powers he continues to be a personage of considerable might in the life of the nation, both temporal and spiritual, because most Japanese still respect him. He has little authority on paper, but traditions as venerable as those associated with Hirohito die hard.

CHAPTER 15

≋≋≋≋≋

Generalissimo Chiang Kai-shek

Chiang Kai-shek was—and still is—an extraordinarily difficult person to write about. What appears here is part of a chapter of Inside Asia *(1939), which was also published in* Current History *(April, 1939). I have had to cut it considerably in its present appearance because as originally written it was one of a group of eight longish chapters on China, all closely interlocked, and it contained a good deal of background material which hardly seems relevant today in regard to Chiang Kai-shek himself.*

That background was, however, not only vividly colorful but it helped inevitably to produce the China of today, and so we should have a brief word about it. China in pre-Chiang days was in a state of violent revolutionary flux. It was still a kind of riotous porridge, a carnival of mess. Various factors were the surviving fabulous war lords, the foreign concessionaires with their treaty-protected special position on the coast, the Japanese who had been nipping off bits and pieces of northern China for some years, and, above all, the miserably starved, crushed, and illiterate peasantry locked immovably to the sparse land. Against this backdrop rose two formidable new elements—Chiang Kai-shek and the Communists.

Chiang Kai-shek, a missionary-reformer type of man who seemed to be a comparatively simple character in the early days, was born in 1887 in Chekiang Province near the sea. He studied to be an officer in Japan, came under the influence of Dr. Sun Yat-sen, the great revolutionary who is the father of modern China, and rose hard and fast. In the 1920's he set out to unify China in a series of military campaigns, and came close to succeeding in doing so—an enormous and altogether unprecedented feat. He was thought to be distinctly a man of the left

[155]

as well as a flaming nationalist at that time; he moved against the white foreign concessions and, in theory, stood by Dr. Sun's three principles— National Unity, Political Democracy, and People's Livelihood—under the banner of the Revolutionary Nationalist Party, the Kuomintang.

Then came troubles. An evolution complicated in the extreme led to a split in the Kuomintang, and civil war broke out between Chiang and the Communists. It lasted for ten weary years (1927-1937). Chiang was never able to win a clear-cut victory and, after their celebrated "Long March," the Communists succeeded in establishing themselves impregnably in northwest China and steadily became stronger. Then in 1937 the Japanese advance into China became a full-scale war, even if this was undeclared. So Chiang found himself in a very tight box indeed, fighting both the Communists and the Japanese.

I met the Generalissimo and most of the members of his remarkable family in Hankow in 1937, while I was doing research for Inside Asia; they had fled up river before the Japanese advance. I remember watching a Japanese air raid from the roof of the American Consulate in Hankow. It was not much of a raid, but frightening and unpleasant just the same. Chinese morale seemed pretty good, but everybody knew that the fabric of the old China was being ruthlessly torn apart. Criticism of Chiang was bitter—mainly because he had spent a whole decade fighting a civil war against his own people instead of confronting the Japanese with any vigor or spirit. His critics said that he had lost one-sixth of China to Japan without firing an effective shot. Meantime the Communists, who were actively fighting the Japanese in the north, steadily rose in power.

In the text that follows I make frequent reference to an episode known as the Sian kidnaping. This had better be explained because it was the root of much that was going on; it was a cardinal as well as wildly bizarre event then, but has faded now. It occurred late in 1936. Chiang had sent Chang Hsueh-liang, the fantastic youth who was the son of the old Manchurian war lord Chang Tso-lin and who was universally known as the "Young Marshal," up to Sian in the heart of the Communist area as his "Pacification Commissioner." But instead of obeying Chiang's orders and attempting to subdue the Communists, the Young Marshal fraternized with them. The Generalissimo, furious at this insubordination, flew alone to Sian to investigate the situation and straighten things out, an act which took great courage. When he arrived (December 12, 1936) the Young Marshal, apparently acting for the Communists, promptly arrested and kidnaped him.

Chiang was held prisoner for thirteen days, which provided one of the most piquant dramas in recent Chinese or any other history. W. H.

Donald, the Generalissimo's Australian adviser, who had also been for some years in the service of the Young Marshal, flew out as a negotiator-rescuer, and so, at the very end, did Madame Chiang. The upshot was that the Generalissimo won his freedom by his own sheer force of character. The details of this story are inordinately complex. To put it together is like threading needles blindfolded. One detail was that the Young Marshal presented Chiang with a formal list of demands including a promise to end the civil war, make resistance against Japan effective, and go easy on the Communists. Chiang accepted these demands. Thus arose a United Front between Chiang and the Communists, and a theoretical end to the civil war. The United Front did not last long.

~~~~~~

If we perspire more in times of peace, we will bleed less in times of war.
                    —GENERALISSIMO CHIANG KAI-SHEK

CHIANG KAI-SHEK, the inconspicuous son of a village merchant who became leader of China's four hundred and fifty million people, is commander-in-chief of army, navy, and air force, president of the Supreme War Council and the National Military Council, president of the National Aviation Commission, and director-general of the Kuomintang, China's single political party. He is also a psychological puzzle of considerable magnitude.

He is the strongest man China has produced for generations, and a terrific disciplinarian; but the enemies he has forgiven—and given jobs to—are many. His dominating mission is to unite China, consolidate it, and indeed he has united it more than any man in centuries of history—but he spent ten years fighting civil wars against his own people. Like that of Masaryk, whom he doesn't otherwise resemble, his life is shot full of paradox. He is a popular leader of formidable stature, but he is a bad politician, the last possible alternative to rabble-rouser or back-slapper. He is a strong Chinese nationalist—but he got much of his education in Japan. He is an extremely typical Chinese—who nevertheless believes in Christianity and the Y.M.C.A.

Mr. Gandhi, the Indian nationalist leader, is a great politician who makes much use of mysticism. The Emperor of Japan is an imperial puppet, whose mystical characteristics are utilized by politicians. Chiang Kai-shek's mysticism is of a peculiar kind. He has no supernatural qualities. One might almost call him supernormal. He does not serve a religion, as do Gandhi and the Emperor of Japan; he makes religion serve him. Chiang Kai-shek is almost a missionary. He is certainly a reformer.

Boundary Stone and Central Righteousness

He is slight, straight, wiry, with delicate features. He carries himself with a curious elastic grace, but stiffly. He is quite tall—five feet nine—but is rather short-legged, and likes to be photographed sitting down, or wearing the broad black cloak that is his favorite costume. He weighs 141 pounds. He dresses in a simple khaki uniform almost always, and likes big-brimmed hats. His eyes are remarkable: a very dark gray, deep, both piercing and luminous, and never at rest. His face, his speech seem somewhat arid, until the eyes light them up. He was severely injured by a fall during the Sian kidnaping, but now his health is excellent.

He rises early—at dawn usually—and works hard till nightfall. He thinks that the time between dawn and breakfast is the best hour of the day. After lunch he takes a brief nap, usually falling asleep to the tune of a wheezy gramophone. His favorite record is Schubert's *Ave Maria;* his friends in the next room know that he is asleep when the record stops. After tea he has half an hour for prayer or meditation. He goes to bed early. He likes to lie down, and does as much work as he can on a sofa.

He is abstemious and methodical. He does not drink or smoke, and he avoids even coffee and tea. For many years he has kept a full diary. (The Emperor of Japan shares several of these qualities, incidentally; he too gets up at dawn, keeps a diary, and doesn't drink or smoke.) Chiang's diary, it might fairly be said, once saved his life; the mutineers at Sian read it, together with some of the Generalissimo's letters to his wife, and were impressed enough to change their attitude toward him. The Generalissimo eats both Chinese and European food, the latter in particular when he is dieting.

The things he likes best are poetry, mountains, and his wife. His idea of a really good time, if he ever has time to have a good time, is to walk in hilly country on a sunny day, or to have a picnic lunch outdoors. His friends can make him do almost anything by promising him a day outdoors. When he walks he recites poetry. His favorite abode is Kuling, in the mountains near Kiukiang, where he has a small cottage; he hasn't been able to visit it since the [Japanese] war. His family life is happy, and Madame Chiang, one of the celebrated Soong sisters, is his indispensable and beloved associate, but he is definitely a lonely man, a person who admires solitude.

The Generalissimo is sensitive and stand-offish. He seldom sees people socially, and he never gives himself away. When touring the provinces he gives the proper official dinner to the local dignitaries, and then makes no further attempt to see them. When thousands of deliriously happy Chinese sought to celebrate a victorious battle at Taierchwang in March, 1938, by gathering outside his house in Wuchang and cheering, he wanted to send them home without a word; his advisers had to appeal to him not to clear the streets. He does not like people in the abstract—or even the particular.

But when the Generalissimo and Madame Chiang see a foreign visitor, as I had occasion to find out myself, they are conspicuously urbane. Madame Chiang receives her guests; after a brief introduction the Generalissimo comes in, and tea is served. Usually Chiang stays just half an hour; then Madame Chiang may carry the conversation further. She interprets for him, since his only foreign language is Japanese; I had the feeling, however, that he knew more English than he admitted. The interpretation is so fluently expert that it is hard to determine who is speaking; Madame (everywhere in China she is known simply as "Madame") knows his mind so well that there are no pauses, no interruptions. The Generalissimo is not a time waster. When I met him he first paid a pleasant compliment to my [then] wife, Frances Gunther, and then asked if I would explain the "European situation" in "one or two" sentences. I did my best. He talks deliberately and interrupts his remarks with a queer guttural snap. He receives journalists for official interviews only very rarely; I was the first foreigner he had seen for a long interview since the war. When the conversation was over, he gave me a Chinese translation of the written questions and answers which had been previously prepared, and signed it with an imposing flourish.

On occasion the Generalissimo is closely guarded—for instance, he has a bullet-proof limousine—but on that same day I had occasion to see that the stories were not true that he never moved without a strong armed guard, never showed himself among the people. My wife and I, leaving his villa, went to call on Dr. Kung, the prime minister, in the Bank of China Building. The scene was the Hankow Bund; a rough analogy would be the Thames Embankment. There, walking along, apparently quite alone, was the Generalissimo, who himself had just visited Dr. Kung, his brother-in-law. He was so inconspicuous in the crowd that he saw us before we saw him, and stopped and greeted us. Then, as he walked deliberately toward the jetty, we noticed that members of his bodyguard did accompany him, but about twenty feet away. Very few people in the crowd noticed that the Generalissimo was there.

The Generalissimo's name is a source of much confusion. His family name was Chiang, and as a boy he was called "Jui-tai"; Chinese children are usually given a temporary name, so that when they grow up they can change it if they wish—a pleasant convention! Reaching adolescence, Chiang decided that the name he wanted was "Kai-shek," which means "boundary stone," an interesting choice psychologically

in that it forecasts the idea of a fixed frontier. But the Chinese ideographs for "Kai-shek" may be rendered in two different ways: the Mandarins would say "Chieh-shih," the Cantonese "Kai-shek." In some books
the Generalissimo is called "Chiang Chieh-shih," and many people in
China still pronounce his name thus.

When he became prominent, he adopted, as most Chinese do, quite
another name, his "courtesy" name. This is Chiang Chung-cheng, which
means, according to one translation, "central righteousness"; note that
he retained part of his original family name, which not all Chinese do.
His adoption of the word "central" and "righteousness" is an obvious
clue to his character. In official proclamations, in signing government
papers, even in reference books, his name is given as "Chiang Chung-
cheng."

In conversation, he is officially addressed as *Weiyuanchang* (Mr.
President), or *Chungszeling* (Generalissimo). In the party, according
to Madame Chiang, he is called "Mr. Chiang"; some old soldiers call
him "Mr. Principal." A considerable source of power has been the
group of officers whom he trained at the Whampoa Academy, a closely
knit clique which was the nucleus of his army. Sometimes he is called
"Lao [old] Chiang," an affectionate diminutive. Madame as a rule
calls him "Kai"; [his adviser W. H.] Donald, who cannot take time to
pronounce all of Generalissimo, says "Jissimo."

Chiang has several times been chairman of the Executive Yuan, that
is, prime minister of the Chinese government, and for a time he was
"President" of China, that is, official head of the Chinese state. But
his main occupation, like the main bent of his mind, has always been
military; since 1926 he has been commander-in-chief of the armed
forces, and head of various military bureaus and commissions, except
during brief intervals. In March, 1938, he became general director
(*Tsungtsai*) of the Kuomintang party; this step had importance
beyond its prestige value, since for the first time Chiang became *party*
as well as military and governmental leader. The Kuomintang, in other
words, merged with the state.

Chiang has no hobbies, no relaxations, except reading. He plays no
games, but he likes to read, especially the Chinese classics. His
favorite passage from Confucius—note the tendency to "uplift"—is the
following:

In order to propagate virtue to the world, one must first rule one's country,
In order to rule the country, one must first rule one's family.
In order to rule the family, one must first regulate one's body by moral
    training,
In order to regulate the body, one must first regulate one's mind.

In order to regulate the mind, one must first be sincere in one's intentions,
In order to be sincere in intentions, one must first increase one's knowledge.
(Quoted in Hollington K. Tong's official biography, p. 606)

Among character traits of the Generalissimo one must mention first,
and above all, his stubbornness, his tenacity. This delicately featured
Chinese soldier is a bulldog. He has no tact. Anyone who has read his
diary describing the Sian kidnaping knows what I mean. He dug himself in, emotionally, physically, morally, and never budged—and kept
begging his captors to kill him.

There is a strong note of cruelty in his character, and the ruthlessness of his war against the Communists is well known. Thousands of
people were executed, many of them for no crime except that they
disagreed with him.

He has a kind of inflexible inner egoism, an egoism so enormous
that it becomes almost *im*personal. For instance, he gravely noted in
his Sian diary that Shao, the civil governor, advised him to be more
"lenient" in his next conversation with the Young Marshal, his captor!
Chiang talked to the Young Marshal with complete unmitigated confidence, and never glossed over his contempt for those who had captured
him.

He is shrewd, suspicious, calculating, and not above the use of
guile. On the other hand, both his physical and moral courage are
indisputable. He has proved more than once that he has no fear of
death.

Another quality which is a source of power is his peculiar concept
of responsibility to the nation. Continually he emphasizes the factor
of discipline, and the necessity for those above to be responsible for
the behavior of their inferiors. It is characteristic that, at Sian, he
"assumed responsibility" for the mutineers who kidnaped him.

He makes wonderful use of enemies. He has a knack of making
them work for him. He resents hotly any aspersion on the characters
of his associates, even if they attempt to betray him; he forgives—
and doesn't forget. This is caused not merely by loyalty or by calculation that the enemy, in the unstable condition of China, may turn out
to be useful, but by a curious *moral* attitude; Chiang feels that he
knows himself to be right, and is willing to wait until the others see
their errors, admit that he is right, and come to him repentant. He
likes to have everyone, even those whom he dislikes, dependent on him.
He is so sure of himself that, in time, he is convinced that he can
convert anybody, or that the power of events will effect conversion.
Thus the extraordinary succession of war lords and such who, after
revolts, have been pardoned, paid soundly, and sent abroad to "recuperate their health."

Another characteristic is his almost illimitable, dogged patience. He develops slowly. Early in 1934 he delivered three lectures to the officers school at Kuling which today make amazing reading—such amazing reading, in fact, that unfriendly critics have hinted that they might be bogus. The lectures, secret and confidential at the time they were delivered, have now been published. At the time they were delivered Chiang was submissively bowing to Japanese attacks and demands. He lost Manchuria; he lost Jehol; he saw the Japanese entrench themselves in North China; he saw Inner Mongolia threatened; yet for years he stood aloof, made no resistance, said nothing against the Japanese, and, indeed, punished Chinese who did. Several of his best officers, appalled at what they called his weakness, his pro-Japanese policy, flared up in civil wars. Still Chiang did nothing. Then the war of 1937 came. Chiang fought. But the lectures prove that even in 1934 he was passionately telling his best officers in confidence that eventually they must fight Japan; he cited Japan as the flagrant and inevitable enemy; he implored them to prepare themselves for the fight that was bound to come; he turned his whole mind to one pitch—the implacable necessity of winning it. How may this apparent paradox be explained? Only by assuming that Chiang knew that, in the early thirties, successful Chinese resistance was impossible; that at all costs the Chinese must do everything possible to appease and mollify the Japanese until they were ready, and had some chance of fighting a successful war; that at all costs, at the risk of any indignity, the Chinese must buy off Japanese attack until the last, the final, the uttermost minute, at which time they might have a chance to win.

He has a distinct tendency to jealousy, and his sense of humor may be described as occasional. He does not laugh much. Once in Sian, at a moment of terrible tension, his great friend W. H. Donald whipped a pack of cards from his pocket, and said to the Generalissimo, "Let's play casino!" (Occasionally Donald and Madame play casino or rummy for golf balls.) The Generalissimo was so stunned that he burst into incredulous laughter. Once he and Donald were motoring in Chekiang, and Donald exploded, "Good heavens, some damned fool has taken down the English road signs!" He was surprised then to hear Chiang chuckling. It had been he who had ordered the English signs to be removed. The Generalissimo likes to collect Scotch jokes, which he tells "on" Donald.

The humor is bitter sometimes. Once Donald said, "What you've got to do is shoot all the crooks and traitors in China."

The Generalissimo sighed, "Unfortunately there is not ammunition enough."

Attitude Toward Money

The Generalissimo's salary is $1,000 (Chinese) per month. His private fortune is not believed to be great, though he made money freely in his early Shanghai days; the fortune of the Soong family into which he married is quite another matter; the Soongs are among the richest folk in China. The General and Madame do not need much money, and do not have to spend much. They do not live like coolies, but their tastes are frugal.

Chiang has a house in his native village, Chikow, and a cottage in the mountains near Fenghua. His residence in the French Concession in Shanghai is unostentatious. The lodge at Kuling, which he likes best, he rents from missionaries. The government built an official residence for the head of state at Nanking, a kind of White House, but the Generalissimo and Madame lived instead in a small bungalow borrowed from the military academy nearby.

The Chinese are not prone to flamboyant demonstration of wealth. The best houses have, as a rule, tawdry exteriors, which are a form of protective coloration. A high official in Nanking bought a cream-colored limousine just before the war; hurriedly he painted it over— black—when it became clear that having such an an ostentatious car might tempt gangsters to do away with him. . . . On the other hand, the Chinese, sensible people, realize that successful generals must have private fortunes, because otherwise they could not pay their troops. Money has always been a vital adjunct to political power—which, for that matter, it is in most other countries.

Attitude Toward Religion

On October 23, 1930, Chiang Kai-shek was baptized into the Christian church. The Rev. Z. T. Kiang, a Methodist minister in Shanghai, performed the ceremony, which took place in the Soong family home. All the Soongs are strong Christians, and it was largely the influence of his wife that led to his conversion. Indeed, when the Generalissimo was courting Madame, his suit was rejected at first, because he was not a Christian. Old Madame Soong demanded that he adopt Christianity; the General, stubborn as always, said that she would think less of him if he assumed a new religion merely to make marriage possible. She was impressed by this; then he promised that if the marriage took place he would study Christianity seriously for a long period and become a convert if he came to believe in it.

His turning Christian is not quite so sensational as it sounds. It has been said that an analogy would be for President Roosevelt suddenly to become a Buddhist, or Hitler a Jew; this is not quite correct, because the Chinese care little for religious stratifications.

The Generalissimo is asserted to be a devout and even ardent believer in Christianity. He and Madame pray daily, the first thing every morning; they say grace before all meals, and observe Sunday fairly strictly. In his speeches Chiang talks incessantly about Christ; he chose "Why We Believe in Jesus" as the text for an important radio address in 1938. When he was kidnaped at Sian, he delivered himself into the arms of the Lord, and prayed for strength from Jesus; when Madame arrived to rescue him, his first impulse was to quote Scripture: "Jehovah will now do a new thing, and that is, He will make a woman protect a man."

Nevertheless, the Generalissimo still reveres his ancestors, like all good Chinese. This raises a nice theological point, because strictly speaking it would not appear that an orthodox Christian, who should believe in hellfire and salvation, can also believe that his ancestors survive as physical entities, to be worshiped and adored. Chinese ancestor worship has no place for hell, purgatory, or a sense of sin, which is one reason why most Chinese are the amiable people that they are.

Schoolmaster Dictator

Every Monday morning at Chiang's headquarters occurs a remarkable ceremony. It gives sharp insight into the Generalissimo's character. About six hundred men walk briskly into the big building and wait. They do not have to wait long. The Generalissimo is punctual. He arrives and mounts the platform. The military band plays a march, and the audience comes to attention.

The music stops, whereupon everyone in the hall uncovers and bows three times to a portrait of Dr. Sun Yat-sen, the creator of modern China. One—two—three. The bows are made with precision and *éclat*. Officers put caps on again. The Generalissimo then reads the testament of Dr. Sun Yat-sen, uttering it a sentence at a time, which the audience repeats. It is exactly like a prayer meeting and the reading of the gospels.

The Generalissimo asks silent meditation for three minutes and then delivers a lecture which lasts at least an hour, and may last two hours or longer. He discusses the military situation, exhorts his officers and civilian ministers to further efforts, scolds slackers, points out abuses, and issues moral injunctions. One recent lecture developed the theme that not only must soldiers be trained to make good officers; good officers, on their side, must learn to be good soldiers. During the entire performance, the audience—which includes everyone of consequence in the government, even cabinet ministers—must remain standing. When it is over, the Generalissimo does not say thank you, or au revoir, but simply a single abrupt word: "Completed!"

~~~~~~

Came World War II in 1939 and Pearl Harbor in 1941. I have not the space to describe the vicissitudes, outrages, spoliations, heroisms, degradations, conflicts in personality, depradations, and rifts in the allied structure which distinguished the situation in China until 1945 when victory came. Chiang became more and more the prisoner of forces he could not control. His command of himself deteriorated as well. The upshot, after sinuous evolutions, was that Chiang, the victorious partner of the western allies, threw victory away. The Communists, still impregnable in the west and north, could not be quelled. Corruption, inflation, and the "reactionary clique" surrounding Chiang destroyed the morale of the rest of the nation. There was no will on the part of most citizens to fight another civil war. Tragedy on a continental scale worked its way toward a fantastic climax. Of course factors other than Chinese contributed to these developments, including the American State Department which, disgusted by Chiang's lack of grip, withdrew aid from him in August, 1949. This is to foreshorten a highly intricate as well as controversial story. Meantime the Communists won victory after victory, although Chiang's forces vastly outnumbered them. Their dogged armies took Peiping, Nanking, and Shanghai. Chiang, his own forces shattered, fled to Taiwan (Formosa), where he still is, and in September, 1949, the Communists proclaimed the People's Republic of China and set about consolidating their regime.

This enormous process still grinds its way along, while Chiang continues to sit stubbornly in Formosa as head of the Chinese "national" government.

When I visited Hankow in 1937 during the short-lived United Front between Chiang and the Communists I met several times a young Chinese officer-politician who impressed me considerably. His name was Chou En-lai, and he is, as everybody knows, prime minister of Communist China today—more than a quarter of a century later. At that time Chou's job was to represent the Communist high command at the Generalissimos headquarters. I had several long talks with him, and I asked him how such a remarkable development as cooperation between Chiang and the Communists had become a reality, even though this might well turn out to be temporary. His reply was that Chiang, in that period, was the one person indispensable to Chinese unity, and who might be able to hold the country together.

Ironic this seems now!

CHAPTER 16

~~~~~~~~~

The Mahatma

This chapter from Inside Asia *appeared first in the* Reader's Digest, *December, 1938, in abbreviated form. The reader may be puzzled by allusions I make to the comparatively good relations existing between Mr. Gandhi and the British. But 1938 was a peculiar year of lull. Certainly Mr. Gandhi was the leader and hero of the Indian independence movement, and, as such, the man who led the mammoth subcontinent of India to freedom from British rule, but he moved by eccentric fits and starts. When I visited India he stood on the moderate side of the independence movement and was trying to take advantage of a period of compromise.*

~~~~~~

> *I am not a visionary. I claim to be a practical idealist.*
> —M. K. GANDHI

MR. GANDHI, who is an incredible combination of Jesus Christ, Tammany Hall, and your father, is the greatest Indian since Buddha. Like Buddha, he will be worshiped as a god when he dies. Indeed, he is literally worshiped by thousands of his people. I have seen peasants kiss the sand his feet have trod.

No more difficult or enigmatic character can easily be conceived. He is a slippery fellow. I mean no disrespect. But consider some of the contradictions, some of the puzzling points of contrast in his career and character. This man who is at once a saint and a politician, a prophet and a superb opportunist, defies ordinary categories.

For instance, his great contribution to India was the theory and practice of nonviolence or civil disobedience. But at the very time that nonviolence was the deepest thing he believed in, he was supporting Britain in the First World War. The concept of nonviolence is a perfect example of Gandhi's familiar usage of moral weapons to achieve practical results, of his combination of spiritual and temporal powers. India, an unarmed state, could make a revolution only by nonviolent means. Nonviolence was a spiritual concept, but it made revolution practicable.

There is again the matter of his celebrated fasts. He fasted purely for moral reasons, but they served a considerable practical convenience, because if he began a fast in jail the British had to let him out. A sort of etherealized Houdini, he was in a position to escape from prison any time he chose because the British would not accept the onus of his death from starvation while in confinement. Yet—the point is important— Gandhi himself never consciously thought of fasting as a method of escape.

His inconsistencies seem remarkable, until you note that his objective seldom varies, but that he is willing to compromise on contributory details. He is interested in substance, not form. For instance, he devoted the major portion of his career to a titanic struggle with Britain, yet later he cooperated more or less freely with Britain under the new constitution. His point in this case was that his objective, Indian independence, could more easily be achieved by cooperation than by struggle, once civil disobedience was over. Yet the paradox is enormous: Mr. Gandhi, who fought the British Empire to a standstill in the 1920's, was almost the best friend the British had in India in 1938.

Another great paradox is his attitude to caste and the Untouchables. Mr. Gandhi devotes the largest share of his energy nowadays to uplifting the Untouchables, but he resisted with his life an attempt to remove Untouchability from Hinduism, which would have been the effect of the British plan (which he succeeded in modifying) to give Untouchables a separate electorate. He adores the Untouchables, and would do anything for them—except remove them from Hinduism, which makes them what they are.

There are other paradoxes and contradictions. To Gandhi modern science is anathema, but nevertheless he uses a thermometer and wears eyeglasses. He pleads for Hindu-Moslem unity, but he wouldn't gladly see a member of his family become a Moslem. For years he was the soul, backbone, eyes, and fingers of the Indian National Congress, but he was not a member of it. His approach to everything is religious, but aside from Hinduism it is difficult to tell what his religion is.

Nevertheless, Mr. Gandhi adds up to a great deal. The record of his life is heroic in the best sense of that word. This tough and rubbery little man, dressed in a loincloth and sitting by his spinning wheel, who weighs 112 pounds, took on the greatest empire the world has ever known—an empire with every recourse in man power, accumulated wealth, tradition, skill and strategy in administration—and almost vanquished it. He fought fate—and what used to be stronger than fate— the British Empire.

Nowadays people are apt to assume that Mr. Gandhi, with his score of great years behind him, is played out; they even think that he no longer counts in India. Nothing could be farther from the truth. He is still the most important living Indian. One cannot be in India two hours without finding out that he still somehow manages to rule the Congress, the nationalist political organization, which is the strongest in India, devoted to Indian independence.

Many young nationalists are impatient at his mysticism, and even his most devoted admirers occasionally blink at his unpredictable vagaries. But his hold on the great mass of the Indian people is unshaken. He is a unique kind of dictator, one who rules by love. He is adored as well as worshiped. His photograph is enshrined in a million cottages; children, sick, are touched with his likeness to make them well. Peasants may come twenty miles simply to see his train pass, even if it does not stop and he is not visible. To the submerged masses, the "dumb half-starved millions" as he frequently calls them, he is a man of miracles. All over India I noticed how the faces of people lit up when his name was mentioned. And he is the only man in India who by a single word, by lifting his little finger, could instigate a new national revolt, who could start civil disobedience again among more than 350,000,000 people— roughly one-fifth of the human race.

What explains the hold Mr. Gandhi has on India? What has he done for India? The outline of his career is known to everyone, but we must sketch it briefly. Let us try to take this extraordinary man apart, and see what it is that controls his unique behavior.

St. Francis in South Africa

Mohandas Karamchand Gandhi was born in Porbander, one of the small native states in the Kathiawar peninsula, on October 2, 1869. Thus he is seventy, which is old for an Indian, whereas it may be comfortable maturity to a Japanese. He came of a solid official family, members of the third or Vaisya caste; both his father and grandfather were *Dewans*, that is, prime ministers, of local Kathiawar states. The name "Gandhi" means "grocer" in his native language. His father, whom he describes as being brave and incorruptible, married four times, and Gandhi was the youngest child of the fourth wife. His mother, a passionately devout woman, given to strict observance of Hindu fasts and customs, profoundly influenced him.

The best source of material for Gandhi's early years is his autobiography, called *The Story of My Experiments with Truth*.[1] It is a work
of very peculiar and original texture. I know no autobiography quite
like it. Artlessly it sets down details of almost shocking intimacy; peacefully it explores the origins of Gandhi's character, like a brook rising to
a river. It gives an impression of almost Biblical restraint, and yet is full
of naïve candor. It varies between passages of great nobility and literary
force and preoccupation with idiosyncrasies almost meaningless to a
western reader. Its last words are—after 1,090 pages—"I must reduce
myself to zero."

His picture of his mother is worth recording:

> The outstanding impression my mother has left on my memory is that
> of saintliness. She was deeply religious. She would not think of taking her
> meals without her daily prayers. As far as my memory goes back, I do not re-
> member her having ever missed the *Chaturmas* [a semi-fast period that lasts
> four months during the rains]. She would take the hardest vows and keep
> them without flinching. . . . To keep two or three consecutive fasts was
> nothing to her. Living on one meal a day during *Chaturmas* was a habit
> with her. Not content with that she fasted every alternate day during one
> *Chaturmas*. During another *Chaturmas* she vowed not to have food without
> seeing the sun. We children on those days would stand, staring at the sky,
> waiting to announce the appearance of the sun to our mother. . . . She
> would run out to see with her own eyes, but by that time the fugitive
> sun would be gone, thus depriving her of her meal. "That does not matter," she
> would say cheerfully. "God did not want me to eat today."

A friend told young Gandhi that Indians are a weak people because
they did not eat meat. "The English are able to rule over us, because they
are meat-eaters." Secretly Gandhi decided to taste the forbidden substance, but a furtive meal of goat's meat made him sick. That night he
had a horrible nightmare, in which a live goat kept bleating inside his
stomach. . . . At about the same time a friend took him to a brothel.
Gandhi says, "I was almost struck dumb and blind in this den of vice. I
went into the jaws of sin, but God in His infinite mercy protected me."
He fled, "saved." On another occasion he smoked a forbidden cigarette,
and almost committed suicide in remorse. He says that he never told a
lie in childhood.

He married at thirteen. Before this he had been betrothed three
times, but the little girls all died. His ten-year-old wife was chosen from
a neighbor's family, and he was married in a joint ceremony with his
elder brother and a cousin. Marriage is a complicated festival to Hindus,

---

[1] Gandhi wrote the book in his native tongue, Gujerati, and his faithful secretary Mahadev Desai translated it into English. It has been published in India but
it is difficult to procure in England or the United States. Gandhi records his hesitation to write it, because "writing an autobiography is a practice peculiar to the
West."

and it was cheaper and more expedient to have the three weddings together. Gandhi writes, "Little did I dream then, that one day I should severely criticise my father for having married me as a child. Everything on that day seemed to me right and proper and pleasing. There was also my own eagerness to get married." He "draws the curtain" over the first encounter of the two nervous, frightened children, and then says that he lost no time in "assuming the authority of a husband."

His wife, Kasturbai, was illiterate. "I was very anxious to teach her, but lustful love left no time. . . ." As a result Kasturbai today—a half-century later—can only barely read and write. "I am sure, that had my love for her been absolutely untainted with lust, she would have been a learned lady today; for I could then have conquered her dislike for studies."

When he was fifteen, Kasturbai had their first child, who died. His father died at about the same period; the event, in addition to its normal consequences, had tremendous moral significance for Gandhi, because at the moment of his father's death he and Kasturbai were in bed together. His "shame" at this is "a blot I have never been able to efface or forget."

The sexual motif is strong throughout Gandhi's book. He continually writes of his carnal impulses and desires; as late as 1933 he says that he has not finally conquered them. Four times God saved him from going to brothels. His first great struggle for emancipation from earthly needs, earthly wants, was in regard to sex; all his fantastic experiments with diet, and his final choice of goat's milk as an ideal food, were caused by his desire to diminish sexual ardor. In 1900, when he was thirty-one, he gave up sexual intercourse; in 1906, he confirmed this abstention with a perpetual vow of continence. This he considered his first step forward to self-mastery; it was the essential preliminary to the doctrine of *ahimsa*, nonviolence.

Having finished high school and the University of Ahmedabad, young Gandhi decided to go to London and study law. This was a very unconventional thing to do in those days. Orthodox Hindus are supposed to be defiled by crossing water and especially by ocean travel, and he had to seek permission for the voyage from his uncle. Reluctantly the uncle gave consent—incidentally, Gandhi had to travel five days by bullock cart and camel to see him—but the subcaste of his community excommunicated him. Note the strength of character of this young man. The worst social consequences could not deter him from the trip. He calmly relates how he sold his wife's trinkets to help pay his way—he left her behind—and he describes his solemn vow to his mother to eat no meat, drink no wine, and have no women. At this period his ultimate ambition was to become a *Dewan*, like his father.

His adventures in London—he arrived there in September, 1888—make strange reading now. He set about learning the ways of this remarkable island people who kept his own people in subjection. An Indian friend told him, "Do not touch other people's things"—(this after he had innocently stroked a silk hat the wrong way)—"Do not ask questions on first acquaintance; do not talk loudly; never address people as 'sir' as we do in India." Young Gandhi bought a dress suit for £10, learned French and Latin, took dancing lessons, and went through miseries trying to find palatable vegetarian food. (He would not eat eggs, or even sauces made of eggs, and had to question waiters to find out how the food was cooked.) He made many friends in the Indian colony in London, became a member of the executive committee of the Vegetarian Society, and was so frightened and shy that he could not talk—he was unable even to read from manuscript—at his first public speech.

Three years later he returned to India, and set up legal practice in Bombay. In his first case, when he rose to cross-examine a witness, he was too timid to speak, and had to sit down again without asking a question. A little later came a disconcerting experience: he was bodily thrown out of an Englishman's office when he came to ask a favor on behalf of his brother. Directly he sought to bring suit against the Englishman—note his pepperiness—but he was prevailed upon not to do so. He swallowed the insult, but profited from it as well.

In 1893, feeling himself a failure in India, he went to South Africa, where the large Indian colony offered him the chance of a good practice. Almost before he knew it he was a leader of the community, and he remained in South Africa, hardly realizing how the time slipped by, for more than twenty years. These were his great years of preparation. South Africa was a rehearsal for what was coming.

When he arrived in South Africa, and indeed for a long time thereafter, he was a loyal citizen of the British Empire. He early became interested in Indian Home Rule through the influence of Gokhale and other leaders, but he was distinctly a gradualist. Indeed, he helped organize medical work during the Boer War and the Zulu rebellion, supporting the British forces; he received citations for bravery in the front line, and in 1914 went straight to London to offer his services for establishing an Indian ambulance corps. This, too, despite the indignities he and his compatriots suffered owing to race and color prejudice in South Africa. In the early days he was kicked, beaten, spat upon as a coolie. He could find no rooms in hotels, no restaurants to eat in.

Gradually in South Africa the two main streams in his life came forth. Later in India they converged. First was his conversion to the doctrine of nonviolence. He read Ruskin, Tolstoi, Thoreau, and set himself to follow their example. He was a highly successful barrister, earning £5,000 a year, but he dropped commercial practice to found an agricultural colony devoted to poverty, nonviolence, and the simple virtues. Second was his growing interest in Indian nationalism. He did not fight the British directly, but he roused a tremendous tumult in defense of Indian rights. He founded a newspaper, *Indian Opinion,* and wrote his first book, *Hind Swaraj* (Indian Independence), showing that he had not forgotten the great peninsula to which he must return. He became the undisputed leader of the nationalist Indians in South Africa, following a series of semipolitical campaigns and efforts to remove discriminations against Indians. He tested out his theory of passive resistance as early as 1906, and three times went to jail.

Meantime he was broadening, developing, both spiritually and practically. The autobiography contains fascinating nuggets from these forgotten days.

For instance, he decided that he was not well enough grounded in the Hindu scriptures. But he was busy, with little time to spare. So he copied out the Gita verses, hung them on a wall, and memorized them during the fifteen minutes each morning he devoted to cleaning his teeth.

He discovered a good deal about the law. From the beginning he refused to take any case the justice of which he doubted. He learned that if he were sure of his facts, the law was apt to take care of itself. "Facts mean truth, and once we adhere to truth, the law comes to our aid naturally." Also he saw that the winning party seldom recovered all his costs, and that compromise was an excellent technique. "The true function of a lawyer is to unite parties riven asunder. A large part of my time during the twenty years of my practice was occupied in bringing about private compromises."

One of his early spiritual struggles was over life insurance. "Man," he told himself, "you have sold almost all the ornaments of your wife. If something were to happen to you, the burden of supporting her and the children would fall on your poor brother." So he took out 10,000 rupees ($3,700) of life insurance. Then he canceled it. What reason, he asked himself, had he to assume that death would claim him earlier than the others? The real protector was, he decided, not his brother, but God Almighty. Then he concluded, "In getting my life insured I had robbed my wife and children of their self-reliance. Why should they not be expected to take care of themselves? What happened to the familites of the numberless poor of the world? Why should I not count myself among them?"

Note the curious emphasis here. He is willing that even his family should suffer provided that his conscience is square with the Almighty. We shall meet this trait again. Mr. Gandhi is a supreme egotist, willing to shoulder this difficult responsibility, because of his conception of mankind, under God, as a whole.

He had many political tussles and tumbles. He learned to handle men, and to handle crowds. He was absolutely inflexible on any matter of principle, and wonderfully supple on minor details.

He was continually exasperated by diet. He tried countless experiments. Finally he gave up salt, tea, and meals after sunset. He began, too, to observe Monday as a day of silence. Goat's milk seemed an ideal food for the observation of *brahmacharya* (self-restraint), but it was only after a terrific struggle that he consented to take it, since, after all, it was not strictly a vegetarian substance. Meantime, he struggled to maintain his vow of continence.

Such was the man, aged forty-five, who returned to India in 1914. Then the great years, the tremendous years, began.

Entrance to India

Out of South Africa there came a wizard across the seas.
                              —MRS. SAROJINI NAIDU

Mr. Gandhi, smelling his native soil again, spent a year in travel and social work, getting close to Indian affairs, and in 1915 founded his *Satyagraha* hermitage near Ahmedabad. This word, *Satyagraha*, needs careful definition. Gandhi invented it. Literally it means no more than "right effort," but "force of truth" or "soul force" is the usual translation, and later is was used loosely to indicate "non-cooperation," "passive resistance," and "civil disobedience." To the hermitage he brought the poor, including a group of Untouchables; he founded a colony, much like his colony in South Africa, devoted to poverty and the law of love. His word swept India. Also he was tackling practical jobs in investigating and helping to redress the grievances of peasants in several districts. By 1917, at least, he was already known as the Mahatma (literally "Great Soul"), a title not directly given him by anyone, but spontaneously bestowed by a willing people.

At the end of the war the political situation was boiling over. India loyally supported Britain during the war; in fact, she sent 1,215,000 men overseas, of whom more than 100,000 were casualties. In return the Indians, Mr. Gandhi among them, assumed that Britain would lighten the burden of its rule. And indeed the British did introduce the Montagu-Chelmsford reforms which gave India a limited—a very limited—measure of self-government. Mr. Montagu, the secretary of state for India, announced in 1917 that

the policy of His Majesty's Government . . . is that of increasing association of Indians in every branch of the administration, and the gradual development of self-governing institutions with a view to the progressive realization of responsible government in India as an integral part of the British Empire.

But the "dyarchy" system, by which Indian ministers in the provinces had rights over certain minor subjects, didn't work well. The Indian movement for home rule continued to grow. To check the rising tide of political discontent, the British introduced the Rowlatt bill, giving the police special powers; it was furiously resented. The country seethed, and Gandhi became the head of the nationalist movement. Even the Moslems joined him. He declared a *hartal,* general strike, in protest at the Rowlatt bill; then in April, 1919, came the grotesque tragedy at Amritsar, when a British general gave the order to fire on a crowd of mostly unarmed Indians—men, women, children— who had no method of escape, and killed and wounded hundreds of them. India rose—but not with a roar. It rose with *Satyagraha.*

Commonly it is said that Amritsar[2] turned Gandhi finally against the British. But already the machinery of civil disobedience—in 1919- 1920 it was called "non-cooperation"—was in motion. Amritsar hurried up the policy, made it inevitable, and to the great mass of Indians gave civil disobedience a tragic reality, a tragic necessity, that it might otherwise have taken longer to achieve. *Satyagraha* swept the country. Mr. Gandhi made it a political weapon as well as a spiritual force. It was as if his teaching struck deep through the skin of India, and touched a sensitive nerve long concealed. The people were on the brink of revolution; the Mahatma showed them the way. The call of non-violence, of self-mastery through abnegation, was something that the majority of Hindus—who are inclined to masochism—instinctively understood. It appealed directly to their religious nature; it made lions out of Hindus.

The British were bewildered. What could they do with people who let themselves be beaten to a pulp without lifting their hands? What could they do when literally thousands of young Indians besieged the jails, demanding to be arrested? Mr. Gandhi's precepts to his *Satyagrahi,* as the passive resisters were called, are almost more than the western mind can comprehend. The Mahatma insisted that *Satyagrahi* must harbor no anger, must not swear or curse, must never retaliate to attacks, must voluntarily submit to arrest, must never insult an opponent, and must *assist* British officials assaulted by forgetful Indians.

Mr. Gandhi broke off relations with the British. He wrote to the Viceroy:

---

[2] The British, too, were profoundly influenced by Amritsar. It might be argued that what reforms have come to India since 1919 have been penance for the Amritsar shame.

It is not without a pang that I return the Kaisar-i-Hind Gold Medal granted to me by your predecessor for my humanitarian work in South Africa, the Zulu War medal for my services as an officer in charge of the Indian Volunteer Ambulance Corps in 1906, and the Boer War Medal for my services as assistant superintendent of the Indian Volunteer Stretcher-bearer Corps during the Boer War of 1899-1900.

I can retain neither respect nor affection for a Government which has been moving from wrong to wrong in order to defend its immorality. . . . The Government must be moved to repentance.

I have therefore ventured to suggest non-coöperation, which enables those who wish to disassociate themselves from the Government and which, if unattended by violence, must compel the Government to retrace its steps and undo the wrongs.

The Mahatma was wrong; the government did not retrace its steps. Instead, the lines of battle were marked out. The Indian Congress declared for *Swaraj* (home rule—literally, "oneself-country") "by all legitimate and peaceful means" and worked out a practical program under Mr. Gandhi's guidance. He became dictator of the Congress. Nationalist Indians agreed to boycott British goods, to take their children from government schools, to withdraw from the law courts, to give up public jobs, to pay no taxes, to surrender titles and honors, and, above all, to use *khaddar*, i.e., homespun cotton. This, like the invention of *Satyagraha,* was another example of Gandhi's astute political sense. Nothing so dramatized the movement—down to the remotest village in the peninsula—as the revival of home spinning and weaving. It at once starved British imports, revived village economy, and gave the Congress a badge, a uniform.

In 1921 came the episode of Chauri-Chaura. An infuriated mob of Indians hacked and burned to death a group of police. Gandhi was horrified. He was about to push civil disobedience further, but he suddenly and startlingly called off the entire campaign. It is difficult to know who were the most astonished by this *volte-face,* the British or the Indians. Gandhi said simply that Chauri-Chaura proved that India was not ready for *Satyagraha.* The people could not yet be fully trusted with this new weapon. He talked of his bitter humiliation, his "Himalayan blunder"; he denounced mob violence and said that he, the person responsible, must undergo cleansing; he set himself the penance of his first great fast.

In 1922, he was arrested. He knew this would come. Listen to his logic:

What can be the motive of the Government in arresting me? The Government are not my enemy; I have not a grain of enmity toward them. But they believe that I am the soul of all this agitation, that if I am removed, the ruled and ruler will be left in peace. Not only the Government but some of our leaders also share this belief. How then can the Government put the people to the test? How can the Government ascertain whether the people do understand my advice or are simply dazzled by my utterances?

The only way left for them is to arrest me. . . . I desire that the people shall maintain perfect self-control and consider the day of my arrest as a day of rejoicing.

(*Speeches and Writings of Mahatma Gandhi*, p. 690)

The trial was a tableau to stagger the imagination. Mr. Gandhi told the prosecutor that his crimes were greater than those in the indictment; gravely, placidly, he pleaded with the judge to give him the maximum sentence. The judge rose to the occasion, and matched the Mahatma's courtesy with his own. The testimony reads like the proceedings of some court of honor under a code of chivalry. The judge sentenced Mr. Gandhi to six years' imprisonment, and the Indian leader courteously thanked him.

He adored jail. It gave him rest and seclusion. His own words are that he was "happy as a bird" in confinement. After a sudden operation for appendicitis, he was released in 1924.

The next year he undertook a twenty-one-day fast following an outbreak of trouble in Kohat between Hindus and Moslems. By his example, he hoped to bring friendship between the two. He wrote, "I was writhing in deep pain. News of Kohat set the smouldering mass aflame. I passed two nights of restlessness. I knew the remedy . . . My fast is a matter between God and myself. My penance is the prayer of a bleeding heart for forgiveness, for sins unwittingly committed. It is a warning to Hindus and Moslems who have professed to love me." Breathless, a whole continent waited the three weeks in anguish. When finally the Mahatma, on the twenty-first day, took a sip of orange juice, he was too weak to talk.

Came then five years of tension, feeling for position, and delay. The British sent the Simon Commission to India to prepare the way for a new constitution, and the Congress steadily expanded in strength and spirit; in 1930, Congress came out flatly for Complete Independence (*purna Swaraj*, which is more than just *Swaraj*), at about the same time that Lord Irwin, the viceroy,[3] announced that the British government considered that the natural issue of India's constitutional progress was merely dominion status. Battle lines were drawn again, and tempers rose. Gandhi wrote Irwin, even though he always addressed him as "Dear Friend," that he considered British rule to be "a curse." He opened a renewed course of implacable opposition. He presented demands to the "satanic" government, which were rejected; thereupon, in 1930, civil disobedience began again—more vigorously than before.

It opened with Gandhi's "salt march" to Dandi on the sea. Salt

[3] Now Lord Halifax, who later became British foreign secretary.

was—and is—a government monopoly; the tax on it bore especially hard on the poorer people, and Gandhi chose it as a symbol that everyone could grasp. The march—except perhaps that of the Red Army in China—is the most remarkable in modern history. With a group of volunteers, the Mahatma slowly traversed the country, and a fire of rebellion followed in his wake. When he began it, he said, "On bended knee I asked the Government for bread, and I got a stone instead." With his friends bowed beside him, he finally reached the sea, and scooped illegal salt from the water, saying, "I would rather die a dog's death and have my bones licked by dogs than that I should return broken."

But he was broken. Rather, since he is Mr. Gandhi who makes his own rules, he was broken and patched up again. Civil disobedience became a great national revolution, but it did not win victory. By 1934, it had fizzled out; thousands of people were in jail, the British ruled by pure repression, and the country was prostrate. What happened then was a double course of events. First, the British hammered out the new constitution at the Round Table Conferences and in meetings of the Joint Select Committee, a constitution which did very considerably advance India toward self-government; second, the Congress, under Mr. Gandhi's lead, came around, by 1937, to reluctant participation in its working. So the net result of civil disobedience was a compromise. The British gave way to some extent; the Indians grudgingly consented to work with them. This is the present situation.

Daily Life of the Modern Saint

Nowadays the Mahatma lives most of the year in a remote village called Segaon, near Wardha, in the very center of the most backward part of India. He chose it, with his customary combination of foresight and crankiness, just because it was peculiarly inaccessible, surrounded by mud and dust, and populated largely by *Harijans* (children of God), which is the name he has given the Untouchables. He wanted to demonstrate that even the most unbelievably backward village in India—and he searched hard to find it—could benefit by Gandhiism.

He rises every day at 4:30 for his morning prayers, and then takes a brisk walk, rain or shine. He did this even in London, when he exhausted the two detectives assigned to guard him. When I write "brisk," I mean "brisk." He walks as Paavo Nurmi runs. I have enjoyed watching Europeans in good condition try to keep up with him. He sails along, carrying a long staff, like some extraordinary bird.

The prayers are very important, even more important than the ritual of stiff daily exercise. In London he would interrupt any meeting without a trace of self-consciousness to sit down on the floor and pray—even in a committee room of the House of Commons. He prays twice a day, in the morning and at sunset. The sunset prayers are in the nature of a public ceremony, because his household joins him, together with the villagers. First his attendants lay a rectangle of straw mats on the ground. Quietly the people gather, squatting on the periphery of the open rectangle, and lamps are lit. The evening I saw the prayers on Juhu Beach (Mr. Gandhi was having a holiday near Bombay) a Japanese priest joined the ceremony, and Miss Madeline Slade, the daughter of an English admiral who is the faithful manager of his household, sang from the Hindu scriptures. The moon rose at one end of the beach just as the sun was setting; the night was calm, still, and very beautiful. Mr. and Mrs. Gandhi walked quietly up, and the Mahatma took his place at the short end of the rectangle, facing the sea. He sat there cross-legged, head bowed, for precisely thirty minutes. There was no other ceremony. No one spoke; no one moved; but the Hindu chants continued plangently. Suddenly he rose; the enchantment broke, and the prayers were over.

He eats no meat, of course, and in fact only seldom takes any cooked food; but it is not quite correct to say that he eats very little. A mug of goat's milk, dates, nuts, a tablespoon of honey, garlic, a bowl of chopped fresh vegetables, and plenty of fruit—oranges, pineapples, mangoes, peaches—this is the general menu.

He works very hard, seeing people incessantly, receiving visitors, consulting subordinates, even when in retirement. Any particularly interesting conversations appear later in his newspaper, the *Harijan*. So no words are wasted. He keeps up a considerable correspondence with people all over the world. His chief relaxation is his bath; he bathes in very hot water for forty minutes before retiring, and usually reads in the tub.

Monday is his day of silence. He will not interrupt it no matter what urgent business is clamoring outside the door.

His work nowadays centers mostly on the village. To revive the village, and thus prevent the countrymen from being sucked into the terrible slums of the towns, is his plan. He has a five-point program for village welfare and economy. Encourage home spinning. Make village education vocational. Improve sanitation. Bring the Untouchables into the community. Above all, stimulate village industry. He is doing his best, for instance, to create work from by-products of dead cattle, fertilizers and the like. Of course no Hindu would kill a cow, which is sacred in India, but the Mahatma is trying to persuade the villagers to utilize those that die naturally—not an easy thing to persuade them to do.

Gandhi has very little need of money, and the financing of his household doesn't seem to be a problem, because what he needs he gets from charity. Rich friends flock across his path. He has small interest in economics in the abstract, and has driven young Congress socialists to despair by his refusal to think in economic terms. Once he told a socialist friend that he believed in both private property *and* nationalization. "I purchase a mill, for example," he explained. "Then I give the people good wages; that is socialism!"

His epistolary style is quite his own. Consider this telegram of condolence to his friend Pandit Jawaharlal Nehru, who succeeded him as Congress leader, when Nehru's mother died:

Mother lived nobly, has died nobly. She was model wife, mother. No sorrow. Let our women copy her example. Love. Bapu.

"Bapu" is what his friends and intimates call him; it is the Gujerati word for father. In his early days he was called "Bhai"—brother. Few people in India call him "Mahatma"; he has always been embarrassed by the phrase. Ordinarily—in fact, universally—he is called "Gandhiji," "ji" being an untranslatable suffix which informally means "Mr." but which connotes affection also. Sometimes he is called "Bapuji" or even "Mahatmaji." When I arrived in India and talked to Congress people, I was puzzled by frequent use of the phrase "High Command." This means —or meant—Mr. Gandhi, too.

His health is quite good, except that he suffers intermittently from high blood pressure. He looks made of rubber. He is not nearly as frail, as brittle, as his photographs indicate; the torso is well-formed, and the muscles hard and smooth. His personal physician, Dr. Roy, one of the first doctors of India, told me that he was "superbly normal." But then Dr. Roy admitted that Gandhiji could do things that normal men could not do.

His experience of fasting has, for instance, given him peculiar powers over his body. Once—indication that he is not given to self-delusion—he noted that fasting could be "as great a weapon of indulgence as restraint." Once he was down to ninety-seven pounds and eating only 400 calories a day. Dr. Roy said he must get up to 104 pounds, and that he could do this only by doubling his intake of food. Gandhi listened patiently, refused to change his diet, and asserted that he could take on the necessary seven pounds in one week without changing his diet by one calorie. Which he did.

He will say, "I will go to sleep for twenty-five minutes." Then he can fall asleep instantly, and sleep for twenty-five minutes and no more. On the trains his attendants know that he will be asleep within thirty seconds of getting into the compartment. Once he was asleep in an automobile, returning from Pandit Motilal Nehru's funeral. The car overturned. Mr. Gandhi was thrown out, but when his worried friends went to him on the roadside he was asleep again.

He owes much to Roy and other doctors, but he detests modern medicine. He calls medicine "the concentrated essence of black magic"; he once argued quite seriously that modern medical science created more tuberculosis and venereal disease than it cured. He once studied nursing, and he has made a hobby of home cures. There are pages in his autobiography about the "earth cure" for constipation, which he invented; it consists of wrapping some good clean dirt around the tummy.

Mr. Gandhi is much less oppressive a personality than most people think. He loves laughter. He bubbles and chuckles in talk. Once he told a friend that he might have killed himself long ago but for his sense of humor.

His tributes to Kasturbai, his wife, are touching. She is a small, round, cheerful woman, with a face like a Dresden china shepherdess, close to him but never obtrusive; he quite calmly notes the wide difference between them intellectually, and says that he has no doubt that she does not approve of many things he does. "She is blessed with one great quality . . . willingly or unwillingly, consciously or unconsciously, she has considered herself blessed in following in my footsteps, and has never stood in the way of my endeavor to lead a life of restraint." In another passage, he writes, "I can no more describe my feeling for Hinduism than for my own wife. She moves me as no other woman in the world can. Not that she has no faults. I daresay that she has many more than I see myself. But the feeling of indissoluble bond is there."

The Gandhis have four sons and several grandchildren. In his autobiography he criticizes himself for not having given his children a better education. One son, indeed, has been a disappointment, but two others have made excellent careers as journalists. The fourth son married the daughter of Chakravarti Rajagopalacharia, the prime minister of Madras. This caused a great commotion, because the Gandhis are not Brahmans, and the Rajagopalacharias distinctly are. Another Gandhi contradiction—the good Hindu thus breaking the laws of caste!

The Gandhi Gambit

Means and ends are convertible terms in my philosophy of life.
—MR. GANDHI

The record of Gandhiji's positive qualities is a long one. The brief narrative I have given of his career indicates some. There are many others, which perhaps help to explain his enormous power and hold on Indians.

For one thing, his unbelievable simplicity. This sometimes reaches the borderline of comedy. Once he went through a minor spiritual crisis before allowing his wife, a third-class passenger, to use a second-class bathroom. Once on shipboard he persuaded a friend to toss into the

sea an expensive pair of binoculars. In prison in South Africa he offered
to clean the latrines himself, although the warder asked him to choose
someone else for the job. In South Africa he learned laundering, starched
his own collars, and taught himself to cut his own hair. One possibly
apocryphal story describes the Englishman who shouted "Coolie" at him
at a railway station. Obediently Mr. Gandhi picked up the Englishman's
bags and took them to the train.

Again there is his very considerable charm. He hasn't had sexual
intercourse for almost forty years, but he adores the company of women,
and he likes to flirt.

His intelligence is quick and shrewd. One could write a thousand
words about Miss Mayo's *Mother India* and not describe it better than
did Gandhi with his famous remark, "It is a book that no European
and every Indian should read." His political sense is acute on other
than merely Indian questions. He called the Munich agreement "peace
without honor," and doubted that it would bring peace.

He is uncommonly intuitive, and not only catches the moods of
people very quickly, but is capable of quick changes of mood himself.
He senses it instantly if his friends are tired; he talks nonsense,
laughs, gossips, makes jokes. But he can resume serious discussion
instantly.

His consideration for others is very detailed. Nehru records how
he found time during a serious crisis to send word to him that his
little daughter had taken on weight. (Nehru was in jail at the time.)
When, after the Round Table Conference, he wanted to give presents
to the two detectives who had risen at 4:30 to jog with him through
Kensington Gardens, he didn't know what to select, since Congress
was boycotting British goods; so he sent for two Swiss watches.
Once, leaving Bombay on a long trip, he saw a friend's wife among the
concourse of people seeing him off; he remembered to tell her not to
buy a new house she was interested in—this was his method of hint-
ing that civil disobedience might begin again, and that none of them
would need new houses. Another woman friend told me that Gandhiji
had certainly saved her life, merely by seeing her occasionally, talking
to her, during a severe nervous breakdown.

He has this tact, charm, consideration, but he can be brutal for a
principle. Consider for instance the story of the illness of his ten-year-
old child Manilal.

The doctor found Manilal with a high fever, caused by pneumonia
after typhoid. He said that eggs and chicken broth might save him,
but Mr. Gandhi refused to allow him either. "Manilal was only ten
years old. To consult his wishes was out of the question. I had to
decide." The doctors implored Gandhi to give the boy nourishing food,

since his life was in grave danger, but the father continued to refuse.
He told the doctor that he would treat Manilal in his own way, if the
doctor would consent to come in from time to time and examine him.
He gave Manilal hip baths and orange juice, and Manilal bravely said,
"I will not have eggs or chicken broth." But the boy grew worse. His
fever reach 104°. Gandhi proceeds:

> I began to get anxious. What would people say of me? What right had
> parents to inflict their fads on their children? . . . I was haunted by thoughts
> like these. Then a contrary current would start. God would surely be pleased
> to see that I was giving the same treatment to my son as I would give
> myself. . . . The doctor could not guarantee recovery. At best he could ex-
> periment. The thread of life was in the hands of God. . . .
> It was night. My mind was torn between these conflicting thoughts. I
> was in Manilal's bed lying by his side. I decided to give him a wet sheet
> pack. To the head I applied a wet towel. . . . The whole body was burning
> like hot iron, and quite parched. There was absolutely no perspiration . . .
> I was sorely tired. I left Manilal in charge of his mother, and went out
> for a walk. . . . Very few pedestrians were out. Plunged in deep thought I
> scarcely looked at them. "My honor is in Thy keeping, oh Lord, in this
> hour of trial," I repeated to myself. . . . After a short time I returned, my
> heart beating in my breast.
> No sooner had I returned, than Manilal said, "You have returned, Bapu?"
> "Yes, darling."
> "Do please pull me out. I am burning."
> "Are you perspiring, my boy?"
> "I am simply soaked. Do please take me out."
> I felt his forehead. It was covered with beads of perspiration. The tem-
> perature was going down. I thanked God. . . . I undid the pack, dried his
> body, and father and son fell asleep in the same bed.
> (*Story of My Experiments with Truth,* Vol. I, pp. 571-577)

The point of this story is, of course, that his honor, his faith, were
more important to the Mahatma than the life of his son. Years later
an almost identical episode occurred, when Kasturbai was taken ill.
The doctors said she would certainly die unless she got nourishing
food. Gandhi consulted with her; they decided that she would not take
it. And she got well, after a harrowing experience.

Another source of power is his tremendous knowledge of India.
There are 700,000 villages in India, and Gandhiji has visited an extraordinary number of them. His travels have been epochal. In the
third-class trains and especially on foot, he has covered the entire
peninsula.

The things Gandhi likes most are children, fresh air, laughter,
friends, the truth. What he dislikes most is a lie.

This is another source of power. People cannot lie to him. I heard
this all over India: as if the Mahatma had some supernatural quality

which overcame temptation to falsehood in other people. His own sincerity, his own love of truth, is so great that he brings out truth in others. Jawaharlal Nehru, who admits that his language is sometimes incomprehensible, talks of his wonderful "knack of reaching the hearts of the people" by this means.

His colossal spiritual integrity on the one hand; his earthly command of politics on the other—this is the Gandhi gambit.

He invented *khaddar* and village spinning, which plunged his revolution into the heart of the countryside; he *walked* to Dandi and the sea, and behind him spread the wildfire of revolt. He likes to choose a small concrete objective that the starved, illiterate millions can easily grasp. Recently the Bombay government wondered how to reach the peasants quickly with concrete proof of the Congress program. Gandhi suggested abolition of a grazing fee that hampered movements of their cattle, and in a few days word of the new program had spread widely. When he decided to hold the annual sessions of Congress, where a hundred thousand people congregate, in tiny villages instead of the great towns, people said that it would be impossible. They pointed to the lack of sanitary arrangements; they were terrified of cholera. But Mr. Gandhi simply let cholera go hang, and nobody got sick—at least not of cholera.

When he left Congress in 1934, he did so in order to make himself more honest, more neutral. He wanted to be in a position to adjudicate, not merely between different factions within Congress, but between Congress and the British. This is as if Abraham Lincoln, say, had quit the presidency in the middle of the Civil War, in order to see that the North behaved with proper honor to the South.

Science of Mahatmatics

When people in India talk about Mr. Gandhi's defects, they are apt to mention half a dozen things.

First, he is dictatorial. "If you choose to follow my lead, you must accept my conditions," he said once. He went to the Round Table Conference in London as the *sole* representative of the Congress, and as a result was drowned in detail and outmaneuvered—and he stated once that he *alone* must decide whether or not civil disobedience is ever to be renewed.

Second, his medievalism. Even his closest friends object to his extravagant use of religious symbolism. There was a great earthquake in Behar in 1934; Mr. Gandhi promptly announced that this was punishment sent to India for the sin of Untouchability; Nehru has a wonderful passage describing how this staggered him.

Third, his meekness, his masochism, have played into the hands of the British in negotiation.

Fourth, his sense of proportion is off-balance. He will stop work all day to deal with any sudden small problem, for instance a forlorn mother in a village, or a crying child. His friends were horrified at several of his fasts, in which he risked his life for what modern minds thought were minor issues. He twice canceled nationwide civil disobedience because of isolated cases of impurity or violence. (But, with wonderful political instinct, he knew that each campaign was lost, and that it was wise to recede at just that time.) One story is that he held up negotiations for the Gandhi-Irwin truce because an officer in Gujerat impounded a peasant's cow. The Mahatma stopped everything until that cow was released.

Fifth, and above all, his inveterate love of compromise. He is a stanch antagonist, but he infinitely prefers settlement to struggle. Gandhiji wants compromise with the socialists, with the princes, with the industrial magnates, with the government in Delhi. Surely no man has ever so quickly and easily let bygones be bygones. He has no hatreds, no resentments; once a settlement is made, he cooperates with enemies as vigorously as he fought them.

Associated with this quality of compromise is his dislike of hard and fast definitions. Once during the Round Table Conference he offered the Moslems a blank check in settlement of communal[4] difficulties, provided they would subscribe to the Congress program of complete independence. Thereupon Mr. Jinnah, the Moslem leader, confronted the Mahatma with seven different definitions of independence which he had at one time or other made. No one in India knows precisely, beyond shadow of a doubt, where the Mahatma draws the line between "dominion status" and "independence." He seldom defines his terms. Once he was asked by a political writer of the *Times of India* to give an important statement on provincial autonomy. He dictated it rapidly, and the writer was delighted with his scoop. He took the statement back to the office—there were only four sentences—whereupon it was discovered that each of the four sentences could be interpreted in different ways.

There are important nuances even to his concept of civil disobedience. He abhors violence, but he admits that some things are worse than violence—cowardice, for example. He dislikes "passive resistance" as a synonym for *Satyagraha,* because he feels that *Satyagraha* is not passive; it is nonviolent resistance, which is quite a different thing from nonresistance *per se.*

He adores formulas. When the Working Committee of the Congress

4 This tricky word doesn't refer to "communism" but to "communities."

meets these days, Mr. Gandhi stays away, waits until the members are in disagreement, and then finds a formula for straightening them out. This science is known throughout India as "Mahatmatics."

Grace Notes

In London his friends took him to see Charlie Chaplin. He noted the considerable crowds around Chaplin's hotel. The two had an amitable talk. Leaving, Gandhi asked his companions, "Who was that delightful man?" He had never heard of Chaplin before.

Once a snake dropped on his ankle, and involuntarily he twitched and shook it off. He has regretted this ever since, because it showed that his devotion to nonviolence was not really perfect.

One of his friends was accused of complicity in a minor scandal. Gandhi heard about it, summoned the friend, and said, "Tell me the whole truth by tomorrow morning." Then he added that if the friend denied the charges, he would investigate them anyway. The friend confessed, whereupon the Mahatma forgave him.

A Congress prisoner behaved badly in Bijapur jail. The British warder threatened to inform Mr. Gandhi, who would start a new fast if the congressman didn't reform. The congressman reformed.

Once he was tempted to ask his followers to eat fruit only after it had fallen from the tree. To pick it while it was still on the branch might touch the borderline of violence.

The Religious Factor

The attitude of the Mahatma toward religion is obviously of supreme importance, but it is not easy to define. No one knows just what faith he believes in. His insistence on rendering good for evil, his feeling that one can win justice only by giving justice to the enemy, his injunction to hate the sin but not the sinner, are the essence of practical Christianity. He believes in original sin, and is probably more like Christ than any man in the political sphere who has ever lived. But he does not call himself a Christian. When, watching him pray, I asked his intimate friends whom he prayed to, they did not know.

The following passage is illuminating:[5]

I do perceive that whilst everything around me is ever-changing and ever-dying, there is, underlying all that change, a living Power that is changeless, that holds all together, that creates, dissolves, and re-creates. That informing Power and Spirit is God. . . . I see it as purely benevolent, for I can see that, in the midst of death, life persists; in the midst of untruth, truth persists; in the midst of darkness, light persists. Hence I gather that God is life, truth, and light. He is love, He is the Supreme Good. . . .

[5] Made in, of all places, a record for the Columbia Gramophone Company.

Gandhi is a devout Hindu, but he believes that the scriptures of *all* the great religions are equally the word of God—Bible, Talmud, Zend-Avesta, Koran, and the Buddhist canon.

He writes:

I cannot account for the existence of evil by any rational method. To want to do so is to be co-equal with God. I am, therefore, humble enough to recognize evil as such, and I call God long-suffering and patient precisely because He permits evil in the world. I know that He has no evil in Himself and yet if there is evil He is the author of it and yet untouched by it.

In an article written in 1920 he says:

Why should we be upset when children or young men or old men die? Not a moment passes when someone is not born or is not dead in this world. We should feel the stupidity of rejoicing in a birth and lamenting a death. Those who believe in the soul—and what Hindu, Mussulman or Parsi does not?—know that the soul never dies. The souls of the living as well as the dead are all one.

Then there is the famous passage about suffering:

Suffering is the mark of the human tribe. It is an eternal law. The mother suffers so that her child may live. Life comes out of death. The condition of wheat growing is that the seed grain should perish. No country has ever risen without being purified through the fire of suffering. . . . It is impossible to do away with the law of suffering which is the one indispensable condition of our being. Progress is to be measured by the amount of suffering undergone . . . the purer the suffering, the greater is the progress.

Swaraj is the ordinary word used by Indians to denote "independence." Lately the Mahatma has used *Ramraj* instead. *Ram* means "God."

~~~~~~

Independence came to India on August 15, 1947, a little less than a decade after I wrote this chapter, at the cost of the loss of Pakistan. The Indian continent had to be partitioned before freedom was attained. Mr. Gandhi was shot and killed the next year by a Hindu nationalist—one of those whom he had liberated—and one of the supreme characters of modern times thus left the scene which he had so richly and eccentrically ennobled. But he still lives in the hearts of millions, if only because he gave the Indian people new spirit, unity, and hope.

〰〰〰〰

Have You Seen Jawaharlal?

I have been told that this was the first "substantial" study of Mr. Nehru ever to appear in English and that it introduced him, so to speak, to the western world. In actual fact he was perfectly well known and widely admired in England by the middle 1930's, although many Americans had perhaps not heard enough about him. In any case my article appeared in Asia Magazine *(February, 1939), and then formed a chapter in* Inside Asia. *Later, in collaboration with Frances Gunther, I wrote another article, "Nehru of India," which came out in* Life *after the outbreak of World War II.*

I might also mention that I, as it happened, was the mechanism or excuse for the first speech Mr. Nehru ever made on the Indian radio— not that this has any importance. He had only recently been released from prison and had never had the experience of talking on the air before. When, traveling for Inside Asia, *I arrived in Bombay late in 1937, friends asked me to make a speech. I was reluctant to do so, but finally agreed. Then a British official of the Indian Broadcasting Services cajoled Mr. Nehru into introducing me. A splendid time was had by all, but I do not think that Mr. Nehru approved of the substance of my talk, which was to the effect that war was bound to come in Europe soon. My lecture, drawn from a magazine article I had just written for the* Saturday Evening Post, *was called "This Peace Is a Cheat." Jawaharlal did not like to think that any peace could be a cheat.*

The backdrop to the text that follows is the same as that of the Gandhi chapter. India was in a state of temporary truce; both sides were girding themselves for the test to come.

~~~~~~

Believe me, if Jawaharlal is not in jail today, it is not because he is afraid of it. He is quite capable of mounting the gallows with a smile on his lips.
                                                                  —MR. GANDHI

THE REMARKABLE HUMAN BEING whose name is Pandit Jawaharlal Nehru is, next to Mr. Gandhi, the most interesting Indian in India. This handsome, cultivated, and exceptionally fastidious and sensitive Kashmiri Brahman, who is the Mahatma's successor in the nationalist movement, is not so baffling a creature as Mr. Gandhi, but he has complexities enough. The struggle in Nehru is triple. He is an Indian who became a westerner; an aristocrat who became a socialist; an individualist who became a great mass leader. More than this, he is a man with a modern mind, a man of reason, a devout—if this is the proper adjective—rationalist. And in India!—the continent of caste and holy cattle, of religious fanaticism to an extreme degree—India, which is a sort of cesspool of rival faiths, but in which faith, any faith, is a paramount desideratum. Nehru the agnostic, Nehru the modern man, faces the colossal medievalism of India. He fights the British, but he fights the entrenched ritualism of his own people too. His position— in reverse—is roughly that of an American politician, say, who dared to come out *against* radios and two-car garages. His struggle is that of a twentieth-century mind trying to make a revolution of material that goes back beyond the middle ages.

* * *

Nehru was born in Allahabad on November 14, 1889, the son of Motilal Nehru, one of the greatest lawyers and richest men in India. It is difficult to call him "Nehru," because in India he is universally known just as "Jawaharlal." Possibly this use of his first name became common in the early days to distinguish him from his father. Sometimes he is referred to as "Panditji" but as a rule the diminutive "ji" is not used with Nehru. Jawaharlal is enough. One thinks of him only as Jawaharlal. "Pindit," incidentally, which means "wise man," is a Kashmiri title he took from his father.

The Nehru family, originating in the hills of Kashmir, settled first in Delhi, then Allahabad. One ancestor, Raj Kaul, was a Persian scholar in the good graces of the Mogul emperor of the time. The family name was Kaul for several hundred years; Nehru, which means "canal," was added later. Nehru's grandfather and great-grandfather both held posts under the last Moguls, and one of his uncles (like Gandhi's father) was a *Dewan* or prime minister of a small native state.

When one says that Jawaharlal is a Kashmiri Brahman and the son of Motilal Nehru, it is as if one were to say that a man was a Boston Cabot or Lowell whose father was like Mr. Justice Holmes. He comes not only from the bluest blood in India, with a tremendous pride of race and heritage, but of a family with a deep tradition of public service and utility to the community.

Young Nehru had an English tutor from his earliest years; in 1905, at sixteen, he went to England, where he studied at Harrow and Cambridge and read for the bar—curious background for an Indian revolutionary! During this period his influences were largely literary. He was shy and lonely; he read Pater and Wilde and was devoted to what he calls a "vague kind of Cyrenaicism," though he came early in contact with social and scientific ideas.

Nehru, like Gandhi, has written an autobiography[1]—but it is a very different kind of book. The Mahatma's placid story compares to Nehru's as a cornflower to an orchid, a rhyming couplet to a sonnet by MacLeish or Auden, a water pistol to a machine gun. Nehru's autobiography is subtle, complex, discriminating, infinitely cultivated, steeped in doubt, suffused with intellectual passion. Lord Halifax once said that no one could understand India without reading it; it is a kind of Indian *Education of Henry Adams*, written in superlative prose— hardly a dozen men alive write English as well as Nehru—and it is not only an autobiography of the most searching kind, but the story of a whole society, the story of the life and development of a nation.

In 1912, when he was twenty-three, Jawaharlal returned to India. Life smote him promptly. It was in any case impossible for him not to be close to politics—for instance the coalition between the Congress and the Moslem League in 1916 was made in his father's house— and he joined the nationalist movement. He met Mr. Gandhi ("All of us admired him for his heroic fight in South Africa, but he seemed very distant and different and unpolitical to many of us young men") and soon made his first speech. He was dumb with shyness and doubtful of his capacity even to speak his own tongue, Hindustani.

Then came the Rowlatt bills and the Amritsar massacre. Nehru writes:

Toward the end of that year (1919) I travelled from Amritsar to Delhi by the night train. The compartment I entered was almost full and all the

[1] *Jawaharlal Nehru: An Autobiography*. London: John Lane. It was published in America under the title *Toward Freedom*.

berths, except one upper one, were occupied by sleeping passengers. I took the vacant upper berth. In the morning I discovered that all my fellow passengers were military officers. They conversed with each other in loud voices which I could not help overhearing. One of them was holding forth in an aggressive and triumphant tone and soon I discovered that he was Dyer, the hero of Jallianwala Bagh and he was describing his Amritsar experiences. He pointed out how he had the whole town at his mercy and he had felt like reducing the rebellious city to a heap of ashes, but he took pity on it and refrained. . . . I was greatly shocked to hear his conversation and to observe his callous manner. He descended at Delhi station in pajamas with bright pink stripes, and a dressing gown.

(Autobiography, pp. 43-44)

Soon after, a turning point in Nehru's life occurred. He took his mother and wife, both of whom were ill, to Mussoorie in the north. It happened that an Afghan delegation, negotiating peace with Britain after the 1919 Afghan war, was housed in the same hotel. Nehru never talked to any of the Afghan plenipotentiaries, but after a month he was asked by the local police not to have any dealings with them. This struck him as being unreasonable; he had no intention of talking to the Afghans, but—a young man of fiber—he refused on principle to obey the order. Thereupon he was formally "externed" from the Mussoorie district. This was his first conflict with British authority. In the next two weeks he had nothing much to do, and as a result became aware of the *kisans,* peasants, and their grievances. The incident at Mussoorie helped turn him to the land.

Already he had had vague socialist leanings. Now these began to be entrenched. With some colleagues he visited the peasants on the little farms. He saw their sufferings firsthand, and heard their grievances. He learned to survive the Indian sun, and to speak to large gatherings. He discovered his capacity to arouse people. He even— indirectly—sent several peasants to jail, because when they had been guilty of looting homes of landlords he—filled with *Satyagraha* spirit—suggested that they should give themselves up to the police. "Many received long sentences and in later years, when I went to prison, I came across some of them, boys and young men, spending their youth in prison."

Here is his first picture of the peasants in their "miserable rags" fighting the lords of the land:

They showered their affection on us and looked on us with loving and hopeful eyes, as if we were the bearers of good tidings, the guides who were to lead them to the promised land. Looking at them and their misery and overflowing gratitude, I was filled with shame and sorrow, shame at my own easy-going and comfortable life and our petty politics of the city which ignored this vast multitude of semi-naked sons and daughters of

India, sorrow at the degradation and overwhelming poverty of India. A new picture of India seemed to rise before me, naked, starving, crushed, and utterly miserable.

(*Autobiography*, p. 52)

Nehru first went to jail during the 1921 non-cooperation campaign. This was the time of the first tremendous enthusiasm for civil disobedience, and hundreds of Indians, guilty of no crime or misdemeanor, fought for the privilege of being arrested. Young men and women mobbed the police lorries going through the streets, and scrambled to get inside the jails.

Next he was arrested in a native state called Nabha, where a British administrator ruled in place of a deposed Maharaja. With two comrades Nehru went to investigate conditions there; they were arrested, led down the street handcuffed, and thrown into a filthy jail. Apparently the charge was that they did not have permission to enter Nabha territory. Nehru was handcuffed to one of his companions for twenty-four hours; at night, as he slept on a muddy floor, rats crawled over his face. It took two weeks before he was released. The "trial," before a judge who knew neither English nor Hindustani, was an unbelievable farce, and Nehru was sentenced to two and a half *years'* imprisonment. Luckily the sentence was suspended—but Nehru and his comrades all came down with typhoid fever, caught from the foul drinking water in the hovel where they were confined.

"The state of Nabha was under a British administrator, a member of the Indian Civil Service, and he had the full powers of an autocrat, subject only to the Government of India," Nehru writes. "And yet at every turn we were referred to Nabha laws and procedure to justify the denial of the most ordinary rights. We had to face a combination of feudalism and the modern bureaucratic machine with the disadvantages of both and the advantages of neither."

Altogether Jawaharlal has served seven terms in prison. Jail or threat of jail took the best years of his life. He was sentenced to an aggregate of fourteen and a half years; several sentences were suspended, however, and he was discharged before time, so that he actually served about six years in all. The last sentence came as late as 1934, after civil disobedience had been called off; he was arrested following an alleged seditious speech in Calcutta, and given two years.

Mr. Ghandi (who only served four brief terms) adored prison; Jawaharlal did not. But he is seldom bitter. There are beautiful passages in his book, describing the stars he managed to see, peering upward from the compound, and the animals—squirrels and monkeys and parrots—he learned to play with. He knows the emotional starvation of jail, the chafing of steady confinement, the terrible dreariness

of day after day, season after season, without change. With wistful
eye he looked

> Upon that little tent of blue
> Which prisoners call the sky,
> And at every drifting cloud that went
> With sails of silver by.

In one jail he lived in a large barrack, with holes in the roof and
crannies in doors and windows. "I lived in solitary grandeur. But I
was not quite alone, for at least two score sparrows had made their
home in the broken-down roof. Sometimes a wandering cloud would
visit me, its many arms creeping in through the numerous openings
and filling the place with a damp mist." It is in this passage that he
writes that suffering, even if it may be necessary for clear thought,
will cloud the brain in excess. He does not like suffering as Gandhi
does. He was not an introvert by nature, he says, but prison made
him so. Jail has deeply marked and pitted this man. He cannot bear
cruelty.

Continually he brooded not merely on the nature of repression but
on the fundamental reasons for it—reasons even beyond the political
struggle in India. To test his courage he withstood a *lathi*[2] charge,
and was bruised and beaten; his own mother was likewise hit on the
head with canes, and knocked down by the police; his wife followed
him to jail. He heard of such incredible sentences as that of the youth
who got nine *years'* rigorous imprisonment for carrying a revolver
and he knew schoolboys who were flogged in jail for political offenses.
But his mind kept ranging above the particular.

Jail alone did not make him a socialist, but it gave him the time
and opportunity for exhaustive political study and introspection. Generally he was well treated in jail; he was permitted books and writing
materials. His ideas on socialism took concrete form, and merged
gradually with his nationalism. He began to see the Indian problem
as more than a struggle between rebel nationalists and British nationalists. He became convinced that British imperialism as a capitalist
growth was the real enemy, and that it must be fought from the socialist
as well as from the nationalist point of view. British imperialism rests
on capitalist profit-making as well as on the political demands of
empire; therefore a logical opponent of British imperialism must be
not merely a nationalist but a socialist too.

This is the root of Nehru's creed. In every possible way he tried
to hammer it home to the Indian people.

Most Indians are distinctly not socialists, but Nehru rapidly became, next to Gandhi, the most important Indian leader. It is a question,

---

[2] A *lathi* is a long bamboo staff, the familiar weapon of the Indian police.

however, if most of his followers are devoted to him because he is a socialist, or in spite of it. At any rate for ten solid years he was either secretary or president of the Congress; he is the only man who has ever been president of Congress three times. He was powerfully instrumental in making Gandhi come out for *purna Swaraj* (complete independence) at the Lahore Congress; at Karachi in 1931 he persuaded the Working Committee to accept a few vaguely and guardedly socialist planks. In 1937, he opposed the taking of office by Congress, but then he went to the country and, in an unparalleled stumping campaign, almost single-handed brought victory to Congress in seven provinces.

"This My True-Begotten Father!"

His father, Motilal, was a very important influence on Jawaharlal, which is not surprising considering how sensitive Jawaharlal was and considering the vitality of the old man. The equation in the Nehru family worked both ways; Jawaharlal influenced Motilal almost as much as vice versa. One is reminded of the psychoanalytic phenomenon of counter-transference, wherein the patient attracts and influences the doctor, instead of the doctor attracting the patient.

The story of Jawaharlal and Motilal, their love, their conflict, their hunger to understand each other, their eventual community of ideas, is well told in the autobiography. Motilal was solidly rich, a lawyer with an extensive practice, an intimate friend of governors and viceroys. He had, in Jawaharlal's words, "strong feelings, strong passions, tremendous pride, and great strength of will." Jawaharlal paints a beautifully revealing portrait of him as man, patriot, father.

The youth, barely twenty, began to drift toward extremism, toward rebellion. Motilal strove to understand his son, to check this drift away from him which horrified him. At that time Motilal was a moderate; he had been a member of Congress for years, but Congress was a very pale body in those days. Motilal wrote an article which Jawaharlal disagreed with; he chided his father by saying that the British would approve it highly. Motilal was wild with rage. Yet Motilal's career depended largely on British policy and peace.

Came Gandhi and non-cooperation. Jawaharlal joined up. Motilal was dumbfounded. "He was not in the habit of being swept away by new proposals." He wasn't at all sure that civil disobedience would work; he resented it that his precious and beloved son should risk jail. The conflict grew. "We tried to be as considerate to each other as possible . . . night after night I wandered about alone, tortured in mind and trying to grope my way out." Then Jawaharlal discovered that Motilal was sleeping on the floor—to see what life in jail would be like for his son!

Within the year Motilal came over completely to his son's side. He took his stand with Gandhi and civil disobedience. This meant giving up his great house in Allahabad, his wealth, his practice; it meant giving up most of the friends, the political acquaintances with Indians and British alike, of a generation; it meant complete remaking of his life at sixty. And promptly old Motilal became the lion of the movement. When Jawaharlal went to jail, his father went with him.

For nine years the two worked together, fought together. Motilal was treated with the utmost consideration in prison, but imprisonment hurt his health. By 1930 he was an invalid. "He pulled himself together and banged a table in front of him, saying that he had made up his mind to be an invalid no longer." But the machine was burned out. "There he sat like an old lion mortally wounded and with his physical strength almost gone, but still very leonine and kingly." Sometime later Gandhi came to see him. Motilal said, "I am going soon, Mahatmaji, and I shall not be here to see *Swaraj*. But I know that you have won it." Early in 1931 he died.

Jawaharlal writes:

I was watching by his bedside. He had had a troublesome and restless night; suddenly I noticed that his face grew calm and the sense of struggle vanished from it. I thought that he had fallen asleep, and I was glad of it. But my mother's perceptions were keener, and she uttered a cry. I turned to her and begged her not to disturb him as he had fallen asleep. But that sleep was his last long sleep, and from it there was no awakening.

Then:

There were some ceremonies at home, and then the last journey to the Ganges with a mighty concourse of people. As evening fell on the river bank that winter day, the great flames leapt up and consumed that body which had meant so much to us who were close to him as well as to millions in India. Gandhiji said a few moving words to the multitude, and then all of us crept silently home. The stars were out and shining brightly when we returned, lonely and desolate.

Later:

I found it difficult to realize that he had gone. Three months later I was in Ceylon with my wife and daughter, and we were spending a few quiet and restful days. . . . I liked the place, and it struck me suddenly that it would suit Father. Why not send for him? He must be tired out, and rest would do him good. I was on the point of sending a telegram to him in Allahabad.

(*Autobiography*, pp. 247-248)

Finally a curious thing happened. Returning home Nehru found a letter from his father awaiting him. It had been sent many months before, and had been forwarded and reforwarded without ever reaching the destination. And it was a letter of farewell.

Word of Legend

Legends aplenty grew up about the Nehrus. One was that Motilal, a highly fastidious person, sent his laundry weekly all the way to Paris. It was nonsensical, of course. Another to the effect that the Viceroy (who had a very high regard for him) sent him champagne in jail is equally without foundation.

Another story, which has been widely garbled and distorted, has it that Motilal's sudden turn away from the British began when Jawaharlal was blackballed by an English club. The facts are these. Many years before, when Motilal was beginning his practice, an English friend offered to nominate him, Motilal, for membership in the European club in Allahabad. Motilal thanked his friend courteously, but declined the offer, because he did not want to risk rejection and because election of an Indian might make English members uncomfortable.

Another story of a different category is that Jawaharlal is a Communist and that he has frequently been to Moscow, there to listen to the party line. But in fact he is not a Communist, but a kind of social democrat; he has been in Moscow only once, and then for a few days in company with his father. They went as tourists to see the tenth anniversary festivities in 1927.

The Man Jawaharlal

At forty-nine Nehru is strikingly handsome—especially when he wears the Gandhi cap, a sort of white forage cap—and he is one of those fortunate people who photograph even better than they look. Usually he wears the Congress uniform—white *khadder*—and manages to appear courtly and impressive even when shrouded with yards of cheesecloth apron. His friends say that he aged a good deal in the past two or three years, mostly as the result of fatigue, incessant traveling, and the giving out of energy. He is tall for an Indian—about five feet ten—with excellent bearing. He exercises methodically, and loves winter sports and swimming.

He lives as a rule in a house called the Anand Bhavan at Allahabad. Motilal gave his tremendous house to the nation, renaming it Swaraj Bhavan; for the family he then built what was to have been a simple cottage, but Motilal was an exceptionally expansive personality, and the simple cottage—the Anand Bhavan where Nehru lives—turned into a house almost as big as the original one. The big house is now the headquarters of the Congress party; part of it is used as a hospital.

But Jawaharlal isn't in Allahabad very often. His travels are formidable. He lives on the railway trains, and by choice travels third class. Anyone who has been in India knows what an ordeal this is. India—Indian India—has no capital. Gandhi is in Wardha, Nehru in Allahabad; Bombay and Calcutta are important centers to Congress, and so are Lucknow and Madras. The Working Committee of Congress —its executive body—meets once every six weeks or so. As a rule it rotates between different cities. The annual session is held nowadays in a remote village. So Congress committee members are incessantly, unendingly traveling. The trains roar across dusty India, bringing them together.

Nehru's wife, Kamala, who came from a Kashmir Brahman family like his own, died in 1936. She had been in ill health for many years, and he was released from one term of imprisonment in order to visit her in Switzerland. Previously, when she was in India, the British volunteered to free him so that he might see her if he would pledge himself informally to give up politics for the period corresponding to the rest of his term. He refused. She begged him to refuse. Their only child, twenty-year-old Indira, went to school in England. Nehru has two sisters; one, Lakshmi, married Ranjit S. Pandit and has been the thoroughly competent minister for local self-government and health in the United Provinces government—the first Congresswoman to reach ministerial rank. As a child she was called Sarup (the Beautiful One), and nicknamed Nan.

Nehru keeps closely in touch with the outside world. He subscribes —when not in jail—to the *New Statesman*, the *Manchester Guardian Weekly*, *Time & Tide*, the New York *Nation*, *The New Republic*, the *Living Age*, and *Vendredi* and *L'Europe Nouvelle* from Paris. Additionally he would like to see regularly several leftist magazines which are forbidden circulation in India. Recently he went for a brief vacation in the Himalayas. The books he took with him were Aldous Huxley's *Ends and Means*, Bertrand Russell's *Which Way to Peace*, John Dewey's *The Quest for Certainty*. J. R. Firth's *The Tongues of Man* (a book on comparative philology), and Levy's *Philosophy for a Modern Man*.

His knowledge of English poetry is profound, and his love for it passionate. Incessantly he quotes classic verse.

He has a great number of acquaintances, but very few intimate friends. He speaks often of his loneliness. He loves children, lightheartedness, laughter, but he is no back-slapper; he hates promiscuous effusiveness; he is moody and ingrown, and finds it hard to meet people halfway. They must come to *him*. He made even his father come to him: to meet his growing mind and soul. In one passage he says that he took to the crowd and the crowd took to him, but that he was never able to lose himself completely to it; he was in it always, and *of* it never.

He is the furthest possible contrast to the mob leader like Hitler or Mussolini. American newspapers tag him with the adjective "fiery," which is singularly inappropriate, though he is capable of flashes of temperament. When he talks, he deliberately understates his case; he sounds like a lecturer at Oxford, even at a political meeting. Frequently he confesses his failings; he is sometimes bored by politics; he is the victim of competitive emotions; occasionally he is unsure of himself and divided in judgment. Dogmatism does not become him. He talks frankly of his inner conflict, of "subconscious depths struggling with outer circumstances, of an inner hunger unsatisfied."

In one despondent moment he wrote that he represented no one. "I have become a queer mixture of the East and West, out of place everywhere, at home nowhere." Much in India disheartens him, and he confesses "retreating into his shell."

He detests ritualism and mysticism, except perhaps in poetry. Religion he calls a killjoy. He is all for modernization, westernization. "The spectacle of what is called religion, or at any rate organized religion, in India and elsewhere, has filled me with horror and I have frequently condemned it and wished to make a clean sweep of it." This— from an Indian leader! And there are some who say that his hatred of religion will keep him from supreme heights in India, because it is inconceivable that India should surrender herself to an agnostic.

He has no faddisms, like the Mahatma. He ate meat from childhood, but gave it up under Gandhi's influence in 1920. He reverted to meat again in Europe, though he felt that it "coarsened him"; now (like Hitler, whom he in no other way resembles) he is "more or less" a vegetarian. He smokes occasionally, and outside India may even take a little light wine. His father drank wine; in fact young Jawaharlal saw him with a glass once, and was thunderstruck; he thought that old Motilal was drinking blood.

His general health is so good that even in jail he had no insomnia, he says. He has, however, recorded some curious dreams. A favorite dream is of flying over open country. He gets no salary for political work, and the family fortune has gone mostly to the cause. What little money he needs he gets from writing.

The things he likes most are mountains, running water, children, glaciers, good conversation, and all animals except bats and centi-pedes. Once he had a moment of intense enjoyment in prison: the temperature was 116° F. and his wife sent him a thermos flask filled with sherbet. The things he dislikes most are "exploitation, cruelty, and people who, in the name of God, truth, and the public good, are busy feathering their nests"; in a word, most politicians.

He wrote to me in 1938, "I suppose my father and Gandhiji have been the chief personal influences in my life. But outside influences do not carry me away. There is a tendency to resist being influenced. Still influences do work slowly and unconsciously. My wife influenced me considerably in many ways, though unobtrusively." He was influenced for a time by Bertrand Russell, and then found him ineffective. He disliked Spengler at first, but found a "certain fascination" in his book.

Nehru proceeded to say that Marx and Lenin had a powerful effect on him, partly from the content of their writings, even more by reason of the way they wrote. He was tired of mysticism and metaphysics; he liked the unadorned, scientific, analytical point of view. He says that he is certainly a socialist in that he believes in socialist theory and method. His general approach is Marxist. But he wrote me, "I am not a communist chiefly because I resist the communist tendency to treat communism as holy doctrine; I do not like being told what to think and do. I suppose I am too much of an individualist. . . . I feel also that too much violence is associated with communist methods. The ends cannot be separated from the means."

He likes moderation. He believes in the rational approach. He says of the Hindu-Urdu controversy: "Open the way to both scripts everywhere." As to communal troubles, which he thinks the British deliberately keep to the forefront, he says that the real struggle is not between Hindu and Moslem, but between both and modern ideas.

One of his defects, people say, is that he is too decent, too honorable, to be a good politician. He is a gentleman. Worse, he is an English gentleman! He has devoted his life to freeing India from Britain, but the British imprint is deep upon him. The old-school tie has turned to homespun cheesecloth, but he still follows a code of chivalry.

The sources of his power are numerous. Consider, for instance, his courage and obvious strength of character. Then there is his technical competence at a job; he was, for instance, a successful mayor of Allahabad for a time. Consider too his industry, both intellectual and physical. In jail he not only wrote most of a closely printed 617-page autobiography, but a history of the world in the form of letters to his daughter, 1,569 pages long. During the last election campaign, he traveled 110,000 miles in twenty-two months, and reached villages everywhere in India. He used vehicles ranging from bullock carts to airplanes; he had to give up airplanes because peasants in remote parts of the peninsula, never having seen a plane before, would overrun the landing fields. Once he made 150 speeches in one week.

Then again there is his modesty and complete honesty with himself. By 1929, he was a hero, almost inundated by the applause and enthusiasm of the masses; by 1930, he had to face hero worship such as no man in India, Gandhi alone excepted, had ever known. He writes that "only a saint or inhuman monster could survive" the praise that came his way without being a little affected. He was distrustful of his popularity but he couldn't help being exhilarated and impressed by it. His family quickly chastened him with raillery; his wife and sisters, and even his small daughter, began to call him at home the names he was given by the crowd. They would say, "Oh Jewel of India, what time is it?" or "Oh Embodiment of Sacrifice, please pass the bread."

His political integrity is unshakable. Nothing can deflect him from the path he has chosen, if he believes it to be right; he dislikes compromises and he has nothing of the occasional slipperiness of Mr. Gandhi. He makes definitions scrupulously, and abides by them.

One small anecdote is to the point. In 1928 came a crucial vote in the Calcutta Congress session, over which his father was presiding. Gandhi and Motilal were strongly backing a proposal that Congress should adopt officially what was known as the "Nehru Report," a document prepared by Motilal. Jawaharlal and his group—he was at the time head of a separate organization, the Independence League, as well as secretary of Congress—opposed this. The vote was close; Jawaharlal's side won. Then he discovered that there had been a technical error in the voting. As Secretary of the Congress he brought this to the attention of the meeting, even though he knew that it would mean overriding his victory and that in the next vote his group would lose.

He has great detachment. Recently—this is a curious oblique sidelight on his character—he wrote a character sketch of himself, and let it be published in a magazine anonymously. No one knew that he was the author until he let the secret out to a few friends months later.

It begins with a resounding "*Rashtrapati Jawaharlal Ki Jai!*" (Long Live Jawaharlal, Chief of State), and describes in somewhat indignant detail his manner as a conqueror of the multitude.

The Rashtrapati looked up as he passed swiftly through the waiting crowds, his hands went up and his pale hard face was lit up with a smile. . . . The smile passed away and the face became stern and sad. Almost it seemed that the smile and gesture accompanying it had little reality; they were just tricks of the trade to gain the goodwill of the crowd whose darling he had become. Was it so? . . . Watch him again.

Is all this natural or the carefully thought-out trickery of the public man? Perhaps it is both and long habit has become second nature now. The most effective pose is one in which there seems to be the least posing, and Jawaharlal has learned well to act without the paint and powder of the actor. . . . Whither is this going to lead him and the country? What is he aiming at with all his apparent want of aim?

For nearly two years now he has been President of Congress. Steadily and persistently he goes on increasing his personal prestige and influence. . . . From the far North to Cape Comorin he has gone like some triumphant Caesar, leaving a trail of glory and a legend behind him. Is all this just a passing fancy which amuses him . . . or is it his will to power that is driving him from crowd to crowd and making him whisper to himself:

"I drew these tides of men into my hands and wrote my will across the sky in stars."

What if the fancy turns? Men like Jawaharlal with all their great capacity for great and good work are unsafe in a democracy. He calls himself a demo-crat and a socialist, and no doubt he does so in all earnestness . . . but a little twist and he might turn into a dictator. He might still use the language of democracy and socialism, but we all know how Fascism has fattened on this language and then cast it away as useless number.

Jawaharlal cannot become a Fascist. . . . He is far too much an aristocrat for the crudity and vulgarity of Fascism. His very face and voice tell us that. His face and voice are definitely private. . . . And yet he has all the makings of a dictator in him—vast popularity, a strong will, energy, pride . . . and with all his love of the crowd an intolerance of others and a certain contempt for the weak and inefficient. His flashes of temper are well known. His overwhelming desire to get things done, to sweep away what he dislikes and build anew, will hardly brook for long the slow processes of democracy.

The article—Jawaharlal must have had a good time writing it—ends with a stirring appeal that he be defeated if he runs again for Congress president. In the document he was outlining possible dangers of the future quite unconnected with himself. He was anxious *not* to be presi-dent of Congress for another term.

Attitude to Gandhiji

Jawaharlal's relations to Gandhi are more complex than those of a disciple to a master. Poles apart as they are mentally and emotionally, they are devoted to each other and they complement each other nicely. Nehru needs Gandhi because Gandhi alone can carry the mass of the Indian people. Gandhi needs Nehru because he is his indispensable second-in-command.

When Nehru first came in close contact with the Mahatma, he thought that in time Gandhi would turn gradually toward socialism. Years went by, and he saw his mistake. He worried terribly about it. It seemed to him an unreasonable paradox that Gandhiji, with all his "love and solicitude for the underdog," should "yet support a system which inevitably produces it and crushes it." He was impatient with Gandhi's ideas of trusteeship by the upper classes; he could not endure it that the Mahatma, who believed in nonviolence, could support a system, capitalism, which was so much associated with violence.

Nehru, strictly speaking, is not the leader of the left in Congress. There are many others much more to the left than he is. He is not, oddly enough, even a member of the Congress Socialist party, a sort of autonomous block within Congress. This—another Indian paradox—is partly because the organized and official Socialists fear that his identification with them might embarrass his leadership of Congress as a whole. Jawaharlal holds an approximate left center position, just as Mr. Gandhi is right center. There are many Congressmen to the right of Gandhi. Likewise he differs basically from the Mahatma in that he cannot follow him all the way on nonviolence. He admits the political value of nonviolence, but he says frankly that nonviolence *alone* cannot carry India to the final goal.

But what a beautifully warm and compelling picture he draws of Gandhi, what a waterfall of tribute his pages are! He talks of his tremendous debt to Gandhi, his "amazing and almost irresistible charm and subtle power over people," his capacity to make "heroes out of clay," his "inexhaustible reservoir of spiritual power." He defends him vigorously against the socialists who call him a reactionary. "Reactionary or revolutionary, he has changed the face of India, given pride and character to a cringing and demoralized people, built up strength and consciousness in the masses, and made the Indian problem a world problem."

Relations to the British

Nehru doesn't hate the British. He hates British imperialism and its exploitation of India, but he freely admits his intellectual debt to British culture. When he takes a holiday, he heads straight for England. He has tried to forget the long agony of jail, to dissociate the responsibility for it from Britain as a whole.

Nor do the British, a few retired Colonel Blimps aside, really hate Nehru. But they *fear* him deeply. It is enlightening to compare British opinions of Gandhi and Nehru; very few Englishmen are worried about the Mahatma any more, but for Nehru they have a healthy apprehension. They attack him as a socialist as a blind for their alarm of him on purely nationalist grounds.

The British are enormously curious about Nehru. They all know Gandhiji; rather few know Jawaharlal. The present Viceroy, for instance, until the end of 1938 at least, had never met him. Everywhere one goes in India, the first political question is, "Have you seen Jawaharlal? What's he like—what's he doing—what's he up to now?"

~~~~~~

I do not think that when I wrote this article many years ago I emphasized sufficiently Nehru's drive and power, nor did I put enough stress on how passionately he was adored, even then, by the great masses of the Indian people.

Of course Nehru's truly great years had not even begun in 1938. He succeeded Mr. Gandhi as head of the Indian National Congress in 1942, and once more was sentenced to jail by the British authorities during the course of the war. He became prime minister in 1947 when India, at long last, obtained her independence, and held this post un-interruptedly for fourteen years until his death, aged seventy-five, in May, 1964. He was also foreign minister and minister for atomic energy and on several occasions acted as minister of defense and finance as well. Internationally he became famous as the creator and principal champion of neutralism.

Bitter disappointments—even tragedies—smote him in his last years. In an almost literal sense he ran India, with its 450,000,000 people, single-handed. Think what his country might have been like "if a man who had not believed fervently in democracy had been at the helm during those intensely critical years." Until the last moment he continued to fight against "poverty, regionalism, superstition, caste, and the abuses of power," as a British writer puts it. The Chinese attack on India in 1962 was probably the worst blow Mr. Nehru ever suffered. Curiously enough I do not think that he had a close enough knowledge of Asia. He took Asia for granted. What interested him to the exclusion of almost everything else in the realm of foreign affairs was the power struggle between the United States and the Soviet Union. Once, in 1950, I had dinner with him in New Delhi after having visited Japan and it struck me that he seemed extraordinarily innocent about things Japanese and events elsewhere in Asia.

Excerpts from his will (June, 1964) are these:

When I die I should like my body to be cremated. . . . A small handful of [my] ashes should be thrown into the Ganga [Ganges] and the major portion of them disposed of in the manner indicated below. No part of these ashes should be retained or preserved.

My desire to have a handful of my ashes thrown into the Ganga at Allahabad has no religious significance so far as I am concerned. I have no religious sentiment in the matter. I have been attached to the Ganga and Ganuna Rivers in Allahabad ever since my childhood. . . . I have watched their varying moods as the seasons changed and have often thought of the history and myth and tradition and song and story that have become attached to them through the long ages and become part of their flowing waters. . . .

The Ganga . . . has been a symbol of India's age-long culture and civiliza-tion, ever changing, ever flowing, and yet ever the same Ganga. . . . Smiling and dancing in the morning sunlight and dark and gloomy and full of mysteries as evening shadows fall, a narrow, slow and graceful stream in winter, and a vast, roaring thing during the monsoon, broad-bosomed almost to the sea and with something of the sea's power to destroy, the Ganga has *been to me a symbol and a memory of the past of India, running into the present, and flowing on to the great ocean of the future.*

The major portion of my ashes should, however, be disposed of otherwise. I want these to be carried high up into the air in an airplane and scattered from that height over the fields where the peasants of India toil, so that they might mingle with the dust and soil of India, and become an indistinguishable part of India.

I would like to conclude on a lower, lighter note. As I mention in the foreword to this chapter, I first met Mr. Nehru in 1937 in Bombay. In 1949 he visited the United States for the first time and, while in New York, came to tea with my wife and me. I asked him a question, "Did you, Mr. Nehru, think even in your wildest dreams when we met in Bombay twelve years ago that within a decade you would be prime minister of a sovereign, independent India?" With some asperity he answered, "No!"

CHAPTER 18

~~~~~~~~~

Kings of the Middle East

It makes me feel mildly old to say so, but I first began to hear stories about Ibn Saud in 1926, almost forty years ago. At that time I was a junior European correspondent of that admirable newspaper the Chicago Daily News. *My boss in Paris sent me to Egypt on a story which did not altogether pan out, and so I went on to visit Palestine, as it was then called, Transjordan, and other countries in the area. Informed people in various cities and outposts kept telling me about Ibn Saud, who was almost completely unknown in the West at that time, and I wrote a series of brief articles about him (August, 1926) which duly appeared in the* Chicago Daily News. *The present chapter about him was published in* Inside Asia *a good many years later in 1939.*

I mention Hussein and the Sherifians. These names should be explained. During World War I the Arabian Peninsula, still subject to the Turks and part of the Ottoman Empire, saw the growth to power of two rival potentates. One was Hussein, the Grand Sherif of Mecca (hence the term "Sherifian") and a lineal descendant of the Prophet Mohammed, who held the holy cities and the coastal strip. The other was Ibn Saud, the mysterious reformist chieftain who lived in the interior of the bleak, inpenetrable peninsula. These two men became bitter enemies and the course of Arabian history for many years was the feud between their rival houses.

Hussein (1856-1931) had several sons. One, Feisal, an extremely distinguished man, was King of Syria for a brief time and then the first King of Iraq. Another, Abdullah, who was lesser stuff, became the ruler of Transjordan.

I BN SAUD[1] is a terrific fellow. He is a full six foot four and correspondingly broad; he weighs 230 pounds, every ounce of it bone and
muscle. He is a complete picture of the vigorous old-time Arab; the only
western touch is his steel-rimmed spectacles. He has a magnificent voice,
deep and plangent, and he likes to bellow. During one series of negotiations with the British, the interpreters were terrified by his interrupting shouts of the Arab equivalent of "What the hell!" They were
measuring a new frontier in miles, and Ibn Saud wanted the distance
explained in terms of the speed of fast or slow camels, the criterion he
best understood.

He has married between one hundred and one hundred twenty wives;
he has several score of sons and unnumbered daughters. The laws of the
Prophet, and Ibn Saud is a very devout man, permit a husband only four
wives, but the King of Arabia gets around this rule by marrying his wives
seriatim. When he travels he takes three wives with him, so that there is
always room for a fourth maiden who may catch his royal eye. Then he
divorces one of the others. He is never married to more than four wives at
the same time. After a wife bears a child, he ships her back to her native
oasis or village, where she is a proud ornament to the community. Marriage, with Ibn Saud, is an instrumentality for the unification of Arabia.
He said recently, "In my youth and manhood I made a nation. Now in
my declining years I make men for its population."

Ibn Saud is a Wahabi. This means that he subscribes fervently to an
extreme reformist subdivision of Islam; the Wahabis are fundamentalists
who interpret the doctrines of Mohammed with great rigor, and add
strictures of their own. No Wahabi may drink, smoke, or gamble.
They wear no gold, silk, or ornaments, and they forbid prayer before
images. Ibn Saud's men created a stir throughout the Moslem world,
when, taking Mecca and Medina, they attempted to destroy some
precious Moslem shrines; they even contemplated demolition of the tomb
of the Prophet itself. Wahabis, believing in the untrammeled essence of
Mohammedanism, do not even mention the Prophet's name in their
prayers; they forbid the presence of women at funerals because the
women, not Spartan enough, may weep. The main reason why Ibn Saud
detested Hussein and his Sherifian brood was that he considered them
impious, soft, intolerably decadent, and corrupt.

[1] Correctly this doughty king's full name is 'Abdul 'Aziz Ibn 'Abdu'r-Rahman
Al-Feisal Al Sa'ūd. Shortened, it is correctly Ibn Sa'ūd. Arabs have no family
names; "ibn" means "son of"; Ibn Sa'ūd means simply "Son of Sa'ūd." Correctly
Iraq is 'Iraq, Abdullah is 'Abdullah, Shia is 'Sh'ia, Maan is 'Ma'an, and so on. The
apostrophe, known as a "glottal stop," represents the unpronounceable Arabic
consonant 'Ain.

Ibn Saud's career may be said to have begun with his great-great-great-grandfather, Mohammed Ibn Saud, who was converted to the Wahabite faith by a wandering mendicant, Abd-el Wahab, 150 years ago, and who set about imposing Wahabism on the Arabian peninsula. He was a fanatic puritan; he wanted to subdue and purify the entire Moslem world. And the campaigns of this long-forgotten Mohammed Ibn Saud in the early nineteenth century were considerable. He captured Mecca and Medina, like his great-great-great-grandson; he invaded Egypt and took Damascus; when he died in 1814, he was ready to attack Mesopotamia and Persia.

The contemporary Ibn Saud was born in Riadh, the chief city of Nejd —which is the desolate and impregnable inner heart of Arabia—about sixty-five years ago. No one knows his exact age. His family had fallen on hard times. As a very young man he assisted his father in ousting a rival chieftain, Ibn Rashid, from power in Nejd; his father was so impressed by his prowess that he abdicated in his favor. This was as early as 1900, when Ibn Saud could not have been more than twenty-six or twenty-seven. He spent a quarter century then in subduing rival tribesmen and consolidating his power; in 1926, having taken Mecca and rid himself of the Sherifians, he proclaimed himself King of Arabia; in 1932, he gave the country a new name—his own.

Ibn Saud was shrewd enough to take money from the British when he needed it, and from other sources too. But Saudi Arabia is an authentic, if primitive, national state, and Britain and the other powers fully recognize its sovereignty. The British respect Ibn Saud, and know his power; they are particularly appreciative that, during [a recent] Palestine crisis, he gave no overt or flamboyant support to the Palestine Arabs. He could have caused much trouble, so great is his prestige, had he done so. Ibn Saud may expect a quid pro quo for this, namely, rectification in his favor of the frontier between his country and Transjordan, which is still not finally demarcated. So the British are very, very polite to him.

Ibn Saud has a good robust sense of humor. He wanted to reward some Egyptian emissaries. So he gave them trophies that they themselves had once brought from Egypt for Hussein, and which he had captured on taking Hussein's capital.

His official car was for some years a battered Studebaker, which, when it went to meet a guest, carried six armed riders on the running boards who at intermittent junctures got out and pushed.

He eats, Arab fashion, with his fingers, from a colossal tray on which several sheep may repose; but he knows what knives and forks are, and he keeps them for his occasional—very occasional—foreign guests. (A Christian foreigner could not, of course, enter Mecca to see him there, but might be received at some city, Jeddah for instance, not so holy.)

The ordinary people of the town and desert greet him without ceremony by addressing him with his first name, Abdul Aziz, and nothing
else; but his courtiers, who are terrified of him, call him "Oh Thou Whose
Name Is Law."

He prays three times a day, and obeys with scrupulous fidelity the
Wahabite injunctions against liquor, tobacco, jewels, gambling, and
fancy dress. Cigarettes are, however, kept in the royal palaces or camp-
ing sites for foreign guests. They are forbidden, of course, to the Wahabis
themselves.

Once when a subordinate officer delayed giving food to a poverty-
blanched and unknown nomad, who had stumbled into camp, Ibn Saud
ordered the offending officer to be flogged, and, after giving the nomad
a regal feast, himself harnessed and led the nomad's camel—the highest
honor that can be paid to anyone in Arabia.

He has almost supernatural knowledge of the terrain and climatology
of Arabia. He can "smell" rain. He knows the intimate stigmata of every
tribe. He is marvelously informed. Once in a raid he conquered a small
force (when he was also facing a big force) by judging at a well how
many enemies had drunk, thereupon determining which group of his
enemies was the smaller.

He lives in the remote interior of Arabia by choice, and has never
been outside the country, but when members of one British mission
arrived to see him they found bottles of Evian water on their luncheon
tray. Their first meal consisted of six courses, all mutton. Slaves outside
the tent noiselessly answered any command.

He imposed a form of conscription on Arabia by means of his Ikh-
wan, or military colonies; he was the first Arab leader to make successful
military use of the Bedouin Arabs (Bedouins are those without homes,
vagrants who follow the grass); he created the first standing army in
Arab history.

Ibn Saud's greatest accomplishment is the unification of the Arabian
peninsula, a few peripheral states and Aden excluded. He belongs to the
modern tradition of nationalist leaders, like Chiang Kai-shek, to whom
national unity is overwhelmingly the first consideration. Other achievements have been marked, too. He tried to bring something of the modern
world to Arabia in the form of radio and motor transport; he reformed
the civil administration, attacked corruption, and punished raiders; he
eased the way of pilgrims to Mecca, who formerly had been fleeced even
for drinking water; he sought to lay the basis of a modern state. Which,
in Arabia, is a job.

Ibn Saud has never received a foreign journalist, and indeed the
number of white men he has seen in his life, mostly British emissaries,
may be counted on the fingers of two hands. A great friend, however, is

H. St. J. B. Philby, the English explorer and author, who has known him well for years. Ibn Saud has grown enormously since the time that he was a simple tribal warrior. He has come closer to western influence, even if indirectly, which has made him more cunning perhaps, less the simon-pure warrior chieftain.

His greatest personal tragedy was the death, from fever some years ago, of his favorite son, who was to have been his heir. Other sons are now being trained for kingship.

~~~~~~

Ibn Saud, the founder of Saudi Arabia, died in 1953. He was certainly one of the most formidable men of modern times. The recent history of his country has been distinguished by three factors—ferocious enmity to Israel, struggles for the succession, and fantastic wealth caused by the discovery of oil. One story is that, as of today, the multitudinous members of the royal family put in their own pockets more than 10 percent of the total national income, which is enormous. Ibn Saud's immediate successor was his oldest son at the time, Saud Ibn Abdul Aziz Al Saud (b. 1902), but Saud's half-brother, Crown Prince Feisal, who was more progressively inclined, acted as his premier and held the real reins of power. Feisal made a coup in March, 1964, which greatly reduced Saud's authority and then in November, 1964, proceeded to appropriate the throne himself.

I made one nice little bloomer in the chapter in Inside Asia *from which this material is drawn. Describing the small Arab principalities along the Persian Gulf, I mention Kuwait, one of "a group of sub-states dominated by the British, operating largely through the India office." I also say that Kuwait, near the frontiers of Iraq and Iran, has a certain strategic value, "but little wealth." I did not know that oil would be discovered there. Neither did anybody else thirty years ago. Today Kuwait is probably the richest tract of territory per square mile in the entire world, and the income of its ruler, the richest head of state on earth, has been estimated at four hundred million dollars a year in a good year.*

~~~~~~

Abdullah of T. J.

Why must the Moslem countries always quarrel? Why can't they live peacefully like the Christian nations?

—EMIR ABDULLAH IBN HUSSEIN

Transjordan is important. It looks like an ax, with the head chopping into Arabia. It is the British land and air bridge between Palestine and Baghdad, and even though its territory is mostly lava and desert, it is of paramount interest in British communications.

The origin of Transjordan as a separate state is curious, and its exact political status was for a long time obscure. In 1919, the British evacuated most of Transjordan, which was considered to be part of Syria; but friction came bewteen France and Britain when Feisal [then King of Syria] was expelled from Damascus, and the British planted him in Baghdad. Then Abdullah, Feisal's brother, marched into Transjordan on the way to Damascus, where he intended to fight the French to avenge Feisal, and perhaps take the Syrian throne himself. The British were embarrassed at this incursion of Arab warriors. Quietly the Royal Air Force reoccupied Transjordan, and Abdullah halted in its capital, Amman. Winston Churchill and Sir Herbert Samuel put their heads together. They "invited Abdullah to remain in Transjordan—partly as a threat to the French, partly to keep him from entering Palestine. And Abdullah has remained in Transjordan ever since—an amiable British puppet.

Abdullah, son of Hussein, brother of Feisal, is a squat, humorous, rather sly, and very astute man in his late fifties, whose salary is $75,000 per year. He is not technically a king, because Transjordan has a special mandatory status, but merely an emir. In his youth he was the most politically active of Hussein's sons: he first got in touch with Sir Henry McMahon during the war, and was a prominent figure in the Arab revolt, though Colonel T. E. Lawrence did not like him as well as Feisal. Abdullah speaks no western language. He likes to laugh. Once he went to the movies in Jerusalem, and saw pretty girls unveiled; he rolled with laughter, muttering, "God is great!" In the entrance hall of his palace in Amman, while waiting to be received in audience, I encountered the most extraordinary object I have ever seen outside an amusement park, a gigantic concave-convex mirror, which produces astoundingly distorted reflections of those who—as all must—look into it.

Transjordan was declared part of the British mandate for Palestine in 1922; but in 1923 it was decided that the articles in the mandate referring to Zionism—the creation of the Jewish National Home in Palestine—should not apply to Transjordan. The Zionists have resented this bitterly ever since. They consider it a serious injustice that the mandate should have such half-and-half application, especially since Transjordan is big enough and undeveloped enough—even though it is the poorest of all the Arab countries—to absorb a considerable Jewish immigration.

Since it is part of the Palestine Mandate—with Zionism omitted— Transjordan is ruled in effect by the British High Commissioner in Palestine (who is represented by a resident in Amman), that is to say, by the British colonial office in London. Public security comes from the strong Royal Air Force station, and from two remarkable native armies, officered partly by the British, the Transjordan Frontier Force and the Arab Legion.

The British do this sort of thing extremely well. Gold is much cheaper than gunfire; don't shoot but buy. The Arab Legion, a superb body of men, which is technically responsible to the emir, has exactly two British officers. One is the legendary Peake Pasha, who was an able assistant to Colonel Lawrence. The Transjordan Frontier Force, which is under the Palestine government, is officered by a handful of British. Not more than twenty or thirty admirably competent young Englishmen keep the peace all the way from Palestine to the Euphrates.

~~~~~~

They didn't keep it long. Abdullah, who was born in Mecca in 1882, became elevated to full kingship in 1946, and served as the first king of Jordan until his assassination five years later. He led the Arab forces against Israel in the border war of 1948, and acquired considerable areas in Palestine. The present ruler is Abdullah's grandson, King Hussein I, an amiable young man whom Colonel Nasser of Egypt and others have put severely to test in recent years.

CHAPTER 19

≈≈≈≈≈≈

First Citizen of the Jews

Like everything else in this section of the present book, "First Citizen of the Jews" was part of Inside Asia *(1939). It also appeared in* Life, *June 12, 1939.*

≈≈≈≈≈≈≈≈≈≈≈≈≈≈≈≈≈≈≈≈≈≈≈≈≈≈≈≈≈≈

Yes, I am a Jew, and when the ancestors of the Right Honorable Gentleman were brutal savages in an unknown island, mine were priests in the Temple of Solomon.

—DISRAELI

Y EARS AGO, when the late Lord Balfour was visiting Manchester during an electoral campaign, he met a young Jewish chemist named Chaim Weizmann. They liked each other at once, and Weizmann talked vividly of the great dream of his life—Zionism. Balfour was moved and impressed. Already he was interested in the Zionist project, and there had been talk of making Uganda, in Africa, a Jewish colony. Balfour turned to Weizmann, as the young man, with perfect poise, argued his point that only Palestine could be the proper national home. "Tell me, Dr. Weizmann, are there many Zionists like you?" Balfour asked. Weizmann smiled and replied, "Mr. Balfour, the roads of Pinsk are paved with them."

Weizmann was referring to his birthplace. The Zionist leader, who is one of the considerable men of the modern world, was born on November 28, 1874, in the village of Motele, near Pinsk, Russia. He was the third child of a family of fifteen, eleven of whom are alive today. His father was a timber merchant of modest means; his mother was an exceptionally devoted and courageous woman. She managed, for instance, to send no fewer than nine of her children to universities, though the family was poor, and the road to education for Jews in Russia in those days was arduous.

In that same early conversation with Balfour, Weizmann showed his ingrown, innate, unshakable conviction that Zionism and Palestine were one. Weizmann asked Balfour, who was still thinking of Uganda, "Would you give up London to live in Saskatchewan?" "But we have always lived in London!" Balfour exclaimed. "Yes," Weizmann replied, "and we lived in Jerusalem when London was still a marsh."

Not only has Weizmann, like most men of politics in the modern age, been dominated all his life by one idea; that idea—Zionism—was from his earliest years associated with the hope of British help. For instance, a letter exists today, which he wrote to a teacher when he was eleven years old, stating that the salvation of the Jews was Palestine, and that only the English could help get them there. Weizmann has been consistently pro-British all his career. This has not kept him from being a passionately good Jew, and it necessarily made him a master of political maneuver.

Young Weizmann went to the *cheder* (religious private school) in his village, then to the *Gymnasium* in Pinsk. He was a brilliant student of science and mathematics, and his mother's favorite child.[1] He progressed to the University of Freiburg, supporting himself at odd jobs, and finally got his doctor's degree in science at the University of Berlin. He returned to Pinsk in the holidays, and was a devoted son. The family was spiritedly intellectual. The other sons became doctors or scientists, and the atmosphere at home was agitated with political and literary talk. Weizmann's father was an early Jewish nationalist.

Weizmann got a job as a lecturer's assistant in chemistry at Geneva, and lived there several years. He met a young woman, Vera (Veratchke) Chatzman, who was studying medicine and who became an M.D., fell in love with her, and married her. She has been his attractive and devoted companion ever since. They have two sons, Benjamin, a businessman in London, and Michael, a science student at Cambridge. Weizmann left Geneva in 1903, when he was offered a lectureship at the University of Manchester, and England—plus Palestine—has been his home for thirty-five years. He still looks back with affection on his Geneva days. When he visits Geneva today he takes friends from the Hotel Beau Rivage, where he usually stays, to the laboratory in the basement of

---

[1] Her maiden name was Rachel Tchemetinsky. She is alive today, and lives in a modest house Weizmann built for her in Haifa, at the foot of Mt. Carmel. He brought her out of Russia in 1926, when his father died. When he comes to Palestine he visits her at once, and the whole family celebrates Passover every year in the aged lady's house.

the University College building, near the Parc de la Reformation, and shows them where he got his start.

Weizmann probably met Lenin in those days. He is not sure. But Lenin lived in Geneva at the time, and most of the Russian students frequented the same cafés. More than once Weizmann sat in the coffee house, unable to pay for the modest drink he had bought, waiting for some friend to come and bail him out. Most of his companions were scientists, not politicians. In any event, whether he met Lenin or not, one fact is extraordinary, if purely coincidental—and that is his facial resemblance to Lenin. He is darker than Lenin was, and his face is broader, but the similarity is exceptional. Once, when Weizmann happened to be at an international conference, the Russian delegates—this was in 1923 or thereabouts—kept staring at him as if he were a ghost, and the Swiss detectives set up a guard at his hotel door thinking that he *was* Lenin.

Long before the Manchester period Weizmann became a Zionist. He had—unlike most political leaders—two lives. He was a chemist by day, and a Zionist by night. Rather, since he is a genius, he was both a chemist and a Zionist twenty-four hours a day; he survived—and enjoyed—a compelling double activity. The only Zionist conference he ever failed to attend was the first one, in 1897. He was in Pinsk, too poor to make the trip directly. He worked his way on a timber boat as far as Danzig, and then rushed overland to Basle, where the conference was held; but he got there two days late.

I cannot treat in any detail the complex inner history of Weizmann's relations with the Zionist movement from 1897 to the present. Suffice it to say that, from the beginning, he was marked for leadership; that as a youth of twenty-seven he dared to oppose Herzl, the founder of political Zionism, whom he considered to be too visionary; that from the outset he took a practical attitude, urging the training of Jews in colonization and agricultural work; that in his maiden speech to the biennial Zionist congress (1903), he conceived and put forward the project of a Hebrew University in Jerusalem; that for fifteen years he was the leader of the "Manchester Group" of British Zionists; that, finally, in 1921, he became president of the World Zionist Organization. Many trials, many crises and counter-crises, and many moments of elation and despair are masked by this brief record.

In 1916 came the greatest moment of Weizmann's life. Chemistry and Zionism merged, though he did not know it then.

David Lloyd George, the British prime minister, was searching for technical assistance in the preparation of explosives. There was an acute shortage of acetone, a substance indispensable to cordite manufacture. This was in the darkest period of the [first great] war. Disaster loomed. Synthetic acetone—and much else—was an imperative necessity. Lloyd George called a conference, and asked the advice of C. P. Scott, the editor of the Manchester *Guardian*. Scott said to Lloyd George, "I know a remarkable professor of chemistry at Manchester University. He comes from somewhere near the Vistula; I don't know which side. I will ask him if he will place himself at the disposal of the state."

Weizmann went to London to see Lloyd George. He was then put in charge of the Admiralty laboratories.

Lloyd George said, "I need immediate action, immediate results."

Weizmann said, "How long can you give me? I'll work night and day."

Within some weeks Weismann had discovered a method of synthesizing acetone. He studied the composition of cereals, and found a method of isolating organisms which permitted him to make acetone out of—horse chestnuts! The method was developed on a large scale. A sufficient supply of acetone, and thus cordite, was assured Great Britain. Lloyd George called for Weizmann again. He said in effect, "Dr. Weizmann, you have rendered great service to the state. I will recommend you to His Majesty for any honors you may wish."

"There is nothing I want for myself," Weizmann said.

Lloyd George hinted at a viscountcy, a monetary grant.

Weizmann shook his head. "There is only one thing I want," he said, "and that is a national home for my people."

A few months later came the Balfour Declaration, which—in theory —provided it. The cause of Zionism—it seemed then—was won. Of course, other factors contributed to the announcement of the Declaration. But Lloyd George himself says that the acetone incident led him to support the Zionist thesis, and that he brought Weizmann into contact with his old friend Balfour, in order to open negotiations. When Balfour saw him, he said, "I need no introduction to Dr. Weizmann. He converted me to Zionism ten years ago." Lloyd George has stated that Weizmann will rank with Nehemiah "in the fascinating and inspiring story of the children of Israel."

The Zionist Colossus

Weizmann's home in Palestine is at Rehovoth, near Tel Aviv. His house is surrounded by citrus groves, and is exquisitely appointed. Weizmann is a lover of life. He is a great host. He is not, like most nationalist leaders, arid in temperament, frugal in habit; he loves good food, good laughter, good conversation. He is a resonant and capacious human being, with a delight in every aspect of experience.

But he works hard. He works hard at Zionism, and at his chemistry still. The chief ornament of the colony at Rehovoth is not the glorious

Ming porcelain inside his house, but his spare, squat laboratory across the grove. In this building, known as the Daniel Sieff Research Laboratory, his staff conducts various experiments, most of them of a practical nature associated with Palestinian agriculture. Weizmann guides them, and he works himself on the by-products of orange peel, in order to increase the value of Palestine's citrus crop.

Weizmann adores Rehovoth. The land on which his house and laboratory were built belonged at one time—a remarkable example of the unity of his life and career—to the first settler who left Pinsk, Weizmann's home town, for Palestine. When Weizmann was a boy of ten, he saw this settler off at the Pinsk railway station, not by any stretch of the imagination conceiving that forty years later he would happen to buy this same man's Palestine property.

When the partition scheme [for Palestine] was being discussed, it was discovered that Rehovoth was on the very edge of the projected Arab state. "Put it in the Palestine area at once," said the British boundary maker. "Palestine without Weizmann is impossible."

Once Weizmann was showing Rehovoth to Sir Arthur Wauchope, then the High Commissioner. Wauchope admired it. "You have a very beautiful place here, Dr. Weizmann," he said. "Yes," Weizmann replied, "and it wasn't built as a summer palace for the Grand Mufti, either."

Weizmann, a complex character—he is first of all a scientist, then a politician, but there is also a good deal of the artist in his nature— has some defects in temperament. He is sometimes moody. Occasionally he sulks. He is stubborn. For millions of Jews, he is Zionism, and Zionism is Weizmann, but he has a certain contempt—like Nehru in India—for the masses as a whole. He is not a good man in a crowd, though his wit, his elegance, his persuasive power in private conversation, are pronounced.

He dislikes documents. He is apt to say, discussing administrative details, "If Shertok is agreed, let's go on from there." (Moshe Shertok is the "foreign secretary" of the Zionist movement.) He will stay up all night to read a scientific paper, but not a political paper. He hates to dictate letters. He writes everything in longhand, in tiny characters, in green ink on blue paper. He seldom keeps carbons of his correspondence, and a good many interesting records of his life have consequently been lost.

The most serious charge against Weizmann is that, a prisoner of tradition and environment, he is too pro-British. He is called too prudent, too old-fashioned, and "too much a gentleman." Another is that for years he apparently did not understand that it was not enough for Jews to be passive, that it was no longer any use fighting fire (the Arabs) with water, that they must be fought with fire. He does not, it is said, appreciate the modern activitist position of Jewry; he does not realize that very many youthful Jews are willing to fight—and die—for their homeland. In London recently Malcolm MacDonald, the colonial secretary, asked him in effect, "Are you willing that Zionism should rest indefinitely on Britain for support?" Weizmann said that he would have to consider the question before answering. But almost any modern Zionist would have replied that, given a fair chance, the Zionists were perfectly capable of defending themselves, and would be delighted to have the opportunity.

The major point of forward-looking Zionists early in 1939 was that a securely established and numerous Zionist majority in Palestine—to put it bluntly, a really Jewish Palestine—would be an infinitely more valuable asset to Britain than Palestine in its present state of turmoil. The Jews would bring stability to Palestine, plus essential and incontrovertible friendship for England, whereas the Arabs continually provoke trouble, and give the enemies of England—Hitler and Mussolini—incessant opportunity for fishing in a troubled desert. This is the point that activist Jews want Weizmann to make—no matter how often the British say that they must remember their responsibilities to the whole Moslem world, for instance to the Mussulmans of India.

Weizmann's positive qualities are many. He has, first of all, courage. Second, like Mr. Gandhi, he has considerable facility for compromise; he is a subtle and competent negotiator. He may be a bit of a prima donna, but his intellectual stature is undisputed. He has a beautiful sense of humor. He reads, talks, and writes six languages with complete fluency, of which his favorite is Yiddish; he can perform wonderful tricks with the Yiddish tongue. A famous chemist once said that he would throw away his whole life's work to have written one page of Weizmann. Above all, he is a man of reason, a man of faith founded on rationality, and superbly honest; he never exaggerates, and always tends to understate rather than overstate a case. His eloquent voice is low. For emphasis, he lowers it. Some of his speeches are first-rate political literature. Finally, Weizmann is a man who has contributed so much to his cause that he has become indispensable. Movement and leader are, at the present juncture, one.

I knew Weizmann better and over a longer period than any other character in this book. After Adlai E. Stevenson and Mr. Nehru I think he is probably the finest person I have ever known in public life. I met him for the first time in London in the early 1930's, and I still remember what a superb host he was—Lucullan. Once, dining with him in London, Frances Gunther and I were served a magnificent plat consisting of a whole salmon baked inside a large, delicate shell of pastry. Fifteen years later we took him and Mrs. Weizmann to lunch in a somewhat splendid New York restaurant and by an extraordinary chance the same dish was on the menu. Weizmann's was better.

During World War II, both in 1939 and 1941, I saw Weizmann in London a good many times. We were both staying at the Hotel Dorchester. The exigencies of the war had forced him to close his beautiful London house. Once we went through an air raid alarm together, and talked most of the night in the shelter at the Dorchester. The company was distinguished, because several sophisticated British men and women of affairs were using the Dorchester as a temporary residence.

Weizmann was mildly nettled because I had called him a "sybarite" in something I had written. He denounced me with great amiability. He was restless and impatient because he could not get a priority to get back to Jerusalem. He had appealed to Mr. Churchill himself for permission to proceed, and was awaiting word. He was asking for a priority for Mrs. Weizmann too, which compounded the difficulty; women were not supposed to travel with official priorities in the dark shambles of those days, but Chaim would not go without her. He said something that struck me profoundly, namely that one of the reasons why the British attitude toward Palestine was so hopelessly obscurantist and equivocal was that the British had an active fear of Jews, whereas they knew that they could always handle Arabs. He also said that the secretary of state for India at the time, Mr. Amery, wanted to be "much more liberal about India than Winston would let him be."

On another occasion he told me an anecdote about Lord Halifax, the foreign minister and a leading figure in the British government. A boatload of Jews could not get into the harbor at Haifa. Weizmann called on Halifax to plead for them. Halifax said that their entry, under the circumstances, would be clearly illegal and thus could not be permitted. Weizmann, lowering his marvelous resonant voice, then said that he had always been given to understand that whereas Mosaic law was inflexible, Christian law was traditionally distinguished by being tempered with considerations of mercy. He repeated the word "mercy," whispering. The word went through the room with the vibration of a note struck on a tuning fork. Halifax picked up the telephone and gave the order that the Jews should be permitted to land in Haifa then and there.

Palestine became free in 1948 and entered the UN as the Republic of Israel on May 11, 1949. I rendered Dr. Weizmann a small service in New York that day by helping him get in touch with the representative of a Latin American country the vote of which was crucial. Weizmann, as was inevitable, became the first President of Israel. But his health had broken down, and he died in 1952.

Part Five

~~~~~~~~

SOUTH OF THE BORDER

CHAPTER 20

<img>~~~~~~~~</img>

Cárdenas Days and Years

*In 1940-1941 I visited all twenty of the Latin American republics,
Puerto Rico, and Trinidad for* Inside Latin America, *from which this
excerpt is taken. It was published in 1941. I have added a word or two
and transposed a few sentences to make the background clearer.*

GENERAL LÁZARO CÁRDENAS Y DEL RIO, who has been justly called the
greatest Mexican since Benito Juárez and who was President of
Mexico from 1934 to 1940, is shaped something like a top—an enormous round chest tapers to a less conspicuous waist and slender hips.
His hair is jet black, his eyes a pure olive green. He has thick red lips,
from which come his nickname—the Trumpeter. His manners are infinitely polite and gracious. He sits on the very edge of his chair, and—
a curious point—keeps his small feet on tiptoe. He is seldom angry;
when he does lose his temper, his face flushes darkly, he remains absolutely silent for a moment, and then speaks in a strained, subdued
voice.

His physical endurance is enormous, and he drives his secretaries
mad. They are afraid to sleep—especially when they are on the road
with him—because they know he will be off at three or four in the
morning, and they seldom know where he's going. He cannot stand to
remain long in town; he is possessed by a necessity to be *close* to the
people. He drinks mildly—a little beer in the evening—but never
smokes. His appetites are healthy and normal. He takes no exercise.
He seldom reads. His handwriting is close-packed, decisive, and illegible.
His married life has been happy. His son, aged ten—who has an

American tutoress—is named for the last Aztec emperor, Cuauhtémoc.

He lives entirely without ostentation, and even when he was President he almost never attended official functions. His caretaker in his Michoacán house is his former barber. When, as President, he lived at Los Pinos, the small lodge near Chapultepec Castle, he liked to point to his swimming pool. "It is my most economical investment," he would say. "I ask my guests to join me in a dip at 6 A.M., and no one ever accepts a second invitation to visit me."

He likes best to live at Eréndira, his property at Pátzcuaro, in the Tarascan province, Michoacán. Here he feels really at home; he has a small boat, and he loves to cruise on the high frigid waters of the lake. The house is named for a heroine in Tarascan legend; the Tarascans were a hardy tribe never conquered by the Aztecs. Cárdenas likes to saunter into the village, put up at a wonderful old hotel called the Ocampo, and eat his favorite native dishes—a kind of pork cooked with chilis, *chicharrón* (crisp pig's skin broiled until the fat disappears), and *chilaquiles*, a humble dish of tortillas diced and cooked with chili sauce.

A man of the camp, he has many friends, but if you ask five different people who are those closest to him, you get widely different answers.

When I saw General Cárdenas—just before he gave up the presidency—the thing that impressed me most was his profound simplicity. He was almost naïve. He does not often give interviews; in fact, he is probably the most elusive head of state I ever pursued. When finally I was received in the President's room in the National Palace, with its glossy floors and green leather chairs and the huge map of Mexico at one end, I found that Cárdenas was interviewing me, not vice versa.

He disconnected his two telephones to prevent interruptions, and then talked about the coming administration and his work for the land and the peasants. When I had asked my questions he said politely, *"Terminado?"* and I rose to go. But he motioned me to remain, and then went on to ask questions for half an hour—about the presidential campaign in the United States, about problems of American labor, about Japan's attitude to the war in Europe, about agrarian problems in the Philippines. His knowledge of world affairs was discerning. When I left, he said, "You are young. Do good work for the world."

General Cárdenas was born in a village called Jiquilpán, in the province of Michoacán, on April 21, 1895. His father was a shopkeeper, a full-blooded Tarascan Indian, who died young. The Cárdenas family was grindingly poor. Young Lázaro had a few years of elementary education, and then set out to earn a living. He worked in a printer's shop for a time, and picked up a few pesos as assistant to the village jailer. Came the [great Mexican] revolution of 1913. Young Lázaro joined up—

and took his solitary prisoner with him, the legend says. This was in 1914, when he was nineteen.

His military career was rapid and fairly distinguished, though he was never an inspired officer like his chief, General Obregón. By 1920 he was a colonel, and by 1924, when the civil wars were over, a general of brigade. Like all Mexican generals he was a politician, but his honesty and powerful civic sense made him an unusual type. Very unusual. He was an odd fellow, this big Indian.

Once when he was stationed in the Tampico district an oil-company go-between reputedly handed him an envelope containing 25,000 pesos, explaining that this was always given to the local general for "protecting the properties." Cárdenas refused the bribe, saying that the oil belonged to the people of Mexico—and has hated the oil companies ever since. Once, after helping to defeat the Escobar rebellion against former President Plutarco Elías Calles, he returned to the military authorities 93,000 out of the 100,000 pesos that had been given him for expenses of the campaign.[1] Other generals thought him a simpleton—if they could bear to think.

But Calles admired him, and his career advanced. He became successively governor of Michoacán, president of the National Revolutionary party (which he later transformed into the present P.R.M.) and minister of the interior. Then Calles picked him to be President of the Republic because he thought this unassuming and competent officer would do a good routine job without daring to threaten his own position behind the scenes. Calles had been *jefe máximo* (supreme chief) for ten years.

Calles got fooled. Within a year Cárdenas smoothly, gravely, quietly, threw him out. He performed this miracle by saying with conviction and authority, "I am the President of Mexico, and I intend to maintain the position the constitution gives me." He added, "I don't think the Congress will refuse support to any President who fulfills his obligations in good faith." The "simpleton" again!—who knew just what he was doing.

Sources of Power of Cárdenas

Of the Cárdenas qualities and sources of power one may mention several. First is his instinctive kinship with the common people, and the way his aims, his ideals, have expressed the inarticulate aspiration of the Indian masses. Cárdenas is never so happy as when he sits on his haunches along a roadside, talking with the peasants for long hours. His travels in Mexico have been epochal, like those of Mr. Gandhi—whom he in some respects resembles—in India. When he was nominated for Presi-

[1] *The Reconquest of Mexico.* By Nathaniel and Sylvia Weyl, p. 94.

dent in 1934, no one thought he would make an extensive campaign, since his election was assured by the backing of the government machine. But he set out and visited thousands of villages in all the thirty-three Mexican states. Probably he has seen more of Mexico with his own eyes than any other living Mexican.

He likes to travel alone, except for one aide-de-camp and a chauffeur. He never carries arms. Once, visiting Guadalajara a few years ago, he all but gave the local governor a nervous breakdown. He refused any escort, and thousands of Indians came in from the countryside to see him. The President of the Republic would sit on the curb, alone, unguarded, hearing complaints, adjusting grievances, listening. He once told Waldo Frank, "It is important that the people know I come among them without fear."

Once, when he was traveling in the north, someone fired at the olive presidential train. Cárdenas asked that the train be stopped and backed into the station. He got off, alone, unarmed, and walked into the station yard, to ask who had done the shooting.

One of the defects sometimes noted in Cárdenas may derive from *too* close association with the Indians, *too* intimate an identification of his own career with theirs—that is, a certain groping quality, a certain naïve tendency to rely purely on intuition rather than calculation, in tackling administrative problems.

Another quality that Cárdenas possessed as President—and still possesses—is, as is clear, his moral sense. His policies were more revolutionary than those of any President since Juárez; he touched thousands of people in that very sensitive spot, the pocketbook; yet he was never threatened or molested. One reason is that almost everyone conceded his absolute integrity and sense of justice. Once he is reported to have said sadly, "Whenever I put my hand in a basket I pull out a thief." What he sought above all was to encourage moral values.

In Sonora a general once remonstrated with him for his incessant attention to detail, his sixteen-hour working day. The general said, "Don't wear yourself out. Tomorrow is another day. And tomorrow everyone will forget what you have done today." Cárdenas replied sternly, "The duty of a public official is to serve the people in every way he can, with no thought of reward, without even thought of appreciation."[2]

He hates cruelty and bloodshed. In his six years of office not one political execution took place, a record unique in Mexico. When the

[2] One expression of Cárdenas' moral sense was a hatred of gambling; more than one prominent politician got rich on gambling concessions, and the poor—some of the rich too—were perpetually being fleeced. In older days big officials often recouped their losses out of the federal treasury. Cárdenas forbade all gambling in Mexico, even card playing in clubs and private homes. Of course the law was not strictly enforced.

insurrectionary General Cedillo was shot (on the field of battle) the officer who killed this troublesome rebel proudly asked for promotion. But Cárdenas was horrified at Cedillo's death, and he *de*moted the officer.

Another quality Cárdenas possesses is great peasant shrewdness. He seldom directly refuses anything to anybody. Nor does he ever attack anyone openly if he can possibly help it.

Once a delegation of villagers accosted him when he was inspecting the Laredo highway near Tasquillo. They asked that the road be moved ten miles so that they would have the use of it. Mockingly Cárdenas remarked, "So you want the outside world to see your unkempt doorsteps, your dirty bedraggled streets . . . ?" The village elders swore that they would compel the citizenry to improve their habits. Cárdenas rejoined: "No. Do not compel. Simply persuade."

As to defects, he had—and has—several. He tried to do things too fast. He never cared for problems of administration—he spent at least two-thirds of his time out of Mexico City—and he hated to delegate responsibility. He wanted to do everything himself—and much of the time his own entourage couldn't find him. He was secretive and vain and he thought that he alone could adjust the grievances of twenty million Mexicans. He perplexed his admirers by permitting equivocal responsibility in various departments; he liked to have *two* men in charge of each separate show. This was caused partly by his hatred of bureaucratic rigidity, partly by his deep inner belief that the best man would come out on top. Finally (like President Roosevelt) he was far too tolerant. He hated to get rid of friends even if they were manifestly incompetent.

His accomplishments will, nevertheless, live in Mexican history. He put through the greatest advance in land reform ever known in Mexico, expropriated foreign oil, allied his government with the Mexican labor federation, the C.T.M., and in general improved the lot of both peasant and worker beyond measure. As to the land reform Cárdenas distributed more land—thirty million acres in six years—than any President in the history of Mexico. Hardly any of the old *haciendas* survive intact. His effort to transform the agrarian system of the country in less than a decade, to abolish feudalism, to give the land of Mexico back to its own landless, was a stupendous undertaking.

[*I remember Cárdenas saying to me eloquently, "The Indian's conception of life depends on having his own land. For the Indian, land is life. An Indian without land is an outcast. Ownership of land produces a harmony with environment which is essential to life in Mexico."*]

Second, he gave Mexico political stability and order of a kind not seen since Porfirio Díaz, without any infringement whatever on civil liberties. There were no political prisoners, no suppressions of free speech, under Cárdenas. Associated with this was the new value on human life his regime inspired. Mexico had swarmed with bloodshed for savage year after savage year. Under Cárdenas, killing stopped.

Third, his education and public works program brought roads, schools, water supply, sanitation, to thousands of villages. He built more schools than all governments since 1911 combined. Coupled with this came a gradual elevation in the standard of living. More people began to drink beer instead of pulque, to wear blue overalls instead of cotton shirts, to wear shoes or sandals instead of going barefoot.

Fourth, he helped reduce the power of the army by breaking up the old provincial armies and transferring recruits and troops from one part of Mexico to another. I heard it said that he had so shaken up the army—most of the higher officers disliked him—that no single general was sure of the support of more than two or three hundred men.

Above all, he gave the Mexican people a sense of national participation in affairs. He sought strenuously to uplift the masses, so that *they* could henceforth keep power, and themselves check the inroads of plunder and reaction.

~~~~~~

Presidents of Mexico are not allowed to serve more than one six-year term and Cárdenas, for this and other reasons, has not been at the top since 1940. He is, however, still a substantial if shadowy influence both in the country at large and in the councils of the PRI (Partido Revolucionario Institucional), the sprawling hold-all party, formerly known as the PRM, which he helped to create and which still completely dominates Mexican affairs. For a time Cárdenas served as minister of war under President Avila Camacho, his successor, and he was brought into the government again as recently as December, 1961, when President Adolfo López Mateos invited all the six living ex-Presidents of the country into his administration. His only official position today is that of executive director of the Balsas River development project. Cárdenas is still distinctly a man of the left. He has been a patron of the leading Communist front organization in the country, and won a Stalin Peace Prize in 1955.

I wanted very much to include in this book sketches of several other Latin American politicians whom I met and liked—for instance Haya de la Torre in Peru and the late Getulio Vargas in Brazil—but my publishers amiably overruled me because of lack of space.

Part Six

～～～～～

WAR IN SICILY

CHAPTER 21

~~~~~

Montgomery and Alexander

In 1943 I had glimpses of the war in the Mediterranean, the Middle East, and Africa. The result was a book called D Day *of which this is a chapter.*

~~~~~~

BOTH THESE EMINENT GENERALS are lean, steel-hard, spare, blue-eyed; both are in their fifties, and both, like so many top officers in the British army, are North Irishmen.[1] Everybody calls Montgomery simply "Monty." The nickname is universal. Almost everybody calls Alexander *General* Alex." The name is shortened, as a token of affection, but it is rarely used without the title, which shows the great respect in which Alexander is held. "General Alex" is younger in years, but he is Montgomery's superior officer. Monty, the showman, takes the bows; Alexander, the director, hovers in the wings. They say that only Alexander can "handle" Monty, or call him "Monty" to his face. Even though he is his junior, Alexander has toward him the attitude of a teacher proud of a brilliant student.

Half the fun of covering the Sicilian campaign was hearing stories about Montgomery. Maybe some are apocryphal; it is always so with men packed with bounce and color. Their personalities are so strong that they create a kind of folklore, and the tinges of distortion add a queer legendary touch to the essential truth, which makes it truer.

Montgomery looks something like a hawk, something—I don't mean this disparagingly—like a fox. He has extraordinarily piercing and lu-

[1] Field Marshal Sir Alan Brooke, chief of the Imperial General Staff, and Field Marshal Sir John Dill, British representative on the Combined Chiefs of Staff in Washington, come from North Ireland too.

[229]

minous blue eyes. He is very alert and clipped in conversation, and his most striking verbal mannerism is the way he repeats himself. When he talks, he puts the second finger of his right hand on the little finger of the left, and ticks off his points with mathematical precision, "One . . . two . . ." He recapitulates phrase after phrase, like this: "The point is," he will say, "Now, the point is . . ." Or, "You will remember. You will remember." Or, "The tanks will go through. Will go through. The tanks will proceed to their destination. Will proceed . . ."

Montgomery has a tremendous healthy ego, and is sometimes difficult to get along with. This is not merely a matter of conceit or vanity; it is based on complete self-confidence and an utter confidence in his men. He never refers to the Eighth Army as such, but always to "*my* army"; never to troops in such-and-such a unit, but to "*my* troops."

The King of England visited Tunisia last spring, inspecting the battle fronts. One afternoon the somewhat inarticulate monarch saw a patch of sunlight on a strip of sand; deeply taken by the color, a rich burnished tan, he said that he would like it for the ribbon of a new decoration to commemorate the African campaign. When the King received General Montgomery the next day he mentioned this. Montgomery looked up.

"Would Your Majesty kindly describe that color again?" the general asked.

The King did so.

"Why!" exclaimed Montgomery. "That's *my* color, that's Eighth Army yellow!"

Monty turned to his military assistant. "It's the exact color of my car. Paint up a sample for His Majesty. Or better, tear a strip off the car!"

But no story about Montgomery can be half so effective in print as in life. One must see and hear the general himself: the quick upward intonation of the sentences, the touch of style and dash he gives to every word.

When I met him [in the field in Sicily] and presented a letter of introduction from Wendell Willkie, he looked it over calmly. "Ah, ah!" he exclaimed. "Willkie, Willkie . . . of course I know Willkie. He was my guest at Alamein. Ha, Willkie! Why, I showed him a battle once!"

Later he gave me a longhand letter to carry back to Mr. Willkie. He made the good score of misspelling *both* Willkie's names on the scrawled envelope.

The general's talk that day was a wonderful mixture of curiosity, incomprehension of any world not his own ("Have you ever heard of an American publication called *Life*, yes, that's it, a publication called *Life*, I believe that was the name, *Life*."), solid wisdom about military affairs, zest in the battle to come, respect and affection for the army he has created, and a courteous interest in such nonmilitary occupations as the writing of books.

He told me that he has kept a diary for years, that he posted it every day, that he kept it under lock and key ("No one in the world knows where it is except myself"), and that it would "blow off everybody's head between Alamein and London." I summoned what little courage I have and told him that I thought he was making a great mistake not to give someone else access to it, because no future historian could write a true history of the African war without knowing what it contained.

"Tell me, would I get any money for my diary?" he asked smiling.

I replied, very deadpan: "About a hundred thousand dollars, General."

He turned to Lieutenant Colonel "Bill" Williams, his aide. "A hundred thousand dollars? What's that?"

"That's twenty-five thousand pounds, sir," answered Colonel Williams, solemnly.

"Well," Montgomery grinned. "Guess won't die in poorhouse after all." (His speech is so clipped that you can only give an impression of it by leaving the pronouns and articles out.)

Like any good actor, he likes to make his effects in his own manner, and many of his more outrageous statements are not to be taken literally. There is a certain waggishness about Montgomery. Once a group of correspondents approached him before Mount Etna, and asked him how the battle was going. "Ha!" he replied. "I have never fought under the eye of a volcano before!"

Montgomery's self-confidence and ego are one of the great sources of his power. When his own back was to the wall, just before Alamein in August, 1942, with the enemy only forty miles from Alexandria, he had the cool effrontery to tell Mr. Willkie, "It is now mathematically certain that *I* will eventually destroy Rommel."

But for all his self-confidence let no one think that Montgomery is one of those men who never listen, who cannot bear to be countermanded. He loathes Yes men. The officers of his staff have tea with him every day, and they talk almost as equals, with complete liberty to discuss, to criticize, to argue. One of his aides—a youngster in his thirties—told me that his own particular job was to tell the general, in no uncertain terms, exactly what he could *not* do. "I'm the No man," said the aide.

Nor, despite the waggishness, should anyone think that Montgomery is anything but austere. In fact, next to self-confidence, the dominating note in his complex character is, as everybody knows, a rigid and compelling asceticism. He is given to odd quirks and idiosyncrasies; for instance he carries a big cage of chickens with him everywhere he goes, so that he will always have fresh eggs. But at bottom his character is as stern as that of Cromwell, with whom he has often been compared. His father was a bishop, and he himself reads the lesson to his troops every Sunday morning. When time permits, he leads his own officers in exhausting five-mile runs, before breakfast. He eats sparingly, he doesn't drink, and he doesn't smoke. Nor will he tolerate anybody smoking near him. I told him that this was a characteristic he shared with Adolf Hitler—which considerably astonished him. Officers approaching toss their cigarettes away quickly and hide their pipes; I watched this happen in Sicily several times, when he was in the open field.

Montgomery has several rules for keeping himself on the razor edge of fitness. For one thing, he told me, he refuses absolutely to do any work after dinner. He goes to bed at about nine-thirty in the evening, without fail, and then spends an hour reading or, in his own words, just "thinking." He said that two other basic rules govern his behavior. First, never worry. Second, never bother with details. Details should be left to the staff, he told me. And also worries. "That's what a staff is for."

The general was born of an Ulster family in 1887. He is a widower, with one child. He served in France in the First World War, and was wounded and decorated; he had some years in Palestine, Transjordan, and India; when World War II broke out, he was in England commanding a division. It was Alexander who brought him to the command of the Eighth Army, in the black summer of 1942. But his appointment was based partly on accident; in fact his later career is a first-rate example of the importance of accidents in history. The officer originally chosen for his command, General W. H. E. ("Strafer") Gott, was killed in an airplane accident, and Montgomery took over as second choice.

He was heartily disliked when he first arrived in Cairo. He was cavalier about his predecessors, which was considered bad form in the extreme, and many officers thought him insolent. Monty paid no attention. He went up forward and wandered around for a day or two, inspecting every position, talking to every man he met, making intimate personal contact with the troops. What he had to pray for was time. "Give me a fortnight," he said, "and I can resist the German attack. Give me three weeks, and I can defeat the Boche. Give me a month, and I can chase him out of Africa." Meantime, he *took hold*. Within forty-eight hours the difference in spirit at the Alamein front was prodigious. The previous commander had scarcely ever visited or even talked to his own men. But within forty-eight hours of Monty's arrival, every man in Egypt knew that a fresh new wind was blowing, that their new commander was something quite different, something unique. He instilled into them, magically, his own magnificent superconfidence.

The plans for the Alamein battle, which opened on October 23, 1942, were made originally by General Wavell when the Italians were attacking in 1940; Wavell selected Alamein as a good position for a last stand, if a last stand should become necessary. Oddly enough, the original Wavell plans were unaccountably lost; when the Germans threatened Egypt two years later, they were unearthed just in time. The actual conception of the 1942 battle was Alexander's. Montgomery was simply the executant. But he executed the job supremely well.

On his arrival in Egypt Monty knew very little about desert warfare. But he was flexible; he was quick to learn. On one of his first tours to the front, he saw men sleeping. They had been doing night patrols, and were worn out. Nevertheless he muttered, "Remarkable . . . Remarkable. *My* men . . . asleep by day. Get them up! Let them train!" But he soon found out that even *his* men could not work by night and train by day and still maintain efficiency. So he softened. He made several mistakes in the early phases of the Alamein battle, the nature of which are still military secrets. But, elastic, he reconsidered his original orders, rescinded his first directives, and started over again on a new track.

In Malta I asked the general what his rules for leadership were, and he replied that he had three. First, no failure can be tolerated. Since failure is inadmissible, the scope of operations must be limited to what it practicable. Second, the general in command must not be prodded into anything too grandiose for the means at his disposal. Third, the general must refuse to be rushed. He must be allowed to pick his own time. No matter what the pressure may be—and sometimes pressure is enormous—he must set himself against anything premature.

Then Montgomery added something like this: "It's a life work to make an army. A life work. An army is a tool, a weapon. You have to forge it, temper it, sharpen it, before you wield it. The first imperative is morale. Morale depends on confidence. On confidence. Also morale depends on victory. Men like an army that is winning." He smiled. "So do the politicians."

Montgomery has the most profound respect for Rommel, his greatest adversary, and one story is that for a long time he kept a photograph of him above his mirror. He would dearly love to meet Rommel when the war is over, and talk about the campaign, trace over the maps again and see why he and Rommel had done thus and so at such and such a time. He thinks that the Germans may have collapsed in North Africa because Rommel, ill at the time, was not "fit." "A man must be fit."

The general is not always respectful of certain eminent colleagues in his own army. He heard not long ago that a fellow officer had become a full general. "That man!" he hissed. "That man a full general! Bastardization of the rank!"

"General Alex" is a man of totally different character. When you mention Monty to people, they may curse or grin. Every time I asked anybody about Alexander, I got a reaction of pleasure, genuine warmth, and admiration.

General Sir Harold Rupert Leofric George Alexander, D.S.O., M.C., etc., was born in North Ireland in 1891. He was the son of an earl, and his mother was the daughter of an earl; he married an earl's daughter, by whom he has three children. Both his grandfather and father were in the army, as is one of his three brothers. He went to Harrow and Sandhurst. For many years he served with the Irish Guards. You note the Irish in him right away—his sense of wry humor, his subtle charm. Also you note the aristocracy. Take one look at him— the serene poised head, the carefully immaculate manner—and you instantly say to yourself the word "aristocrat." Nor do I mean this in the snobbish sense of the term. I mean aristocracy in the sense of personal, not social, superiority—superiority in brains, courage, taste, and style.

Alexander has served thirty-three years in the British army. They sit lightly. He is youthful-looking and extraordinarily handsome. He was a famous athlete in his day; a champion miler in 1914, he would have represented Great Britain at the next Olympic Games had they not been called off. He listens well, and thinks carefully before he talks. This is not so much for reasons of prudence as shyness. "Shyness" in many Englishmen is simply a device whereby somebody with nothing to say has an excuse for not saying it. It is a shield for inertia, for lack of imagination, sometimes for stupidity. But Alexander's shyness is quite different. It is a kind of serenity, a deliberateness founded on tact and good manners.

I met a newspaper friend who went through the disastrous retreat in Burma with Alexander early in 1942. "I've seen more 'flap' [panic, disorder] in peacetime maneuvers," said my friend succinctly. Nothing ever ruffles Alexander. He was the last man off the beach at Dunkirk; he coasted about in a motorboat, seeing that everybody else was off. But he did it in his usual quiet way. He is as unspectacular as Montgomery is spectacular.

This general does not wear his heart on his sleeve, but no one should think he is dry-as-dust. Quite the contrary. As a young man he was an exceptionally dashing officer; he always carried an Irish flag hidden in his pocket, which he wanted to be the first to plant in Berlin. For a time he was in command of the Lettish Landwehr, in Riga, against the Bolsheviks. But even though vividly fighting them in the field he was delighted to acquire some Russian characteristics. He learned to ride straight-legged; he grew an enormous bushy mustache and wore his helmet deep over his nose.

As with so many British officers of high rank, the variety of his interests is astonishing. Once he learned tap dancing. He speaks four or five languages, including Russian and Hindustani. His hobby is water-color painting, and like Mr. Churchill he is good at it. He likes to fly his own airplane; he owns a little puddle jumper. The variety of his friendships, too, is considerable. In Riga many years ago he met Walter Duranty, who later became the Moscow correspondent of the New York *Times*. He liked and admired Duranty extremely, and gave him many of his early scoops. Duranty was the only newspaperman he would talk to, and I imagine they must have had terrific times together. During the middle of the Tunisian campaign, more than two decades later, he telegraphed Duranty asking why he wasn't there.

The outline of General Alexander's career is exceptional, in that he got his present command after being in charge of two defeats, Dunkirk and Burma. In France, during World War I, his record for pure personal bravery, courage, was—without exaggeration—extraordinary. During the years after 1919, Alexander served variously in Constantinople, Waziristan, and the northwest frontier of India. In 1938, at forty-five, he became the youngest major general in the British army, and was given command of the First Division at Aldershot. In France, early in 1940, he was promoted to lieutenant general, in command of the First Army Corps. After Dunkirk, Alexander returned to England and took the Southern command, that is, the command that would have to bear the brunt of the Nazi invasion of England, if it came. It didn't come. But lots of other things did. In February, 1942, "Alex" went out to Burma, taking over there at the worst possible moment, when Rangoon was surrounded. He had to fly in, over the enemy's lines, in order to reach his headquarters. Forty-eight hours later the Japanese took Rangoon. And he had to fight his way out. Then in August, 1942, he was promoted to Cairo and the command of the Middle East; he promptly summoned Montgomery from England, as we have seen. On February 20, 1943, after the miracle of Alamein and after Monty had chased Rommel across Africa, he was given command of Allied land forces in the Mediterranean, under Eisenhower.

I talked to several British officers about Alexander. One said, "He's the most unselfish man I ever met. He always gives praise to the other chap. He'll give anything away. My God, I remember how things were in Burma. We were in a really tight spot. There were a million refugees all around. How Alex bucked everybody up! If a woman would stop and ask for water, he'd halt and give it to her. He gave away things that were really important, you know. I took quite a dim view of it. I didn't approve at all."

The general's tastes and habits are, as one may guess, simple. In Sicily, he lived under a roof for the first time since Burma; even so, he liked to slip out and make his bed outside. From Cairo to Tunisia, he lived (like Monty) in a "caravan"; Alexander's is a three-ton, specially built four-wheel-drive Chevrolet. It looks like a ship's cabin, with a bunk at one end, a big desk at the other. He likes open cars, and occasionally he would leave the caravan to drive alone in a jeep. Like every British officer I met, he is crazy about our jeep, and he hopes to get one for hunting after the war, but he is afraid that it may be too expensive to maintain. "They use a great deal of petrol, you know." He told me once that driving a jeep fast on the desert was like skiing.

Alexander and Montgomery, who are very close friends, are something more than a team. They have been a kind of entity; the great point about their careers is the way they interlock and complement each other. They worked together for years; Alex commanded a brigade when Monty commanded one of his regiments; Alex commanded a division when Monty had a brigade; Alex had a corps when Monty had a division; then Alex got a whole army group, with Monty as his army commander. Neither has ever done so well separately as together. One of their best officers put it nicely: "Alexander is the cannon, and Montgomery is his shell."

In a single sentence Sir Winston Churchill once called Montgomery "vehement," "formidable," "austere," "severe," "accomplished," and "tireless." He rose to splendid—if controversial—heights after the campaign in Sicily and later in the war. Everybody knows about his spirited disagreements with Eisenhower, Bradley, and Patton in France in 1944 and 1945. His asperity increased with the years and his autobiography, which he told me would blow off everybody's heads from Alamein to London, did indeed cause a few to shake and rock when it appeared in 1958. Lord Montgomery still maintains his capacity for being dramatic, unexpected, and unconventional. He was sitting in the House of Lords one day recently and, turning to the man next to him, said casually, without a trace of pain showing on his features, "Excuse me, but I am having a coronary thrombosis." He marched away to find medical care, and indeed it was discovered that he had just had a heart attack.

Field Marshal Lord Alexander also had a distinguished career after Sicily, not only in military affairs but in politics as well. He was governor-general of Canada for a time. Self-effacing mildness and chivalry continued to mark him. "Not a glory hopper," is the way he was once characterized by Sir Winston Churchill.

Part Seven

~~~~~~~~~

A GALLERY OF AMERICANS

CHAPTER 22

~~~~~~~~

FDR: The Historical Perspective

This is the first chapter of Roosevelt in Retrospect, *published in 1950. But I began work on it as early as 1944, when I started research for my* Inside U.S.A. *Originally I planned to include Mr. Roosevelt in the U.S.A. book, but this turned out to be impossible because of the weight of the material I accumulated, so FDR became a book on its own. A small point —it can do no harm now to reveal that the source for the remark that "the President never 'thinks' " was Eleanor Roosevelt.*

~~~~~~

> *It takes a long long time to build the past up to the present.*
> —FRANKLIN DELANO ROOSEVELT

FRANKLIN DELANO ROOSEVELT, thirty-second President of the United States and Chief Executive from 1933 to 1945, the architect of the New Deal and the director of victory in World War II, Franklin Delano Roosevelt who is still both loved and hated as passionately as if he were still alive, was born in Hyde Park, New York, in 1882, and died in Warm Springs, Georgia, in 1945. It was his fate, through what concentration of forces no man can know, to be President during both the greatest depression and the greatest war the world has ever known. He was a cripple—and he licked them both.

Was he a great man? Of course. But what made him so? How did the greatness arise? His career, by almost any criterion, is one of the most extraordinary in modern times. But exactly why? What controlled his character? What did Roosevelt himself contribute to his own proliferating destiny? What transformed him from a not very exceptional young man into a mature colossus? What came from the *Zeitgeist*, what from him?

I once heard it said that Roosevelt's most effective quality was receptivity. But also he transmitted. He was like a kind of universal joint, or rather a switchboard, a transformer. The whole energy of the country, the whole power of one hundred and forty million people, flowed into him and through him; he not only felt this power, but he utilized it, he retransmitted it.

Why does a country, if lucky, produce a great man when he is most needed? Because it really believes in something and focuses the entire energy of its national desires into a single human being; the supreme forces of the time converge into a single vessel. Roosevelt could manipulate this power, shooting it out at almost any angle, to provoke response, to irradiate ideas and men, to search out enormous issues. He was like a needle, always quivering, oscillating, responding to new impulses, throbbing at the slightest variation in current—a magnetic instrument measuring ceaselessly the tone and intensity of public impact. But no matter how much the needle quivered and oscillated, it seldom varied far from its own true north.

But this analysis, however suggestive, is too artificial for my taste, because the essence of FDR was not mechanistic, but sublimely (and sometimes ridiculously) human. Of all his multifarious qualities the dominant was probably his extreme humanity. The term "humanity" covers a wide arc—from amiability to compassion, from fertility in ideas to subtlety in personal relationships, from the happy expression of animal vitality to the deepest cognizance of suffering and primitive despair. The President was inveterately personal, and people were inveterately personal about him. A lady I know, by no means a sentimentalist, said two or three years after his death, "He made me glad I am a woman. I miss him actively, personally, every day." At least a dozen people all over the country told me early in 1945—the remark became almost trite—"I never met him, but I feel as if I had lost my greatest friend."

His radiant, energetic smile—even with the touch of glucose in it, even when it seemed contrived—stirred people with confidence and hope. His lustrous voice, so soothing, so resonant, so alive, said, "My friends . . ."—and the people were. They were not merely his followers, but partners. He led by following, which was one of the most distinctive sources of his power. He lifted people above themselves—he gave them a goal—and hence no one was ever able to take the masses away from him. He gave citizens the sense that they, we, the country, were going forward, that life was still the kind of adventure it had been in pioneer days, that the pace was fast and that substantial rewards were attainable.

Yet, more than any modern President, he split the country—which is one of the more obvious Roosevelt paradoxes. Why was he hated so, defamed and calumniated so? Because he took from the rich and gave to the poor. But that is only one explanation. Why, five years after his death, is he still hated so? Because what he did lives after him. But that too is only part of the story.

Roosevelt stood for the "common man" (though this ambiguous phrase is a cliché earnestly to be avoided) but he was certainly not common himself. In fact he was a storybook Prince Charming, a fairytale hero to the millions; he ruled with a wand—even if it was an ivory cigarette holder. Out in the rain, men and women strove—literally—to touch the hem of his cape as he passed, this man who could not walk. The "common" people chose him, a prince, to lead them, and he did things for them, as a good prince should. What was the New Deal except a vast exercise in *noblesse oblige*?[1]

To a supreme degree Roosevelt had five qualifications for statesmanship: (a) courage; (b) patience, and an infinitely subtle sense of timing; (c) the capacity to see the very great in the very small, to relate the infinitesimal particular to the all-embracing general; (d) idealism, and a sense of fixed objectives; (e) ability to give resolution to the minds of men. Also he had plenty of bad qualities—dilatoriness, two-sidedness (some critics would say plain dishonesty), pettiness in some personal relationships, a cardinal lack of frankness (for which, however, there was often good reason), inability to say No, love of improvisation, garrulousness, amateurism, and what has been called "cheerful vindictiveness." Amateurism?—in a peculiar way, yes. But do not forget that he was the most masterfully expert practical politician ever to function in this republic.

Observations on Whether or Not He was a Great Man

I have said that "of course" he was a great man. He fulfilled a concrete historical function, his career epitomized the cardinal pressures of his era, he was what Emerson might have called a Yea Sayer, a world man, and no erosion by history will ever efface some of the things he did. He was admired and loved all over the world, not just in the United States; his appeal was universal.

Yet it is difficult to summarize in a single word what he stood for, as

[1] A good many writers on FDR have used this *noblesse oblige* analogy, but it should not be pushed too far. Certainly the early New Dealers themselves never thought of the New Deal in *noblesse oblige* terms, nor, I think, did Roosevelt himself. They thought in terms of emergency and social justice.

one may say that Socrates stood for Reason or Napoleon for Conquest. In a sense Roosevelt was an instrument, not a creator. He was not a true Original. He was not pure, like Joan of Arc, nor profound, like Dante, nor did he breathe fire, like Shelley. He had plenty of moral grandeur, but he was multiplex and multiform. He was neither a poet, a philosopher, an artist, a mystic, nor even an intellectual. He had few Ideas. In sheer brain power, he was outweighed by several of his contemporaries, and somehow he lacked wholeness of soul, in the way that St. Augustine, let us say, had wholeness of soul, or, on a different level, Cromwell or Spinoza. He called himself a Christian and a democrat, but one does not associate with him the overwhelming, overpowering creative impulse that comes to a man with a permanent, absolute devotion to a single principle. Roosevelt was never a man obsessed. He was not a Goethe, whose whole career may be crystallized by the use of a single word, Nature, or even a Gladstone (Liberalism), or a Bismarck (Prussia).

Probably what it all boils down to is the matter of contribution. He did not create a country, as did Masaryk, or a continent of the imagination, like Beethoven, or a new world of science, like Freud. He may not have been as stupendous a human being as, say, Michelangelo or Tolstoy, but if you measure a man practically by the work he leaves, FDR ranks very high. A Roosevelt advocate might say: (1) Almost single-handed he saved democracy in the United States; (2) he brought the United States to world leadership for the first time. Certainly he belongs in the category of Washington and Lincoln as one of the three greatest presidents in American history, whether you like all he did or not. And think how he is missed!

Greatness? What is greatness? Consider on a different level the peculiarly revealing item that, though he was as much of a cripple as if both legs had been sawed off at the hip, it was inconceivable that anyone should ever have thought of him as an invalid.

Conservative or Liberal?

An easy definition is that a conservative is someone who wishes to conserve things; a liberal is someone who wishes to liberate. Of course this definition breaks down at once when we consider that, in order to conserve, the conservative may have to liberate; he may be unable to conserve the larger order except by liberalizing various institutions. Conversely, the liberal will have nothing left to liberate if he does not conserve the rudimentary essentials. Roosevelt was a liberal about old-age pensions; but he was a conservative about the Bill of Rights. He was a liberal on issues like social security, child labor, and a hundred others; but he was an extreme conservative about democracy. It goes without saying that he belongs to the line of progressive Presidents: Jackson, Theodore Roosevelt, Wilson. Yet it should not be forgotten that some reforms of the New Deal helped to strengthen and even preserve the free-enterprise system in this country, and considered from this angle FDR was one of the most conservative Presidents in our history.

Roosevelt himself thought in terms of action and results, not abstractly. In fact one of the most extraordinary things about his mental structure was that he almost never had abstract thoughts at all.

Once I asked someone very much on his side who was as well qualified to know as anybody, "Just how does the President *think?*" The answer was, "My dear Mr. Gunther, the President never 'thinks'!"

Roosevelt and Roosevelt

If anybody had ever predicted to Theodore Roosevelt that Franklin Delano Roosevelt, his fifth cousin and nephew-in-law, would be elected President of the United States once, let alone four times, the response would probably have been an indignant snort. Nevertheless TR had a considerable regard for FDR when Franklin was a youngster, and FDR had a deep respect and admiration for TR. The first vote for President FDR ever cast was for TR—probably his only vote for someone not a Democrat. Later Woodrow Wilson became FDR's leader, but, the late Josephus Daniels told me once, they were never particularly close; even when FDR became Wilson's assistant secretary of the Navy, he was still much more under the influence of his great cousin Theodore. Most Roosevelts have a habit of sticking together, politics aside.

The two Roosevelts had strikingly parallel lives to a point. Both came of prosperous and sturdy Dutch stock, both were born in New York State, both went to Harvard (Theodore, '80; Franklin, '04), both opened their careers in the New York legislature, both were assistant secretaries of the Navy,[2] both were governors of New York, both ultimately reached the Presidency. Their policies were often similar too. TR waved "the big stick" at "malefactors of great wealth" and spoke with pugnacious contempt of the "vested interests," one of many phrases invented by him that have become fixed in the language; FDR—his words were milder—talked of "economic royalists" and "driving the money changers from the temple." Both were Big Navy men, and pursued an extremely active foreign policy; TR acquired Panama, sent the fleet around the world, and was an international hell raiser in general. Also TR worked out the Peace of Portsmouth between Russia and Japan;

[2] Actually five different members of the Roosevelt family have at one time or other filled this post in this century, a remarkable fact that should have interest for the historians. The other three were Theodore Roosevelt, Jr. (under Harding and Coolidge), Henry L. Roosevelt (under FDR), and Theodore Douglas Robinson, a cousin, under Coolidge.

FDR had peace problems at Casablanca, Teheran, Quebec, and Yalta. But the strongest analogies remain domestic; for instance both men were ardent conservationists. TR stood for the "Square" Deal; FDR for the "New" Deal. The very phrase New Deal derives from the concepts of two former Presidents, Woodrow Wilson's "New" Freedom and the Square "Deal" of Theodore.

Similarities in temperament between the two Roosevelts are also marked, but one must withstand a temptation to exaggerate them. The same family background produced certain common traits, though not those that might be most easily imagined; both were rich men, with deeply ingrained aristocratic impulses, and both stood for social justice. There is a strong reformer streak in Roosevelts. Another item is that both surmounted onerous physical handicaps, though at different ages; TR's asthma, however, even though it threatened to make him an invalid, can hardly be ranked as a catastrophe with FDR's paralysis. Another point is the intense interest both men had in natural history and the outdoors, and their somewhat infantile delight in shooting birds and beasts. FDR had a considerable bent for natural science, particularly in childhood, but he never developed it as TR did; even if he had not been paralyzed, it is almost inconceivable that he could have written such a muscular book as *African Game Trails*. FDR's passion for ships and water is widely known; not so well known is that TR once wrote a history of the Naval War of 1812. Still another item: both had a deep and adhesive family sense, and loved children. Still another: both were immensely curious, with agile fresh minds and variegated interests. Still others (we are getting down to minutiae): both loved to read aloud, to do business at meals, to go on picnics, and to pamper dogs.

But there were differences too. TR was like a dragon; FDR was like a faun, at least as a youth. There was much more buncombe and bluster in TR. He was less urbane and graceful, and more bellicose. He was, Henry Stimson records, "the most commanding natural leader" he had ever known; certainly FDR was a great leader too, but not in quite that way.

Of course FDR never had the opportunity to toughen himself in the west on the fist fights and hand-to-hand brawls that TR loved. One cannot quite imagine him saying, as TR did, "I am as strong as a bull moose, and you can use me to the limit!" The accent is gentler— for instance consider FDR's words in the 1944 campaign, "I am an old campaigner, and I enjoy a good fight." He did—but he used his head more than his fists. He did not have the elder Roosevelt's fierce industry: for instance TR wrote more than 100,000 letters during his seven years in the White House, incredible as this feat may seem, and Ike Hoover, author of *Forty-two Years in the White House*, tells us that he often read "three or four" books a night. But also FDR had qualities that TR didn't have—resilience, a magical serenity, and consummate delicacy of political approach. FDR envied TR his vitality. Once he sighed to an interviewer, "TR needed only six hours' sleep a night, but I have to have eight."

At Campobello, FDR's summer camp in New Brunswick, Canada, one trail was tough in the extreme. It led along the shore and then over precipitous rocks and broken hills; in one place you had to swim a few yards where the path broke off, and the water was icy cold. FDR, before illness struck him, made a point of taking this hike just once every summer. But TR would have done it every day, and before breakfast at that. (Incidentally Eleanor Roosevelt told me once that one of TR's own hikes near Oyster Bay was so rugged and difficult that it terrified her when she was a child.) TR loved obstacles. He loved to overcome something just for the sake of doing so. FDR preferred to go around an obstacle rather than blast it off the road, if he could get to the other side just as expeditiously.

Bonds between the two men remained close for a long time if only because of their abstrusely interlocked family relationship. When Eleanor Roosevelt married Franklin, it was TR, then the President of the United States, who gave the bride away; Eleanor was TR's godchild and favorite niece. One detail is that when the ceremony was over TR turned to Eleanor with the words, "You've done well to stick by the name of Roosevelt!"

Recently I asked one of FDR's sons, Franklin, Jr., if he had any childhood memories of TR; he replied that when he was growing up in Washington "Uncle Ted" was at Sagamore Hill most of the time, but that when he visited the capital he would usually drop in on the Franklin Roosevelts for tea and that he was always boisterous, jovial, and aggressive. In fact, he would rush up to the room where the small Roosevelts were getting ready for bed, grab young Franklin with one arm and his brother John with the other, and then haul them across the room, roaring, "I'm taking two little pigs to market!" Franklin was scared half to death (he was about five at the time) because he thought, first, that Uncle Ted might well be actually carting them off to a butcher shop, and second, that he might slip and drop them down the stairs.

Roosevelt and Wilson

Likewise, the influence of Woodrow Wilson on Franklin Roosevelt was profound; likewise, these two Presidents shared some striking traits. Each was of the upper gentry; yet each was a people's man. The career of each can be stratified into four clear periods—domestic preoccupations, a foreign crisis, war, and interest in the future peace. Each was a gentleman; each had qualities of grace and gallantry; each had charm and courage. But, whereas FDR's charm was natural and spontaneous, Wilson's was more sporadic; he had to turn it on. Wilson was much more intellectual than Roosevelt; he really used his beautifully articulated mind. It would have been unimaginable for Wilson to use a dozen collaborators on a single speech, as FDR often did. Nor did Roosevelt have Wilson's ear for cadenced prose. Wilson was more austere than FDR, brittler, and less fluid and receptive. Wilson was a Scots Covenanter; FDR a Dutchman of good will. Both men were idealists, who believed firmly in Right; but FDR was much less doctrinaire. FDR was of course the better politician, sensitive whereas Wilson was stubborn and dogmatic, relaxed whereas Wilson was often hurt and tense. Wilson was never a backslapper or a hail-fellow-well-met; he seldom called anybody outside his family by a Christian name, whereas, as is notorious, FDR used first names at sight. Wilson feared people; Roosevelt loved them. Wilson, a genuinely shy man, never really *liked* politics, whereas FDR adored every nuance of the art and science of political maneuver.

One analogy, not often thought of these days, is that Wilson, too, was paralyzed after his stroke on October 2, 1919. And it is a pungent forgotten detail that, before the stroke, Roosevelt flirted with the idea of trying to persuade Wilson to run for a third term.

Another analogy, on quite a different level, is that neither ever told anybody *everything*. (But does any President?) Another is the way each used people. But Wilson gave men orders; FDR cajoled them. FDR sent Harry Hopkins to Europe almost exactly as Wilson sent Colonel House; but whereas House was a kind of supermessenger, Hopkins was a friend, a genuine intimate. Also FDR—so complex, so given to several motives—thought that the trip would be useful for Hopkins's own education and development.

Wilson was, we know, more orderly than FDR. But when he played golf he never kept score—something which would have shocked Roosevelt profoundly. One point of difference, which tells a good deal about their contrasting attitudes toward social affairs, is that whereas FDR belonged to a covey of clubs at Harvard Wilson set out to abolish clubs at Princeton. Wilson, with his stern aloofness, was a creature devoid of personal emotion—so one might think. But it is unlikely in the extreme that FDR could ever have behaved as Wilson did when he was courting Mrs. Galt, when, for days on end, the business of government all but stopped while the President pressed his torrential, neurotic suit.

Yet the bond between the two men is unmistakable. FDR often quoted Wilson, as he quoted Theodore; one Wilson maxim he used was, "Reactionaries can always present a front because their program is so negative." And one can easily imagine FDR reading with satisfaction Wilson's definition of statesmanship: "The resolute and vigorous advance towards the realization of high, definite, and consistent aims, which issue from the unreserved devotion of a strong intellect to the service of the State." One can imagine, too, how indulgently he might have smiled at such an example of Wilson's frosty humor as his remark on bureaucracy, "I shall create no more boards. I find that most of them are long, wooden, and narrow."

Then, too, FDR might well have been amused—and impressed—by Wilson's instruction to one emissary he sent abroad: "Pay no attention to our ambassador there. If you get along too well with him, we will know that you yourself are doing nothing; but if you get into too much trouble, remember that we will call you home."

World War I took Wilson by surprise, and at the outbreak of hostilities in 1914 he appealed to the American people to be neutral "even in thought"—something FDR would never have done. Indeed FDR did the exact opposite. Wilson thought that the war was caused "by nothing in particular" and for a considerable interval he saw little to choose between the British and German varieties of illegality. FDR, as we all know, took a sharply different line.

In domestic fields Wilson was a definite precursor of FDR's New Deal, though people are apt to forget this now. Under Wilson came the Federal Reserve banking system, attacks on monopoly in big business, women's suffrage, federal loans to farmers, the eight-hour day for railway workers, much miscellaneous social legislation, and, above all, the income tax. Also Wilson created an "ethical climate," as it has been aptly defined, which Roosevelt inherited after a long and dreary gap. But the more important analogies are in the realm of foreign policy; both Wilson and FDR helped carry America out of international provincialism. One reason why FDR did prepare for war is that Wilson had not prepared; this is probably Wilson's chief gift to him. Wilson created the League; FDR helped create the United Nations. But FDR learned well from Wilson's supreme mistake: Wilson cared so much for the United States of the World that he forgot the United States of America. This classic blunder FDR never made. Painstakingly, never-endingly, from the beginning of the crisis over isolation in the mid-1930's until his final preparation for the San Francisco Conference in 1945, FDR kept in mind Wilson's defeat by the Senate. "The tragedy of Wilson was always somewhere within the rim of his consciousness," as Sherwood[3] points out. Wilson was, in short, his stop sign, his warning signal, for year after crowded year. He took no steps at all for

[3] *Roosevelt and Hopkins,* by Robert E. Sherwood (New York, Harper & Brothers, 1948), the best book on FDR yet written.

bringing the United States into world commitments without the most scrupulously calculating eye to Congress, because the red light that was Wilson always shone.

Roosevelt and Churchill

One may easily forecast the weight of dissertation that will come about these two prodigious virtuosos and their equally prodigious interrelation in future years, as more and more documents become available.

A celebrated ambassador once said mischievously to an equally celebrated Washington hostess, "What do you think you would find if you cut Roosevelt open?" The reply was, "What would you find if you cut open a paper doll. Nothing." This is not to be taken seriously of course, but in point of fact Roosevelt sometimes did give the impression of being two-dimensional. Churchill seems fuller-bodied, with greater depth; one thinks of him as all one color, the scarlet of the beefeater guardsman or the purple of the Renaissance; FDR had a multiplicity of shadow tones and reflecting surfaces. Churchill, one feels, is always one man, though astoundingly various within his single frame; Roosevelt was every sort of man.

Many obvious points of similarity exist between the two, but Churchill was probably a better gambler, and took chances more; also he was a better bargainer. It is unlikely that FDR would ever have put up such a bluff as, for instance, Churchill did in 1943, when he tried to bludgeon the Turks into entering the war by threatening to "give" the Dardanelles to Russia. Churchill wrote more eloquent and brilliant prose. He had a deeper apperception of historical realities. He trusted his experts more, and avoided government-by-crony. He was more accessible to controversy. It is interesting that Henry Stimson records that he "could cut loose at the Englishman as he never felt free to do with his chief"; he argued with Churchill much more freely than with FDR. A minor point is their relation to the scientists in their entourage. Roosevelt bears more responsibility for the atomic bomb than any single man, but he did not like scientists much and never had them close by. Churchill and his chief scientific consultant, Lord Cherwell, were inseparable.

Oddly enough FDR and Churchill were eighth cousins once removed. Both men, it appears, can trace a common descent from a personage known as John Cooke, who came to America on the *Mayflower*. John married Sarah Warren; one of their daughters was the great-great-great-great-great-great-grandmother of Sara Delano, FDR's mother, and another was a direct ancestress of Churchill's American-born mother, Jennie Jerome.

Some confusion has existed as to exactly where and when the two men first met. Churchill himself says that, when Roosevelt visited England during World War I, they encountered one another at a dinner at Gray's Inn; Churchill was "struck by his magnificent presence." But, remarkably enough, he appears to have forgotten this episode when the two leaders saw one another for the first time in World War II; it irked Roosevelt that Churchill apparently had no recollection of their previous meeting.

As one reminiscence follows another we learn more of the profound complexity and scope of the Roosevelt-Churchill intercourse during World War II. Between them something like seventeen hundred telegrams, letters, and other communications passed in five and a half years, starting with Roosevelt's sympathetic initiative to the "Naval Person" when Churchill became first lord of the Admiralty in 1939. Churchill's letters to Roosevelt from this date until Pearl Harbor constitute one of the supreme feats of political argument of all time. He "armed" FDR with patient lessons; he laid the framework for the destroyer transfer; he ceaselessly cajoled, explored, exhorted; he wheedled him, encouraged him, and called out sternly, "Do it now"; he prompted Roosevelt to the idea for Lend-Lease in the celebrated nineteen-point letter of December, 1940; he kept at him artfully through his ambassador in Washington; he analyzed history for him as he made it, in documents of unprecedented insight, brilliance, variety, and vigor. But one must not think that Roosevelt was a dupe or that he played second fiddle. The Churchill salesmanship was masterly; but FDR did not need to be persuaded on the major premises.

The President and prime minister met ten or twelve times during the course of the war—on the *Augusta* (where the Atlantic Charter was drawn up), four times in Washington, twice in Quebec, and at Casablanca, Cairo, Teheran, and Yalta. According to Churchill's own calculation they had 120 days of close personal contact in all. Nothing in contemporary—or other—annals quite matches the dramatic intensity and importance of this series of monumental conferences; it is quite safe to say that never before has talk between two men so influenced the course of world history, both military and political. Roosevelt once telegraphed to Churchill, "It is fun to be in the same decade with you," which would appear to be one of the more massive understatements of the age.

After the Atlantic Charter meeting, when the two leaders returned to their respective ships, each immediately asked one of his adjutants, "What did *he* think of me?" FDR was inclined to be boastful later. He told a friend, "I had thirteen warships at that meeting, but Winston had only two or three. One of his broke down, and I had to *lend* him a destroyer!"

General Eisenhower met Churchill at Casablanca in 1943. Roosevelt hardly knew Eisenhower then, but the President turned to him when the prime minister left the room: "Isn't he a wonderful old Tory to have on our side?"

FDR and Churchill bickered and bargained and nettled one another as the strain of waging coalition war became almost intolerable, and often this issue of Toryism was at the bottom of their difficulties. Roosevelt exasperated the prime minister almost beyond speech by pushing for the independence of India, by constantly adducing the need of colonial peoples for self-development. FDR stated openly at one press conference late in the war that Winston was "mid-Victorian on all things like that" (i.e., things having to do with the British Empire), and that "he would never learn." Once—at Teheran—they had a spat over the status of Newfoundland, and Sherwood and Elliott Roosevelt recount some other lively episodes. Think what the prime minister must have felt when FDR quite casually urged the British to give up Hong Kong! Eleanor Roosevelt writes, "He [FDR] never minced words in telling Mr. Churchill that he did not think the British had done enough in any one of the colonial areas in really improving the lot of the native peoples."[4] FDR had an extremely generous and copious imagination about anything to do with improving anybody's future.

Another important point of difference was the Second Front; the British did not want to risk a major operation across the Channel until 1944. Of course this issue involved the Russians, who thought that they were being bled white in the east while the western allies stalled. At one of their conferences, trying to break through Stalin's implacable suspiciousness and reserve, FDR "ganged up" on Churchill (having given him due warning), and proceeded to bait him in the Russian dictator's presence. But the baiting went a little far. I asked someone who was present if this episode actually had taken place as frequently described. "You bet it did, and it wasn't funny, either!"

On smaller counts, personal counts, there were other irritants. For one thing Churchill, as is notorious, liked to take gargantuan naps in the afternoon, "naps" sometimes two or three hours long, and then stay up most of the night, whereas FDR worked straight through the day and wanted to be in bed by midnight. And Churchill was puzzled and irritated by the President's discursiveness. The prime minister annoyed Roosevelt by bringing his own map room to the White House; FDR, who was good at tit for tat, retaliated by bringing *his* own map room to Quebec. Churchill, the record would indicate, was much more generous than Roosevelt in comments of each about the other. Modestly

---

[4] The quotation from Mrs. Roosevelt is from her second volume of autobiography, *This I Remember* (New York, Harper & Brothers, 1949).

he would describe himself as the President's "first lieutenant." He was the elder; yet he liked to address him as "Mr. President," though of course FDR called him "Winston" practically from the moment they met.

Churchill began to be worried about Roosevelt's health at Quebec. Shortly thereafter, in the campaign against Dewey, FDR made his famous campaign ride through the streets of New York in icy rain; at once Churchill telegraphed him, appealing to him to take better care of himself. Once the prime minister (at Quebec) said that to encounter Roosevelt, with all his buoyant sparkle, his iridescence, was like opening a bottle of champagne. Roosevelt was not so given to such pleasant compliments. It is recorded that, in their last meetings together, Churchill always looked "as if he were going to get hit," and Roosevelt is once supposed to have said, "Yes, I *am* tired! So would you be if you had spent the last five years pushing Winston uphill in a wheelbarrow."

James F. Byrnes writes in *Speaking Frankly* that the President complained at Yalta about Churchill's too frequent and lengthy speeches, "which held up business." Byrnes replied, "Yes, but they were good speeches." Then FDR chuckled and admitted, "Winston doesn't make any other kind." On the other hand Edward R. Stettinius, who was also present at Yalta, reproduces in his book a handwritten chit FDR passed across to him on one occasion when the prime minister began to speak, "Now we are in for ½ hour of it," which would seem to be a comment somewhat snide.

Astonishing things occurred at the second Quebec meeting, according to Henry Morgenthau. Roosevelt took Morgenthau with him to Quebec, because the agenda included the British monetary situation— "Churchill keeps saying he [not personally of course] is broke," Morgenthau records. The conferees had a violent argument about the status of Germany after the war, and Churchill attacked Morgenthau ("I never had such a verbal lashing in my life") for his projected scheme of transforming Germany into a pastoral, industryless state. "The President . . . said very little. This was part of his way of managing Churchill. He let the Prime Minister wear himself out attacking me. . . . Then, when the time came, he could move in with his superb and infectious humor and compose the situation." Churchill demanded, "What are we going to have between the white snows of Russia and the white cliffs of Dover?" (i.e., if Germany were destroyed) and Morgenthau asked the President what to do. FDR replied simply, "Give me thirty minutes with Churchill." He was sure that he could "handle" him.

David Lloyd George was another British statesman whom Roosevelt strikingly resembled; like Lloyd George, FDR greatly modified the structure of capitalism, and as a result was hated and vilified by the "ruling" classes; like Lloyd George (and Churchill), he organized victory in a tremendous war. The Lloyd George reforms paved the way indirectly for the rise of British socialism to political power; the remark has been made about him, "He saved capitalism, but by so doing made socialism certain."

A final point: Roosevelt may have been cavalier to Churchill on occasion, and perhaps he did speed up, despite him, the disintegration of the British Empire; yet it cannot be denied that, the prime minister aside, Roosevelt deserves more credit for keeping Britain herself alive after Dunkirk than any Englishman. He was one of the best American friends Britain has ever had, and during the blackest period of the Battle of Britain he was almost as important in maintaining *British* morale as Churchill himself, which is to say a lot.

Roosevelt and Hitler

Surely no two men who played supreme roles in the same supreme drama could have been more unlike. But Hitler is worth brief mention for two reasons. (He came to power, incidentally, on January 30, 1933, which was Roosevelt's birthday, and just five weeks before the first inaugural.) First, several of the forces propelling Hitler into power were much the same as those that put Mr. Roosevelt into office—mass despair in the midst of unprecedented economic crisis, impassioned hatred of the *status quo,* and a burning desire by the great majority of people to find a savior who might bring luck. Roosevelt won in 1932 partly because Mr. Hoover was so discredited and unpopular; similarly the electorate in Germany, though of course tricked and deluded and beaten down by terror, voted not merely for Hitler but *against* the feebleness and ineptitude of the previous regime.

But, second, Mr. Roosevelt never became a dictator. He was often called a dictator, as he was called a Communist, by people too stupid, too dishonest, or too prejudiced to be able to tell good from bad, white from black, fish from fowl. . . . [But he] might easily have tried to make himself dictator, and moreover a dictator like Hitler, who was legally *voted* into office, had he been crudely ambitious or unscrupulous. Roosevelt had the votes; what is more he had the actual power—and chose never to exercise it. We are apt to forget nowadays the immense, unprecedented, overwhelming authority conferred on FDR by an enthusiastically willing Congress during the first hundred days of his first administration. The Reichstag did not give Hitler much more. Suppose Roosevelt had *not* been a democrat at heart. Merely by pressing the analogy to Hitler, we may toll off what we might have lost, but did not—the existence of opposition parties, a free judiciary, independence of the civil service, the rule of law, freedom of religion and education, the Bill of Rights, the Constitution itself—to say nothing of the

right of Americans to think freely, talk freely, breathe freely, throughout the land.

~~~~~~

*I met President Roosevelt only four or five times but, as was the
case with Mr. Churchill, each meeting produced at least one ineffaceable
impression—a line of talk, an anecdote, a gesture. The first time was at
a press conference in the White House on December 7, 1934, midway
through the all-but-forgotten pressures and turmoils of the first term,
and seven years to a day before Pearl Harbor. I was then the Vienna
correspondent of the Chicago* Daily News, *I was home in the United
States on leave, and I was permitted as a matter of routine courtesy
to be present.*

*I had never been to a presidential press conference before, nor had
I ever seen Mr. Roosevelt before. I was startled and amazed. I had been
used to the stuffy, useless kind of press conferences we got in Budapest
or Paris; this was something new to my experience. But it was not Mr.
Roosevelt's talk and manner that impressed me most: what struck
me with such force and delight was that here was the President of the
United States, the most powerful man in the world, sitting casually at
a desk with his back to a broad window.*

*At once I knew that I was home. I had left the world of the police
state, terror, tyranny, and oppression, the dark world of Hitler, Stalin,
and Mussolini. No European dictator would ever possibly sit with his
back to a window.*

*Eighteen years later I sat in that same gracious oval room and talked
to President John F. Kennedy. Because I thought it would amuse him, I
told him about my first encounter with Mr. Roosevelt in this same room
with all its ease, harmony, lack of posture, lack of pressure—no trooping
of the colors, no frock-coated underlings, no obsequious secretaries, no
cordons of police—above all its indifference to security. I went on to
mention how the windows back of the President's desk had impressed
me. I saw a glint in Mr. Kennedy's smile. He had caught up with me.
Indeed he was ahead of me. Before I could finish my sentence he interrupted with a wry grin, "Yes—same windows, but they're bullet-
proof now!"*

*Some months after this and after Mr. Kennedy's assassination in
Dallas I ran into Judge Sam Rosenman, one of Roosevelt's most intimate advisors. I told him this little story, which has such tragic implications now, and a peculiar expression came into Rosenman's bland
face, at once knowledgeable and cryptic. He said, "The windows were
bullet-proof then."*

I saw Mr. Roosevelt for the last time in Washington at the inauguration in 1945. Orson Welles, Quentin Reynolds, Mark Van Doren, and I had done a broadcast that he liked, and so we were all asked down. The President almost always gave thanks for favors indirectly, and without mentioning them. I was terrified when I saw his face. I felt certain that he was going to die. All the light had gone out underneath the skin. It was like a parchment shade on a bulb that had been dimmed. He sat alone in one corner of a big room in the White House as two or three hundred guests passed near an informally arranged table laid with a somewhat scant buffet. (Dorothy Thompson said immediately after we were presented to the President, "Let's go out and get something to eat!") One by one, men and women were led forward in a long, crooked file, while a secretary whispered, "Don't hold him up. Let him finish his lunch." Mr. Roosevelt shook everybody by the hand, and the handshake was firm enough, but I could not get over the ravaged expression on his face. It was putty-colored, gaunt, and sagging, and the muscles controlling the lips seemed to have lost part of their function.

The next morning, January 20, 1945, we joined the crowd, not a big crowd, on the snowy White House lawn. Seldom have I been so moved. We saw the White House children and grandchildren strolling and scampering around the open porch in winter clothes—red scarves, blue mittens, white stocking caps—while eminent dignitaries of the Republic mingled with them. Down below, we stamped our feet in the snow, moving about in small circles and craning forward. The scene was like a Brueghel, with the sharply colored figures etched on the new snow, the throng of tall men in dark clothes above, and the fluid, informal movements of the listeners. James Roosevelt helped FDR to his feet, Chief Justice Stone administered the oath, and the President delivered a short, taut speech. There was no pomp at all; the whole affair might have been a high school graduation. I kept thinking how an occasion like this would be organized in one of the Axis countries, or even in England. Yet the United States was the greatest nation on earth. Maybe, I thought, the way this simple and colossal ceremony took place helped tell me why.

CHAPTER 23

≈≈≈≈≈

Coast to Coast

Late in 1944 I set out to write Inside U.S.A. *It took me thirteen months to visit Washington, D.C., and all the forty-eight states, and fifteen more to write the book, which was published in May, 1947. A revised edition appeared in 1951. Most of the next three chapters of the present book come out of it.* Inside U.S.A., *which in its original edition was more than half a million words long, paid somewhat less attention to personalities than its predecessors. I did not anchor it on people as I anchored* Europe *and* Asia. *My interest in people had not abated but, though I did not plan it that way,* Inside U.S.A. *turned out to be a kind of broad survey of the country state by state rather than a series of personal studies. But this is not to say that personalities were neglected. There were passages, long and short, on at least thirty characters, including presidential candidates like Thomas E. Dewey and Harold Stassen, labor leaders like Walter Reuther and Harry Bridges, industrial giants like Henry Ford and Henry Kaiser, newspaper proprietors like Colonel Mc-Cormick of the Chicago* Tribune, *governors all the way from "Alfalfa Bill" Murray of Oklahoma to Ellis Arnall of Georgia, and a covey of senators including Arthur Vandenberg, Burton K. Wheeler, Robert A. Taft, and John Bricker, whom I described as being like interstellar space—a vast vacuum occasionally crossed by homeless, wandering clichés.*

I have had to leave all of these out of the present book because of considerations of space. The few that I do include here, like a couple of square inches clipped out of a blanket, are chosen largely to give some indication of the extraordinary variety of the United States, its incomparable vitality, diversity, and color—also to give a taste of bizarre confusions of its politics.

"The Man from Missouri" was written for Reader's Digest, *and ap-*

peared there in June, 1945, shortly after Mr. Truman became President. It was written in a hurry, and obviously does little but peck at the surface. People grossly underestimated the Vice-President at the time, which is one reason why I tried to point up his virtues. He had been ignored in high places. For instance, incredibly enough, FDR talked with him only once between the nominating convention in the summer of 1944 and the inauguration in 1945.

No one, in a word, knew much at that early date about Mr. Truman's qualities of grit and pepper. Nor could anybody have known that this modest man would have courage enough to make three of the most formidable decisions in American history—dropping the first atomic bomb, launching the Marshall Plan, and standing up to the Communists in Korea.

Nor did I value Earl Warren highly enough when I wrote about him in Inside U.S.A. *Of course this was a long time before he became a sturdily liberal Chief Justice of the Supreme Court associated with some of the most momentous decisions in its history, including that of May 17, 1954, which ruled that racial segregation in the public schools was unconstitutional. Ever since, reactionary crackpots and the more rancid Negro haters have reached a summit of silliness by saying that Warren should be "impeached." He goes right on doing good work. Let the crackpots crack their pots.*

The Man from Missouri

Two senators who disagree on practically everything on earth—except their respect for Harry S. Truman—told me early this year [1945] that, if he became President, he would (a) choose as able a cabinet as any in our history, and (b) let it alone. Harry S. Truman's single most valuable quality is his knack of picking good men—and then backing them up. His greatest asset is that he knows what he doesn't know.

Like General Eisenhower, whom he strongly resembles in some respects, Mr. Truman is a perfect "chairman of a committee." He listens and takes advice; he correlates divergent points of view; he gives everybody an even break or better; he encourages those who need encouragement; and he can, if necessary, be tough in making decisions.

One of Harry Truman's best friends, Barnet Nover, the distinguished foreign affairs editor of the Washington *Post*, gave a dinner party last March and, since the then-Vice-President of the United States was coming, our hostess had place cards at each table arranged with proper regard to protocol. First to arrive, the Vice-President paid not the slightest attention to this formality. He circulated around in as comfortable, unpretentious, and agreeable a manner as could be. He was lively and animated; he was simply a guest among other guests.

I had an impression of what you might call bright grayness. Both the clothes and hair were neat and gray. The gray-framed spectacles magnified the gray-hazel eyes, but there was no grayness in the mind. His manner held a combination of contented humor, alertness, a wide and fluid range of interests, playfulness, and, above all, a deep human interest in everything that went on.

His voice is reasonable, very reassuring, and without much Missouri twang. His conversational manner is alert and poised. He talks very swiftly, yet with concision. You have to listen hard to get it all.

I asked him when he had first met Mr. Roosevelt.

"In 1929, when I was a county judge in Missouri. Roosevelt was then governor of New York, and I thought he was the greatest man I ever met." Pause. "And I still think so."

Later there was a contrary note [about somebody else]. The Vice-President happened to mention an eminent politico. "He's an ass. You understand me? You know the word? An *ass!*"

Mr. Truman evidenced not the slightest sense of the importance he might feel as Vice-President. "They elevated me to this job, that's all, and here I am."

Mr. Truman served in the Senate from 1934 to 1944, and of all ninety-six senators he became probably the most popular. One anecdote tells the story. On the day he took over as Vice-President, no fewer than forty of his colleagues dropped into his office. It was like old-home week. It is no derogation of Henry Wallace, Truman's predecessor, to say that, in all his four years, he had not similarly been greeted. Mr. Wallace never quite got to be "a member of the club."

One of the new President's closest associates told me: "Whatever he undertakes to do, he does well. And you can be sure there's absolutely no difference between him now and when he was a county judge. He hates stuffed shirts." Another comment was the following: "If you busted the door in and said, 'Harry, what the hell, you're nuts!' he'd quietly ask you to come in and explain exactly why." This same friend added, after a serious pause, "If you bounced him in the nose, hard, he might blink, but you'd never see him *weave!*"

Let it not be forgotten that, while he was senator, a poll of Washington correspondents by *Look Magazine* named Harry Truman as one of the ten most valuable men in Washington. He was the only member of either branch of Congress to make the first ten.

The new President's chief relaxation—if he has any time to relax nowadays—is music. He learned to play the piano as a boy, and he plays quite well, although he calls it "messing around at the keyboard." His tastes are Chopinesque. What he likes most is to play the piano while his twenty-one-year-old daughter Mary Margaret sings. Mr. Truman is also fond of reading. When he was a boy he read straight through the public library of his home town, Independence, Missouri. For years he read the Congressional Record every night before going to bed.

His mother—who is still alive, a staunch old lady of ninety-two—taught him to read, Mr. Truman told me. A book she gave him when he was twelve, *Great Men and Famous Women*, had signal influence on him. It taught him something of the relationship of men to government, and how political leaders were shaped and made, though he had absolutely no idea of ever becoming one.

The President was born on a Missouri farm in 1884. He is of Scotch-Irish descent, with a little French mixed in. His grandparents had come west in about 1840, out of Kentucky. He met his wife, Bess Wallace, in Sunday school, when she was five, and says he has been in love with her ever since. It is an extraordinary thing that, in this day of universal education, the President of the United States should not have gone to college. The reason is of the best; his family was too poor, and he had to earn a living. For ten years, after high school, Harry worked on a six-hundred-acre farm that "grew everything"; these years, he says, were the best of his life. After that came jobs in a drugstore and a small bank, and command of a field artillery battery in France during World War I.

The President has never had much money. When he arrived in Washington he was in debt; he has since paid off every cent, while living on his salary.

Mr. Truman didn't engage in sports as a boy, because of defective eyesight. "So they made me an umpire," is the way he laughs it off. One eyeball is flat. But with glasses, the Chief Executive sees perfectly. His health is, in general, excellent.

Mr. Truman has been accustomed to getting to work very early. His executive secretary, Matthew J. Connelly, told me that in years he had "beaten the boss to the office only once." Mr. Connelly added: "And he always took the day home with him too."

After Pearl Harbor Mr. Truman went to General Marshall and asked how he could be of service. Truman hoped to get into uniform again. But Marshall told him, in effect, while appreciating his gesture, "Senator, you're fifty-five. This is a young man's war. We can't use you."

Truman respected Marshall's point of view, but he was hurt. He hated to think that he was too old to be of use. In the winter of 1940, he made a tour of Army camps then being built throughout the country. He traveled in his own car, at his own expense; he covered about thirty thousand miles. As a county commissioner in Missouri he had spent some $60,000,000 on roads—"the best darned roads in the United

States." He knew a lot about contracts and construction. And what he saw being built didn't please him.

So Mr. Truman made one of his rare Senate speeches. He introduced a resolution calling for an investigating committee. This was approved, and in April, 1941, the committee got to work. It has been estimated that the Truman Committee probably saved the country between two and three billion dollars, and a good many thousand lives, by its insistence on strict standards in war contracts and the like.

Mr. Truman did not want the job of Vice-President. He went to the 1944 convention in Chicago with a speech nominating James F. Byrnes in his pocket. He still had it in his pocket when, trying to think fast, he had to make a speech of acceptance on getting the job himself.

He hated to leave the Senate. "I liked being a senator. I wanted to stay in the Senate all my life. But when I get a job, I try to work at it." A month before the convention, Truman chatted with a newspaper friend about the impending nominations. Truman said, "I wouldn't be President of the United States for a million dollars."

Mr. Truman has been solidly in favor of world cooperation from the time he entered public life. He looks back to his historical reading as one chief source of his internationalist ideas. The greatest political experiment in the history of all government was, Mr. Truman thinks, the American Constitutional Convention of 1787. He hopes—though he didn't say so in so many words—that the work of this convention can, in our times, be somehow projected on an international scale in full maturity.

President Truman had a good deal to do with the B_2H_2 resolution in 1943, pledging the Senate to international cooperation. Burton, Ball, and Hatch were all members of his own committee; all were close friends, and it was easy for all to meet under his baton. And it was Truman who, in the earliest negotiations, suggested that if anything at all was to come of the effort, it must be bipartisan.

Immediately after his inauguration as Vice-President, Mr. Truman held a lunch for the freshmen senators. At the lunch, Truman was careful to invite all the B_2H_2 men, and also Tom Connally, chairman of the Foreign Relations Committee. The idea was to let Ball and Hill and Hatch talk to the newcomers about Dumbarton Oaks. Then Truman, mostly by personal persuasion, got all sixteen freshmen (including Capehart of Indiana and Hickenlooper of Iowa, strong midwest Republicans) to sign a round robin to the President, pledging support of the Administration's foreign policy.

One day last March I dropped in at the Senate Office Building for an appointment with the then Vice-President. His receptionist said that, having had to go to the dentist, he was a bit "off schedule." At 9:58 he sailed in. "Late, late," he muttered, whizzing through the outer office. He called me in, and talked till a little after twelve. Once a secretary interrupted. He twinkled at her, "Want to see if I'm really working?" Once Mr. Connally dropped in. "This son of a gun," Mr. Truman pointed to me, "is trying to find out what kind of a son of a gun *I* am!"

I asked Mr. Truman what he believed in most. He said right away, "The Sermon on the Mount—and that isn't just a religious answer." He went on to assert that no individuals, communities, or countries ever got anywhere that didn't observe the Golden Rule, that didn't maintain "a sense of decency" about other individuals, communities, and countries. "Look at Hitler. His word wasn't good, so he got nowhere, finally." He added somewhat ruefully that, human nature being what it is, a lot of folks just can't help being "pirates at heart." But "let's try to help 'em get over it."

I asked him what he liked most. He answered without any hesitation, "People—and to do things for people." Then (with a laugh): "Without expecting anything much by way of reward, either!"

But what Mr. Truman talked about most was Missouri, and he talks of it with loving pride. He stood for a quarter of an hour before a large map of Missouri, demonstrating points in its geography, history, and agriculture, with zealous erudition. Missouri is, according to its most eminent living son, the only state in the Union which could get along self-contained if you built a fence around it. And Missourians are, he laughed, "ornery folks, against everybody." "What are they *for?*" I asked. "Missouri!" Mr. Truman was delighted to reply.

〰〰〰〰〰〰〰〰〰〰〰〰〰〰〰〰〰〰〰〰〰〰

I saw Mr. Truman at the White House twice when he was President. The first talk came on November 16, 1945. Tiny lines had grown around his mouth. He looked tired, perplexed, and annoyed. "This is a thankless job," he sighed. He wanted to know how it could be that Congress stood so far behind the people. Taking over a program in midstream had been a grinding task. Everywhere there were worlds within worlds—114 of them! Mr. Truman gave a wry chuckle. "Why did I say 114? Because that's the number of counties in Missouri!" The Russian problem was a persistent headache. He vouchsafed the prophecy that the Russia of 1950 would be very different from the Russia of the day, and hinted vaguely that there might be some kind of "loosening up"; he said that the people of Russia wanted peace—"but how to get at 'em?" He talked frankly about colloquies he had had at Potsdam with Stalin, and added that one of Stalin's chief adjutants was "the most pigheaded man" he had ever met. At the end Mr. Truman mentioned the bomb. Maybe it would turn the world into a "cold star." I said it would be hot first. The President added that the decision to drop it was "terrible." But, he concluded, it saved a quarter of a million American lives.

I saw the President again on December 8, 1947, between 12:05 and 12:27 P.M. Mr. Truman looked much better; he was fresh, confident, and relaxed as well as full of sass. He looked ten years younger than two years before, and obviously the Presidency was agreeing with him. He said that if it were not for the fact that 1948 was an election year he could clear up "this Russian thing," straighten Europe out, and stabilize China. But he thought that the opposition would play politics on foreign policy to a large degree, and that this would hamper his hand. He talked with the warmest possible admiration about General George C. Marshall and expressed great confidence in General Dwight D. Eisenhower. He said that he had several times "invited" General Douglas MacArthur to return to the United States, but that MacArthur had refused to come. "I want to pin a decoration on him," Mr. Truman said. Then came a little story. Eisenhower had recently returned from a trip to the Far East. Reporting to the President, he told Mr. Truman that he'd better look out, because MacArthur was already "running for President" against him. In the same week another eminent officer arrived from Tokyo to give the President a message from MacArthur—to warn him that Eisenhower was running for President against him! Then he added that he had told Ike some time before that if he, Eisenhower, wanted to run for the Presidency, he himself would be delighted to step aside.

Leaving the Oval Room I asked a question, "How do you take the load off?" Answer: "I never take it off."

~~~~~~

Earl Warren of California

California, more than any other part of the Union, is a country by itself, and San Francisco a capital.
—LORD BRYCE

Warren's victory over James Roosevelt in 1950 made him the first governor in California history ever to be elected to three terms. Previously (when he crushed Robert W. Kenny in 1946) he set up another record by being the first governor of the state ever to win both party nominations; this was made possible by the anarchic California electoral system which permitted him to file on both the Republican and Democratic tickets. Warren took his third oath of office on January 8, 1951, and told the legislature that the civilian defense program—against air raids and the like—must of necessity be the state's first preoccupation. A Third World War, he indicated, was "probable," following Chinese intervention in Korea.

Earl Warren is honest, likable, and clean; he will never set the world on fire or even make it smoke; he is a man who has probably never bothered with abstract thought twice in his life; a kindly man, with the best of social instincts, stable, and well balanced; a man devoted to his handsome wife and six splendid children; not greedy, not a politician of the raucous, grasping kind that has despoiled so much in the United States; a "typical" American in his bluffness, heartiness, healthy apple-pie atmosphere and love for joining things; a man glad to carry a bundle for his missus in the neighborhood supermarket and have an evening out with the boys once in a while; a man with nothing of a "grand line" and little inner force, to throw out centrifugal or illuminating sparks; a friendly, pleasant, average Californian; and a man who, quite possibly and with luck, could make a quite tolerable President of the United States.

Warren won in 1950 as in 1946 even though Democratic registration in the state far exceeds Republican. But the great influx of migrants into California in recent years not only added vastly to the electorate; it steadily caused shifts of population within the state, which means that registration does not always mean what it ought to mean.

California was for years overwhelmingly Republican. Under Roosevelt it was as overwhelmingly Democratic; FDR carried it all four times he ran. Many times in this book, *Inside U.S.A.*, we shall allude to this phenomenon, that in state after state the enormous magnetic, polarizing force of Roosevelt caused a complete political turnabout in 1932, 1936, 1940, and 1944. FDR's death, and the subsequent breakdown of the broad dikes channeling his coalition, released forces which are not yet fully resolved. Mr. Truman carried California narrowly in 1948, but the Republicans won resoundingly in 1950.

Warren was born in Los Angeles in 1891. He worked at every kind of job as a young man, from selling papers to playing the clarinet. His father, a railway mechanic, was murdered some years ago—in a crime that had no political significance but which is an indication that California's tradition of frontier violence is not far away. Warren entered political life as a committee clerk in Sacramento after a brief period of law practice, and rose slowly. He was district attorney for Alameda County (which includes Oakland and Berkeley) from 1925 to 1938, and then attorney general of the state. Little is remembered for or against him in those jobs except the *Point Lobos* case, which is too complex for treatment here.

In 1942 Warren ran for governor for the first time; he won largely because California was so fed up with his Democratic predecessor. Also, he was running in a nonpresidential year, and hence did not have a Roosevelt ticket to oppose. Technically he stood as a nonpartisan and he won handsomely. By 1944 he was a national figure, and he was offered the Republican vice-presidential nomination under Dewey; he turned it down. There were two reasons for this: first, he has no private fortune, and with a large family to support and his children at the most expensive age, he could not afford the office; second, he shrewdly sensed that Roosevelt could not be beaten and that if FDR carried California it would be quite a black eye for Mr. Warren. His caution did not endear him to the Republican hierarchy, and during the campaign he was accused of being lukewarm to Dewey. Then in 1948, after a dark-horse attempt for the Presidency himself, he did run for Vice-President on the Dewey ticket, and was beaten. His subsequent California victory in 1950 emphatically restored him to national prominence; he is almost certain to be a prominent contender for the Presidency in 1952.

As governor Warren has always been fair-minded, conscientious, tolerant, and liberal. He lifted old-age pensions from forty to fifty dollars a month; he tried to push through a compulsory health insurance bill, which the lobbies beat; he set about a program of prison reform; he worked hard for a state Fair Employment Practices Commission, and to augment unemployment insurance; he greatly improved the governmental machinery of the state, and created a Reconstruction and Reemployment Commission that did admirable work. He played for AF of L support (which he now has); hence, he tended as a rule to support everything the AF of L asked for. Finally, he "reduced taxes." But beware of this cliché. It can be said of a dozen governors in a dozen states that, to their credit, they "reduced taxes." But to "reduce taxes" is the simplest thing in the world in years when tax receipts are greater than ever before in history; most states have enormous surpluses today, not deficits. The real point is why taxes were not reduced more.

Warren's dominant note is, to sum up, decency, stability, sincerity, liberalism, and lack of genuine intellectual distinction. But how many American governors have genuine intellectual distinction?

〰〰〰〰〰〰〰〰〰〰〰〰〰〰〰〰〰〰〰〰〰〰〰〰〰〰〰〰〰〰〰〰

A Freshman from the Mountain Slopes

I will not wear another man's collar.
—WAYNE L. MORSE

Wayne Lyman Morse, Republican senator from Oregon, whom his opponents call a "secret New Dealer" and a "labor stooge," is a tall lean man with a sharp nose and sharp dark mustache, tough, talented, and emphatic. When making his first campaign in 1944, he found that he was getting nowhere in the conservative ranch country in the eastern part of the state. Morse had an idea. His whole career has been that of an intellectual, but he decided to ride with the ranchers. He was a professor of law, but he knew plenty about horse flesh. So he visited Pendleton during its famous roundup, and though this was the home town of his opponent he made no speeches. He simply spent three days riding. His horse, which he raised himself, is a prize-winning stallion named Spice of Life. Then Morse—and horse—made a little tour of the ranch country. One of his hosts, a feudal baron to whom he had been anathema, finally burst out, "Any guy who can raise a horse like that and ride like that can't be the son of a bitch I always thought he was!"

This story went all over the state, and helped the young professor of law considerably in what turned out to be an easy victory. Morse carried every county in Oregon, something that had never happened in its history.

Spice of Life is still with Morse in Washington, D.C. So is another prize winner, Oreganna Bourbon. Morse came east by Ford and trailer, taking with him both horses, his wife, and three baby girls.

The senator comes by his horsiness honestly. He was born on a three-hundred-acre homestead farm near Madison, Wisconsin, in 1900. The family is of old Yankee stock, and one forebear was Samuel F. B. Morse; several of his ancestors fought in 1776, and he carefully keeps up his membership in the Sons of the American Revolution. Both his grandfather and father were practical farmers, specialists in livestock and horse and sheep breeders. Wayne never forgot, and still likes to quote to this day, something his father told him when he was only knee high, "The outside of a horse is good for the inside of a boy."

But it is more than merely horses that brought Wayne Morse to Washington, and made him one of the most outspoken and conscientious legislators in the country. Here is an honest man, with a good mind, good will, and guts.

Morse's dominant characteristic, outside his obvious brain power and wire-taut nervous energy, is courage. He told me once, "You know, people like a scrapper. I always try to be good-natured, but I certainly punch hell out of a lot of people."

Morse practically never equivocates or straddles. He speaks out for what he thinks is right, and lets the chips fall where they may. For instance he fought Harry Bridges, the California labor leader, to a standstill in an arbitration case, and then appeared as a character witness *for* him in one of the Bridges trials. He tries to decide every issue on its merit, without regard to party label. For instance he once told the Senate that the OPA "needed a housecleaning from top to bottom and I would start with Chester Bowles and send him back to the advertising business." But at about the same time he voted *for* the confirmation of Henry Wallace as secretary of commerce and Aubrey Williams as REA administrator.

Early in 1946 Morse vigorously attacked Senator Taft as a survivor of the old Ohio gang that had destroyed the traditional liberalism of the Republican party, and then a few weeks later snapped briskly and impartially at Mr. Truman, saying that the President's speech to Congress about the railway strike was "one of the cheapest exhibitions of ham acting" ever known.

The outline of Morse's career is simple. He went to the Madison public schools and then the University of Wisconsin; he got his bachelor of arts degree in 1923 and became a master of arts a year later. A good student, he worked hard on the debating team and also found time to get a commission in the Field Artillery Reserve, after four years of military training. He decided to be a teacher, and went to the University of Minnesota, where he was instructor in argumentation and coach to the debating team; here he received a law degree in 1928.

Meantime, in 1924, he married Miss Mildred Downie, who had been a classmate at Wisconsin. Mrs. Morse was a crack student in home economics; and while her husband was studying law she taught home economics in a Minneapolis high school. This too is part of a familiar American pattern, that of the brilliant-but-poor young student ably assisted by a young woman with her own job as well as the job of raising a family and washing dishes. Incidentally, when Morse became senator, and although he needed the money badly, he refused to put her on his pay roll, though most senators have long sanctified this practice. Morse is a stickler on such financial matters.

The Morses went out to Oregon in 1929. He had never seen the state before, and his antagonists sometimes call him a carpetbagger, since he has only been an Oregon resident a mere twenty-two years. First he was assistant professor of law at the University of Oregon in Eugene. Two years later, at the age of thirty-one, he became professor of law and dean of the law school, one of the youngest law deans in the country. He held this post until he resigned to run for the Senate— the first time he ever ran for anything—in 1944.

Meantime, Roosevelt had made him a public member of the National War Labor Board. During twenty-five months he wrote more than half of all the opinions the board made. He quit in disgust because of a complex quarrel over coal involving Harold Ickes, John L. Lewis, and the President. He thought that the President should have been willing to meet Lewis head-on, instead of giving way to him. Before this he had

had a vivid fight with James F. Byrnes, who was then head of the Office of Emergency Management. Roosevelt, as reward for his work on the WLB, had promised him a judgeship in the circuit court of appeals. Morse is a poor man, and this would have meant a good job for life. But when he refused to kowtow to Byrnes and Ickes, the President reneged on the appointment, and he never got the job.

Early in 1944, Morse met the persuasive E. Palmer ("Ep") Hoyt, who was then editor of the *Oregonian*.[1]

"You ought to run for senator," Hoyt said.

"Ridiculous," Morse replied. "I've never run for office in my life."

"We all think you ought to run," Hoyt said.

"Who's we?" Morse asked.

"We" meant the progressive Republicans of the community—especially those who loathed the incumbent senator, Rufus C. Holman. Holman was a pronounced isolationist who had voted against practically every major national defense measure. So Morse had two fights on his hands—the Republican primaries against Holman, and then the general election against a Democrat. He won both handily, even though Roosevelt carried the state. The situation had elements of the picturesque. Morse, a former Roosevelt appointee, was fighting against FDR, who however was being backed by almost all those backing Morse.

Morse has never had any money but his modest salary. His campaign cost plenty, but he kept turning campaign contributions down. He refused to be beholden to anybody. He told all comers that, if elected, he would vote as he pleased, with no debts at all to any special interests. He rejected one offer of $3,500 from the liquor interests, and $4,100 from the CIO.

His record in Washington continued to be ornery from the conventional Republican point of view. An ardent believer in civil rights for Negroes, he came within an ace of putting over a sensational coup—a bill abolishing the poll tax. By a hair, the southern Democrats managed to defeat it. And he filibustered for ten hours and two minutes against the Taft-Hartley Act; this speech was the longest the Senate had heard since Huey Long, but is by no means the longest on record. Old Bob La Follette of Wisconsin, back in 1908, talked on one occasion for eighteen hours.

Mr. Morse has continued for the past fifteen years to be one of the most stubborn, high-minded, independent, and hard-hitting men in

[1] Hoyt later moved on to Denver, where he stirred up the entire population as publisher of the Denver *Post*.

American public life, and his orneriness has not diminished. He has even
gone so far as to switch parties in midstream, something rare in U.S.
politics. (Some British leaders have switched twice, like Winston
Churchill.) The only other outstanding contemporary American I can
think of who has turned from one party to the other is that admirable
public servant W. Averell Harriman. As to Senator Morse, a Republican,
he refused in 1952 to support Eisenhower as the presidential candidate,
and became an independent; then four years later he formally "crossed
the floor" and became a Democrat. Traditionally Oregon is a strong Re-
publican state, but Morse, running as a Democrat, has been re-elected
to the Senate twice.

Saltonstall of Massachusetts

Leverett Saltonstall, three times governor of Massachusetts and senator
from Massachusetts since January, 1945, is a tall, swift, skinny man
of fifty-four with hard red cheeks, absolute honesty, and the gift of being
popular. He is practically the nicest person anybody ever met. I never
heard of anybody who disliked him—after years of hurly-burly in one
of the toughest political states in the union. He has, it seems, everything: wealth, industriousness, Yankee shrewdness, and, above all, character. Then you discover that in 1944 he won the greatest vote in Massachusetts history up to that time; the cliché has it that when Saltonstall
is running, you don't count the votes, you simply weigh them.

Saltonstall, a blue blood of blue bloods, is the most complete possible
contrast to the popular conception of the successful American politician.
How did he get that way? Let us explore.

For one thing, he has the precious gift of modesty; for another, he
gets on well with almost all kinds of people. When he was still governor
he took me out to Needham, where he made a noonday speech. Afterward I overheard two bits of dialogue. One man said, "Governor, thanks
for your check." Saltonstall looked puzzled. "I'm your electrician," came
the response. At the same moment another guest called out, "Any chance
of playing tennis sometime this week, Lev?"

A few days later I ran into him in the lobby of the Somerset Club.
Nobody who has ever seen him could possibly forget him; his face is
extraordinarily distinctive. But before I could say a word he strode up,
and introduced himself. "Maybe you've forgotten me," he said with complete genuineness, "I'm Leverett Saltonstall."

One hears much of Cabots, Lowells, Adamses, but actually from the
point of view of seniority the two greatest families in New England are
not these; only the Winthrops and Saltonstalls are, as the phrase is,

"arms-bearing"; they brought their coats of arms from England. "My God, they *are* a family!" one friend told me, explaining that they were so impeccably sure of their perpetuity that they named their children for their grandparents, not the parents.

The Saltonstalls trace descent back to 1343. Sir Richard Saltonstall founded the Boston suburb of Watertown in 1630, and on his death left his fortune to Harvard College; for ten successive generations the Saltonstalls, father and son, have gone to Harvard. During the Revolutionary days the family—very intelligent and prescient—supported the American side. Leverett's great-grandfather was once president of the Massachusetts senate and mayor of Salem; his grandfather was collector of the Port of Boston by appointment of Grover Cleveland. Both grandfather and father were Democrats, odd as this may seem.

I talked to Saltonstall several times and each time I tried to explore the pattern of his convictions. The central core is always, it seems, associated with his family: the family that produced him and the family he produced. And he has reached a simple philosophy more or less to the effect that a good family spirit is what produces good communities, which in turn is what should produce good government. Naïve? Perhaps. When I asked him, "What do you believe in most?" he scratched his head and looked puzzled. "Well, it might sound more impressive if I said something like 'democracy' or 'the country,' but let's not be pretentious—what I believe in most is Harvard and my family."

Saltonstall was conventionally graduated from Harvard in 1914, and was secretary of his class; his scholastic record was not distinguished. He read for the bar, and worked for a few years as an attorney and—of course, Boston being Boston—as a "trustee."

But politics bit and scorched him early. It is in the blood. I asked him how his political life began, but I do not vouch for all the details that follow—he is both so swift in speech and so shy that it is somewhat difficult to nail him down. It seems that one of his uncles, Endicott Peabody Saltonstall (the whole story is pivoted on family relationships), once set out to run for district attorney. When James Michael Curley, the celebrated Irish boss of Boston, heard that Endicott Peabody Saltonstall might get this job, he snorted, "What! All three of him?" But Uncle Endicott got in. Then Leverett became an alderman. Endicott gave him a post in the district attorney's office, and in 1923 he ran for the Massachusetts legislature and won.

In 1936, having risen to be speaker, Saltonstall entered for the lieutenant governorship; he was defeated in a close race by an Irishman who, ever since, has lived on the reputation of being the one man who ever beat him. For Saltonstall has never lost another election. He ran for governor in 1938 against Curley, and won by a tremendous vote—

in part because so many Bostonians had become sick of that grotesque old man. Running for re-election in 1940 and 1942, he won again. Then came the senatorial race in 1944.

This election filled the seat originally held by Henry Cabot Lodge, Jr., who, a capable and highly complex and ambitious young man, resigned in February to enter the Army. Saltonstall might easily have quit as governor, whereupon the lieutenant governor could have appointed him to the Lodge vacancy—which would have meant a senate seat without a fight. But, says Saltonstall, "I didn't quite like to do it." So he decided to stay on as governor until his term was finished, and take his chances running as a regular candidate. His victory in the race that followed was prodigious. He ran ahead of his ticket by three hundred thousand votes, and carried Massachusetts by a 2-to-1 majority—something all but unprecedented.

Why did Saltonstall run so far ahead of the ticket? What accounts for his hold on Massachusetts voters? It appears that there are several reasons:

1. His obvious merit. He gave the state six years of excellent administration. People liked him because he was wholesome and upright. His popularity overran party lines.

2. He was careful not to say anything much against Roosevelt. He always worked closely with Washington on national defense.

3. A moderate liberal, he caught most of the middle-roaders. Some of his speeches sound as if they had been written for, not against, the New Deal.

4. His labor record was good, and although the Political Action Committee of the CIO, which was very strong in the state at the time, did not overtly support him, it did little to oppose him. (The CIO, incidentally, did support him in 1942.)

5. Above all, the Irish-descended community did not fight him with much punch. Motives for this date back a long way. Many honest Irish were mortified by the records of previous Democratic governors; they wanted a decent upstanding man. And some Irish, looking up to the Yankees, voted for Saltonstall out of a curious inverted snobbery— they enjoyed being on the Brahmin side for a change; they were eager to line up with Beacon Hill.

6. A last complex point. *Some* of the Irish voted for him, even if this meant a diminished vote for the Democratic ticket, because they hated FDR.

Saltonstall has come a long way quickly and he still has much to learn, his friends say. At the beginning, because of his shyness, he didn't like rough give-and-take; he was the world's worst public greeter. The legend is that two friends hired a suite in the Parker House, installed a soap box in a locked room, ripped off Lev's coat and shirt, hoisted him up on the box, and kept him there shouting and gesticulating till he got used to it. Another story is that one adviser sought to curb him from ever saying anything extemporaneous; Saltonstall had made some wisecrack that didn't quite catch fire. The adviser cautioned him, "Lev, any time you ever think of another quickie, call me up, and next day I'll let you know whether or not to use it."

There is a cliché about Saltonstall: that he has everything—except brains and top-flight intellect. But good senators are seldom "brilliant" or "profound." His chief defect, if you can put it that way, is what I would describe as a lack of essential bulk. He does not lack stamina; but his shoulders are not very broad. He could never be like Theodore Roosevelt, say—a prodigiously full man capable of taking violent risks, of making tremendous mistakes, of creating explosive cataclysms. He is not an Olympian; he will never mimic Prometheus. The blasting fires of creation do not rage in his lean belly.

Nevertheless, in recapitulation, we may summarize the chief sources of his considerable power. First, integrity. He never pretends to be what he isn't. Second, modesty and friendliness. Third, a canny man, he never promises anything. He told me that in three campaigns for governor, he had made only one specific promise, to repair a stretch of local road near Holyoke. Fourth, he draws support from both sides, because of his essential moderation. Fifth, though wealthy, he is very frugal, and he gave Massachusetts the strictest financial administration since Coolidge. He has never in his life wasted a cent—something which appeals to Yankees. Sixth, he has a kind of naïveté more precious than the most refined sophistication. I heard him say once that he had sent two chickens from his farm to Washington by air express, so that a relative might have them for Thanksgiving. The express bill was $3.88. He added quite seriously, "The chickens weren't worth $3.88 themselves, but I sent them anyway."

~~~~~~

One reason why I include Saltonstall here is that his background represents such a contrasting element to others familiar on the American political scene—the urban melting pot and, out in the countryside, the tradition of the barefoot boy and old red schoolhouse. Saltonstall has continued to be elected senator from Massachusetts with huge majorities. But he never made much of a mark in the Senate. It was typical of him that he waited for more than a year, on first being elected, before making a major speech.

Inside U.S.A. was, I repeat, first published in 1947 and revised in

1951. I looked up two men in it the other day because they were relatively inconspicuous then and I could not remember whether I had included them or not—John F. Kennedy and Lyndon B. Johnson. Mr. Johnson gets a bare mention in the original edition of Inside U.S.A. *as "an able representative" who belongs, I wrote, "to the national rather than the peculiarly Texas scene." Then in the revised edition I describe briefly his fantastic campaign for the Senate in 1948, which he won by 87 votes out of 988,295.*

John F. Kennedy does not appear in the original U.S.A. *but there is a one-line footnote about him in the revised edition. Discussing Massachusetts politics in general and the influence of the Irish I mention Joseph P. Kennedy, the father of the late President, and "the splendid war record of his sons." The footnote reads, "One son, John F. Kennedy, an attractive youngster of 29, ran for Congress in 1946 and won James Michael Curley's former seat."*

I wish very much that there could be passages about Kennedy, Johnson, and several other illustrious contemporary Americans—for instance Adlai E. Stevenson—in the present book, Procession, *but I never wrote character sketches about them.*

CHAPTER 24

≈≈≈≈

The Not-So-Little Flower

This, written in February, 1945, is another fragment from Inside U.S.A.
*Mr. La Guardia was then at the height of his rambunctious power. Per-
haps the reader may think this chapter has little relevance today, but
I include it here partly because it is an old favorite of mine and partly
because I think it demonstrates something of the fierce complexity of
our urban civilization and the fantastic variety of details still involved in
governing a great city.*

≈≈≈≈≈≈≈≈≈≈≈≈≈≈≈≈≈≈≈≈≈≈≈≈

THE MAYOR asked me if I'd like to come down to City Hall and spend
a day with him. I sat at a corner of his desk for eight consecutive
hours and twenty minutes, and took as full notes as I could on everything that happened.

Fiorello Henrico La Guardia, the most spectacular mayor the greatest city in the world ever had, has characteristics and qualities so obvious that they are known to everyone—the volatile realism, the rubber-
supple grin, the flamboyant energy, the occasional vulgarisms. But the
mayor I spent these uninterrupted hours with showed more conspicuously some qualities for which he is not so widely known. He picked
what he called a "desk day" for me to sit in on. He did not inspect a
single fish market or visit a single fire. What he did was work at his
major job, administration of the city of New York. What he did was
to govern, to put in a routine day as an executive. Routine? Yes—but
wait.

"Everybody talks about the mayor's 'temperament'—which doesn't
exist!" Reuben A. Lazarus, one of his closest associates and his legisla-

tive aide, told me. Mr. La Guardia really runs the entire machinery of New York City, in all its dazzling complexity, single-handed or, let us say, with his own two good hands. Temperament? There is no time for it—unless it happens to serve a useful purpose.

Just once during my ten hours the mayor lost his temper (ten because I had two more hours with him after his official day was done). Then in a second he was grinning. "When I get excited and blow off like that," he winked, "it was all planned two days ago."

The mayor said that he would pick me up at my apartment, and his car came by at 9:12 A.M. With him was Robert Moses, commissioner of parks. It was seventeen above zero outside; the mayor wore no overcoat but he kept a warm rug on his knees. We swept downtown while Moses went through a pile of papers and the mayor rapidly gave his decision on point after point.

Sample of the talk:

Moses: "You can't do that. There's a constitutional inhibition." The mayor: "Can't I? Well, work it out yourself." Moses congratulated him about something mildly. The mayor: "I know I'm good. Go on." Then a difficult decision. The mayor: "Okay! But God Almighty!"

Then—in six or seven minutes as we rolled along—rapid questions and answers on subjects ranging from Brooklyn tenements to how to build a playground.

Mr. La Guardia's car is something. A steel desk swings out over the back seat, and a reading lamp that looks like a small searchlight can focus on it. A special radio of course—which intermittently barks out news of police alarms and fires. A fan, a locked compartment full of guns, and a telephone. I asked the mayor if it worked. He told me about an occasion when he had called the lord mayor of London, from the moving automobile in the streets of New York, to invite him over for a visit. "My dear fellow," replied the lord mayor (and Mr. La Guardia reproduced his accent with ripe and luscious flavor), "I'm only in office for a year, don't-you-know, and I have twenty-five hundred social engagements already!"

We arrived at City Hall at 9:29. A man was waiting for La Guardia on the outside steps. The mayor bounced right past him; one might say he bounced right through him. Bits of conversation floated behind "Hizzonor" like darting minnows. "I want to talk to Patterson about that. Bob will follow up. Write him a sympathetic letter." We were in the mayor's office by 9:31.

It is one of the pleasantest offices I've ever seen—a large room painted white, with a coal fire at one end; though on the ground floor, it is extraordinarily quiet. Also it was hot—very hot. The mayor dislikes too much fresh air. The fire boiled and bubbled. On one wall hangs a

portrait of President James Monroe, and on an easel is a charcoal sketch
of Puccini. Next to the desk is an immense wooden contraption built like
a trough; it contains the active files for which there is no room downstairs. Then on a mantel I noticed a violin, a gift from Jascha Heifetz.
It is made of aluminum and is the substitute violin Heifetz used when
traveling in the tropics.

The mayor's technique of work is this. First, he has no telephone
—at least none is on his desk. During eight hours and twenty minutes,
he used the phone only once. When he does use it, the call comes outside in the anteroom where Miss Betty Cohen, a secretary, who reads
his mind with electric swiftness, stands faithful guard; the door between the office and this anteroom is always open, and the mayor
marches briskly in to take the call. Miss Cohen leaves her cubbyhole
and walks to Mr. La Guardia's desk fifty or sixty times a day. The mayor
seldom leaves his chair. But, while seated, he goes through a considerable amount of movement. He sits back, pounces forward, swings
around. He leans back so far that his feet leave the ground. Without
actually leaving the chair, he goes through practically every physical
motion known to man. Meantime his face and hands are perpetually
active. His glasses fly up over his forehead; he shoots his fists out; he
grimaces, chortles, frowns, nods, shrugs, beckons, leers. There is never
a lost second between one appointment and the next. I was fascinated
to see how this was arranged, because there are no audible buzzers or
bells. But a light flashes on Miss Cohen's desk when the mayor wants
something. A new visitor is announced by the expedient of Miss Cohen
walking into the room and slipping a piece of paper with a name on
it on top of the appointment pad. The name is never mentioned aloud.
So there is no interruption of talk with whatever visitor is with him at
the time.

I sat most of the day at the corner of the big desk. No one paid any
attention to me except to smile. Sometimes the mayor introduced me;
sometimes he did not. Only seldom did I get a chance to ask him some
of the questions I badly wanted to ask. There was never enough time.

From this point on I shall try to give a picture of the La Guardia day
by listing each appointment and activity exactly as it came.

9:43. "Get me Judge Wallace on the phone." This to Miss Cohen.
9:43. He started going through his mail. He gets five hundred to
six hundred letters a day, which his secretaries winnow to forty or fifty.
They attach to each of these a pink slip, summarizing the contents.
The mayor goes through the forty or fifty with intent and conscientious
care, but swiftly. Three secretaries stand by the desk. Miss Cohen superintends operations generally, and two other girls take the dictation.
This is the way the mayor's talk went. "Tell him to work up some-

thing, quick." "I'll want to write to Stimson on this." "Memo. Ed. see me."
"Tell Jones to come in today." "All fixed for tomorrow at two?" (The
mayor was going to Washington.) "When are you returning me?" Then
picking up a letter he scowled and paused. It was from someone in San
Francisco, asking advice on crime prevention. He dictated a succinct
reply. Of twenty-odd letters this was the first he answered.

9:47. Judge Wallace was on the phone and the mayor left the room
to talk to him.

9:49. More letters. He sorted them like playing cards. "I'll want to
talk to Anna Rosenberg about this." "No." "This is for Brundage." "You
can reach him in Washington if you want to." "Write a pleasant answer."
Then a long pause; he read a four-page letter, and put it aside carefully
without comment. More short letters. "If it's on the sidewalk, it's the duty
of the abutting owners to clear the sidewalk." "It's my impression I
asked you to comment on this tax memo, *in re* schools. Please return,
with constructive suggestions." A gesture of scornful dismissal: "Never
heard of this guy." Then: "Please investigate. Police to move for revoca-
tion." "Give this to Newbold Morris." "I don't know if this is a police
job or FBI job. Deserves careful study, skillful investigation." Then
(rattling a paper): "Please remember this name. Underline it. I want
you to be able to identify him." On something else: "Let it sleep." Then:
"Children's Museum, Brooklyn." "Breaks in water main. Let's get a
special file on this. I want a comparison for the last ten years." "Oh,
for goodness' sake, we never answered this. 'My dear Mrs. X . . .' "

10:27. Letters seemingly finished. Then came one more, to his good
friend Montemezzi, composer of the opera *Love of the Three Kings.*
"Okay, girls, that cleans us up." As the secretaries left the room, he
called to Miss Cohen, "I want to see Chester Bowles tomorrow. If he says
lunch, say 'No'; it's hard on him." Then a second instruction: "Can I
see Ickes? Tell him it wouldn't be a bad idea to have X. X. there." Then
to somebody new who popped into the room and whom I was not able
to identify. "This is manpower. This is testimony. This is very good on
police."

10:28. The mayor leaned back. I asked him about the big trough of
files. "I'll tell you a little story. Files are the curse of modern civilization.
I had a young secretary once. Just out of school. I told her, 'If you can
keep these files straight, I'll marry you.' She did, and so I married her."

10:35. Instructions to Miss Truda T. Weil, his education aide. "We've
been planning a vocational high school for the maritime trades, to train
stewards for the Merchant Marine and so on. . . . But will this be necessary after the war, considering the number of men to whom the Navy
will have given training?" He and Miss Weil talked it over. He ordered
her to dig up background.

10:39. Press conference. Eight or ten reporters, the men regularly assigned to City Hall, came in and asked questions about gambling in connection with basketball. The mayor demonstrated a fierce puritanism. "We *must* protect amateur sports; we can't have people corrupting kids who are playing *games!*" Then a violent onslaught against the "tin-horn chiselers, the big mouths, the procurers." "What's wrong with the newspapers and the courts? People abuse the police for doing their duty and enforcing the law; they abuse me when what I am doing is to protect the home." Then an onslaught again. "Dirty little pimps who say their constitutional rights are being violated when as a matter of fact all they've got is good connections!"

10:55. The mayor said, "This is a lull. I had planned to open a tunnel." So I had a chance to ask some questions. But not many. The lull lasted until 10:58.

JG: "What's the hardest decision you ever had to make?"

La G: "Damn it all, I've never been able to keep a diary. The days are too crowded. There are tough decisions every day. I could write a book, about twenty of 'em. . . . When I came into office this city was bankrupt. Its revenue was hypothecated. I had to put it on a pay-as-you-go basis. Taxes. Everybody thought, 'That damn fool of a new mayor is committing suicide.' . . . I didn't give it a thought. Usually when you ask a public official what he plans to do, he'll think in terms of the next election. I've never worried about the next election. I've never belonged to any political party for more than fifteen minutes. . . . Why do good public servants break with political parties? It's so simple. The political people never ask you to do anything that's *right*—and that you're going to do anyway! No. What they want you to do is all the things that are wrong."

10:58. Dr. Ernest L. Stebbins, commissioner of health, and Judge Robert McCurdy Marsh. Discussion of meatless days. The mayor was silent for six or seven minutes, listening to Stebbins hard; this was his longest period of silence during the entire day. The judge was about to be sworn in as a member of the board of health. Someone asked, "Are you going to ask the press?" and the mayor replied, "Let's not make a secret of it." The newspapermen entered, and he swore Judge Marsh into office.

11:35. I asked the mayor how he accounted for his own hold on the electorate. "There's a fundamental political fact about the city of New York. The stratification isn't by parties. Ultraradicals, ultraconservatives: they both vote *for* me! Otherwise I could never break through. A well-informed electorate understands that the essence of municipal government is housekeeping, to make a city clean and keep it that way. What am I proudest of? Oh, well!" He grinned, and then became serious. "That I raised the standard of municipal government everywhere in this country, by raising it in New York and so proving it could be raised!"

11:37. Man announced. "Oh, I don't want to see him now." Pause. "Well if he's here, let him in." Man entered. "Hello, Fiorello." Five minutes' chat on textbooks, leading to the point that "education must *not* be rationed," and on the curious fact that there seemed to be plenty of paper for racing sheets and stock market reports, but none for reprints of modern classics for the schools. "What I'm thinking of is the class of 1957. Teach 'em English from Grade 1A up. Proper English."

11:47. Miss Weil again. She said, "I drafted the report. Thought you wouldn't have time to look. But . . ." The mayor read through the draft. Miss Cohen came in. Signing checks, fixing up petty cash. Then a minor crisis. The mayor (an angry mutter): "If they don't know my stand on that by *this* time!—"

11:50. Mary Dillon, president of the board of education. To me in parenthesis: "Remember, you're to write about the city, not the mayor." Then fifteen minutes of vivid argument with Miss Dillon. Expostulating, "Mary—after what we've gone through together!—" Points at issue: lunchroom situation; centralized purchase of food; transfer of personnel. "Let me handle him. You'd have trouble with that hombre." Then a quarrel full of violent comedy about whether somebody should, or should not, be hired for a job which would entail raising his salary from $6,500 to $7,500 a year. The mayor fought like a tiger to keep the figure down. But Miss Dillon explained patiently that the man was, at the moment, indispensable and his appointment an absolute necessity. The mayor kept refusing. Miss Dillon suggested a compromise at $7,000. The mayor scornfully kept on saying "No!" Then she left the room after discussion of other matters and at the very last moment, at the door, she called over her shoulder, "$7,000?" The mayor grunted, "Well—okay!"

12:05. Dictated a memo on books. "Pick your books as you would your friends. Have Emerson in your home. Ever see a movie that was a bit over your head? Well—it was because you haven't read enough."

12:12. Henry M. Brundage, commissioner of markets. Quickly followed by—

12:15. Delegation of eleven retail butchers and chain store representatives. But interrupted by—

12:16. An official whom I did not identify. He popped in for exactly thirty seconds, breathless, saying only "How about ODT?" and then adding a quick interjection, "Yes but the road to Rockaway!"

12:16½. Butchers' delegation resumed. Long, tangled, tortuous discussion on the meat shortage. Problems: How about kosher stores? Can chain stores just close their meat counters on meatless days? What about the unions? What about fish? ("Anybody here know anything on fish?") How about the men who boned the meat the night before? "We've screamed our heads off at OPA!" Why weren't cod and haddock available at the retail prices the mayor gave during his last broadcast? Why can't you use the neck bones that the Army discards? Long argument with butchers on just how a neck is boned. The mayor showed them how.

12:50. Miss Cohen and Miss Resnick. Dictation. "How do you spell calisthenics?"

12:53. Resumption of talk with me on municipal politics and what really makes power in New York. Everybody said in 1934 it was hopeless. Corruption and contagion. But was it hopeless? Look how municipal government has improved everywhere. A sudden bursting but modest smile. Politicians don't like it. Of course not. "*Why* are the machine politicians against me?" (A bray of laughter.) "They've been on a very strict diet, and you know what it is to starve!" Basis of New York politics used to be patronage. Favoritism in contracts; fortunes out of nepotism. "But I harass the bums!" New York City today has $1,126,-000,000 in war contracts. Think of the loot—if old-time crooks and gangsters could get their hands on it!

12:54. Lunch. That is, the mayor had a cup of black coffee, nothing else, and I had a sandwich (of cheese, since it was a meatless day).

12:56. Last year, in 127 days of racing, $400 million was spent on gambling in New York. Most of it in little bets—two-dollar bets and so on. "So—I keep after it." Why? "Because those two-dollar bets should have been spent on food, clothes, shelter, and a smile at the family table in the evening. A guy loses his money; he's ashamed to face his wife; so he drinks; he gets arrogant and they quarrel in front of their kids."

1:09. A representative of the Carey Coach Company. Talk on local transportation, how to ease the rush near Pennsylvania and Grand Central stations.

1:15. Four physicians, led by Dr. Edward C. Costelloe of the fire department. Discussion about men discharged from the Army returning to work. After Dr. Costelloe left I asked, "Don't you ever get tired, Mr. La Guardia?"

"Toward sundown."

1:58. Patrick Walsh, fire commissioner. A man with a lovely brogue: "So your specific orders, mayor, are—?" "My suggestion is to get a court decision." But—"If we go into court on this with one of those political judges, we'll get it in the neck!"

2:05. Miss Weil again. More statistics about maritime trades, and a projected curriculum for the school. I walked with Miss Weil to the door. She whispered in admiration, "All day long—just to get the proper background for whatever decision he will take. What a field he covers! What a grasp he has!"

2:06. Edwin A. Salmon, chairman of the city planning commission and city fuel administrator. Report on fuel supply. Orders: "Get in touch with K. before he has kittens. Then see me once more." Other complicated details. "Damned good, Salmon!"

2:09. An aide in shirt sleeves came in with a bag of tobacco to fill the humidor. "I didn't want to disturb you before." The mayor tossed him half a dollar and said, "Get me some matches."

2:15. William Wilson, commissioner of housing and buildings. He stood while talking. "Well, major." (Lots of people call the mayor "major.") Up to this point, incidentally, except for one phone call and when he swore in Judge Marsh, La Guardia himself had not once left his chair. Mr. Wilson leaned over the desk, shuffled, paced, edged forward on tiptoe, and presented about thirty different matters for attention, judgment, and decision. Most were in the personal sphere, like cases of dispossession and wrangles over property; the mayor took the most prodigious pains to be fair. "Interesting case here, major. Thought you'd like to hear about it." La Guardia looked at a chart describing a certain property, showing the sun area at 9 A.M., 6 P.M., and so on, for different days of the year. Then he took time out to dictate a memorandum to Reuben Lazarus, his aide in Albany: "Keep your eye on all bills affecting multiple tenancy." Then to Wilson: "Call your file Special War File, Pending Availability, Impending Material." Zoning orders. "God damn it, I don't want to hear about it." But he listened. He began to be restless, tapping his knuckles on the desk. Wilson: "Here's a little headache." La Guardia: "Okay, you stick your neck out." Wilson: "I have my budget. I hope you won't trim it." La Guardia: "I won't trim it much." Wilson: "I'm still coming back for more money on demolition, but the budget is smaller than last year." La Guardia: "I'll give you every break I can." Wilson: "You bawled me out over this last time, but listen, the man is over seventy; forty-two years in the service, an absolutely clean record. Here's his card." The mayor looked at the photograph attached. "When this picture taken?" Wilson shrugged. "Okay," the mayor sighed. "If you want him another year, keep him on."

2:38. A lull, arranged for my benefit.

JG: "Whom do you hate most?"

La G (grunting): "Hitler."

"What do you like most?"

La G: "Music."

"What do you believe in most?"

La G (smiling): "Children."

2:44. John McKenzie, commissioner of marine and aviation. Everything from the latest plans for Idlewild, which will be the biggest airport in the world, to an alleged injustice to a blacksmith. "Let's smoke 'em out." "Put a burr under that guy's tail."

3:03. Miss Cohen brought in a letter. "Well, for God's sake! It's from Eleanor!" He spoke warmly and admiringly of Mrs. Roosevelt. Then fished in his desk, pulled out the small green Official Directory of New York City, and carefully checked a detail.

3:03½. Inquiry from WPB, Washington, on statement about restricted lighting.

3:04. (By this time all appointments were about half an hour late). William W. Mills, president of tax commission. Made his report. La Guardia (swiftly): "Congratulations!"

3:06. He rose abruptly, and retired for about a minute.

3:07. Brundage again. What's to be given to the newspapers on meat crisis? Quick dictation of a memo.

3:10. Arthur Popper and Adrian Burke, representing Youth House. What to do with tough kids, thirteen or so. Very volatile; you can't reason with them as you can with delinquents a few years older. Report on Public School Number X, which seems to have more incorrigible boys than any other. The mayor broods: "I'm thinking big along those lines." Then a quick change of mood and a funny story.

3:36. Meeting of the Mayor's Committee on Race and Religion; chairman, Charles Evans Hughes, Jr. Points discussed: Pushcart peddlers and a new Harlem market; problems involving pickles in fancy glasses; savings bank mortgages and their relation to housing projects; discrimination against Negroes in employment; origin of Irish and Italian gangs; how to build a proper community spirit. During this appointment (the longest of the day) the mayor ran every gamut of emotion and expression. He was arch—as when he said to Mr. Hughes, "Can I talk to the committee about the things you thought I was so emotional about last time?" He was gloomy—as when he wrapped his hands about his head and groaned about the need for social workers. He was anecdotal—as when he told a spirited and irreverent story about General Charles de Gaulle. He was ironic—as when he said, "Now, let's be good Anglo-Saxons; don't lose our heads like all those Latins up in Albany!" He was contemptuous—and with highly appropriate gestures—talking about "the fakers in the housing racket, experts who couldn't build a doghouse!" He was gay—again with fitting gestures—when he tantalized the committee by saying, "Now go ahead and make your own mistakes!" He was enigmatic—as when he said blandly, "The publishers say, 'We have to print the news.' But there are two ways to print it!" He was sacerdotal—as when he murmured, "I believe in what you will find in St. Luke, but don't ask me what it is." He was impish with paradox when he grinned wickedly, "The Republicans didn't know me very well then, so they thought I was a member of their party, when I was!" And finally, he was intensely sober. His fist smashed down on the desk, and he called out angrily, "So long as I'm the mayor, regardless of race or religion, everybody in this city gets treated on merit and alike!"

4:42. A secretary entered the room and paused pointedly at the door, as if to indicate that time was slipping by. This was the only time this happened all day.

4:43. John Delaney, chairman of the board of transportation, and Newbold Morris, president of the council. Talk on budget. The mayor rapped an envelope. "There's $72 million in this stack of paper!" Then his feet went up on the desk and he yawned. He smiled at me questioningly: "Tired?"

5:01. Grover Whalen and a delegation. Whalen was the only man all day for whom the mayor rose. Civilian defense. Ice show at Rockefeller Center. Building projects. Gossip.

5:32. Signing the day's letters; Miss Cohen and Miss Resnick stood next to him as he went through the pile. An official popped in. "Talk fast," the mayor said. Then, not seriously, "What do you mean by coming in at this unseemly hour?" The official grunted, "I've been waiting since four-fifteen, major." Then last-minute details. Miss Cohen to remind him about something regarding the St. Lawrence Waterway. Somebody dismissed as a *Dummkopf*. Wild rage—a literal frenzy—on discovering that liverwurst sandwiches had been available in the municipal cafeteria today, though it was a meatless day. Then good humor again: "Betty . . . change this. I said I wanted to write a sharp letter . . . well, never mind."

5:39. C. R. Beardsley, commerce department. Last appointment. Then a final call to Miss Cohen. "What do I have to take home with me? Oh, say, don't forget, prepare that second thing for Bowles."

5:46. The mayor stretched and said to me, "Come on, let's go." Then to various aides and secretaries: "Have a car ready. No curb interviews."

5:58. Silly item from a news agency that demanded last-minute attention. Then: "I guess I'm tired too."

5:59. Out of the building and into the car. The mayor took me home with him to have a drink, eat some antipasto, and meet his wife and children. We rolled up the East River Drive and suddenly he grabbed the telephone, calling Miss Cohen on something he had forgotten. We could hear her, but she couldn't hear us; La Guardia was as disappointed as a child that the phone didn't work. We reached Gracie Mansion. Then we talked till 7:55 about Tom Dewey, good food, the sources of Mr. Roosevelt's power, summer camps for kids, Russian foreign policy, and the Atlantic Charter.

I left at about eight. The mayor was going to have a bite of supper. Then he had paper work facing him till midnight and beyond. I felt that I had had one of the most remarkable—and remarkably full—days I have ever gone through. And that Fiorello H. La Guardia is one of the most original, most useful, and most stimulating men American public life has ever known.

~~~~~~

Mr. La Guardia retired from the mayoralty of New York City soon after this was written and died on September 20, 1947, of cancer of the pancreas. Many people in the chapter have gone, but the problems and issues remain much the same.

CHAPTER 25

~~~~~~~~~

The Case of Mr. Crump

This article appeared first in the Reader's Digest, *May,* 1947, *just before
its publication in* Inside U.S.A. *I include it here because Mr. Crump
provides such a remarkable contrast to La Guardia, and also because the
exercise of finding out about this mysterious personage and writing
about him was fun. The era of old-style urban bosses was beginning to
die out when I wrote this. Curley in Boston, Pendergast in Kansas City,
Hague ("I am the Law!") in Jersey City, and varied caitiffs and gorillas
in Chicago and elsewhere were still legendary figures, but their power
was being drastically cut down. Now they are largely no more than
memories of a fragrant past, and bosses today are for the most part
housebroken.*

~~~~~~

M<small>R. CRUMP</small> was the last of the great city bosses to function unim-
paired in the United States. Actually he was more than just a city
boss; he not only ran Memphis, he ran the state of Tennessee.

Two fine old Negroes heard some time ago that the Pope had died.
"Who was he?" one asked the other.

"Oh, a big fellow very important—in a county east o' heah."

"He died, you say? Who do you reckon Mr. Crump is goin' to put in
his place?"

On another occasion Mr. Crump arrived at a political rally and took
his place on the rostrum. A Negro leader made an impassioned speech,
and in his peroration pointed to Crump with the words, "There he sits,
ladies and gemmun, and though his skin is white his ole heart's as black
as your'n or mine."

How did E. H. ("Ed") Crump run Tennessee? The answer could not be simpler. First, the state is usually Democratic by two to one; the total vote runs about 400,000, of which some 260,000 is normally Democratic; in other words, to win any Tennessee election, all you need is something over 130,000 votes. Of these, Crump customarily had 100,000. Sixty thousand of Crump's 100,000 votes were concentrated in Shelby County, of which Memphis is the county seat. Time and again opposition candidates were well ahead until the Shelby vote was counted; then the great Memphis vote drowned them under. Technically, Crump controlled this through the kind of organization and behavior familiar in several American cities, but Memphis, 41 percent Negro, is a special case; it has the largest proportionate Negro population of any southern city. Tennessee is not a white primary state, and the Negro vote is consequently of very considerable value; Crump controlled it for years, absolutely. Tennessee is, on the other hand, most distinctly a poll-tax state, and the poll tax was the chief single element serving to perpetuate the Crump regime.

Beyond all this was much else: Mr. Crump had famous exoteric and esoteric methods. Suppose, like Edward W. Carmack[1] in 1946, you were running against a Crump candidate, who in this instance happened to be Senator Kenneth M. McKellar. You would have found several obstacles in your path, to put it mildly. For one thing, Mr. Crump would have bought advertisements in most of the state's newspapers at considerable cost, in which he called you anything from a "donkey" to a "vulture," with assorted adjectives like "cruel," "treacherous," and "venomous," and said that you had "no more right to public office than a skunk has to be foreman in a perfume factory." You would find, as Mr. Carmack did, that you could find no arena or other site in downtown Memphis available for speechmaking, and that no printer dared make your campaign posters.[2]

Let no one doubt the concrete blistering efficacy of all this. Once the present governor of Tennessee, Gordon Browning, running for governor with Crump's backing, won Shelby County by sixty thousand votes. They fell out, and two years later Crump opposed him when he ran for re-election. Browning then *lost* Shelby County by sixty thousand votes!

In a more personal field Mr. Crump did things with real zest. He donated boat rides to cripples and shut-ins, organized opossum hunts for the faithful, and gave a prodigious annual picnic at the fairgrounds; at a recent one he distributed—free—thirty thousand frankfurters and sixteen hundred gallons of lemonade. He liked to roam around with fire-

[1] Mr. Carmack's father was a famous Tennessee editor, who was murdered in Nashville in 1908 by a political opponent. The tradition of political violence in Tennessee is, as in Kentucky, never far away.

[2] See a series of columns of Thomas L. Stokes in the Scripps-Howard papers, July, 1946.

crackers in his pocket, which he tossed to the children, under pennants and banners streaming with the words THANK YOU, MR. CRUMP.

Not long ago a well-known young attorney who was running for the legislature went to an outing given by one of Crump's cronies; he happened to be playing gin rummy when it was announced that all guests would join up in softball teams. The young man, not dreaming that he was committing political suicide, said lightly, "When the boss says you gotta do something, you gotta do it." This remark was reported back, and incredible as it may seem the would-be legislator was compelled to resign his candidacy and in fact soon found Memphis so uncomfortable that he moved to Nashville. Crump was very sensitive about being a boss; the legislator's remark was not only considered to be *lèse-majesté,* but also an intrusion into the forbidden. The fact that the wretched creature apologized, saying, "I didn't realize what I had said," made no difference. One of the Crump lieutenants dismissed the whole episode by announcing, "Our friend made a mistake; he can now go on his way." Such magnanimity!

Of course the machine could not have existed unless it did "deliver the goods." A minor instance of this is that, the day I met Mr. Crump, he had spent the entire morning in the Memphis streetcars, riding up and down as an ordinary passenger, because he wanted to check on complaints about inefficiency. There is no doubt that Crump gave Memphis good government at low cost; the city had admirable public services cheap. This was no Kansas City. There was no graft, no corruption; Crump never took a cent from the public treasury, nor did he permit anybody else to do so. He was relentless, yes, if anybody really got under his skin; once an entire county was redistricted to get rid of a magistrate he disliked, and once the legislature went to the length of writing specific legislation purely to embarrass one of his enemies. Yet there was little atmosphere of tension or reprisal. One of Crump's most consistent critics, on good and legitimate grounds, was Edward J. Meeman, who has ably edited the *Press-Scimitar* for many years. Crump wrote fantastically vituperative letters to him, signed with a giant floriferous scrawl, but Meeman was never threatened or otherwise interfered with.[3]

Crump, aged seventy-six, looks like three apples. He is a very tall lean man, and under a streaming mop of pure white, cotton-wool hair, his hard, round, red cheeks stand out like apples and so does the hard, round, red chin. He is a vegetarian, and doesn't swear, drink, or smoke. He is president of E. H. Crump & Company, investment bankers, one of the most prosperous real estate and insurance firms in the South. He was born in a Mississippi village in 1875, with traces of Scottish and Nor-

[3] One of these letters began, "Your stupidity at times defeats the cold cruelty and cunning evil with which you seek to inject [*sic*] in your news articles and editorials." Meeman replied by printing it.

wegian ancestry. After working on a farm, Crump moved to Memphis when he was seventeen to make his way in the world; soon he organized a buggy and harness company, and then branched out into real estate. He was about twenty-six when he first went into politics; he was red-headed in those days, and gained the nickname "the red snapper." He was elected to several minor municipal posts, and in 1909 became mayor of Memphis. His hold on the city never slackened for almost forty years; he ran for office twenty-six different times, and was never once defeated; he "assisted" in eighty-seven other elections which his men won. Once he sent out petitions for a mayoralty election with the candidate's name left blank; even so, everybody signed them. In 1940 he ran for mayor; four minutes after his inauguration he resigned the post and took off for New Orleans to see a football game. One odd point is that he has never made a public speech in his life.

Mr. Crump writes famous letters to the newspapers. Those he sends Meeman are soft as silk compared to the philippics received by Silliman Evans, the estimable publisher of the Nashville *Tennessean*. For Mr. Evans, who organized and led the poll-tax fight against him, he reserves the really sulphurous thunder. Mr. Evans once showed me some of these letters. They are really quite remarkable. Crump delivered one in January, 1945, by messenger, in order to avoid possible violation of the postal laws, and after causing it to be read in the legislature as "privileged" matter. He called Evans a man "with a foul mind and wicked heart," with "ventosity" [*sic*] as his chief stock in trade. He called Jennings Perry, then the editor of the *Tennessean* and one of the ablest liberals in the South, "unworthy, despicable, a venal and licentious scribbler . . . with the brains of a quagga," who writes unintelligently on any subject "just as one would expect of a wanderoo." Of a third *Tennessean* victim, the political columnist Joe Hatcher, Crump said simply that he had "a low, filthy, diseased mind" full of "ululation" [*sic*]. The three together—I am choosing only the mildest language—were called "mangy, bubonic rats, yellow to the core." Evans is a doughty character with no mean sense of humor. What he did was simply print on his front page Crump's full and unexpurgated text, under pictures set side by side of Crump, one of Crump's cronies, a "wanderoo" (purple-faced ape), and a "quagga" (a kind of African wild donkey).

No one should think that Mr. Crump is crazy or even some type of monster. Actually—the kind of paradox that so often happens—he is a man of considerable erudition and, when he wants to turn it on, of the most engaging charm. I had no particular desire to meet him. I said to a newspaper interviewer that I didn't care much about how Boss Crump bossed Memphis since the pattern is the same in most cities, but that I would be interested in what forces, if any, bossed the boss.

The phone rang the next day, and it was Mr. Crump himself speaking gently, "So you want to know who bosses *me!*" He said flattering things about my books, and asked me to come right over. I hesitated and he went on, "Really, I don't think you can write about Tennessee without seeing me." Then we had a fascinating couple of hours. When I asked about his organization he laughed in deprecating reply, "Oh, we have friends all over the state," and murmured that he merely likes to "assist things"; he averred that his only real interest was in building a good community, and talked of the work he had done for Negroes.

Mr. Crump's downfall and collapse came in 1948. There were three main reasons, disintegration within the machine itself (state employees were tired of having to kickback percentages of their salaries), liberalizing elements at large, and the personality of a stunning new arrival on the national scene, Estes Kefauver. Crump threw everything he had into the struggle to beat Kefauver, particularly in the primaries. This was open insurrection, and had to be crushed. He took out inflammatory advertisements in the newspapers, tried to smear Kefauver as a "Communist," and employed every trick and shady device known to the politics of Tennessee. But Kefauver came in handsomely (so did the anti-Crump candidate for governor) and the Crump dictatorship wilted into the shadows.

It may be said that Boss Crump gave Memphis "good" government.[4] But almost all the creditable items were the equivalent of Mussolini making the trains in Italy run on time. Perhaps they did run on time, and a good thing too. But at what sacrifice—at what cost to things much more important? Memphis had not really functioned as a democratic community for a third of a century; a whole generation grew up without fulfilling the first and simplest duty of citizenship, that of exercising political choice. Out of laziness and fear, participation in the American democratic process passed Memphis by, and for this civic infantilism Mr. Crump was alone responsible. Stanley Baldwin once wrote that dictatorship is like a giant beech tree—very fine to look at, but nothing grows underneath.

〜〜〜〜〜〜〜〜〜〜〜〜〜〜〜〜〜〜〜〜〜〜〜〜〜〜〜〜〜

I thought that Mr. Crump would be hotly annoyed by this article. Not at all. He wrote me commending it in floriferous terms, and otherwise expressing his appreciation. Politicians, here as elsewhere in the world, have certain unvarying characteristics, among which self-blindness stands high.

[4] Mr. Crump told an interviewer after this article appeared in the *Reader's Digest*, "John Gunther said I bribed the people with good government. Who could want anything better than that?" But people did.

CHAPTER 26

∿∿∿

Caesar of the Pacific

Look *sent me to Japan in June, 1950, to write about MacArthur and the American occupation. The result was a small book,* The Riddle of Mac-Arthur, *which was published early in 1951, as well as a group of articles for* Look. *My wife, Jane Perry Gunther, and I happened to arrive in Japan at an interesting moment—a few days before the Korean War broke out. At that time and for some months thereafter MacArthur was at the summit of his prestige and power. It pleases me now that I saw him when he was at his dazzling best—before the fall.*

In November, 1950, as everybody will remember, the war seemed won. American Marines made a brilliant landing at Inchon and our forces reached the Manchurian border. Then came a devastating counter-attack by Communist Chinese troops, in support of the North Koreans, from their "privileged sanctuary" above the Yalu River. This forced a painful American retreat, changed the whole course of the war, produced an angry military deadlock, and led indirectly to MacArthur's dismissal. President Truman fired him on April 11, 1951.

MacArthur is, I think, the most difficult character I have ever had to write about except possibly Chiang Kai-shek. He irritated and alienated many people. For one thing his superiorities, which he did little to damp down, were almost insupportable. He was first in his class at West Point; his performance there was the most brilliant in many years, and in some details has never been surpassed. His overall scholastic record for the four-year run was 98.14 percent, and in several courses he was the only cadet in the history of the Academy to make perfect marks—a flat 100 percent. He was the youngest divisional commander in France in World War I, the youngest superintendent West Point ever had, the youngest active major general in the Army, the youngest chief of staff, and the youngest man ever to become a full general. He was the only soldier in American history whose father was also chief of staff, and the first full general ever to win the Congressional Medal of Honor—his father won it too. He was the first American ever to become a field marshal in another nation's army, and the first American commander to fly the flag of the United Nations. He was also one of the few soldiers in American history dismissed from his command by a President of the United States while he was in the field in the very middle of an inordinately complex and fluid military operation.

What follows is drawn from several chapters of The Riddle of Mac-Arthur.

WHEN General MacArthur's plane first came into sight of Japan on August 30, 1945, the General was dozing quietly. The softly symmetrical white cone of Mt. Fujiyama became visible, and General Courtney Whitney, his chief political adviser, whispered to another general, "Wake the old man up." The other general was not rash enough to do so, and Whitney took the risk himself. He tapped MacArthur on the arm gently, then pointed to the sacred mountain outside the window. MacArthur woke up, murmured, "Well! Good old Fuji!" paid no more attention, and promptly fell asleep again.

The plane was the *Bataan*, the same private plane that took him to Korea five years later, and then—as now—it was unarmed. No other aircraft escorted it, and none of the passengers carried anything but side arms, even though few other Americans had arrived in Japan as yet, and nobody knew what they would find.

Nobody could guess what treachery there might or might not be. A fierce army of 2,500,000 Japanese, completely untouched by battle, still existed in the home islands. Fanatic militarists had just made a brief abortive revolt against the Emperor for surrendering. MacArthur's decision to accept the Japanese capitulation on the *Missouri* in Tokyo Bay before more than a handful of American air-borne troops arrived has been called the greatest gamble in modern history.

Anybody who enjoys laughter at the discomfiture of experts has only to glance back at some journalism of the period. Professors who studied Japan all their lives, military experts who knew every nook and cranny of the Japanese character thought that MacArthur was taking a frightful risk. There were some—in those days—who in fact believed that the concept of any kind of occupation in Japan would turn out to be impossible. There would be guerrilla warfare for years within ten miles of Tokyo. No American administrator would be safe without permanent heavy guard. The Japanese would devote themselves to passive resistance mingled with the most savage type of organized brigandage. The country would blaze with a permanent flame of hatred for the conquering Americans. And so on.

The MacArthur party landed at a pockmarked airport called Atsugi, used by the Japanese as a Kamikaze strip until a few days before. The General put up for the night in the New Grand Hotel in Yokohama, the only one in operation. It was filthy, decrepit, and alive with small animal life. The Japanese staff, petrified at what was going on, managed to dig up a steak for dinner. General Whitney, sitting next to MacArthur, thought that the food might be poisoned; only by vigorously restraining himself did he resist the spontaneous impulse to snatch the meat away as MacArthur started to eat. MacArthur simply ate.

The Supreme Commander had ordered the Japanese to provide fifty motorcars for the trip into Tokyo the next day, to take care of other members of his staff who came in by air that night. It was a revelation to the Americans to discover that fifty automobiles that actually ran did not exist in the entire Tokyo-Yokohama area.

The party set out for the enemy capital, after signal and radio crews had gone ahead. MacArthur saw several of his officers carrying arms. "Put all guns away," he said.

A few weeks later the General returned to Atsugi to meet Mrs. MacArthur, who came with their son Arthur and his Chinese *amah* (nurse), Ah Chu. Mrs. MacArthur, who knows her husband well, was astonished to discover that there was no guard at all at the airport. The General, unarmed, with one aide, unarmed, constituted the entire reception committee. The group drove back to Tokyo through the broken streets, still packed with rubble, unlighted, and menacingly deserted. "Isn't it dangerous?" Mrs. MacArthur whispered. "Not at all," the General smiled.

These episodes, minor as they are, tell a good deal about MacArthur. They demonstrate his undoubted courage, his instinct for understanding the Japanese, his simplicity in some respects, his fatalism, his fixed sense of objective, and something else that has led him into danger on occasion —a tendency to exaggerated optimism, based on his unalterable conviction that he is a man of destiny.

I heard someone who admires him greatly say, "In the abstract, would you say that it is wise to have a Supreme Commander who never had a single moment of pessimism in his entire life?" Of course great egoists are almost always optimists.

Cracking Down

Some people in Japan, even after the occupation had been going on for several months, did not fully realize that MacArthur was the boss; they thought that the American administration would, in time, go soft. Mac-Arthur's gloves were so coated with kid that the Japanese were tempted to neglect what was underneath. On January 4, 1946, came the first "purge" order, and this was a stark awakening. Three or four members of the cabinet had to be dismissed, because they had been [found to be] militarists, i.e., war criminals, before the war.

The prime minister at the time was the venerable Baron Kijuro Shidehara, a fine old liberal who had always stood out against the war-mongers so far as any Japanese could dare to do. His foreign minister was Shigeru Yoshida, the prime minister today. Both, even though they had opposed the war, thought that MacArthur's purge went too far, and, full of Japanese pride and the instinct to reach for every advantage, de-cided to risk a showdown with MacArthur and announce the resignation of the [whole] cabinet in protest.

Shidehara, fearful of a personal encounter with MacArthur, had a diplomatic "illness," and sent the wily Mr. Yoshida to represent him. The Supreme Commander received Yoshida at once, with General Whitney present. Yoshida thereupon proceeded to say that the cabinet would present its resignation to the Emperor the next day, and the Emperor would then presumably charge Baron Shidehara with forming a new government.

MacArthur, affixing Mr. Yoshida with his famous burning (but cold) stare, said the following: "Mr. Minister, I have the highest regard for Baron Shidehara, and I know of no one better qualified to carry out the terms of MY directive [about the purge], but if the Cabinet resigns en masse tomorrow it can only be interpreted by the Japanese people to mean that it is unable to implement my directives. Thereafter Baron Shidehara may be acceptable to the Emperor for reappointment as prime minister, but he will not be acceptable to ME." There followed, in the words of an official account, "a moment of profound silence." Mr. Yoshida said finally and falteringly that he would transmit this message to the prime minister; General Whitney accompanied him down the corridor to the elevator.

"You understand what the Supreme Commander said, did you not, Mr. Minister?" Whitney asked politely.

Yoshida replied, "Too well, too well!"

The cabinet did not resign. The purged ministers resigned, their places were taken by others acceptable to MacArthur, and the govern-ment continued to function without crisis or interruption, carrying out the Supreme Commander's further orders.

A somewhat subtle point arises here. It might be thought that the episode proves that as of that date the Japanese cabinet was totally sub-servient to MacArthur. Actually the General took the course he did partly because of his policy to let the Japanese themselves run their own show and deal with their own problems in their own way so far as possible. MacArthur did not want to become subject to the charge that he had made the cabinet resign. He wanted it to continue in office, after it had purged itself.

But, from that date to this, no Japanese prime minister or other high official has ever dared to take any major political step without carefully sounding out MacArthur's headquarters first.

Why Doesn't He Come Home?

MacArthur has not been in the continental United States since May, 1937, when he returned briefly to New York (in order to get married there) from the Philippines. Why has he never come back since? How shall one account for the fact that he has stayed out of his own country for almost fourteen years? How can one explain the fact that his son, now aged twelve, has never even seen the United States? Of course travel was difficult for MacArthur during the war; he was a busy theater commander, always short of men and supplies. But other American commanders returned to Washington, if only for consultation, during the war, and several returned a number of times. Since 1945 MacArthur can justly plead the fact that he has been too heavily submerged in duties in Japan, but even so his prolonged absence without even a brief holiday is remarkable.

I asked at least a dozen people in Tokyo and elsewhere, both friendly and unfriendly, how they explained this, and I got a wide variety of answers.

1. Duty. He has the feeling that there is a job to do in Tokyo, just as there was a job to be done in the Pacific during the war, and that it is not right for him to leave until it is completed.

2. His ego. He has an obsession that he is utterly indispensable and that the whole structure of SCAP [Supreme Commander Allied Powers] might fall to pieces if he left even for a month or so. Contrariwise, he is afraid to go home, for fear that his absence might prove that he is *not* indispensable.

3. He identifies himself with the United States and fears that, if he should leave Japan, millions of Asiatics will interpret this as meaning that America is pulling out of Asia.

4. He waited too long. A triumphal return to the United States might be an anticlimax now.

5. Back in America (if he stayed) he would be no more than a retired general—and in Tokyo he is a [virtual] emperor.

Some Tokyo observers believe that MacArthur has so convinced himself of his "divine" mission in Japan that he will stay there till he dies.

(Even so, this would not seem to preclude a short vacation home some-day.) Others believe that he wants to come home now and that it is an acute personal sacrifice for him to have to stay on in Tokyo, but that events in China and Korea make him remain.

If the General ever does leave Japan, those indisputably in a position to know say that he will do two things he has never done before: (a) address a joint session of the Diet; (b) call on the Emperor.

He Almost Never Leaves Tokyo

MacArthur practically never leaves Tokyo, which is another odd and suggestive point. Between September, 1945, and the outbreak of the Korean War in June, 1950, he left Tokyo or its environs exactly twice. He went to Manila for the celebration of the Filipino Independence Day on July 4, 1946, and to Seoul for the proclamation of the Korean Republic in August, 1948. When he journeyed to Manila, he planned to proceed to Baguio and spend a lazy week there; but abruptly after the ceremonies he changed his mind and decided to fly back to Japan at once. Similarly on his first trips to Korea in 1950 he invariably contrived to return to Tokyo by nightfall of the day he left.

What is more, in Tokyo itself, he almost never varies from a fixed routine. Twice a day he drives the short distance from the American embassy, where he lives, to the Dai-Ichi Building, where he works, and back. Occasionally of course there are visiting dignitaries to meet or see off at Haneda Airport, military functions to attend, and the like. But by and large the mile and a quarter between the embassy and the Dai-Ichi constitutes the entire physical experience of his life in Tokyo. This—and only this—is the sum total of his arc.

Something even more extraordinary is that he meets very few Japan-ese. He never, under any circumstances, sees *any* Japanese socially, and his professional acquaintance is limited to a handful. He will receive the Emperor, the prime minister, the foreign minister, the heads of both houses of parliament, and the chief justice of the supreme court, on official business. *Nobody* else. Thus, astonishing as the fact may seem, MacArthur in his five years in Tokyo has never talked at length to more than, let us say, a dozen or so Japanese officials. He carries this policy of exclusion to the most extreme lengths. For instance, Mrs. MacArthur has never met either Emperor or Empress, and he himself has never met the Empress.

For that matter he sees comparatively few Americans. In the early days of the Korean fighting his trips to the front did a great deal to lift up morale, if only because so few G.I.'s had ever seen him before. He seldom reviewed troops in Tokyo; he almost never paid visits of inspection to military posts. One of the chief show places of contemporary Japan is the naval base at Yokosuka, where Admiral Benton W. Decker did magnificent work for several years; it is only thirty-eight miles from Tokyo, but never once did MacArthur visit it.

Why does the Supreme Commander keep himself so rigidly aloof? One reason is that, over seventy, he wants to conserve his energy; he hopes to live a long, long time, and sets his pace accordingly. Another, more important, is that he feels he understands Oriental "psychology," and that the Japanese will respect him more if he is seldom seen. Mac-Arthur has almost become a Japanese himself, particularly in the matter of self-discipline. By being unapproachable, almost invisible, he elevates his own prestige. And, of course, his ego plays a role. God does not choose often to expose himself.

MacArthur's habits of seclusion put, it goes without saying, an oner-ous burden on his subordinates, since he is dependent on them for the quality of the information he receives. Seeing little himself, he has to rely on the eyes (and ears) of others. Are they good enough? This is a hotly disputed topic in Tokyo.

If only in the realms of pleasure and the delights of the picturesque the General pays a considerable price for his austerity. He has not had much fun in Japan, a country in which a great deal of fun is available. MacArthur has never (during this tour of duty at least) squatted on a *tatami* mat to have a ceremonial Japanese dinner. He has never seen at first hand the way the Japanese make stairs steep in order to save space, the exquisiteness of Japanese gardens where perspectives of the broadest scope are imprisoned in a tiny area, or the way a Japanese servant cooks water for a bath. He has never met Mr. Yamashita, the bearded dignitary who superintends the bizarre spectacle of cormorant fishing at Gifu, or seen the tissue-paper messages tied to the trees outside the Kiyumizo Temple in Kyoto. He has never bought a ten-cent fountain pen on the Ginza, or gazed at the autumnal landscape through the bland windows of mountain villas near Nikko. He has never listened to a geisha play the samisen, walked through the dark aisles of the cryptomerias in the deer park at Nara, or eaten raw fish with chopsticks.

But do not think that MacArthur does not know a great deal about the Japanese. He does. Many Americans in Japan are lamentably, al-most grotesquely, deficient in knowledge and understanding of the peo-ple they rule; some of his chief subordinates have scarcely ever met any Japanese at all. But there is little lacking in the Supreme Commander's own basic grasp and intuition.

MacArthur and Roosevelt

The General's antipathy to the New Deal is well known, and it is gen-erally assumed that he heartily disliked Mr. Roosevelt. In actual fact this was not the case. He disapproved of much that FDR did, and, during the war, like most theater commanders, he felt that he was being starved while other fronts were favored; also MacArthur would probably have adopted a different strategy for the war as a whole. But his personal regard for Roosevelt was always high, and the two men were good friends for many years.

MacArthur, though this is not well known, owes a great deal of his career to Roosevelt:

1. When he became President in 1933 FDR kept him on as chief of staff, though it was unprecedented for a chief of staff to serve an extra year.

2. Roosevelt encouraged MacArthur to accept the offer from the Philippine government [to command its armed forces] whereby he was enabled to go to Manila in 1936, although this meant his temporary retirement as a U.S. officer.

3. Above all, well before Pearl Harbor (on July 26, 1941, to be precise), FDR drew MacArthur back into active service, and appointed him Commanding General, United States Army Forces in the Far East.

4. It was FDR who ordered MacArthur out of Bataan in 1942, and so, indirectly at least, made possible the long march back.

5. Roosevelt took MacArthur's side in the Honolulu conference held in the summer of 1944, when it was decided (over spirited Navy objections) to push for reconquest of the Philippines rather than attempt to land on the coast of China and elsewhere.

To hear MacArthur reminisce about Roosevelt is a fascinating experience, as I am lucky enough to know. The Hawaii conference just mentioned has been neglected in Roosevelt literature and when I met MacArthur I asked him if he could throw some light on it. He talked for twenty minutes without a stop. As he describes the occasion a great array of admirals—Leahy, King, Nimitz, Halsey—were on one side: he himself was alone on the other. Roosevelt listened to the Navy, and appeared to be committed to its point of view. Then MacArthur put forward his case, and did so with such pertinacity and fervor that FDR began to swing over. Before a final decision was made Admiral King returned to Washington, thinking that *his* policy had been accepted. Roosevelt then called MacArthur in, and told him that he, MacArthur, was the winner after all, and that the Philippines would be the next great target. MacArthur, as he relates this anecdote, does so with the most vivid relish, suggesting rather than overtly stating the weight of forces set against him, and how subtly he managed to overcome them. Roosevelt's last words were, "Well, Douglas, you win! But I am going to have a hell of a time over this with that old bear Ernie King!"

MacArthur had planned to leave Honolulu the next day, because he had a new amphibious operation to superintend thousands of miles away. FDR turned to him, "Douglas, would you mind staying with me one more day?" Of course MacArthur consented, and the two men spent most of the next twenty-four hours together. Most of FDR's talk was about the past, and his mood was poignant. They took a drive out of the city and saw hundreds of tanks ready for dispatch to the Pacific front; Roosevelt asked MacArthur if he remembered the day in 1933 when they had asked Congress for just twenty tanks for the defense of Hawaii, and Congress had refused. And here were tanks massed wheel to wheel as far as the eye could reach.

MacArthur was convinced during this meeting that FDR was dying. Only his spirit, his inner fire, his reservoir of soul, kept him alive even then, the General thinks. When he returned to his headquarters in Australia he told his wife, "Jean, the President will be dead within six months." He was only two months wrong.

A good many analogies exist between FDR and MacArthur. Roosevelt was well-born, devoted to the American tradition, and a gentleman to his fingertips; so is MacArthur. Both were, in a sense, mama's boys; the mother of each lived to a great age, doting on her son. Roosevelt's character was full of dash—even bravado—and he loved to talk; ditto MacArthur. FDR was more of a "fixer" perhaps; MacArthur has a simpler force. Roosevelt was a more subtle person with far deeper sensitiveness to the major pressures of his time; MacArthur is more apocalyptic, and also a good deal fancier and showier. Politically FDR was of course much further to the left than MacArthur. He was a broader person, with more social vision. Yet—strange as it may seem—there are strong traces of the New Deal in SCAP, MacArthur's administration.

MacArthur has several times been compared to Caesar, and there are several analogies worth making, even if they are a bit farfetched— prolonged absences from his native country; subordinates not in his own class; strong will, imperiousness, narcissism; an acute interest in history; great military skill and valor; patriotism complicated by merciless ambition; administrative capacity and the ability to make use of conquered peoples; desire to leave behind him a structure of law; and a taste for benevolent autocracy.

Several other proconsuls whom MacArthur calls to mind, if the necessary allowances are made, may be mentioned. One is Marshal Lyautey, the great French soldier-administrator who created modern Morocco. Lyautey, before his prodigious accomplishments in North Africa, also had much to do with the development of Indochina and Madagascar. He was both a pacifier and a colonizer. Like MacArthur he ruled in part by making full use of the native population; like MacArthur, too, he was used as a catspaw by reactionaries at home.

MacArthur, even though he may be as vain as the Earl of Essex (another proconsul—in Ireland), has great virtues. Mainly they are virtues of a somewhat antique type, more notable in classic ages than our own—strict honorableness, belief in the right, moral courage, and dedication to an ideal. But he has plenty of defects, and is fiercely hated as well as loved. Nobody in American public life is so controversial. One reason is that he seems to personify so rigidly, so flamboyantly, the idea of military caste. Another is his theatricality: what can only be called his hamminess. If you pin down people who dislike him, it is this theatricality that they dislike most.

Still another, since the disaster implicit in Chinese intervention in Korea, is that MacArthur is too "dangerous." Many Americans felt in the grim days of early December, 1950, that his strutting and bombast, his imperiousness and dislike of adjusting himself to external advice— together with shockingly gross blunders in the realm of information— might get us deeper into war. [Of course] he was in an extraordinarily difficult position, since he could not bomb the enemy above the Yalu frontier. Even so, the way he was caught by surprise and the consequent retreat of his stupefied armies can hardly be excused.

What MacArthur Is

First let us put straight certain technical and terminological matters. General MacArthur wears, as the saying goes, several hats. He is:

1. Supreme Commander for (not "of") the Allied Powers, or SCAP. In this role he has become curiously depersonalized, since he is an institution as well as a man. In Tokyo you hear the word SCAP forty or fifty times a day, and occasionally somebody will say "the Scap," meaning MacArthur himself, but generally the term has come to mean headquarters.

2. Commander in Chief, Far East (CINCFE). As such MacArthur is commander of all United States Army, Navy, and Air forces in the area of the Far East Command. His authority in this capacity goes far beyond Japan itself; even before the Korean War it embraced Okinawa and the Ryukyu Islands, the Philippines, the Marianas, and other island groups including Guam.

To whom is MacArthur responsible in his United States Army function? It is often assumed that he has no boss at all, but this is not correct. Like any American general in the field he has at least four superiors: General Collins (Chief of Staff), General Bradley (Joint Chiefs), Mr. Marshall (Secretary of Defense), and Mr. Truman, the President of the United States. A five-star general can, of course, pretty well make his own rules, and nobody has ever excelled MacArthur in his capacity to tear the guts out of a directive, but by and large he is scrupulously careful to maintain the military proprieties. There may be occasions when he communicates secretly with the President, over anybody's head; nobody would know except a few signal officers and technicians. Mostly, however, he proceeds "by the book." After all, as I heard it said, "He himself helped write the book."

One striking—indeed unprecedented—point is that MacArthur has no deputy either as SCAP or CINCFE. His chain of command includes, of course, a chief of staff, but there is no second man in the MacArthur organization, and never has been.

3. Since July 8, 1950, MacArthur has been United Nations commander in the Korean fighting, under the blue-and-white United Nations flag.

4. MacArthur is not head of state (the Emperor is) but he assumes several of the functions of a head of state. The government of Japan has, for instance, no relations whatsoever with the outside world except through SCAP. A foreign diplomat assigned to Tokyo is accredited, not to the Emperor, but to SCAP, and it is MacArthur, not the Emperor, who receives ambassadors, heads of missions, and the like. He is a kind of baby sitter for the entire nation.

In blunt fact MacArthur's authority is so great and his powers so sweeping that he is the actual *ruler* of Japan. The manner of rule is often indirect, and a semitransparent façade is carefully maintained behind which Japanese authority is exerted in many fields, but MacArthur is in fact the all-powerful boss of eighty-three million Japanese, and will remain so until a peace treaty is signed.

Operating through the channels of the Japanese government itself, MacArthur by a single word can outlaw from public life any Japanese; he can disband any Japanese political party, order new elections, dissolve parliament, set aside the government, and rule by direct military order if necessary. Constitutional authorities differ on the question whether or not he could actually fire the Emperor.

Powers of this formidable nature are unique in American history, and it is a tribute to MacArthur that he has used them with such moderation. The British have been accustomed to producing viceroys for generations, and men like Clive, Curzon, Warren Hastings, and Cecil Rhodes are known to every schoolboy, but no American has ever held quite the job MacArthur holds. Not the least amazing fact is that he reached this unprecedented power through a series of circumstances partly haphazard and fortuitous.

Aspects of the MacArthur Character

Against this backdrop we proceed to explore some of the Supreme Commander's personal qualities, his root sources of power and attributes.

His dominating characteristic, next to courage, is probably ego. Out of this ego, which is measureless, come some of his most useful characteristics, like confidence, magnetism, and the capacity to inspire utter devotion in his followers. Out of it, too, come some negative traits like his touchiness and sensitiveness to criticism, which are accentuated by the extreme touchiness of his staff. Also he has a conspicuous tendency to reward loyalty too much for its own sake—to count too much on old comrades in arms who have grown with him during the years. There should be newer blood around MacArthur. But he will not tolerate anybody near him being too big. I even heard it said, "None of MacArthur's men can *risk* being first-rate."

Everybody knows about the tilt of his gilt-edged cap, the carefully pressed uniforms and shining boots, the open-throated profile flung at cameras. The General has terrific style. If, in the abstract, you set out to draw a picture of the quintessentially ideal commander, the perfect type of composite soldier-hero, it might turn out to be astonishingly like MacArthur. Even the fact that he unostentatiously wears *no* decorations whatever is part of his ostentation.

An eminent officer of World War I, General Enoch Crowder, once told a high official of the State Department, "I thought that Arthur Mac-Arthur [the General's father] was the most flamboyantly egotistic man I had ever seen—until I met his son."

Perhaps it is his sense of duty that makes MacArthur egotistic. He can be—and often is—relaxed, gay, and even shy. He carries the plumage of a flamingo, but his voice can be modest too. By no means is he always stern, pontifical, defiant. He is, in fact, almost as notable a winner-over of the reluctant as Roosevelt; persuasiveness is one of his paramount qualities. Still, few people outside his immediate entourage really *like* him. They may respect him, admire him, emulate him, or even worship him (as many Japanese and Filipinos undoubtedly do) but it is hard to imagine him as a universal mass leader, at least so far as the rank and file of the American public are concerned.

But by his own men, the rockfast inner circle, he is adulated. Tokyo is full of retired oldsters who practically stand on street corners to tell you with pride how intimate they are with him even if they haven't laid eyes on him for a year. I have heard him seriously compared to Alexander the Great by a member of his staff, to Alexander's disadvantage. Another officer told me with absolute seriousness that he considered MacArthur to be the greatest man who ever lived.

Another MacArthur trait is his signal tendency to overoptimism and wishful thinking. For instance he did genuinely think in the late 1930's that the Philippines, given time, could successfully defend themselves against Japan. And—to come up to date—he most distinctly did *not* anticipate major Chinese intervention in Korea in 1950. He is, most people in Tokyo believe, far from realistic about the future course of Japanese affairs. MacArthur wants desperately to believe that the democratization of Japan will progress and stick, if only because this would be his own supreme accomplishment. But how much of the SCAP reformation *will* endure no man can know.

It is hardly necessary to recapitulate here the story of MacArthur in World War II. By the summer of 1941 practically everybody knew that war was coming—sometime. Mr. Roosevelt recalled him to active status as a major general on July 26, 1941, and promoted him to lieutenant general the next day, in command of all U.S. Army Forces in the Far East, and the Philippine Army became part of the American command. MacArthur was severely embarrassed by the destruction of his planes on Clark Field [near Manila] on Pearl Harbor day. The Japanese caught him in exactly the same naked and exposed state as they caught the Americans in in Hawaii, though he had ample warning, since the Pearl Harbor attack had come ten hours before.

One may bring this story up to the present again by mentioning that MacArthur has several times made serious blunders in judgment, based on faulty information. The attack on South Korea on June 25 apparently took him by complete surprise, and he thought that the Korean War was won after the landing at Inchon on September 15. Then (though he tried to wriggle out of this by saying that the remark had only been "jocular") he predicted flatly that the American troops would be home by Christmas —only three or four days before they were caught by surprise and hammered back by the Chinese. MacArthur, having scouted the ground personally for what was to have been his final advance, crashed into a colossal trap.

MacArthur had thought—another error—that Manila could be held for a long period, because Corregidor was "the strongest single fortified point in the world." He did not think that the Japanese, or anybody, were capable of the type of attack they launched. Moreover he felt that the Japanese would by-pass the Philippines in favor of softer spots to the south. He was wrong.

MacArthur's positive qualities and merits are, of course, many. For one thing, he is packed with brains even if his judgments have been sometimes wrong. For another, let nobody underestimate his sheer, immense force of character. An American officer who was a cadet when he was superintendent of West Point was asked his opinion of the general. Reply: "He's the only man in the world who could walk into a room full of drunks and all would be stone sober within five minutes."

His memory is photographic, and he is blessed with one of the most useful advantages that mortal man can possess—he reads very quickly.

He has a profound knowledge of military history, and loves to quote from old historians. The story has been told that he got the idea for the Inchon landing by rereading accounts of Wolfe's campaign against Quebec in 1759. Apparently he never forgets *any*thing. It is only a minor sidelight, but it certainly impressed me that in Tokyo in 1950 he recalled vividly and accurately some details of a conversation I had with him in Manila in 1938. Once he was discussing proposals to modify the original plans for the American invasion of Honshu, the main island of Japan. On his own authority MacArthur was working over the directives that had been sent him from Washington, and he wanted to land in a different place, north of Tokyo. Someone pointed out that the surf along that particular stretch of beach was apt to be nasty. "Certainly," the General said. "I remember seeing it when I came out to Japan with my father in 1905."

Dennis McEvoy, the representative in Tokyo of the *Reader's Digest*, presented his wife to the Supreme Commander some time ago. MacArthur began to reminisce about a prize fight he had seen in company with her grandfather, M. H. De Young, in San Francisco *forty-seven* years before. The General remembered who had won the fight, who had fought in the semifinals, and what other guests were in the party.

He has a pleasant wit. At lunch in Tokyo, when he happened to be talking about the Prince of Wales, I asked him if he had seen an article in *Life* wherein the Duke of Windsor describes a golf match he had played with Emperor Hirohito in the 1920's. Both these regal figures were crown princes then. It became clear to the Prince of Wales that Hirohito had never had a golf club in his hand before, and so the Prince politely pretended that he too could not hit the ball. MacArthur laughed and then seized the point at once. "How pleasant that two men destined to be heads of state should be gentlemen with each other!"

That he talks a great deal—and eloquently—is famous. I have seldom met anybody who gives such a sense of the richness and flexibility of the English language; he draws out of it—like Winston Churchill—as out of some inexhaustible reservoir. His manner of delivery is somewhat jerky; his choice of words, again as with Mr. Churchill, is often archaic. Of course, like many great talkers, he never stops; he is an old-fashioned monologist par excellence.

General Eisenhower called on him in Tokyo during the period when both men were being conspicuously mentioned for the Presidency. Eisenhower was before the war a junior member of MacArthur's staff in Manila. The two generals respect one another heartily. In Tokyo, however, members of the MacArthur entourage are blindly, savagely jealous of Eisenhower and his political prestige and popularity. Eisenhower could not get a word in for three-quarters of an hour, while MacArthur reminisced about old times. Then Eisenhower interrupted to say, with emphasis and much elaboration, that he did not think that any military man should be President of the United States. His sincerity was manifest. But MacArthur cocked a wary eye at him and said, "That's the way to play it, Ike."

Finally, MacArthur's physical courage is legendary; it is quite safe to say that no general officer in modern history, let alone a theater commander, ever took such risks. Time and again, in both world wars, he has exposed himself to brutal fire in a manner reckless—but casual— almost beyond belief. He never wears a steel helmet, and seldom carries arms. He stalks a battlefront like a man hardly human, not only arrogantly but lazily. The attitude is Napoleonic; the bullet that will strike him has not yet been cast. Japan is a country notorious (until recently at least) for its addiction to political assassination; but MacArthur never takes any but the most primitive precautions. He enters and leaves the Dai-Ichi four times a day, every day of the year, and invariably a crowd of from fifty to a hundred Japanese assembles by the doorway to watch him. Traffic is not permitted on the streets while he moves, and an elevator is held for him within the building, but the crowd itself is not watched, and MacArthur is never (nowadays) accompanied by a guard of any kind. Any crank could throw a bomb or grenade. He pays no attention.

A distinguished American admiral and specialist in the newly developed art of amphibious warfare was sent to MacArthur's headquarters in 1943. The General greeted him with considerable coldness, cast indirect aspersions on his ability, and then flatly warned him—without quite going so far as to insinuate that he was a "spy"—that he must not communicate directly in any way with his bosses in Washington, King and Leahy. "If you do," MacArthur intoned, "ECHOES WILL BE HEARD!" The admiral considered himself insulted, and was bitterly resentful, as indeed he had claim to be; he knew that MacArthur had a perfect right to demand loyalty, but not to forbid him proper contact with his own superiors.

For some months their relations were of the stoniest, though the admiral, a good soul, dutifully proceeded with his job. Then came an important landing, and the admiral accompanied MacArthur onto the beach immediately behind the first assault wave. MacArthur was so impeccably uniformed, so polished, creased, and immaculate, that the admiral became doubly furious—especially when, under hot fire, he summoned photographers to come up and take their pictures. A shell exploded a few yards from the group. The admiral—and the photographers—instantly fell flat on their faces. A few seconds later, he peeked up. There was MacArthur, in the midst of smoke from the shell, standing straight as a staff, his chin high, his arms calmly akimbo. The ad-

miral slowly crawled to his feet, and wondered in trepidation how Mac-
Arthur would greet him. There was a pause, and then came the Supreme
Commander's voice, "Damned glad, admiral, that *some*body on my staff
has sense enough to lie flat!" From that moment to this, the admiral has
adored him.

MacArthur: Personal

MacArthur's first wife, whom he married in 1922 when he was forty-two,
was Louise Cromwell Brooks, the stepdaughter of the Philadelphia millionaire Edward T. Stotesbury and sister of the James Cromwell who
married Doris Duke. MacArthur met her when he was superintendent
at West Point. His family, though comfortably fixed, was an Army family
and not rich; now he was hurled upward into multimillionaire society.
He did not like it much. MacArthur is not gregarious; he is austere; he
does not care for upper-bracket excesses and trivialities. Nor did Mrs.
MacArthur enjoy life in the Philippines, which she apparently thought
was the equivalent of transalpine Gaul. She divorced him in Reno in
1929; thereafter she married, first, Lionel Atwill, the well-known actor,
and second, Alf Heiberg of Washington, D.C. MacArthur does not mention her in his biography in *Who's Who*.

In 1935 Mrs. Arthur MacArthur, the General's aged mother, journeyed out to Manila to see her son, and on shipboard met a youthful,
charming southern lady named Jean Marie Faircloth, of Murfreesboro,
Tennessee. Miss Faircloth, born to wealth, was taking a cruise around
the world. MacArthur's mother, a southerner herself, liked her, thought
that she would be an ideal wife for her son, and asked her to stop off in
Manila. The General and Miss Faircloth fell in love, and were married
in New York (at the City Hall) on April 30, 1937. Mrs. MacArthur is
nineteen years younger than her husband. They have one son, Arthur,
born in Manila, who is twelve.

Mrs. MacArthur is animated, dark, neat, pretty, and alert. She misses
nothing. She is vitally important to her husband's life; he is crazy about
her, and she worships him. She calls him not "Douglas" nor by any nickname, but "General," but this is not an example of stuffiness or awe of
her husband; rather it represents a type of traditional southern courtesy.
Nevertheless it is something of a shock to hear her address him as
"General" across an informal luncheon table. Mrs. MacArthur takes a
good deal of the load off the Supreme Commander's shoulders. She
represents him at multitudinous social functions (to which he never
goes at all), pays his respects to various dignitaries, and, when he entertains at the embassy, is a perceptive hostess. As a rule she awaits her
luncheon guests in the large embassy drawing room, and talks to them
with cheerful high spirits till—sometimes half an hour later—the Su-

preme Commander enters. As he comes in the door, which is a tidy distance away, she utters a mild exclamation like, "Why, there is the General"—almost as if he were an unexpected visitor. He advances rapidly, grasps her, says, "Jeanie . . . Darling!" and kisses her warmly, in front of the guests, as if they had not seen one another for weeks, though they have in all probability not been separated for more than two or three hours. During lunch she carefully assists in giving the guests voice, in case they are too timid to talk or in the event that the General's eloquence is in full majestic flow, by interrupting gently and saying, "But General, Mr. X wants to ask you about this-or-that." Previously, before he has entered, she has found out tactfully what subjects the guest is most eager to discuss.

Mrs. MacArthur maintains her role without the slightest pretension. At parties she does nothing to differentiate herself from other officers' wives, though, of course, people new to Tokyo feel a certain thrill when she enters and the assemblage whispers, "Mrs. MacArthur has arrived." She stands in line to cash a check at the bank like anybody else, shops at the PX, asks no special privileges, and is universally admired.

My wife and I had the good fortune to attend a MacArthur lunch, and we were the only guests. What struck me first was that the General was not so tall as I had remembered him, or as his photographs seem to show. He is extraordinarily handsome—beyond doubt one of the best-looking men of our time; handsome not merely from the point of view of conventional good looks, but with a magnetism, a vitality, that come from within. Also he looks amazingly young. His hands—sensitive, slim hands, those of an artist or a surgeon—look somewhat frail, and they tremble slightly, but the appearance as a whole (I am not exaggerating) is that of a man of fifty, not seventy, moreover, a man of fifty in the very best physical condition and at the top of his form.

I asked Lt. Col. C. C. Canada, his personal physician, if MacArthur was a good patient. Answer: "I don't know. He's never sick." And in plain fact he has not lost a day on account of illness for almost thirty years.

This is the more remarkable in that he works so hard. But he has established a peculiar routine, which gives him plenty of time to relax. He gets up rather late, has a leisurely breakfast, does some (but not much) paper work, and sets out for the Dai-Ichi at about 11 in the morning, sometimes later. He works till 1:45 or 2, and then returns to the embassy for lunch. After lunch, every day of the year, if possible, he takes a nap, a good nap, for an hour or so, as Winston Churchill does. Then he returns to the Dai-Ichi at about 5 or 5:30, and works till evening—9 or later. Dinner is when he gets home, invariably with Mrs. MacArthur alone. There are no social distractions of any kind. The

General *never* pays calls, goes to parties, sees any outsiders socially, or entertains except at lunch.

MacArthur himself attributes his superb physical condition to three things. First, the daily nap. Second, his abstemiousness. He eats very little, and has not had a drink (except rarely on ceremonial occasions) since he was called back to active service in 1941. He smokes in moderation; his corncob pipes are well known. Third, he has the wonderful advantage—like Roosevelt—of being able to fall asleep almost instantly. He never worries about a problem once the day's work is done.

He takes no exercise whatever, which some people think is odd. But, talking to people in his office, he paces a great deal; his friends say, in fact, that he covers three or four miles a day pacing, though this can hardly be true.

His routine may seem comparatively easy, but on the other hand he never has a day off. I mean this literally. He works Sundays. He works Easter. He works New Year's Day. He works Christmas. There has not been a single day away from work since he took over in Japan. This is hard on his staff. In fact it is murderous. His leading officers have to keep *his* hours, in addition to doing the work of their own sections, which may mean that, year in and year out, they are on duty from eight in the morning till nine or even later at night, with never one day off— not even July fourth. Nobody on MacArthur's immediate staff can possibly have any social life, because the General is apt to demand their presence at any time, and of course they cannot accept normal luncheon or dinner engagements because his own dining hours are so late. When they want to get home to their wives at 6 P.M., after a long hard day, MacArthur pops into the office and work starts all over again. Someone once brought up to MacArthur himself the fact that he worked his men too hard, that he was "killing" them. The Supreme Commander snapped in reply, "What better fate for a man than to die in performance of his duty?"

MacArthur almost never uses the telephone once he is in his office— indeed there is no telephone on his desk or even in his own room—has no secretary, and seldom dictates anything. He does his correspondence by scribbling in longhand, often on the back of the letter he is answering. He had about three hundred cables from all over the world on his seventieth birthday; he wrote an individual acknowledgement of each. He writes his own speeches, laboriously and in longhand, after a staff member prepares a draft. He seldom speaks in public, and hates to speak ad lib.

When he issues a statement Japanese newspapers are obliged to print it in full, without cuts. One odd point is that, reproducing anything from MacArthur, the Japanese (and local English) papers always print his name twice, once to represent his actual signature, once to confirm that the name was typed on the original document. "Douglas MacArthur" (signature) is printed in blackface, "DOUGLAS MACARTHUR" (nonsignature) in caps.

He reads all his own mail. This he insists upon. No letter addressed to him personally may be opened by anybody else. To preserve the spirit of his instructions, and at the same time save him effort, his aides slit open *half* the edge of each envelope addressed to him. He then rips it open, and proceeds to read. The General is from this point of view extremely accessible. All anybody needs do to gain his attention is to write a letter.

MacArthur's chief failing as administrator is that he tries to do too much himself. Like most clever people he is inclined to be distrustful. He wants to keep everything close in his own hands, and he passionately loves detail. He himself makes the decision even on such a matter as, say, whether or not a visitor will be housed at the Hotel Imperial, or, if not, where. His principal overall defect is that he does not understand the storms and stresses of the *modern* world.

To return to our lunch. Actual quotations from the General's talk are, of course, not permissible, though there is no harm in giving a rough impression of what he said. What struck me most was his lightness, humor, and give-and-take. The *mystique* of the great commander so surrounds MacArthur that one is apt to forget how human he is. I expected him to be oracular, volcanic, and unceasing. He was all that, but something else too; he laughed a good deal, enjoyed jokes, told some pretty good ones, permitted interruptions, and listened well. This is not say that his talk was fluff. It was not. He talked of the differences between Japan and Germany, of the way the situation of Japan has changed because the situation of the allies has changed, of the face of a girl he remembered in Yokohama fifty years ago, of the "thought police" in former days and how they even terrorized children, of a prostitute who won a recent election because all her clients (some fifty thousand in all!) voted for her, of the way the Japanese had believed that the Americans would come as pillagers with fire and sword, of Eisenhower and the denazification program in Germany, of Vincent Sheean, of the Japanese war trials and how below a certain level a war "criminal" was just a patriot, of the Kabuki theater, of the sad state of American journalism, of the decency of the blood and breeding in the Japanese royal family, and of how the Japanese, humiliated and humble, having lost faith and face by the terrible sting of their defeat, will never, *never*, NEVER revert to a life deprived of freedom, because they have now tasted that most immeasurably precious of all human attributes, the right of the free man to stay free.

MacArthur ate almost nothing during lunch, but drank several cups of coffee with heaping spoonfuls of sugar. Part of the time he looked directly at us or his wife; part of the time he talked with his face gazing steadily, fixedly, out of the window to his right. What was he looking for, looking at?

~~~~~~

I think that he was looking at himself. And it was pride, hubris, ego, which finally brought him down. His relations with President Truman and the Pentagon became grievously strained as the military situation in Korea worsened, and, as I have said above, Truman dismissed him from his command in April, 1951. MacArthur wanted to fight the war strictly in his own way, against the wishes of the Administration, and the principle had to be reasserted and established once and for all that in the United States civilian authority is superior to the military. MacArthur, on returning to America, was welcomed by enormous crowds, made a famous address to a joint session of Congress, and testified at length in the congressional investigation that followed. Controversy raged. But the fact could not be gainsaid that the MacArthur career was ruined. He was dead.

Actually he did not die until thirteen years later in 1964. His reputation for military and political sagacity as well as regard for human conditions at large and interrelations between the world's peoples underwent a severe blow immediately after his death, when several interviewers revealed what his plans had been for ending the Korean War.

One of these interviews was given to Bob Considine of the Hearst Press on January 27, 1954. MacArthur told him that he could have won the war in Korea in a "maximum of ten days" in spite of the enormous Chinese concentrations above the Yalu. He said that he would have first taken out the enemy's air power by dropping "between thirty to fifty atomic bombs" on his air bases and other depots strung across the neck of Manchuria, and then sent in 500,000 of Chiang Kai-shek's troops from Taiwan "sweetened by two U.S. Marine divisions." Then it was his plan to spread a belt of radioactive cobalt from the Sea of Japan to the Yellow Sea on the northern rim of the battlefront. Radioactive cobalt, he indicated, is not an expensive material and has an active life of between 60 and 120 years. It could have been spread "from wagons, carts, trucks and planes," and for at least 60 years there could have been no land invasion of Korea from the north. Such is the legacy which Douglas MacArthur would have given to the world.

CHAPTER 27

〜〜〜〜

Ike

A year after our trip to Japan and the Far East Look *sent my wife and me
to Paris to do a story or two about Dwight D. Eisenhower. These articles
appeared on December 4 and December 18, 1951, and presently I expanded them into a small book,* Eisenhower, the Man and the Symbol,
published in 1952. What follows is part of its first chapter.

*Eisenhower was, like MacArthur, at the peak of his military career
when we saw him. He was confronting a momentous decision, whether
or not to return to the United States and run for President. At this time
he had not yet even made it clear beyond doubt whether he was a Republican or a Democrat, but the popular demand for his participation in the
impending American presidential race was overwhelming.*

*Eisenhower provided in several respects the sharpest possible con-
trast to MacArthur. For one thing he did not like war.*

〜〜〜〜〜〜〜〜〜〜〜〜〜〜〜〜〜

EISENHOWER is probably the most popular American who has ever
lived and worked in Europe, with Americans and Europeans both.
This sandy-haired, warm, magnetic man of sixty-one from Abilene,
Kansas, became head of SHAPE (Supreme Headquarters, Allied Powers in
Europe) early in 1951. SHAPE is a kind of "little Pentagon" out in the
woods near Paris, and a case may be made that running it is the most
important job in the democratic world, next to one. The other one is also
something that Eisenhower is interested in, the Presidency of the United
States.

Whether or not Eisenhower will run for President is unknown at the
moment of writing, for the simple reason that the General himself has

not yet finally made up his own mind. Probably he will have come to a decision on this, the most difficult of all decisions ever to afflict him, before these pages appear in print. He is one of the few Americans in history of whom it can be said with a fair chance of being accurate that if he wants the Presidency, from either party, it is his.

As commander of SHAPE Eisenhower is strictly an international official, holding a post for which there is no peacetime precedent. The joke is sometimes made that he is only one twelfth American, since he is theoretically responsible not to Mr. Truman or the Joint Chiefs of Staff in Washington but to a council comprising twelve different nations, of which the United States is only one.

In any case it is Eisenhower who is on the firing line. His is the finger in the dike. If the Russians attack in Europe, it is he who will be responsible for holding them. By pushing a button, he can set into motion troops (not just American troops, but European troops) from the northern tip of Norway to Sicily in the Mediterranean. Nobody has ever had exactly this power before. I asked one of his officers a question about Eisenhower and defense. Perhaps the reply was an exaggeration: "Without Eisenhower there would be no European defense."

But what Europeans like most about General of the Army Dwight David Eisenhower is his marked civilian-mindedness. He has been a soldier all his life, but believes in peace. He does not stand for war, but for defense against war. He does not seem to represent the military class at all, and several times in Europe I heard him described as that odd type, a "peace general."

Eisenhower's popularity is phenomenal even in France, a country not strongly given to the admiration of exterior heroes. Early last year the General made one of his rare trips into Paris, to attend a dinner given to Miss Margaret Truman by President Auriol. After dinner at the Elysée the company went to a performance of *Antigone* at the Comédie Française, the formal, brittle shrine of French dramatic art. The blasé audience paid only the minimum of polite attention to Miss Truman and the President of the Republic; then, a few seconds later, Eisenhower entered the presidential box. There had been no announcement that he would be there but he was instantly recognized, and the entire house rose spontaneously and cheered. No greater tribute could be paid in France to *any*body.

Personal

Eisenhower at sixty-one looks energetically fit. Years may have accumulated in his face, but they do not show much. His face is as pink-and-tan as ever, his high forehead as unwrinkled, and his skin as glossy. His mobile, decisive grin is still practically as broad as the English Channel, and his friendly eyes are so bright a sea-blue that they look like spoonfuls of it.

When I met him in his office for an hour's talk he wore no decorations at all. The room is airy, well lit, and comfortable. He rose several times while talking animatedly, picked up a golf club, and, carefully giving himself enough room, practiced a few swings. He puts on and takes off intermittently a pair of steel-rimmed spectacles. On his desk was one book—Gibbon—and a copy of an American magazine notable for its extreme reactionary views. When I mentioned this he made a gesture of distaste, but I do not know whether he was shrugging off my remark or the magazine. Incidentally visitors are told, before stepping into the inner office, to take off the identification badges which, for security reasons, they must wear on their lapels while within SHAPE. Eisenhower knows that they are necessary, but thinks them unsightly.

A day or two later we had another talk, when the General asked my wife and me to have drinks with him and Mrs. Eisenhower on a Sunday afternoon. Our car pulled up and scratched the gravel in the dim rain (this was near Paris, so of course it was raining) and a GI servant ducked out with a red umbrella. But before we could get out of the car, there was the General himself quietly waiting in the doorway, standing pink and immaculate to say a greeting. No aides, no secretaries, no doorman, no fuss, no protocol, no pomp. I thought what a contrast this made to some other headquarters I have visited—for instance, MacArthur's.

The Eisenhowers live in a fairly big but unpretentious refurbished house. The French government insisted on providing the General with it, and gave him a selection of those available in the region. This one (its official name in American Army parlance is "Quarters No. 1") lies in the Parc de Marnes, near the forest of Marly, which since the eighteenth century has been a hunting preserve of the Kings—and later the Presidents—of France; it is about four and a half miles from SHAPE, and about half an hour from Paris. The nearest village, Marnes–La Coquette, has been painted by many artists.

The Eisenhower house, called the Villa St. Pierre by the French, was built around 1850. A slope of luminous green lawn stretches out from the white porch. Mrs. Eisenhower, in a black-over-rose tea gown, made us welcome. She is a woman of medium height, pretty, with dark hair, bangs, and a nice voice. Only rarely does she meet outsiders. She plays no role at all in the General's official life, except on occasional trips, and has no relish for formal ceremonial entertainment. As a matter of fact the Eisenhowers entertain extremely little; the only people they see socially are members of their immediate entourage, or very close friends visiting Paris.

Once a well-meaning American tycoon wrote a prominent friend in Paris suggesting that he invite the Eisenhowers to a cocktail party, so that he, the tycoon, could meet Ike informally. The party did not take place. Or, if it did, the Eisenhowers were not present. There is about as much chance of getting the General and Mamie to a cocktail party as of getting Stalin or the Pope to a fancy-dress ball at the Ritz.

Presently Eisenhower whisked me out of the room to show me some recent samples of his painting, and to see the house. This is decorated in a simple, semimodern style. The French government offered Mrs. Eisenhower any of the exquisite period furniture that is housed in the *Mobilier National* (a kind of repository of the national art, used to decorate French government buildings, embassies, and the like) but she preferred something nonantique and in the American manner. Similarly she was offered paintings out of the national collections, but she said no.

The servants are American Negro GI's, even the cook. It may seem odd, in the heart of France, where cooking is an advanced and exquisite art of arts, that the General should not have a French chef. But he doesn't, for two good reasons: (a) his simplicity and Mrs. Eisenhower's complete Americanism; (b) security reasons. In the house of the commander-in-chief the important servants must be American. Otherwise all conversations at table would have to be guarded, and nobody could risk leaving documents around.

In blunt fact it would be inaccurate to say that the Eisenhowers live in "France." They live at a comfortable American Army post that happens to be in French territory. Neither they, nor most members of their staff, have any real participation in the life of France. This is a pity. I met one member of the entourage who had only been in Paris twice since his arrival, though the most gracious, civilized, and rewarding city in the world is scarcely half an hour away.

Office Routine and Habits

The General gets up early, like most Army people, and is usually out of the villa by eight-fifteen and at his desk at SHAPE a few minutes later. He usually sees General Alfred M. Gruenther, his chief of staff, first, consults his aides, and is ready for the first appointment of the day at eight-thirty. As a rule he sees twenty to twenty-five people a day, though some of these may be grouped together, as at lunch. The General always (when in France) lunches in his own modest dining room at SHAPE, and almost always there are business guests. Lunch is a strictly utilitarian occasion. "I use lunch," he told me, "to get my basic ideas off." He does not like particularly to see women in his office, and is apt to resent it slightly if a distinguished visitor brings anybody female along. He feels that with women present he cannot talk as informally as he might like, or let off steam. Eisenhower is an extremely loquacious man—much more so than is generally known—and his conversation is sometimes flavored with mild profanity. The range of his visitors is astonishing. I have just seen the appointment sheet for a week. It includes, aside from multitudinous members of his staff, the American high commissioner to Germany, the president of an American university, the Belgian minister of national defense, the head of ECA in Europe, the chairman of the board of a big American steel company, a German politician, several United States congressmen and newspaper owners, the chief of staff of the armed forces of Denmark, an American bishop, the SHAPE historian (in whose work he is intensely interested), the American ambassador to Great Britain, and several old cronies from back home.

Eisenhower hates to read any document longer than a page, and his staff knows this well. He likes to say, "If a man can't get what he wants to say on a single page, then it isn't worth reading. He hasn't crystallized his own thinking." Sometimes, when his aides think that he simply *must* read a report that is longer, they contrive by careful artifice to read it aloud, or, better, to get him to read it aloud himself at a meeting.

He is often frank to the point of indiscretion in casual conversation. During the war he often commented picturesquely on the shortcomings of his own generals and members of his staff. If he sometimes talks too much, it is to avoid saying anything. Sometimes, to feel a person out, he plays dumb. Or, if somebody is trying to get something from him that he does not want to give, he pretends not to understand. He has a marked capacity to delegate authority, and he lets his subordinates make most of their own decisions. But if an officer doesn't seem to know his job, the General can crack down fiercely. There are some things for which he will not forgive an officer. The first is incompetence; the next, being slow. His character is buoyant, but he has a lively, decisive temper, and knows full well how to bang a desk, though he seldom does so. When he loses his temper he is apt to spell out words in an angry yell. He will say, "Where is that memo—MEMO?"

He sandwiches in his paper work and dictation between appointments, or sometimes late in the afternoon. He never—absolutely never—takes paper work home. When the day's work in the office is done, it is done.

Eisenhower is usually referred to by members of his staff as "the General," "the Boss," or just plain "Ike." Never once did I hear anybody use the phrase "Supreme Commander," though that is what he is. Such high-flown terminology is discouraged. This is sharply at variance with the atmosphere around MacArthur, as any visitor to Tokyo will attest. Hundreds of people call Eisenhower "Ike" to his face, but mostly these are civilians. His officers never do, unless they are alone with him or in an intimate small group, and not always then. Even Field Marshal Lord Montgomery, his first deputy, addresses him as "Sir" when they are in conference. Incidentally General Marshall has never once used the expression "Ike." When Marshall writes to him these days, the salutation is still what it always was, "My Dear Eisenhower."

* * *

His talent for conciliation, for welding a team, is one of his salient characteristics. When he is a member of a group not devoted strictly to military matters (as at Columbia University) he is sometimes apt to give his opinions—at considerable length—too early in the discussion; he is overeager, and occasionally naïve. An almost innocent impatience leads him to talk too much. But later, as he sees other points of view developed, he is commendably quick to modify his own. There is nothing static or cramped about Eisenhower. His attitude is always supple and aware. He is open-minded and likes to take advice.

Time and time again, when for instance he met with the Joint Chiefs, he would pull together a meeting that was fraying with words like "Gentlemen! We have been asked a question, and we are not facing it!" People in lower echelons would say, "If we can only get this issue to Ike, it will be all right." On the other hand he has several times been criticized —for instance by members of congressional committees before whom he testified—for being too easygoing. Partly because of his eagerness to please, he would on occasion seem to shift his views unduly, and fail to take a firm enough stand for what he believed in.

Once, in 1947, a friend came back from Tokyo and passed the word to him that men around MacArthur, jealous because he, Eisenhower, was being talked of for the Presidency, castigated him as a "compromiser." Eisenhower was furious. He banged the table. "Compromiser? Ask the Germans if I compromised on Omaha Beach!"

Eisenhower proceeded to analyze the implications of this charge. "If anybody said during the war that I was a compromiser, it really means that they thought I was too pro-British." Then, in rebuttal, he proceeded to outline some important differences he had had with the British. Continually he pressed them to be more enthusiastic in regard to OVERLORD, the invasion of France across the Channel; continually he promoted the subsequent complementary invasion from Marseilles, which the British opposed; continually he fought against any diversions that would have diluted the force of his master attack, such as the Balkan campaigns that Churchill wanted. On the eve of D Day in 1944 he rejected British proposals to call off full-scale airborne support of the operation, which Air Chief Marshal Leigh-Mallory thought would cause disastrous losses. Once, in blunt fact, his opposition to Churchill was so forceful that the prime minister threatened to resign. This was because Ike insisted on going ahead with ANVIL, the landing in southern France, on the date planned in spite of Churchill's prolonged and bitter opposition. Churchill said that he might have to go to the King and "lay down the mantle of my high office," but, even so, Eisenhower refused to budge.[1]

Some American officers, however, thought definitely that Eisenhower leaned too far to the British side in later operations. General Omar N. Bradley voices this complaint forthrightly in his recent memoirs. Eisenhower's staff at SHAEF was "British dominated" and he several times appeared to favor Montgomery against his American commanders. Of course circumstances forced this. Eisenhower had imperatively to keep all his subordinates in balance, and some of these were as temperamental as tenors with sore throats. To keep them scrupulously in check was his job as Supreme Commander.

As a matter of fact the General's ability to compromise was one of the most valuable of all his qualities. In waging coalition warfare—or for that matter in most fields of military or human endeavor—compromise of some sort is necessary almost every moment of the day. Eisenhower became, during the war, the most successful "chairman of a committee" in military history. This was because he had a superlative gift for smooth, energetic tact—for achieving unity among the most widely separated and rival elements. He had the inhumanly difficult task of melting down into a single amalgam the American Army, the American Navy, the American Air Force, the British Army, the Royal Navy, the Royal Air Force, the Canadian Army, various French contingents, Poles, Greeks, South Africans, Italians, Norwegians, Australians, New Zealanders, and heaven knows what else. The amount of skillful leadership this took, if measured in decibels, would make enough noise to split Gibraltar. Consider merely the fact that until 1942 Eisenhower had never held a fighting command. Yet he had to give orders to veterans like Air Marshal Tedder and Admiral Cunningham.

Eisenhower and the Fourth Estate

Eisenhower probably has better relations with newspapermen individually as well as with the press as a whole than any American since Roosevelt. This is the more remarkable in that he does not play favorites, practically never gives interviews, and—strangely enough—is not particularly accessible. Contrary to legend, he is not altogether easy to see. Since he took the SHAPE job he has held only one press conference; this took place on the day that the headquarters became operational. If some-

---

[1] *My Three Years with Eisenhower*, by Captain Harry C. Butcher, USNR (New York: Simon and Schuster, 1946), p. 639. This book is a mine of information about Eisenhower.

body of the stature of Edward R. Murrow, say, or Quentin Reynolds arrives in Paris, the General will receive him for an off-the-record chat, but such occasions do not happen often. To most correspondents resident in France, Eisenhower is almost completely aloof. When a new bureau head arrives for an important agency or newspaper he will see him for a brief courtesy call, but such visits are not encouraged.

At a press conference the General is direct, forceful, man-to-man, and above all modest. The late Stephen Early, than whom there has never been a greater expert in such matters, said after attending an Eisenhower press conference in 1945, "It was the most magnificent performance of any man at a press conference I have ever seen." Eisenhower is almost too modest in his approach. He said at one press conference during the war that all correspondents should pass any direct quotes to the censor, "so that you can correct any errors I might make, at least in grammar." Several European newspapermen, never having seen Eisenhower before, got a lively shock at the SHAPE conference in April, 1951—shock because the General was so unprecedentedly informal. He gave those who did not understand English perfectly permission to interrupt him at any point, and almost seemed to be asking for as much guidance as he gave.

Eisenhower disliked—and dislikes—censorship, and his theater during the war was signally lenient in this field. The contrast to MacArthur and affairs in the Pacific during the same period is remarkable. There news was either controlled at the source, or built up to the personal aggrandizement of the commander. Nothing remotely like this was ever permitted to occur in Europe. One of Ike's rules was, "Nothing about me personally." Censorship on security and strictly military matters was of course necessary, but Eisenhower's press officers held it to a minimum. Political censorship was seldom imposed. During the early days of the North African campaign it was imperative to clamp down on the fierce fratricidal quarrels of de Gaulle and Giraud, but Eisenhower records now that he thinks that even this was an error, and regrets having had to do it.

I met Eisenhower at a press conference in July, 1943, in Malta, and was stunned. Here was the commander-in-chief of one of the most stupendous operations in military history, on the very day before it was to take place; yet he spent sixty-five minutes in solid, earnest, friendly give-and-take with a group of newspapermen and press officers, discussing matters so utterly remote from his own direct responsibilities as radio routes to Tunis and the like. His frankness was exceptional. He said, "Now listen: I want to cooperate with you fellows, and I want you to cooperate with me. You could all gang up and bust me, but I could bust you too."

Some details of this talk were fairly technical from a newspaperman's point of view, such as the differences between the four different types of censorship which existed in Malta at that time. Eisenhower caught most points like a flash. When he failed to understand something, he said so at once. He turned to one of his assistants, General Whiteley, and remarked, "Sorry, Jock, I didn't get that." Once he said to a public relations officer who was pressing him hard, "Maybe I'm dumb; repeat that, please." He wanted to cut all the red tape. I continued to marvel that an officer with, shall we say, several other things on his mind should be giving so much detailed, close attention to such a comparatively minor matter as press communications. He won us all. One of the American censors, a youthful captain, pointed out that one of Eisenhower's own suggestions would not work. "I'm sorry, sir," the captain kept saying, "you cannot do that, because it would violate security, sir." It was refreshing in the extreme to hear such a junior officer tell the commander-in-chief what he could and could not do, and Eisenhower accepted it.

On July 10, two days after the Sicily landings, we had another talk. He was working in a damp cubicle not bigger than ten feet by fourteen; there was a single table covered by a gray blanket and a white blotter; an oil heater was burning, but the clay floor was wet and cold. The General tossed away one of his cigarettes and asked, "You fellows got a dry cigarette?" None of us had. He seemed very pleased at the way the campaign was going. "By golly," he kept muttering, "I don't understand it! By golly, I think we've done it again!" By this he meant that the amphibious operations had taken the enemy completely unawares, and that there had been no serious attack on our landing craft though they were sitting ducks. The General rocked back on his wicker chair, his heels caught in the lower rung. He grinned from cheek to cheek, and told us something altogether new. His grin kept on expanding. "Every once in a while I like to tell you something like this, because you might hear it from somebody else, and if *I* tell you, it shuts you up!"

Some Intellectual Patterns

Not by any stretch of the imagination could Eisenhower be called a highbrow or an "intellectual." His main mental characteristic is drive. He is practical-minded; he hates what he calls "forensics"; theory irritates him and he believes in first things first.

He wrote *Crusade in Europe* in seven weeks, a record any professional writer may well envy. He does not know how to use a typewriter; in the old days he wrote longhand, and now he dictates. *Crusade in Europe* is (unlike so many recent books by generals) strictly his own production. He wrote—or rather dictated—every word. Two friends helped him, however, in editorial revision—Joseph Barnes, then the foreign editor of the New York *Herald Tribune*, and Ken McCormick, representing Doubleday & Company, his publishers.

Eisenhower reads little these days in the realm of serious literature; he has never been of a particularly studious temperament. The coarse joke was heard, when he became president of Columbia, that he was the first president in the history of that estimable institution who had never read a book. As a matter of fact I asked him once what books had influenced him as a young man; he responded with an oddly assorted but typically American list that included *Pilgrim's Progress,* Conan Doyle's *The White Company,* and Mark Twain's *Connecticut Yankee at King Arthur's Court.* As a boy he read a great deal of history, and his favorite hero was the Roman citizen Cincinnatus, which has an interesting relevance today. He still likes to reel off famous dates in ancient history—like 490 B.C., Battle of Marathon—and does it accurately.

What Eisenhower does read today is Westerns, pulp Westerns, the gaudier the better. He is seldom without a pile of these monstrous products. He hates flashbacks in fiction. Always he wants drive, directness. Also he loathes foreign words or phrases in a book in English. "By jiminy, our own language is rich enough, why don't we learn to use it!" His favorite adverb is "instantly"; he uses it all the time, both in speech and writing. His favorite maxim, which he quotes often, is Benjamin Franklin's "We must all hang together, or assuredly we shall all hang separately." Another is from Woodrow Wilson, "The highest form of efficiency is the spontaneous cooperation of a free people," and still another, Lincoln's "Among men there can be no successful appeal from the ballot to the bullet, and they who make such appeal are sure to lose their case."

Once I was sitting with him in Malta when he suddenly had the idea of dictating a brief memorandum congratulating the people of Malta on their heroic resistance to the forces of the Axis; the time had come when the role Malta played in the allied invasion of Sicily could be made publicly known. It was a Sunday and his aides were taking time off. So the General dictated his memorandum to me. He worked on it over and over again, changing a word here, a word there, as he paced up and down the room, nervously excited. "Let's make it epigrammatic; let's make it exquisite!" he exclaimed. Then he paused with a chuckle. "I suppose you think 'exquisite' is a hell of a word for a soldier to be using."

All his life Eisenhower has been interested in the art of writing. His grades were never particularly good in high school or at West Point except in English; in English he was always near the top. He spent some years in the War Department as a kind of sublimated ghost writer, little known as this fact may be. He was put to the task of preparing various papers for his superiors, and did this so well that several officers asked for his services. Also he went to France for a period (few people recall that the Eisenhowers had their first taste of Paris life in 1929) for duty with the American Battle Monuments Commission, and he was author of the admirable guidebook this body issued. Then in 1930, when he was a lowly major, his work came to the august eye of Douglas MacArthur, who had just become chief of staff. For several years thereafter Eisenhower helped MacArthur substantially with his speeches and written work. Great kudos came to MacArthur in particular for his reports as chief of staff during this period, which have been described as the most "classic" documents of their type ever written. Mostly these were written with the competent aid of Dwight Eisenhower. Also Eisenhower wrote part of MacArthur's celebrated "Farewell to the Army" speech when he, MacArthur, resigned as chief of staff in 1935.

Recently a friend happened to ask him what generals he admired most. The first answer was William Tecumseh Sherman, which is fascinating on at least three counts. Sherman said, "War is hell"; he also became president of a university (Louisiana); and he rejected the Presidency of the United States in terms more forthright than have been heard since. Eisenhower proceeded to say that the question of a favorite general had two aspects. From the point of view of affectionate regard, as well as for qualities of leadership in the field, he chose Washington and Lee; from the strictly military point of view, and without regard to personalities, Napoleon and Hannibal. Once he said of Napoleon, "I sure would have liked to have tangled with that fellow!"

Food, Drink, Games, and the Art of Painting

Eisenhower does not need much sleep, but customarily he goes to bed early. He never dozes in the afternoon; one of his aides told me that in seven years he had never known him to take a nap. He drinks sparingly, and never drinks during the day.

For years he smoked like a furnace—sixty cigarettes a day or more. I remember lunching with him in Washington when he was chief of staff, and between 12:45 and 3 P.M. he certainly smoked at least fifteen cigarettes. (It was at this meal, incidentally, that he demonstrated a favorite dessert—hot coffee from the luncheon cup poured over vanilla ice cream.) I asked him what brand of cigarettes he liked and he replied that it didn't matter in the slightest—he smoked anything. I asked him how he managed to endure long official dinners in London where smoking is forbidden until after the King has been toasted—which may be two hours after the meal has begun. He replied that he always tried to persuade the chairman of the dinner to have the toasts right after the soup. I asked him what he did in those eclectic London clubs where smoking is forbidden in the dining room at any time. "Oh, I'd never show myself in a club like that!"

While he was at Columbia the General's pulse rose suddenly, and on doctor's orders he gave up tobacco. He stopped on the instant. Within a week, his pulse had returned to a normal seventy-two, and he has never smoked since. I asked him if he minded it when people smoked in his office. He laughed, "Oh, no. It gives me a sense of moral superiority. I had enough will power to stop smoking, but they have not."[2]

His attitude toward money is to be prudent, but not to be much interested in it for its own sake. When he resigned as chief of staff in 1948 he had no money at all; he didn't even own an automobile. He told me that an old comrade in arms asked him for an emergency loan of $500, and he had the greatest difficulty in scraping this sum together. He disliked the prospect of living in the president's imposing house at Columbia, and fell in love with a small house in Bronxville that he wanted to buy; but it cost $60,000—far too much. "I'd have been paying for it all my life," he said. He was horrified at the expense of maintaining the Columbia house (which required a staff of half a dozen servants); also—a significant point—he refused to take any salary from Columbia. So he had to earn a modest fortune quickly. This he did by writing *Crusade in Europe*. He sold it as a "package," and, since he was not a professional author, the Treasury permitted him to pay taxes on it on a capital gains basis, which saved him a very large sum on income tax.

He has no expensive tastes, and is extraordinarily unsophisticated about most worldly matters. He told me once that he had not seen a Broadway show for years, and [I discovered in Malta that] he had never even heard the name of one of the best known of living American playwrights. For a long period he avoided New York City itself, and spent only one night in it in twenty years. Its Babylonian grandeurs depressed and in fact frightened him. "I'm scared of that darned town," he said.

The General has three basic hobbies—bridge, golf, and painting. One expert told me that he is not a really great bridge player, which he might easily be, because he does not compete regularly enough with extremely good players—the only way to maintain the highest degree of excellence. On the other hand, his favorite antagonist is General Gruenther, who is incontestably one of the best bridge players in the world. But he is too busy to play often. When he does play, stakes are modest. One story is that Gruenther slyly tries all sorts of tricks to improve his game, so as to make him a stronger competitor. Eisenhower is a first-rate poker player—his poker is probably as good as his bridge—but nowadays he plays seldom. Once, before the war, his annual poker winnings amounted to $3,900, roughly what his army salary was. As a result he gave up playing seriously. He did not want to think of it as a business, or become dependent on poker earnings.[3]

[2] The General made the same response to several people, and this story has been widely publicized.

[3] According to Raymond Daniell in the New York *Times*, "He Is Our Eisen and This Is Our Hour," November 1, 1942.

He likes fishing, but aside from golf takes little other exercise.[4] During the war he played everything from badminton to ping-pong at odd moments to relax from strain, and General Marshall persistently ordered him to go riding. Nowadays he does not ride much. Years ago— at West Point—he wrenched a knee badly playing football, and then hurt it again when a stupid instructor forced him to do exercises getting on and off a horse. The injury was so serious that it almost kept him from getting a commission. Also it ended his athletic career, which was a savage blow. He had liked games above all as a boy. The injured knee troubled him for years. He felt ashamed of it. He told me once, "I was like a man with his nose cut off going out into society!"

Whether or not he is a good shot is a moot point. Several of his biographers mentioned a comedy episode that occurred at Caserta, Italy, late in 1943. His advance headquarters had just been set up there, and a rat was discovered in the General's bathroom by Telek, his famous Scottie. The rat was, according to observers, sitting placidly on the toilet seat, and Eisenhower determined to dispose of it himself. He took out his pistol, put on spectacles, and began shooting. He missed four or five times, as the rat became mobile, and finally it had to be dispatched by someone else.

Finally, painting. The General started to paint some years ago, and has been at it enthusiastically ever since. Painting relaxes him and gives him the challenge of a problem in a field utterly unrelated to his daily work; often he has found out, while doing a canvas, that his subconscious mind keeps on working on some military issue that has been bothering him, and when the canvas is done the military issue is settled too. He paints mostly at night; the lack of natural light does not trouble him. Sometimes, particularly if he is at work on a landscape, he refers to colored photographs taken previously of the same scene. Once, surveying the lawn outside his house, he told a guest that he would like to paint it, but that "the greens were too much for him." He showed me in Paris several portraits he has done recently, one of his two grandchildren, the other of his close friend Louis Marx, the New York toy manufacturer. The children are painted together, like twin cameos, against a flat background; that of Mr. Marx is on beige. "Never tried that color before!" the General exclaimed with satisfaction. Eyes are sometimes difficult, but the mouth is the hardest feature to paint, Eisenhower thinks.

[4] His French hosts, knowing that he cannot easily go fishing elsewhere, recently stocked a pool nearby. Then they played a mild joke by instructing the groundkeeper to feed the fish to capacity. "Make the General," they said, "fight for his fish." As a result he scarcely got a nibble the first time he went fishing there; the fish were too full of food.

Basic Qualities: Modesty and the Civilian Touch

One of Eisenhower's principal sources of power is his obvious integrity, his sincerity and capacity to inspire confidence. Years ago I met a British general in Algiers who had just had his first contact with him as commander in chief. His words were, "By Jove, what a person to rely on!" The General's liking for people, his spontaneity, his instinctive ability to understand the other person's point of view, make him little short of a prodigy at personal relationships, though he sometimes seems to lack humor. And his charm is legendary. When he enters a room, almost any room, a ripple of emotion seizes those present; they catch his glow.

Another quality is his directness. Nothing in his whole life so revolted him as his first glimpse of a Nazi "horror camp"—the concentration camp at Ohrdruf, near Gotha, which he saw just after its liberation by American forces, before the piles of bones could be hidden or the last of the starving, miserable, incredibly emaciated prisoners done to death. Within an hour, he dispatched a message to the Secretary of War in Washington asking that a delegation of American publicists and politicians be flown to Europe at once so that they could see these unbelievable horrors firsthand, before the camp was cleaned up. Then—an acute Eisenhower idea—he forced German *civilians* (not soldiers, who might be expected to be in tune with such savagery) in the nearby towns to bury the dead. The mayor of one such town, who had never known that such things existed in his neighborhood, committed suicide with his wife that night. Eisenhower, when he heard this, exclaimed "Good!" He was delighted to find that some Germans at least had a sense of shame and "a few sensibilities left."

Eisenhower is indisputably one of the most modest men who ever attained a great station, but this does not mean that he is not sure of himself. One of his most valuable qualities—practicality—arises out of this assurance. But the humility is genuine; the modesty is not mock. He said to a friend once, "My only satisfaction in life is to hope that my effort means something to the other fellow. What can I do to repay society for the wonderful opportunities it has given me?" In the great Guildhall speech in London in June, 1945, he said, "Humility must always be the portion of any man who receives acclaim earned in the blood of his followers and the sacrifices of his friends."

In strict contradistinction to some other commanders, he never permitted correspondents during the war to dateline their stories "General Eisenhower's Headquarters." The term had to be "Allied Headquarters."

One story, which members of his staff today neither confirm nor deny, is that, when offered the Congressional Medal of Honor by Mr. Roosevelt, he turned it down. He had done nothing in the realm of personal heroism to deserve it, he insisted. If this legend is correct, Eisenhower is certainly the only man in American history ever to have refused this supreme decoration. Of course for a man to have no vanity at all would be the greatest of all vanities. Therefore it is a pleasure to report that Eisenhower did, once or twice, behave quite normally and register his delight at an accomplishment, or confess to a legitimate ambition. For some days in November, 1942, he was in operational command of the fortress of Gibraltar; this excited him so much that he scribbled a memorandum about it longhand. His permanent rank at that time was, incredibly enough, only lieutenant colonel; yet he was bossing British field marshals, and he could not help being amazed at his own position. On another occasion he confessed that he had always hoped that he would be promoted to the grade of four-star general, if he ever reached this grade, on the actual field of battle.

Finally we come back to the essential master point that Eisenhower is so civilian-minded. In fact, though he has spent his whole life as a soldier, he actually seems to *be* a civilian; he wears civilian clothes quite often, and even likes to make cracks about "the Pentagon mind." One of my French friends, meeting him for the first time, burst out recently with the words "But he is such a nonmilitary general!" Plenty of Europeans think that some crazy American officer may drop one of our atomic bombs for fun someday. They know that Eisenhower won't.

His speeches are to a remarkable extent packed with antiwar sentiment. He harps again and again on the fact that our generation has been twice defaced by war, and that war must not come again. He talks about the "crime" and "waste" of war and its "beastliness." He said on one occasion, "I hate war as only a soldier who has lived it can, only as one who has seen its brutality, its futility, its *stupidity*." He talks of the "dark ground of prejudice, fear, hysteria—the soil in which the evil seeds of war flourish." On another occasion he told a graduating class (of civilians), "Your business is to put me out of business."

Here are some further Eisenhower sentiments on the subject:

Total war would be the suicide of our generation.
We must train the youth of America to avert World War III, not to refight World War II.
Belligerence is the hallmark of insecurity.
There is no glory in battle worth the blood it costs.

His prestige, which was great anyway, has as a result of all this become greater, particularly in Europe. He has become the first citizen of Europe. Many on the continent grab his words as if they were meat, bread, and guns, because he is the general who is going to *prevent* a war, not make one. Europe's prevailing mood these days is to hope for peace; and Eisenhower, though he would be the first to resist attack, is an eloquent symbol of this mood. He gives people confidence that he really *believes* in peace; more than this, and above all, that peace is a reasonable objective that he is strong enough to attain.

Field Marshal Lord Montgomery is supposed to have made a little joke recently: "If Ike returns to the United States to run for President, I'll have to go there too and campaign against him, in order to keep him here."

~~~~~~

As is clear, there is little appraisal in this chapter. I was trying to do a straight-out reporting job about Ike in Paris. Perhaps I should add that I knew Eisenhower fairly well from earlier days and had been at close quarters with him during one brief period of the war; he contributed in Sicily to one of the best small adventures I ever had in my life. Actually I met Eisenhower for the first time in Manila as far back as 1938. I had an appointment with General MacArthur, who at that time was a field marshal in the Philippine Army, in his penthouse in the Hotel Manila. The bright-eyed, widely smiling young officer who greeted me and took me to MacArthur's doorstep was, believe it or not, none other than Ike. I am not sure of his rank but I believe that he was a major. Anyway he was a junior member of MacArthur's staff, and served him well. In later years I have several times heard Ike reminisce about Mac-Arthur, and his memories are rich and rare.

Eisenhower is so well known today there is no point in dwelling upon details of his career. He returned to the United States early in 1952, resigned from the Army, made it clear at last that he was a Republican, and ran for President and won in 1952 and again in 1956. During all this time he remained one of the nicest—if somewhat cloudy—men anybody had ever met. Politics and the routine of administration bored and baffled him. During the war he seemed to be surpassingly clean-cut; as President he often appeared to be working in fields that irritated him and threw him off.

One key to his popularity during both his terms in the White House was certainly the factor which I stress strongly in passages above. He wanted peace. He stood for peace. He straddled and equivocated on various issues and tried to deal with others—for instance Senator Mc-Carthy—like an ostrich, but citizens at large felt reasonably sure that he would not make war, and this is what counted. He was not fixed and stapled to military attitudes as MacArthur was.

A hint to much else in Eisenhower's later career may be seen in another passage in the material above. I mention his "eagerness to please" and the fact that he failed "to take a firm enough stand for what he believed in." This trait was one of the reasons for the appalling muddle over Senator Goldwater in midsummer, 1964, when he contradicted himself, floundered, and gave up all the normal characteristics of leadership. Eisenhower wanted above all to be all things to all men, and so ended up by being nothing to anybody.

As a matter of fact several of his views on domestic matters have been ill-shaped and woolly from the beginning. He had a gelatinous "middle of the road" attitude without ever defining where the curbs were. As to affairs abroad he was much more cogent. One fascinating document which is not widely known, although it was published in the Saturday Review *(January 21, 1961), is the speech Ike prepared in advance for delivery in Leningrad when he was about to visit the Soviet Union in 1960, after the Summit Conference. His trip had to be canceled because of the storm created by the U-2 incident, when an American espionage plane was shot down over the Soviet Union in extraordinary circumstances, thus provoking Mr. Khrushchev to great wrath. Eisenhower's undelivered speech is a model of what a speech written for such an occasion should be. It does not kowtow to the Russians in the least, nor does it contain any hint of appeasement. It is soundly, eloquently American. But Ike makes a stirring appeal for friendship with the Russian people. He talks about community of interests between Russia and America in older days. He asks his Russian listeners to see for themselves how America has changed. He says that if the American system is described as merely being "capitalist" its whole essence is missed. He sets out to convince his audience that above all else in the world the American people want peace with all nations. One nuggety sentence is "I hope that you [his presumptive Russian listeners] will come to my country in tens of thousands, as Americans have come here, to see and examine our way of life in America."*

I would like to add one detail not in the political realm. When my wife and I visited the Eisenhowers near Paris and the General showed us his paintings, he was asked if he had ever painted an abstraction. He looked horrified, and shot at us the words "Abstractions are immoral!"

Part Eight

~~~~~~~~

BEHIND THE CURTAIN

CHAPTER 28

~~~~~~

Tito of Yugoslavia

In 1948 my wife and I visited four of the Iron Curtain countries for Look *and the New York* Herald Tribune *and then I wrote a book called* Behind the Curtain, *which was published in 1949. What follows here is a condensation and amalgam of two chapters.*

~~~~~~

YUGOSLAVIA, the brawniest and most stubborn of the Balkan states, a lusty country containing 15,320,000 Serbs, Croats, Macedonians, Bosnians, Slovenes, Montenegrins, and other commingled folk, is ruled by Marshal Tito. Its uniqueness—as of the moment of writing—is that it is flanked not by one Iron Curtain, but by two. Marshal Tito is probably the most isolated political phenomenon on earth. Since June 28, 1948, when his government was formally cast out of the Soviet orbit, the Yugoslavs have had to hew out their own path, and a thorny and difficult path it may well prove to be.

We shall go into the reasons for this formidable quarrel between Tito and the Cominform and its ramifications and results below. The details are as complexly fascinating—even bewildering—as, say, a verbatim report of one of the great Russian treason trials before the war. Certainly the mere fact of the rupture is the most important and pregnant development in Russian relations with the rest of the world since the Hitler-Stalin pact of 1939. But by way of introduction there is something else to say, which is that Yugoslavia is still very much a Communist state despite the quarrel, its government follows the Soviet model more closely than does that of any other satellite, and its temper and spirit are much closer to Moscow than to us.

This contradiction, I warn the reader, will haunt the pages following.

Belgrade has split off from Moscow and a great quarrel rages. But by far the easiest way to describe Belgrade is to say that it is a Moscow in miniature. Poverty and drabness; a severely moral atmosphere and a lack of elegance and grace; long queues everywhere; terrible shortages in consumer goods; emphasis on industrialization together with wildly inflated prices; intense xenophobia and suspicion of foreigners; inaccessibility of most officials and a heavy pall of bureaucratic secrecy—these are characteristics common to both capitals.

But also one gets the same sense of brutal forthrightness that Moscow gives, a sense of power and change, of a world being utterly reborn for good or ill, pulled out by the roots, everything topsy-turvy, with a transvaluation of all values, everything being tried for good or ill in a radically different way.

Here I must mention a second contradiction. Poverty? Suspiciousness? Brutality? Yes. It is incontestable that Yugoslavia is a police state, afflicted by some savage miseries human and political. But on the other hand any visitor is almost bound to feel a strong impression of confidence, *élan*, and above all patriotism and vitality, as well as of duress. The government certainly represses the bulk of the people—in theory for their own future well-being—but Tito himself is far from being unpopular. The mass of people are made to bear the most appalling hardships, and any overt expression of discontent would be ruthlessly stamped out; yet a great many Yugoslavs continue to think of Tito as an authentic national hero.

Journalism is not, we well know, an exact science. It would be a brave soul who would be dogmatic about Yugoslavia. Innumerable shades of gray lie between the black and white. Privation, disgruntlement, hatred, hope, discipline, fear, faith—all these qualities are intermingled.

Then, let us mention Yugoslav stamina and durability. This has nothing to do with communism; it has to do with the national character. One feels that nothing is going to stop or thwart these people. They are tough as leather, with a terrific capacity to take punishment.

Tito, Human Being and Statesman

There has been immense publicity about Tito; actually, comparatively little authentic is known about him, and long passages in his career are still soaked in mystery. It is an odd point: no official biography of him exists. Tito today is seven things: (1) the only marshal of the Yugoslav army and commander-in-chief; (2) minister of national defense with control of the Army, Navy, Air Force, and police; (3) secretary general of the Yugoslav Communist party and member of the Presidium; (4) chairman of the Central Committee of the Communist party, its leading body; (5) head of the Yugoslav Politburo, the organ by which it runs the country; (6) chief of the People's Front; (7) prime minister of the federal government of Yugoslavia.

All this sounds sharp and concrete enough, but even about Tito's very name there is mystery. His actual name—probably—was and is Josip Broz, though variants are sometimes used, like Brozevic. I have a pamphlet before me, issued by a Yugoslav group in New York in 1944, in which he signs himself "J. B. Tito." Officially nowadays his signature is J. Broz-Tito, Marshal of Yugoslavia; more familiarly he is addressed as "Comrade Marshal." Like almost all Communist conspirators, he used several names in his underground days; one was "Valter," and this still crops up occasionally. There are several theories, all fanciful, about his choice of "Tito" as a cognomen: (a) he named himself out of admiration for the Roman Emperor Titus, of which Tito is the Serbo-Croat form; (b) ditto, but the Titus involved is St. Titus, an early Balkan missionary; (c) the initials stand for *Tajna Internacionalna Terroristicka Organizacija* (Secret International Terrorist Organization); (d) the sound "Tito" is fairly close to that of the Yugoslav words "you" and "do"; the legend has arisen that Tito gave orders, "You do this!" and his followers got into the habit of calling him by a similar locution. Actually Tito picked the name himself in his underground revolutionary days simply because he liked it; it stuck, and it is impossible to think of him today as anything else.

The leading sources of Marshal Tito's power are, I should say, the following. He is a practical man, not an intellectual, which appeals to the people. He has courage, and Serbs like bravery. Also he is proud, stubborn, and patient, three qualities that cardinally reflect the national character. People say, "This Tito of ours is a real *Yugoslav;* he shows how superior we are to the Bulgars and Hungarians and Albanians." Then again he appears to be an excellent judge of human nature; he has picked his assistants ably, and he arouses intense devotion in his subordinates. Above and beyond all this is the basic historical fact that it was he who mainly built up the Partisan organization, who directed it through the most bitter years, and who liberated his country in large measure himself. Yugoslavia is the only country in the Soviet orbit where the government was not handpicked and installed by Moscow.[1]

[1] Soviet orbit? Let me go into this puzzling business once more, since the reader may still be confused by this double-edged attitude of Yugoslavia to the rest of the world. I have said that although the split between Moscow and Belgrade is yawningly wide and so far unbridged, the Yugoslavs still consider themselves in the Russian sphere. This may sound like a violent paradox. As a matter of fact, it is a violent paradox. All I can say is that it is also true. Moscow may consider Yugoslavia heretical and unreliable. But Yugoslavia, even though cast out—and even though unyielding to Russian pressure—still thinks of itself as an ally of the Soviet Union and a full sympathizer with basic Communist aims. For instance, despite the split the Yugoslavs still cooperate closely with the USSR at UN meetings and in other

The political basis of Tito's support is, first and foremost, the party organization. Second, military folk who admire him as a soldier. Of course the rank and file of the military have no choice—as of the moment—but to support Tito. Third, many citizens who think that, following the Cominform split, the West may be persuaded to help Yugoslavia. Fourth, many non-Serbs, who like him because he ended the old Serb hegemony. Fifth, citizens at large who hated the confusions, corruptions, and exploitations of the old regime, and welcomed any new strong hand with a broom.

Then atop this are personal qualities. Tito is no great intellectual; but this does not mean that he is not intelligent. He plays good chess. He knows six or seven languages well, including Russian, Bulgarian, Czech, and an obscure Asiatic tongue he picked up when he was a prisoner of war in Turkestan. His German is excellent; he speaks it with a good rough Vienna accent. Some Serbs say, incidentally, that he speaks his own language, Serbo-Croat, with a strong Russian intonation. He reads French and Italian, and, as we shall see, his knowledge of English is far from imperfect. Tito writes little. Profundities in ideology have never interested him particularly. But I have seen several of his early pamphlets, which are direct and forceful but which were possibly written for him, and he is credited with being the author of one book, *Borba za Osobodjenje Jugoslavije, 1941-45, The Struggle for the Liberation of Yugoslavia.*

Most dictators are monsters—either distorted ascetics, frustrated egomaniacs, or men with pathologically bitter resentments against society. But Tito appears to be a calm, friendly, and fairly normal person. He likes to eat and drink copiously. He likes people. He likes to swim and take long walks in the hills carrying a staff. Another quality is his very considerable personal charm, about which people "warned" us in Belgrade. They said, "Look out—don't be taken in!" Women in particular are strongly attracted to him, and he likes them; at a party, he is courtly and gallant, and he exerts a great hypnotic appeal on women when he speaks in public. Also he is one of the very few dictators with a lively sense of humor; one of his most interesting mannerisms is a running chuckle while he talks.

Tito, who is very closely guarded, lives in Belgrade in undisclosed whereabouts. For official entertaining he uses the so-called "white" palace in Dedinje (an outlying residential section of Belgrade) which was the home of the former regent Paul; in summer he goes as a rule to Bled, an enchanting lakeside town in the Julian Alps, where he lives in the former royal villa. Also he has quarters in Zagreb—or, for that matter, anywhere

---

international fields. Also, a point not to be minimized, it is just conceivable that the rift may be healed in time.

he wants to have them. Driving out from Belgrade one day we passed another of his houses, on a farm on the Novy Sad road. It was once a tile factory. A short round watch tower now commands the site.

The four main centers of opposition to Tito, on the domestic side, are, first, the old Serbs, who despise him as a Croat interloper; second, the "rich" peasants, if any still exist; third, the Catholic Church in Slovenia and Croatia; and fourth, members of secret reactionary groups. These last exist in all the Balkan and Central European countries. They are the only Europeans we met who actively want a war, because they know that they are finished unless the United States of America sends an army in to rescue them. It may shock Americans to hear it, but an upper crust of surviving oligarchy in this part of the world would, if it could, foment any kind of internal trouble, in the hope that this might in turn produce American intervention. Their only hope is war. And they want the United States to fight it.

Finally, the Russians are of course out to get Tito. But he is very ably guarded; he learned the technique of taking precautions in a thoroughly efficient school, that of Moscow itself. When he makes a public appearance, the streets are cut off to traffic and houses are searched along his route; his movements are never made public and only a few intimates know where he is at any given moment; I even heard that all his food is tasted. Even so, some people think that the Russians will eventually succeed in getting rid of him. I even heard well-informed people (but not Yugoslavs) make wagers in a café that he would be dead within a year.

Career of the Stout Marshal

No one knows exactly where or when Tito was born or of what parents. He came of peasant stock, and in this part of Europe nobody bothers much about birth certificates. Apparently his father was a Croat, his mother a Slovene or possibly a Czech. They are never spoken of. He was brought up as a Catholic. An "official" birthplace has now been bestowed on Tito; it is in the wild region near Zagreb called Zagorije and known colloquially as "Behind the Mountain." Certainly he springs from somewhere in the Zagreb area. The date of his birth is usually given as sometime in May, 1892.

Tito, then known as Josip Broz, got a job as a metal worker, which was apparently his father's trade. In 1914 or 1915 he was drafted into the Austro-Hungarian Army; he was made prisoner by the Russians in the Galician campaign of 1915—or perhaps he simply crossed over to their side—and then spent several years in Russia as a prisoner of war. Came the Russian Revolution. Perhaps Tito was already a Communist at this period. At any rate the vast upheaval of 1917 freed him, and he fought in the Russian civil wars. Apparently he did not return to Yugoslavia till about 1923, when he resumed his old trade of metal worker. He worked in Zagreb and the industrial town of Kraljevica and became secretary of the metal workers' union. In 1924 he was arrested as a Communist conspirator and agitator, and was sentenced to five years in prison (practically all the Iron Curtain luminaries are political jailbirds), which he spent in the famous Mitrovica jail; here he met and commingled with most of the people who are still his close associates. He was released in 1929. Then till 1934 there is scarcely any trace or record of him; what he did in these years is still a mystery.

But I met one Austrian Communist who told me he had known Tito well in Vienna, and also it appears that he lived in Paris for an interval. He must have returned to Yugoslavia, secretly and at great risk, several times. He denies having actually fought in the Spanish Civil War, but he seemingly worked for the Loyalists in France as a recruiting officer. By 1937 he was prominent enough to become secretary general of the outlawed Yugoslav Communist party and a member of its secret Politburo. But he was still Broz and still utterly unknown to the world at large. One must try to keep in mind what the life of underground Communists was during this period. They lived in a surreptitious world of stealth, conspiracy, continual harassment by the police of a dozen countries, privation, and dedication. Underneath the calm external surface of Europe, they had an interlocked and explosive secret life all their own.

Came World War II. When the Germans attacked Yugoslavia in 1941 Tito was in Zagreb using the name Tomanek. He was smuggled, the story goes, by Czech engineers—not out of the country—but farther in, so that he managed to get to Belgrade and help organize the first Partisan resistance there. The rest of Tito's story, including the tragic quarrel with Draja Mikhailovic, his rival as a nationalist leader, is well known. Of course there is no doubt that he took advantage of the patriotic war to further his own Communist ends. One story is that his real identity was first disclosed to his followers at a famous secret conclave at Bihacs late in 1942; the guerrilla from the mountains, Tito, was found to be none other than the old revolutionist Josip Broz. In November, 1943, the title of Marshal was conferred on him, as president of the National Liberation Movement. In 1944, when his Partisans had liberated more than half the country, he met Churchill and other Allied leaders for a conference in Italy; the reason Churchill was so impressed by him was, of course, predominantly military. Tito, not Mikhailovic, was the man who was really delivering; Churchill would have made a deal with Satan himself, if Satan were killing enough Germans and driving them out of Yugoslavia. Then came abstruse and labored negotiations between Tito and the Yugoslav leaders outside, culminating in a secret agreement with Ivan Subašic, who was prime minister of the government in exile in London, for a regime of national unity after the war. Tito has been in the saddle ever since.

Of course very little indeed was known about any of this at the time. Operations in Yugoslavia were necessarily cloaked by the most steely censorship. Nobody—not even Allied leaders—was allowed to know much about what was happening in the dark Yugoslav byways, in order to avoid giving anything at all away to the Germans. The Nazis, be it remembered, had offered 100,000 gold reichsmarks for Tito's capture, and they had flooded the country with posters bearing what they thought was his photograph. But nobody was sure of his identity. His name first began to be printed in American and British newspaper stories late in 1943, and these make fascinating reading now. One of the best was by Cyrus L. Sulzberger in the New York *Times* on December 5, 1943; it was written in Cairo, and contained this passage:

> Anybody who states with flat positiveness who Tito is, is talking through his hat. Not even the Allied liaison officers now stationed with him have that knowledge. The secret of Tito's identity is one of the best kept of this war, and there are reasons for this. Use of an anonymous fighting name is a common practice in the Partisan army. . . . This method avoids the enemy's learning the exact identity of the leaders of the patriots and making reprisals against their families. . . . Furthermore . . . it unquestionably has a certain romantic appeal.

Two of the legends about Tito that I heard in Belgrade years later appear in Mr. Sulzberger's article. One is that there have been several Titos—that different people operated under the same name. I am inclined to dismiss this as unlikely, because the main line of Tito's personality and works (part of which can now be confirmed by captured police records and the like) is so consistent. But it would not have been beyond the realm of the collective Partisan imagination to have given successive leaders the same name, Tito, in order to confuse the enemy. People may die; the name is permanent and immortal; this seems to be the theory. The second legend is in a comedy vein, and it is to the effect that Tito (the Tito of early Partisan days anyway) was in reality a woman. A British officer in Yugoslavia, none other than Evelyn Waugh, is supposed to have asked Tito facetiously if this was true. Tito, a lusty type, is reputed to have answered, "Well, if you *were* one, I could quickly prove that I am not."

Tito's sense of humor, though perhaps crude, is quite advanced. Last summer Randolph Churchill, son of Winston, tried vainly to get a visa to visit Yugoslavia. He finally appealed by telegram direct to Tito, ending with the words "Don't you know who I am?" The story goes—probably it isn't true—that Tito telegraphed back, "Certainly, you are Vic Oliver's ex-brother-in-law."

The terrific heroism and romance of Partisan days have left a strong impact on all those who shared them. Even retrospective articles written today by eye-witnesses who hate Tito's politics are warm with personal admiration; apparently nobody who ever fought closely with this doughty chieftain will ever forget him. And most of his wartime comrades and associates never seem to think of him as a Communist at all, but as an undivided Yugoslav and nationalist.

Impressions of Our Talk

En route to an interview with Tito, my wife and I were met at the Zagreb railway station by a young and courteous official. He carted us off in a modest car to a nearby hotel and said that he would telephone in an hour or so, after we had breakfast, to tell us the exact time of our appointment with the marshal. I noticed that this young man's use of western languages was extremely limited. In fact he was the only person I have ever met in my life who accomplished the feat of using monosyllables of three different languages in a three-word sentence; he pointed to a street and said, "*Très* big *weg*." (Very big road.) When he announced that he himself would take us in to Tito I asked as tactfully as possible if he could bring along someone else as interpreter.

He picked us up as arranged, and there in the car was someone who looked like a longshoreman out of a job for years—wearing a coarse cap and sweater, without a necktie, unshaved and dilapidated. I asked politely, "You speak English?" and he replied, "Please, you are very welcome." So far as I ever learned this was his total command of English. The nervous official who met us must have assumed that he *had* to find, on the shortest notice, someone who knew at least a word of English, and had simply picked up this worthy citizen—who had perhaps once been in America—off the streets. It was all rather disarming, alarming, and engaging.

We were whisked through a park until we found ourselves before a villa in a garden on the outskirts of Zagreb. A soldier not very conspicuously armed opened a gate in a wooden lath fence, and passed us through a second gate without formality. Here, at the doorstep of the villa, we were met by someone who—apparently without the knowledge of the official who met us—had already been given the job of being interpreter for the occasion. He was a Belgrade newspaperman. So our official disappeared like a streak of lightning, and with him the longshoreman picked up on the street, whom we never saw again.

A very large dog—an Alsatian crossbreed—leaped out as we climbed to the front door. This is Tito's famous Tiger, an animal with a great Partisan history. Tito captured him from an S.S. colonel during the war.

We were led briskly through a couple of rooms furnished in a somewhat heavy Middle European manner and there was the Marshal coming across a third room to greet us. He led us out on a terrace after shaking hands. There he asked us to sit with him in comfortable chairs at a small table. I was fascinated to observe that the interpreter—and also a secretary whom we were never able to identify—were made to sit on straight chairs about eight or ten feet away. This made conversation somewhat laborious. It isn't easy to have an informal chat with a dictator when you have to talk through people who are kept off at such a respectful distance. Both the interpreter and secretary held pads of paper on their knees. They wrote very little down, however.

Conversation was difficult for another reason too; there were language troubles. Tito speaks good German but my own German is not too fluent and my wife knows none. The interpreter's English—though a bit more copious than that of the man off the street—was about on a par with my German. Then we found that Tito himself knew English quite well. He appeared to understand almost everything—once he interrupted to say that he hadn't quite got the last word in one sentence, and the word was a fairly difficult one, "fathom." Another time, he corrected the interpreter by pointing out that the correct English for a word he himself had used in Serbo-Croat was not "epoch" but "episode," which shows that his knowledge of English is, indeed, quite sensitive. But he was loath to speak it. My wife spoke French, and I did some translating from German into English. The interpreter was useful only when Tito broke into Serbo-Croat, which he did when he was expressing himself at length on a serious political point.

But the first thing that the marshal said, after we sat down amiably, was that there could be no talk of politics at all. This was a blow indeed. We prepared ourselves for a nice half hour of discussion of the birds, the beasts, and the flowers; a terrible floundering moment came in which nobody said anything at all in any language. Then somehow—I swear I do not know how—I asked some sort of question that must have at least approached the political field; it interested Tito and we were off. From then on we were in politics and nothing but politics up to our necks with no holds barred.

Something may have aided this. A servant arrived with a tray of drinks. We had *slivovitz*, white wine in very large gold goblets, and Turkish coffee. It was still only about eleven in the morning, and alcohol at this hour is notorious for what it will do to improve conversation. Tito, however, drank nothing but a sip of wine. My wife and I had a *slivovitz* or two. The secretary and interpreter were offered nothing. Tito, by the way, smoked cigarettes steadily, using a very small holder in the shape of a pipe. This is one of his best known mannerisms.

The Marshal looked well. He gave the appearance of being calm, relaxed, and solid. He has no nervous gestures of any kind. The Soviet press has been portraying him as a cowering wreck, which he certainly is not.

He is a heavy-set man, rather short, very handsome, and possessed of much of the charm we had been told about. His eyes are small, somewhat cold, and very blue; his hair, once blond, is graying. He has good-looking teeth, and he laughed a great deal—a laugh good-humored, tolerant of the questions we were asking, not at all guarded or ironical, and sometimes—yes—bored. He wore a white suit with a dark red polka-dot tie, with a single medal in the lapel. He has often been accused of flamboyance in dress and manner and there has been much talk of a huge diamond ring he always wears. Indeed he wore it, but it did not seem to us very big or unnaturally conspicuous.

The range of talk covered everything from the United States presidential campaign to whether or not Mr. Dewey was an isolationist; from trade relations between Yugoslavia and the Soviet satellites to the work Tito has done to ameliorate the old frictions between Serbs and Croats; from the Marshall Plan to whether America ever interfered in the domestic politics of foreign countries; from the role of the new "People's Democracies" in European economy to whether or not communism and capitalism could eventually survive together in the same small world.

Also we, on our side, tried to tell him something about the United States—about the kind of nation the United States is, what it believes in, what it likes, what it doesn't like, how it responds to incidents, how it is both extremely powerful and extremely sensitive, how it is puzzled by Russian ignorance and bad behavior, how it is in Europe for a long time to come. And Marshal Tito listened with what appeared to be attentive curiosity and interest. Another point is that just before we left, after an hour, I asked if, looking back at everything broadly, he thought that Marx had ever made any mistakes. He chuckled, but did not answer.

In summary I would say the following. Marshal Tito and his closest associates seem to believe: (1) There will be no war. (2) If there is a war, it will be the United States that starts it. (3) If there is a war, Russia will win it. (4) One reason for this is that aggressors usually lose wars. (5) Despite the Cominform split Yugoslavia would prefer to fight on Russia's side rather than ours. (6) The Marshall Plan is distasteful to Yugoslavia because of its "political" motivation. (7) If the peace can be held countries like Yugoslavia may well turn out to be bridges between East and West. (8) Yugoslavia hopes to continue to have good relations with the other satellites in spite of the Moscow quarrel. (9) Good relations are possible between the United States and Yugoslavia on the basis of improved trade relations if the United States doesn't attempt any political interference in Yugoslav affairs.

The Cominform Split

It is time now to tell the detailed story of the rupture. This became public on June 28, 1948, but we know now, by the published correspondence, that friction began to develop much earlier, and had reached ignition point by March. Tito's first letter to Molotov is dated March 20. But hardly a dozen people in the world knew that this letter had been sent.

So far as the general public is concerned the first intimation that something very odd was happening was the announcement on May 8 that two important Yugoslav ministers, Andrija Hebrang (Light Industry) and Sreten Zujvic (Finance) had been dismissed from their posts. The charge was "deviationism," but nobody knew quite how or in what direction the deviation had taken place. It is always so in a Communist state: policy is made in secret by a tight clique at the top, and nobody as a rule knows which side anybody is on; moreover, the most exiguously narrow dialectical points, so subtle as to be almost beyond the comprehension of an outsider, may determine the issue one way or another.

Then on May 25, Tito's official birthday, some bright spirits in Belgrade noted that Stalin had sent him no congratulations, though the year before the papers had been full of them. Still, this might have been an accident. Next rumors spread that the Cominform meeting scheduled to take place in June was not going to be held in Belgrade, as planned, but in Prague, and that the deliberations would be secret.[2] Then the Manchester *Guardian* correspondent in Budapest got a clear scoop by reporting on June 26 that a crisis was impending between Yugoslavia and the Soviet Union. On June 28, finally, the Cominform resolution excommunicating Yugoslavia came out. It was printed in a Prague newspaper, the official party organ *Rudé Právo*. Probably the first notification to the Yugoslavs themselves was this release. They answered, via Radio Belgrade, on the night of June 30, and the whole world suddenly became privy to this unprecedented family quarrel—to the spectacle, moreover, of a satellite refusing to kowtow to its master, and defying Kremlin infallibility.

But for some time dense mystery attended most details. Then, about

[2] Belgrade was at that time the headquarters of the Cominform. (Nowadays it meets in Bucharest.) "Cominform" is an abbreviation of Communist Information Bureau. This was set up in 1947 by the Communist parties of the chief European countries, under Moscow supervision, as a kind of extension of the old Comintern or Communist International, which was dissolved in 1943.

July 25, clandestine pamphlets began to appear on the streets of Belgrade, which had been printed in the Serbo-Croat language *in Moscow*. The Yugoslav police did their best to prevent the circulation of these, but plenty were distributed; they gave the Soviet side of the case, and were in effect an appeal to the Yugoslavs over the head of their own leaders. A fortnight later the Belgrade government released a pamphlet of its own, which was at first made available only to party members; later it was put on sale in the official bookshops, while, of course, the Russian pamphlet continued to be suppressed.

The letters read like the angry recriminations of a man and wife long and happily married who are plunged suddenly into an acrimonious divorce. Indeed a principal theme is infidelity. And money is a subordinate exacerbating irritant, as in most divorces. The Yugoslavs are the defendants and their tone is hurt, horrified, and at the same time respectful—even deferential—as if hoping that the plaintiff will have mercy and call off the suit.

The Russian letters are so appallingly brutal, dogmatic, and unreasoning that one is completely at a loss at first to explain why Moscow should ever have taken the lead in releasing them. They are by far the most revealing evidences of Communist psychology since testimony in the great purge trials of the 1930's. But the temper they show—an almost insane arrogance plus misinformation and ignorance positively stupefying—precisely explains why they *were* released. Moscow was so ill-informed and superconfident as to assume that, once the whole affair became public, the Yugoslav people would rise, throw Tito out, and lumber over to its side.

Belgrade took the shock of Soviet excommunication calmly. There was no disorder, and experienced observers could see no sign that any new measures of public security were in force. Tito carried with him the party apparatus and the People's Front, and any known opponents must have been quietly submerged. There was no hint whatever of the one thing that could have displaced him, armed insurrection. Nevertheless an episode like this has its effects, if only by leaving an emptiness, or scar. Yugoslav Communists feel that they are living in a kind of vacuum.

The ferocity of the Soviet press campaign against Tito has mounted steadily, and is shared fully by the other satellites. He is denounced nowadays in terms worse than Moscow ever used for Goering or Hitler. But harsh words don't break bones. What counts is the Soviet economic boycott, which has been merciless. And the other puppet states, on Moscow orders of course, have joined this attempt to crush Tito by economic means. For instance the Czechoslovaks went so far as to withdraw their tourists from Dalmatia, which for generations was their traditional favorite spot for summer holidays.

But Moscow suffered too, if only because the unity of the satellite ring was shattered and the Kremlin lost irretrievable prestige. One wonders again and again how the Russians could have made such a blunder, and, having made it, persisted in their course. They forced their own hand, I heard it said, by prematurely disclosing details of the quarrel to the other CP's. Then they couldn't back out. But the basic reason for their behavior, as the Yugoslavs themselves point out, remains conceit, ignorance, and bad nerves. And the net result is of incalculable importance—that the international front of world communism has for the first time been broken.

I would not say, however real and serious it is today, that the break is irrevocable on an extremely long-time basis. I do not think that the Yugoslavs can easily back down now, but strange and unforeseen things happen often in the Marxist ethos. Then too—in time to come— Moscow might conceivably have to change its own tune. Remember the Hitler-Stalin pact.

Prominent Yugoslavs, when they talk about the break, do so with considerable detachment. They say that the particular and specific items referred to in the correspondence were nothing but contributory irritants. The sole fundamental issue, as a member of the Yugoslav government expressed it to me, was simply whether or not Belgrade had to dot every Russian *i* and cross every Russian *t* on command. The Yugoslav conception was different. It was that a group of independent socialist republics, some big, some small, could develop freely together as friendly and cooperating equals. The Moscow conception was that everything had to be under the spreading iron thumb of Moscow.

Tito rebelled against this; therefore Tito had to be destroyed. It was not so much a question of nationalism as of simple authority and obedience. The Soviet allegation of faulty party "democracy" was simply an attempt to get more latitude for their own sympathizers in Yugoslavia to undermine Tito. The charge of "anti-Soviet bias" was a device whereby the Russians hoped to obtain an easier atmosphere for agents to work in. The derogation of the Partisans was an attempt to diminish Tito's military and political prestige. The charge of neglect of the class struggle was a deliberate ruse to set Tito off on a witless adventure against his own peasants. And so on.

"We resented it that we were not trusted. It was as simple as all that," one Yugoslav told me. "Our belief was that a free socialist state should be permitted to grow up according to its own inherent instincts." This conception, the Yugoslavs cogently add, might well help rather than hinder future Socialist aims, in that Communist revolutions in France, Italy, and so on will be much more likely to come about if each country is (a) given some trust and free rein; (b) allowed to build out of its own specific national institutions.

Was the Break on the Level?

Yes. Some folk, particularly those who think that if it doesn't rain in
Kansas or if the aurora borealis changes color it is the result of a deep-
seated and nefarious Communist plot, assert that the Stalin-Tito break
is bogus. I cannot agree. Travel behind the Curtain half an inch, and you
will get from every side evidence of the sharp and conclusive reality of
this conflict. Let me repeat that it may possibly be patched up in time,
if there are more big changes in Moscow and the Kremlin reverses
itself, or if Tito himself is liquidated. But as of the moment the break
is absolutely genuine.

Surely a careful reading of the full correspondence is enough to
disprove the "phony" theory. The suggestion that the entire affair was
a plot, designed to pull wool over the eyes of the West, has been
dismissed as impossible by every Balkan expert. The theory that the
whole thing was contrived out of the full cloth simply will not hold
water, if I may mix a metaphor. Moreover, as far as the Russians are
concerned, let it be remembered that Moscow Communists believe in two
things above all: discipline and prestige. The Kremlin would never have
risked the very serious infractions of the former and very serious damage
to the latter that the split was bound to produce, unless impelled by the
most urgent of imperatives.

The breaking off of an important satellite from Moscow, in this
era of expanding international communism, is an event of supreme interest. Merely to weigh the long-range philosophical involvements, to
judge what leverage these may bear on political developments tomorrow
—for instance in places so remote as China—might well require months
of careful study. What we have here is the first sign of breakup in the
Soviet empire. We have demonstration of bad brains in Moscow, and
the blunt revelation that a basic division exists, within Communist
ranks, between ideas of international and national sovereignty. Again
consider what stupendous importance it will have for us if the new
China (to say nothing of other regions in Asia) is Titoist, not Stalinist.

〰〰〰〰〰〰〰〰〰〰〰〰〰〰〰〰〰〰〰〰

*Today, sixteen years after I wrote this, relations between Marshal
Tito and the Kremlin are still peculiar. Yugoslavia is not a Soviet satellite, but remains firmly Communist. Tito and the Kremlin have, so to
speak, kissed and made up several times, but Yugoslavia still pursues its
own policies. Polemics have continued to be intermittently venomous,
but Khrushchev and Tito have had cordial talks. The stout Marshal
once declared that Belgrade and Moscow had "identical views on the*

most important issues of the day," and Mr. K. told an interviewer, "Yugoslavia is neutral, but I believe it would fight on the Soviet side if the USSR were attacked."

One result of this situation has been to throw Tito into close touch with the other neutrals. He built up intimate relations with Nehru, Nasser, and Sukarno, and made two extended trips to the uncommitted nations of the Afro-Asia bloc, India, the United Arab Republic, and Indonesia.

Meantime, his contribution to contemporary history remains solid. My text above does not give sufficient emphasis to Tito's work in cementing Yugoslav unity. To all intents and purposes he has ended the ravaging quarrel between the Serbs and the Croats which tortured the Yugoslav state during the first forty years of its existence. Early tendencies to separatism on the part of the Macedonians, Slovenes, Dalmatians, Bosnians (who are largely Moslem), and the idiosyncratic mountaineers of Montenegro have also been for the most part forgotten. Of course all this has taken place under a ruthless political dictatorship.

But the major episode that will always be associated with Marshal Tito's name is, of course, the fissure with the Kremlin. One can only express amazement once more at what the rupture reveals of old Stalinist attributes—sensitiveness, unforgivingness, suspicion, secretiveness, and autocracy. And the monolithic solidarity of the Communist bloc was indeed splintered, and the great rasping break between Moscow and Tito was followed in time by the defection of Albania, the ferocious (but on-again-off-again) quarrel with China, as I was lucky enough to foretell, and, above all, the present evolution whereby most of the European satellites are stirring toward Tito's thesis that communism should be allowed to develop along the particular nationalist lines suited to each country.

I have seen Tito several times since I wrote this chapter. As I write today in 1964 he is seventy-two and has been secretary general of the Yugoslav League of Communists, the body that counts, for twenty-seven uninterrupted years. And he still fulfills a triple role unusual in the extreme, being at once head of the state, the government, and the party. Tito has mellowed with the years. He is still implacably tough, but he manages to remain bland, hearty, youthful, and good-looking.

The coincidence has utterly no significance, but for some reason or other I still remember vividly that I happened to be received in Rome by Pope Pius XII on the very day in 1948 when news of the Kremlin-Tito split first reached the newspapers. I dared to ask His Holiness his opinion of this thorny and epochal event and the unconventionality of his reply startled me—"I have not heard from my informants in Belgrade yet."

Part Nine

~~~~~~~~~

I HOLD THEE FAST, AFRICA

CHAPTER 29

The Northern Tier

These pieces that follow are all fragments out of Inside Africa. *I did the roadwork for this long book in company with Jane Perry Gunther in 1952–1953, and spent a good two years writing it. Publication came in the autumn of 1955. Africa, it need hardly be said, has changed immeasurably in the past decade. It was clear enough when we visited the so-called Dark Continent in 1952–1953 that, even then, emergent nationalism was the heart of the storm, the fulcrum of the story. But nobody knew then that national independence would come so quickly and in so many countries from one end of Africa to the other. If anybody had told me in 1952 when I visited Tangier, Rabat, Algiers, and Tunis that Morocco and Tunisia would have thrown out their French rulers and become free nations by 1956 I would have said that they were crazy.*

In 1955 when I closed proofs on Inside Africa *there were only four independent African states on the entire vast continent (Liberia, Ethiopia, Libya, Egypt). Today (1964) there are thirty-seven, with several more to come. Almost the whole of Africa has repudiated the old colonial rule and torn itself stridently free. Thus the following sketches of the Pasha of Marrakesh and the Bey of Tunis are, in a sense, period pieces, but they show something of the extraordinary medievalism of the Africa of that day. This was the backdrop against which contemporary nationalist Africa, with all its faults and failings, had to struggle to emerge.*

Lord of the Atlas

WE HAVE MENTIONED El Glaoui, the Pasha of Marrakesh, a splendidly romantic city in southern Morocco, several times in these chapters [of *Inside Africa*], and now we must treat of him in more detail. This picturesque old chieftain is one of the most remarkable characters we met in all Africa. He is a kind of Oriental Charles the Bold, who fought 121 pitched battles in his youth, has been wounded thirty-two times, and is proud of the number of men he has killed with his own hand. Also he has a dark, almost feline quality of grace. He has been called the Metternich of Morocco, and has the sophistication of a really first-rate cardinal. The key to his policy is that, like good cardinals, he has always been consistent.

The Glaoui is called other things too—"Lord of the Atlas," "the Black Sultan," and "the Gazelle of the Sus," the Sus being the rich, fertile valley below Marrakesh, between the Atlas ranges, which he holds in fief. His full name is correctly Hadj Thami Glaoui el Mezouari; "Thami" is his given name, and "Glaoui" that of his tribe. His domains cover several thousand square miles, in which live at least a million Berbers, perhaps more; his private "army" of Berber warriors, who owe him unequivocal fealty, numbers about 300,000. Probably the Glaoui is the last feudal lord on earth with so many armed men at his disposal. (They are not, however, armed in the modern fashion, but carry romantically old muskets.) Then too as Pasha of Marrakesh he is chief administrator—for the French—of much of southern Morocco. It is as if, in the United States, a subpresident with his own militia had virtually autonomous authority over Texas, Arizona, and New Mexico.

The Pasha's political strength lies mostly in the fact that he has always played the French side. But he would resent hotly being called a puppet. He likes the French, and they like him, a valued ally. He is proud of his position. I will not forget his expression when a tactless French lady told him patronizingly in a mixed group that France could always count on him because he knew on which side his bread was buttered. He was not only angry, but deeply hurt.

The Pasha is tall, very dark, gaunt, and with a handsome face that carries an engaging note of rascality. His antique hands are wrinkled like walnuts, and he has a winning smile. He is over eighty now, but still fit physically. Eighty is no age at all for a Moor. He has an elder brother, Sidi Hassi, who is ninety-six, and who is still an active administrative officer—his title is "Pasha of the Kasbah."

The Glaoui is a devout Moslem, and has made the pilgrimage to Mecca no fewer than five times. He has never touched alcohol in his life, but he has no objection to serving it profusely to European guests. He plays good golf, and his private course near Marrakesh is supposedly the best in North Africa. He is renowned for his physical prowess as well as courage and gift for direct action; once he broke up a riot in the *medina* by laying about him with a whip. He knows French, but speaks it haltingly; as a rule he talks in Arabic (or Berber) through an interpreter. His efficient secretary, Albert E. Berdugo, comes from Tangier, and is of an old Jewish family; that the Pasha of Marrakesh should have a Jewish aide surprises people who do not know how well the Moorish and Jewish communities generally get along in Morocco.

One of the Pasha's great enthusiasms is Winston Churchill, who has several times visited him in Marrakesh, and partaken of his sumptuous hospitality. He admires in particular how much Sir Winston can eat and drink. The Pasha is a very rich man indeed. One of his palaces, which he uses as a guest house for European visitors, is unexampledly ornate, furnished in what Oriental taste considers to be the correct manner. One of the bathrooms has two huge tubs. The Pasha's idea was that a husband and wife visiting him might enjoy the experience of bathing together in the same room. The source of his wealth is, of course, the people. His official biographers say that he maintains substantial agricultural properties in southern Morocco, and the legend is that every shopkeeper in Marrakesh works for him one day a week; he owns manganese, cobalt, asbestos, lead, uranium, and gold mines. An unfriendly critic, the well-known French writer Claude Bourdet, says that the Glaoui grinds down his serfs like an old-time robber baron, and is a merciless exploiter through the mechanism of his own police and tax collectors. The peasants have to give him what is called "spice"—gifts whenever he sets out on a trip, or on the occasion of holidays and feasts—as well as free labor when he demands it. He has a complete personal monopoly of the local output of saffron, almonds, and olives, and pays for these articles only 50 percent of the normal market price. Mint may not be sold by others until he has disposed of his own mint crop.[1]

El Glaoui rose out of the Imézouaren family, and his forebears have been powerful locally for more than two hundred years. At the turn of this century three different feudal families fought to control the Atlas passes. The young Glaoui became Pasha of Marrakesh in 1908, and except for one short interval he has held this position ever since. He was Pasha when the French came in 1912, and decided to welcome rather than resist them. The Glaoui and Marshal Lyautey, the great French administrative-colonizer, became close friends. When World War I broke out Lyautey summoned him to say that he might have to send the French garrison in Morocco back to Europe to fight against the Germans, and asked him what would happen in Marrakesh if the French withdrew. The Pasha replied in effect, "Leave it to me." Lyautey did so, and the whole of the Sus stayed quiet, although French pacification of the Berber tribes had only just begun. Oddly enough the garrison of Marrakesh itself consisted in 1914 mostly of *Germans* in the French Foreign Legion!

Later the Glaoui became a principal instrument of the French "paci-

[1] *Temps Moderne*, Paris, July, 1953.

fication" of Morocco. He fought and subjugated his own countrymen on behalf of France. In World War II he worked hard and cleverly for the Allied cause. He refused to have anything to do with the German Armistice Commission during the Vichy period, kept his tribesmen back in the hills with their arms secure, and staunchly welcomed the American landings at Casablanca in 1942.

Naturally the Glaoui's family connections ramify through the whole of Moroccan official society. His elder brother El Madani was once Grand Vizier, and he is a son-in-law of the present Grand Vizier, El Mokri.

The Glaoui himself has at present, it is believed, four wives and four principal concubines. Probably he has had twenty or thirty children, but nobody would be likely to know for sure. Of these, six sons and two daughters are well known, though the daughters are, of course, never seen by outsiders. I heard them described as "wilted flowers"; they sit indoors most of the time, and are seldom even permitted into the palace courtyards, lest they be tainted by the glimpse of some unauthorized male. When they take an automobile ride not only are they heavily veiled, but the windows of the car are screened.

The Glaoui's household, as we observed it, seemed harmonious. The father dotes on his sons, while ruling them with a fibrous hand. Sometimes visitors see a homely scene—one of the boys sitting casually on the balcony outside his office, waiting for him to appear, and then greeting him with devoted respect and affection. The wives are not veiled within the palace, and mix freely with the children, whether they are *their* children or not. The Pasha seldom has a meal with them—or even with his grown sons—but he is never far away, and knows all that goes on. The boys went to good French schools, and were made to learn French from infancy. In fact, to improve their French, they were even forbidden to speak Arabic to each other at home. Similarly in India in the old days potentates insisted that their children speak only English.

The eldest son, whose mother was a Circassian, is Si Brahim, the Caid of Telouet.[2] He is in his early thirties, and is a complex youngster, who appears to be as strong and delicately turned as a spring; he is pale, good-looking, and reserved to an almost sinister-seeming degree. Telouet is the ancestral fortress of the Glaoui tribe, and Brahim, as its caid, has considerable local power. Probably he will be his father's successor as Pasha, but nobody can be sure.

Si Sadek, another son, is a judge in the Pasha's court at Marrakesh— an attractive young man with a highly refined, acute, and serene intelligence. He wanted to go to Harvard Law School, but his father kept him so busy that he could not get away. (To become a judge under Koranic law takes eleven years of study.) Recently the Pasha asked

[2] "Si" means "Mister," more or less.

Sadek what he would like most for a birthday present; he expected some such answer as a Cadillac, but Sadek's reply was, "A pilgrimage to Mecca with my mother." Si Hassan, another son, is a painter of distinction, who recently had a succesful one-man show at the Wildenstein gallery in New York, after several exhibitions in Paris. He and Sadek have the same mother. Hassan, like Sadek, is exceptionally cultivated and attractive, and his paintings have gaiety, sweep, and color.

* * *

Visiting the Pasha is, naturally, an experience of the most piquant quality. We were summoned to the Marrakesh palace. Outside the walls were rough-looking guards, dressed in the ragamuffin way of most Moors, without arms or uniforms. They reminded me of retainers outside palaces in Mexico, who are similarly nondescript and look like the most menacing of loafers. Penetrating one gate, we walked through three successive courtyards, each paved only with dirt (to make easier footing for the horses) and of a strange irregular shape. The impression is of a kind of slipshod crazy quilt—a miniature Hampton Court cut out of angular mud. On the porch of the Pasha's own residence squatted an enormously fat unveiled Negro woman, chatting casually with a high official. The appointments inside are astonishing. I felt as if I were in the Alhambra redecorated by a dealer in Victorian antiques. Rooms are tiled in yellow, pale blue, and an insidiously brilliant green, with high wooden ceilings painted in gilt and other colors. Sèvres porcelain, Imari chinaware, Turkish clocks are part of the décor. There are narrow benches set against the walls, and practically no other furniture.

The Glaoui received us for our first visit in his business quarters, and these are modest. Against one wall I saw a painting of Marrakesh by Mr. Churchill, placed atop a very large iron safe. The safe had a nice cozy look. Then the Pasha showed us a set of leather-bound autographed books, kept on a special shelf, that the British prime minister had sent him, together with—of all odd things—a portrait of Churchill and Stalin, autographed by the former but not the latter.[3] The Pasha looked ageless. He looked like a black tulip made of steel. He wore a striped brown-and-white *djellaba* over an inexpensive American-style soft shirt and foulard tie. With one eye half closed, the Pasha addressed us soberly. He has strong opinions. The main thing he said was that, if the French ever leave Morocco, the result will be anarchy and bedlam. He is for France because he thinks French rule is the best. He gave me the impression of a man individualistic and completely fearless, a cross between Robin Hood and Rupert of Hentzau, who did not comprehend, spry as his in-

[3] This was one of the few times I ever saw any books in an Arab or Moorish household. Arabs do not go in much for libraries.

tellect is, anything at all of the pressures of the modern world. But we did not talk long. Our host just wanted to look us over. Then we were asked to dinner.

* * *

Nothing in gastronomy is more exotically enticing than an Arab *diffa* or banquet. We went to several. First Hassan and Sadek gave us a "simple" lunch as a kind of dress rehearsal, so that we could learn in privacy what to expect and how to comport ourselves. Then General Guillaume, the French High Commissioner, drove us one day to a town called Demnat, where he was bestowing a decoration on a venerable caid. This was a full-dress feast. At the gates of the city armed horsemen on white chargers fired their muskets in salute, and pranced in fierce display. We were given ceremonial offerings of dates and milk, and heard for the first time the most extraordinary sound that North Africa provides—the high sibilant whistle, which is almost a whinny, a neigh, made by the long files of women from the town, who line the castle walls, and, as they begin to oscillate in a slow rhythmic dance, let loose this penetrating horselike chant.

Guests at a Moorish meal sit on cushions or low divans, with a large white napkin laid over their knees. You may use this, but not too conspicuously, to clean the lips, but not the fingers.[4] You may hold bread in your left hand—bread is in large soft chunks—but otherwise the left hand is not supposed to touch food, because of a Moslem custom having to do with bodily cleanliness. Except in special cases there are no knives, forks, spoons, plates, or other implements. The tablecloth is put on the floor, to catch crumbs. You eat with your right hand, taking everything from a common dish, and if you are a purist you use only the thumb and first two fingers. These fingers are not supposed to touch the mouth. To lick the fingers, no matter how greasy they may become, is bad form; but I have seen it done. These procedures are simple enough with some types of food, but not all. *Couscous* is difficult. Or try picking up a blazingly hot fried egg with three fingers and get it into your mouth without touching the lips or spilling. Unskilled people use wads of bread as a cleanser. Bones and similar debris are tossed on the floor or table.

First—at a typical feast—a servant arrives with a copper kettle, or pitcher with a thin spout, and pours water into a bowl over the hands of each guest. (At the conclusion of the meal, this ceremony takes place again, and soap is provided.) Next comes mint tea, thick and sticky. Then *plat* after *plat* arrives; each makes a separate course. Then, as in a

---

[4] Even in the best houses napkins are apt to be old and full of rough darns; cloth is precious in North Africa. Sometimes they do not match. Africa is the continent where nothing matches.

Chinese meal properly served, you reach over to the common dish, which all share, and choose a morsel to your taste. Women of the household are never present at a *diffa*. Each dish, if anything is left, is passed on down to the women, who are waiting in a different part of the castle or dwelling. When the wives and concubines have finished, it goes on in turn to male servants, then to female servants, and finally to retainers, hangers-on, or slaves.

It was interesting to watch French people of the most impeccable refinement, who might have been characters out of Marcel Proust, eat Moorish meals. They ate with their fingers with the most obvious gusto and relish; in fact they seemed to be possessed by a mad glee while tearing a hot slippery chicken apart with their bare hands. I offered the remark at one dinner that eating without implements was a simple enough indication of a suppressed tendency to revert to childhood, and a lady replied that, indeed, in the Faubourg St. Germain where she was brought up she had been strictly forbidden ever to touch food with her hands, had always yearned to do so, and now took a special perverse joy in doing it.[5]

But let me proceed to our dinner *chez* the Pasha. Twenty bearded retainers, looking like a line of owls, saluted our arrival at the palace. We entered a small room with maroon-striped settees, green curtains, and a flaming yellow carpet—Moslems love clashing colors—and with arched windows and a vaulted ceiling. One guest this evening was a celebrated French official, the Préfet of Casablanca; another was a barefooted, white-robed Arab octogenarian, the Caid of Mogador. A cold wind whipped through the doors and windows, which are usually kept open at ceremonies of this kind. (At luncheon birds may fly in and out.) The Glaoui, who had been sitting alone on a hassock, rose to greet us. He wore Arab dress (and carried a poniard) except for Argyle socks and a bright red necktie. At once we moved across a courtyard filled with orange trees to another division of the palace, where an American-style bar was functioning. Of course the Glaoui and the Caid did not drink the cocktails that were offered, which were a brilliant pink in color. Dinner was announced by a major-domo who entered abruptly and twitched the Glaoui's elbow, in the peculiar informal manner of Moorish servants. We went outdoors again, crossed another courtyard, and emerged finally into a room big enough to seat two hundred. The chief colors here were pink, lettuce-green, white, and purple. The Pasha, with a chortle of satisfaction, slid out of his slippers unobtrusively, climbed gaily over a

[5] One lady I know cannot always quite manage to swallow some of the odd delicacies that may be provided at a *diffa*, like certain internal organs. Such items she surreptitiously sticks away into her slab of bread, hoping that this evasion will not be seen.

hassock, sat down on a divan, and invited us to sit around him. This is what we ate:

First, a pale green soup composed of almonds, peas, and bits of white fish. (This was a concession to the uncouth West. We were even allowed plates and spoons. Moors know full well that existence is impossible to a Frenchman unless dinner begins with soup.)

Second, a whole roast lamb, served naked and intact. This, the staple course at an elaborate Moorish meal, is known as a *mechoui*. With infinite dexterity the Glaoui broke into the hot crackling skin, and seized from underneath specially tender morsels, which he passed on with his fingers to my wife. Often a lively competition occurs among guests to get the meat deepest down, from the ribs, where it is particularly fat and tender. This procedure may sound gross, but is not. Nobody tears off big chunks of flesh. People eat slivers and delicate strips. Sometimes at a big *diffa* the course following this is *another* whole roasted lamb, prepared with some sort of sauce to differentiate it from the first.

Third, a *pastilla*. This *plat*, which takes a full forty-eight hours to prepare, is the pride of a good Moorish cook. It is a pie, almost three feet in diameter, the crust of which is an inordinately fine, flaky *mille-feuilles*, on which a design is made with powdered sugar. Underneath, as a bold guest dents the crust, and usually burns his finger doing so, will be found a miscellany of shrimp, tripe, sweetbreads, olives, liver, *cervelles*, mussels, and fried eggs. It is a veritable treasure nest, and delicious beyond speech.

After this we had four more main courses in sober succession—squabs with a sauce like none other I have ever tasted before or since, a kind of hot, liquid and milky hollandaise; a covey of whole roast chickens, stuffed with olives and swimming in a lemon dressing; a ragout of lamb, onions, eggplant, and hard-boiled eggs; and a second, different ragout—slices of lamb laid tenderly atop a bed of peas and almonds. Then came a dish of strangely shaped pretzels seasoned with molasses, the equivalent of the sherbet still served occasionally at formal dinners in the West; it is sweet, and a refresher before what is to come.

Couscous was next. This, the basic food of Morocco for rich and poor alike, is made of semolina. The mound of grain may contain anything else from cool-skinned grapes to chunks of mutton; that of the Pasha came with turnips, carrots, and hazelnuts. *Couscous*, like rice in Japan, is always served toward the end of the meal so that you can fill up if you are still hungry, and it is bad manners to take too much. It is hard to manage with the fingers, since it is almost as dry as sand. The Glaoui is one of the world's foremost manipulators of *couscous* balls. We watched him fascinated. He picks up a handful of the hot grain, tosses this in his palm without touching it with the fingers, and gently bounces it in the hollow of his hand until by some miracle it forms a cohesive ball; this he then pops into his mouth, catching it on the fly. It was like watching a man with one hand make and eat golf balls.

At last came a cake made of frozen figs and tangerines. The Pasha picked up his napkin, and with a flourish dropped it on the tablecloth; this is the conventional gesture to indicate that the meal, any meal, is over. During all this we of the West drank champagne. The old Caid, who never said a word during dinner, sipped lemonade steadily with a peculiar hissing gurgle. Finally—the end is the beginning—we had mint tea again, the universal drink of North Africa, which is supposed to be an aphrodisiac.

* * *

After dinner ladies of the harem danced for us, first five Berber girls, then five Arabs. That we should be allowed to see them (and they to see us) was an exceptional experience. The Berber girls were somewhat stout and danced what is known as an *Aouache.* One had golden casta-nets, which made a bell-like sound. In the background, a male musician played something that seemed to be a musical saw set athwart a long mandolin; the sound was like no other I have ever heard. The dancers had their shoulders and arms covered, but with sleeves slit so that the skin was visible; legs and ankles were completely concealed, and this gave a curious provocative quality to the rhythm of the dance. The move-ment, as the girls made a vibrating circle, was mostly with the hips and feet.

Then came the Arabs, who were slimmer, prettier, and more sophis-ticated. The musician was a violinist and the performance more deliber-ately erotic. The girls wore turbans, draped so that the hair could be seen (or it was caught up with bright ribbons), blouses with the arms bare, and clanking golden chains and bracelets. They carried small drums, called *gambri,* the beating of which accentuated the flexing of their bodies. Their movements spread from the belly both up and down; even the head oscillated in a sexual motion, and the dance came to a climax when each girl, bending forward and back sharply, while still rotating her torso, plucked at her sash.

～～～～～～～～～～～～～～～～～～～～～～～～～～～～～～～～

All of this the Pasha of Marrakesh watched with alert appreciation. So did we. Hard times came to the Pasha—in the political sense—soon after these pages were written. He fell as French rule fell, and died at just about the time Morocco became an independent nation, in 1956. Perhaps it was just as well. Several of his sons do useful work with the new Moroccan government.

~~~~~~

The Grand Vizier

One remarkable personage in Morocco is the venerable prime minister or grand vizier, Hadj Mohammed El Mokri. He is, as of the moment of writing, not less than 103 years old. None the less he is still spry and in fair command of his faculties; he took his usual holiday in France last year, exactly as if he were a youth of seventy, still smokes cigars, and still runs the Sultan's personal government. This old and durable gentleman—the facts are incredible—was born in 1851, when Millard Fillmore was President of the United States and Louis Napoleon was Emperor of France. He represented Morocco at the Algeciras Conference in 1906, and was considered at that time to be one of the country's mature statesmen. He has been grand vizier without interruption since 1920— in five different sultanates; sultans come and go, but the ancient and indestructible grand vizier remains. Few politicians in history can rival the record of thirty-four solid years in office. He has always been staunchly pro-French. Naturally the old man's personal as well as political influence is profound, if only through the labyrinthian web of his family relationships. One of his daughters married El Glaoui, the Pasha of Marrakesh; another married a former sultan, Moulay Hafid; one of his sons is Pasha of Casablanca. The grand vizier has a marked sense of humor, and is apt to be coquettish about his age. He asked a visitor recently, "How old do you think I am?" The visitor replied that he did not look a day over eighty, and the grand vizier was vastly pleased. A French official said of him once, "In this man death has died."

Bey of Tunis

Few people of consequence in the contemporary world can have more medieval characteristics than the Bey of Tunis. He positively reeks of the Dark Ages—and not merely those of Europe, but of Asia. It happens that he is of amiable disposition; otherwise he might be a Turkish despot of the murderous thirteenth century. This elderly gentleman (he was born in 1881) must be the last monarch left in the world to maintain a private troupe of dwarfs. One of his passions is alchemy; he likes to mix secret brews and potions in his laboratory. He is also fascinated by astrology, and is an enthusiastic astronomer. His knowledge of science cannot, however, be highly advanced, since he knows no western language, and even his Arabic is primitive.[6]

I asked a French official if the Bey, like the Sultan of Morocco, made

[6] See "The Bey of Tunis," by George W. Herald, *United Nations World*, December, 1952. Sacheverell Sitwell also mentions the dwarfs in his enthralling book *Mauretania*.

a Speech from the Throne every year; the answer was, "Ridiculous!—
How could he?—He cannot read or write." One rumor is that the Bey
began life as an artisan, and he still likes to do things with his hands;
his palaces contain thousands of clocks, with which he tinkers constantly. He looks like an Oriental version of the late Kaiser Wilhelm, with
a soaring but stiff mustache. I asked if he dined in the western or eastern
fashion, and received the answer, "No one would know." President
Eisenhower's salary would be roughly $12,000,000 per year if he, Eisen-
hower, were paid the same percentage of the national budget that goes
to the Bey. But oddly enough the beylical group does not exhibit marked
signs of extravagance; the French say that its members are too stupid
and unimaginative even to know how to spend money. What I liked most
when we visited the throne room in the Dar El Bey (palace) in Tunis—
a monstrously Victorian structure—was a small projecting alcove with
low windows. Directly underneath this lies a route into the bazaar, and
here the Bey, unobserved, can watch the passers-by, like a child playing
at being a spy.

The Bey is properly called Sidi Mohammed Lamine Pasha; he is a
"sovereign" but not a king, and is addressed as His Highness, not His
Majesty. Officially, by French style, he is *Possesseur du Royaume de
Tunis, Souverain actuel,* and the throne is described as his *dépositoire.*
He has ruled since 1943, when his predecessor, a personage named
Mohammed El Moncef Bey, was rudely kicked out of office and exiled to
Pau. The Bey comes of a Greek or Cretan family that has been in power
in Tunis uninterruptedly since 1705; it replaced a truly fabulous cut-
throat dynasty founded by a renegade Corsican named Murad. The
Bey's father was also a Bey, but there were two others in between.

Here we reach something inordinately strange. The beys do not inherit by primogeniture, nor are they chosen by a *ulema,* or council, as in
Morocco. The succession goes to the *oldest*—not the youngest—properly
accredited member of the beylical family. This anomaly derives from
Turkish days, when a child or youth, if heir apparent, was almost certain
to be assassinated. A brochure available in Tunis names eighty-three
royal personages with the rank of *prince du sang de la famille beylicale
actuelle,* listed by date of birth; the oldest was born in 1862, and the
youngest in 1941. The present Bey was number four on this list when he
reached the throne. In addition to the eighty-three princes there are about
160 other beylical individuals. Mostly these make a slatternly if gilded
crew. Because of their prestige and position they are forbidden to work,
and must be supported by the public payroll. The Bey's eldest son is Sidi
Chedley Ben Mohammed Lamine Bey; he was born in 1910 and is number twenty-eight on the inheritance list. It is extremely unlikely that he
will ever accede to the throne, if only because he is an ardent national-

ist and the French hate him. The heir presumptive at present is a dignitary known as the "Bey du Camp." This title was bestowed traditionally on the most prominent person likely to succeed the Bey; then he was given a military command and packed off into the hinterland to keep him from making trouble at home. The present Bey du Camp is named Azzedine Bey, and was born in 1882. He is supposed to be insane. The new monarch, if it turns out to be Azzedine, will be almost as old as the present one. Following Azzedine on the list are three other princes now in their sixties. The ruler of Tunis is almost always an *old* man before he can reach the throne. Sons have no chance.[7]

The present Bey has, so far as is known, only one wife, who is never seen; she is a Negress, and is called the "Beza." Commonly she is said to descend from stock not distinguished; in fact she is supposed to have come out of a *gourbi,* or mud hut. The Bey and his consort have nine daughters and three sons. One daughter, Princess Zakia, is the wife of Dr. Ben Salem, a former minister of health and an outspoken nationalist; he was arrested and interned by the French in 1952. The princess herself has been accused of being a member of a ring of conspirators providing weapons for terrorists. Modern times have, it seems, even reached the family of the sovereign. Most emancipated Tunisian nationalists do not like the royal circle, on the ground that most of its members are worthless parasites; they concede, however, that it has a certain value as an instrument to reach the masses.

The Bey of Tunis differs from the Sultan of Morocco in several important respects. (a) He is not a Sherifian, not a descendant of the Prophet. (b) Politically, he is much more inert. (c) He has no religious authority over the community, since Tunisia is not a theocratic state.

The French do not have much regard for the Bey, but, since they want to preserve the fiction that Tunisia is a "sovereign" state, they cannot do without him. This has not prevented them from surrounding his palace with troops and threatening the use of force when, on occasion, he has refused to sign decrees. But they are loath to use too much force because this would throw him further into the nationalist camp, nor can they possibly afford to eject him from office at the moment and replace him with somebody else. The Bey is, on the other side of the fence, under considerable steady pressure from intellectuals in Cairo—also Pakistan —to take the nationalist side more firmly. He becomes more nationalist all the time, if covertly. To sum up, both the French and nationalists find this anachronistic old gentleman useful, but they both know well that the whole beylical hierarchy is an outrageous excrescence and bar to Tunisian progress.

[7] Azzedine Bey was assassinated by a nationalist terrorist after these lines were written.

His Majesty King Idris I of Libya

The name of the King of Libya is officially al-Sayyid Mohammed Idris al-Mahdi es Senussi. "Idris" means "Enoch." The monarch is in his middle sixties now, and is a thoughtful, somewhat frail old gentleman. His dominating characteristics are erudition, piety, and suspiciousness. Nothing has ever mattered much to him except freedom, if not for all of Libya, at least for that part of it known as Cyrenaica. He has considerable elevation of character and a subtle intelligence. He knows no western language, but is an Arabic scholar of advanced attainments, and is probably the most sophisticated as well as learned head of state in the Moslem world. His chief defect is lack of force.

We saw him not in Tripoli or Benghazi but in Cairo, where he was recuperating from a recent illness. That he had been away in Cairo for an extended period—"an absentee monarch"—caused much criticism in Libya. He makes plans with a good deal of secrecy, and moves by sudden whim. King Idris and his suite lived in Cairo at the Mena House, a celebrated hotel near the Pyramids. He had elaborate quarters there—most of one floor. Outside his rooms sat a delegation of magnificent white-robed tribal sheikhs, slim, cloudily silent, and immobile; they looked like white fingers, with nails for faces. They had been waiting to see him (he had been too ill to receive anybody) for three solid weeks. A page summoned us and I thought that we were being led to some ante-room where a chamberlain would prepare us for the audience with His Majesty. But we were ushered, without intermediation, directly into the royal presence. Of course an interpreter was present. Idris has a bushy mustache and gold-rimmed glasses; he wore a blue cloak and tarboosh. He sat in the middle of a sofa, and we faced him in chairs a few feet away. My first impression was that this was an extremely gentle man. I have always, for some reason, had difficulty talking to Arab potentates; they do not give out readily, and Idris has the reputation of being even more reticent than most. So it was a welcome surprise to find that he talked readily—and with charm and humor. A chuckle runs in his voice. Idris may be frail, but his wits are still sharp. Talking about Morocco he said that French policy was bound to produce—unfortunately—exactly that which it wanted to prevent, namely, a permanent state of disorder which the Communists would exploit. Talking about the United States, he asked us—with a bright gleam—why we worked so hard to liberate countries behind the Iron Curtain, which would probably turn out to be enemies no matter what, while we neglected countries that would always be our friends, like Tunisia and Morocco.

King Idris fills a double role—he is both the secular monarch and religious head of his people. In the familiar Moslem pattern, as old as

Islam itself, he was a religious figure first, and then turned to politics. Idris is the grandson of the founder of the Senussi order, and hereditary leader of the Senussis. We must have a word about these peculiar people. They are dervishes, with a tradition both fiery and devout. Like the Wahabis in Saudi Arabia, they are extremely strict Moslems, reformists who want to return to the original hard-and-fast purity of Islam. The movement was founded by "the Grand Senussi" (grandfather of Idris), who was born near Tlemçen, in Algeria, in 1787; it spread out into the desert among the Bedouin so strongly that, by the end of the nineteenth century, the Senussis had established what has been called "a theocratic empire," spilling over political frontiers. This was then broken up by the British, French, and Italians. But the Senussis continued to maintain their cohesion and identity, partly by reason of a remarkable institution known as the *zawia*. The *zawias* are a combination of town hall and seminary, where the teachings of the fraternity are kept alive; almost every village and oasis has one, though the Italians destroyed a great number of them in the Senussi wars.

King Idris was born in 1889 in the Jaghbub oasis in Cyrenaica, and has been head of the Senussi order since 1917. During World War II he assisted the British greatly in their desert campaigns, and, after the Axis forces were chased out of Libya in 1943, he returned to his country after twenty-one uninterrupted years of exile. In 1949 the British made him Emir of Cyrenaica again, while waiting for a final UN decision on Libya as a whole. A national constituent assembly proclaimed him King of Libya in 1950, although the country did not yet formally exist.[8]

King Idris has no male heir, which is a tragedy for the country. He was married first in 1897, when he was only eight years old; this was a purely ceremonial wedding, made for family reasons. He has never had more than one wife at a time. Two subsequent marriages ended in divorce, when they produced no living issue. Then in 1932 Idris married again; his wife was a cousin (born in 1911), named Al Sayyida Fatima Al Shifa bint al-Sayyid Ahmad al-Sharif. She has had no fewer than fourteen miscarriages. As a result of all this Idris has designated his brother, by name Rida, as crown prince and heir to the throne, with the succession going then to Rida's eldest son. Rida, who is known as Deputy King and who lives in Tripoli, is a jovial, socially minded man, quite different from the retiring Idris. The royal family, which has thirty-eight male members—all of whom have to be supported by the state—is fiercely split.

[8] During the final negotiations one UN delegate is supposed to have said to a colleague, "At three o'clock this afternoon we free Libya." His colleague replied, "Impossible. We freed Libya yesterday." From "The Newest State and Monarch," by Judd L. Teller, *The Reporter*, March 4, 1952.

Idris and Queen Fatima (who of course is never seen) live most of the time at Leyte, a few miles from Benghazi. Here an underground stream flows, which was the original River of Forgetfulness of the ancient Greeks, and which contributed the word "lethal" to the English language. The royal palace was formerly an Italian casino. Also the King has a summer capital at El Baida, in a hilly region 140 miles east of Benghazi. When Idris visits Tripoli he uses the palace once occupied by Marshal Balbo, who ran the country for Mussolini. All this means that Libya, a country with fewer people than Arkansas, has in effect four capitals. Moreover Idris has lately been spending most of his time in Tobruk, near the Egyptian border—presumably to make it easier to get away if he should have to leave the country quickly.

Recently Libya got its own national currency for the first time, but the issue had to be withdrawn and another substituted, because Idris objected to the use of his effigy on the banknotes; strict Moslems do not like to have their faces portrayed. The King's Speech from the Throne last year showed, more than ever before, the strong influence of Egypt on his domain. Idris did not get on well with Farouk (who was pro-Italian and thought that Idris was too pro-British) but he has a close relation with the Nasser regime.

In October, 1954, Ibrahim Ahmed Al Shalhi, the minister of palace affairs, and by all odds the man closest to the King, was murdered. He was *nazir* of the Royal Household, and had almost unlimited power; his origins were obscure, and one story is that he was a slave brought up by members of the Senussi family and trained to be Idris' bodyguard; he was barely literate, but even so became the undisputed *éminence grise* of the regime. Al Shalhi was assassinated by a young man named Sherif Mohieddin Al Senussi, a nephew of both Idris and Queen Fatima. A similar sensation would occur if, let us say, the prime minister of Japan should be murdered by one of the Emperor's cousins.

Some episodes extraordinary even for an Oriental monarchy took place after Al Shalhi's death. Idris purged several members of the government. Then the *entire royal family* (except the Queen and the Crown Prince) were deprived of their titles and privileges, and nine conspicuous princes including the son of the Crown Prince were packed off to exile in a forlorn oasis 150 miles south of Benghazi. The nineteen-year-old prince who murdered Shalhi was, despite his youth and royal blood, executed in February, 1955.

To sum up: In the present phase Idris is the only person capable of holding Libya together, but he himself hardly seems capable of doing so. At least he steadily favors his native Cyrenaica over Tripolitania, and as a result resentment by the richer and more advanced Tripolitanians has become the chief political issue of the country. Earnest Libyan patriots who want above all to make the federal system work are caught in a cruel dilemma, because if they attack the King they defeat their own best interests by making the country weaker.

〰〰〰〰〰〰〰〰〰〰〰〰〰〰〰〰〰〰〰〰〰〰〰

I have no idea what ever happened to El Mokri, the Moroccan grand vizier. He must be dead by this time. Nor do I know what ever happened to the Bey of Tunis, except that he was deposed. Tunisia became free in 1956 under the leadership of one of the most competent of modern African men of state, Habib Bourguiba, who proclaimed a republic and assumed office as President on July 25, 1957. He still holds this post and holds it ably, and his relations with the French, who imprisoned him for long periods, are good. Almost everywhere in Africa the French have managed to retain close bonds with their former dependencies.

Similarly the venerable Idris is still King of Libya ten years after these pages were written. At that time his country was often called "a box of sand." Today it has become impressively rich, like several of the new middle eastern states, as a result of the discovery of oil. American influence is strong, but the Libyans are not happy about the presence of a large American military air base, Wheelus Field, near Tripoli.

CHAPTER 30

〰〰〰

Nasser

The most important event in the history of modern Egypt occurred on July 23, 1952, when a handful of youthful military zealots seized power. Ever since, events have moved on with precipitous velocity. The long and short of the situation today is that Colonel Nasser still rules the country. During the first period of the revolution his partner and theoretical chief was General Mohammed Naguib, but they broke apart and since November, 1954, Nasser has run the show alone.

For thirty years or more the struggle for power in Egypt was triple— between the British, the palace, and the WAFD, or nationalist party. The 1952 coup d'état cut across all three of these traditional elements of force, and as a result Egypt has had to adjust itself to an altogether different equilibrium. The army mutineers struck, in a sense, against the British, the palace, and the WAFD.

For a long time the British had run Egypt outright, or at least tried to do so. Then came the period when it served their purpose to rule by means of Egyptian governments but to keep these as soft and pliable as possible so that they could be easily manipulated. Any quarrel among Egyptians always played into the British hand. All this has been ended. The chief claim to fame of Nasser and Naguib is, in fact, that Britain is no longer a direct power in Egypt at all. Two events of surpassing international importance have occurred since the military clique took office—the agreement of February 12, 1953, providing for self-government in the Sudan (largely negotiated by Naguib) and the subsequent agreement of October 19, 1954 (largely negotiated by Nasser) whereby the British promised to evacuate the Suez area. Later came the crisis over the canal. Egypt was on its own—at last.

As to things domestic, Nasser-Naguib ousted the fat king, abolished the titles of Pasha and Bey, proclaimed a republic, dissolved the old political parties, built up the Liberation Rally as a new supra-party machine, struck against feudalism, staked out a land reform, and sought to punish those guilty of corruption. In a word they sought to give Egypt a new face.

When my text below was written in 1954 Colonel Nasser was only thirty-seven years old, an inconspicuous and little-known lieutenant colonel. It was by no means certain that he would survive in power. I wrote that he could conceivably "be forced out of office or assassinated before these lines reach print," but also that he was "a man of force, acumen, and deep moral and intellectual conviction," who might well "evolve into a kind of Egyptian Ataturk, and remain in power for years to come." Nasser has cardinal faults—of course—and he has made mistakes. But his chief source of strength is his simplicity and that he still stands for something, the liberation and advancement of the masses. He gave people what they seldom had before, hope. No wonder Egyptians have called his movement the "blessed" revolution. But progress has been agonizingly slow and the case may well be made, as British observers sometimes do, that the fellaheen, or peasants, are still not much better off than they were ten years ago.

What follows is a consolidation of two chapters in Inside Africa *(1955). Part of it appeared in magazine form in April, 1955.*

〰〰〰〰〰〰〰〰〰〰〰〰〰〰〰〰〰〰〰〰〰〰〰〰

> *It [the Arab world] has known what it wanted to do away with, but it has not known what it wanted to build. . . . The problem was to restore human dignity to Egypt.*
>
> —GAMAL ABDAL NASSER

L IEUTENANT COLONEL GAMAL ABDAL NASSER (correctly Gamel Abd Al Nasir) was born on January 5, 1918, and is of modest bourgeois background. His father was a post-office clerk in Alexandria; his mother was the daughter of a businessman. From the age of seventeen Nasser had strong revolutionary tendencies. He was several times arrested for participation in student riots. He went to the Renaissance Secondary School in Cairo, studied law for a time, and then decided to devote himself to the army. He was commissioned in 1938, served for a time in the Sudan, and fought against the Jews in Israel. But even while campaigning in Palestine he records that he was fully aware that the "real" battleground would be Egypt itself. One turning point of his life came in February, 1942, when the British unleashed tanks and machine guns against King Farouk's palace. Nasser had no particular use for Farouk, even in those days, but he was the monarch, and that he should be humiliated and browbeaten so flagrantly seemed to Nasser an intolerable affront to Egyptian dignity. What an irony it is that it should have been the same Nasser who, ten years later, destooled the profligate King and hurled him out of the country!

Nasser is a tall, large, gracefully built man with remarkable eyes and a big rudder of a nose. His personal habits are exemplary. He lives with complete lack of ostentation in a modest Cairo villa, and his personal life has been happy. He has five youthful children. He is a devout Moslem, and does not touch alcohol. He has acute interest in politics all over the world, and is one of the few African—or European—statesmen who subscribe to such periodicals as *Foreign Affairs* not by ordinary post but by airmail. The dominating aspect of his character is disinterestedness plus force. He cares nothing for himself; all that interests him is the life of Egypt. He is much more reserved and less turbulent than most Egyptians, and his businesslike clarity of manner shows little of the inferiority-superiority sensitiveness and lack of poise that distinguish many of his compatriots.

This is not to say that he has ever lacked emotion. I heard him described as a man of ice—and fire. He took part during the war in an attempt to force the release of a deposed nationalist prime minister, Aly Maher, from detention; he looked for guidance for a time to such notorious extremists as Hadj Amin El Husseini, the exiled Grand Mufti of Jerusalem; he was an early member of an inflammatory organization known as the Moslem Brotherhood, and on one occasion even flirted with the idea of assassinating the King.

What is more, Nasser took active part in another murder plot which, however, miscarried. He has described this himself, in a series of three articles for the Egyptian magazine *Akher Saa,* entitled "The Philosophy of the Egyptian Revolution," which he wrote in 1953.[1] Few documents of our time are more revealing. It is a rare thing, to understate the case, for a man who is running a country to confess that only a few years before he had been leader of a murder squad. He does not reveal the name of the intended victim, but describes in considerable detail his own emotions. At this time he and his fellows were convinced that nothing but "positive action," that is, political assassination, could save Egypt. His prose is somewhat flowery:

I remember one night which marked the turning point of my ideas and dreams on this score. We had prepared a group for action and selected a person who we decided must cease to exist. We observed his habits and laid

[1] I have had access to a privately circulated translation of these. They were printed in part in the London *Observer,* October 10, 17, and 24, 1954.

down a detailed plan. We were going to shoot him down as he returned to his home in the night.

We set up an attack group to do the shooting, a covering force to protect the attack group, and a third group to organize the getaway. The appointed night came, and I went out with the attack group. Everything went according to plan. . . .

The squads concealed themselves in their chosen positions; and when the marked man came by, bullets were sent in his direction. The execution squad withdrew while the covering force protected its retreat, and the getaway to safety began. I started the motor of my car, and drove away from the theater of the positive action we had organized.

But suddenly there resounded in my ear the sounds of screaming and lamentation and the wailing of a woman, the crying of a baby, and then a continuous agitated call for help. . . .

I arrived at my house and threw myself on my bed, my mind in a furor and unceasing turmoil in my heart and conscience. The sounds of screaming and lamentation, wailing, and the calls for help continued to ring in my ears.

I didn't sleep all night. . . .

Was I right? I answered myself with conviction: I acted for the sake of my country.

Were these the only possible means? I replied, in some doubt: What else could we do?

Is it really possible to change the future of our country by eliminating this or that person, or is the problem deeper than this? . . .

We dream of the glory of the nation. But which is more important, to eliminate those who ought to be eliminated or to bring forward those who should be brought forward?

Then Nasser describes his violent emotion of relief the next morning when he learned that the shots had gone wild, and the victim had escaped without serious injury.

Nasser's articles are of absorbing interest, showing as they do the convulsion of agony that gripped his mind, and also how half-baked some of his thinking was. Ceaselessly he reflected on the weakness of his country, its degradation and shame. Egypt had to be redeemed; it had to be saved not merely from the British[2] but from itself; it had to be made strong, united, free, with a new cleanliness of spirit, with corruption and selfishness abolished. But how?

He took the lead at last in organizing the Free Officers Committee, composed of some four hundred youthful men, most of them under the rank of major. In effect, it is still this body that rules Egypt today. At the top were nine or ten of his closest comrades, who came to be called the *Binbashi* ("major" in Turkish). But even while he was creating this hard core of revolutionary organization, he continued to be harassed by torturing self-doubt. In his articles he stresses the point over and over again that his role—and the Army's—was dictated by fate, by circumstance.

[2] Nasser uses the locution "the Imperialism" as a synonym for "British."

Events were looking for a man, not vice versa. "It was not the army that defined its role in the events that took place; the opposite is closer to the truth. The events and their ramifications defined the role of the army in the great struggle to free the nation." Yet he asks himself—was it *necessary* for the Army to do what it did?

Conscientiously he seeks to explore the philosophical background to his action, as well as his own motives. He asks himself, "When did I discover the seeds of revolution within myself?" He thinks that they must have been planted in his subconscious in early childhood, put there "by the generation before us." He records that even as a child he burst into a rebellious shout every time he saw an airplane in the sky:

> Ya 'Azeez, Ya 'Azeez
> Dihiya takhud al-Ingleez!

> Oh Almighty, Oh Almighty,
> Disaster take the English!

A Word of Background

After severe rioting in Cairo on January 26, 1952, the Farouk regime crumbled fast. The desperate King tried one futile expedient after another. Corruption was positively orchidaceous. One item making for bitterness was a scandal—shocking even for Egypt—over munitions. Profiteers in Cairo had deliberately supplied the Army at the front in the Palestinian War with defective or worthless arms and ammunition, and had made huge profits by this evil enterprise. Senior officers showed their displeasure by electing as chairman of the Officers Club a general almost unknown to the country at large, but one who had made a reputation for decency and courage in the fighting in Israel—Mohammed Naguib—against the King's candidate. Nasser says in his articles that these events were subsidiary—that the coup was inevitable, and was bound to have come in any case—but they played nicely into his hand. Once the King lost the loyalty of the Army, he was doomed.

Nine officers composed Nasser's original Revolutionary Council, which grew out of the original Free Officers Committee. Naguib was not among them, but was brought into it because the clique needed an older man, a soldier with authority and prestige, to give it respectability. Nasser plotted the coup, and then sold it to Naguib. The junta, under Nasser's guidance, moved in the early hours of July 23 with force and precision. Tanks commanded strategic points in Cairo, and radio broadcasts announced to the nation that the Army had moved "to purify itself." There was no bloodshed or disorder. There were no demonstrations against foreigners—if only because Nasser did not want to give the British any pretext for stepping in. An incidental point is that the plotters maintained close contact with the American Embassy as soon as the coup got underway, and got strong sympathy from Americans in Cairo.

Farouk was forced to abdicate on July 26, and left the country. For a time a regency ruled and then, on June 18, 1953, the monarchy was abolished. The junta set up Aly Maher as its first prime minister, but he did not last long; Naguib replaced him as prime minister and then became President as well.

What ailed Farouk? First, greed; second, lasciviousness. Cairo gossip has it that, following an injury in an automobile accident some years ago, his whole character suddenly changed. From being a slim, handsome young man he became very fat; from being a personage reasonably serious—if spoiled—he turned into a self-indulgent playboy. I met him in Cairo several times during the war. He showed a good deal of dash and spirit—also vanity and capriciousness. Like most kings, he lived in a peculiar private world of his own. Some of his mannerisms were, even then, excessive. Leaving a night club one evening he reached in his pocket for a handful of coins and slithered them over the dance floor with the gesture of a child skipping stones across water; no doubt this was his manner of tipping the waiters. The thing he talked to me about most, politics aside, was whether or not he would be a success in Hollywood and how, above everything else in life, he wanted to meet Miss Ginger Rogers. His income was around £2,000,000 per year, and he had four palaces, two yachts, a squadron of "personal aviation," and carloads of erotica. One thing may be said about Farouk with the utmost assurance: not a soul in Egypt regretted his departure outside of his own small loop of henchmen, and probably not a soul survives who wants him back.

What Cairo—and Egypt—live on mostly is cotton; without cotton (and the Nile) the country would die; Egypt produces the finest long-staple cotton in the world, and from cotton it gets not less than *four-fifths* of its foreign exchange, i.e., its imports; few countries have an economy more vulnerable. The cotton yield per acre is 438 pounds as against 339 in the United States. Cotton was introduced into Egypt by Mohammed Ali in the 1820's, and, strangely enough, the American Civil War forty years later made it the basis of Egyptian wealth; when Lancashire could not buy cotton from the American south, the British textile industry had to turn to Egypt instead.[3] For years the British played politics with Egyptian cotton; they were by far the best customer and—until recently—could always keep the country in line by limiting their cotton purchases. The Nasser regime wants, if possible, to broaden the

[3] See Emil Ludwig, *The Nile*, p. 545.

basis of Egyptian economy, and make it less critically dependent on one export crop. For instance, a big petroleum hunt is going on, with several American companies participating. To have permitted this marks a substantial reversal in Cario policy. For a long time the Egyptians, being on the point of getting rid of the hated British at last, would not tolerate even the faintest idea of letting other "imperialist" interests enter the country. But Nasser wants above all to bridge the yawning, desolate gap in Egypt between rich and poor.

His plans are so ambitiously wide in this direction as to be almost grandiose. Political consolidation must come first, but Nasser and his men never cease to think in terms of future long-range economic development, so that the standard of living of the masses as a whole may be raised. General Naguib, when he was still prime minister, told me pithily that "underexploitation can be worse than overexploitation." He added, "*Egyptians* have been exploited, but not Egypt. Let us try to make the great wealth of Egypt available to the *people*." I asked four different Egyptians of the most varied background what the country needed most. All answered with a single identical word, "Production." One huge project, which will cost more than $500,000,000 and take ten years to build, is a new dam, the Saad el Ali (High Dam) scheme. This will be in the form of a "pyramidal granite rock field half a kilometer thick," to be situated near Aswan; if all goes well, it will increase the total arable land in the country from six to eight million acres, and increase national production by $450 million per year.

Egypt had by the 1947 census a population of 19,087,304. Today the figure is probably between 21 and 22 million. Practically all of these millions are squeezed into the green fertile thread of the Nile valley, with the result that the density of population here is the highest in the world, about 1,600 per square mile.[4] Moreover the population has for years grown at an astonishing pace, and will presumably continue to do so. It has increased by 100 percent in forty years, and soars nowadays at the unbelievable rate of 350,000 per year. "The only thing that grows in Egypt and stays in the country," a university professor told me, "is the population. We are a nation smothered by ourselves." He paused with an ironic chuckle. "One fault is that most of our four thousand villages do not have electric light. There is nothing for the people to do after sundown except have sexual intercourse."

Make more land. Make fewer people. Either of these solutions would alleviate the problem, but neither is easy. The desert is difficult to irrigate, and the rank and file of Egyptians are not educated enough to

[4] The density of population per square mile of cultivated land in the United States is 210.

understand the necessity for birth control.[5] A possible future remedy may be industrialization. The lesson of history is that as industrialization increases and the standard of living goes up, the birthrate tends to diminish. As things stand today the only check on the irresistible advance of population is infant mortality. This reaches in Egypt the staggering figure of 129 per 1,000 (as against 29.2 per 1,000 in the United States). The average life expectancy of an Egyptian at birth is only about thirty-seven years.

Not only are millions of Egyptians jammed together in the narrowest of spaces; inequalities in the ownership of land are extreme. There are about 2,700,000 landowners in all; of these more than 2,000,000 own less than an acre each. Eighty-five percent of the total population of Egypt is altogether landless. But 2,000 rich pashas own no fewer than 1,200,000 acres; *36 percent of all cultivable land in the country is in the hands of one-half of one percent of the population.*

The Egyptian pashas were—until recently—not only probably the richest class of their kind in the world, in comparison to the rest of the people, but the most corrupt. During the war when I visited Egypt the saying was that forty new millionaires were created every month, largely through graft. Ex-King Farouk derived from a tradition opulent and extravagant beyond belief; his grandfather the Khedive Ismail owned one-fifth of *all* cultivable property in the entire country, and nevertheless borrowed from Europe the neat sum of $495 million in a reign lasting sixteen years. Another exacerbating factor was that the landowning aristocracy had, by and large, practically no interest in the country (except to draw money out of it); it sprang from the Turks and did not even consider itself to be Egyptian.

In contrast the lot of the submerged millions of fellaheen on the soil (*fellah*=plowman) was miserable beyond description. It still is. The fellah lives with his water buffalo in mud, slime, and penury. A recent survey by Rockefeller Foundation scientists found that living standards in Egyptian villages were lower than anywhere else in the civilized world, and that the *average* income in Egypt is only about $87 per year.

Nasser-Naguib on reaching power set out at once to make a land reform. In principle the big estates are to be broken up, and all individual land holdings limited to two hundred acres. What the lush aristocracy thought of this can easily be imagined. Screams of bloody murder reverberated up and down the Nile. Some people were even

[5] Strikingly enough the rector of Alexandria University recently made a public pronouncement to the effect that nothing in Moslem theology forbids birth control. Many patriotic young Egyptians—instead of marrying several wives before they are twenty—now defer marriage until they are in their mid-thirties and then remain monogamous. They do not want to add the burden of surplus children to the nation.

stupid enough to whisper balefully the word "Communism!" Of course
nothing could possibly be a more fruitful hotbed for Communist agitation than Egyptian society unreformed, with the fellah permanently
glued to his mire. Reforms like those that Colonel Nasser seeks to put
into effect are, it is only too manifest to people of good will, the best
possible defense *against* future Communist advance.

Nasser in Power

Nasser apparently hoped that, once he threw out the King and set up
a new government, the people would automatically rally to him and
stay rallied, in pursuit of the shining ideals of the revolutionary movement. Indeed mass demonstrations of unprecedented size and enthusiasm—demonstrations such as Egypt had never seen before, with hundreds of thousands of people massed in the streets—did take place.
This was when Naguib was titular leader of the junta. But to have a lot
of people out in the streets is not the same thing as successful government. To re-create a country overnight is not easy, or, as Nasser puts it,
"to develop the mature political consciousness that is an indispensable
preliminary for a sound democracy." There had to be the sternest kind
of activity on at least three fronts—first to get the mechanics of government into smooth operation, second to clean out and punish personages
guilty of corruption and other crimes in the previous regime, and third
to make the new government secure against the danger of a counter
coup.

The Council of Revolutionary Command—executive body of the
junta—was increased in membership from nine to fourteen, and then
pared down to eleven. Its motto was Unity, Order, Work. But even here
at the very top, trouble came. Two at least of the original group have
been ousted and either exiled or imprisoned. One of these was a Communist. The council contains several red-hot socialists today, but no
Communists. The word in Cairo at the beginning—among bitter enemies
of Nasser-Naguib—was that the junta was "90 percent Fascist, 10 percent Communist." This was a gross exaggeration, if only because the
inner struggle for power was based on personalities, not ideology. If the
government took measures that savored strongly of state capitalism, it
was because private capitalism had ceased to function fruitfully. Things
were astoundingly mixed up.

Nasser-Naguib borrowed ideas from Fascism, but they were much
less totalitarian and extremist than those who opposed them. Their
methods may have been totalitarian, but not the basic aim. Membership
in the new Liberation Rally was voluntary, not obligatory. There was no
accent on force for force's sake. Almost at once every effort was made to
work out a system of constitutional reform, and pave the way for free

elections and the resumption of democratic government. The army was the protector of the people, and the revolution was in the people's name.

One early watchword was "Clean up!" The junta set out to rub some of the slime off Egypt's oily surface. A three-man revolutionary tribunal was set up, more or less on the model of the French Revolution, under the chairmanship of a youthful air officer. The sentences it meted out were mild on the whole—except in a few instances of outright treason. The purge affected almost every sphere of Egyptian society, and a weird collection of characters met judgment. All political leaders of the Wafd, Liberal Constitutional, and Saadist parties who had held ministerial office betwen 1942 and 1952 were deprived of all political rights until 1964. This made a clean sweep of the old politicians. Dozens of Army officers, career diplomats, and university professors were purged. Nahas Pasha [a conspicuous former prime minister] was jailed, and his wife, Zeinab el Wakil, who had been one of the real rulers of Egypt in the last days of the monarchy, was found guilty of fraud and corruption and had some $3,000,000 worth of property confiscated. Another ex-prime minister, Ibrahim Abdel Hadi, who had been involved in scandals during the Palestine war, was actually sentenced to death for "high treason and conspiracy with a foreign power." This sentence was, however, later commuted. Several personages in Farouk's entourage got long sentences, as did one member of the short-lived regency council and at least two Wafdist ministers.

One persistent, almost ineradicable source of dissidence and turmoil was the Moslem Brotherhood. This, a body which combined extreme nationalist aims with a kind of fundamentalist religious fanaticism, was not so much a party as a movement. It grew up after World War II, and had several million members at the height of its power. It wanted freedom from Britain above all, believed in political terrorism, and assassinated two Egyptian prime ministers. At one time Nasser, as I have already mentioned, belonged to this organization, and so probably did several other members of the cabinet and the Council of Revolutionary Command. Also it was penetrated strongly by Communists. Nasser-Naguib tried to co-operate with the Brotherhood at first. But they were bound to come into conflict, if only because there was not room in Egypt for two revolutionary mass movements. The Brotherhood began to make agitation against the government, and in January, 1954, it was suppressed; 450 of its leaders were arrested, two thousand local headquarters were shut down, and $8,500,000 of its funds were confiscated. But it refused to stay suppressed. Its supreme "guide," Hassan El Hodeiby, was released from jail after a time and trouble began anew. In October came an attempt by members of the Brotherhood to assassinate Nasser; eight shots were fired against him, but he escaped untouched. This time the government moved against the Brotherhood in real earnest, and it was crushed and broken up to such an extent that it is doubtful if it can ever rise again.

The October episode also served to end General Naguib as a political force. He was removed from office (November, 1954) and placed under house arrest. Probably he had nothing to do with the plot against Nasser, but Brotherhood terrorists said that they planned to make a new revolutionary government under his (Naguib's) leadership. Whether or not the General was aware of this conspiracy to make use of him is unknown.

The consequent breakup of the Nasser-Naguib relationship is one of the saddest of contemporary political episodes. Naguib had great quality and brought much to the revolution. The two men complemented each other nicely. Nasser was the brain, the theoretician, the organizer; Naguib was the doughty and incorruptible man of action, wildly popular with the masses. For a time there was a profound fondness between the two partners as well as close political affiliation. What, in the end, caused the split? First, pressures within the army. Second, Naguib wanted a quick return to a normal parliamentary regime, but Nasser thought that the people were not yet ready. Naguib is much more moderate than Nasser, much less inclined to push through a truly revolutionary program on a long-range basis. Third, temperamental differences growing into acute bitterness and jealousy.

Nasser for a long time stoutly denied reports that he intended to get rid of Naguib and take over his functions. He said, "I am too young. Besides, I am too fond of him."

As of the time I visited Egypt in preparation for this book [*Inside Africa*] Nasser had no public post at all; Naguib had everything. He was prime minister, commander-in-chief of the Armed Forces, minister of defense, head of the Army Revolution, leader of the National Liberation Rally, and chairman of the Council of Revolutionary Command.

Nasser first emerged into public view on July 18, 1953, when he became deputy prime minister and minister of the interior. Before that, very few people indeed outside the inner circle even knew his name. What he needs most, as is only too obvious, are time and political tranquillity. He cannot get the former without the latter. To rule successfully he must hold the good will of the people at large, and not let his government degenerate into a purely military junta, exercising authority capriciously. But to rule at all he has to hold the reins firm, and this he cannot do—for the time being at least—without maintaining arbitrary rule.

[6] *World Today*, February, 1955.

One thing can be said without question—already he has done more for Egypt in a couple of years than the royal family did in a hundred and fifty. He is absolutely honest and has never asked anything for himself. The very fact that he is both dedicated and honest is a phenomenon so puzzling to old-style Egyptians that they cannot "understand" him. I heard him described as a "simple man with a complex mind." But, after all, that is better than being a complex man with a simple mind.

What Nasser and his men lack most is concrete managerial experience. No doubt they have made mistakes, but it would be a tragic day for Egypt and the world if they should be overturned and the country should succumb to forces more revolutionary or, worse, be sucked back into the sloth, greed, and infamy of the old regime.

~~~~~~

Much has happened in Egypt since I wrote these passages. But Nasser still holds power. He has been furiously attacked and condemned by various elements in the world outside. Some of his Arab brethren detest him almost as much as they detest the Jews, and his neutralist policies have not—to put it mildly—endeared him to Washington or most of the chancelleries of Western Europe. Nobody is likely to forget that he nationalized the Suez Canal, which precipitated the great fracas of October, 1956, when an Anglo-French-Israeli military attack on Egypt was aborted in what was probably the most formidable international crisis since World War II. Two years later Egypt and Syria merged (except geographically) to form the United Arab Republic, with Nasser as its President. The union was short-lived. Meantime his flirtatiousness toward the Soviet Union increased, and if I were a citizen of Israel I would look at Nasser with an extremely cold eye if only because of the German nuclear scientists he has imported into Egypt. In fact in this connection I, as a good American, look at him with an extremely cold eye. In 1962 he bitterly alienated Jordan and Saudi Arabia by supporting anti-royalist revolutionists in the Yemen. He broke up Arab unity all over the Middle East, while retaining his monstrously obscurantist attitude to Israel. In the domestic sphere he continues to have to deal with such pressing problems as the Aswan Dam, the land reform, population (he has instituted a government program of birth control), and nationalization of industry, under an ambitious blanket program called "Arab socialism." Typical of him still is one of his early apothegms, "Every one of us is able in his own way to perform a miracle."

Certainly he needs them. The United States has pumped something like a billion dollars into Egypt in the past eight years, and we supply surplus food to the country worth an estimated $140 million a year. It *has been calculated that "one quarter of all food eaten by Egyptians" comes to them free from America. This has not prevented some recent highly unpleasant nationalist demonstrations against the U.S., including the wanton burning of the American library in Cairo. Meantime, in the accepted neutralist manner, Nasser accepts help from the Communist bloc as well. The Soviets and their satellites are, in fact, contributing no less than $500 million in credits to Cairo for the second Egyptian Five Year Plan.*

CHAPTER 31

~~~~~~~

The King of Kings

A condensation of this treatment of Haile Selassie, Emperor of Ethiopia, appeared in Reader's Digest, July, 1954. *Then the full version was printed the next year in* Inside Africa. *The Emperor at this time was at the zenith of his power.*

~~~~~~

> *The Aethiopians slept near a thousand years, forgetful of the world, by whom they were forgotten.*
> —EDWARD GIBBON

W E REACH now a country utterly unlike any we have seen in Africa so far. Ethiopia, sometimes called Abyssinia, is a mountain fastness, a fortress, cut off to a large extent from the adjacent world by the mere fact of its altitude, an impregnable feudal kindgom lost in space. The thing that struck us most politically was, of course, the person of the Emperor. Haile Selassie strides the immense wastes of the Ethiopian plateau—like a gnome.

One might almost say that the chief issue in Ethiopia is a struggle between this frail, tenacious little man *and* his country. The note he sounds is of progress, modernization, at least to the extent that difficult circumstances make this possible. Haile Selassie has committed himself to a carefully calculated effort to conquer the backwardness of his domain, and bring it into the embrace of civilization overnight. No struggle in Africa is more challenging.

A generation has grown up since the Italian conquest of Ethiopia [in the 1930's], when Haile Selassie's proud, dainty, and adhesive figure commanded the liberal conscience of mankind. A visitor does not have to be in Addis Ababa long to find out that he is still Emperor of Ethopia and King of Kings. In fact he runs his country, both blessed and tortured as it is by some of the most titanic forces ever let loose by nature, almost as if it were a kindergarten.

When we arrived in Addis Ababa friends drove us in from the airport. "My God, the Emperor!" exclaimed our escort—not sacrilegiously, but in the tone of a man confronted suddenly with an overpowering natural phenomenon. A big green Rolls-Royce, flying the imperial flag, shot toward us around a corner. Donkeys scattered, and, almost as if they were bending before some invisible wind, passers-by flattened themselves on the road, not merely bowing, but in full prostration. Our car—and all other cars—jerked to a stop, and our companions jumped out to the street, bowing stiffly as the imperial limousine darted past. The King of Kings, perched on cushions, bowed back politely, and then swept on. This ceremony of recognition of the Emperor is *de rigueur* in Ethiopian society.

The Emperor himself, however, takes protocol somewhat less seriously than do members of his entourage. Recently he visited Massawa, the Eritrean seaport. A group of diplomats saw him approach, and smartly jumped out of their own cars to salute him. He wagged his finger at them as if they were children behaving *too* properly.

A few days after our arrival in Addis Ababa my wife and I had the honor of being received by His Imperial Majesty (few people ever say merely "His Majesty"). I have met a good many kings, but never one like this. The extreme stiffness of the Ethiopian court dates from a tradition centuries old; even in comparatively recent times courtiers were supposed to approach the Emperor by crawling across the room. In earlier days the penalty for disrespect was cutting off the lips and tongue of the offender. When etiquette began to take on a western character, during the present Emperor's reign, the model chosen was Swedish, and Sweden has the strictest court in Europe.

I faced minor sartorial difficulties, since I had been told that I must wear a morning coat and striped trousers; I did not possess these articles, and could find nobody in Addis Ababa who had them to fit my size. Eventually I was permitted to penetrate into the imperial presence in nothing more formal than a dark suit, and nothing untoward happened. The kingdom is still standing. Carefully friends briefed us about what we had to do. On entering the Emperor's chamber three separate bows are necessary, one at the threshold, one halfway across the room, and one on being presented—on the part of my wife three curtsies. Similarly one must bow or curtsy three times on departure, while walking backward.

Haile Selassie sat placidly on a small French-style sofa, wearing a khaki uniform with a placard of decorations. He rose as his principal private secretary, Ato Tafarra Worq Kidane Wold, introduced us; Mr. Worq is one of the most important dignitaries in Ethiopia.[1] His Imperial Majesty knows English quite well but prefers not to speak it; he talked in his native Amharic, and Mr. Worq translated expertly. After twenty minutes Mr. Worq left the room for a moment, to fetch a gift for us; while he was absent the Emperor went right on talking—in French much better than mine. There was no need to have had any interpretation at all! But when Mr. Worq returned we instantly reverted to a laborious combination of English and Amharic. Such is the royal custom.

Almost everything about Haile Selassie has a quality of grace, as well as impeccable dignity. Everybody has seen his photograph, but I had not realized before how exceptionally short he is. He looks like an aristocrat from the Levant. On the sofa were two tiny brown dogs, which he fondled as we talked. The Emperor's conversation was simple and direct, but I had the feeling that he was a complex character. He said that he knew well that the United States was a traditional friend of nationalism, since it had never recognized the Italian occupation of Ethiopia, and (while we were talking in French) that it was his *rêve* to visit America.[2] He told us that he had ordered Ethiopian troops to fight in Korea because other countries had helped *him* during the Italian invasion. He denied that there was any danger of communism in Ethiopia and said that he would like very much to see a common defense program established for the Middle East, with American participation.

One of His Imperial Majesty's duties this morning was inspection of the Imperial Police Staff College at Aba Dina, where a class of officers was graduating, and we were invited to attend this ceremony. The school, which is run by Swedes, proudly demonstrated its achievements. The program told us what we would see. "Brief examination in investigation of the scene of crime, with saving traces." "Demonstration of a modern equipped rushing-out-car with police and radio." Cadets did exercises in ju-jitsu, and showed us that they knew how to take fingerprints. Haile Selassie walked from exhibit to exhibit, in the piercing sunshine, amid swarms of angry and pertinacious flies. He wore a long khaki cape and a large beige-colored pith sun helmet, which made him look something like a mushroom.

When he entered the main room, where a throne had been set up, he

[1] Once he was a translator in the British embassy.

[2] This dream was soon fulfilled. In 1954 His Imperial Majesty took a five months' trip abroad, visiting the United States for the first time. He received a resounding welcome. America fascinated him. Also he went to England (where Queen Elizabeth II conferred on him the Order of the Garter) and several countries on the continent, including Yugoslavia, where he got on well with Marshal Tito.

rested his tiny feet on a cushion; otherwise they would not have reached the floor. He never smiled, nor looked to the right or left. Each cadet had to walk up four carpeted steps, salute in a complicated manner, and then descend backward. The Emperor shook hands with no one but a senior Swedish officer. He made a short speech, and a band played the wild, soaring notes of the Ethiopian imperial anthem. The feeble ineptness of much that we saw was heartbreaking. One boy, chosen to demonstrate his skill in mechanics, could not make the gears of a car work; another who gave a lecture on crime prevention was so dazed—numb— that he could scarcely talk. Yet it is out of beginnings like this, no matter how clumsy, that Haile Selassie's Ethiopia is being built. A loyal, honest, and efficient police is a necessity in Ethiopia—just as it should be in New York—and it cannot be created without education, education, education.

What Makes Ethiopia Unique

Four interesting phenomena are these: (1) Ethiopia is not only an independent state, but has by far the longest record of independence of any country in Africa except Egypt, and it differs strikingly from Egypt in that it has *never* been under foreign domination, except during the Italian occupation from 1936 to 1941. (2) It is Christian—indigenously Christian from the most ancient times, not Christianized by modern missionaries. (3) It is *not* a "black" or Negro nation, as most people think. Some of its people are black as Vulcan, and some have Negro blood, but Ethiopians most distinctly do not think of themselves as Negro or Negroid. (4) In Ethiopia, the equation characteristic of colonial Africa is reversed—Europeans work for Africans, not vice versa.

Let us elaborate on these four points in turn.

1. Ethiopia remained unconquered—until Mussolini—for almost three thousand years, even during the heyday of the European scramble for Africa, for the simplest of reasons—it was too inaccessible, too mountainous and impregnable, to attack. Even in Homeric times Ethiopians were known as "the farthest away of all mankind"; their country was the place where the sun was supposed to set. Ethiopia was, however, several times penetrated—but not conquered—by Europeans. The Portuguese, seeking the legendary Prester John, touched on its coasts; then in the sixteenth century came the Turks, who brought in Islam. The British sent the Napier expedition into the country in 1868, to rescue a handful of British subjects held in captivity; the operation was a success, but cost £9,000,000. In 1895 the Italians attacked Ethiopia, but they were so badly mauled at the celebrated Battle of Adowa that they retired and left the country severely alone—as did the other great powers—till 1935.

Ethiopian history goes back all the way to Solomon and the Queen of

Sheba. Their son Menelik became the first ruler of the kingdom, and all Ethiopian kings—ever since—are believed to be his lineal descendants. The name "Menelik" is so revered that no monarch ever dared adopt it as his own first name, although it occurred in family names, for interminable centuries, until the great Menelik II (1889–1908), who was Haile Selassie's granduncle and the victor of Adowa. Myths that describe the origin of the dynasty are picturesque, and have been the subject of innumerable Ethiopian works of art. Sheba was Queen in the ancient Ethiopian city of Axum; she heard of Solomon's wisdom, determined to visit him, and organized a safari to Jerusalem. At a sumptuous banquet, Solomon assured her that he would not seize her virtue, since she was so highly born, if she promised in return to take nothing that belonged to him. They dined together and he saw to it that she ate amply of foods highly spiced; then he slept in a canopied tent nearby. She woke up, thirsty, and surreptitiously took a drink of water. So Solomon said that she had broken her word, and must surrender herself to his embraces. Thus the first Menelik was conceived, and the Solomonic line brought into being. The throne is still called the Solomonic throne.[3]

Four principal provinces or "kingdoms"—Amhara, Shoa, Tigrai, and Gojjam—grew up on the isolated wilderness of the Ethiopian plateau during the Middle Ages, and fought each other perpetually. Axum was the capital from prehistoric times until 1538. The imperial crown is still kept at Axum, and this remote village was—and is—the site of some of the most stunning and mysterious objects of antiquity in the world, giant obelisks made of single blocks of granite, larger than Egyptian obelisks, the origin of which is unknown. Ethiopia needs archeologists today almost as much as it needs adding machines. Until modern times the Ethiopians were mostly a savage people. That is to say, they were probably as savage as the Visigoths, the Angles, or the Franks. They were peculiarly addicted to mutilation, and liked to cut off the hands or feet of enemies captured in battle; even today, in some remote regions, a man is not supposed to be worthy of marriage until he has killed somebody and given his fiancée the sexual organs of the victim. But let us keep in mind that as late as the reign of Queen Elizabeth I people in England were publicly hanged, drawn, and quartered, a form of execution much worse than any ever devised in Africa.

2. The statement that Ethiopia is "Christian" needs modification, in that probably half the total population (there are no reliable statistics) is Moslem or pagan. But the government and ruling classes are almost solidly Christian (Coptic). The country might almost be called a theocracy, and Haile Selassie himself, an extremely devout Christian, more or

---

[3] Margery Perham's indispensable *The Government of Ethiopia*, p. 403, contains a full and flavorsome account of this old legend.

less runs the Ethiopian national church. Remote Coptic monasteries have been functioning in Ethiopia without interruption for almost fifteen hundred years. The clergy is fantastically numerous—one authority says that one out of every five adult males is a priest—and fantastically backward; it is probably the most illiterate clergy in the world.

The Church plays such an exceptional role in Ethiopia, economically and politically, that we must tell something of its origin. In about A.D. 340 two Phoenician boys, both Christian, were shipwrecked in the Red Sea, made their way into Ethiopia, became favorites of the King, and converted him to the Christian faith. One boy, whose name has come down to us as St. Frumentius, traveled back and forth between Ethiopia and Egypt, and in time became the Abuna (roughly, archbishop or metropolitan) of Ethiopia, under the authority of the Patriarch of Alexandria. When Frumentius died, the King asked the Patriarch to send him a new Abuna. This system—appointment of the head of the Ethiopian church by the Coptic patriarch in Egypt—went on without serious interruption from the fourth century till 1950. The head of the Ethiopian church, with vast powers, was always an *Egyptian* Copt, even though he might be a man well beyond middle age who had never been in Ethiopia before and who knew not a word of any Ethiopian language. It was as if, throughout the course of British history, the Archbishop of Canterbury always had to be a Finn or Dane. There came, inevitably, incessant struggles for power between various kings and their Abunas. To exercise influence in the secular field, the Abuna had to keep on good terms with the King. The King, on his side, had little authority if the Abuna was against him. And neither could kick the other out.

Haile Selassie set about ending this anomalous situation after his return from exile, and when the last Egyptian Abuna died he refused to accept a new one. He wanted the leadership of the church to be Ethiopian. Delicate and protracted negotiations with the Alexandrian patriarch were necessary before he had his way. He had to tread carefully because he did not want to break too sharply with tradition. In the end a new system was set up. The church became national, and the Abuna must always be Ethiopian hereafter. The Emperor nominates a man suggested by the local clergy, and this nomination is then "confirmed" by the Patriarch in Alexandria, who no longer has any role in the actual choice. Many hard-shell Copts bitterly resented the Emperor's course of action, but there was nothing they could do about it.

3. Ethiopians of the ruling class—the Amharas who live in the high central province—consider themselves to be "white" no matter what their color is, and are a terrifically proud people. The "blacks" are slaves from the Sudan or other Negroes; Europeans (including Americans) are thought of as "pink." Once the rumor spread that the United States in-

tended to send an American Negro as ambassador to Ethiopia; this
would have been a hideous *faux pas,* and luckily did not happen. Most
Amharas still have features markedly Caucasoid; it is only their dark
skin that makes them look like Negroes. They do *not* as a rule have
squat noses or bulbous lips.

Nowadays Ethiopians like to call themselves a "Sabaean" people;
"Saba" means "Sheba," and the Red Sea is known locally as the "Sabaean"
Sea. They look north and east rather than south or west. Even if they
concede they are "African," they belong to another world too, that of
the Middle East. There is practically no contact, cultural or economic,
with Black Africa. Kenya, although it borders on Ethiopia, seems further
away than Saskatchewan. But the Sabaean peoples, the Greeks, the
Arabs, the mixed folk of the Levant, have close bonds.

Ethiopian Jews exist; they are called Falashas, and make influential
small communities in several areas, particularly near Lake Tana. They
were great warriors as well as traders, and at one remote time even took
over the dynasty; they think of themselves as exiles from the Promised
Land, but do not know Hebrew. Certainly Haile Selassie himself must
own to some faint tincture of Jewish blood, since he claims descent from
Solomon.

4. Foreign influence in Ethiopia is profound. Hiring foreigners for
government jobs is, of course, necessary because so few trained Ethiopians are available. Swedes train some of the police, the imperial guard,
and the military air force. The Emperor's two closest political advisors
are American. Among other officials the chief justice of the High
Court is British, as is the commissioner of police. The French own the
railroad which connects Addis Ababa with the sea at Djibouti—the only
railroad in the country. It spans 486 miles, and has been called the most
expensive railway in the world; it costs three times more to ship a con-
signment of hides from Addis Ababa to Djibouti than from Djibouti to
New York. The chief trading company, A. Besse and Company, famous
throughout the Red Sea world, is French, domiciled in Aden. Another
important company, Mosvald, is Norwegian. There are Canadian officials
in the Ministries of Finance and Commerce, and an Israeli, born in
Hungary, is advocate general and chief prosecutor. A Czech is an advisor to the Foreign Office, an Austrian is head of the Development Bank,
and one important judge is a Free Pole. A Greek doctor is physician to
His Imperial Majesty, and is one of the very few foreigners ever given
the title "Bitwoded" (Well-Beloved). A Swiss is director of the telecom-
munications training center being established by the Technical Assistance Administration of the UN. A spaghetti factory is Italian. The
brewmaster in the St. George Brewery is, fittingly enough, a Czech from
Pilsen, and the conspicuous King George Bar on the central plaza of

Addis Ababa is run by a Greek. The bandmaster of the imperial guard is
(again fittingly) a Viennese.

Still More Background

The word "Amhara" (mountain people) comes from Hebrew, and the
language, Amharic, has its own script (as do Armenian and Georgian),
and is inordinately complex; I could not find anybody who would say with
certainty whether its fantastic alphabet contained 247, 256, or 259 different letters. But the Emperor has resisted attempts to Latinize it. The only
place in the world, I was told, where this abstruse language is taught
outside Ethiopia is the School of Oriental Studies in Paris. Few books
exist in Amharic—even in Ethiopia itself—except the Bible, and it took
many years before this was translated successfully.[4] Most proper names
in Ethiopia have a Biblical derivation. For instance, Haile Selassie means
"Power of Trinity."

Ethiopia has substantial reserves of subsoil wealth, but the surface
has hardly been touched. Coffee is the most important crop; our word
"coffee" comes, in fact, from the Ethiopian name "Kaffa." American Point Four experts take one look at the land and can scarcely believe
what they see; the plateau near Addis Ababa has a fertility probably
unmatched in the world except by the American corn belt, and could
become one of the greatest granaries on earth. Of course communications
(except by air) are primitive in the extreme, and make progress difficult. All but one or two Ethiopian roads have approximately the status
of British roads at the time of Stonehenge; in the whole country, only
2,300 miles of road exist at all. The distance from Addis Ababa to Harar,
the chief town of the Emperor's home district, is 240 miles; the trip will
take two full days if you have a car with four-wheel drive. Large parts
of the country can only be reached by jeep, and only six cities in the entire kingdom are connected by telegraph. A scant ten others can be
reached by radio—if the radio is working.

Parts of Ethiopia are still semi-savage; it is one of the few countries
in Africa where, in some areas, it is distinctly unsafe for a person to go
about alone. (There are similar areas, of course, in New York City.)
Some Ethiopian women—until quite recently—wore their hair plaited
with the bowels of oxen, and among the Gallas dead children may be
hung on trees instead of being buried. Not long ago a British customs
official on the Ethiopia-Kenya frontier complained to his Ethiopian colleague that his dog kept him awake by howling all night. A few days
later the dog appeared without ears. Horrified, the Briton asked what

---

[4] The ancient Coptic language, displaced by Amharic, is Geez, which is variously
spelled Ghis, Gheez, and Ge'ez. Some priests still use it on occasion, as priests in
western lands may use Latin.

had happened. The Ethiopian officer replied, "The dog did not listen when I told it to be quiet, and so I cut its ears off."

Ethiopia had, as of the time I went there, exactly seven movie theaters and two newspapers. Both papers were weeklies under government control; one appeared in English and Amharic, the other in French and Amharic. A British editor[5] has described recently some of his tribulations in the wild, wonderful field of Ethiopian journalism. His news stories were mercilessly cut, and political comment forbidden. Here are some stipulations laid down by the censorship:

1. Whenever the Emperor is mentioned his name must appear at the beginning of the article, and no other name must appear before his.
2. All references to the Emperor, including all pronouns, must be capitalized.

Ethiopians are not only extraordinarily proud but sensitive in the extreme. I heard a *Ferengi* (foreigner) who knows the country well and likes it very much say, "These are the most arrogant people in the world, and this is their most endearing quality." Social life is difficult, because officials simply forget to turn up for a dinner party, and never bother to explain. It is almost as hard to get good servants as in New York; people are too supercilious to work, unless they obtain a feudal or semi-family status.

We were warned not to photograph street scenes—the only place in Africa where this happened. It is not that people fear the evil eye, which the camera represents in some African communities; the authorities do not like Ethiopian primitiveness to be exposed. Passports of all visitors are impounded for a day or two, and in Addis Ababa strict curfew closes off the streets at night. Nobody is allowed out of doors without a pass.

Ethiopia has never had a true election, and nobody would pretend that it is a democracy. There are no political parties, no trade unions, no vehicles for the expression of opinion, and no civil liberties in our sense. A "parliament" exists, but it is altogether rudimentary; the Emperor picks the membership of the upper house himself. No political opposition is permitted. If an important official falls into disfavor, a difficult problem is created—what to do with him? In the United States a defeated senator, or a retiring member of the cabinet, can go back to his law practice or other occupation, but in Ethiopia there is no place to go, because no good jobs exist outside the government. Some fifty politicians of rank are believed, as of the moment, to be in *confino*, or forced exile, out in the desolate wastes of the plateau. They have their own servants (or slaves) and a certain liberty of action and movement; but

5 William H. Seed, "Censorship in Ethiopia," *Manchester Guardian*, October 7, 1952.

they cannot return to Addis Ababa. In the old days the authorities waited till a prisoner was forgotten, whereupon he would be poisoned. I asked, "Can prisoners write letters?" Laughter greeted the naïveté of this remark. "Of course not. Most cannot read or write. If they dictate a letter to a scribe, the scribe will write what *he* feels like writing, and send the document to whomever *he* may gain favor from. Or he may send several contradictory letters."

Everything—any progress—depends ultimately on education, and the Emperor's program in this regard is the best thing in the kingdom. Nobody is "minister" of education—a vice-minister is in charge of this department—because the Emperor himself acts as minister. Approximately one-third of the budget goes to education (a large percentage for Africa—and for several countries not in Africa), and Haile Selassie has spent immense sums out of his personal fortune to support educational effort. About eighty thousand Ethiopian children go to school. Teachers have a heartbreaking job. Children learn slowly, and overvalue what they learn; a high-school graduate will think that he is competent to be a minister. One curious point is that few children ever have toys to play with; as a result they never learn to do things with their hands as American youngsters do, and are apt to be clumsy, with no manual dexterity, in later life.

Finally, one should mention that the Emperor has to do practically everything himself. He is "the sole source of power and initiative" in a country which till recently had hardly "a semblance of modern administration."

The Negus: His Life and Times

Haile Selassie I, Elect of God, Conquering Lion of the Tribe of Judah, King of Zion, *Negusa Nagast* (King of Kings), and Emperor of Ethiopia, was born in Harar Province in 1892. He has been the most powerful person in the country since 1917; in other words his authority has persisted undiminished for more than thirty-five years, except of course during the Italian occupation. Haile Selassie spent five years to a day, from May 5, 1936, to May 5, 1941, in exile. Mussolini cost him his throne, but he regained it in a manner of speaking because of Hitler; had not Hitler made World War II, provoking British intervention in Ethiopia, he might still be sitting in Bath, England, where he spent part of his forced sojourn abroad.

He was grandson of [the great Emperor] Menelik II, and inherits royal blood from both father and mother. The British embassy in Addis Ababa has a chart of the imperial family that covers several square yards; Ethiopian genealogy is abstruce. Young Haile Selassie got a western education from a French Catholic mission in Harar, and showed outstanding qualities—including ambition—very early. Menelik (before his dotage) took careful note of him, pushed him hard, and made him a *ras* when he was still a youth. *Ras*dom is not inherited; the title corresponds more to "Marshal" than to "Duke" or "Prince." Haile Selassie was called Ras Tafari at this time, and, after Menelik had tried him out in various posts, he became vice-governor of Harar before he was twenty-five. Menelik died, and was succeeded as Emperor by Lij Yasu (Jesus), one of his grandsons. Yasu's reign was a disaster. He offended the priestly hierarchy by embracing Islam, which is as if a King of England should suddenly become Buddhist, and committed other indiscretions. World War I was going on then, and Turkish and German influence grew steeply in Ethiopia. Came a palace revolution (1916) made mostly by the Church, but in which the British and French (who wanted to frustrate Yasu) certainly played a hand. Yasu was deposed, and Haile Selassie brought forward to replace him. But he could not be made Emperor yet. The succession went to an aged and incompetent lady, the Empress Zauditu, one of Menelik's daughters, but Haile Selassie became regent and heir to the throne. Three forces favored him: the Church, his imperial lineage, and one wing of the army. Even so civil war took place until he fought and won a pitched battle with Yasu's forces. A decade of subterranean struggle followed—mostly with intractable *rases*—before he gained a firm, final grip on power. Such intrigues went on as made even Ethiopian hair stand on end. Then (he was still known as Ras Tafari) he negotiated Ethiopia's entrance into the League of Nations, which brought him marked prestige, and wrote a new constitution giving himself wide powers. In 1928 he became King of Shoa (an important province), and in 1930, when Zauditu died, he was crowned Emperor. Old Yasu was still alive. He was not invited to the ceremony. He was, in fact, still a prisoner in chains—literally—and remained so until his death in 1935.

Haile Selassie's appearances before the League of Nations at Geneva, his defiance of Mussolini and gallant resistance to Italian conquest, are too well known to need description here.

When further resistance against Italy was hopeless the Emperor abandoned his capital (via the French railway), although several of the tough old *rases* fought on for some months, like Ras Imru, who later became Ethiopian ambassador to Washington, and Ras Desta. A major influence in persuading him to go—after the front collapsed and further military operations were impossible—was his wife. The Emperor's justification for his departure was that nobody else could possibly represent Ethiopia in the outside world, and lead successful efforts for its resurrection. In this he was perfectly right. He spent difficult years. He went to Jerusalem first, where Abyssinian monks live in the

Church of the Holy Sepulchre; the British were busy conciliating the Italians at that time, after the failure of sanctions, and did not want him in the Middle East. France, under Laval, would not have him, and he was unable—on account of Italian pressure—to establish residence in Switzerland. Finally the British took him in, and set him up in a house in Bath. After Munich the British began to see how useful Haile Selassie might, after all, turn out to be. When World War II broke out the reconquest of Ethiopia became an Allied aim, and in August, 1940, the Emperor was flown to Khartoum to further this. The Emperor "organized" the campaign—one of the most remarkable in modern military history—but British and Indian troops did most of the fighting, assisted by Ethiopian guerrillas.

*   *   *

Haile Selassie's Empress, whose name is Manan, is a most striking character. She is a very large woman, almost rhomboidal in shape; she is impassive, uncommunicative, and seldom seen. She comes from a powerful and rich family in the Wallega country, near the Sudan; the marriage had great political significance, since it united two distant groups. Haile Selassie is her second husband. The Empress has, so far as is known, no distinct political views, except a desire to keep the monarchy intact, but in several directions she exercises a signal influence. She is extremely religious and conservative, and has a marked interest in finance.

The Emperor and Empress dine out once a year at each embassy or legation in Addis Ababa; these occasions are, needless to say, marked by the most severe formality. In return the imperial family gives occasional big diplomatic receptions. Foreign guests are sometimes embarrassed because the town palace of His Imperial Majesty, even though it is an imposing structure with gates almost like those at Buckingham Palace, contains few accessible powder rooms.

Haile Selassie's chief quality is probably tenacity. What he believes in most, after Ethiopia, is himself. But he is completely dedicated and selfless in his devotion to his country, and there are few who do not respect him. He is a careful administrator, and an expert at the art of knocking heads together when he presides at cabinet meetings. He has no sports or hobbies. Nothing really interests him except the giant task of holding Ethiopia together, reforming its feudal structure, and bringing it to a self-respecting status in modern society.

Since he trusts nobody's ability fully, the Emperor has to deal with almost everything himself. He will himself scrutinize the contract for a new cook at the palace, and he annotates every important document in the diplomatic bags. One of his dominating traits is curiosity. If he sees a new type of rifle, he wants to take it apart with his own hands. At seven in the morning, say, he will announce that he intends to visit such-and-such a school; then at the school he questions the children on what they learned the day before, and what they think of their teacher.

How far does the Emperor's writ extend? For a long time the answer to this was "Not very far," because Ethiopia had virtually no communications. Today Haile Selassie wields authority over a larger area than anybody who has ever held the throne. There are still areas near the Sudan border where no real administration exists, and from the time of his accession till 1952 he avoided visiting the northern province of Tigrai, which was notorious for being restive. In a sense Haile Selassie has to run his country as pre-Tudor kings ran feudal England. If an obstreperous *ras* refuses to share tax collections with the central government and cannot be brought to heel by force or be influenced by other procedures, it is just too bad.

The Emperor's Chief Sources of Power

We might recapitulate these as follows: (1) The fact that his line—by legend anyway—goes back to Solomon and Sheba. (2) The church. (3) Intense and ceaseless personal scrutiny of every aspect of administration. (4) His gallantry of character and other personal qualities. (5) Nobody exists who could take his place. Ethiopia is a one-man-show.

The basic struggle in Ethiopia is between the feudal interests, who go back to Menelik and beyond, and those more progressive, represented by the Emperor, who is however part of the feudal interests himself.

To sum up: Haile Selassie's government is personal and its curse, like that of all palace governments, is that it is too centralized (something that cannot be helped at present) and lacks competent, trustworthy personnel. But there can be no doubt that, against fantastic obstacles, the Negus has already done more for his people than any emperor in history, by bringing it from barbarism to the threshold of modern times in a generation.

~~~~~~

If I were writing this chapter today I could not stress Ethiopia's isolation from its neighbors and say, for instance, that Kenya, which borders on it, "seems further away than Saskatchewan." Ethiopia has not only come lately much closer to other members of the community of African states, but has risen as a leader. The OAU (Organization of African Unity) was set up in Addis Ababa, the capital of Ethiopia, and had its first meeting there in May, 1963.

The Emperor plays a cautious and watchful game but he is fully

aware of what is implicit in the enormously steep rise in African national-
ism, and wants, within reason, to be one of the boys. Domestically things
go slowly, but Ethiopia has changed considerably for the better since
I visited it. The country still pathetically lack roads, public health ser-
vices, communications, and much else, but there have come advances
in public works and education.

 Disaffection with Haile Selassie broke out into the open in December,
1960. A group of high officers and civilian officials, who thought that
his reforms were far too laggard and ineffectual, took advantage of his
absence on a state visit to Brazil to attempt to make a coup d'état against
him, but the revolt was put down. Its leader, astoundingly enough, turned
out to be Haile Selassie's own eldest son, the Crown Prince Asfa Wassan,
who was born in 1916 and educated at the University of Liverpool. Most
of the conspirators, including several of the country's most conspicuous
young intellectuals, were caught and publicly hanged on trees and posts
in the center of Addis Ababa; the Crown Prince's life was spared.

CHAPTER 32

≈≈≈≈≈≈≈

Showboy

This study of Nkrumah, the President of Ghana, first appeared in Collier's *Magazine, May 28, 1954, after which it became a chapter in* Inside Africa *(1955). When it was written Nkrumah was at the threshold of his career; his title today is Osagyefo, meaning "Messianic Savior," and he is dictator of his country. Much early hope for Ghana has been lost by Europeans who thought it would evolve into a truly democratic state.*

≈≈≈≈≈≈≈≈≈≈≈≈≈≈≈≈≈≈≈≈≈≈≈≈≈≈≈≈

> *I came out of jail and into the Assembly without the slightest feeling of bitterness to Britain.*
>
> —KWAME NKRUMAH

DR. KWAME NKRUMAH, prime minister of the Gold Coast [now called Ghana], is one of the most remarkable personalities in Africa. He is the first Negro ever to become prime minister of a British colony, and as leader of the Gold Coast revolution he personifies the hopes of black nationalism everywhere on the continent where people are educated enough to have heard of him. He has been called "the African Nehru," the "Giant of Ghana"—Ghana being the vernacular name for the Gold Coast—and, depending on the zoological predilections of his admirers, both the "Eagle" and the "Lion" of Africa. His nickname is "Showboy," but not in the sense of "showing off"; it indicates merely that his fanatically devoted followers think of him as a prize demonstration piece.

Dr. Nkrumah was educated largely in the United States, and is forty-six. He is a socialist who flirted with Communist ideas in his youth, but he is not a Communist. His personality and career demands serious study, not only because of his intrinsic interest and importance but because he obviously portends so much. The Gold Coast is the pacemaker for African nationalism, and as it goes so may much of the rest of the continent go in time. Nkrumah's Gold Coast will probably become before long the first Black Dominion in the Commonwealth. Conversely if it blows up and the experiment fails—on account of inexperience, corruption, or what not—independence movements will be set back elsewhere.

Dr. Nkrumah (pronounced En-krooma) reached his present elevated position through a combination of factors: (a) his own personal qualities, which are striking; (b) the evolution of British policy, which gave these qualities substantial play.

Also Gold Coast characteristics played a role. This country is altogether different from Nigeria, for example, although the two have many problems in common and their historical origin is similar. But the Gold Coast is much more homogeneous than Nigeria, smaller, more compact, and far richer. Like Nigeria it is divided into three distinct areas, but these have closer links. There is no risk of fragmentation as in Nigeria. Prime Minister Nkrumah is the creator and head of a *national* party, and has a national following. Politics here are more advanced, stable, and sophisticated, despite perennial sharp crises. Nkrumah can make his own pace, because he has no serious competitor for leadership.

The Gold Coast evolution toward dominion status, or independence within the Commonwealth, is being watched with electric interest by Europeans nearby. For instance, the Gold Coast (including British Togoland) is completely surrounded by French territory except where it faces the sea. What will be the effect of an independent Gold Coast, if it is successful, on these French areas? And what about the Congo? As to British Africa the repercussions may be felt far afield. Already Nkrumah is talking about a future federation of West African free states. If the Gold Coast turns out to be capable of efficient and enlightened self-government, then it will be logically difficult to deny that, given a further period of tutelage long or short, the same thing may be true for Uganda, or Kenya, or even Tanganyika. Open one door; the draft will blow open the other doors.[1]

Nkrumah and the British

I stand for no racialism, no discrimination against any race or individual, but I am unalterably opposed to imperialism in any form.
—KWAME NKRUMAH

Government House in Accra is a marvelous old castle built right up out of the sea so that a lather of surf slaps without pause against the walls. Christiansborg Castle it is called, and it was built by Danish slave traders

[1] Of course it is official British policy that all their territories shall have *eventual* self-government.

in 1661. The stone came from Denmark—ballast in the outgoing slave ships. The structure is the purest, most dazzling white, with tall palms leaning against the crenelated battlements, and kingfishers nesting in the moldy cannon. In the garden are maroon, salmon-pink, scarlet, and pale yellow cannas, as regal as any flowers I ever saw.

Christiansborg has a history almost as romantic as its appearance. The Danes bought the promontory, where it sits in stately radiance, for seven gold bars, from African chiefs in the neighborhood. Then the Portuguese took it from the Danes and then the Danes took it back from the Portuguese. It is the only fort in all Africa which was once recaptured by an intrepid band of Africans themselves. The British, when they took over the Gold Coast, used Christiansborg as a lunatic asylum for a time. Its wild and isolated beauty, the crashing of the waves against its towers, the salt moisture seeping endlessly through the thick walls must have made it almost indecently appropriate for this purpose. It has been Government House since 1900.

The governor, Sir Charles Noble Arden-Clarke, asked Dr. Nkrumah to meet us at dinner. No ban on fraternization between British and Africans at Government House, as it does in some British territories, exists on the Gold Coast. But no one knew, until he arrived, whether the prime minister would actually appear for dinner or not. He would not have been so rude as to have neglected to come without warning, but his secretary might well have sent word at the last moment that, owing to some emergency, he would be unable to be present. Anyway he came. It was interesting to meet the prime minister in such a setting. The Union Jack flew stiffly in the dark breeze on a terrace overhead. Here was an African nationalist, pledged to terminate British rule, breaking bread at the governor's own table. But I do not want to stress unduly the dramatic impact of this. Relations between British and Gold Coasters are gracious on the whole, and the atmosphere of the dinner was cordial, even casual.

Nkrumah has a high, narrow, fully domed forehead, a receding crown of hair, a nose only moderately broadish at the tip, the perfect white teeth typical of Africans, and big lips nicely shaped, like slices of a tangerine. He is of medium height, supple, graceful, and assured. All his movements and gestures have power, ease, and magnetism. He neither struts nor shows exaggerated reserve. People often describe him as having "melancholy" or "brooding" eyes, and perhaps this is true, but we discovered soon enough that he likes to laugh.

Nkrumah wore African dress, which struck me deeply if only because I had never seen anything like it before. The national costume of the Gold Coast differs from any other in Africa; it is a robe worn like a Roman toga, with the left arm and shoulder exposed. Some people, depending on the weather, wear a kind of thin shift under their togas, and the prime minister did so this evening—it was white with an embroidery of tiny gold stars. The toga itself was magnificent. It differed from those worn by people on the streets as a Valentina gown, let us say, differs from one from Seventh Avenue. It was of a dusty golden color, with a rectilinear design in deeper gold, yellow, red, and pale green. The silk that goes into togas like these, which are customarily worn only by chiefs, is called *kente* cloth. It is designed and made locally, and is thus distinguished from the plebeian "mammy cloth" which comes from England or North Carolina. *Kente* cloth is woven in long narrow strips, and these, when sewn together to make the robe, give it a characteristic pattern. It is very costly. Enough for a good robe may cost three hundred dollars, but many people buy them. The rectangular designs always have an esoteric meaning, like Scottish plaids.

We met Nkrumah the next time in his own quarters, and here he wore much simpler, less flamboyant dress. He lives in an Accra suburb in a house strangely named—Luttorodt's Memorial Inn. This belonged, or belongs, to a prosperous African photographer, one of his close friends, and he and his staff have the use of it. It is of European design but has striking African touches. The brick walls are painted the brightest possible pink with thick white stripes on the intervening lines of mortar. The shutters are green on one side of each window, red on the other. In the garage I saw a black Cadillac, which gave rise to a minor scandal lately. Nkrumah, his enemies alleged, may have received this as a gift from somebody of dubious reputation who wanted favors. The prime minister, denying these allegations, says that he bought the car himself with legitimately borrowed money. The controversial vehicle is notable for another and quite different reason. Nkrumah's adherents told me that, whenever he traveled out from Accra into the villages, people would recognize the car as his and polish it with their robes. They did this as a gesture of affection and respect. Nkrumah's simplicity has always been one of his chief qualities. Out in the country, he gives no thought at all to where he sleeps. He will share a beggar's *kenke* (mealie meal) anywhere. He sits on the muddy ground and talks on terms of complete familiarity and equality with any citizen.

Courtyard and corridors at Luttorodt's are full of tatterdemalion retainers, as in the headquarters of any African dignitary. We were led upstairs to a small bare study where the prime minister received us. With him was his secretary, an intelligent and very pretty girl from the British West Indies named Joyce Githens. Sometimes she led the talk when a question did not interest him. I asked him what he did for relaxation, and he replied dryly, "Work." Miss Githens suggested that he should add, "See people." He drives into the hinterland every Sunday, to maintain his close contact with the masses. I asked him what intellectual influences he remembered most, and he replied, "Hegel." Other influences make a mixed bag. Christianity is certainly one; his speeches are peppered with the names of saints. So was Gandhi, who taught him the meaning and power of civil disobedience. So was Roosevelt and the American New Deal.

I asked him if he were a socialist, and he replied, "Of course"; then he added that he was a "Christian Marxist," without, however, defining this peculiar term. He denied firmly that he was, or ever had been, a Communist. Marxism has interested him, he went on, merely as a philosophical point of view, not in the realm of practical political affairs.

The Gold Coast revolution is, Nkrumah thinks, a forerunner of the inevitable emancipation of all Africa, particularly West Africa. His fondest political hope is that the Gold Coast, Nigeria, and the rest of West Africa will, in the future, be able to combine into a free federation; creation of a truly African Africa is his greatest dream. Recently he paid a state visit to Liberia. He wants the closest possible relations with all the nearby territories.

Nkrumah spent fourteen months in prison, but this experience did not, it seems, embitter him against the British. He told us that after independence he would be quite prepared to hire British advisors under contract. He has the greatest respect for men like Arden-Clarke. In jail he was subject to the regular discipline, and got no favors. "But it wasn't too bad. I made fish nets and wove baskets." His behavior in prison was exemplary, as it was in court. The British like him for this—he "plays the game"—and for such minor reasons as that he has amicable relations today with the judge who sentenced him. A British official who gave testimony against him was the one assigned to greet him when he was released from jail. Nkrumah stuck out his hand warmly, laughed, and said, "Well, sir, I'm glad to see you again in God's fresh air!"

When we prepared to leave him after an hour Nkrumah said that he wanted us to meet his mother. She came out of the kitchen downstairs. She is about sixty-five, a tiny, dignified, and immensely proud old lady. The prime minister talked to her affectionately in her native tongue; she knows no English. I asked her (with Nkrumah interpreting) if she had known when her son was a little boy that he was going to be a great man. Tartly she replied, "No one can know things like that. But—" She finished the sentence by putting a hand on Nkrumah's shoulder, in a gesture denoting at once satisfaction, pride, skepticism about the reality of all this, and a cozy confidence that she, at least, was not going to have any nonsense from her son even if he was prime minister.

Personal Qualities of the Prime Minister

Nkrumah is a bachelor. He likes the company of women, including white women, but says that he has no time to get married. One of his best-known remarks is, "Every woman in the Gold Coast is my bride."[2]

He neither smokes nor drinks, though occasionally he may have a sip of champagne. Mostly he is a vegetarian, and when we saw him he did not touch coffee. Many nationalist leaders or dictators in pre-war Europe cultivated similar puritanisms, but they are somewhat rare in Africa, except among Moslems. Nkrumah's salary as prime minister is high—£3,500 per year.[3] He has no interest in sport, worldliness, or the frivolities that waste the time of most men, but he is fond of music, both classical and the local dance music, which resembles calypso and is called Highlife.

He works long hours, but without much sign of strain. His manner is almost always suave. He talks well when he wants to, but is some-times guarded—especially with Europeans—and even inarticulate. He gets up at six, does paper work, and then receives for an hour any-body who wants to see him. This is in the orthodox tradition of African leaders. *Anybody* may walk in. And hundreds do. At about nine he goes for several hours to the headquarters of the Convention People's Party, of which he is president, and then proceeds to the prime minister's office or the Legislative Assembly if it is in session. Here he does his adminis-trative and parliamentary work. He returns home, has a brief dinner, and then has conferences or does more paper work till midnight.

Nkrumah has guts. Consider the cocoa story. Some years ago Gold Coast cocoa, which is by far the country's chief source of wealth, be-came afflicted by a disease called "swollen shoot;" this is caused by an insect known as the mealy bug, and is extremely difficult to extirpate. The only sure way to keep swollen shoot from spreading and ruining the crop is to destroy the diseased trees root and branch. But the trees continue to bear cocoa beans for several years after swollen shoot first attacks them, even though they are bound to die eventually. Orders went out to chop down and burn the infected trees, but the peasant farmers refused to do this. It was like asking them to cut off their own heads. At first Nkrumah opposed obligatory destruction of the trees. He wanted a voluntary system. Then, when he came to realize that the blight of swollen shoot, if unchecked, might ruin the entire cocoa industry, he reversed himself and made the farmers destroy all their diseased growth. Up to 1953 sixteen million trees have been destroyed. For Nkrumah to impose this Draconian measure on his own people, many of whom

---

[2] See a well-informed cover story on Nkrumah in *Time*, February 9, 1953, and "Letter from the Gold Coast," by Oden and Olivia Meeker, *The New Yorker*, December 20, 1952.

[3] Other ministers get £3,000. These figures were suggested by Arden-Clarke. The Colonial Office was reluctant at first to establish salaries on such a high level. But as a matter of fact £3,000 does not go far in Accra if a person lives in the European manner. Also, I heard it put, this figure gives three thousand good reasons for a minister to stick at his job.

were too ignorant to understand why it was necessary, took signal political courage.[4]

Nkrumah's first quality is, people say, his animal spark, his magnetism and vitality. Second, his resilience. He is not in the least fixed or doctrinaire, and can bounce back from almost any blow. He works by intuition more than intellect, and is a highly skilled negotiator. Third, he has more serenity and confidence than most Africans.

But do not forget that the hub of his character is nationalism. What he believes in above all is freedom for his country. He has not, however, committed his party to a specific date for independence. If you ask him, as we did, when the Gold Coast is to be fully free, he will reply warily, "Soon," or "Next year." He knows full well that, before he can rule alone successfully, he needs a better administrative structure and more trained men, and he is far too shrewd to tie himself to any unalterable date.

The Gold Coast revolution has three aspects—youth against age, the people against the feudal chiefs, the nationalists against the British. It is Nkrumah's greatest source of power that he combines in himself leadership in all these spheres.

Most of the men around him are young, in their forties or even younger. They will presumably dominate the Gold Coast for a generation, and they can grow up with it. The situation is unlike that which obtained in India, for example, where the majority of nationalist leaders were old men when independence finally came. One of Nkrumah's biggest assets is that he has captured the imagination of the youth, and works from the bottom up.

His second most important source of power is probably his gift for concrete political organization. He learned a good deal about this in London, by watching the tactics of Herbert Morrison. The CPP (Convention People's Party) is organized throughout the Gold Coast down to the smallest village. Nkrumah handles it like a man winding a watch. The party has loud-speakers, automobile caravans, and other paraphernalia hitherto unknown to Black Africa. It has its own party colors (red, green, and white), its own uniformed brigades of women and youth, its own salute, which is the open palm displayed at arm's length, and its own insignia. Its motto is "Freedom," pronounced with the accent on the second syllable, and its slogan "Forward Ever, Backward Never." Some performances put on by the CPP may seem naïve to Europeans, but they have undeniable effect.

Nkrumah was brought up as a Roman Catholic, but now calls himself a "nondenominational Christian." Some people say that he still

---

[4] Strangely enough, another mortal enemy of the cocoa tree is mistletoe, which strangles the growth of the young shoots.

occasionally consults a *juju* or medicine man, and this is quite possible. Once again we encounter the extraordinarily pungent contrasts of Africa. Few Africans, even those most emancipated, can shake off their tribal heritage overnight. This is, as we know, the basic reason for their self-division, their so-called "schizophrenia." They go to Cambridge, they read the *Times*, they belong to clubs, they even marry white women; but they are rooted nevertheless to a past of which they are often ashamed, but which they can seldom totally exorcise if only because their skin stays black. Color is the core of everything. But Nkrumah shows few signs of self-division or inferiority. What his movement means, in essence, is the substitution of a modern fetish—nationalism —for the tribal fetishes of his fathers. Therefore he must use such symbols as motorcars brightly painted green, red, and white. He has to make the new "mystique" attractive and understandable in *African* terms. As to *juju*, why should he not, if he wants, visit a witch doctor? Similar phenomena are not unknown in the West. Mackenzie King, who was Prime Minister of Canada for twenty years, had crystal balls all over his office, indulged steadily in the fanciest kind of "spiritual" hocus-pocus, and never moved an inch without consulting an astrologer.

Saturday's Child

Dr. Nkrumah was born in 1909 in a small village, Nkroful, in the Nzima area near the frontier of the French Ivory Coast. His native tongue is a dialect of Twi, one of the Akan languages. At the time of his birth there were no roads at all in this region, only tracks through bush. He was named Kwame, which is a word associated with "Saturday," because he was born on that day. Later he was given a Christian name— Francis—but he seldom uses it. His father was a goldsmith, an artisan who made trinkets; his mother was a mammy trader, a small shopkeeper.

Catholic mission schools—first near Nkroful, then at a town called Sekondi—gave him his early education. He was intelligent and ambitious and, when he was about eighteen, became a teacher. He saved enough money to go to Achimota College near Accra. He would have gone to England for further study, but could not get a scholarship. One of his uncles staked him to a trip to the United States, and he entered Lincoln University in Pennsylvania. This is one of the oldest and best-known Negro institutions of learning in America, which has made a specialty of hospitality to African Negroes. Nkrumah worked his way through Lincoln at all manner of jobs, and saw a good deal of America and the West Indies during vacations. He got no fewer than four degrees—in theology and science as well as a B.A and M.A.—and became for a time an instructor at Lincoln. I met recently one of his classmates, who said: "Nkrumah was sober, reserved, and conscientious, as well as brilliant. The main thing about him was that he acted as if his whole life were planned."

An American writer[5] who saw Nkrumah not long ago asked him if he had ever been subjected to any particular racial humiliation in the United States. The prime minister replied that, at a bus station in Baltimore, he once asked where he could get a drink of water, and the clerk pointed to a spittoon. We could be fanciful about the mysterious processes of history and point out what extraordinary personal accidents have influenced events, but anybody who asserted that Great Britain is on the point of losing its richest African colony, the Gold Coast, and that Nkrumah is prime minister today because of the barbarian rudeness of somebody in Maryland twenty years ago would almost certainly be wrong. The incident may have annoyed Nkrumah at the time, but he took it with good humor. His basic philosophy was formed long before this episode. When he was still a youthful undergraduate he was writing to friends in Accra, "If I fail to bring self-government to the Gold Coast, bury me alive!"

He became president of the African Students Association of America and Canada, and his classmates at Lincoln wrote this about him when he got his first degree.

> Africa is the beloved of his dreams;
> Philosopher, thinker, with forceful schemes,
> In aesthetics, politics, he's "in the field,"
> Nkrumah, "très interessant," radiates appeal.

One legend is that Nkrumah was powerfully influenced in the United States by Paul Robeson, but the truth is that he only saw Robeson once, and this was at a public meeting. Later, however, another American Negro did make a strong impact on him—the venerable Dr. W. E. B. Du Bois, whom he met in England. He attended a Pan-African Congress in Manchester organized by Dr. Du Bois, an ardent spokesman for Negro rights who is now far to the left.

Nkrumah spent several years in England; he studied at the London School of Economics, and met a good many British intellectuals, some of them Communists. Indeed it was almost impossible for an impoverished African student in London at that time to have tolerable social relations with anybody who was not a Communist or extreme left-winger. Nkrumah's so-called "Communist period" derives from this. When he was arrested in Accra years later, a membership card in the British Communist party was found among his papers, However, it

[5] Wolfgang Langewiesche in the *Saturday Evening Post*, March 7, 1953. "He Wants to Rule West Africa."

had never been signed. Nkrumah laughs about this today, saying that he had used the card on occasion to get into Communist meetings and the like, but that it had no other significance at all and that he was never an actual party member.

In London, Nkrumah kept in close touch with Gold Coast political developments. Now came the turning point of his life. A political leader named J. B. Danquah was head of the chief nationalist party of that day, the United Gold Coast Convention, or UGCC. This, following an evolution too complex for mention here (Gold Coast nationalism has a long and emphatic history), was expanding strongly. Dr. Danquah needed men, particularly an organizer. So he communicated with Nkrumah—whom he had never met—in London and invited him to become secretary of the organization. Nkrumah accepted, and arrived back in the Gold Coast on December 16, 1947. He had been twelve years away.

Nkrumah in Action

1. He set to work with ruthless drive, enthusiasm, and acumen to consolidate his position in the party. He was nominally under Danquah, but soon supplanted him. Then, he took advantage of an angry local situation to challenge the British. There had been a crisis in the cocoa industry and desperate Africans were boycotting European shops. On February 28, 1948, only two months after Nkrumah's arrival, some Negro war veterans marched toward Government House to demonstrate there. They were dispersed by the police and two were killed, which caused bitter public indignation. Rioting broke out all over the town, mobs burned and pillaged in the streets, and twenty-nine deaths occurred. A British official told me, "On February 27 the Gold Coast was a model colony. On March 1 it was a shambles."

2. On February 29, while rioting still went on, Nkrumah in his capacity as secretary of the UGCC telegraphed an appeal to the Colonial Office in London, saying that the local authorities could no longer maintain order and demanding the immediate recall of the governor, one of Arden-Clarke's predecessors. It is interesting that, in this moment of extreme stress, he found time to send copies of this telegram to a dozen newspapers all over the world, including the London *Daily Worker*, the Associated Negro Press (Chicago), the Moscow *New Times*, and the New York *Times*.

3. The governor assumed emergency powers and on March 13 issued orders sending into exile Danquah, Nkrumah, and other UGCC leaders. There was no trial, and no direct accusation that Nkrumah had any relation with the February bloodshed. His banishment was decreed solely on the ground that this was "expedient for securing the

public safety and the maintenance of order." Nkrumah was at once packed off to a remote village in the Northern Territories.

4. A commission of inquiry was set up to look into the disturbances. This made a long report, which contained various charges against Nkrumah, mainly that between his arrival on the Gold Coast and the outbreak of the riots he had greatly stimulated the organization of nationalist activity. (Of course that had been his job, but it amazed the British that he could have done so much so quickly.) Also it alleged that Nkrumah had organized a society known as the "Circle," a secret body the members of which swore personal fealty to him. The aim of this was national unity and independence for West Africa, and the eventual creation of a Union of West African Socialist (not "Soviet") Republics, but with a pledge not to resort to violence "except as a last resort." Nkrumah, when he gave testimony about the riots, dismissed his plans for this organization as an old "dream"; it was something he had played with in London.

5. In London the Colonial Office did not like the look of things. It did not want anything further to happen that might provoke disorders in the Gold Coast, and after careful investigation issued a policy report which took what was on the whole a strong pro-African line. It said that the Gold Coasters did not have enough share in government (which was Nkrumah's main point) and urged prompt constitutional reform.

6. Then early in 1949 the British made an extraordinary gesture. They appointed an all-African committee of forty, under the chairmanship of an African judge, Sir J. Henley Coussey, to write a new constitution. What the British were doing, it seemed, was to give the Gold Coast away. The people of the Gold Coast were to be given the opportunity to determine for themselves the kind of government they wanted.[6] The Coussey report was accepted by the Colonial Office with certain qualifications, and the way was thus opened to a general election, the first in Gold Coast history.

7. Nkrumah was released from internment in the north. At first he rejected the Coussey proposals because he thought that they did not go far enough. He called the new constitution "bogus and fraudulent," and, not a man to go halfway, demanded immediate dominion status. Later he modified this view, and decided to give the new constitution a try. But at the same time he set up the machinery for a civil disobedience campaign, which he called "Positive Action."[7]

8. Now came an internal fight. Nkrumah thought that the UGCC, under Danquah, was moving much too cautiously. He outmaneuvered

[6] See *The Gold Coast Revolution*, by George Padmore, p. 56.

[7] At about the same time Colonel Nasser in Egypt also put forward the idea of "Positive Action," but he meant a different thing by it.

Danquah, the man who had brought him back to the Gold Coast, and in June, 1949, captured his movement by forming a new party of his own, the Convention People's party, or CPP. This is the party which he still heads, and which runs the government today. At its first mass meetings CPP organizers sang songs like "Lead Kindly Light" and "Onward Christian Soldiers." But their tactics were anything but pious. It was a party with a punch.

9. Meantime Sir Charles Arden-Clarke had come out as governor. He was, and is, as impregnably British as a bulldog or Piccadilly Circus, but he understood the temper of the times. He decided to get into direct touch with Nkrumah, and sent a senior British official to see him. Some old-line Britons were scandalized by this—it shocked them that Arden-Clarke should delegate anybody to *talk* to Nkrumah, "that scalawag." But, if the government did not treat with Nkrumah at once, he was in a position to make a revolution. "The lorry was running wild." The meeting took place on January 5, 1950, and marked the first time that Nkrumah ever had a political meeting with a British official.

The two got along well, but reached no agreement. Nkrumah insisted on going ahead with civil disobedience. The Briton urged prudence. Nkrumah replied, "We are a desperate people, and will adopt desperate measures if necessary." He proceeded to put on a general strike, but it was nonviolent. Arden-Clarke forbade the police to use firearms, and there was no bloodshed. Nkrumah was, however, arrested, on the charge of having fomented an illegal strike, tried (by a correct judicial process this time), and sentenced to two years in jail.

10. His imprisonment made him even more of a hero to his fanatic followers than before. The word spread that the jail could not hold him, and that he slipped out every night in the guise of a white cat.

11. The new constitution was duly promulgated on January 1, 1951, and the election campaign began. The CPP barnstormed the country with great success, even though Nkrumah and most of its other leaders were in jail, and won in February by a tremendous majority. Nkrumah had been chosen to stand for a constituency in Accra, although he was unable to campaign, and got 22,780 out of 23,122 votes. In the country as a whole the CPP won thirty-four out of thirty-eight constituencies, with its slogan of "S.G. Now." ("S.G." meant, of course, self-government.) The voting was completely orderly and conducted with great efficiency, although the Gold Coast had never had an election before, and in some areas as many as 50 percent of the people went to the polls.[8]

12. Now the British were in a quandary. It was clear that the CPP would have an overwhelming majority in the Legislative Assembly just elected. But Nkrumah was in prison. How could a new government func-

[8] Of course the over-all number of citizens eligible to vote was relatively small.

tion with its leader in jail? Arden-Clarke decided to exercise his power of clemency, and let him out. This was a bold and statesmanlike step. On February 12, 1951, Nkrumah was released from the James Town prison in Accra—100,000 people were waiting for him on the streets —and went to Government House to confront Arden-Clarke personally for the first time. It is important to remember that at this time the CPP had had no experience whatever with administration. The legend is that Arden-Clarke, after the first conference, arranged for classes, staffed by teachers at Achimota, to instruct the new ministers in parliamentary procedure. In actual fact well-attended lectures did take place, but the initiative came from Achimota. Arden-Clarke and Nkrumah, after their first encounter, became good friends and established a fruitful relationship. The new Gold Coast owes much to the wisdom, friendly tact, and farseeing firmness of Sir Charles Noble Arden-Clarke.

13. Nkrumah set up three principles for his men to follow. First, African ministers must not live in the choice European bungalows that the British had always provided for members of the government. Second, only a minimum of social admixture with individual Britons would be permitted. Third, members of his cabinet must pay back one-third of their salaries into the party funds.

14. At first Nkrumah was called "Leader of Government Business." A new constitutional advance came in March, 1952, and he assumed the title and position of prime minister.

* * *

The Gold Coast government consisted when we were in Accra of eight African ministers (six of whom were CPP men) and three British members who held their posts ex-officio. These were in charge of the three most important portfolios, finance, justice, and defense and external affairs, but the Africans had the majority and could outvote them. In the Assembly of eighty-four there were only nine Europeans. In theory Nkrumah's men could legislate about anything, subject only to the brake of the governor's reserved powers, which have never been used. This was a genuinely *African* government, although the ultimate power was still British.

As to full independence, that is a matter of timetable. Nkrumah, as I have already pointed out, has not fixed a firm date. The government must first bring the north up to the level of the rest of the country. On the other hand he must keep abreast not only of his own restless followers, but of his African opposition. This explains what happened on July 10, 1953, when he presented to the Assembly an important motion [authorizing] the Gold Coast government—*as soon as the necessary constitutional and administrative arrangements are made*—to request

Her Majesty's government in Britain to pass an act declaring the Gold Coast "to be a Sovereign and Independent State within the Commonwealth." Of course the phrase "as soon as" was the operative clause in this motion. But even so the black peasant boy from the Akan country, the student at Lincoln University and the lonely expatriate in London, has come a long, long way.

~~~~~~

Indeed. And he has continued to march along since these pages were written a decade ago. A new constitution was promulgated in 1954 which provided for an enlarged legislature elected directly by the people, the first fully "responsible parliament" in Black Africa, and an all-African cabinet was appointed, the first ever to be installed in a British colony. Soon the legislature also became all-African. Then, in March, 1957, a historic date for Africa, Ghana reached full independence and thus became the first black dominion in the British Commonwealth, with Nkrumah as prime minister. At last in July, 1960, another historic date, Ghana transformed itself into a republic (although still a member of the Commonwealth), and Nkrumah took office as its first President.

The Osagyefo expanded glossily in other directions as well. He organized the first "All-African People's Congress," held in Accra in 1958, absorbed British Togoland, and made plans for union with Mali and Guinea. His international posture became neutralist, with strong leanings to the Soviet bloc. Meantime he encouraged his own glorification as a public figure and established complete one-man, one-party rule—a ruthless left-wing dictatorship.

Civil liberties have to all intents and purposes disappeared, and opponents of Dr. Nkrumah have been exiled or flung into jail by the hundreds. Ghana more and more takes on the ugly contours of a police state. This is not to be excused, but we of the west should keep in mind that democracy is an extraordinarily difficult and expensive form of government, and many of the new African countries were simply not up to it. The Congo is a tragic case in point.

I said early in this chapter that the effect of an independent Gold Coast on the nearby areas would be considerable. This turned out to be the case. The irreversible movement of Africa toward independence would have taken place in any case, but the example of Ghana probably served to speed up this giant process. "Open one door; the draft will blow open other doors." Nigeria, Kenya, Uganda, Tanganyika, Zanzibar, the Cameroons, Madagascar, Northern Rhodesia, Nyasaland, and a covey of other African states have wrenched themselves free or, in some cases, became free by default.

When I returned from Africa I must have been asked a hundred times by Americans if the emerging African nations were ready for self-government. Of course they were not in the sense that they had enough education, political experience, and wealth. But the question was meaningless. It had little if any relevance. The African states were out to get self-government whether they were ideally ready for it or not, and nothing could stop them. They had the will to be free, and, moreover, the colonial powers were no longer willing to expend the blood, sweat, and money necessary to hold them down. The tragedy is that Africa was too poor, underdeveloped, too grievously undereducated, to be able to take advantage fruitfully of its new freedom. And the old empires bear a large share of responsibility for this misfortune, lamentable as it was.

As to Dr. Nkrumah he has, it would seem, steadily become more mystically inclined as well as dictatorial and absolutist. He calls his new philosophy "Consciencism," and it contains concepts somewhat abstruse and difficult for the westerner to understand. Obviously this development was foreshadowed by some of the early intellectual patterns and experiments mentioned in this chapter. I have often asked myself why Nkrumah, with all his pith and brilliance, his promise and undoubted love for his people, has let himself become a tyrant. I imagine that he himself would answer that circumstances have demanded this. The root, core and pivot of his belief is still hatred and fear of the old colonialism, and governing his every action, no matter how muddled and amorphous his thinking may seem to be, is the compulsion to keep the new Ghana secure in his own hands. His spokesmen will say that dictatorship is, in the present stage, better than chaos; only a strong leadership can keep Ghana free from convulsions like those that have afflicted the Congo. The prime question is one of motive—whether or not the Osagyefo is acting primarily on his country's behalf or his own. And even though he has behaved brutally toward some of his old colleagues and paralyzed some elements of the nation with fear he has managed so far to keep Ghana reasonably stable, prosperous, and secure.

CHAPTER 33

~~~~~~~~

Mr. Tubman of Liberia

What follows is a compilation from two chapters about Liberia in
Inside Africa *(1955). Part of it appeared originally in the* Saturday
Review *under the title "Pepper Coast Republic," September 24, 1955.*
Mr. Tubman at that time was just completing his first decade of power,
and he is still President of the country today.

~~~~~~

THE PRESIDENT OF LIBERIA is a plausible and enterprising man in his
middle fifties named William Vacanarat Shadrach Tubman, sometimes called by the nickname "Shad." The Honorable Mr. Tubman has
been Chief Executive of Liberia since 1944, and will probably remain
President for a considerable time to come. He is a character of the
utmost originality and interest, who gives forth a certain waggish note.

Liberia itself is *sui generis*—unique. I could use any of several adjectives about it—"odd," "wacky," "phenomenal," or even "weird." It is, as
is well known, one of the four independent countries in Africa, and for a
great many years (until Egypt became a republic in 1953) it was the
only republic on the continent. Haiti in the West Indies aside, it is the
only Negro republic in the world.

Monrovia, the capital, was named for President Monroe, and is practically the only city I have ever seen without either taxis or buses. What
is more, it does not even have many bicycles. The people are too poor,
too mercilessly exploited. A village in Uganda or in the wastes of
Northern Nigeria will have bicycles in profusion, but not the capital
of Liberia. There was no succesful public telephone service in Monrovia
until last year, and the system does not extend beyond the city; it
was impossible (at the time of our visit) to telephone to the airport,

Roberts Field, fifty miles away, or even to the Firestone plantation which plays a paramount role in the economic life of the country.[1]

The population of Monrovia is, according to some, seventeen thousand; according to others, thirty-five thousand. Liberians are proud of this city and there are, indeed, a few stately but down-at-the-heel old-style mansions, built in the manner of the American south. The town has one modern office building. A modern port, built during the war by American Lend-Lease funds (cost, $19,000,000), permits liners to be loaded directly from a wharf, instead of by means of lighters plunging through the surf. The port aside, Monrovia looks like something afflicted by scurvy. It is not merely crumbling with rot, but deliquescent. The streets are for the most part slippery ditches oozing with red mud. The hospital, originally the premises of a German cable station, has been called "the worst single sight in Africa." There is no insane asylum or poorhouse. Lebanese and Arab traders run the dank, scrofulous waterfront, and I saw a headline in a local paper, HOGS INFEST THE TOWN— SANITARY INSPECTORS NOT CONCERNED. In the police station men awaiting trial sleep in "pools of urine."

One area not far from the Executive Mansion looked to me like a swamp, but it is apparently the most fashionable part of town. Here, if the mud will permit their passage, one may encounter automobiles of the most flamboyant contemporary cut—cream-colored, chocolate-colored, or painted green-and-silver—carrying important officials or their mistresses on various errands, and which resemble fireflies trying to skip through muck.

Socially Monrovia is reminiscent of what Natchez or Savannah might have been in the old days, except that the leading families are, of course, black instead of white. Everybody knows everybody else, and people have an easy courtesy, with a sense of dignified tradition. They dance the Virginia reel. I heard one lady say, "We took our dances with us to America, and now we have brought them back here." The late secretary of state, Gabriel L. Dennis, was an accomplished performer on the piano and musical saw. Social notes in the daily press are picturesque. A lady may be called her husband's "solar star." A new rum factory opened while we were in Monrovia, and was described as being "aristocratic." An official memorandum, signed by the secretary of state on behalf of the President, announced rules for the behavior of guests at the last Independence Reception and Ball at the Executive Pavilion. "At the ball there should not be any shaking of hands." The report of

---

[1] A postal service exists, but it does not function regularly outside Monrovia. A foreign consul told me that it was the custom for the postmaster to visit new arrivals in town and ask for a loan of $100, more or less, to ensure that mail would be delivered "promptly."

an official picnic at about the same time said that "Tommy guns announced the arrival of guests of honor."

The aristocracy, like all good aristocracies, has close ties to the land. Almost everybody has a patch of rubber. Land is a very serious matter in Liberia, and so is citizenship. Nobody not of Negro blood may become a citizen, and only citizens may purchase land. Liberia does, however, encourage foreign enterprise in certain particular fields. The country has, for instance, considering its poverty and lack of maritime development, an astoundingly large merchant fleet, amounting to not less than 2,349,978 tons. A similar situation exists in Panama. Foreign shipowners register vessels under the Liberian flag, which gives them freedom of movement and unusual advantages.

I asked a Monrovian of consequence a simple question, "Why is Liberia so poor?" His answer was a jovial, "You tell me!"

* * *

Liberia is roughly the size of Ohio or Tennessee, but the entire country has only *ten miles* of paved road, five of which are in the capital. There are no more than 260 miles of "all-weather" roads, and not all these (except in the Firestone area) are actually passable at all times. The total road mileage—including dirt tracks—is only 800. Liberia never had a road at all until 1916, when an enterprising American diplomat built one in Monrovia itself, so that he could use an automobile that had arrived there by mistake, the first ever to be seen in the country.[2] Today Liberia produces enough rubber for thousands of American cars to ride on, but two-thirds of the country cannot be reached except on foot. In the Hinterland,[3] porters carry folk on hammocks; communication is by what people ironically call the "ankle express." My wife and I drove from Monrovia to a village called Totota, perhaps sixty miles away, to have lunch with President Tubman at one of his country estates. An army truck had to escort us—to pull us out of the mud if we got stuck. This was the worst road I have ever been on in my life. It is also Liberia's best road. We traversed on that day about *half* of the total "improved" Liberian road system. Bridges are often slippery planks laid across chasms. Of course this was in the rainy season, and Liberian rains are really something. Last year 260 inches of rain fell in the Monrovia area, all of it in six months.

Consider public health and education. Only two native Liberians have ever become doctors. There are also two naturalized Haitian M.D.'s,

[2] This odd bit of history is mentioned in *Liberia, 1847-1947*, by Charles M. Wilson, p. 91. Also see "Letter from Liberia," by Oden and Olivia Meeker, *The New Yorker*, November 29, 1952.

[3] The back country is officially called the Hinterland, spelled with a capital "H."

but in the whole country there are probably not more than half a dozen reputable physicians, outside of Firestone and the missions. Infant mortality among Africans runs as high as 75 percent in some areas.[4] No public health service at all existed till 1931—and Liberia has been an independent republic since 1847! More than 90 percent of the population is illiterate. In 1946 the total sum allotted to education in the national budget was only around $50,000 (80 percent of education was taken care of by missionaries); it is substantially higher now, roughly $1,500,000 out of a budget of $10,088,810. Liberia College, the chief institution of "higher" learning in the country, where several of its leading contemporary citizens were educated, had for years no library, laboratories, or scientific equipment; a former head of this school calmly appropriated all its funds on one occasion, and with this loot sent his daughters to be educated in Italy.[5] Another institution, the Cuttington College and Divinity School, is run by the Protestant Episcopal Church (which has been established in Liberia since 1836). It operated at a place called Cape Palmas for many years, but the buildings there gradually disintegrated—melted away in the rain. One American missionary group worked in Liberia for seventy-five years without ordaining a single minister.

The poverty of most Liberians is formidable. The average income of a man out in the bush is 25 cents a day. An American businessman got this note from his chief boy one morning:

Dear Sir:
Will you please buy me one Umbrella or Hat? I have already get my Rain's Coat but I did not have Umbrella either hat. So that is the reason why get me so late this morning.

Obediently yours.

Thievery—the cities swarm with thieves—is most conspicuous during the rains. First, rice is short then, and people are hungry. Second, the noise of the rain makes it easy for thieves to get around. Stealing is, however, by no means confined to professional criminals or to the poor. It is almost a national sport. Newspapers talk openly of "wholesale stealing" in government departments. Recently the Italian legation lost, of all things, its safe. Even at a fashionable cocktail party in Monrovia, an unwary guest may have his pocket nimbly picked or his wallet rifled. Liberians love to wear top hats, and the joke is that these are useful as well as decorative in that they are so convenient for the temporary disposal of minor loot. A hostess may even find rolls of her toilet paper missing, and a top hat is an admirable place for concealing objects of this nature.

[4] The rate in the United States is 2.92 percent.
[5] Raymond Leslie Buell, *Liberia: A Century of Survival*, pp. 16-18.

As to corruption in Liberia that, too, like the rains, is really some-thing. It exists on all levels. Money is, let us say, assigned to some gov-ernment department for a worthy project. But it is rare for the entire sum to reach its destination. Underlings help themselves to a share of the appropriation as it moves along, like mice nibbling at a piece of cake. This would not matter much in a rich country, but it is a disaster in one with such a small budget as Liberia. Precious funds are wasted. "Kansas City," I heard it said, "can afford graft; Monrovia cannot." But obviously in a nation so pathetically poor corruption is bound to occur. It cannot be stopped until the standard of living of the people as a whole is raised. Bizarre tales may be heard in this general realm. An American expert came out to train the police; he went home on leave and, when he re-turned, he found that his entire collection of fingerprints had disap-peared. If a man is important enough, he can run up hundreds of dollars' worth of bills in the local shops; maybe he will settle them at some future date, but maybe not. In the field of *political* corruption Liberia has had some wonderful distinctions. One President of the Republic (not Mr. Tubman) got 243,000 votes in a certain election, though only 15,000 persons were privileged to vote. That is really laying it on. It might have happened in Missouri. But not even in Missouri would any politician have quite dared to do what one Liberian candidate for office did in the early 1940's, just for fun—he dressed a monkey in a frock coat, took him to the polls, and let him "vote."

Most educated Africans in neighboring countries pay lip service to Liberia because it is an independent republic, created by freed Negro slaves, but they despise it inwardly, because it constitutes a betrayal of what modern Africans stand for. Even Ethiopia has higher standards. Liberia might almost be called a kind of perverse advertisement for im-perialism, since, although the country is free, the people are so badly off compared to those in most French and British colonies. Liberia has not had the advantages in education and similar fields that enlightened colonialism provides. This does not, however, mean that Africans are not capable of advance, in Liberia or anywhere else. What it does mean is that Liberian governments in the past have not been good enough. Members of the ruling class, which happens to be Negro, have not done a tithe of what they should have done for their own Negro people.

One brief word on Liberian history. Almost everybody knows some-thing of this romantic tale. The area was once called the "Pepper" or "Grain" coast. Liberia was created by the American Colonization Society, a private organization (its first president was a nephew of George Wash-ington) formed in 1816 to transport freed American slaves to Africa, where they might settle and start a new life on their own. The motive was only humanitarian in part. A good many American slaveowners *wanted* to get freed slaves out of the country; it was dangerous to have them around. Also in 1819 the American navy was empowered to seize slave ships on the high seas, free any slaves found, and return them to Africa, as part of an attempt to suppress what remained of the organized slave trade. The American government (under President Monroe) and the American Colonization Society worked together. An expedition was sent out to explore the possibility of settlement on the Liberian coast. The British had already done the same thing in Sierra Leone. The expedition arrived safely in 1822 at a site which the pioneers named Providence, and land was bought. Payment, "after long and tedious palavers with the native kings," consisted among other things of "six muskets, one box beads, two hogsheads of tobacco, one cask gunpowder, six iron bars, six pieces of blue baft, three pairs shoes, one box soap, one barrel rum, one dozen knives and forks, ten iron pots, and a dozen spoons."

The President: Personal

Mr. Tubman, the eighteenth president of his country, derives from an old Americo-Liberian family; his mother's forebears came from Sparta, Georgia, and his father's from Atlanta. It is often said, however, that his heritage also includes admixtures of "native" blood. A Tubman helped finance the first trip of the American Colonization Society to Liberia, and a lady named Harriet Tubman, who lived in Maryland (U.S.A.) in the 1850's is a character well known to American Negro history. Whether or not she was an actual ancestor of President Tubman is uncertain.

Tubman's father was a minister of the gospel, who rose to be speaker of the Liberian House of Representatives. He gave his son as good an education as the country provided in those days, which was not much, and young Tubman became a lawyer. He worked hard, advanced quickly, and served both as a senator and an associate justice of the Liberian Supreme Court, before his rise to the Presidency. He has always been an astute, shrewd, and farseeing politician.

The President is of medium height; he looks tough, shrewd, and supple. He likes the company of women, and has been married several times. His present wife, a cousin of former President's Barclay's, is a pretty, shy, smiling woman. One of his sons went to a Massachusetts preparatory school and entered Harvard in 1954.

Before we met Mr. Tubman we inspected carefully his photographs, which may be seen everywhere. In one he wears a top hat (of course), a morning coat of the most severe and formal cut, and several medals; the President is a Grand Master of the Order of the Star of Africa, among other things. In his right hand is an ebony stick; in his left an exceptionally long cigar. Other manifestations of Mr. Tubman's omnipresence are at once apparent to a visitor to Monrovia. We saw the William V. S. Tubman Bridge and other public monuments. The William V. S. Tubman School of Music exists, as does the President Tubman Dramatic Institute.

Mr. Tubman is a *bon vivant,* and likes to sit around with his cronies. His favorite haunt is the well-known S.A.C. Club, the impregnable inner citadel of the Americo-Liberian aristocracy. It has about thirty members, and is expensive and exclusive; a member told me that (with assessments for parties) it can cost up to $500 per year. I asked, immediately on arriving in Monrovia, what ran Liberia. The universal answer was, "Tubman, the S.A.C. Club, and the 125 leading families." When the President visits the S.A.C. after nightfall the roof (which has four squat towers) is illuminated, to show that he is there.

Mr. Tubman is a staunch Methodist—in fact he is a lay preacher and likes to be called "Doctor"—but he sometimes carries a gun. With this he is, on occasion, playful. By Liberian etiquette, no automobile may pass the presidential vehicle (a Cadillac presented to him by an American businessman) and other cars must draw up to the side of the road and stop if the President is passing. Last summer somebody did not pull over, no doubt because he did not know that it was the Chief Executive behind him. The tale is told—it may well be apocryphal—that Mr. Tubman then drew out his pistol calmly and shot out the rear tires of the offending car. When he saw that the occupants of the automobile he had halted so dramatically were an American and his wife, he gallantly picked them up, and, amid much laughter, drove them to their destination.

Much talk in Liberia centers on Mr. Tubman's yacht, the *President Edward J. Roye.*[6] This 463-ton vessel, which has a passenger capacity of thirty-six, was bought in Holland, where it had been a coastwise steamer. No one knows exactly what it cost, but its upkeep is estimated to be around $125,000 a year, or more than 1 percent of the *total* national budget. Mr. Tubman dispatched no less a personage than the country's secretary of state to shop for it in European marine circles. One story is that the yacht could, in the event of a Liberian revolution (a prospect unlikely in the extreme), be a convenient mechanism for the quick escape from the country of the entire cabinet. Reports that the *President Edward J. Roye* is not seaworthy are manifestly untrue; it carried Prime Minister Nkrumah of the Gold Coast to and from Monrovia on his recent state visit, and in 1952 Mr. Tubman used it—part way— for a trip to Spain. Tubman partisans say that the yacht, far from being

---

[6] Roye was the first all-black President of Liberia (1870-72); his predecessors were mulattoes or octoroons. Mr. Roye was born in Ohio, and had a stormy career in Liberia. He was deposed as President and put into jail. Seeking to escape the country, he was drowned when his canoe capsized in the surf.

a personal luxury on the part of the President, is a national necessity. It is, in fact, the Liberian Navy. When Tubman was a senator he, like everybody, found it appallingly difficult to get around the country; sometimes the Senate had no quorum, simply because the roads were impassable. A yacht, which can fetch people up and down the coast, removes some of these impediments to official travel. Liberia is no longer at the mercy of cargo boats which may, or may not, stop at the local ports. Be this as it may the Tubman yacht has provoked controversy. Liberia has one independent (or more or less independent) newspaper; this printed a dispatch from Washington early in 1953 announcing that President Eisenhower did not intend to keep *his* presidential yacht in commission. There was, of course, no mention of Mr. Tubman's yacht, but that such an article should be printed at all, criticizing the Chief Executive by even the faintest implication, was considered to be extremely daring. Not all has been smooth aboard the yacht itself. According to the authoritative British journal *West Africa*, four of its Dutch officers were suddenly replaced by Germans not long ago. They were alleged "to have been concerned in a mutiny on board."

The President is a jovial and relaxed person socially, but his official life is marked by the most extreme punctilio. At Tubman's second inaugural, which is supposed to have cost a sum truly grandiose, *gray* cutaways and top hats had to be worn. One luckless photographer got into trouble by taking a picture of a Liberian dignitary arriving for a function—the inaugural festivities lasted a whole week—dressed in gray formal clothes of the most impeccable cut, but riding in an open pickup truck; that the truck should have been included in the photograph was deemed tactless. People like to be addressed by their titles as well as names. Almost everybody is an "Honorable," and the proper mode of address is "Mr. Undersecretary" and so on. Life at the Executive Mansion, which is on the corner of Ashmum and Randall streets, is strictly regulated. In the garden of this building, however, I saw something startlingly informal—statutes of an elephant, a leopard, and a bush cow. The elephant's trunk is adorned with a colored electric light, as is the forehead of the bush cow and the leopard's fiercely open mouth.

Liberians are, of course, sensitive about demeanor, exactly like Paraguayans, the ancient Toltecs, or citizens of Fort Worth, Texas. If a member of the *corps diplomatique* should happen inadvertently to affront the President, even on the most trivial matter, his usefulness would be abruptly ended. The Liberian solicitor general, S. R. Horace, lost his job not long ago in circumstances not fully explained. He was discharged for "political and *social* reasons," misconduct in social relations, and "disregard of special considerations due to the Head of the State."

Mr. Tubman can, however, be merciful on occasion. The manager of

the local radio station, by name John West, called on him wearing a
dusty sport shirt; the scene was the presidential farm. Another official,
Mr. Dunbar, had an audience with the Chief Executive at about the
same time, encountered Mr. West, and wrote a letter to the *Listener,*
a local newspaper, saying that Mr. West's improper costume was an
insult to the President. Thereupon Mr. Tubman himself wrote a letter,
which was also published, clearing Mr. West of this charge, and saying
indeed that Mr. Dunbar, who had informed on Mr. West, must have
washed up at the nearest creek before entering the presidential area.
Mr. Tubman proceeded: "You will remember that I was in my disaabilles
[*sic*] when you arrived and that I remained in that condition for the
duration of your stay at the farm; that was for the benefit of relaxation
. . . I consider Mr. Dunbar's letter to be the quintessence of officiousness
and totally unwarranted."

The Chief Executive is a wealthy man, and has property in Monrovia
(several houses said to be his were pointed out to us), a sizable
rubber estate near Cape Palmas, and Konoyale, a cocoa plantation near
Totota.

Of course the President has defects, but he is sharply intelligent,
alert, and accessible; that he keeps his fingers on everything is his
chief source of power. He is certainly the hardest-working man in Liberia, and, I heard it said, the *only* man with the real interests of the
country at heart. He has done more to stamp out petty corruption among
officials than any President in Liberian history. No government payment
over $250 may be made without his personal approval, and, together
with the secretary of the treasury, he signs *all* government requisitions.
When he was in Spain the transfer of an automobile from one government department to another had to await his express authorization.

No President has ever traveled in the Hinterland as much as he;
intermittently he goes upcountry to have palaver with the native chiefs.
Practically all the Liberian tribes support him now, except perhaps some
dissident Krus. Most important of all, a full 20 percent of the national
budget goes nowadays to a new Economic Development Program, which
is being administered with Point Four cooperation. If rubber and iron
ore continue to bring good prices, Mr. Tubman will have more revenue
at his disposal for public improvements and education. He certainly
needs everything he can get if Liberia is to become a mature, self-respecting state.

Mr. Tubman's house at Totota, in the middle of the wettest stretch
of jungle I saw in all Africa, looks something like an Alpine château,
and has a wonderful view of green hills bathed in mist. In the large
salon the furniture was of bamboo, and various ornate trophies stood
against the walls. The President's desk is of the French style, heavily

decorated with gold, and, oddly enough, is informally placed in a corridor near his bedroom. In the main reception room the elaborate large rug was covered with a transparent plastic sheath to keep mud off.

Mr. Tubman greeted us affably, and introduced us to several of his retainers, who sat by in attitudes of extreme stolidity. He was gay and talkative, as if to make up for the total silence of his staff, members of which apparently do not often dare to express themselves if visitors are present. Mr. Tubman drank Bass ale, and offered us hearty slugs of whisky as an *apéritif*. Lunch, when it came, was ample and delicious. We had sherry, red wine, champagne, and half a dozen stoutly substantial courses including corn on the cob. I sat next to Mrs. Tubman, who did not say more than two or three words during the entire meal, which lasted several hours.

The President: Politics

Mr. Tubman was first elected to the Presidency in 1943, and took office early the next year, his term being for eight years. In those days a Liberian President could not succeed himself, but the constitution was amended so that, in 1951, Mr. Tubman was able to stand for a second term, which he won without difficulty. This term was, however, limited to four years. In 1953 the Senate and House passed a petition urging him to accept a national "draft" in 1955, and succeed himself once more, and this he agreed to do. Originally—in the early forties—Mr. Tubman was a "Barclay man," handpicked by the then President, Edwin Barclay, to be his malleable successor. Under Barclay government was a completely closed circle, with the backwoods natives tightly frozen out. But Mr. Tubman, once in office, refused to be a Barclay stand-in. Instead of being a puppet, he broke open the old Barclay clique, pursued his own policy, and became President in fact as well as name.

I have already mentioned that the people of Liberia are sharply divided into two groups (1) the Americo-Liberians and (2) the natives, who are the huge majority. The basic cleavage is that between the ruling Americo-Liberian minority and the overwhelmingly more numerous mass of natives. If there is any struggle for power, it is between these two section of the population. But the natives have practically no power. One can appreciate readily how the first Americo-Liberians, expanding from their original tiny nucleus and seeking to hold themselves together, feared and despised the aborigines in the Hinterland. But as Liberia developed and became stable the natives were treated worse, not better. They were denied the most elementary rights and decencies. The Liberian government behaved toward them even in modern times as backward white colonial powers did fifty years ago.

There was no political fraternization within the bond of color. Here *black* settlers exploited a black countryside.

On the other hand a certain amount of mixing up inevitably took place, and many Americo-Liberians had what are called "outside" children. Tribal youngsters often took the names of their masters in the towns, so that, after a generation or two, nobody could tell with much precision what name meant what. I heard one estimable lady, a leader of Monrovia society, groan aloud, "You cannot tell the wheat from the chaff any more. *Every*body is a native." Hence the ruling caste is extraordinarily sensitive about its aristocratic purity. The leading families among these are almost as interlocked and pervasively powerful as those that ruled prewar France. On the way to visit the President, we passed the rubber estates of several. Most are cousins, and a few names predominate. One Tolbert is vice-president of the republic, another is assistant secretary of agriculture, and another is a senator. One Cooper is ambassador to London, one is secretary of agriculture, and one is (or was) a wealthy businessman. One Barclay is an associate justice of the Supreme Court, and another is one of the two living Liberian MD's.

Take the natives now. Of the estimated total of 1,5000,000 some 60,000, who live along the coast, are considered to be "civilized." There are twenty-three tribal groups, among them the Krus, who are great fishermen, the Bassas (who provide most of the servants in the towns), the Grebos, and the Vais. These latter were the ruling class before the Americo-Liberians came, and were advanced enough to have achieved a written language, one of three written African languages on the entire continent.[7] Liberia also has a considerable number of Moslems, and many of the Hinterland people have become Christianized. Severe scandals occurred in the early 1930's when a League of Nations commission found Liberia guilty of taking part in the slave traffic, i.e., selling its own people abroad for slaves.

The great bulk of natives is still excluded from the fruits of government or business in Liberia, but Tubman has done more for them than any other President ever has. He had the good sense to see that, considerations of justice quite aside, Liberia could not be made into a viable state if something like 1 percent of the nation permanently oppressed 99 percent. He knew, if only as a gesture of political prudence, that he must make some effort to tap the strength of the submerged tribal masses. The natives have not got much from Tubman, but they have got something. For the first time, there are several in the House of

[7] The others are Amharic and Tamachek (Berber). See Duncan MacDougald, Jr., *The Languages and Press of Africa.*

Representatives (but none in the Senate), and a few have lately reached administrative posts. It is fascinating to watch developments like this —Negroes permitting other Negroes to emerge. Liberia feels the same winds, though they are faint as yet, that have blown with such vigor on Nigeria and the Gold Coast. The yeasty tribal masses cannot be permanently kept down.

* * *

The Liberian political system is closely modeled on that of the United States. There are ten senators, two from each county, and thirty-one representatives; the Vice-President presides over the Senate, just as does the Vice-President in Washington. In theory all citizens over twenty-one, including women, are entitled to vote if they are property owners or pay a modest hut tax. But elections, even today, are apt to be a burlesque, because there is seldom any choice of candidate. Liberia is a one-party state. What is known as the True Whig party, the Tubman party, has held power without serious interruption since the 1870's. Mr. Tubman is not only President, head of state, Chief Executive, and commander-in-chief of the army, but party boss.

Not long ago a resident of Monrovia complained to a high Liberian official that a certain person was giving him trouble. "Why not arrest him?" the official suggested. "On what charge?" "Oh, any charge."

Mostly Mr. Tubman rules by means of patronage, exactly as a President of the United States may rule. His enormous, unchallengeable weapon is jobs. The government (Firestone excepted) is by far the largest employer in the country, and all government jobs go—naturally —to members of the True Whig party. The party is financed in turn by a levy on every officer who earns $25 a month or more, amounting to two weeks' salary during normal times, a month's salary in an "election" year. Nobody can possibly get a job if he is known to be in opposition, and no opposition can exist effectively because nobody outside the government has any funds. No neater system of political domination has ever been devised.

Mr. Tubman knows as well as anybody that there are crooks and grafters in Liberia. But he cannot get rid of them all until an educated class arises out of which he can find better men. Close to him are the ablest people in the country. He is careful, however, to see that nobody is an obvious Number Two man. He plays politics by balancing one associate against another, as politicians have done from Pericles to Roosevelt.

Overt criticism of the President is considered to be sedition, and a person guilty of giving information of a deleterious nature to foreigners is, in theory, subject to a jail sentence. As a result people in Monrovia are

somewhat guarded in their expressions of opinion. There is no Gestapo
(as is sometimes alleged) because there is little need to have one; everybody tells Mr. Tubman everything, if only to curry favor. All this being
true, it is astonishing that public criticism, of a veiled sort (and never
aimed at the President directly), is sometimes heard. One newspaper, a
remarkable journalistic phenomenon called the *Friend,* is not against
Tubman, but tries to take its own line. In March, 1953, it wrote that
"high job seekers" were among those urging Mr. Tubman to come out
for a third term. The President issued a statement denying this and saying that the editor was a disappointed job seeker himself. The editor
replied in a front-page editorial, "We feel that we owe it to the public to
correct the statement made by the President in which he alleges that the
editor of the *Friend* is 'disgruntled, mortified, and chagrined' because of
his disappointment in not being appointed consul general to Germany.
We call on High Heaven to refute this statement, and we hasten to make
it cristal [sic] clear that we are not disgruntled, mortified, or chagrined."

On another occasion, when this editor was being attacked by the True
Whig old guard, he replied, "There is one object all these super loyal
citizens seem to have in view, and that is to increase the President's
sensibility and thereby move him to either imprison the editor of the
Friend for life or close down the *Friend* or have the Frontier Force *shoot
the editor down.*" (Italics mine.)

One opposition leader of consequence has, despite all obstacles, managed to rise, a man named Dihdwo Twe. He is a Kru, and for years
sought to represent the crushed masses in the Hinterland. Back in the
1920's he helped bring to light before the League of Nations the role of
leading Liberians of that time in the slave traffic, and the ruling classes
have hated him ever since. In 1951 Mr. Twe achieved something almost
impossible—he organized a genuine opposition party and set out to oppose Tubman for President. A further miracle might have occurred
and he might have won the election, but at the last moment the outraged
True Whig forces managed to prevent him from running owing to "a
technicality." Mr. Twe was then charged with sedition, but managed to
escape from the country. His movement was called "treasonable," and
several of his adherents were arrested. Recently the Institute of Ethnic
Affairs in Washington petitioned the Human Rights Commission of the
UN on behalf of Mr. Twe, who is now living in Sierra Leone. Witch
doctors were employed to try to poison him, this document alleges. Mr.
Twe, who was educated in the United States, wrote Mr. Tubman a perfectly dignified letter (before he fled the country) urging electoral reform. Mr. Tubman's reply was as follows: "For the present time, my
reply to your note is that you are inherently a traitor to your country, a

consummate liar, a senile visionary, a sophisticated bigot, and an un-compromising egotist, the truth of which you will be made to realize."

~~~~~~

Nevertheless it must also be said that Mr. Tubman has done more for Liberians than any President in its history. As in the case of Ethiopia, circumstances and conditions have considerably improved since I wrote these pages. One vital new factor in the country's economic life has been the development of important iron ore reserves in the Bomi Hills, under American direction. Above all Liberia needs revenue, and this enterprise is substantially augmenting the national income.

Politically Mr. Tubman continues to hold all the thongs of power. His character and attitudes have changed little. In January, 1956, came his inauguration for a new term. The festivities went on for a gala week. Little attention was paid to the fact that, at approximately the same time, two leaders of a political party which dared to oppose him were shot by the police and several others convicted of "sedition" and sen-tenced to death. This followed an alleged "assassination attempt" against the President. Several details are macabre. "The legal advisor of the opposition party was arrested and dragged through the streets of Mon-rovia at the end of a chain fixed to a jeep." (Leonard Ingalls in the New York Times, January 6, 1956)

This election was fancy even for Liberia. The official count gave Mr. Tubman 244,873 votes, the opposition candidate 1,182. In Mont-serrado County Mr. Tubman received 55,850 votes, roughly 15,000 more than the county's total population.

I didn't mean to be hard on Liberia when I first wrote this chapter. But the result was that I am not, I would say, quite the most popular author in the world in the opinion of the Tubman circle. I have even been told—though I have no evidence of this myself—that copies of Inside Africa are strictly forbidden entrance into the country, and that possession of it is a crime.

~~~~~~~~~

CHAPTER 34

A Visit to Dr. Albert Schweitzer

*My wife and I spent a week in Lambaréné with Dr. Schweitzer in
1953. A condensation of this chapter appeared in* Reader's Digest *(August, 1954) and then became a part of* Inside Africa, *1955.*

~~~~~~

> *Whatever is reasonable is good. To be truly rational is to
> become ethical.*
> —ALBERT SCHWEITZER
>
> *You can burn a candle at both ends if it is long enough.*
> —ALBERT SCHWEITZER

INCONTESTABLY Schweitzer is a great man—one of the greatest of this
or any time. The majesty of his thought and the breadth and force of
his ethical sense are almost, if not quite, Olympian. Schweitzer is too
lofty, too manifold to grasp easily—a "universal man" in the sense that
Leonardo da Vinci and Goethe were universal men. Everybody knows
that he is a teacher, seer, humanitarian, healer, and practical idealist.
He has had four different professional careers, and is an authentic
quadruple doctor—in philosophy, medicine, theology, and music. He has
written learned books on Bach, Jesus, and the history of civilization, and
is the world's foremost authority on the architecture of organs as well
as a celebrated interpreter of organ music. Also Dr. Schweitzer knows a
great deal—more than many men who have devoted their lives to these
fields—about aesthetics, tropical zoology, anthropology, and agriculture,
and is an expert carpenter, nurse, mason, veterinarian, boat builder,
dentist, architect, repairer of pumps, draughtsman, mechanic, pharmacist, and gardener. Universal man indeed!

He has multitudinous disciples—Schweitzer "addicts"—and these talk about him with an almost frightened reverence, as people at Yasnaya Polyana talked of Tolstoy. Schweitzer's own view of himself is simpler, and partakes of his anthropomorphism. He said once, "I am a tall tree in the Vosges!"

Schweitzer would be intolerable if, together with his overwhelming intellectual and moral virtues, he did not have defects. He himself is quite conscious of these, and mentions in one of his books that he has often been "arrogant" and "lacking in love," and that he has even "hated, slandered, and defrauded." In plain fact the old man—he was turning seventy-nine when we saw him—has several frailties. His venerators are horrified if these are mentioned; they want their Great Man whole, untattered and undiminished. Few people ever visit Lambaréné, the Schweitzer lair in French Equatorial Africa, and dare to write anything except unrestrained eulogies. But he can be cranky on occasion, dictatorial, prejudiced, pedantic in a peculiarly Teutonic manner, irascible, and somewhat vain. And why not? It might even be whispered that Dr. Schweitzer's views on several subjects are obstinately old-fashioned. Again, why not?

Our chief interest was, naturally, to find out something of his relation to Africa. Actually Dr. Schweitzer does not know much about Africa except his own small and isolated corner, as he himself freely concedes. He has made eleven voyages to the continent, but, with the exception of a two-week sojourn in the Cameroons in 1924, he has never visited any African country except French Equatorial Africa. (Of course ships on which he is a passenger make brief stops at various West Coast ports, and these he saw briefly. He has never traveled by air.) He has lived in Lambaréné for an aggregate of twenty-eight years, but has never once even been to Brazzaville, the capital of the territory, which is 420 miles away. This is as if a man should, say, live in Oneida, New York, all his life, and never once go to New York City. It is also an interesting point that, so far as I know, Dr. Schweitzer has never learned any African language or dialect—except a few words of greeting—though of course he knows Latin, Greek, Hebrew, English, French and German.[1] As to his attitude toward Africans en masse, that is a mixture of benevolence, perplexity, irritation, hope, and despair. I would imagine that he has little if any belief in the capability of Africans—at least in his own area —for self-government. He hates oppression, of course, and believes devoutly in the brotherhood of man, but he has, it seems, almost no conception of the volcanic surges and stresses of modern Africa and its hungry zest for political advance. He is, in short, one of those good old

[1] He does not like to speak English, but I had the feeling that he understands it well.

souls who would like to see the white man stay on in "colonial" areas forever.

Also I was much struck by something else. Dr. Schweitzer is a profound moralist, but he has comparatively little interest in human beings as such, African or otherwise. His mind goes in, not out. Basically his interests are art and ideas. The hospital is run in a way somewhat difficult to explain. Some visitors find in it all that they are looking for spiritually; to meet Schweitzer and see his work is a magnificent emotional experience. Others—though they may not say so—do not quite regard it as the model of a Christian community. Discipline, though not overtly exercised, is somewhat strict; everything, as I heard it put, is "noted." Discussion at mealtimes or in the evening hardly exists, and acolytes do not sit at the feet of the master to absorb wisdom—because he seldom talks. His aloofness is remarkable, and he has small contact with most of his workers. If any trouble occurs, the disputants are called into Schweitzer's office one by one. With his eyes closed, the Doctor tells them what his ruling is—"Do this," or "I want no more of that"—without permitting apology or explanation. Schweitzer is always fair, but he simply does not have much interest in minor personal problems. On the other hand he can be magically charming on occasion and is literally worshiped by his old associates. His laughter—when he laughs—is a striking indication of his inner sweetness. It is a shining laugh, a silvery laugh, and it tinkles.

No bush hospital can be tidy, any more than can a farmyard in South Carolina. There will always be things out of place, and innocent litter on the ground. But Schweitzer's hospital was, I thought, the most unkempt place of its kind I saw in all Africa. The sanitary arrangements are —how shall I put it?—picturesque. Of course Schweitzer is totally above such details. Another thing that struck me was that many African workers seemed unhappy and somewhat unfriendly—even surly. They wheedled for tips. Once, a hundred yards away from the hospital, I was openly solicited by two robust, grinning Negro ladies. I laughed and pulled two francs out of my pocket, saying that this was all the money I had. With cheerful contempt they said it was not enough and waved me on. It seemed an odd thing to happen so close to Dr. Schweitzer.

Later we watched him feed one of his pet antelopes; the hospital area swarms with animals, and on these the Doctor bestows the most tender care. He seems to be fonder of the animals in Lambaréné than the human beings, and perhaps—who knows?—they reward him more. As a whole the hospital gives a curious atmosphere of being a kind of abstraction, almost an exercise in penance. Schweitzer does his work for himself before God, as well as out of a sense of duty for the Africans. He is not only saving the bodies of men, but his own immortal soul.

Life and Work of the "Thirteenth Apostle"

The great secret of success is to go through life as a man who never gets used up.

—ALBERT SCHWEITZER

Some sort of demon has always possessed Schweitzer; he pursued both faith and reason, not easy bedfellows. Once he wrote that he belonged proudly to the fellowship of those who bear the Mark of Pain. To make his career at Lambaréné comprehensible we must go back to the roots.

He was born in Upper Alsace in 1875; his father was an evangelical pastor, and his mother the daughter of a pastor. The family moved to an Alsatian village named Gunsbach when Albert was an infant, and this is still his European home. One of his grandfathers was a schoolmaster and organist; three granduncles were also organists. Schweitzer told me, when I asked him about his parents, that he was strongly influenced by his father, but that he remembers his mother more. His mother met death in an extraordinary way; during World War I she was knocked down and trampled to death by German cavalry horses trooping up an Alsatian road.[2]

Puny children, if they survive adolescence, often grow up strong; nature, it seems, hoards her reserves and delays giving full vitality until it is really needed. Schweitzer was a sickly child, with a subsequent robustness that was, and is, phenomenal. Also—more strangely—he was a poor student, slow to read and write. Because of this, as he grew up he *made* himself master subjects that were particularly difficult for him, like Hebrew. He had a stern, glowing sense of duty. Schweitzer says that he lacked self-confidence when he was a youth, but he has certainly never lacked it since.

As a child he hated cruelty and injustice; he would not shoot birds, fish, or track animals as his playmates did; he wore clogs instead of shoes because other Gunsbach boys could not afford shoes. Also his passion for music began early, and in this as well as other fields he was an authentic prodigy. He composed a hymn at seven, and began to play the organ at eight "when his legs were scarcely long enough to reach the pedals." He records that he almost fainted with emotion the first time he ever heard brass instruments playing together—he had to prop himself against a wall to avoid falling. He heard a Wagner opera for the first time when he was sixteen, and was so inexpressibly moved that it was days before he could give "proper attention to his work in school."

In early manhood three of his four professional lives proceeded con-

[2] *Out of My Life and Thought,* one of Schweitzer's best autobiographical works, gives exactly one sentence to this episode.

currently. He studied philosophy at the University of Strassburg, and a thesis on Kant brought him his first doctorate. He studied theology and in 1900, when he was twenty-five, was ordained curate of the St. Nicholas Church in Strassburg. He studied the theory of music, and began his career as an organist. He had degrees in philosophy, theology, and music at twenty-six, and became a *Privatdozent* on the Strassburg faculty.[3] A stream of books began to pour out from him, and has never stopped. In his early thirties appeared the biography of Bach; he wrote it first in French, and then completely rewrote it, much enlarged, in German. Then came his *Quest of the Historical Jesus,* which upset many theological assumptions of the time; a work on organ building, which has similarly remained a classic; a dissertation on the problem of the Last Supper; and a searching study of St. Paul.

His vigor was enormous. He records that sometimes he went to his organ studies early in the morning without having been to bed at all.

I asked Schweitzer in Lambaréné what his family had thought of all this. He answered, "When I was still a young man my father asked me what preoccupied me and I replied, 'A work on eschatology.' My father shook his head, saying, 'My son, I pity you. No one will ever understand a word you write.' "

Schweitzer worked a good deal in both Paris and Berlin in those days —he liked Berlin better—and it is interesting that, so far as I know, there is no mention at all in his work of politics or nationalism, not even Alsatian nationalism. Alsace was German when he was born, but had been French five years before; it became French again in 1918. Schweitzer grew up in both French and German, but is more instinctively at home in German. Even if he had no interest in nationalism, he has been a victim of it. He was a German citizen working in French Equatorial Africa when World War I came; he was promptly interned by the French as an enemy alien, and his hospital was kept under guard by black troops.[4] In 1917 he was brought back to France and spent ten grisly months in camps for enemy internees—concentration camps, we would call them nowadays. This was probably the bitterest experience of his life, and marked the only time when he has ever been severely ill. He never got dysentery in Africa; in France he did.

In Lambaréné, sitting in the garden by the river, I asked him which

[3] See *The Africa of Albert Schweitzer,* by Charles R. Joy and Melvin Arnold. This and Joy's *Albert Schweitzer, An Anthology,* are invaluable works on Schweitzer.

[4] He records that, on the day after he was forbidden to work at the hospital, he at once proceeded to start writing his *Philosophy of Civilization.* Previously, so that his music would not get rusty, he set out to learn *by heart* the organ compositions "of Bach, Mendelssohn, Widor, César Franck, and Max Reger."

he thought himself to be most—French or German. His reply was quick, *"Homo sum!"*

* * *

When Schweitzer was twenty-one he vowed to give himself nine years of fulfillment in art and theological service; after that he would do something else. So, at thirty, seeking complete spiritual self-realization, he abruptly quit his three careers, having reached a very tidy summit in each, in order to become a doctor and go out to Africa for the rest of his life as a medical missionary. No act of renunciation could be more profound.

Why medicine? Would it not have been enough to be a nonmedical missionary? Because, he records, he was tired of talk, and wanted action.

Why Africa? First, because of his father's early conversations. Second, because he had been strongly impressed in his youth by a heroic statue in Colmar, portraying a Negro in chains at the foot of a monument. (This statue, incidentally, was by Bartholdi, the sculptor of the Statue of Liberty.) Third, a communication from the Paris Missionary Society, which reached him at the critical time, emphasized the need of medical service in French Equatorial Africa.

Why Lambaréné? Because it was one of the most inaccessible and primitive spots in all Africa, one of the most dangerous, and one without any doctor at all in the area.

He worked at his medical studies at Strassburg from 1906 to 1912 and finally, aged thirty-eight, became an M.D. His thesis was a psychiatric study of the mind of Jesus, with particular attention to "mental derangements of which other scholars thought He might have been a victim." A period of internship and special courses on tropical medicine in Paris followed. These years were the most difficult and fatiguing he ever spent, he records. A German medical education was a thoroughly grueling process in those days; yet while going through this Schweitzer managed to continue teaching philosophy, kept on with his activity as curate of St. Nicholas, and started work on a definitive edition of Bach's organ music.

He married in 1912. Before this a friendship with an elderly and distinguished noblewoman "rounded off many a hard angle" in his personality, as he puts it. His wife, by name Helene Bresslau, the daughter of a noted Strassburg historian, is Jewish. She learned nursing in order to be able to help him in Africa, and has been his devoted companion and assistant (though for reasons of health she has not been in Lambaréné recently) ever since. The Schweitzers have one daughter, Rhena, and four grandchildren.

Schweitzer assembled his equipment, and paid for the entire expedition himself out of gifts from his parish and his earnings as a lecturer and organist. He records how the preparation of intricate shopping lists gave him high "artistic satisfaction." His theology was so unorthodox that the Paris Missionary Society, which had to give its approval of the venture, asked him to submit to an examination on his beliefs. This he refused to do, but he called on various members of the organization individually, explained his ideas, and was passed. He had to promise, however, to confine his activities solely to the medical field, and be "as silent as a carp" on matters of theology, for fear of "subverting" other missionaries in the field. Finally Schweitzer and his wife were ready. With seventy packing cases of supplies, they sailed for Africa from Bordeaux on March 26, 1913.

* * *

Lambaréné is situated on the River Ogowe fifty miles south of the Equator, in the territory of Gabon. The Ogowe flows roughly parallel to the Congo five hundred miles north of it, and is the largest river between the Congo and the Niger. The easiest way to describe the area is to paraphrase Schweitzer himself, and say that it resembles the beginning of the world—clouds, river, and forest combine and melt into a landscape that seems literally antediluvian. Most of the year the air is like steam coming out of a green mist, and I, for one, would not have been surprised to see prehistoric lizards rise out of the swamps and swallow islets at a gulp.

Lambaréné lies about 175 miles above the mouth of the Ogowe at Port Gentil, and is an island. Further up the river there is little but *brousse*—bush. The island measures approximately ten miles by four, and has a population today of two thousand natives, forty-four French, and one Swiss. Schweitzer's establishment is not on the island, but is a mile or two away on the mainland across a gray-green, soupy branch of the Ogowe. When Schweitzer arrived in 1913 there were already two French missions in the area, one Protestant and one Catholic, but neither had a doctor. One of these had formerly been an American mission.

Every inch of habitable land near Lambaréné has to be seized from the giant forest. The waterways are the roads. The tribesmen in the area had been cannibals not long before, and the forest was—and is—populated thickly with beasts of unamiable disposition, like pythons and gorillas. The rivers are heavy with crocodiles and hippopotamuses, and Schweitzer told us that the hospital was virtually isolated from Lambaréné itself from six every evening until the next morning, because at night hippopotamuses were likely to attack and tip over the *pirogues* (dugout canoes) that are his only means of transport. On the other hand there is no atmosphere at all of danger, active or passive, except from mosquitoes.[5] The forest (it is particularly rich in enormous *okoumé* trees) seems to have been thoroughly intimidated by the Great Doctor, even if it isn't.

Here, then, forty-two years ago, Albert Schweitzer began his work. To build a bush hospital from scratch—and Schweitzer did it practically with his bare hands—is something like swimming the Atlantic in a suit of armor. Once he had to move and rebuild the entire establishment, because the old huts were made untenable by a dysentery epidemic. For one period of eighteen *months*, he says that he scarcely had time to do any medical work at all. His labors were like those of Hercules. One of his books describes with understated vividness how he and Madame Schweitzer had, on one occasion, to fill cavities in each other's teeth. African patients, suffering anything from leprosy to phagedenic ulcers, from strangulated hernia to elephantiasis, were not always easy to handle. For one brief period, after the death of a patient who arrived at the hospital too late for successful treatment, Schweitzer was considered to be a leopard in disguise, who deliberately took lives.

Once he records that he threw himself in a chair and groaned aloud, "What a blockhead I was to come out here to doctor savages like this!" Then his faithful African interpreter replied, "Yes, Doctor, here on earth you are a great blockhead, but not in heaven."[6]

But nobody can be more obstinate, more dogmatically purposeful, than an Alsatian theologian. Even in periods of complete despair Schweitzer was "intoxicated with delight at having to deal with realities which could be determined with exactitude." The plain fact is that, despite everything, he loved Lambaréné, and still loves it. Among other things it taught him his basic ethical concept, which is the root of his philosophy today and which he calls "reverence for life." Once in 1939 he returned to Europe intending to take a long recuperative holiday; after the barest glimpse of Gunsbach he changed his mind and returned to Africa forthwith, traveling back in fact on the return trip of the same boat that brought him to Europe. The demon was still pursuing.

Schweitzer, when he set out for Africa, thought that he was giving up forever what was dearest to him—art and preaching. He prepared to sacrifice three things—"to abandon the organ, to renounce academic teaching, and to lose my financial independence." (He says that, even today, he cannot bear to look at the lecture building at the University of Strassburg, because it calls up poignantly all that he has missed.) But the old Doctor was spared the sacrifice. Or, to put it somewhat differ-

---

[5] But once on the river my wife had to scratch a tsetse fly off her neck.
[6] *More from the Primeval Forest*, by Albert Schweitzer, p. 182.

ently, all the sacrifices have, as it were, paid off. He has always had a piano with him in Africa, and so he has been able to keep up with his music, although it was certainly a deprivation not to have a proper organ. His Bach recordings, made when he was on holiday in Europe, have been a profound artistic success. As to academic work he lectures widely whenever he returns to civilization, and has been honored by universities without number. He became one of the two or three most famous men in the world, and won the Nobel peace prize for 1952.

First Encounter with Le Grand Docteur

Nowadays it is easy enough to get to Schweitzer, if you do not mind old airplanes and eccentric flying. We put down at the airport across the Ogowe from Schweitzer's hospital. I have never seen an airport like this, because there was nothing whatever on it to indicate any connection with flying, except the stepladder on which we descended from the plane—not even a windsleeve or a drum of gasoline. When the plane took off, leaving us there, the stepladder remained where it stood, blankly alone in the middle of the field, stepping up to nothing—a perch to infinity. I asked our pilot what Lambaréné was like. He replied in succinct English, "It stinks." I asked the Negro official representing Air France what it was like. He replied with the utmost solemnity, "It is purgatory on earth, monsieur." (Of course they meant the town, not Schweitzer's installation.)

The hospital startles some visitors because almost everybody thinks beforehand that it will be like an Indian *ashram,* an aseptic harbor of tranquillity, spirituality, and out-of-this-worldness.

Schweitzer sent his assistant, Miss Emma Haussknecht, in a *pirogue* to meet us at the riverbank, but the French authorities insisted on giving us a lift on their official launch. This cut swiftly across the swollen, solid-seeming river. We disembarked at a point where other *pirogues* were clustered, and climbed up a rough, hot, bushy path. Schweitzer's hospital, on first glance, looks like what, in fact, it is—a native village. Patients come from miles around, often with their families. Miss Haussknecht, an Alsatian nurse who has been Schweitzer's dedicated companion since 1925, is general manager to the whole establishment, and serves as interpreter from French or German into English. She wore a white sun helmet and carried a large white umbrella. (It is one of the Doctor's theories that the tsetse fly is less likely to attack white objects than those darker.) This admirable lady is a most determined character —once, many years ago, she *walked* from Lambaréné to the coast. She led us to our room, gave us the key, and told us to be careful always to lock the door. "Please never leave your room unlocked, even for a moment." This remark was something of a shock.

The fear of theft is, of course, natural. There are Africans who steal, just as there are Europeans who steal. But Schweitzer's camp, we found out later, was positively obsessed by fussiness about stealing. It was sharply disillusioning, in this community dedicated to good works, to find that there should be so much overt distrust. *Everything* at Schweitzer's is kept rigidly under lock and key. We even had to give our key to the roomboy each morning when he made up the room. The servants are not permitted to carry keys.

Our building was a long, low, narrow structure, set so closely under trees that it almost seemed to be bearing foliage itself. Schweitzer designed it, and has every reason to be proud of his work. The rooms have cross ventilation, and are cool. The windows are screened, but without glass. Each room has one or two narrow iron beds, a simple washstand, wicker chairs, shelves, and a table. There are no closets, bathrooms, running water, or electric light. Nevertheless it was not only comfortable, but extremely pleasant.

A dozen or more of these narrow cubicles face the long shady veranda. Two doors down from us was a European woman convalescing from sleeping sickness. She was holding a parrot, and she warned us not to play with it, since it was *méchant,* and would bite. We met then a young man, one of Schweitzer's associates, carrying a sick baby mandrill. Most of the African servants, I noticed, had bandages stained with gentian violet on their hands or feet. It did not occur to me then that they were lepers.

Slop basins from the rooms are poured into an open drain flowing directly in front of the veranda, and bits of bandage, broken crockery, scraps of grapefruit peel, and the like, are scattered in it. But somehow this was not offensive, and the building itself gave the impression of being spotlessly clean. Five feet away were three rude wooden crosses; children had put them up to mark the graves of dead animals. Miss Haussknecht led us past a nearby rockpile where a dozen Africans were at work, swinging hammers. These too were lepers. One youth sat alone, without hammer or pick, crooning, while goats, dogs, pigs, and chickens scrambled near him. "He is a mental patient, but not violent," Miss Haussknecht said. "We call him *Petit Poisson,* because those are the only words he understands."

We strode up a dirt path, through brush and fruit trees, for a quarter of an hour. There was a sense of aliveness in the trees; they seemed to vibrate with heavy, hidden, sodden life. This path is nicknamed "Philosopher's Walk," and leads to the new leper village that Schweitzer is building half a mile away. We passed a small cemetery, and saw a homemade monument to an African, one of Schweitzer's first nurses, who had been cook to none other than De Brazza. As always, the generations are close in Africa. Near a ragged clearing Schweitzer himself came forth. He has a powerful aquiline nose, dripping gray mustache, and eyes that really *fix* you. He is strongly built, and wore an open white shirt, tattered pants, and heavy black shoes. Force, repose, command, sensitiveness— all these characteristics are reflected in his proud, grizzled, piercing face. It is a wonderful face, and he is a magnificent-looking man.

Courteously he asked us if his *pirogue* had been comfortable, and Miss Haussknecht explained that we had come by the government launch. Schweitzer seemed to be disconcerted by this, and responded with a curious gesture, a kind of sweeping, mocking bow, as if to indicate ironically that he was delighted that we had received such unusual official hospitality. Then he asked us, horrified, why we were not wearing sun helmets. We discovered later that sun helmets are practically a fetish at Lambaréné. Nobody at the hospital ever stirs out of doors by day without a *casque*, and the Great Doctor even wears a hat—a crumpled old fedora—when he goes out at night. He attributes his good health to the fact that he always covers his head except indoors. At least a dozen times in the next few days people rushed after us every time we stepped out, offering us headgear. Vainly I tried to explain that I had been in Africa for eight months, had visited places much hotter than Lambaréné, and had not worn a hat yet, much less a sun helmet. Then I pointed to the sky. Not a trace of sun was visible. This was June, the dry season in this part of the world; the sky was heavily overcast with low-lying, dirty wool clouds; it was a meteorological certainty that there would be *neither* rain nor a single ray of clear sun until August. But Schweitzer's folk kept pursuing us—for our own good, of course. Sun helmets are completely archaic in most parts of Africa now, but not here. There is a good reason for this. The sun helmet is the badge of the old colonial. Also Schweitzer himself has had several minor sunstrokes (he got them indoors, when he was not wearing a hat, from sunshine piercing holes in thatched roofs) and is excessively sensitive about the subject. When, the next day, he saw that we were still bareheaded, he stared at us as if we obviously must be demented, and then shrugged cheerfully as if to say the responsibility was no longer his.

Schweitzer led us forward briskly to the leper village, where he wants to erect substantial structures, with iron roofs like those at the hospital proper, to replace the present miserable huts which could be blown away by the next tornado. Immediately he got to work, and it was striking to see him devoting himself to this activity, that of being fore-man of a labor gang. But Schweitzer begins and ends each day with this occupation. *Some*body has to do it. A group of lepers stood by. They were, I admit freely, the worst workmen I have ever seen. They used their spades (they were supposed to be digging foundations) with about as much animation as corpses. If they had spines, they were made of blotting paper. They were not too ill to work, but just plain lazy, as well as numb with boredom and indifference, dazed like zombies. Schweitzer strode amongst them with explosive and hortatory grunts. He argued, threatened, and cajoled. He took a spade himself. Then he chanted a kind of tune, to mark time for the digging: *"Allez-vous OPP! Allez-vous OPP-upp-O P P! Hupp, upp, Hup, upp, OPP!"*

We asked Schweitzer a question or two about the workmen, such as what they got to eat.

"Seven bananas a day."

I asked, "Would they work better if they got eight bananas?"

Dr. Schweitzer's eyes flashed. (And they really do flash.) "No. That would disturb discipline and morale. If somebody does particularly good work, I may give him extra fare, but I do so secretly, so that the others will not know."

We toured the village, smoky with little outdoor fires, and with ebony children underfoot in the greenish dusk. We passed some bad leper cases, and Schweitzer asked them to show us their hands. "Do not touch the hands," Dr. Schweitzer said.

Forest Hospital and Its Routine

All thinking men must renounce the attempt to explain the universe.
—ALBERT SCHWEITZER

Schweitzer's encampment lies on a low, sloping bluff and has forty-five or more buildings; these are all home-built, simply made, and serviceable. Everybody knows what a frightful toll the tropical heat and dampness impose on any structure; that Schweitzer's should be so substantial and in such good condition is amazing. And he built most of these with his own hands. The hospital has between 350 and 400 African patients, depending on circumstances, and 75 paid African helpers, mostly lepers. There are some 500 mouths to feed every day. There are of course no paved walks or roads. The French authorities offered to put in a telephone line to connect Schweitzer with Lambaréné, but the old Doctor would not hear of it. There is no running water, no hot water (except what is boiled in pots), no electricity except just enough for the operating room, no radio since the departure some years ago of a physician who had one, no motorboat, and no chapel.

Animals drop their refuse everywhere. One afternoon we saw a sick dog lying in one corner of the dispensary, while an orange-colored cat lay next to the crude board that was the treatment table. The hospital has about 150 goats, which fertilize the fruit trees. Near the dining hall are a wild pig in a cage, and a monkey on a six-foot leash, tied to a tree. Chickens, other birds, goats, and piglets scratch near the rations laid on the ground, before these are distributed to the African help. Four graceful antelope stand in a rough wire enclosure; the Doctor feeds them through the wire after dinner every night. In one cage are both guinea pigs and parrots. One European nurse has a pet civet cat, another a big red pig named Tecla, and another a chimpanzee, by name Fifi. For a time (one visitor to the hospital records) Schweitzer even kept a litter of baby rats, although he did not try to make pets of them. The pets are treated with the utmost affection and at the same time are made useful, if possible. As we walked in to lunch one day Schweitzer encountered Tecla, and calmly wiped his shoes on her. Obviously the pig enjoyed this process, and her stiff bristles gave the Doctor's shoes a formidable shine.

What appears to be the main hospital ward is a long one-story structure, cut apart into narrow dark rooms, each of which opens to a courtway. The patients do not lie actually on the floor, as they do in most bush hospitals, but on wooden bunks covered with matting. I did not see any sheets or pillows. Outside each door a small, smoky fire is burning; here the family of the patient does the cooking. It is good to have these fires; they keep the mosquitoes down, and thus lend to lessen the incidence of malaria and sleeping sickness. (Yellow fever and acute sleeping sickness cases are, incidentally, the province of a new government hospital on the island, and are no longer dealt with by Schweitzer.) If a man has no family, and is too sick to cook for himself, he becomes a serious problem. Most patients will not accept food from anybody not a member of their own tribe out of fear of being poisoned.

Schweitzer has saved thousands of lives, which is the more extraordinary considering the primitiveness of his equipment. There is, so far as I could see, no mechanism at all for sterilizing bandages under pressure; water has to be boiled in kettles propped up on stones, underneath feeble wood fires out in the open. For years drugs and bandages were in short supply. Every safety pin is precious. Things that we would take utterly for granted in a European hospital are objects of wonder, if they exist at all. I was told that Schweitzer did not like elaborate modern gadgets. For one thing they are difficult to maintain or repair in a tropically humid climate. What point is there to having hot-water bags, if they rot in a week? For another, he wants the Africans to feel comfortable, in circumstances that make them think they are at home, so that they will not be timid about coming to him when they are ill.

We came across a nurse at work on a sheet of board that served as a table. Projecting from a blanket was something that looked like the greenish, decayed trunk of a small tree. She was scraping blotches of what appeared to be fungi off this. It was a man's leg.

We peered into the operating room one morning; it was startling to be able to look right in from the courtyard. On the table lay a naked Negro, his abdomen streaming with blood. I looked more closely. It was not blood, but mercurochrome. The doctor who performed the operation —it was a routine hernia—came in to lunch an hour later. He had not had time to wash up completely and, in his shirt sleves, sat down with his arms still scarlet with mercurochrome up to the elbow. I do not mean to indicate by this that surgery at Schweitzer's is rough or incompetent. It is not. Standards are very high.

One bizarre sight is the insane asylum. It is a small square box without windows, with two padlocked cells on each side. A certain amount of light gets in through a criss-cross aperture. There are no sanitary facilities, but at intervals the occupants are led down to the river to bathe. The violently insane must be locked up not only to protect the community, but to keep them from being murdered by their families. Schweitzer records in one of his books his delight that he was able to build this structure, because it replaced one smaller. The smaller one must have been even more ghastly. Yet it is a remarkable tribute to Schweitzer's thoroughness and humanity that there should be room for the insane at all. Most bush hospitals do not have such facilities.

In a crowded open space near the dining hall Africans busily carry produce in rude barrows made by putting short poles on packing crates. Women squat on the ground, binding palm fronds together for roofing; others are busy on sewing machines, and still others iron the wash with primitive irons heated by a lump of wood coal. The Doctor strides back and forth, amid this orderly animation, seeing that everybody works. The bustle and clatter are those of a frontier camp. The great moment here comes when the rations are distributed. Each African entitled to a ration gets seven large bananas a day, plus two sticks of manioc wrapped in leaves, the native equivalent of bread. Also, on occasion, the ration includes palm oil, rice, and soap. The bananas (which are really plantains) are measured out with scrupulous care, so that everybody gets fruit of identical size. Some workers get a cash wage as well as their ration, but this is small, averaging only about 7½ cents a week.

One nurse in the establishment is senior even to Miss Haussknecht; she is another Alsatian, Miss Matilda Kottmann, who came to Lambaréné in 1924. She is a most saintly and delightful person. The chief doctor at present (Schweitzer himself does not do much active medical work nowadays) is Hungarian; another is one of the old man's nephews. The nurses are dedicated utterly to their work. One told me that their health is generally good, but that they are likely to get malaria if they are very tired after taking care of a *European* patient, since these need more attention than Africans. (The Europeans come mostly from the logging camps nearby, and have separate hospital quarters.) It is a most remarkable thing that Schweitzer himself has never once had malaria. For a time, years ago, sores on his feet were apt to become ulcerated, but this aside he has *never* been seriously ill in Africa, which is another proof of how much he likes it.[7]

There are almost always visitors at the Schweitzer board, and some of these—even those who come uninvited—may stay for months or even years. Schweitzer's hospitality is boundless, and nobody is turned away. Usually guests, if they stay any length of time, do some sort of work, like helping call the hospital roll or distributing the bananas.[8]

Miss Haussknecht said one morning that she had arranged an ex-pedition up the river in a *pirogue*. "Four of our best lepers will row you. Do not touch their hands or paddles."

By this time—after only a day or two—we had lost or managed to conceal most of the instinctive apprehension we felt about lepers. To enforce strict segregation of leprous patients would be altogether im-possible in a community like Lambaréné. The worst cases are restricted to a certain area, but others wander about freely. The truth is that leprosy is not nearly so unpleasant a disease as some that are widely prevalent in our western world, and it is not particularly contagious (though, after contact, a person cannot be absolutely sure he has not caught it for five years). Probably it is less contagious than tuberculosis. It is an odd medical point that the bacillus of leprosy is almost indis-tinguishable from that of tuberculosis, even to a skilled eye under the microscope. Incidentally Schweitzer has never seen a case of appendicitis in an African, and cancer is virtually unknown.

The hospital day is regulated by a series of bells—reveille at 6:30 A.M., breakfast at 7:30, and lunch at 12:30. A brief siesta is then sup-posed to be obligatory, but *le Grand Docteur*, which is what the natives call him, seldom sleeps. At 6:30 P.M. a bell announces the end of the day; at 7:30 comes the dinner bell and at 8:30 a final bell after which the *indigènes* are not allowed out of doors. Europeans, too, seldom stir outside after this hour, because of the danger from mosquitoes. But once we joined the whole staff at the riverbank, when Schweitzer cele-brated a saint's day by building a large fire of palm fronds and watching it burn fiercely. That was all that happened, but it was a beautiful and impressive ceremony. The Doctor's face was rapt, and the flames sounded like surf.

The dining table is long enough to hold twenty or more people, and is lit by a row of kerosene lamps. Schweitzer's cook is a Swiss lady, and the meals are simple, ample, and altogether delicious. At breakfast pots of tea and coffee are waiting, with toast and several kinds of jam made

[7] The sunstrokes I mentioned above were minor.
[8] Nothing about Schweitzer impressed me more than his letter asking us to stay with him. It ended with a medical homily advising us not to eat underdone meat while in Africa and always to wash our hands after shaking hands with a native.

out of local fruit. At lunch there will be a vegetable or fruit stew—for instance of papaya and carrots mixed together—plain boiled sweet potatoes in their jackets, noodles, bread-fruit fritters, palm nuts, fresh salad, and steamed bananas. Once we had meat—some lamb sent over by a neighboring mission. Eggs or fish are served every day, sometimes twice a day. At dinner tureens of healthy thick soup are placed on the table as the company assembles, and this is followed by rice or macaroni, other vegetables, and great bowls of fresh fruit cup up into a macédoine.

Schweitzer sits at the middle of the long table flanked by Miss Haussknecht and Miss Kottmann, with guests of honor opposite. Gently the two nurses offer him special delicacies, like radishes from his preciously tended garden, tidbits of salad, or brown beans. At each meal, including breakfast, Schweitzer eats steamed bananas. Sometimes he puts food into a soup plate, and eats with a spoon. When fresh fruit is served he pulls a large penknife out of his pocket, and peels an orange or grapefruit with it.

Immediately before each meal Schweitzer says a brief grace in French; immediately after dinner (no meal takes more than half an hour) he announces a hymn in a decisive voice, and hymnbooks are passed around. He walks to an upright piano at one end of the room, and plays briefly but with great vigor and precision as the company sings. He returns to his place at the table, inspects carefully a list of Bible passages, slowly opens the Bible, and reads a few lines from scripture.

Schweitzer is a most incisive, alert, and authoritative conversationalist. His mind is sharp as a saw, and he gives forth opinions with a wonderful quick dogmatism. The epigrammatic quickness of his mind is as astonishing as its spiritual breadth and profundity. He is a true German "thinker." But he seldom talks much at meals these days—he is too tired.

After dinner doctors and nurses gather at one end of the long room, and have cinnamon tea or some similar mild stimulant. Schweitzer may, or may not, join them. One evening he left the table at once, because an argument—he called it a "palaver"—with some workmen had exhausted him. Another evening he sat with us until after nine, at which time Miss Kottman reminded him that it was time to deal with his mail. Always on leaving the dining hall he takes with him odd bits of food, which he gives to the antelopes. Then—after curfew has descended on the rest of the camp—he will work till midnight or beyond.

Grace Notes

He never wears a necktie (while in Africa) unless he is officiating at a funeral or similar occasion. In fact he owns only one necktie, which he bought in 1928. When questioned about this by one of his biographers he replied, "Why have more than one tie? After all I can only wear one at a time."

When he finishes writing a chapter of whatever book he is working on he loops a string through the pages, and hangs them behind his desk, "like a bag of pheasants." (Of course metal clips cannot be used in Lambaréné, since they rust at once.)

He will not step on a flower needlessly, and would never dream of harming an animal. One reporter in Paris has, however, recorded that he saw Schweitzer, in a moment of irritation, squash a moth that was bothering him.

He saw me writing notes one afternoon, and asked me if I kept a carbon. I said no, and he said that he didn't either, but that when he is working on a manuscript he writes a message on the first page—"Dear Thief: If you happen by chance to *find* this, please return it to the above address, and you will have my eternal gratitude."

He writes everything in a neat round longhand, and can only find time to write at night when the day's work is done. He told me, "Writing costs a man a lot." He shocked the customs officers at Bordeaux on one occasion when he boarded his ship carrying with him some unanswered mail. It filled four potato sacks.

Some Miscellaneous Attitudes

He admires greatly Romain Rolland, the Stoic philosophers, Frederick the Great, Lao-tse, and, among musicians aside from Bach, César Franck (also an organist), Wagner, Schubert, Beethoven, and Mozart. He likes Russian music if it is "real." Somewhat grudgingly he concedes that Shostakovich is real, and he has a certain regard for Rimsky-Korsakoff. He has, or so it seemed from his conversation with us, more appreciation of Goethe than of Shakespeare. He thinks that Socrates was a "demagogue," and that most real progress in Europe has come in periods of enlightened, benevolent despotism. I asked him if he had hated Hitler. Miss Haussknecht answered for him saying that he hated nobody, but that if Hitler had been drowning he, Schweitzer, would have hesitated a moment before taking off his shoes to dive in and rescue him.

Everything, he thinks, must have a moral basis—particularly art. He has profound regard for Tolstoy for this among other reasons. André Gide he cannot understand, because Gide carries self-analysis to such intricate and exasperating lengths. "One day he writes in his journal that he takes tea for breakfast, and the next day coffee. What difference does it make?" When I asked him if he thought that Napoleon was a great man he snorted a rough *"Non!"* He had correspondence with Gandhi on occasion; apparently he thinks that Gandhi was politically naïve. Freud, whom he knew and liked, puzzled him. "He was better as a man than in his work." He had great respect and liking for Dr. Einstein. He mentioned Hegel once, and when I said that Hegel was the father of Marx he replied with a snort of contempt, "Only Marx made Marx!" I asked him whether he thought that any war could ever be justifiable, and he answered that he could not answer—he did not know. I asked him what had given him most pleasure in life, and he replied, "Whatever I am working at."

Africans try Schweitzer's patience sorely, no matter how much he loves them in the abstract. He says that his Negroes have nothing whatever to do after work is finished each afternoon, but that it never occurs to them to fish in the river—yet they complain of protein deficiency. If they get any education at all, they promptly move into the towns, and try to become stenographers. Yet he, Schweitzer, out in the hinterland, cannot for the life of him find a good carpenter, or even somebody to tend a field. He smote himself on the breast telling us this. "I am the only pèasant!"

It shocked him frightfully that there had been recent riots in Port Gentil, with bloodshed. Apparently he attributed these to the free-and-easy ways Africans have been encouraged to assume. Much in contemporary French policy does not please the Doctor. There was even a "revolt" in the Schweitzer hospital itself a year or so ago, which the staff had to put down; he himself was away in Europe at the time. Patients armed with knives marched on the inhabitants of the leper village, saying that the lepers had threatened them.

He did not seem to have much faith in the educability of Africans in his vicinity, or even their good will. He said, "I put a mango here, a banana here, a breadfruit here. The Africans do not know enough to tell which tree is which. I explain. They walk away and by the time they reach the river in ten minutes they have forgotten."

He reported a colloquy with one of his native boys, who asked him why he was not as good as Schweitzer was. "I'll tell you," the Doctor replied. "Each of us goes out into the forest with an ax, a hammer, and a saw. A tornado comes. You drop your tools and run. I retreat more slowly, and pick up the tools you have dropped. So, when we return, I have six tools, you have none. Is that not so?" The boy replied, "Yes." Schweitzer went on, "And does this not prove that I am better than you are?" The boy shook his head, not seeing the point at all.

To be civilized, the Doctor thinks, a person must pass four tests. He must not lie, he must not steal, he must prove that he values property, and he must be kind to animals.

We sat on upturned boxes in the garden, and Schweitzer gave us a little lecture. Boys passed bearing pails of water, which, like much else in the hospital, are marked sternly with the initials A.S.B. (the "B" stands for the maiden name of his wife); Schweitzer saw that the paint was rubbed off one, and he groaned aloud, "Now they will steal it!" A boy moved slowly. The Doctor turned to him with a resigned, exasperated plea: *"Voulez-vous marcher? VOULEZ-vous!"* A moment later he was telling us that the only way to reach the African was "through the heart." We climbed toward the camp and saw a baby chicken with its eyes scratched out. Schweitzer comforted it tenderly.

On our last night at the hospital we were invited after dinner to accompany Schweitzer to his small bedroom and adjoining office. Here is a tatterdemalion assortment of books, papers, stores, tools—a saw was lying across a sheaf of manuscript—empty tins, piles of music, and bits of carpentry. On a wall I saw the portrait of a bearded dignitary—Charles Darwin. I could not have been more surprised if it had been Beelzebub. "Darwin sought the truth," said Schweitzer calmly. We peeked further, and saw his favorite antelope, Theodora, behind a rude net of wire, and two chimpanzees in a cage, Romeo and Juliet. All sleep in close proximity. Schweitzer led us to his celebrated piano, which has organlike pedal attachments; this is lined with zinc to keep termites out, weighs three tons, and was presented to him by the Paris Bach Society when he first set out for Africa forty-two years ago. Schweitzer, my wife, and I all sat squeezed together on the small bench—indeed there was no other place to sit down—and he played some Bach superbly. This brief nocturnal recital was the last touch, the authentic Schweitzer ceremony of farewell. He was not playing for us particularly. He plays every night, especially when his eyes are tired. He said to one recent visitor, "I play for my antelope." But it was a fascinating privilege to hear him play, and it is this picture of him, sitting at that battered old wreck of a piano in the middle of the silent jungle, that I shall always remember as most typical of him—this crusty old Bismarck of the spirit, this magnificent tyrant with a heart of gold.

〜〜〜〜〜〜〜〜〜〜〜〜〜〜〜〜〜〜〜〜〜〜〜〜〜〜〜〜〜〜〜〜〜〜〜〜

A puzzling paradox remains. Dr. Schweitzer's lack of sympathy for the nationalist aspirations of contemporary Africans has become widely known by now, and historians dealing with him in the future will be compelled to face this dilemma squarely and try to account for it. Surely it is the strangest of ironies that this extraordinary man who has given so much of his life to Africa, and who is probably the best known of all living white men in relation to Africa, should have been totally inert— in fact a hostile bystander—to the tumultuous, epochal struggle for liberation and self-government which convulsed Africa in his own time and in so doing transformed its entire face during the very period of his own work on the Dark Continent.

My Schweitzer piece was considered very daring when it came out. I do not think many readers will find it so today. Shortly after its publication in Reader's Digest *I received an angry letter from the Great Doctor himself enclosing pages from the* Digest *and underlining passages he did not like. What appeared to affront him most was that I said that he looked like Buffalo Bill. I still do not think that this was an insult. Buffalo Bill was a handsome man. Moreover I pointed out emphatically that Schweitzer has "a wonderful face" and is "magnificent-looking." But I dutifully cut the Buffalo Bill reference in my final text as printed in* Inside Africa. *I don't know whether Dr. Schweitzer ever saw the book, but I never heard from him again.*

Part Ten

~~~~~~~~

INTO THE SIXTIES

CHAPTER 35

~~~~~~~~

Macmillan

This estimate of Mr. Macmillan first appeared as a magazine article in December, 1958, and then, much extended, became a chapter of Inside Europe Today, *which was published in 1961 and republished in a revised edition in 1962.*

Mr. Macmillan has had a wide variety of nicknames in the British press—so much so that his ups and downs in popular esteem might be measured by them. He rose from "Mr. MacMothballs" to "Non-stop Mac" and "Go-getter Mac," and later fell to "MacMania." In between there were "MacWonder," "MacShuffle," "MacMaster," "MacBland," "MacMartyr," "MacWhim," MacJingo" (during Suez), "MacArtful," "MacWhirl," "Mac-Jekyll," "SuperMac," and even "Tar-Mac, the Great Arterial Engineer." This last came when the government was being troubled by a bizarre snafu in relation to a road.

Mr. Macmillan was prime minister, easing into his second year of office, when I met him in 1958. Not many people thought at that time that he would last at 10 Downing Street five more years until 1963.

~~~~~~

WHEN HAROLD MACMILLAN became prime minister in January, 1957, to the surpirse of practically everybody in the United Kingdom except himself, British fortunes and prestige were at their lowest ebb for a generation. The grim fiasco over Suez had split the country; Anglo-American relations were the worst since 1776 or thereabouts; the Commonwealth was restive and alarmed; morale at home was cracking, and a flight from sterling threatened; the Tory party was frustrated, leaderless, and discouraged.

Today, some five years later, developments have come that are little short of phenomenal. Suez left a lurid scar, but the wound has healed; relations between London and Washington are harmonious and fruitful, and Britain has the largest gold stock in its history; above all, the Rt. Hon. Maurice Harold Macmillan, prime minister and first lord of the Treasury, is undisputed leader of his party, widely popular and respected in the country at large, and at the peak of his considerable powers, although his prestige underwent a good deal of erosion in 1961 and his position is not what it once was.

Mr. Macmillan, a complex character who is half-Scot, half-American, would be the last man to assert that the contemporary rise in the British position has been due exclusively to himself. But he contributed strongly to it, and he symbolizes a new spirit in the Tory party. Interestingly enough he himself has undergone an evolution not unlike that in the country itself. Success has brought him confidence.

When he became prime minister, he was no more than a shadow to the great mass of the public—moreover, an enigmatic, old-fashioned, and almost comical shadow. As often as not he seemed paralyzed by diffidence or inertia, like a parody of the Edwardian county gentleman. The change to the revivified Macmillan of today did not come overnight. In fact, the first months in office were heavy going—for himself as well as for those around him, who despaired at his inability to "communicate" himself to the public.

Although he is a profound Conservative in most of his instincts and leader of the Tory party, Macmillan is by no means an orthodox Tory. He spent more than twenty years in rebellion against stand-pat party principles, flirted with socialism, and was once called a "dangerous" left-winger. No British politician has much future these days unless he pays lip service at least to the principles of the welfare state, and Macmillan's conscientiousness, idealism, and "pink conservatism" have contributed substantially to his rise, as well as such factors as dexterity and cleverness.

I asked one of his best friends how he accounted for the slow but emphatic change in the prime minister, his transformation from a private into a public person. Answer: "As a matter of fact, Macmillan has never been a 'private' person. He has been in public life for well over thirty years. He was relatively unknown, but not 'private.' What happened when he became prime minister was that he wanted to sit down for a while and get his bearings. He knew that there were certain tasks to be tackled, and that he had to tackle them. He said to himself, 'If I'm any good, it will show in time.' He started doing things that were bold and imaginative, and people began to realize that here was a man of unusual vigor, competence, and intelligence."

Then, in May, 1958, came Macmillan's appearance on Edward R.

Murrow's TV show, "See It Now." For many months the prime minister had resisted doing anything on TV; he was loath to be interviewed, and he hated radio. (He has no radio or TV in his country house, and, so far as I know, there is no TV in Downing Street.) Then he awoke, overnight, to find himself a television star. His dry, understated personality, originality of view, candor, modesty, and quiet good humor became for the first time apparent to millions, both in England and the United States. Nobody could say that Murrow "made" Macmillan, but he gave him a big lift upward so far as public relations are concerned, and the prime minister, gratified and astonished, said later that the show was worth five by-elections.

Outline of the Rise to Power

The bare bones of Macmillan's career can best be put on display by mentioning some of the influences that helped shape him.

First, his Scots background. His paternal great-grandfather was a crofter (tenant farmer) on the island of Aran; his grandfather, Daniel, grew up in the most pressing poverty. But Daniel was enterprising enough to make his way down to England, where he became a book salesman. Then, with a brother, he set himself up in a bookshop in Cambridge, and eventually moved to London and founded (1843) the great publishing house of Macmillan, which is still one of the foremost in the world. Maurice, the prime minister's father, joined the family business after having been a music student and teacher. He was a somewhat unworldly character, diffident, introspective, and religious.

Harold Macmillan's mother was an American, Helen (Nellie) Belles, the daughter of a Kentucky doctor who practiced medicine for many years in a small town in Indiana. A woman of commanding grace and push, she married an artist named John Bayliss Hill in 1874, at eighteen; he died a few months later, and Nellie made her way to Paris to study music, an adventurous thing for such a young woman to do in those days. Here she met Maurice Macmillan, and they were married in 1883. Harold, their third son, was born in 1894.

The prime minister has always revered her. He told me, when we talked in Downing Street not long ago, that she had been by far the strongest influence on his life. Like Franklin D. Roosevelt's mother, she adored her son, but took no nonsense from him. She wanted him to be ambitious; she wanted him to be a success, even if he cultivated a languid pose. Whether, when she died in 1937, she could have guessed that he would ever be prime minister is open to question. One important point is that Nellie was an ardent Francophile. Harold was made to learn French in the nursery before he learned English, and he has been fond of things French ever since.

Macmillan narrowly escaped death in an air crash in North Africa in 1943; he woke up in a hospital, badly burnt, without any idea of what had happened to him. His first words were, "Tell my mother that I'm alive and well." She had been dead six years.

Undiscriminating writers on Macmillan talk about his "aristocracy," as if he were a Churchill or Salisbury. Indeed, he married far up into the aristocracy and many of his attributes are aristocratic, but he is not an aristocrat by birth at all. He comes of peasant Scots blood mixed with middle-class American stock, and is mostly a product of what has been aptly called the "commercial intelligentsia."

Second, education. Probably Macmillan is the best-educated prime minister since Balfour or Asquith, although he is not an intellectual of their standing. He went to Eton and Balliol College, Oxford, loved the classics, and was a good (if somewhat lazy) student. Once, during World War I, when he was seriously wounded and cut off from his troops, his men found him in a shell hole reading Aeschylus—in Greek.

Today, he is still inveterately bookish. Returning recently from Australia on the first all-Commonwealth tour ever taken by a British prime minister, he amused himself by reading all fourteen volumes of Froude's *History of England.* When John Hay Whitney, the American ambassador to the Court of St. James's, met him for the first time he was busily occupied with a history (in French) of the Quai d'Orsay. When he was exhausted after one long cabinet session a colleague asked him what he was going to do to relax; his somewhat defiant answer was, "Read a *good* novel!"

Actually, however, the prime minister does not read much fiction these days, although he is—and always has been—a Trollope addict. He told me that he turns more and more to history and biography. He likes long, pithy lives—particularly about illustrious predecessors in British history—full of documents. The day I met him he was reading a life of Palmerston. He likes Latin, and sometimes bewilders people by making jokes in Latin, or scribbling Latin puns on official minutes.

Third, World War I. Young Macmillan left Balliol to take a commission in the Grenadier Guards, and served in France for several years. He was wounded three times, and his last wound—a shattered pelvis—kept him in bed for twenty months. His friends thought that he would never walk again. The meditation forced upon him by this prolonged immobility, as well as the suffering it caused, cut a strong groove in his character. He served ably, but was never decorated or even mentioned in dispatches. He did not, in his younger days, seem to leave much of a mark on his contemporaries, either at school or in the army. Memoirs of the period, even by those who knew him well, seldom refer to him.

Fourth, marriage. Macmillan went to Canada in 1920 as an A.D.C. to the governor general, the ninth Duke of Devonshire, and married his daughter, Lady Dorothy Evelyn Cavendish. This was an epochal event. At once he entered the patrician inner circle. The Queen Dowager, Alexandra, came to his wedding, and so (and this may have pleased him more) did Thomas Hardy.

The Devonshires have proliferated for generations through the tight upper fabric of British social, political, and court life, and, on entering politics, Macmillan found that he was related by marriage to no fewer than sixteen members of the House of Commons. Later it was calculated that he had blood ties with seven out of the nineteen members of the cabinet, and with no fewer than thirty of the total number of men (eighty-five) in the government. (In British terminology "cabinet" and "government" are different; the cabinet is the small central core of the government. A man can rise to be a "minister," i.e., a member of the government, without being a member of the cabinet.)

The Macmillan situation *in re* his relatives was much compounded in later years. After a cabinet reshuffle in November, 1960, Julian Amery, his son-in-law, became secretary of state for air, and Lady Dorothy's nephew, the eleventh Duke of Devonshire, became parliamentary undersecretary in the Commonwealth Relations Office. At least three other men with ministerial rank were related either to the prime minister or his wife. David Ormsby-Gore, who recently became ambassador to Washington after having served ably as minister of state for foreign affairs, is the brother-in-law of Maurice Macmillan, the P.M.'s only son, who is also in the Commons. When these appointments were announced, Hugh Gaitskell, the leader of the Opposition, commented good-humoredly, "The prime minister has staunchly refused to allow any unfair discrimination against his relatives." Other comment was a bit stiffer, and the *New Statesman* (December 10, 1960) acidly pointed out that the Macmillan government contained one duke, one marquess, six earls, two viscounts, and no fewer than seven barons.

Fifth, business. Macmillan went into the family publishing business in 1924, and for many years, with his elder brother Daniel, was joint managing director of the company. As a publisher, he paid more attention to business than to the editorial side; nevertheless, he was active on the literary front as well. One of his decisions was to publish *Black Lamb and Grey Falcon,* by Rebecca West, even though it was a thousand pages long, in a period of acute paper shortage.

The Macmillan roster of authors through the 118 years of the company's existence is impressive; Henry James, Shaw, Wells, Kipling, Yeats, and a multitude of other distinguished men were all published by Macmillan at one time or other. The company had a special penchant for poetry, and also—oddly enough—for left-wing economists and historians, like J. M. Keynes.

Sixth, politics and public affairs. Macmillan felt, in the good old

British way, that it was his duty to fulfill his obligation to the community. Besides, he wanted to get ahead, and to enter politics was the natural thing to do. He stood for Stockton, an industrial and shipbuilding constituency, in 1923, soon after his return from Canada, and lost in his first run—by seventy-three votes. But he ran again the next year, won handsomely, and has been in the House of Commons—with interruptions—ever since.

Stockton taught him a lot, particularly in the depression years. Later he moved on to a safer constituency, Bromley. Unemployment was an agonizing problem, and young Macmillan came to grips for the first time in his life with the common man. In the mid-1930's he wrote a book, *The Middle Way,* which caused a considerable stir; it advocated a kind of modified New Deal for England, and Macmillan became anathema to the hardshell Conservatives. He replied in kind, and some of his remarks, criticizing the conservative leadership of the time, are still quoted. He called the Bank of England a "permanent tyranny," talked with contempt of "casino capitalism" and "the aristocracy of second class brewers and company promoters," and said that members of the Conservative front bench were "disused slag heaps."

He even went so far as to vote against his own party on a matter having to do with unemployment relief, and on one occasion campaigned momentarily for a socialist against one of his own Tory colleagues. For a time he advocated a coalition with labor, and talked of building up a "synthesis between socialism and capitalism."

Meantime, foreign affairs came to dominate British politics. During the Baldwin-Chamberlain period Macmillan pursued an independent line. He "refused the party whip," which was tantamount to temporary resignation from the party, because he favored sanctions against Italy during the Ethiopian War, and vigorously (although politely) opposed Munich and appeasement. Altogether he spent long years in the "wilderness," was snubbed by the Tory leadership, and never got a ministerial post until 1940, when he was forty-six.

Then success came fast. Winston Churchill became prime minister, and in 1942 sent him to Algiers as minister resident; here he formed friendships with two men whom he had plenty of occasion to work with later—Dwight D. Eisenhower and Charles de Gaulle. One reason why Churchill gave him the Algiers job was that he had been, in a modest way, a Churchill "man"; another was that he knew French so well. The nursery pays off.

Macmillan then became secretary of state for air, and after that minister of housing; this was a lesser job, but he worked at it loyally and was a marked success. There followed terms as minister of defense for six months in 1954-55, foreign secretary from April to December,

1955, and chancellor of the exchequer from December, 1955, to January, 1957. In all these posts his tenure was short, and in none did he make much of a record, except housing. He was a disappointing foreign minister, and left little mark on the Treasury. How, then, did Harold Macmillan happen to become prime minister in January, 1957, when Anthony Eden resigned?

Historians will be writing about the minutiae of this for a long time to come. Churchill and Lord Salisbury, who was at that time the *éminence grise* of the Conservative party, put in for Macmillan as against R. A. Butler, his principal rival. The Tory rank and file thought that Macmillan was safer, more resolute, and had more stamina, although he was still an eccentric character, an odd type, in the eyes of many.

Macmillan's role in the Suez fiasco has aroused bitter controversy. First, he was a strong backer of Eden's ruinous policy of going into Suez by force of arms. Second, he was the most influential minister to urge withdrawal when it was seen that the military adventure was a fiasco. His main motive, his friends say, was not so much worry about the reactions to Suez in America, Russia, or the Commonwealth, but fear that the disaster might cause a run on sterling.

A somewhat cynical observer put it this way when the grisly affair was over. "After all, we have to have a leader. And we might as well have one who leads both ways. Macmillan led us into Suez, and then led us out again!" Later, a jingle was composed:

> When Eden bombed that old canal,
> Our hero Mack the Knife,
> Said I'll stick by you, Tony,
> And be your friend for life.[1]

Personal

Macmillan is a tall man, taller than most of his photographs indicate—about six feet one. For some years he cultivated what can only be called a "droopy" look; the joke was that Eden was a rabbit trying to look like a man, whereas Macmillan was a man trying to look like a rabbit. He has large hands, and a softish handshake. One of his peculiarities is that his handwriting is very small, and his secretaries have a hard time deciphering it.

He has a perceptive face, longish graying hair brushed back in a pompadour, and luminous dark eyes. The lids are heavy, and hang sharply down at the outer corners; he has sometimes been called "the hooded wonder." His manners are, of course, effortlessly good, even bland. One of his ministers told me that his chief single source of power was his calmness, that he was "unflappable."

[1] New York *Post*, June 13, 1960.

Macmillan is notorious for being the worst-dressed man ever to sit in Downing Street. He hates to go shopping, and, as Franklin Roosevelt did, likes to wear tweed jackets thirty years old. His attitude toward dress has been called "appalling," and he has not bought a new suit for years. Instead of a waistcoat, which is considered to be *de rigueur* in British official life, he usually wears an old cardigan sweater which he may, or may not, remember to button. Instead of a hat he prefers a tweed cap, which looks like something that might have been discarded by Sherlock Holmes.

He eats abstemiously, and at formal parties seldom does more than nibble; his favorite dish is cold meat. Also he is fond of savories, the sharp combinations of cheese, eggs, bacon, mushrooms, or anchovies that the British like to serve after dessert. He smokes anything, preferably a pipe. He is one of those wise men who thinks that alcohol is a benign substance, if only because it loosens the tongue, and he drinks in moderation.

He is healthy, sleeps well, and, although obviously a sensitive person, does not seem to have a nerve in his body. No matter how late it may be, he always reads for an hour before going to bed. He seldom takes holidays, and in his first eighteen months as prime minister had exactly seventeen days off. Unlike almost all Englishmen of his class, he is not much interested in sport or games, although he likes the outdoors—trees particularly—and sometimes has time to shoot. He shoots left-handed, and is a tolerable shot.

Some people think that the prime minister gives forth a note of sadness, as if he were nursing a secret sorrow, and he is certainly not what anybody would call an ebullient man. He has, however, an alert sense of humor, and loves to make jokes, some of them very sharp.

The word "shy," which is sometimes applied to him, demands qualification in the case of Macmillan. He hates hurly-burly, never slaps backs, and dislikes contact with people he does not know, but in his own circle is far from shy. What he likes best in the world, next to England, books, gossip, and his family, is conversation, and he is a fast fluent talker.

Occasionally he would go to fashionable London cocktail parties before he became prime minister; he would stand alone in a corner as a rule, polite but bored, until somebody came up who interested him. He can run into an old acquaintance at a club, and, if full of his own thoughts, not even recognize him. Then he will, as it were, wake up, and call out a greeting. Macmillan's mild adventures in various clubs give rise to almost as many anecdotes as his bookishness. Time and time again, members of the Beefsteak (a dining club) or Buck's are astonished to see the prime minister walk in unannounced and alone. He sits down at the common table, greets those present, and joins the talk.

I asked somebody who has known Macmillan all his life if he had ever thought that he would be prime minister. The answer was suggestive. "No. But now that he is prime minister, it seems natural that he should be."

In a recent speech, Macmillan said, "When you are a prime minister everything becomes a bit larger than life." He proceeded, "It's really quite surprising. A week's holiday with one's in-laws becomes a life addicted to shooting on ducal grouse moors. A couple of weekend study groups with one's colleagues becomes country house government. A modest cheerfulness becomes a reckless flippancy. But don't mistake me. No politician would feel happy without this sort of thing."

Some people say of him critically that he is an "actor," and one discerning French lady of my acquaintance calls him a *cabotin,* a word difficult to translate. It can mean anything from overacting ham to wandering minstrel. Much of his life has been a series of poses. Indeed, he has cultivated an air of off-beat cynicism, perhaps to save himself from disappointment; he is not so much of a cynic as he pretends to be, but part of what began as a pose has stuck. There is something curiously unreal about him, as if he were not made of real flesh and blood; he seems masked.

A prominent Labour M.P. was asked recently to name Macmillan's outstanding characteristic, and replied, "Pomposity!" Another answered, "Superciliousness." Others think, beyond this, that his chief defect is lack of deep inner conviction, that he is too detached, too clever. Macmillan, on his side, has often seemed to be unwarrantedly rude to Labour members. This is not good policy, because the Opposition will always be there the next day; it divides the country; moreover, to show disrespect for the Opposition is to show disrespect for the House of Commons itself, the symbol and repository of all that is best in British democracy.

The Prime Minister at Work

Remarkably enough, Mr. Macmillan has no office in the business premises of Downing Street—not even a desk. He works on a long table, which can seat about twenty men, in the ground-floor cabinet room. Upstairs he has a small study, and it is true that this does contain a small, fragile desk of sorts, but it is not at all the kind that an important executive would be expected to use. I asked him what on earth he did with his papers, since there were no drawers or filing cases anywhere, and he replied airily that "they went into boxes."

The Downing Street establishment is small, and the prime minister's secretariat does not consist of more than seven or eight people, most of them youngish civil servants. Macmillan was stupefied, on a recent visit to Washington, at the size and ramifying extent of the presidential establishment. The British procedure is much less complex and grandiose.

Moreover the atmosphere at No. 10 is astoundingly informal. A bobby stands at the door; otherwise there are no precautions that one can see, no security check of any kind. The prime minister is mildly formal during actual meetings of the cabinet (which normally take place twice a week), but otherwise he is almost disconcertingly casual, relaxed, and familylike. Macmillan seldom rings for anybody. Instead he scurries out into the tiny rooms that house the staff, wanders around alone like a mother hen pursuing chicks, and says to somebody, "I'm having trouble with this memorandum—please help me draft it."

The doorway leading from the office of the principal private secretary to the cabinet room has tacked on it a note in the prime minister's handwriting: "Quiet Calm Deliberation Untangles Every Knot." This is from the Gilbert and Sullivan operetta *The Gondoliers*, and Macmillan put it up there with his own hand to indicate that this should be the mood of the entire establishment. Once, years ago, the author of *Tom Brown's School Days*, Thomas Hughes, came on hard times and wrote the Macmillan company for a job. The reply by Harold Macmillan's grandfather laid down certain conditions, one of which was that the firm expected every employee "to do the day's job in the day." The maxim has been carried over to rule Downing Street today, and the P.M. tells his staff about it any time that anybody will listen.

I asked him if he liked being prime minister, and he answered with an emphatic, cheerful affirmative. He has a philosophic attitude toward the unfolding of history. I asked him how he took the load off, and he indicated lightly that he had others to do that for him—which was a nice little compliment to his able secretaries. In fact, Macmillan takes decisions easily, without weighing inconvenient or embarrassing consequences too much, and is an excellent leader of a team. "If you take all decisions too seriously, you never take them," he says to friends. His favorite phrase is, "Let's think it over," and he never lets himself be overpressed.

He gets a dispatch box full of papers every night, and acts on them after dinner—sometimes while relaxing with his family. Most ministers "play the box" with a group of secretaries standing by, to whom they dictate instructions. Macmillan—as a rule—prefers to do this work alone. He writes a minute on each paper in red ink (only the prime minister may use red ink on a cabinet document) ordering whatever action he recommends.

I came in to see the prime minister at three one afternoon, and was told that I would have fifteen minutes with him. I left Downing Street around five—two hours later! The prime minister (like Roosevelt) likes to talk. When I was ushered casually into the cabinet room, with its stimulating historic associations, Mr. Macmillan reached out to grasp and show me a silver candlestick he had just received. It had previously belonged to five other prime ministers—Walpole, the younger Pitt, Peel, Disraeli, and Lord Rosebery.

Mostly, at the beginning, he talked about British history, the British past. (He did not mention his exertions as prime minister; among other things he had traveled eighty thousand miles in eighteen months, not bad for a man of his age.) He took me out in the garden, told an anecdote about Mr. Gladstone, and hustled me around No. 10 and the adjoining No. 11, residence of the chancellor of the exchequer, pointing out various associations. Then we scooted up to the Treasury Board Room, in an adjacent building, where the cabinet once met with the monarch in the chair. The custom had to be given up after Queen Anne—because George I, her successor, did not understand any English.

Macmillan talked about how difficult it is to take adequate notes on a telephone conversation, probably because you do not see the person you are talking to; how newspapers in London once printed editions all night; about Russian policy in Central Asia before World War I, and much else concerning Russia, including details of a trip he took there, as a tourist, in 1929; about what a wonderful face Disraeli had; about the proper pronunciation of Polish names; about the joy of rereading old books instead of taking a risk with a new one; about Asquith, Lloyd George, Nehru, Adenauer, Father Knox, and Lytton Strachey; above all, about England in the years just before 1914—the glow and throb of the England that was, the gallantry and peculiarly innocent ardor, valor, of those lost, silken, quivering days, and how a whole generation was cut off, sacrificed, exterminated.

At the end I asked him what he believed in most. I have asked this question of many eminent men and have had a vivid anthology of responses. The prime minister might have replied England, himself, the Anglo-American alliance, change, standards, the august routine of old-style aristocratic life, or the people. His answer was God.

To Sum Up

Mr. Macmillan is, like all prime ministers, a complicated human being, but one of his principal assets is that his approach to a problem is almost always direct—refreshingly so. Three items come to mind. First, the prime minister became convinced early in 1959 that the international situation was deteriorating so seriously and at such a pace that something must be done at once to stop the possibility of open conflict; so he decided to go to Moscow himself, have a look around, and investigate the possibility of getting along with Mr. Khrushchev. Second, he took an eighteen-thousand-mile trip through Africa in January, 1960, and, visiting the Union of South Africa, made one of the best speeches of his life there, referring to the "strength of African national conscience," and accepting it blandly as the most natural of facts that "a wind of change" should be blowing through the continent, even though he knew that this would meet sharp disfavor from his audience. Third, after the collapse of the Summit in the summer of 1960, he tried once more to unravel the international logjam over Russia. Khrushchev was being at his most provocative in relation to the Congo, disarmament, and other issues. Macmillan sat down and wrote him a personal letter which contained the phrase, "I simply do not understand what your purpose is today." Seldom has a communication about great political affairs been addressed to a Russian premier in such personal, informal language, and it had an immediate effect.

Word About the Establishment

I lived in England for six months in 1958, and I don't think I ever heard the word "Establishment." Then, when I returned to London in 1960, it seemed to be on every other lip. Actually the term was invented some years ago by Henry Fairlie, a provocative columnist and TV commentator, in an article in the *Spectator*. As a matter of fact, the elusive concept that Mr. Fairlie sought to define is no new thing in England. I myself, feeling my way toward the same idea and trying to analyze what ran England, called it (with no originality whatever) "an inner circle" back in 1936. Those I nominated as immovable members of this included Stanley Baldwin, Lord Tyrrell, Geoffrey Dawson of the *Times*, Lord Salisbury (father of the present one), Montagu Norman, then governor of the Bank of England, Lord Derby, and Sir Maurice Hankey.

But I added that no two observers would agree on the names to be included, Baldwin aside. One should never be tempted to think that the ruling classes in the United Kingdom comprise a body which could meet in a room, elect a chairman, or otherwise perform the organic functions of domination. The "ring" is not a ring. Indeed—I am still paraphrasing what I wrote in 1936—the overriding strength of the British ruling classes is its fluidity. It is quite possible to belong to one of the oldest families in the British Isles and yet not be "in." Brains are certainly not the sole criterion for entrance, nor is wealth, nor is position, although all three will help.

How, then, does one define the inner circle, or Establishment? Who *does* run England? Mr. Fairlie's definition emphasizes a desire to perpetuate forms, with "reverence for the orders, privileges, and mysteries of a conservative society," and he adds that the Establishment is *not* a "power elite." For instance, a big newspaper publisher can exert enormous power but would no more be accepted by the Establishment than Heliogabalus. I doubt that any member of the Labour party would consider himself to be an authentic member of the Establishment, even while in office. Also one must think in terms of religion; almost all in the Establishment pay at least nominal allegiance to the Anglican Church. I do not think that there are any Jews in the Establishment, and Roman Catholics are few and far between.

Nor does membership in the Establishment necessarily depend on class, or even money. Class does not matter as much as one might think. If a poor boy out of the Midlands rises to be speaker of the House of Commons or secretary of the cabinet he will be "in," no matter how humble his origin. Conversely, the richest blueblood in the City may be out. A poet, like John Betjeman, may well be regarded as a highly important (if irreverent) Establishment voice, and scholars, if, for instance, they happen to be masters or dons in a distinguished Oxford or Cambridge college, are often favored. In a way institutions are more important than individuals. Institutions, after all, persist when men are gone. But *some* individuals will remain members of the Establishment forever, even when they have lost political power, like the present Salisbury. Another point to make is that almost anybody who enters the Establishment has, even if not rich, been a success in whatever his field happens to be. Above all it is an organization of those who have *arrived*.

Anyway, omitting names, I will risk severe argument and rebuke by listing those who, by reason of their position, have almost automatic membership in this indefinable holy of holies today. First, the prime minister [in a Conservative government]. Second, the permanent under-secretary of the treasury, who is head of the civil service. A flamboyant foreign minister or a stuffy, docile chancellor of the exchequer may very well not be "in," but it would be impossible to keep the head of the civil service out. Third, the Archbishop of Canterbury, and possibly the Archbishop of York as well. Fourth, the governor of the Bank of England. After this the field becomes somewhat more open. Most people would certainly include the editor of the *Times*, the head of the BBC, the private secretary to the monarch, and a scattering of fellows of All Souls, the post-graduate Oxford college restricted to fifty scholars of outstanding intellect. Also distinguished economists are apt to be included, though no economist today has the rank of Sir Josiah Stamp, as an example, before the war. One might even throw in a hostess or two.

But again one must urge caution; these elevated figures do not sit down in a room together, have a cozy or conspiratorial drink, blackball aspirants, or make policy. Far from it. Several wings of the Establishment do not like other wings, and have small contact. It is all very mysterious, like so much in England—a country given to stylistic enigma. For instance, I was enchanted to hear, on the most expert authority, that the recent election for the chancellorship of Oxford University, in which Mr. Macmillan vanquished Sir Oliver Franks, the former British ambassador to Washington, was a *defeat* for the Establishment, not the opposite. But of course Mr. Macmillan is titular head of the whole Establishment, the whole bag of tricks. How then could his election (by the narrow margin of 279 votes) be regarded as a defeat? The answer seems to be that the masters, fellows, dons, and so on at Oxford form their own special rarefied segment of the Establishment, and hotly wanted Franks, one of their own, for the job as against a rank outsider—on academic terms—like Macmillan.

Certain cardinal events become landmarks in the evolution of the Establishment, on which it stands fast. One was the abdication crisis in 1936. The Establishment, personified at that time by Mr. Baldwin and the then Archbishop of Canterbury, preferred to have Edward VIII leave the throne rather than accept Mrs. Simpson. So Edward—and Mrs. Simpson—went. Another was Suez. The Establishment was badly shaken by this, but held firm. I have met eminent members of the Establishment who like argument and even, in their strange British way, welcome defeat once in a while. Their theory is that "it is good for the Establishment to realize that it is not omnipotent"—even if it runs the country.

More about Macmillan may be found in Chapter 39 below. After he resigned the prime ministership he resumed active work as a publisher and set about writing an autobiography.

CHAPTER 36

~~~~~~~~~

The Old Man on the Rhine

In 1960 I went to Western Europe to cover the ill-fated Summit Con-
ference in Paris. These brief sketches of Adenauer, Erhard and Brandt
were by-products of the trip, and later became a chapter in Inside Europe
Today *(1961), revised 1962. My overall impressions about Germany were*
two. First, unification was of course the greatest German problem by far,
but nobody seemed to be pushing it hard. Second, German economic re-
covery and prosperity were positively dazzling. It certainly seems to pay
to lose a war.

~~~~~~~~~~~~~~~~~~

WHEN I SAW Dr. Konrad Adenauer early in 1960 I thought that he looked fifty-five, although he was eighty-four. He has the ageless-ness of old Chinese mandarins, and, indeed, the cast of his features is faintly Chinese—broad cheekbones, taut ivory skin, eyebrows almost invisible, and a long nose pushed inward at the bottom, a tapir's nose. He looks so youthful, comparatively speaking, that the quaint legend has arisen that he had his face lifted. This is, of course, untrue, but he suffered severe facial injuries in an automobile accident many years ago, and had to undergo elaborate surgery, which accounts, among other things, for the Oriental slant of his glistening small eyes.

In any case Dr. Adenauer seems indestructible, although his posi-tion was gravely shaken by events in 1961. This tenacious old gentle-man was born in 1876, when Ulysses S. Grant was President of the United States, when Queen Victoria was only halfway through her reign, and when Alexander II ruled Russia. His eyesight is still good; so is his hearing, and he still works a hard, lively day. He insists, however, on

[453]

a sound nap after lunch, and if he is traveling abroad and has a public function to attend, he sometimes asks for a bed in a room close to where he will be speaking, so that he can rest briefly before he appears.

Dr. Adenauer, the great years of whose career did not even begin till he was seventy-two, does not live in Bonn itself, the capital of the Federal Republic of Germany, as West Germany is officially called, but in Rhoendorf, a suburb a few miles away across the Rhine, where he has had his home for many years. Here fifty-four stone steps lead from the road to the gate of his villa, and these he climbs every day—well, not so briskly as a boy, but he does climb them, sometimes faster than his visitors. If the day has been exhausting, a turn among his rosebushes revives him, or a bottle of sound Rhine wine. He likes to play a game called *boccie* (an Italian version of bowls), and has alleys for playing it both at home and in the garden of the Chancellery, the Schaumburg Palace in Bonn. Altogether, Dr. Adenauer is an astounding physical phenomenon. His manner is still sharp, direct, and bold. People talk unendingly about what will happen in Germany when *Der Alte* dies, as if this were about to happen tomorrow, but it is quite possible that he still has half a dozen good years left in him.

Adenauer's basic sources of power are several:

First, the very fact of his age. He has become a kind of "grandfather image"—not necessarily loved, because he is too severe, too obstinate, too authoritarian, too wily, to arouse much love. "He is a grandfather who tells us fairy stories," one of his political adversaries put it to me. Another said, "He is not a grandfather image, but a *ghost* image." Be this as it may, Dr. Adenauer, even if not loved, is almost universally respected and admired. He has a strong ethical appeal. Moreover, his age is a veneer, an armor, serving to make him untouchable. One of his major political opponents, a Social Democrat, told me that he no longer felt free to press him closely in a political attack; it didn't seem sporting to tilt the lance too sharply, even though the Chancellor is amply able to take care of himself in debate. Finally, one increment of age is, or should be, experience, and Dr. Adenauer has an unrivaled treasury of political lore to draw on.

Second, his *success*—even if this is beginning to pale now. Of course he has made mistakes, but in his twelve uninterrupted years of rule, he has transformed West Germany from a broken wreck, a shambles, into the most powerful, prosperous, and confident nation on the continent. This country has risen from complete destitution in 1946 to have a gross national product of $70 billion in 1960, and its gold reserve, $2,139,000,000, is the second largest in the world. Its *total* reserves of gold and foreign currency amount to almost $7 billion, and its industrial production has risen 85 percent since 1953.

Third, American support.

Fourth, nobody else in Germany holds a candle to him as a political manipulator. There are plenty of able German politicians, but Adenauer puts them all into shadow. He is, be it remembered, not merely administrative head of the government but legislative leader as well, and his skill in both capacities is unparalleled.

Fifth, Adenauer stands for what most West Germans seem to want today—peace, stability, rapprochement with France, and integration into Europe. Needless to say, these items are particularly welcome after the inadequacies of the Weimar Republic, twelve years of militant savagery under Hitler, and the catastrophe of World War II.

One eminent German told me, "I do not like Adenauer. But he ended the tragic feud across the Rhine, and I will feel naked when he is gone."

The Chancellor's chief quality, aside from durability, courage, and political sagacity, is probably his power of simplification. This is a trait somewhat unusual among Germans, but Hitler (whom Adenauer in no other way resembles) had it too. Hitler based almost the whole of his ferocious crusades on half a dozen points simply stated and easily grasped—*Lebensraum*, anti-Semitism, repeal of the Versailles Treaty, and concepts such as *"Ein Reich, ein Volk, ein Führer."* Adenauer is also a man of comparatively few ideas, and has a marked gift for making them clearly understandable to the people at large. He likes to explain his policies in the simplest terms, and is a man of reason, who can make long sentences short (another quality unusual in a German). One of his favorite maxims is, "As soon as you are complicated, you are ineffectual."

On the other hand, he has what I have heard described as a "dark" mind. This does not refer merely to his conservatism, which is profound, but to his suspiciousness—his exaggerated sensitiveness to imaginary plots, conspiracies, and stratagems.

Dr. Adenauer once wrote a brief article for *Reader's Digest* in which he said that, when tired, he had learned that he could recuperate quickly by putting his feet in a basin of ice water, which drove the blood to his head. Another item that I find appealing is that he has a sweet tooth, and, during long cabinet meetings, nibbles at chocolate bars.[1] But no one should be misled by such trivialities. This is a man strong, unbending, and undivided, and the subsurface hull of his character is impermeable.

* * *

The story of Adenauer's career is well known, and three forces which helped to shape him—class, religion, geography—are fundamental. He came of middle-class stock (one of his grandfathers was a baker) with

[1] Terence Prittie, "Konrad Adenauer," *Atlantic Monthly,* September, 1957.

strong roots in the bureaucracy. He is, of course, a devout Roman Catholic, who likes to think that God is a conservative. Above all, Adenauer is a Rhinelander, that is to say a German who can look back to a rich European as well as a purely Teutonic heritage. The story is always denied officially, but there seems good reason to believe that, after World War I, he joined the Rhineland Separatist movement briefly —that is, he was willing to give up Germany for France. As to his attitude toward Prussia and eastern Germany, the antithesis of the Rhineland, a favorite story about him is that, whenever he took the train to Berlin in the old days and crossed the Elbe, he would mutter darkly, "Now we enter Asia!" He didn't go so far as to think that Prussia, Pomerania, Brandenburg and so on were actually populated by Mongol nomads, but, even then, he regarded the Elbe as what it is in fact today, a frontier.

Adenauer was born in Cologne on January 5, 1876, the son of a minor official. A dutiful student (but no blazing intellectual), he got a degree in law after study at several universities, and followed his father into the civil service, becoming a clerk in the Cologne Rathaus. He was thirty-eight when World War I broke out, and never saw military service. In 1917, aged forty-one, he reached the first climax of his career, and became lord mayor of Cologne. This post he held for sixteen uninterrupted years, until 1933; meantime, he became a leading member of the old Zentrum (Catholic) party. He lost his job as *Oberbürgermeister* when the Nazis came into power, and, during the next grim years, was arrested twice by the Gestapo. Mostly, however, he sat out the Nazi regime placidly enough at Rhoendorf, cultivating roses, about which he is erudite, amusing himself with various hobbies (he loves to tinker with antique clocks), and biding his time.[2] His personal life was happy. He has married twice, and is now a widower; he is the father of seven children, and has no fewer than twenty-one grandchildren. Twenty of these attended his eighty-fifth birthday celebration on January 5, 1961. One of his sons, Paul, is a priest, and lives with him today at Rhoendorf; another has followed in his footsteps (and those of his father) to become an administrative officer in the Cologne mayoralty.

When the Americans took Cologne toward the end of World War II Adenauer was called out of retirement and reinstated in his old post of mayor of Cologne. This was in 1945, and he was sixty-nine. The allies desperately needed "clean" administrators, who had never had any dealings with the Nazis, and men of experience and stature were hard to find; Adenauer was a perfect choice, although he was thought to be somewhat old. But when the Cologne area was assigned to British occupation, things did not go well, and a British officer fired him for "in-

[2] Flora Lewis, "Der Alte at 83," New York Times Magazine, January 4, 1959.

competence" in 1947. What this meant was that he was too authoritarian for the local British taste. Adenauer determined to go into national politics, and set out to create and build up the Christian Democratic Union, the party which he still leads today. He became Chancellor in 1949, as representative of a coalition which had a majority of only two in the Bundestag; there have been three general elections since, in 1953, 1957, and 1961. Adenauer won the first two, but slipped in 1961.

The Chancellor has always thought, with his logical and somewhat pedantic mind, in terms of a fixed, strict timetable. First (he was his own foreign minister from 1949 to 1955, and in effect continued to be so until 1961), he sought to unify the three allied zones of occupation in West Germany, as a bridge to freedom from foreign control; second, to consolidate the position of the new Federal Republic when it became a sovereign state on May 5, 1955; third, to regain the esteem of the victors in World War II, and become their firm ally; fourth, to rearm West Germany and join NATO. All this he has achieved on schedule. The fifth great objective—reunification of the two Germanys—is not yet attained.

We must have a word about the general election which took place on September 16, 1961, after three months of hot campaigning. The main antagonists were Adenauer, leading the CDU, and Willy Brandt, the able and attractive mayor of West Berlin, who is leader of the SPD (Social Democrats). The CDU dropped from 50.2 percent of the total vote in 1957 to 45.3 percent, and lost its majority in the Bundestag. This was a stinging personal defeat for Adenauer, the worst in many years. Willy Brandt's socialists got 36.3 percent of the vote as against 31.8 in 1957, and gained twenty-two seats while Adenauer was losing forty, but this was not enough to give the SPD control. A party known as the Free Democrats (FDP), headed by a strong parliamentarian comparatively new to the national scene, Dr. Erich Mende, rose from 7.7 percent of the poll to 12.7 percent, and from 42 deputies to 67 in an assembly numbering 497.

Thus the Free Democrats held the balance of power, and at once announced that Adenauer must go. Their first candidate to succeed him was the stout Dr. Ludwig Erhard, who has served Adenauer for many years as minister of economics, but who is anathema to him as his successor. Brandt, on his side, wanted a three-way coalition. Adenauer, tough and spry as a combination of bulldog and fox terrier, and fighting now for his political life, struggled to hold on to office and eventually— at the cost of having to drop his foreign minister, Dr. Heinrich von Brentano, and of other losses—managed to stay on top, after seven weeks of wrangling. On November 7 he was elected Chancellor by the Bundestag, and began his fourth term as leader of a coalition government composed of the CDU and FDP. But his majority in the Bundestag, even so, was reduced to only eight, and it was persistently reported that, in return for being allowed to continue to rule, *Der Alte* promised to step down after two more years in office, instead of staying the full course of four.

* * *

Dr. Adenauer has, of course, defects and limitations. In the old days his rule was almost defiantly personal, and he laid down the law to cabinet ministers and other associates in no uncertain terms. Everything so largely depended on the will—or even whim—of the Chancellor that nobody else dared to assert much authority; government became "ramshackle." The head was strong, the legs weak. Liaison was faulty and one ministry could be totally ignorant of what another was doing in a common field next door. Nowadays Adenauer's power is not quite so undiluted. He has to listen to Dr. Mende and others. Even so, the old man seeks to hold his own to the last breath.

One peculiarity about *Der Alte* is that he has little taste for economics, on which politics must so often depend. "Somebody *must* go to the Chancellor," one of his associates whispered to another recently, "and tell him what a tariff *is*." His indifference to economics in the abstract has not, however, kept him from being an enthusiastic advocate of the European Economic Community, or Common Market, even though this brought him into sharp conflict with Dr. Erhard, who opposes certain aspects of the Common Market because membership means that Germany must raise some of its tariffs. This, Dr. Erhard thinks, will hurt German industry. But Dr. Adenauer overruled him, and Erhard sank—on this issue—like a pinnace in the wake of a battleship. One of the Chancellor's most trusted friends, Dr. Walter Hallstein, a former official in the German Foreign Office, is president of the executive committee of the Common Market organization in Brussels, and Adenauer helped put him there. Adenauer saw the Common Market as a supremely important instrumentation for furthering his dearest wish, the *political* integration of Germany, France, Italy, and the Benelux countries. He said to a friend recently, "I want to stay alive longer for only one reason —to see a United States of Europe in my time."

This statement would have been more in consonance with Dr. Adenauer's inner beliefs if he had said, "A United States of *western* Europe." As is well known, the Chancellor's enmity to the Soviet Union is fixed, implacable and irreversible. A mild little joke is that his name is really John Foster Adenauer. To a great many liberal-minded people his ideas on Russia seem obscurantist and old-fashioned; his mind, so his critics say, is not only closed, but sterile. It does not seem to occur to him that a third of the world is Communist, and that in the long run the alternative to war must be some kind of accommodation with the Soviet Union, no matter how brutal and ill-mannered its policies may be. De Gaulle in France and Macmillan in England both believe that a *détente* with Russia is essential, on decent terms, and, even after the failure of the Summit Conference in May, 1960, and the sharpening of polemical struggle between the U.S. and the Soviet Union in 1961, must be energetically pursued; but not Adenauer. The old man has been as immovable as the Drachenfels forests near his home.

Who Runs the Federal Republic?

1. Adenauer and the Christian Democratic Union, despite the sharp recent reduction in its parliamentary majority.

2. The great Rhineland-Ruhr industrialists. They support the CDU heavily, and have a massive lobby in the Bundestag; roughly seventy deputies are supposed to be direct representatives of big industry. It should not, however, be thought that the Chancellor is under the thumb of the industrialists. They are in his pocket more than the reverse. Nobody in Germany tells Adenauer what to do, not even Alfried Krupp. Some of the very biggest Ruhr magnates lean over backward, as a matter of fact, to avoid intermingling at all with politics; they do not have too good a name in the Germany of today (many supported Hitler), and they know that if they become too conspicuous publicly they will have the Social Democrats snapping at their heels.

3. The *Länder*, or states which comprise the Federal Republic. There are ten of these, which are represented in the upper house of parliament or Bundesrat. Like American states they have a considerable local pride and identity as well as influence, and are autonomous in respect to a good many functions, for instance education. Three *Länder* have Social Democratic governments at present. It is important to mention in this connection that Prussia, which dominated Germany for two hundred years, has been broken up. It no longer exists even as a place name on the maps.

4. Both the churches—Catholic and Evangelical (Protestant). Sometimes people assume that because Adenauer is a Catholic the CDU is exclusively a Catholic party, like the Christian Democrats in Italy; this is not true. When *Der Alte* created the party he deliberately chose *not* to follow the example of the old purely Catholic Zentrum; instead he played hard for Protestant support as well. He knew that he had to have Protestant backing, for the obvious reason that Protestants comprise 51.1 percent of the nation. Bremen, Hamburg, Schleswig-Holstein, Lower Saxony, and parts of Hesse and northern Westphalia are all strongly Protestant. Today—an interesting phenomenon—an effort is made in

high government circles to keep a close balance between Catholics and Protestants; if Mr. A. in a certain ministry is Catholic, then Mr. B., the next in line, must be Protestant, Mr. C. Catholic again, Mr. D. Protestant again, and so on down to the bottom.

5. The trade unions, which present a mixed picture, and the agricultural vote, which is predominantly conservative. Farmers number about 12 percent of the population of West Germany.

6. "Senior citizens"—that is, the pensioned class together with hundreds of thousands of others who are "beneficiaries of social security." Most of these are zealous to protect their considerable emoluments.

* * *

It is, however, far from easy to list, much less appraise, all the forces at work in contemporary Germany. Nobody should be categorical. A chief reason for this is the astounding fact that approximately one out of every four West Germans is either a refugee or an "escapee" (or "expellee," the term most frequently used in Germany), and many of the recent arrivals are unassimilated. Of the total population of fifty-three million about thirteen million did not even live in West Germany before the war. Some, the "escapees" or "expellees," were forced out of those territories, once German, which lie east of the Oder-Neisse line and which were annexed by the Russians and Poles (East Prussia, western Poland, Silesia, and so on) at the conclusion of the war; the indigenous German populations were weeded out to the last man and forcibly expelled. The others were the copious stream of refugees fleeing from the Communist regime in East Germany until recently. Obviously, the Federal Republic, with no fewer than thirteen million new citizens, is in a state of flux, of physical as well as emotional commotion, of unpredictably volatile development. Today's West Germany is a new country—and a frontier country at that.

Among Other Leaders

Of the men under Adenauer I met several; the most interesting, I thought, was Dr. Ludwig Erhard, the Vice Chancellor and minister of economics, who is the author of the *Wirtschaftswunder* (economic miracle, i.e., German recovery). He is a very large, energetic man with a face almost the color and, it seems, the size of a harvest moon; his tiny mouth looks like a hole drilled into a pumpkin. Dr. Erhard likes to eat and drink, is a vigorous conversationalist, and chain-smokes cigars in paper holders. During a conference, one of his secretaries supplies and lights these one by one. Although his background is Bavarian, Erhard is a Protestant. I asked him how he happened to get into politics. He replied cheerfully that an American jeep drove up to his apartment in Munich one morning in 1945, and without explanation carried him away. Dr. Erhard was a professor of economics, and thought that, for some mysterious reason, he was being arrested. No. The Americans had heard that he was one of the few economic specialists in the country who bore no taint of Nazism, and were carting him off to be a member of the new Bavarian government they were setting up.

Erhard is an old-fashioned free-trader in economic approach, and a passionately devoted believer in laissez-faire. What he seeks to build up in West Germany is "a socially minded free-market economy." As things stand at the moment, he is still the chief contender for succession to the chancellorship if Dr. Adenauer retires, despite Adenauer's own hostility to the idea and in spite of the new—and fluid—situation caused by the new coalition between the Chancellor and Dr. Mende's Free Democrats. For a long time the *Alte Herr's* choice as crown prince was not Erhard, but the minister of finance, Franz Etzel, because the latter is supposed to be more "Europe-minded" than Erhard, and thus more to the Chancellor's international taste. But Etzel cannot even begin to rival Erhard as a vote getter, and has pretty much passed out of the picture.

What caused the economic miracle which Erhard has so brilliantly brought to pass? (1) Germans are a notoriously industrious people; they work hard, and are thrifty. Despair ruled the nation in 1946; hard work was not merely something expected of every citizen, but salvation—a way out of a stultifying blind alley. (2) Much of the prewar German industrial plant was destroyed by allied bombing, or dismantled by the French and British after the war; hence most German factories are comparatively new, built from scratch, and highly modern and efficient. (3) Marshall Plan aid poured roughly three billion dollars into the country. (4) The massive stream of refugees from East Germany and expellees from beyond the Oder-Neisse provided an almost inexhaustible labor market. Even today unemployment scarcely exists; in fact, shortage of labor is acute. (5) Until comparatively recently Germany was disarmed and, like Japan, did not have to allocate a large percentage of its budget to armament.

Willy Brandt and the Berlin Deadlock

Willy Brandt, the *Oberbürgermeister* or governing mayor of West Berlin (in effect, prime minister of the West Berlin government), is one of the most attractive men I have ever met in public life. A friendly person, he projects candor and confidence, and is without a trace of humbug, the curse of most professional politicians. I have seldom known a man more satisfactory to interview; he answers questions straight on the nail, without pettifoggery or evasion, and is quick-witted, eloquent, and honest. He stimulates and gives out. To an extent he reminded me of Wendell

Willkie, in both his abundant physical magnetism and square-jawed, tousled good looks.

Brandt stands on the moderate right wing of his party. Roughly his position is that of Giuseppe Saragat in Italy, or, to a degree, of Hugh Gaitskell in Britain. He is not particularly interested in theory; what does interest him is power. Let the SPD gain office; then it will be time to talk about controversial items in socialist theory. Brandt's sources of strength and qualities are several, like his youth (he is only forty-seven), tough energy, and vote-getting appeal to the middle class. Above all he is the man on the firing line, the man on the spot in Berlin, a city permanently in trouble, and the heart of the most dangerous crisis in the world.

Mayor Brandt was born in Lübeck, and purists in the German language sometimes scoff mildly at his accent, which has a salty Baltic tang (even as they laugh at Adenauer for his soft Rhenish purr). He managed to flee from Germany after the rise of Hitler, and, unlike most of his Social Democrat comrades who escaped to the south or east, went north and headed for Norway: he worked as a journalist, did political liaison work with the Norwegian resistance, and later rose to the honorary rank of major; after the war he returned to Berlin (in Norwegian uniform and with a handsome Norwegian wife), got a job in the Rathaus, and became a protégé of the late Ernst Reuter, the indomitable prowestern, prodemocratic mayor of West Berlin during the airlift in 1948.[3] Brandt was never what the socialists call a "Schumacher man," that is, a fanatic nationalist. Probably on most issues in foreign affairs his position does not differ greatly from that of Dr. Adenauer, though neither would like to hear this. He was beaten in his first try for the Berlin mayoralty, and won the second. He speaks excellent English, enjoys many friendships, and lives in a small flat in circumstances of the utmost modesty.

Again I permit myself a trite remark—what an odd, baffling, convoluted, mysteriously perverse people the Germans are! What prompts me to say this is that a principal point of Brandt's opponents in the 1961 electoral campaign was the very fact that he fled to Norway and joined the anti-Nazi resistance there during the war. Today's Germany has, after all, repudiated Hitler. Dr. Adenauer and numerous others, like Dr. Erhard, who were anti-Nazi but who sat out the war in comparative tranquillity, are applauded; yet Herr Brandt, who risked his life in actual combat against the Nazis, was called a "traitor." That he adopted Norwegian citizenship was termed a "betrayal." Nothing more odiously unfair can be imagined. Also a smear campaign was launched against Brandt by the CDU, in which Adenauer demeaned himself by taking part, on the ground that he was illegitimate, which he has conceded in

---

[3] Reuter was—interestingly enough—an ex-Communist.

a perfectly straightforward fashion. His father deserted his mother shortly after he was born, and he changed his name to Willy Brandt many years later.

In an hour with us Mr. Brandt covered a wide range of topics. One of his special interests is education. Nothing is more remarkable in Germany, he thinks, than the profound, almost revolutionary difference between the present generation of youngsters and the last. Thirty years ago the youth of the land was almost insanely nationalist, but not today. Thirty years ago students fought duels; today they ride scooters, drink *espresso,* read paperbacks, and take holidays in France. Herr Brandt would like to see the level of teaching made higher—to get rid of the teachers who are old enough to have been Nazis during the war, and who still feel "subjective guilt" about Hitler. He does not think that neo-Nazism, either among young or old, plays any role at all in contemporary Germany; in the whole of Berlin he doubts if there are more than two thousand people connected with any extreme rightist movement. Dr. Adenauer's greatest contribution, he considers, is that his government has, so to speak, *absorbed* the surviving Nazis, thus rendering them impotent.

Communism? "It doesn't command one percent of the electorate." Anti-Semitism? "Maybe we have here in Berlin gangs of hooligans; if a gang has thirty members it is a big gang and half a dozen of the thirty will be spies that we have planted there." Unification? He smiled shrewdly: "History does not recognize the word 'never.' "

About the position of Berlin Mayor Brandt seemed fairly optimistic from a long-range point of view. He does not think that the Russians will dare to impose another formal blockade, if only because "even Khrushchev must have public relations advisers and to use the weapon of starvation against a city is not a technique that will gain him friends" —he does not want the Soviet Union to be more isolated than it is. As to Germany in general, the *Oberbürgermeister* puts a certain amount of hope in the possibility of disarmament. The German problem and the security problem are inextricably mixed together. If Russia and the West could ever achieve some modicum of agreement on disarmament, this might reduce the necessity felt by both sides to keep troops on German soil. East Germany? The Communist regime, as of today, would not get ten percent of the vote in a free election. But this statement means little, since nobody is going to give the people a free election. As time goes on two contrary forces will gain ground: first, more East German citizens will want the truth, but second, those who have roots with the past and know what non-Communist life was like will begin to die out.

A good many Germans, Mr. Brandt thinks, still feel torn between East and West. Nowadays young people in particular want to belong to the

West, although many do not go quite so far in their desire for European integration as Chancellor Adenauer, but to some the East is a constant temptation, as well as threat. Citizens feel that they cannot sit forever between the two forces; they must be on one side or the other. "The struggle is not between the extremes at each end, but in the middle of the minds of men in the middle."

~~~~~~

Chancellor Adenauer, aged eighty-seven, was finally squeezed out of office on October 15, 1963, after fourteen years in power. He retained his position, however, as national chairman of the Christian Democratic Union, and has never ceased trying to influence events both as a member of the Bundestag and privately. He has certainly been one of the most adhesive personalities of our time. It is difficult to like him but his contributions should not be ignored. It was Adenauer, still full of sap and sting in his late seventies, who made possible an orderly transition from the shabby horrors of the Nazi regime to parliamentary government. He brought Germany out of an evil dictatorship, defeat, and burning chaos into the embrace of the democratic world, although some of his own views are reactionary in the extreme.

Dr. Erhard succeeded Adenauer as Chancellor. Adenauer did everything possible to keep him from getting the job, but failed. Adenauer's age was such that Erhard, in comparison, seemed to be a mere youth. But he is sixty-seven. A man to watch is Dr. Gerhard Schroeder, the foreign minister, in his middle fifties. Shroeder is a Saarlander who, beginning a career in law, joined the Nazi party in 1933 when Hitler reached power. Then in 1941 he was courageous enough to marry a young lady partly Jewish, and to quit the Nazi movement. He has been bitterly attacked for his allegiance to the Nazis for a period, but no charge of any wrong-doing was ever brought against him, and he was cleared by a de-Nazification court. This is a tough, able, and cunning man.

CHAPTER 37

~~~~~~

The Person of de Gaulle

This chapter, like the two preceding, grew out of a Reader's Digest *assignment. Then I included it in* Inside Europe Today, *published in 1961 and republished the next year. At the time I wrote France was still fiercely gripped by the conflict in Algeria, which colored indelibly most public—and private—thinking about de Gaulle. Algeria became independent from France after seven years of bitter civil war on July, 3, 1962. But France, so to speak, won the war as well, because it was rid of the Algerian agony at last and was free, under de Gaulle, to pursue its normal path.*

~~~~~~

If it be true, as I hold, that a nation, like an individual, has a soul, a conscience and a mission, it follows that there are some desertions, some denials, which no "sacred egotism," as it is called, can justify. It is for this reason that those whose concern is for the soul of France and the integrity of her conscience, who are convinced that France must carry out her immemorial mission, have not recognized and will never recognize the capitulation of June, 1940.

—GENERAL CHARLES DE GAULLE

TWENTY-SIX YEARS AGO I wrote in *Inside Europe* that whereas Germany was one person, Hitler, France was a whole lot of people. Today almost exactly the opposite is true, for, although Adenauer is the dominant character in the Germany of 1962 the country is divided and there are a good many other consequential Germans in both West and East; but in France today nobody—nobody at all—really counts except Charles André Joseph Marie de Gaulle.

[465]

In 1936, when *Inside Europe* first appeared, Léon Blum was just about to succeed the unspeakable Pierre Laval as prime minister; Laval was executed in 1945, and Blum died in 1950. There is no mention of de Gaulle in *Inside Europe*. He was at that time an inconspicuous colonel of infantry in his middle forties; few outside his immediate circle had ever heard of him. Within four years he was to become leader of the French nation in exile, organizer of the Free French, and commander of the Fighting French. By the end of the war he was a world figure—contentious, cranky, unpopular in many quarters, but a supreme, indomitable world figure just the same.

I have met General de Gaulle several times, dating back to London in 1941; if he chooses, he can be the rudest man alive. He can also be winning. Whenever I have seen him I have gone away thinking that his chief characteristic is inflexibility. It is impossible to ignore his aloofness, his Olympian quality of detached grandeur. He is positively lunar, although not necessarily cold.

Once in the middle 1950's when he was out of power I called on him in the sterile-looking headquarters he maintained on the Rue Solferino at that time—a kind of hideout office. He asked me what French political figures I had been seeing, and I named one or two. A curious smile wrinkled his lips and he commented, "Ah! But you have met nobody but the pro-Americans!" I replied, "Who else is there?" to which he answered instantly, *"Moi!"* Of course he did not mean this altogether seriously. (When I told this story later to a celebrated British lady, her comment was, "It's a wonder he didn't, like a king, say 'Nous!'")

The General is somewhat stout these days, and looks, with his formidable height, like a slightly swollen obelisk. He is seventy-one and his eyesight has weakened with the years, but otherwise he is in quite good health.

De Gaulle is impervious to all except the closest of personal relationships, such as to his family, but he does have friends of course—old comrades in the Resistance, or men whose intellect he genuinely respects, like André Malraux, the author and art critic, who fought with the Loyalists in Spain a quarter of a century ago, and who is his minister of cultural expansion, and Louis Joxe, a former ambassador to Moscow and minister of education, who became minister of state for Algerian affairs. But the President seldom unbends to anybody; his relation to his associates is almost that of a monarch, a somewhat arrogant monarch at that. Almost never does he take advice, and only seldom does he communicate his intentions to subordinates. Nobody has influence on him. "The only trouble with the General," one of his cabinet officers is reputed to have said on one occasion, "is that he is not a human being." A principal minister was once asked what French policy on a certain issue was. He replied, "I know what it was half an hour ago, when I left the General. I do not know what it is now."

De Gaulle is almost totally inaccessible to outsiders. Adenauer, a gregarious man at heart, will see almost anybody; so will Khrushchev, if it will serve a purpose; but de Gaulle is probably the head of state hardest to meet on the continent, with the possible exception of Dr. Salazar in Portugal. It is wrong, however, to assume that he despises people. It is simply, as one observer who has studied him closely for years put it to me, that he has a somewhat pessimistic view of human values. He hesitates to share himself, because he feels that humanity is weak, that it is the nature of man to be frail, and that even the best of men cannot be expected to live up to their promise. Therefore it is better not to trust human nature fully, not to give members of his entourage his unqualified confidence. This deeply ingrained characteristic in de Gaulle, which also serves to make him magnanimous when somebody does fail him, is probably the principal reason why nobody—not a soul— is in discernible view as his successor. Nobody is being trained to take on his responsibilties. There are some heads of state who persistently avoid having first-class men around them because of fear of being over-shadowed; they are jealous of the man just outside the door, or enjoy playing one aspirant for power off against another. Stalin and Hitler were prime cases in point. This is not at all the reason for de Gaulle's diffidence. He has no jealousy of anybody, no fear of anybody else rising to the succession; what he does fear is that potential candidates for power do not have the necessary status or capacity. Quite recently a deputy to the National Assembly asked him point-blank what the future was going to be. De Gaulle replied calmly, "Well, you will have to find another de Gaulle."

This egoism is rocklike, unswerving from first to last, and almost sublimely absolute. Once, during his retirement, he was looking back to an early episode in his career and said, with perfect seriousness, "Ah! That was when I *was* France!" As recently as January, 1961, when one of his friends suggested that he should thank those who had voted for him in the Algeria referendum just concluded, he replied, "How can France thank France?"[1]

With his incomparable arrogance goes a marvelously sensitive touch. In September, 1961, right-wing conspirators attempted to blow up his car when the President was en route to his home at Colombey-les-Deux-

[1] A different version of one of these anecdotes appears in Edward Ashcroft, "Return of the Warrior," *Sunday Times* (London), May 15, 1960. Also see the New York *Herald Tribune*, July 12, 1960, and *Time*, January 20, 1961.

Eglises, but this plot to assassinate him failed. Who but de Gaulle would have brushed off the incident with five words—"*Une plaisanterie de mauvis goût!*"—"A joke in bad taste"?

I have heard it said that the difference between de Gaulle and Adenauer is that the former is a Frenchman, the latter a European. I do not think this is quite accurate. Certainly de Gaulle is a Frenchman above all else; and detests most aspects of supranational policy, but in some respects he is a better European than Adenauer, because his arc is broader. Adenauer is, in fact, a kind of Eisenhower-era American. De Gaulle has a much bigger conception of Europe; he considers that it stretches to the Urals, and he was the first statesman after the crash of the Summit in 1960 to point out the absolute necessity (on acceptable terms) of seeking some kind of accommodation with Russia, no matter how disagreeable and aggressive Khrushchev was. During 1961 and the crisis over Berlin, however, his attitude to negotiations with the Kremlin stiffened. Meantime, he has developed an unfortunate blunt enmity toward the UN.

There has been some talk that de Gaulle will leave a testament, as Lenin did, listing and assaying various candidates for the succession. Commenting on this one of the wisest Frenchmen I know remarked, "Nonsense! Kindly remember that this is France. When de Gaulle dies he will be dead, and no Frenchman would pay the slightest attention to any testament he leaves." There are two things, somewhat paradoxical, that should always be remembered about France; it consists of forty-five million people most of whom are (a) hard-headed realists, and (b) anarchists at heart.

* * *

One legend is that, on moving into the Elysée, the General and Madame de Gaulle tactfully, quietly, eased out of their jobs every person on the domestic staff—there weren't many—who had been divorced. The General, a good Catholic, did not think it proper that he and his family should be served by a divorced person. Another is that exactly one vote is supposed to have been registered against the General in his own village of Colombey-les-Deux-Eglises (population about five hundred) in the election which made him President. The lone dissident was the de Gaulle cook. She thought that moving to Paris and assuming the duties of President would tire the elderly General too much.

The pattern of de Gaulle's thinking may be judged from these excerpts from a press conference which he gave in Washington on April 25, 1960, during a visit to the United States. Of course this took place before the Summit Conference:

Q.—Mr. President, do you anticipate another summit conference besides the meeting this year in Paris, perhaps in Moscow when President Eisenhower will visit Russia?

A.—If we do not wage war, we must certainly wage peace. In order to wage peace, we must negotiate. And in order to negotiate, we must meet together.

Q.—Mr. President, the curiosity of the press is all-consuming. Who is your favorite French poet?

A.—My favorite French poet is the one that I am reading at the time that I am reading him. There are many whom I like and admire. I ask all of you for permission not to hurt the feelings of any of them—even those who have long been dead—by making choices.

*   *   *

De Gaulle was born in Lille on November 22, 1890; his father was a professor of philosophy at a Jesuit college; his paternal and maternal strains both represented the *petite noblesse,* and such qualities as rigidity, prudence, frugality, and correctness were born into him. Also born into him was a highly suggestive name—de Gaulle, which can be stretched to mean "of France." He decided to choose a military career, and was graduated with honors from Saint-Cyr, the French equivalent of West Point. He had—ironically enough—a passionate admiration for his first commanding officer, Henri Philippe Pétain, then a colonel; he dedicated his first book to Pétain, and Pétain was godfather to his only son. Twenty-odd years later, the Vichy government headed by the miserable Pétain was to sentence him to death for treason. De Gaulle was a good officer, but rose slowly; and he was one of those comparatively rare birds among officers who realize that the pen is mightier than the sword. In 1934 he published *The Army of the Future,* which advanced the thesis that attack was better than defense—a most unorthodox view at the time, when France was crouching behind its supposedly impregnable Maginot Line—and appealed for the creation of a new type of highly mobile, mechanized army, which would be characterized by the mass use of large numbers of tanks. The French paid not the slightest attention to these views—but the Germans did. The book was, in fact, much taken up in military circles in Berlin, and de Gaulle, it might almost be said, was the unwitting father of the Nazi Panzer divisions which, when war came to the West in 1940, crushed France, the Low Countries, and the British expeditionary force with appalling speed. At any rate de Gaulle's military theories were certainly proved right.

De Gaulle fled to London after the collapse of France and, on June 18, 1940, made one of the most celebrated speeches in contemporary history. He was unknown; he was forlorn and penniless; he was alone, a man without a country; and he was magnificent. His words, saying in effect that France had lost a battle but not the war, and that Frenchmen everywhere should rally to his standard (his opening words were, "I, General de Gaulle . . ."), rang like trumpet blasts around the world. The subsequent years were stormy. He created the Free French movement; had grisly quarrels with the Americans and British during the Vichy period; suffered various ignominies in Algiers when the allies could not decide to back him or not; entered Paris as a conqueror in 1944, and set up a provisional government; supervised the birth of the Fourth Republic; outlined a sensible policy for French Africa; went to Moscow (when the Americans and British dawdled over recognizing his regime), negotiated a Franco-Russian treaty, and brought several French Communists into his government; was meantime denounced as a Fascist by the ill-informed; resigned office early in 1946 because the multiplicity of French political parties made government unworkable; stood in the wings for a while, and created his own party, the Rassemblement du Peuple Français; hoped to be called back to power, and was not; retired from active politics and buried himself for years at Colombey, biding his time, proving his mastery of French prose in a superb autobiography, and consolidating his long view of life; was called back to save the republic in the great crisis of May, 1958, when the army revolt in Algeria, led by the parachutist General Jacques Massu, came close to making civil war; took the prime ministership, superintended the formation of the Fifth Republic, and put this before the people; and finally became first President of the Fifth Republic and of the newly formed French Community on January 8, 1959.

* * *

What does de Gaulle believe in most? First, of course, France. Second, himself, but as a symbol of France.

What does he want most? To restore France to indisputably accepted status as a first-class power, which it has not been since Munich. This is why he has been such a thorn in the flesh of NATO, and why he has insisted that France shall have its own nuclear weapons.

What does he need most? Time. Yet he is seventy-one.

What are the chief sources of his power, aside from such obvious personal qualities as endurance, an extraordinary logical mind, and intelligence?

First, his "mystique," or identity with the spirit of France. The leader, the cause, the nation have become one. He has a hand, it has been written, *"pure, sure, dure."*[2] What Frenchman can resist him when he says that the three things that count most in leadership are "concision, precision, decision"?

No man could be more gnarled with ego, but associated with this is

[2] Sonia Tomara in the New York *Herald Tribune*, February 29, 1944.

a curious and altogether genuine humility. He answers fan letters himself—longhand!

He memorizes his speeches, and can talk for an hour on the most difficult matters without departing from his text by a jot or tittle, and for some inexplicable reason the French admire this. He is called a *"cerveau"*—a brain. (Marshal Foch was similarly a *cerveau*, but not Joffre, Pétain, or Weygand.) His TV speech delivered on Algeria on January 29, 1960, was, a good many people of consequence believe, the best heard in Europe since the great Churchill speeches during the war. For pure and scintillating power of logic, it even surpassed Churchill. As is often the case, he refers to himself both as "I" and in the third person. His opening words were: "If I have put on my uniform today to address you on television, it is in order to show that it is General de Gaulle who speaks, as well as the Chief of State."

Second, the fact that history has, after all, so far proved him right. He said that France would come back to life, and it came back to life. He said that the Algerian "ultras" would be beaten in 1958 and 1960, and they were beaten. Moreover he was right vis-à-vis other *Frenchmen;* which means much more to the French than if he had merely been proved right against such barbarians as the British or Americans.

Third, his disinterestedness. Almost every citizen knows that he cares for nothing except the public good. A friend put it this way: "His patriotism is as indisputable as his prescience; thus he appeals not only to whatever instincts for gratitude that the French may have, but to their capacity for imagination."

Fourth, the regime that preceded him was utterly discredited. He filled an arena desperately confused.

Finally, although de Gaulle's demerits and defects are obvious, and although he suffered a marked decline in prestige and popularity in 1961, there can be little doubt about the extent of his contribution. Of few statesmen can it be said that they saved a country; Lincoln was one; Churchill is another; but de Gaulle goes them one better, in that he saved his country not once but *twice* in his lifetime—which must be one of the rarest phenomena in history. Without de Gaulle, there would have been no Free France in 1940; and without de Gaulle the country would probably have succumbed to civil war in 1958 as a result of the crisis in Algeria. Once Charles André Joseph Marie de Gaulle saved France from Germany, and once he saved it from itself.

Radical Socialists and the Deux Cent Familles

The first two questions I asked when I arrived in Paris in 1960 were: "What has happened to the Radical Socialist party?" and "What happened to the *deux cent familles?*" In prewar days France was run, if it was run at all, by an unstable combination of these two factors—the Radical Socialists, who were neither radical nor socialist, but who represented the solid block of middle French citizens who were the heart of the nation and who always voted against "the church and the château"; and, second, the *"deux cent familles,"* or two hundred families, who constituted the financial oligarchy centering on the regents of the Bank of France.

Neither is an important factor today, and this is what makes the biggest of all changes in contemporary France, next to the emergence of de Gaulle.

The Radical Socialists, the party of giants like Clemenceau and Herriot in their great days, were wiped out as a serious instrument by three factors:

First, Hitler. The Radical Socialists were the root and pillar of the Third Republic; hence, when Hitler conquered France the party was discredited, and it never regained its place in the Fourth Republic, which ruled from 1946 to 1958. Of course the moral collapse of the party and its diminution of prestige predated the war; it was a Radical Socialist, Edouard Daladier, who betrayed the Czechs at Munich.

Second, internal dissension. This is a complicated story. Its gist is that Pierre Mendès-France, the Radical Socialist prime minister in 1954–1955, set out to reform the party, clear away its dead wood, and bring it up to date by eliminating the bureaucrats who ran the local machines. This caused furious resentment; the party split up, and Mendès formed a leftist splinter group of his own. Also one should mention the suicidal tendencies toward fragmentation which marked the French political system. The Radicals were not exclusively responsible for this by any means, but they took a large share of the onus for the incessant rotation of cabinets that distinguished France before and immediately after the war.

Third, de Gaulle. The Fifth Republic came into being, and both Mendès (who was one of the ablest and most courageous premiers France ever had) and the conservative wing of the Radical Socialists lost much of their *raison d'être*.

As to the financial oligarchy, it still exists, but its power is much attenuated. This is not merely because it has become inherently weaker itself, but because the state has become so much stronger. The upper bourgeoisie hangs on to its wealth; but the real direction of affairs is in the hands of a new managerial caste. The government—the state—operates under a series of Four-Year Plans, and plays a substantially greater role in financial and industrial matters than before the war. It was, in short, nationalization which killed the old oligarchy. Few outsiders realize how much of the French economy has been nationalized. The state owns and operates the railways, coal mining, gas and electric power, the oil industry in part, the largest automobile works in France (Renault), the five biggest credit banks, several of the large insurance companies, atomic energy, most of the aviation industry (for instance, Air France), the biggest steamship line, and of course—from long back —tobacco, the Opéra, and posts and telegraphs.[3]

These examples of nationalization are not quite so revolutionary as they may seem. For one thing, state intervention in industry has a long and honorable history in France; a state, or rather royal, monopoly on the manufacture of such items as Sèvres porcelain, as an example, started centuries ago. For another, nationalization of some companies took place as a result of special circumstances; Renault was nationalized because it collaborated. For another, although various industries may be owned by the state, the management still has wide powers; several state companies are virtually autonomous, like Air France, and are certainly not run like ministries even though they are under theoretical public—not private—control. Air France is, incidentally, the largest airline in the world.

Another trend not generally appreciated abroad is the development of the social security system; next to England, Austria, and the Scandinavian countries, France is probably closer to being a full welfare state than any in Europe. Not only are ordinary benefits in force, but a variety of special stipends. As an example, the government pays an allowance to newlyweds, and the birth of children is handsomely subsidized. Social security includes "housewife allowance," health insurance, and prenatal care; parents get copious supplements to their social security for each child, up to 33 percent of the father's salary for families with more than three children, and the state provides further handsome contribution to the support of children as they grow up. The more children, the bigger the benefits; perhaps this is another reason why the French birth rate climbs.

Who does run France, if the Radical Socialists and the financial oligarchy count no longer? This is a difficult question, but three elements at least must be mentioned: (1) de Gaulle; (2) the civil service; (3) survivors of the Resistance.

〰〰〰〰〰〰〰〰〰〰〰〰〰〰〰〰〰〰〰〰〰〰〰〰〰〰〰

I was lucky enough to meet General de Gaulle three or four times in the autumn of 1941, when he was an exile in London, consolidating his leadership of the Free French. He was much less Olympian and

---

[3] Steel, however, the most important item of all, is not nationalized.

abrasive in those old days. But the jib of his mind has remained the same. Many of the British and Americans in London did not like or trust him. One complaint was that he was "too mechanical," and another was that he never mentioned "democracy." He was, however, already a marked man. One eminent Briton told me that it was certain that "he would lead his troops into Paris within four or five years," and a lady of my acquaintance also made a good prophecy when she said, "But he has become a name instead of a man, and so we will never be able to get rid of him."

I have just looked through some notes I made in London. I thought that he was a great man. I was also impressed by the way he smoked, with a cigarette perpetually stuck to his lip, even while he talked. One day I went to a large formal luncheon given him by a journalists' association. Every guest had a mimeographed copy of the speech he was about to deliver. He rose and talked for eighteen minutes. He had no manuscript with him so far as I could see; at any rate he made no use of it. I read my copy of his speech as he delivered it, keeping up with him word by word. He had memorized it down to the last line. Never for eighteen minutes did he vary by a single word from the text he had prepared.

To get down to the present, I mention above that nobody in France is being trained to take on de Gaulle's responsibilities and that nobody is in discernible view as his successor. This situation has, I think, recently become modified. The coming man is, it would seem today, Georges Jean Raymond Pompidou, a nonparty man who became prime minister on November 28, 1962. Pompidou, aged fifty-three, ran the Rothschild banking interests for some years, and has been a Resistance fighter, teacher, and writer as well as highly successful banker and businessman. Rothschilds never choose the mediocre, nor does de Gaulle.

CHAPTER 38

~~~~~~~~

Mr. K.

I *went to Soviet Russia, my fourth trip there, in 1956 for* Collier's
Magazine. Collier's *died while I was en route and* Look *took over my
contract and printed what I wrote. It was the longest article* Look *had ever
published as of that date. This chapter is also abstracted from what
I have written about Khrushchev in four different books—*Inside
Russia Today *(1958),* Inside Europe Today *(1961), a revised edition of*
Russia, *and a book for children called* Meet Soviet Russia.

I met Mr. Khrushchev for the first time in 1956 at a reception given
in Moscow by the Turkish embassy. The American ambassador, Charles
E. Bohlen, introduced me, saying that I was a writer and journalist.
Mr. K. instantly gave it as his opinion, vividly stated, that journalists
were an extremely low breed of cats. Then I happened to see Dimitri T.
Shepilov, who was at that time the foreign minister, standing nearby.
For some years Shepilov had been editor of Pravda, and I had the
temerity to say to Mr. K., "If you have such a low opinion of journalists,
why did you make a journalist your foreign minister?"

Khrushchev replied with a peculiar dark, airy gesture, "He's the only
good journalist in Russia, and so we had to give him a job!"

Watching Mr. K. and members of the Presidium at receptions in
Moscow became an interesting indoor sport. Khrushchev held no governmental post at this time but he dominated almost everything—including every room he entered. I will never forget the expression on the face
of Lazar M. Kaganovitch one afternoon when Khrushchev was making
a rough off-the-cuff speech at the Polish embassy. Kaganovitch, who was
high in power at that time, listened to Khrushchev with an air compounded of satisfaction, bewilderment, amusement, approval, and
dismay. He put out his hands, palms up, with his head wagging, and

*you could almost see the words form on his lips as Khrushchev kept
on blasting away, "What can you do with a man like that! But what a
man!"*

*And at another party of this sort I once saw Mr. K. drink eleven
glasses of champagne. Then he changed to tomato juice.*

〰〰〰〰〰〰〰〰〰〰〰〰〰〰〰〰〰〰〰〰〰〰〰〰〰〰

NIKITA S. KHRUSHCHEV, the foremost political personality in the world
today after John Fitzgerald Kennedy, was born on April 17, 1894,
in a hamlet named Kalinovka, near Kursk, close to the Ukraine. He is,
however, Russian in origin, not Ukrainian as is sometimes thought. As
of the moment of writing his jobs are three: first secretary of the Central
Committee of the CPSU (Communist Party Soviet Union), chairman of
the Council of Ministers of the Union of Soviet Socialist Republics (that
is, prime minister), and chairman of the Party Bureau for the RSFSR,
or Russia proper. He controls both party and state, and is undisputed
leader of the largest political organism in the world, which covers one-
sixth of the land surface of the globe.

No man of politics has ever had his name spelled in so many ways
in so many different languages:

French:	Khrouchtchev
German:	Chruschtschow
	(But in Viennese newspapers this
	sometimes becomes Chruschtchew)
Italian:	Krusciov or Kruscev
Spanish:	Khrushchev
Portuguese:	Khruchtchev
Dutch:	Chroesjtjew
Swedish:	Chrusjtjov
Danish:	Chrustjov
Polish:	Chruszczew

The British popular press incontinently lops off a few h's and spells
him simply "Kruschev." Gutter newspapers in America call him "Khrush,"
"Krush," or even "Krushy," and he is universally known, even in the most
respectable circles, as "Mr. K." He is also variously pronounced. In Russian the correct pronunciation is "crew-shove," with a light accent on the
"shove." Most Europeans alter this to "cruse-shove." To call him "crew-
shef" or "crews-chef" is, to purists, incorrect.

Khrushchev's father was a miner who eked out a living by shepherd-
ing flocks; the family was dirt-poor. He had practically no education as

a child, and Edward Crankshaw, one of the best-informed British authorities on Russia, says in a recent authoritative book that he still *could not read or write at twenty-three*. Another British expert, writing anonymously in the London *Observer* (May 15, 1960), says flatly that he first learned to read at the age of twenty-six. If this is true one can say fairly that the need to have formal education in childhood may be exaggerated, or, at the least, that Khrushchev's capacity for absorbing education as an adult was little short of spectacular. There may be gaps in his knowledge, but he is extraordinarily well informed on a large variety of subjects, and, even if his use of language is pedantic on occasion, few politicians have ever learned to express themselves with more articulateness, command of idiom, and punch. Incidentally, his love of peasant tales and vast fund of folklore and proverbs, which he quotes abundantly, are characteristic of one who has learned by ear in childhood, not from books.

The Russian Revolution came in 1917, when Khrushchev was twenty-three. He was a locksmith by trade, and also worked as a shepherd. He joined the Bolshevik forces, did well, and, immediately after the civil war, was sent to a party school in the Donbas region. Here some elements of education were pumped into him, and he was sent thereafter to a Workers' School at the Donetz Industrial Institute. Then in 1929, when he was thirty-five, he entered the Stalin Industrial Academy, now called the Moscow Industrial Academy, in Moscow for further study. This habit of picking out promising young men and giving them opportunity for specialized adult education is a characteristic—and admirable—Soviet trait.

In the 1930's Khrushchev rose like a rocket. He became a strong party member, lifted himself in the hierarchy, and, when he was still under forty, was secretary of the Moscow District Party Committee, a vital post. One of his sponsors, a man whom he later deposed, was Kaganovitch, a historic early figure of the Revolution. By 1939 Khrushchev had become a full member of the Politburo, now called the Presidium, the ruling body of the party, and he has been a member of this organization, the most important in the USSR, ever since. He was the first man ever admitted to this holy of holies who grew up after the Revolution, and, as such, has always symbolized the new generation of leaders. He has no record of pre-Soviet activity and, as has been aptly stated, is "totally a product of the Soviet era."

When World War II broke out he was chief of the party in the Ukraine; he was promptly made a lieutenant general in the armed forces, and took part both in the formal defense of Stalingrad and in guerrilla fighting in the neighborhood. While still retaining the Ukraine post, he maintained his position as head of the party organization in Moscow as well and, in the immediate postwar period, divided his time between Moscow and Kiev, the capital of the Ukraine. He was responsible for the odious anti-Stalinist purges that afflicted the Ukraine after the war, managed to avoid being purged by Stalin himself, and advanced to become one of the half-dozen Kremlin leaders closest to Stalin in the ugly period when Russia was ruled by black terror and when the Cold War got under way, between 1946 and 1953.

But the Kremlin guards its secrets well. When Stalin died on March 5, 1953, after almost thirty years of iron rule, Khrushchev was little known outside Russia and not particularly well known—except in the inner circle—within the country. The turning point of his life came immediately after Stalin's death. The full story of what happened is still unknown. But a decision was reached by those closest to Stalin, probably while his body was still warm, to abolish one-man rule, establish collective leadership, and reinstate the *party* as the chief organ of Soviet power. A motive for this was self-protection; the epigones huddled together to keep safe. For many years Stalin had not ruled through the party at all, but through the police and his own sinister private secretariat. Now a triumvirate was formed to *reinstitutionalize* the regime; it consisted of Vyacheslav M. Molotov, the former prime minister, Georgi Malenkov, who had been Stalin's principal secretary for years, and the notorious Lavrenti P. Beria, the boss of the secret police. Khrushchev himself was not, in the first instance, a member of this triumvirate. He was, however, still party boss in both Moscow and the Ukraine, and was given the job of superintending arrangements for Stalin's funeral. Malenkov became both prime minister and head of the party, as Stalin had been, on March 9. He held this double post for only eight days, however. Then, in circumstances which have never been satisfactorily explained, he decided to give up the party secretaryship but to remain prime minister. Malenkov must have known that the first of these positions held vastly more power than the second; therefore the supposition is that he was forced to divide his functions. By whom? We do not know. But we do know that it was Khrushchev who replaced him in the party post, and, a few months later, Mr. K. was formally installed as first secretary of the CPSU, which job he still holds, and which is the most powerful in the Soviet Union. All of Khrushchev's subsequent career derives from this.

Malenkov, as prime minister, was much weakened. The triumvirate was now a quadrumvirate. But soon Malenkov, Molotov, and Khrushchev turned like jaguars on Beria; he was arrested, condemned to death, and shot on Christmas Eve, 1953.

This ended the era of outright police rule, and the way was now open for the rubbery Khrushchev (one of his nicknames in Moscow is the "Football"), with his unparalleled powers of maneuver and political sense, to consolidate his own position. Malenkov was deposed as prime minister in February, 1955, and was replaced by Marshal Nikolai Bulganin, one of Mr. K.'s closest associates; Malenkov himself was demoted to become minister of electric power stations. Next came the crisis of June, 1957, when Khrushchev, in one remarkable swoop, got rid of Molotov, Kaganovitch, Shepilov, and several other semi-titans, when they were attempting to get rid of *him*. Malenkov was dispatched to exile in a remote eastern region and put in charge of a factory there, and Molotov became ambassador to Outer Mongolia—also a long way from Moscow—for a time. Interestingly enough, none of those whom Mr. K. displaced were, so far as we know, sentenced to any term of imprisonment; certainly none were shot. Khrushchev was able to nip the Malenkov-Molotov plot in the bud by his control of the *party* apparatus, even though old-line Stalinists resented—and may still resent—his attitudes and policy. The next step came when Marshal Georgi K. Zhukov, minister of defense and boss of the Red Army, was sensationally eased out of office in October, 1957. Many so-called experts on Soviet affairs held for a long time that Zhukov "ran" Khrushchev; they were wrong. Mr. K. now had the field to himself, and in February, 1958, replaced the placid Bulganin as prime minister. Though he was sixty-four, he had never until that minute held anything but a party post—he had never been a cabinet minister or head of a government department.

For several years, however, it had been clearly apparent to those who had eyes in their heads that it was he who was running Russia. The 1958 reshuffle did no more than eliminate Bulganin and make the structure tidier.

The Personal Side

Photographs exaggerate Mr. K.'s ugliness—he is certainly ugly, but not so gross, so porcine, as some pictures indicate. People who see him on television miss something; the TV cameras take his mobility away, his pepperiness and color. He is one of those roly-poly stout little men— not really fat—who are fast on their feet, almost airy. He leans forward alertly, almost as if he were on tiptoe, when he talks, and his supple mouth is as a rule a tiny bit open, as if his eagerness to devour whatever experience is coming cannot be checked. He has a silver fringe of hair, an upturned nose, three small chins, and twinkling, very dark small eyes set widely apart and deep. It is hard to tell their color—probably deep brown. Two gold teeth shine when he smiles, and a gap is noticeable between the two upper front teeth; he has one mole, or wart, next to his nose on the left cheek, and another under his right eye.

Khrushchev wears as a rule pale suits and a peculiar sort of nylon-type shirt—off-white or cream in color, with a low-lying collar, almost like that of a sport shirt, but with full-length sleeves and cuffs, which are fastened with formal links. He looks, even in winter, as if he had planned to go to a yachting party, and then changed his mind when half dressed.

Khrushchev's manner is that of a rogue who, except when in one of his rages, enjoys being roguish. He is a kind of monster, but not an unattractive monster—what the British call a "card."

He speaks out as he pleases—straight out—and has been guilty of all manner of indiscretions. He is the only member of the Kremlin "team" who cares, or dares, to be indiscreet, and out of this arises his reputation not merely for bluntness, but for crudity. But he is good-humored as a rule, and anecdotes about him sound coarser than they really are. Once he meandered amiably across a crowded room [in Moscow,] went up to a foreign lady of great rank notable for her dignified aloofness, nuzzled her on the neck, and murmured, "My little white pigeon!"

He can betray truly horrible lack of taste. At a Yugoslav reception late in 1956 he called out to a French journalist in a loud voice, "I've just heard a good joke. Eden is sick. Do you know what he's suffering from? Inflammation of the Canal!"

At one party, when a member of a visiting delegation commented on the fact that so many Russian women work, Khrushchev horrified the guests by replying cheerfully, "Yes, our women work, and they are honest women—not like women in France, who are all whores!"

Khrushchev is a tough egg, and understands tough talk. He said to his host, after one particularly noisy reception, "This has been too crowded and confused." The host, who represented a quite important country, replied icily, "In that case don't bother to come again." Khrushchev was startled, but accepted the rebuff with good humor.

When arrangements were being made for the visit of Marshal Tito of Yugoslavia to the Crimea, correspondents at a press conference tried to worm details out of Khrushchev. Daniel Schorr of the Columbia Broadcasting System, a lively and penetrating interlocutor, fished around with various questions, trying to pin Khrushchev down as to the date, so that he could be there. Khrushchev turned to him finally with exasperated irony, "Mr. Schorr, I think that we will manage to have our meeting without you!" One cannot imagine any other figure in Soviet history indulging in conversation of quite this sort. Certainly it is impossible to imagine the Napoleonic Stalin doing so.

And, of course, during his trips to the United States, he displayed elements of personality ranging all the way from the crude and outrageous to the prankish. He is like some monstrous jellyfish with every tentacle vibrating.

But in making an estimate of Khrushchev one should not pay too much attention to the antics and the effervescence. The chief constituents of his character are robust common sense, ruthlessness, a drive to get things done, and, above all, optimism and confidence. He is supple, wily, and enjoys his job. Another quality is quickness. In India he promised to set up in Moscow a school for the study of Indian languages; it was done at once. He is peppery, practical, and likes projects. John Fischer, editor of *Harper's Magazine,* served on the UNRRA mission to the Ukraine, and had opportunity to watch Khrushchev in action there; he was much struck with the way he seemed "to get his main fun out of life out of conceiving and pushing through a variety of grandiose schemes." Finally, his political canniness and intuition are advanced. When the Israeli attack on Egypt got under way in 1956, Khrushchev told K. P. S. Menon, the Indian ambassador, that the British were certain within a matter of hours to deliver ultimata to *both* Israel and Egypt. He had the future moves worked out. And, an hour later, news came through that the British had indeed done just what Khrushchev predicted. Mr. Menon was so impressed by this that he wondered if Khrushchev could possibly have had secret information about it, but he had not.

Khrushchev is extraordinarily articulate and well informed on an abundant variety of matters. In London he attended several conferences at 10 Downing Street, thrashing out issues with members of the British government. Most of those present were flanked with advisors, and had large stacks of printed matter before them. Khrushchev talked, and talked well, without ever referring to a single note, or asking advice from anyone.

On the other hand, largely because he is a prisoner of dogma and therefore crazily suspicious of western methods and institutions, he can be remarkably obtuse at times. He was convinced for instance that the British could not possibly have undertaken the Suez adventure without American foreknowledge and approval; he flatly refused to believe Ambassador Charles E. Bohlen when Bohlen told him that President Eisenhower knew nothing whatever of the British invasion plans, and was much surprised when presently the United States insisted on the cease-fire.

Then too his ignorance is marked in several fields. For instance he was extremely impressed by the fact that when he and Bulganin went out in the streets of London, the crowds behaved respectfully, but without much excitement or enthusiasm. Later Khrushchev turned to one of his British friends and said how much he admired the way the British authorities had arranged with the police to see to it that the crowds behaved in exactly this manner! He simply could not believe it when he was told that no instruction had been given to the police—or to the crowds—and that the way people reacted to him was perfectly genuine and spontaneous.

Historical details from the past always interest him. When he went

out to Chequers, the weekend country house used by British prime ministers, he could not take his eyes off a drawing which showed the way
Chequers looked in the seventeenth century. (It hasn't changed much
since.) Khrushchev was astounded at this example of British continuity,
and kept muttering about what a sharp contrast it made to Russia. For
instance, when Chequers was already a comfortable place to live in, the
city of St. Petersburg did not even exist, and Moscow was still an unkempt combination of oriental village, fort, and trading post.

Also, one should not neglect his irascibility. When Mr. Macmillan,
visiting Moscow on the trip which opened the way to the Summit Conference, happened one morning to say that he had a high regard for
Chancellor Adenauer, Mr. K. at once erupted into fury—so much so that
the visit came close to being terminated on the spot. And, once more, we
must mention his outrageousness. Who but Khrushchev, on a trip to
Yugoslavia, would confound the Yugoslav authorities by inviting all the
plain-clothes men assigned to guard him, who had been pretending not
to be plain-clothes men, into his chambers to have a round of convivial
drinks? Who else, when he went to England, would have thought of
bringing a live bear cub as a gift to the Queen? And what other Communist leader would have said in his first public speech in New York,
"If you like capitalism—and I know that you like it—carry on and God
bless you!"[1]

His view is almost always practical. Once, according to Max Frankel
of the New York *Times*, he went so far as to say, "You cannot force
people into paradise," referring doubtless to the fact that there were
bound to be setbacks in the development of Soviet domestic policy.
However, it might well be noted that it is Khrushchev who decides what
"paradise" (presumably socialism) is, and he is certainly no stranger to
the use of force.

When Khrushchev first emerged on the public scene and made his
first forays abroad, usually in company with Bulganin, who looks like
a derelict Virginia landowner addicted to mint juleps, people were apt
to think that he was a clown, a drunkard, a buffoon. He likes to drink,
and has certainly been drunk on occasion; but just as certainly he is
not a drunkard. And, behind the fireworks, his hard core of belief and
utter fixity of aim were always evident if you chose to look for them.
Crankshaw tells a characteristic little story in his *Khrushchev's Russia*.
The prime minister, engaging a group of western diplomats in discussion
at a Moscow reception, clearly bested them. "Look at me!" he proceeded

---

[1] Of course, this remark must be judged in its context. Khrushchev also
said, "I speak bluntly so that you will know who you are dealing with. Such
clarity improves relations. But remember that a new social system, the socialist
system, has come into being. It is already treading on your heels and we are
reckoning on overtaking and outdistancing you."

to exclaim. "Here am I, a simple Communist. I worked with my hands. I never went to school. You great gentlemen went to the best schools in the world. You are trained professionals. And yet I make rings around you. Tell me why!"

Mr. K. and Mr. S.

The question is often asked, granting that Khrushchev will stay on top for some little time, whether he is more "dangerous" (to the free world) than Stalin was. The answer depends on definition. He is certainly less dangerous than Stalin in that he does not rule by iron caprice, and is more moderate, more flexible. Khrushchev is not likely to set off any such adventure as the Korean War. On the other hand, he is less cautious than Stalin, more indulgent. Also his very flexibility and moderation may, in the long run, serve to make the Soviet Union stronger vis-à-vis the United States, rather than weaker; relaxations may increase its power, not diminish it. Again the point might be made that by "respectabilizing" the Soviet Union, so to speak, Khrushchev is in a better position than Stalin to pull wool over the world's eyes, and delude neutrals and opponents.

Mr. K. was thickly tarred with Stalin's evil brush, but a major landmark of his career was certainly the spectacular six-hour speech he made to the Twentieth Party Congress in February, 1956, in which he repudiated the Stalinist cult of personality, re-expressed the policy of collective leadership, and, making sensational disclosures about the Stalinist terror, drew the veil off some of the most heinous of his predecessor's crimes. Then at the Twenty-second Party Congress in October, 1961, this process went even further. Stalin was not only defamed, but posthumously dethroned, and the decision was taken to remove his body from the mausoleum in Red Square where it had reposed next to Lenin's—both neatly embalmed and on public view—since 1953.

The 1956 speech, though it has dominated most of Communist thinking ever since all over the world, has never to this day been published in full in the Soviet Union—a suggestive commentary on Soviet methods. But the 1961 attack on Stalin became public knowledge almost at once, and, in their extraordinary way, the Russians dutifully switched around and began pulling down statues of Stalin which still survived all over the place, began the laborious task of rewriting encyclopedias and schoolbooks, and renamed various cities, even including Stalingrad.

De Gaulle on Khrushchev

When President Charles de Gaulle visited New York in April, 1960, the following colloquy took place at a press conference:

Q. A fundamental question, Mr. President, do you consider Khrushchev a man of good will, or does it make no difference?

A. I have had the advantage of personal contacts with Chairman Khrushchev recently when he was in France. We have talked a great deal and at great length on all the subjects in which the world is concerned and even passionately interested in at the present time. If you would like to know what I can see about the impression I drew from these contacts, I would tell you that Mr. Khrushchev seemed to me to be a strong personality. He is a man who has fought all his life for his ideas, and that has necesarily left a mark on him.

Actually I have the impression that at the level where he finds himself, he realizes, and he has realized, that the problems of the world are perhaps less simple than one thinks when one considers them from a single point of view. Moreover he is a man who is very knowledgeable on current problems, very well informed of people and things. In short . . . I do not think the Soviet Union could be represented by a man who better expresses what Russia is today, which, in my opinion—and this is my opinion—is no longer the Russia of yesterday, not even the Russia of ten years ago.[2]

Sources of Power, Attitudes, and the Character in Summary

Mr. K.'s basic sources of power are, I should say, six. First, the sheer overpowering force of his personality. Second, his painstakingly well-informed and ruthless control of the party machine. Third, the fact that most Soviet citizens are better off materially than they have ever been before. Fourth, he symbolizes termination of the terror—release from the depravities of Stalin's police. Fifth, he stands for peace, which every Russian wants. Sixth, he personifies vividly the stamina and extraordinary singleness of purpose of the Soviet regime.

One of the things that struck Americans most in Khrushchev's television interview on CBS was his remark that the grandchildren of his listeners would be living under socialism. This is an old line of his, and he really believes it, devoutly. He said the same thing to the British in London. In other words he expects the socialization of the world within about fifty years. After all, about a third of it is socialized already. But this marks a recession in his thinking; a few years ago, he was wont to say that the *children*, not grandchildren, of present-day citizens of the West would be socialist.

Khrushchev believes in peace and coexistence, if only because such concepts, in his opinion, favor his ultimate goal [which is to win the world without a war]. But let no one think that he will withdraw one inch from several elements in Marxism. Some time ago a newspaperman asked him if the "new look" of Soviet foreign policy was genuine. He replied that he wanted peace, cooperation, and good relations with the West, yes, and then added what has become the most famous of all his

[2] New York *Times*, April 26, 1960.

off-the-cuff remarks: "If you think that peace means giving up socialism, you can wait until the shrimp learns to whistle."

What Khrushchev hates most is NATO and the American overseas bases, because these confront him with the possibility of retaliation in the event of war. What he fears most, basic American strength aside, is West German rearmament. What he wants most, next to Soviet advance, is disarmament. What annoys him most is the situation in Berlin and West Germany.

One aspect of his character can be clarified by keeping in mind always that he is, above everything, a peasant—cunning, tenacious, glib, impertinent, proud—always so proud!—with a gift for coarse repartee and wearing chips on his shoulders as big as epaulets.

Elements in the Power Pattern

Mr. K. certainly runs the Soviet Union today, but it is important to point out that government is still collegial. Khrushchev dominates, but he dominates through consultation: there is no doubt that, in the last analysis, he is "accountable to a power entity,"[3] namely the 135 members of the Central Committee of the party and its Presidium (14 full members, 7 alternates). He can bully the party; cajole it; pack it; talk it into doing things it doesn't like; and conduct extraordinarily intricate maneuvers within its body—but he cannot ignore it. One proof of this is that, if government were *not* collective, Khrushchev would not dare leave Moscow so often and for such extended trips. Dictators never let their thrones get cold. Stalin did not leave Russia more than once or twice in thirty years. But Mr. K. sails all over the place without care, to the most distant points, which can only mean that he has no fear of being eliminated in his absence—also that the regime has been institutionalized to the extent that his associates can take important routine decisions no matter where he is.

As a matter of fact, not merely has the dictatorship become liberalized to an extent, but severe opposition may be expressed to the prime minister on occasion. To the surviving Stalinist element Mr. K. is still a highly unorthodox type, and the right-wing dogmatists, like Mikhail A. Suslov, have never accepted fully his volatility, tendency to improvise, and willingness to negotiate with heretics like Tito.

There are several dangerous points at issue. One is China. The Chinese Communists, dogmatists to the bone, can still quote the orthodox litany of Marx and Lenin, which Khrushchev cannot, because he has cut himself off from the support of traditional dogma. Second, agriculture. Two disastrous crop failures in a row have come to the Virgin Lands,

[3] Richard H. Rovere, "Letter from Below the Summit," *The New Yorker*, May 28, 1960.

and agriculture is, as always, the sorest subject in the Soviet Union. If further crop failures should occur in Kazakhstan or elsewhere Krushchev might very easily find himself in grave trouble. Finally, quite without regard to dogma or concrete issues, there are always questions of power politics to consider—outs wanting to be in. All this being said, Khrushchev is an extremely wary operator, his control of the party machine is firm, and he dominates most of his fellows like a giant among pygmies.

~~~~~~

Mr. K. was ousted from power in October, 1964. All three of the points at issue which I mention immediately above played a role. Obviously Khrushchev was astounded at being dismissed. His optimism and confidence were, right up to the last moment, undimmed. Once, when Mr. K. was visiting New York, a reporter asked him "who ran the store while he was away"; he replied with a kind of gay contempt, seeming to be perfectly sure of his own position, "My grandsons—Nikita, Alexei, and my third grandson who is also a Nikita." But that bit of talk took place in 1961, and by 1964 much of Khrushchev's power had been ground away.

No matter how grossly Mr. K. may be condemned later, in the well-known Soviet manner, his place in Russian history will be secure in the mind of any reasonably objective historian for a long time to come, if only because he was the man who made the transition from Stalinism at its bleakest to the technocrat-oligarchs of the future. He is not a nice man, but his gifts are great and his accomplishments distinct. For one thing he put Soviet theory on a new tack by repudiating to a degree two formerly basic Marxist tenets—that parliamentary government is never anything more than a mockery, and that violence is essential for the transformation of society.

This is not to say that violence may not come. But in the perspective of today, 1964, it should be remembered that (a) Mr. K. stepped down before President Kennedy's bold and vigorous stance in the great crisis over Cuba in 1962, and (b) signed the test ban treaty. Moreover, as is mentioned above, he scrapped the Leninist hypothesis that war between the Communist and capitalist countries is inevitable, and espoused (on his own terms, of course) the cause of "peaceful," competitive coexistence.

General Eisenhower once said something quite pertinent about Mr. K. (New York Times, *February 17, 1962) "I think he very much wants peace . . . he would make as good an agreement as he could, as long as he didn't have to open up his country."*

To conclude let me mention the prodigious coup de théâtre *Mr. K.*

put on during the UN General Assembly in New York in September, 1960. This was Mr. K.'s second visit to the United States and he came (by slow boat) uninvited. Rather he appointed himself chairman of the USSR delegation to the Fifteenth Assembly, and thus could not be kept away. American authorities restricted his movements to Manhattan and the Soviet enclave on Long Island; but this, even if it was an annoyance, did not daunt him, and from the balcony of the Soviet embassy on Park Avenue he made naughty little quips about "being under house arrest." I watched him closely at several receptions. The picture was always the same. Nehru, Nasser, Tito, Sukarno, Castro, Gomulka, Macmillan, Hammarskjöld, Eisenhower were all in New York at one time or other, but Khrushchev was the star. No matter who else turned up at a party, few guests had eyes for anybody except Mr. K. He would bounce into the room, pudgy and smiling, leaning earnestly forward, to be swallowed up instantly by a pushing, shouldering mob of the curious. One of Khrushchev's prime qualities, which all true stars have, is magnetism. In New York he was not only crude, outrageous, and prankish, but resilient, unquenchable, ribald, tenacious, and a man with a positive genius for saying the last word. At times he seemed to have forgotten all about the collapse of the Summit four months before, and it did not even occur to him that there were good reasons why President Eisenhower, whom he had wantonly insulted, might not be happy to receive him.

Mr. K. described the Security Council as a spittoon, and, as became famous, tore off his shoe during a speech at the Assembly, waving it and banging with it on his desk. In shirtsleeves he conducted nocturnal interviews from his perch at the Soviet embassy with newspapermen clamoring on the street twenty feet below, sang one night a few bars of the Communist hymn, "The International," and even, in a mock gesture of respect, pretended to be leading an orchestra and "conducted" a few passages from "The Star-Spangled Banner." He joked with Edmund Stevens, the correspondent in Moscow of Time, *about his beard, compared some hostile demonstrators in the street to the material that one may find under a horse, and, when he was roundly booed by a group of fashionable dowagers at the Hotel Plaza, roundly shouted "Boo!" to them in return.*

He scooted up to Harlem to visit Dr. Fidel Castro, denounced the Monroe Doctrine, and solicitously asked Marguerite Higgins of the New York Herald Tribune, *who had recently given birth to a child, whether the infant was a boy or a girl. He conceded that the police in New York behaved well, in the manner of good police everywhere, said that he felt that he ought to stay long enough in America to justify his expense account, and told journalists that he did not expect to start a war that night so that they could go home and sleep in peace. When a reporter asked him if the Russian government was elected by the people he replied, "Didn't you know that in our country we have no trousers to wear? Really, run quick and find out."*

It is just possible that, in addition to the reasons I have already given, hi-jinks of this playful type contributed to Mr. K.'s downfall. The Kremlin has no sense of humor, and does not approve of jinks high or low. In any case the irony is conspicuous. Khrushchev, who had repudiated the Stalinist cult of personality, fell from power when his own personality became too marked.

CHAPTER 39

〰〰

Inside England 1964

〰〰〰〰〰〰〰〰〰〰〰〰〰〰〰〰〰〰

I went to England to do this article for Look *in the autumn of 1963. It was printed in April, 1964.*

───────────────────────────────

Against a backdrop of unprecedented complexity, two men, comparatively untried, comparatively unknown, have begun an implacable struggle for the future of Britain. Seldom in a British contest for power have two antagonists been so sharply antithetical in character, or represented such diametrically opposing views.

One of these two men is, of course, the new Conservative prime minister, formerly the Earl of Home. He tossed his coronet into the Thames in October, 1963, in order to be able to sit in the House of Commons. Thus surrendering a peerage that went back six centuries, he became Sir Alexander Frederick Douglas-Home, a commoner, but he continued to be a millionaire aristocrat, great landowner, hunter of grouse and fisher for salmon, suave, balanced, cultivated, and a quintessential embodiment of what many people consider to be the curse of modern Britain—class.

The other, Harold Wilson, leader of the Labour party, is almost as archetypical of the new world as Home appears to be of the old. Wilson, the son of an industrial chemist in Yorkshire, is totally self-made—an intellectual, a man with devout belief in technical proficiency, a social scientist, brilliant, cool, lonely, anticlass, antiprivilege, antiaristocracy, a creature not of moors and thistle, but of blueprints and economic design.

Sir Alec Frederick Douglas-Home is perfectly tempered, the exquisitely carved end product of fourteen generations of Scottish lairds. Wilson has called him an "elegant anachronism." But it would probably be an error to think that, just because he is an aristocrat, Home has the weaknesses common to most worn-out aristocracies—effeteness, decay, the air of being exempt. In actual fact, he has pith, fiber, and a clean, hard intellect, as well as charm. His predecessor as prime minister, Harold Macmillan, once said of Sir Alec, "A wonderful little man—iron painted to look like wood." But how much he concretely knows about the angry pressures of the modern world remains to be seen.

He has also been described as looking like an "important senior faun." He is gaunt, almost frail, and displays a twinkle. Wilson, by contrast, resembles a cherub—compact, bright, brisk, with rosy cheeks under thick silver hair.

The forthcoming election, which must take place before November, 1964, has been characterized by an able British commentator as a struggle between the Establishment and the multitude. But this is perhaps an oversimplification. Certainly, Douglas-Home represents the Establishment, but the dominant factor of the Tory party is not as obscurantist or reactionary as it sometimes seems to be. The fact is that when Macmillan was forced to give up the leadership because of sudden illness, it was split open like a kidney on a skewer over the leadership issue. This explains the fantastic charade of last October, when the Tories found themselves unable to pick a new leader. Candidates like R. A. (Rab) Butler, Lord Hailsham and Reginald Maudling failed. Macmillan, conducting almost intolerably dramatic negotiations from his sickbed, sounded out the party, and Home emerged as his personal last-ditch candidate.

Wilson, on his side, is certainly a people's man, but not exactly a member of the "multitude." He is too choosy for that—by no means a burly representative of the crowds at large, a mob orator or demagogue. His mind is cold, and his posture dry. What Wilson stands for mostly is a concept that, in a peculiar way, overrides the old categories of right and left, although he is obviously more leftist than rightist. He stands for education, reform, and, above all, the application of science to government. Clearly, the Labour party does not command a monopoly on such subjects, but Wilson, a devout and dedicated Labour man, thinks that his party will really get results. His approach is not theoretical, but pragmatic.

To understand the programs the two party leaders offer, we must take a close look at the Britain they hope to lead. Most of the economic indicators are favorable, trade is lively, and people have money to spend, although the overall rate of economic growth lags behind that of the Common Market, and unemployment—even though patchy and only 2 percent of the total labor force—is more pressing a problem in some areas than at any time since World War II.

The railways are in ghastly shape, and the country's narrow, twisting roads, to say nothing of city streets, can no longer bear the fierce burden of traffic imposed on them. A great deal of poverty remains, although wages are way up. Britain still has shameful slums, obsolete housing, and derelict dockyards. Some industrial plants and procedures are almost inconceivably antiquated.

But many Britons are enjoying luxuries. More than three million of them take holidays on the continent every year. Hotels are full, restaurants crowded, taxis hard to get, and everybody who wants a drink seems to be having one—provided that the grotesquely out-of-date licensing hours permit. Money spent on gambling is at a fantastic high—the equivalent of more than $3.5 billion, or about $68 per person per year. Above all, people dress better. The kitchen where your maid works may still be in a noisome cellar, but the youthful maid, even if her clothes are cheap, looks chic. Upper-class British women seem to be as well dressed as Frenchwomen. The legend of the "dowdy British" is no more.

For all this, I do not think that the British are in an altogether happy state. Generalizations are risky, but the rank and file of citizens seem apathetic about the future, despondent, or confused. Deep heart-searching goes on among the intellectuals. A perspicacious Frenchman told me in Paris, before I set out for London, "You will find England quite revealing—it is having a nervous breakdown." Most of the classic symptoms of nervous breakdown are indeed discernible—depression, self-doubt, unsettlement, fatigue. A German told me, "Yes, the British are prosperous, so much so that they do not realize as yet that they are swimming in ice water."

During last fall's Blackpool conference of the Tory party, I was startled by a headline in the *Sunday Telegraph,* a distinguished Conservative newspaper, reporting a speech by a leading minister: PLEDGE TO KEEP BRITAIN A FIRST-CLASS NATION. Such a headline would have been almost inconceivable in the leonine days of British power.

The wits are merciless in their jibes at the Establishment—and practically everything else as well. What England seems to lack, above all, is an objective. Hence, unity is lacking.

I asked one high-standing civil servant, a former don, what his children, aged eighteen and sixteen, talked about, and he replied, without showing much pleasure in the reply, "Nothing!" Compared to American youngsters, London boys and girls seem to be less fresh, more supercilious, tired, bored. Those in their twenties seem to have little, if any, interest in politics—unlike their parents, who, at the same age, were fighting the war against Hitler. This phenomenon has led several British thinkers to express alarm about the lack of rapport between the older and younger generations. Perhaps there is a good reason for this—the older generation did not transmit the vital essence of what England was. Anyway, tell today's youngsters that the Empire is gone, and they yawn.

What all this adds up to is that the British are in a period of transition—painful transition. The last twelve or fourteen months have been among the cruelest and most disillusioning in recent history. But anybody who thinks that Britain is "done" or "finished" as a result of its recent tribulations is just plain silly. Back in the 1930's, Oxford boys by the carload signed pledges not to fight for king or country. A few years later came the Battle of Britain—and they fought, and fought superbly.

However, let us examine the present record. All through 1963, the British suffered mishap after mishap—in almost every sphere, even the weather. The winter was abnormally severe. Power services broke down, electricity ran short, industry creaked, people shivered. It seemed that the country could no longer physically run itself; the antique machine proved unable to withstand a prolonged emergency. There came a variety of other shocks. The great Buckinghamshire train robbery seemed to cast doubt on the efficiency of one of the most revered of all British institutions, Scotland Yard. Then—something altogether unprecedented in this century—a British monarch was publicly booed in the streets. This occurred when Queen Elizabeth and the Duke of Edinburgh attended a theatrical performance accompanied by King Paul and Queen Frederika of Greece. The event had little, if any, significance in the large, since it derived from resentment by a minuscule group protesting developments in Greek—not British—politics. The British Royal Family is the most unshakable of institutions. Nevertheless, the fact remains: The Queen of England was booed, hissed, and greeted with cries associating her companions with fascism.

Then consider Skybolt. This was the air-to-ground missile which was to have been the core of Britain's nuclear defense. At the Nassau conference between President Kennedy and Prime Minister Macmillan, the United States decided to abandon further development of Skybolt, and communicated this decision to the British in no uncertain terms. To soften the blow, the U.S. offered to sell Britain the Polaris missile instead. Polaris, as everybody knows, is a missile designed primarily to be fired from nuclear-powered submarines.

No doubt Polaris is a better weapon than Skybolt, but the British were profoundly shocked. They have no Polaris-firing submarine at present, and their first one will not be ready for service until 1968. So they found themselves out on a long limb on a prime matter of defense. What the loss of Skybolt meant, even though Skybolt itself was by no means ready for use, was that they could no longer look forward to an effective nuclear deterrent of their own. This is a complex and fiercely controversial subject; plenty of Britons do not want to have any nuclear deterrent of their own. Nevertheless, the Skybolt decision was a blow. "The Skybolt did more damage to Anglo-American relations than anything since the war," a senior M.P. told me. "Our nuclear capacity, that is, our status as a great power, was mortally damaged, and now depends on you. Yet, because you failed to carry on with Skybolt, we cannot get over the feeling that you, the Americans, no longer need us and hence are not reliable."

Next came an even greater blow. President Charles de Gaulle knocked Britain out of the European Economic Community, or Common Market, just as negotiations for British entrance had finally come to a head—after years of on-again, off-again parleying. The shock was penetrating. To be black-balled by a Frenchman!—it was almost too much to bear. But, in the view of many, the British got no more than they deserved. They had vigorously opposed the Common Market in the first instance, attempted to sabotage it, set up a rival organization, and shilly-shallied interminably about joining until it became clear that it was to their advantage to do so. For the British themselves had been sharply divided on the Common Market. In the end, the Tory party took a pro-Common Market position; Labour was split.

For the time being at least, de Gaulle's veto annulled what would have been a great and seminal event—British adhesion to a continental system. It shut Britain off from closer economic association with Europe. The Atlantic Alliance was shaken, because de Gaulle, acting against the British, was also acting against the United States, and British relations with France were severely damaged.

Next came the Profumo-Keeler scandal, which in its grisly turn followed the Vassall scandal. The Profumo affair is supposed to be dead and decently buried, but when I was in Britain people still talked about it with extreme vociferousness. In September, 1963, came publication of the Denning Report, which was supposed to liquidate the business once for all. As soon as it appeared I asked almost every Londoner I met, "Granted that the Profumo affair hurt the government, does the Denning Report redress this situation?" Answers were mixed. The report allayed certain fears about security, dissipated to an extent an enormous mass of fantastically ugly and salacious rumors about other (unnamed) ministers, and made it clear that Macmillan and other leading members of the Tory party had been hoodwinked by John Profumo's first protestations of innocence. But Lord Denning left several questions unanswered, opened others, and did not altogether put to rest the apprehension that things were very, very rotten in some of the best circles in Britain.

One little joke—clean enough to print—is that the initials "B.C."

and "A.D." acquired new meanings—"Before Christine" and "After Denning."

Mr. Profumo himself, it seems, was not so much blamed by the public at large for moral dereliction as he was for flagrantly lying in the House of Commons. That he had lied to his wife, his friends, and his colleagues in the government might be forgiven, but not that he had lied to the House of Commons. *That,* as I heard it put, was spitting on the floor of the club. One limerick that went the rounds was:

> There was a young lady, Christine,
> Who upset the party machine.
> They knew it was lewd
> To lie in the nude,
> But to lie in the House is obscene.

The significance of the Profumo affair was not so much that, along with the Argyll case, it exposed some lively shenanigans in British society, but that the authorities handled it with such incompetence and lack of savvy. Moreover it was a blow to good old British pride that a British *government* could have been shaken to its roots—almost made to fall— by so squalid and undignified an affair. How could leaders be trusted in great affairs of the realm when they had been so ostrichlike and inept in dealing with a secretary of state for war who had slept with a tart?

Finally, in this general area of British discomfiture, comes the most important item of all—loss of the Empire, which began in a large way when India became independent in 1947. Everybody has been aware for a long time that Burma is gone, Eire is gone, Cyprus is gone, Egypt and the Sudan are gone, Singapore is gone, most of British Africa is gone. But it seems that this prodigious evolution is only now beginning to sink in and become an emotional reality to the average Briton. Citizens are beginning to recognize at last the consequences of the loss in the simplest human terms. In the old days, elite youngsters went into the Foreign Office, Colonial Office or armed forces to serve the Empire. Now they go into insurance companies, public relations or TV. Conversely, men who have given thirty years of their professional lives as devoted, seasoned civil servants in former colonial territories, or, for that matter, as hardworking plantation owners in East Africa or Malaya, are trickling back to London—not to be promoted to governorships or important positions in the City, but to become—secretary of the local golf club. Bewildered, they don't know where else to go.

The Empire meant not only physical panoply, but power and purpose. It was lucrative. It was also very useful strategically and as a repository of military manpower. Few Britons, except a minority of extreme diehards, think it possible to regain the old imperial power. With grace, the British have made the best of their demotion. Mr. Mac-

millan wants to go down into history as "the deliverer of Africa." Patterns
change quickly. During my recent stay in London, the British embassy
in Jakarta was burned down by a howling mob. Thirty years ago, that
would have meant the instantaneous dispatch of a British gunboat—
at the very least—to Indonesian shores. Today, the incident went almost unnoticed.

Often, in talking about the tremendous readjustment made necessary by the loss of Empire, the Briton will say, "Ah, but we have the
Commonwealth instead!" But have they? The Commonwealth is still
there, and is a strong emotional reality, but it is certainly not the Commonwealth that was. Ties are still close between Britain and the so-
called "White Commonwealth," or old dominions—Canada, Australia,
and New Zealand—but the story is not quite the same with newly
emerging states in Africa that have risen to Commonwealth membership. For one thing, the new countries tend to become republics; hence,
the symbol of the British monarch as a unifying force is weaker. For
another, a country like Ghana, let us say, is apt to have closer ties to its
African neighbors than to other members of the Commonwealth, and
is much more likely to vote at the UN with the new Afro-Asia bloc. In
fact, the Commonwealth "bloc" at the UN can scarcely be said to exist
any longer.

Britain is, in plain fact, no longer as necessary to various Commonwealth members as it was. Even the "White Dominions" do not have as
intimate an association with the mother country as before. Putting things
very roughly, the basis of association in former days was the exchange
of industrial goods provided by Britain for raw materials produced by
the Commonwealth. But now, Canada, Australia, and even New Zealand, although still closely linked to Britain emotionally, are eager to
achieve their own industrialization. Australia is moving closer to Asia
in matters of trade day by day, and Canada (despite some harsh political quarrels) to the U.S. A final point is that several Commonwealth
members bitterly resented the British attempt to dive at the last moment
into the Common Market. They felt snubbed and put at a disadvantage.

Where, then, are the British going to go? Former Secretary of State
Dean Acheson said in a recent speech that "Great Britain has lost an
empire and has not yet found a role." Harold Wilson thinks that the new
role will be scientific leadership—intensification of scientific and technical development, the application of scientific research to industry, and
planning. Science is to be the British "new frontier."

In an effort to discover what course Britain might follow if Labour
were returned to power, I had a vivid forty-minute talk with Wilson.
This is a most exceptional man. His manner is disarmingly casual, but
his eyes shine like blue marbles, and his talk goes fast—very fast.

Smooth, chunky, fit, he puffed intermittently at the pipe that is one of his trademarks. Wilson is forty-eight.

His outstanding characteristics and sources of power are, I would say, (a) fixity of aim, (b) brains, and (c) equanimity. Some people say that he is "bloodless," but I do not find him so. I have known him from previous years and have always found him friendly in the extreme, although he is perhaps hard to reach. He is quite capable of playing rough if necessary. One of his adversaries told me that he was an "unpleasantly" first-rate operator, and people complain that they do not know where they stand with him, that he hates to take unpopular decisions, and that his ambition leads him to opportunism. He is accused of having been politically shifty in 1960 when he contested unsuccessfully for the leadership of the Labour party against the late Hugh Gaitskell, one of the most decent and high-minded as well as ablest men of modern times.

Gaitskell did not like Wilson. The party was badly split. After severe infighting, Wilson, who has the inestimably valuable political asset of being lucky, inherited Gaitskell's position when Gaitskell died early in 1963. I asked a dozen Labourites if, in their opinion, the party is better equipped to win the election under Wilson now than it was under Gaitskell. The answer was generally yes, although Gaitskell is grievously missed. Gaitskell was much more elevated than Wilson, but, most of my friends said, he could not have given Labour the effective leadership that Wilson, with his hard drive and ability, is providing.

One curiosity about Wilson is that he and his wife almost never entertain at home—this, too, in a country extravagantly given to mixed dining-out and social gregariousness. I met man after man, including several of his closest associates, who had never been inside his modest house in Hampstead. Another oddity is his method of exercising. Occasionally, he snatches an hour and plays golf—alone!

Something else little known about him is his close acquaintanceship with Soviet Russia. Not even remotely has he any Communist affiliations or sympathies, but he has visited Russia ten or eleven times, because of a job. For some years he was economic advisor to the Montague-Meyer timber interests and went to Moscow regularly to negotiate for British purchases of Russian timber. Wilson knows the Russians, understands them, and is not likely to be misled by them—or anybody else. His alertness and adroitness have led to the comment that he is the only Englishman alive with "built-in radar."

James Harold Wilson is a man dominated by facts. There are no stars in his eyes—only figures. One of his closest friends told me that he typifies the anonymous white-collar middle class much more than the conventional Labourite. He personifies the nameless bank clerk, the traveling salesman, the accountant slowly climbing the long ladder in an insurance company, the hard-working bureaucrat in a government office.

Wilson never went to what the British call a "public" (i.e., private) school. He won a scholarship at Oxford, and became a don at the astoundingly early age of twenty-one. He taught economics, but he is altogether nondoctrinaire, nonideological, and economics in the abstract did not interest him. Essentially, I heard it put, Wilson is a statistician. He thinks not in terms of social theory, but of making the best possible use of the present economy and expanding it under scientific controls.

The things he believes in are the Labour party, himself as an instrument of the Labour party and, above all, progress and reform. He wants to reform practically everything in Britain—from the educational system to the pattern whereby junior brains in industry and government are only seldom able to penetrate upward through the crusty, outmoded, antiscientific "old boy" layers of the powerful British Establishment.

Wilson began political life as a Liberal. He became a Labourite, won a seat in Parliament in 1945, and became president of the Board of Trade at the age of thirty-one, the youngest cabinet minister since the second William Pitt. As such, he says jokingly, he was "Minister for Private Enterprise." A strong socialist, he nevertheless got on well with business. His position in the party today is left of center, approximately to the degree that Gaitskell was right of center, but if he becomes prime minister, circumstances may force him to become less leftish. A man has to be bigger than himself to be prime minister.

Wilson took a strong line against the Common Market, and is thought to be vaguely anti-European. He wants at all costs to keep nuclear weapons out of German hands and is extremely skeptical about the possibility that Britain can maintain its own nuclear deterrent. But he supports NATO and is a profound believer in the Commonwealth. What about his attitude toward the United States? One of his closest associates puts it this way: "Harold's view is roughly the same as that of Wladyslaw Gomulka, the Communist leader of Poland, in regard to Russia. He thinks that we certainly have to get along with the Americans, and that it is therefore good policy to try to humor and please them. Moreover, if we want to be able to exert any influence on them, we've got to accept the fact that they're the boss, while doing our best to maintain our own policy."

Labour's chief talking points in this year's election will be: (1) The Tory party is utterly played out, unfit to govern; (2) after thirteen years, it is high time for a change; (3) the two-party system demands alternations in government if democracy itself is to survive. The chief Tory point that Labour, to win, must rebut is that Labour's seminationalization program will take good times away. The Tories will assert that they must "save Britain from socialism."

Both parties have, of course, been thrown off course by the uncharted currents flowing through today's world. "Labour," I heard it said, not altogether seriously, "looks back yearningly to the bad old days —before the affluent society." The Tories, on their side, look back to the "good old days" when the British fleet ruled the seas, and there were no such nasty things as nuclear deterrents. As a matter of fact, Labour has taken on rightist tinges, and progressive Tories have moved steadily toward the left. It was Labour that joined the United States in Korea and started work on the British atomic bomb, and it was the Tories who gave Africa away. (But a Labour Government had taken the lead in the process of imperial breakup by giving freedom to India.)

The deepest domestic issue facing both parties is education. Almost everybody agrees that something must be done sooner or later so that the equivalent of a good public-school education (Eton, Winchester, Harrow) becomes available to the rank and file. Britain simply has not got enough educated men and women to make the machine work. Only 4 percent of British students go on to college. Analogous figures for the USSR are 15 percent; France, 22 percent; the U.S., 28 percent. Moreover, Britain's two levels of school and university education, one for the rich, one for the poor, make no sense in a modern society and are acutely damaging to the nation at large. Only by extension of education can Britain rid itself of caste—the class system. (The change is already under way, and seven new universities are to be created soon.)

Labour and the Tories do not differ much in foreign policy, although it is interesting—another example of how topsy-turvy things have become—that Labour, which usually takes an international position, tended on the whole to oppose the Common Market, whereas the traditionally nationalist Tories supported it. As to defense, the Conservatives think that Britain should maintain its own nuclear deterrent, however frail, at all costs. Labour wants to drop the deterrent, but maintain loyalty to NATO and the American alliance.

Now let us take a brief look at Sir Alec Frederick Douglas-Home. He became prime minister and leader of the Conservative party late in 1963 partly because of a double negative. Neither R. A. Butler, the deputy prime minister, nor Lord Hailsham, the cracklingly bright minister for science, was able to form a government in the shattering crisis of last October, as I have mentioned earlier. If Home had not been fished out by Macmillan and forced down everybody's throat as an acceptable compromise candidate, and if Butler had not agreed in the end to support him, a "dissolution" might have been necessary—adjournment of Parliament and the calling of a new general election at once. This would have meant that the Tories would have had to go into the electoral fight without any leader at all, and the result might well have been a catastrophe. Home was the alternative to disaster.

Even so, when he first emerged as a long-shot possibility during the Blackpool conference, it was difficult to take his candidature seriously. No peer had been prime minister since Lord Salisbury in 1902. Home had to surrender his peerage and seek a seat in the Commons, because the convention has become absolutely fixed that the British prime minister must be a commoner. (The title "Sir" in Home's present name does not count.) Lord Hailsham, trying desperately for the prime ministership himself, had just announced that he would give up *his* peerage and stand for the Commons, but Hailsham's viscountcy only went back one generation, and presumably meant little to him. Home's peerage, on the other hand, meant much. He was the fourteenth earl, and his barony dates from 1473. People thought at first he would not give all this up, and, moreover, that it would be "vulgar" for one peer to follow another so precipitously in throwing a peerage away. Then, too, the talk went, Home's renunciation of his title would give Labour the nice point of being able to say that the Tories had to pass over all their 360 MP's in the Commons to find a leader in the Lords. Above all, many felt that Home projected a disconcertingly nonmodern image. Even the *Sunday Times* published his photograph under the title "The Man Within the Ermine."

After a speech at Blackpool, where he was having to follow a very cagy line, Home dared reporters to try to find in his text any clue whatever to his own intentions, and offered as a reward the choice of a week's grouse hunt or a "salmon and whisky" dinner. This struck some critics as being very old-style indeed.

Home was born in London in 1903. He went to Eton, of course, and then Christ Church, Oxford. At Eton he was called "the most unambitious boy in its history," and at Oxford his academic record was not distinguished. He was, however, a stubborn cricketer, and people liked him. He was modest and casual and, despite his heritage, never threw his weight around.

He went into politics as the natural thing to do, and won a seat in the Commons in 1931. His rise was slow, and he left little mark in his sixteen years there. (He had to give up his seat automatically when he succeeded to the earldom upon his father's death.) He did, however, become parliamentary private secretary to Neville Chamberlain, accompanied Chamberlain to Munich, and was a strong Munich man, on the ground that the Communists were a worse danger than Hitler.

In the Lords, Home filled several minor posts and then, in 1955, was chosen by Anthony Eden to be secretary of state for Commonwealth relations. In general, his tendencies were strongly right wing. Next, in 1960, Macmillan made him foreign secretary—an offbeat choice that surprised observers almost as much as his later choice of him as prime minister. At the Foreign Office, Home was competent, but hardly a ball of fire.

Home's chief qualities are probably tenacity, good humor, a wiry Scotch mind, and extreme decency and disinterestedness. This is a man who could never do anything false, tricky, or dishonorable. He is one of the best shots in England, and likes to collect butterflies, putter around the garden, arrange flowers, and watch birds.

Home has a lively and effective wit. When, after being named prime minister—the only prime minister in British history who for an interval did not have a seat in either Lords or Commons—he was chivied by the Labourites for having been the fourteenth Earl of Home, he replied mildly, "But isn't Mr. Wilson the fourteenth Mr. Wilson?"

He had a prolonged period of illness during World War II, when tuberculosis of the spine kept him prostrate, locked in a cast. Surgery cured him, and Sir Alec made a little joke to the effect that this was the first time anybody had ever performed the impossible task of putting a backbone into a politician.

When Home was summoned by the Queen and kissed hands on his appointment, Mrs. Barbara Castle, a well-known Labour M.P., said, "I just cannot believe it. The Tory party is bent on committing suicide." But, though Sir Alec's background may be feudal, he is not necessarily feudal himself, although certainly on the right. The Conservative party has undergone its worst crisis in a generation and is perhaps irremediably split, but Home himself is not to be dismissed lightly. It may even turn out that he will prove to be the hardest of all Tory candidates for Labour to beat.

Wilson won, but by a narrow squeak.

Index

Aba Dina, Ethiopia, 376
Abdullah ibn Hussein, King of Transjordan, 204, 218-10
Abyssinia, *see* Ethiopia
Abyssinian War, 20, 24, 25, 36, 113, 444
Académie Française, 111
Accra, Ghana, 389, 393 n., 395, 396, 399, 400
Acheson, Dean, 495
Achimota College, Accra, 395
Addis Ababa, Ethiopia, 375, 380, 382, 383, 385, 386, 387
Aden, 207, 380
Adenauer, Konrad, 449, 453-60, 461, 462, 464, 465, 467, 468, 482
Adenauer, Paul, 456
Adowa, Battle of, 377, 378
Afghan War (1919), 190
Africa, 126, 132, 345-60, 374-87, 388-402, 417-36, 494, 495, 498; *see also* North Africa
African Game Trails (Roosevelt), 244
African Students Association of America and Canada, 396
Aftermath, The (Churchill), 124, 129
Ah Chu (MacArthur's nursemaid), 290
Ahmedabad, India, 173
Ahmedabad University, 170
Air France, 473
Akher Saa, 363
Alamein, Battle of, 231, 232, 233, 235
Albania, 341
Alexander, Field Marshal Lord Rupert Leofric George, 229, 232, 233, 234-36
Alexander, King of Yugoslavia, 28, 111
Alexander II, Tsar of Russia, 453
Alexandra, Queen of England, 64, 443
Alexandria University, 368 n.
Algeria, 465, 470, 471
Algiers, Algeriam, 321, 345, 444
Allahabad, India, 188, 195, 196, 198, 202

All-African People's Congress (1958), 401
Al Senussi, Sherif Mohieddin, 359
Al Shalhi, Ibrahim Ahmed, 359
American Battle Monuments Commission, 317
American Colonization Society, 407, 408
American Federation of Labor, 263
Amery, Julian, 443
Amery, Leopold C. M. S., 217
Amharic language, 381
Amman, Max, 10
Amman, Transjordan, 209
Amritsar massacre, 174, 189, 190
Andreyev, Communist Party Secretary, 42
Ankara, Turkey, 94, 96
Anschluss, 70, 71, 73
Anti-Semitism, 12, 14, 66
Antwerp, Belgium, 127
Arabia, 204-08
Arab Legion, 210
Arden-Clarke, Sir Charles Noble, 390, 392, 393 n., 399, 400
Arif, Colonel, 94
Arms and the Covenant (Churchill), 128
Armstrong, Hamilton Fish, 15
Army of the Future, The (de Gaulle), 469
Arnall, Ellis, 255
Aryanism, 17
Asfa Wasan, Crown Prince of Ethiopia, 387
Ashcroft, Edward, 407 n.
Asia Magazine, 187
Asquith, Herbert, 122, 127, 442, 449
Associated Negro Press, 397
Astor, Lady Nancy, 41, 57
Aswan Dam, 372
Ataturk, Ghazi Mustafa Kemal, 21, 22, 82, 92-97, 98, 99

Atlanta, Georgia, 408
Atlantic Charter, 249
Atlantic Monthly, 139
Atomic bombs, 248, 256, 261, 307, 322, 498
Atsugi, Japan, 290
Attlee, Lord Clement, 135
Atwill, Lionel, 303
Aubervilliers, France, 108, 109
Augusta, U.S.S., 249
Auriol, Vincent, 309
Australia, 58, 296, 495
Austria, 18, 21, 68-73, 89, 98
Avanti, 22, 23, 25
Axum, Ethiopia, 378
Azaña, Don Manuel, 85
Aztecs, 222
Azzedine Bey, 356

Bagdad, Iraq, 209
Bakhunin, Mikhail A., 82
Baku, Russia, 44
Balabanov, Mme. Angelica, 21, 22
Balbo, Marshal Italo, 34, 359
Baldwin, Stanley, 58, 128, 287, 450, 452
Balfour, Lord Arthur, 135, 211, 212, 214, 442
Balfour Declaration, 214
Balkan states, 19, 327
Baltic states, 83
Baltimore, Maryland, 396
Banque de France, 111, 113
Barbados, 62
Barcelona, Spain, 85
Barclay, Edward, 412
Barnes, Joseph, 316
Barrow, Errol W., 62
Bartholdi, Frédéric Auguste, 422
Barthou, Louis, 111
Bartlett, Vernon, 15
Basle, Switzerland, 213
Bataan Peninsula, 295
Bath, England, 383, 385
Beardsley, C. R., 281
Beckett, Sir Gervase, 58
Bedouin Arans, 207, 358
Behar, India, 183
Behind the Curtain (Gunther), 327
Belgrade, Yugoslavia, 328, 330, 331, 332, 333, 337, 341
Beneš, Eduard, 52, 60, 91
Benghazi, Libya, 359
Benn, Wedgwood, 130
Berchtesgaden, Germany, 8
Berdugo, Albert E., 347
Bergson, Henri, 117
Beria, Laventi P., 478
Berlin, Germany, 57, 58, 59, 69, 82, 93, 234, 421, 461-64, 468, 485
Berlin airlift (1948), 462
Berliner Tageblatt, 58
Berlin University, 212
Bernard, Tristan, 117

Besse and Company, A., 380
Bethmann-Hollweg, Theobald von, 60
Betjeman, John, 451
Bibesco, Princess Elizabeth, 116
Birkenhead, Lord, 131
Bismarck, Prince Otto von, 88, 151, 242
Blackrock College, Dublin, 102
Blood Purge of 1934, 3
Blum, Léon, 111, 115-21, 466
Blum, René, 116
Blum, Thérèse Pereira, 119
Boer War, 126-27, 131, 171, 175
Bogdanoff, Communist Party Secretary, 41
Bohlen, Charles E., 475, 481
Boland Mills, Ireland, 102-03
Bolsheviks and Bolshevism, 24, 45, 50, 51, 132, 234, 477
Bombay, India, 171, 181, 183, 187, 196, 203
Bonn, Germany, 454
Borah, William E., 90
Bordeaux, France, 423, 433
Boston, Massachusetts, 268
Botha, Louis, 126
Bourdet, Claude, 347
Bourguiba, Habib, 360
Bowles, Chester, 265, 275, 281
Bradley, General Omar Nelson, 236, 314
Brahim, Si (Caid of Telourt), 348
Brandt, Willy, 453, 457, 461-64
Bratianu brothers, 64
Braun, Eva, 18
Brazil, 67, 226, 387
Brazzaville, Fr. Eq. Africa, 418
Brenner Pass, 71
Brentano, Heinrich von, 457
Briand, Aristide, 24, 72, 109, 110, 111, 112
Bridges, Harry, 255, 264
Brinker, John, 255
Britain, Battle of, 135, 252, 492
British Africa, 494
British Museum, 116
Bronxville, New York, 319
Brooke, Field Marshal Sir Alan, 229 n.
Browning, Gordon, 284
Brücker, Lieutenant, 8, 12, 15
Brundage, Henry M., 275, 277, 280
Brüning, Heinrich, 111 n.
Bruree, Ireland, 102
Bryce, Lord James, 261
Bubnov, Politboro member, 44
Bucharest, Rumania, 63, 64, 65, 66, 67, 337 n.
Budapest, Hungary, 253, 337
Buddha, 166
Buell, Raymond Leslie, 406 n.
Bukharin, Nikolai Ivanovich, 39, 85
Bulganin, Marshal Nikolai, 479, 481, 482
Bullitt, William C., 52
Burke, Adrian, 280
Burma, 234, 235, 494
Butcher, Captain Harry C., 314 n.

Butler, R. A., 445, 490, 498
Byas, Hugh, 145
Byrnes, James F., 251, 259, 266

Caillaux, Joseph, 110
Cairo, Egypt, 232, 235, 357, 362, 365, 369
Cairo Conference, 249
Calcutta, India, 191, 196
Calles, Plutarco Elías, 223
Camacho, Avila, 226
Cambridge University, 189
Cameroons, 401, 418
Campobello, New Brunswick, Canada, 245
Canada, 58, 236, 245, 395, 442, 495
Canada, Lieut. Colonel C. C., 304
Cannes Conference (1922), 24
Capek, Karel, 90
Cape Palmas, Liberia, 406, 411
Capus, Alfred, 117
Cárdenas, Cuauhtémoc, 221-22
Cárdenas y Del Rio, General Lázaro, 221-26
Cardinal's Mistress, The (Mussolini), 22
Carmack, Edward W., 284
Carnarvon, Lord, 31
Carol, King of Rumania, 63, 64-67
Casablanca Conference, 135, 244, 249, 250, 348
Caserta, Italy, 320
Castle, Barbara, 500
Castro, Fidel, 487
Cazalet, Captain Victor, 61
Cecil, Lord Hugh, 129
Cedillo, General, 225
Celtic, S.S., 103
Chamberlain, Sir Austen, 58, 59, 84
Chamberlain, Houston, 17
Chamberlain, Neville, 61, 91, 122, 128, 129, 499
Chamberlin, W. H., 39, 47
Chambrun, Count René de, 112-13
Chang Hsueh-liang ("Young Marshal"), 156, 157, 161
Chang Tso-lin, 156
Chankaya, Turkey, 96
Chaplin, Charlie, 185
Chatêldon, France, 108, 112
Chauri-Chaura episode, 175
Cherwell, Lord, 248
Chiang Kai-shek, Generalissimo, 155-65, 207, 288, 307
Chiang Kai-shek, Madame, 157, 158, 159, 160, 162, 163, 164
Chicago Daily News, 72, 204, 253
Chikow, China, 163
Chilston, Lord, 52
China, Communist, 87, 139, 148, 165, 202, 261, 262, 288, 300, 307, 341, 485
China, Nationalist, 155-65
China War (1937), 148, 150, 156
Chou En-lai, 87, 165
Christian Democratic Union (CDU), 457, 458, 459, 462, 464

Christiansborg Castle, Accra, 389-90
Churchill, Lady Clementine Ogilvy Hozier, 130, 132
Churchill, Lady Jennie Jerome, 124, 125, 248
Churchill, Lord Randolph, 124, 125
Churchill, Mary (Mrs. Duncan Sandys), 132
Churchill, Randolph, 132, 333
Churchill, Sarah (Mrs. Vic Oliver), 132
Churchill, Winston (American author), 130
Churchill, Sir Winston S., 36, 53, 59, 61, 122-36, 209, 217, 235, 236, 248-52, 253, 267, 301, 304, 313-14, 332, 347, 349, 444, 445, 471
Ciani, Countess Edda Mussolini, 26, 28, 29
Ciani, Count Galeazzo, 26
Clemenceau, Georges, 112, 472
Cleveland, Grover, 268
Clive, Robert, 298
Cody, "Buffalo Bill," 436
Cohen, Betty, 274, 277, 278, 280, 281
Cold War, 478
Collectivization, 47-49
Collier's Magazine, 388, 475
Cologne, Germany, 60, 456
Columbia University, 313, 317, 318, 319
Cominform (Communist Information Bureau), 327, 330, 336, 337-39
Comintern, see Third International
Common Market, European, 458, 490, 493, 495, 497, 498
Commonwealth, the British, 495, 497
Communist International, 38
Communists and Communism, 39, 41, 42, 51, 52, 53, 67, 77-87, 91, 109-10, 118, 121, 155, 156, 161, 165, 195, 198, 226, 256, 327-41, 369, 370, 373, 376, 388, 396-97, 459, 460, 463, 470, 475-88, 499
Comoedia, 118
Confucius, 160-61
Congo, 401, 402
Congress of Industrial Organizations, 266, 269
Coniston (W. Churchill), 130
Connally, Tom, 259, 260
Connelly, Matthew, J., 258
Considine, Bob, 307
Constantinople, Turkey, 92, 95, 235
Convention People's Party (CPP), 394, 399, 400
Cooke, John and Sarah Warren, 248
Coolidge, Calvin, 270
Copenhagen, Denmark, 77
Cosgrave, W. T., 104
Costelloe, Dr. Edward C., 278
Coussey, Sir J. Henley, 398
Cromwell, James, 303
Cromwell, Oliver, 125, 232
Crowder, General Enoch, 299

Crump, E. H. ("Ed"), 283-87
Crump & Company, E. H., 285
Crusade in Europe (Eisenhower), 316, 319
Cuba, 98, 126, 486
Cunningham, Admiral, 314
Curley, James Michael, 268, 271, 283
Current History, 155
Curtis Publishing Company, 85
Curzon, George Nathaniel, 298
Cuttington College and Divinity School, 406
Cyprus, 494
Cyrenaica, Libya, 357, 358, 359
Czechoslovakia, 18, 82, 85, 60, 88-91

Dáil Eireann, 104, 106
Daladier, Edouard, 121, 472
Damascus, Arabia, 206, 209
Daniell, Raymond, 319 n.
Daniels, Josephus, 243
D'Annunzio, Gabriel, 31
Danquah, J. B., 397, 398-99
Danzig, Poland, 17, 213
Dardanelles, 96, 126, 127, 248
Dartmoor Prison, England, 103
Darwin, Charles, 435
Da Vinci, Leonardo, 417
Dawson, Geoffrey, 450
D Day (Gunther), 229
Decker, Admiral Benton W., 294
De Gaulle, General Charles, 315, 444, 459, 465-74, 483-84, 493
Delaney, John, 281
Delhi, India, 188
Dell, Robert, 110 n.
Demnat, Morocco, 350
Denmark and the Danes, 19, 390
Denning, Lord, 493
Denning Report, 493
Dennis, Gabriel L., 404
Depression of the 1930s, 239, 252
Derby, Lord, 450
Desai, Mahadev, 169 n.
Desta, Ras, 384
De Valera, Brian, 100, 101
De Valera, Eamon, 98-107
De Valera, Jeannie O'Flanagan, 100-01
De Valera, Vivian, 100
De Vecchi, Count Cesare Maria, 34
Devonshire, Duke of, 442
Dewey, Thomas E., 251, 255, 263, 281
De Young, M. H., 301
Díaz, Porfirio, 225
Diet, Japanese, 147
Dill, Field Marshal Sir John, 229 n.
Dillon, Mary, 277
Dimitrescu, Poui, 66
Disraeli, Benjamin, 99, 211, 449
Djavid Bey, 94
Djemal Pasha, Ahmed, 95
Dollfuss, Engelbert, 7, 21, 68-73
Donald, W. H., 157, 162

Dostievsky, Fëdor, 90
Douglas-Home, Sir Alexander Frederick, 489-90, 498-500
Dovia di Predappio, Italy, 20
Dreyfus case, 118
Du Barry, Mme., 64
Dublin, Ireland, 124
Du Bois, W. E. B., 396
Duca, Joh, 66
Duff Cooper, Alfred, 61
Dukas, Paul, 119
Duke, Doris, 303
Dumbarton Oaks Conference, 259
Dunbar, Mr., 411
Dunkirk, France, 234, 235, 252
Duranty, Walter, 38, 44, 45, 235
Dzhugashvili, Ekaterina (Stalin's mother), 43

Early, Stephen, 315
East Africa, 494
East Germany, 54, 460, 461, 463
Eastman, Max, 84
East Prussia, 460
Edelman, Maurice, 135 n.
Eden, (Robert) Anthony, 15, 52, 57-62, 115-16, 445, 480, 499
Egypt, 204, 232, 233, 361-73, 403, 481, 494
Egyptian Nationalist Party (WAFD), 361
Eher & Company, Franz, 10
Eighth Army, British, 230, 232
Einstein, Albert, 434
Eisenhower, General Dwight David, 235, 236, 250, 256, 261, 267, 301-02, 306, 308-24, 410, 444, 481, 486, 487
Eisenhower, Mamie, 310, 311
Eisenhower, the Man and the Symbol (Gunther), 308
El Baida, Libya, 359
Elizabeth I, Queen of England, 378
Elizabeth II, Queen of England, 376 n., 492, 500
Emerson, Ralph Waldo, 241
Empire, Britain's loss of, 494-95
Enciclopedia Italiana, 33
Enver Pasha, 95
Erhard, Ludwig, 453, 457, 458, 460-61, 462, 464
Erzerum, Congress of, 95
Establishment, the British, 450-52, 490, 491, 497
Estoril, Portugal, 67
Ethiopia, 26, 36, 113, 114, 374-87, 407, 416; see also Abyssinian War
Eton School, 442, 498, 499
Etzel, Franz, 461
Eugene, Oregon, 265
European Economic Community, *see* Common Market
Evans, Silliman, 286
Ezhov, Communist Party Secretary, 42

Fairlie, Henry, 450
Farouk, King of Egypt, 362-63, 365, 366, 368
Fascists and Fascism, 23, 24, 29, 31, 32-33, 34, 36, 66, 67, 70, 115, 116, 200, 369
Fatima, Queen of Libya, 358, 359
Feisal, King of Syria and Iraq, 204, 208, 209
Fenghua, China, 163
Ferdinand, King of Rumania, 64
Fighting French, 466
Fillmore, Millard, 354
Finer, Dr., 23, 25, 28
Firestone rubber plantation, Liberia, 404, 405, 406, 414
First Army Corps, British, 235
First International, 82
Fischer, John, 481
Fischer, Louis, 41
Fish, Hamilton, Jr., 84
Five-Year Plan, 39, 46-47, 48, 53, 54, 79, 83
Flandin, Pierre-Etienne, 111, 119
Foch, Marshal Ferdinand, 471
Ford, Henry, 255
Forli, Italy, 21, 22, 25, 26
Formosa (Taiwan), 165
Fortune magazine, 31, 141, 153
Forty-two Years in the White House (Hoover), 244
France, Anatole, 112, 117, 118
France and the French, 19, 60, 61, 67, 71, 77, 81, 82, 83, 87, 105, 108-14, 115-21, 129, 134, 209, 232, 235, 313, 345, 346, 347-48, 351, 353, 354, 356, 357, 358, 360, 380, 384, 385, 421, 428, 434, 442, 455, 456, 461, 465-74, 493, 498
Frank, Hans, 71
Frank, Waldo, 224
Frankel, Max, 482
Franklin, Benjamin, 317
Franks, Sir Oliver, 452
Frederika, Queen of Greece, 492
Free Democrats (FDP), 457, 459, 461
Free French, 466, 470, 471, 473
Freiburg University, 212
French Equatorial Africa, 417-36
French Foreign Legion, 347
French Ivory Coast, 395
Freud, Dr. Sigmund, 433-34
Friedjung case, 89
Frumentius, St., 379
Fulton, Missouri, 135

Gaitskell, Hugh, 443, 462, 496, 497
Gandhi, Kasturbai, 170, 180, 182
Gandhi, Manilal, 181-82
Gandhi, Mohandas Karamchand, 157, 166-85, 188, 189, 191, 192, 193, 194, 196, 197, 198, 199, 200-01, 216, 223, 392, 433
Garner, John Nance, 147-48

Garrigue, Charlotte, 90
Gaulle, General Charles de, *see* De Gaulle
Geez language, 381 n.
Geneva, Switzerland, 58, 59, 72, 212-13
Geneva crisis (1935), 28
Genghis Khan, 54
Gentile, Giovanni, 32
George VI, King of England, 230
German Armistice Commission, 348
Germany and the Germans, 3-19, 60, 67, 69, 70, 71, 81, 82, 84, 85, 93, 105, 110, 112, 113, 114, 116, 121, 128, 133-34, 135, 232, 233, 247, 251, 252, 306, 313, 321, 332, 333, 347, 372, 384, 420, 453-64, 465, 469, 485, 497
Ghana, *see* Gold Coast
Gibbon, Edward, 374
Gibraltar, 149, 322
Gibson, Miss, 29
Gide, André, 117, 433
Giolitti, Giovanni, 23
Giraud, General Henri Honoré, 315
Githens, Joyce, 391
Gladstone, William, 242, 449
Glaoui el Mazouari, Hadj Thami (Pasha of Marrakesh), 345-53, 354
Gobineau, Joseph Arthur de, 17
Goebbels, Joseph, 8, 15, 72
Goemboes (Prime Minister of Hungary), 93
Goering, Hermann, 8, 15, 18, 71
Goethe, 417
Gokhale, Gopal Krishna, 171
Gold Coast (Ghana), 388-402, 414, 495
Goldwater, Barry M., 324
Gomulka, Wladyslaw, 487, 497
Gora, Georgia, Russia, 42
Gott, General W. H. E., 232
Grand Fascist Council, 34
Grant, Ulysses S., 453
Great Britain and the British, 19, 57-62, 71, 96, 107, 113-14, 122-36, 166, 167, 168, 171, 173-77, 183, 184, 185, 188, 190, 191, 192, 193, 195, 196, 198, 201, 205, 206, 207-08, 209-10, 212, 214, 215, 216, 217, 229-36, 247, 250, 251-252, 267, 358, 361, 362, 364, 365, 366, 376 n., 377, 378, 383, 384, 385, 388, 389, 392, 396, 397, 398, 399-401, 408, 439-52, 456-57, 461, 462, 470, 474, 481, 489-500
Greece, 85, 94, 96
Gropper, William, 140
Gruenther, General Alfred M., 311, 319
Guadaljara, Mexico, 224
Guillaume, General, 350
Guinea, 401
Guitry, Lucien Germain, 117
Guitry, Sacha, 117
Gunsbach, Alsace, 420
Gunther, Frances, 159, 187, 216
Gunther, Jane Perry, 135, 288, 304, 310, 335, 345
Gwynn, Nell, 64

Hackett, Francis, 22, 28
Hadi, Ibrahim Abdel, 370
Hafid, Dultan Moulay, 354
Hague, Frank, 283
Haifa, Palestine, 212 n., 217
Haile Selassie, Emperor of Ethiopia, 374-387
Hailsham, Lord, 490, 498, 499
Haldane, Lord, 60
Halifax, Lord, 189, 217
Hallstein, Walter, 458
Halsey, Admiral William Frederick, 295
Hammarskjöld, Dag, 487
Hanfstaengl, Putzi, 7, 9
Hankey, Sir Maurice, 450
Hankow, China, 156, 165
Harar, Ethiopia, 381, 384
Hardy, Thomas, 443
Harijan, 178
Harper's Magazine, 3, 20, 37, 73, 77, 139
Harriman, W. Averell, 267
Harrow School, 125, 189, 234, 498
Harvard University, 243, 268, 348, 408
Hassan, Si, 349, 350
Hassi, Sidi (Pasha of Kasbah), 346
Hastings, Warren, 298
Hatcher, Joe, 286
Haussknecht, Emma, 425, 426, 430, 431, 432, 433
Hawaii, 300; see also Pearl Harbor
Haya de la Torre, 226
Hayama, Japan, 147
Hebrew University, Jerusalem, 213
Heiberg, Alf, 303
Heiden, Konrad, 6, 14, 16
Heifetz, Jascha, 274
Heimwehr, 70, 71
Helene of Greece (Queen of Rumania), 64, 65
Henderson, Sir Nevile, 4
Herald, George W., 354 n.
Herr, Lucien, 118
Herriot, Edouard, 111, 117, 120, 472
Herzl, Theodor, 213
Hess, Rudolph, 15
Hickenlooper, Bourke, 259
Higgins, Marguerite, 487
Hill, John Bayless, 441
Hindenburg, Paul von, 3, 7, 18, 26, 93
Hind Swaraj (Indian Independence) (Gandhi), 172
Hindus and Hinduism, 167, 169, 170, 174, 176, 178, 186, 198
Hindu-Urdu controversy, 198
Hirohito, Emperor of Japan, 139-54, 157, 158, 289, 291, 293, 301
History of the Russian Revolution (Trotsky), 87
Hitler, Adolf, 3-19, 21, 27, 29, 30, 32, 34, 36, 38, 39, 41, 43, 50, 53, 54, 57, 58, 60, 68, 69, 70, 71, 91, 93, 98, 99, 107, 113, 115, 121, 128, 132, 135, 197, 216, 232, 260, 383, 433, 455, 459, 462, 463, 464, 465, 467, 472, 499

Hitlerism, 70
Hitler-Stalin Pact (1939), 327, 339
Hoare, Sir Samuel, 114
Hodeiby, Hassan El, 370
Hodonin, Moravia, 90
Holman, Rufus C., 266
Honolulu Conference (1944), 295
Hoover, Herbert C., 111, 252
Hoover, Ike, 244
Hoover moratorium, 111
Hopkins, Harry, 246
House, Colonel Edward M., 246
Hoyt, E. Palmer, 266
Hughes, Charles Evans, Jr., 280
Hughes, Thomas, 448
Humanité, L', 118
Hungaro-Yugoslav dispute (1934), 59
Hungary, 54, 133
Huss, John, 22
Hussein I, King of Jordan, 204, 205, 206, 210
Husseini, Hadj Amin El, 363
Hyde Park, New York, 239

Ibn Saud, Abdul Aziz, King of Arabia, 204, 205-08
Ibn Saud, Mohammed, 206
Ickes, Harold, 265, 266, 275
Idris I, King of Libya, 357-60
Imru, Ras, 384
Inchon, Korea, 300, 301
Independence League, 199
India and the Indians, 126, 131, 166-85, 187-203, 217, 232, 235, 250, 341, 481, 494
Indian Broadcasting Service, 187
Indian Civil Service, 191
Indian Home Rule, 171, 174, 175
Indian National Congress, 167, 168, 175, 176, 177, 179, 181, 183, 184, 189, 193, 196, 199, 200, 202
Indian Opinion, 172
Indians, American, 222, 224, 225
Indochina, 296
Indonesia, 341, 495
Ingalls, Leonard, 416
Inner Mongolia, 162
Inside Africa (Gunther), 345, 362, 374, 388, 403, 416, 417, 436
Inside Asia (Gunther), 139, 155, 156, 166, 187, 204, 208, 211, 255
Inside Europe (Gunther), 3, 4, 19, 20, 37, 88, 92, 98, 108, 115, 122, 255, 465, 466
Inside Europe Today (Gunther), 439, 453, 465, 475
Inside Latin America (Gunther), 221
Inside Russia Today (Gunther), 475
Inside U.S.A. (Gunther), 239, 255, 256, 262, 270-71, 272, 283
Iraq, 204, 205 n.
Ireland, 98-107, 128
Irish Free State, 98, 102, 104, 106-07
Irish Guards, 234

Irish Republic, 102
Irish Treaty (1921), 104
Iron Curtain speech, Churchill's, 135
Iron Guard (Knights of the Archangel Michael), 66, 67
Irwin, Lord, 176
Ise, Japan, shrine at, 144, 145
Islam, 205, 377, 384; *see also* Moslems
Ismail, Khedive, 368
Ismet Pasha (Ismet Inonu), 96, 97
Israel, Republic of, 61, 217, 362, 365, 372, 481
Italo-Turkish War (1911-12), 25
Italy and the Italians, 20-36, 72, 77, 94, 96, 113, 114, 116, 129-30, 233, 332, 358, 374, 376, 377, 384, 385, 406, 444, 462
Ito, Prince, 151

Jackson, Andrew, 243
Jakarta, Java, 495
James, Henry, 443
Japan and the Japanese, 53, 81, 83, 139-154, 156, 157, 162, 202, 235, 288, 289-292, 293-94, 298, 299, 300, 301, 302, 305, 306, 461
Japan: A Short Cultural History (Sansom), 146
Japan Advertiser, 145
Japanese Constitution, 151, 153, 154
Jaurès, Jean, 118
Jeddah, Arabia, 206
Jehol, 162
Jerome, Leonard W., 124
Jerusalem, Palestine, 209, 212, 378, 384
Jews, 12, 19, 66, 89, 95, 116-17, 209, 210, 211-17, 347, 362, 372, 380, 422, 464
Jimmu, Emperor of Japan, 143, 144
Jinnah, Mohammed Ali, 184
Joffre, Marshal Joseph J. C., 471
Johnson, Lyndon B., 271
Jordan, 372
Journal (Renard), 116, 117
Joxe, Louis, 466
Juárez, Benito, 221, 224
Juhu Beach, India, 178

Kaganovitch, Lazar Moiseevich, 39, 42, 50, 52, 475-76, 477, 479
Kaiser, Henry J., 255
Kalaks, 49
Kalinovka, Russia, 476
Kamakura, Japan, 147
Kamenev, Lev Borisovich, 39, 44
Kameyama, Emperor of Japan, 149
Karachi, India, 193
Kaul, Raj, 188
Kefauver, Estes, 287
Kemal, Ali Risa, 95
Kemal, Latifé Hanum, 96
Kemal, Mustafa, *see* Ataturk
Kemal, Zubeida, 94, 95
Kennedy, John Fitzgerald, 253, 271, 476, 486, 492

Kennedy, Joseph P., 271
Kenny, Robert W., 261
Kenya, 386, 389, 401
Keynes, J. M., 443
Khrushchev, Nikita S., 37, 324, 340-41, 450, 463, 467, 468, 475-88
Khrushchev's Russia (Crankshaw), 482
Kiang, Rev. Z. T., 163
Kiev, Russia, 478
King, Admiral Ernest Joseph, 295, 302
King, Mackenzie, 395
Kipling, Rudyard, 443
Kitchener, Lord Horatio Herbert, 123, 126, 132
Knickerbocker, H. R., 15, 43, 133
Knox, Father, 449
Kohat, India, 176
Konoye, Prince, 153
Korean War, 153, 256, 262, 288, 293, 298, 300, 307, 376, 483, 498
Kottmann, Matilda, 430, 432
Kraljevica, Yugoslavia, 332
Kremlin, the, 49, 50
Krestinsky, Communist Party Secretary, 41
Kreuger, Ivar, 8
Krupp, Alfred, 459
Kulaks, 86
Kuling, China, 158, 163
Kung, Dr., 159
Kuni, Prince Kuniyoshi, 151
Kuomintang (Revolutionary Nationalist Party), 156, 157, 160
Kurdistan, 94
Kuwait, 208
Kyoto, Japan, 144, 294
Kyujo (or imperial palace), Tokyo, 146-147

La Corbière, France, 112
Lafayette, Marquis de, 113
La Follette, Robert, 266
La Guardia, Fiorello Henrico, 272-82, 283
Lahore Congress, 193
Lambaréné, Fr. Eq. Africa, 417-36
Lambrino, Zizi, 64
Lamine Bay, Sidi Chedley Ben Mohammed, 355
Lamine Pasha, Sidi Mohammed, 354-56
Langewiesche, Wolfgang, 396 n.
Lateran Treaty (1929), 27
Lausanne, Treaty of, 96
Lausanne Conference (1922), 29
Laval, José (Countess de Chambrun), 112
Laval, Pierre, 52, 108-14, 385, 466
La Vallière, Louise de, 64
Lawrence, Colonel T. E., 30, 209, 210
Lazarus, Reuben A., 272, 279
League of Nations, 22, 58, 59, 62, 113, 247, 384, 413, 415
Leahy, Admiral William D., 295, 302
Leigh-Mallory, Air Chief Marshal, 313
Leipzig, Germany, 90

Lemaître, Jules, 117
Lend-Lease program, 249, 404
Lenin, Nikolai, 21, 38, 39, 41, 42, 44, 45, 46, 83, 85, 129, 198, 213
Leningrad, Russia, 53
Leninism, 39, 45
Lettish Landwehr, 234
Levant, 380
Lewis, John L., 265-66
Leyte, Libya, 359
Liberation Rally, 362, 369
Liberia, 392, 403-16
Liberia College, 406
Liberian Navy, 409-10
Libya, 113, 357-60
Life magazine, 187, 211, 230, 301
Lille, France, 469
Lincoln, Abraham, 317, 471
Lincoln Prison, England, 103
Lincoln University, 395-96, 401
Lippmann, Walter, 12
Liverpool, England, 103
Lloyd George, David, 24, 96, 99, 104, 105, 122, 213-14, 251-52, 449
Locarno Pact (1925), 29, 72
Lodge, Henry Cabot, Jr., 269
London, England, 29, 116, 134, 149, 171, 177, 183, 185, 216, 217, 321, 394, 396, 397, 398, 401, 469, 473, 481, 491, 495, 499
London *Daily Herald*, 29
London *Daily Mail*, 80
London *Daily Worker*, 397
London *Evening Standard*, 132
London *Morning Post*, 80, 126
London *Observer*, 363 n.
London School of Economics, 396
London *Sunday Telegraph*, 491
London *Sunday Times*, 499
London *Times*, 129, 130
Long, Huey, 266
"Long March," the, 156
Longworth, Clara, 113
Look magazine, 257, 288, 308, 475, 489
López Mateos, Adolfo, 226
Los Angeles, California, 262
Lost City, The (Gunther), 73
Lotta di Classi, La (*The Class Struggle*), 22
Louis XIV, 65
Louisiana State University, 318
Louis Napoleon, Emperor, 354
Lübeck, Germany, 462
Lucknow, India, 196
Ludendorff, General Erich F. W., 93
Ludwig, Emil, 27, 28, 34
Ludwig, King of Bavaria, 64
Lunacharsky, Anatoli V., 84
Lupescu, Mme. Magda (Princess Elena), 63-67
Lyautey, Marshal Louis H. G., 296, 347

MacArthur, Arthur, 290, 292, 299, 303
MacArthur, General Arthur, 289

MacArthur, General Douglas, 153, 154, 261, 272-307, 308, 312, 313, 315, 318, 323
MacArthur, Jean Marie Faircloth, 290, 293, 296, 303-04
MacArthur, Louise Cromwell Brooks, 303
MacDermott (Irish revolutionist), 102
MacDonagh, Thomas, 102
MacDonald, Malcolm, 216
MacDonald, Ramsay, 135
Macmillan, Daniel (Harold's brother), 443
Macmillan, Daniel (Harold's grandfather), 441
Macmillan, Lady Dorothy Evelyn Cavendish, 443
Macmillan, (Maurice) Harold, 439-42, 459, 482, 487, 490, 492, 493, 494-95, 498
Macmillan, Helen (Nellie) Belles, 441
Macmillan, Maurice, 441, 443
Macmillan Publishing Company, 441, 443
Madagascar, 296, 401
Madani, El, 348
Madison, Wisconsin, 264, 265
Madras, India, 196
Madrid, Spain, 84
Maglione, Msgr., 121
Magnitogorsk, Siberia, 39
Maher, Aly, 363, 366
Malaparte, Curzio, 78
Malaya, 494
Malenkov, Georgi, 478-79
Mali, 401
Mallarmé, Stéphane, 117, 118
Malraux, André, 466
Malta, 233, 316, 317, 319
Mamund campaign, 131
Manan, Empress of Ethiopia, 385
Manchester, England, 103
Manchester *Guardian*, 35, 214, 337
Manchester University, 212, 214
Manchukuo, 83
Manchuria, 83, 162, 307
Manila, Philippine Islands, 293, 295, 300, 301, 323
Maniu, Julius, 65-66
Mao Tse-tung, 87
March on Rome (1922), 24, 34
Marie, Queen of Rumania, 64
Marlborough, Duke of, 132
Marrakesh, Morocco, 345-53
Marsh, Sir Edward, 130
Marsh, Judge Robert McCurdy, 276, 279
Marshall, General George C., 258, 261
Marshall Plan, 336, 461
Marx, Karl, 82, 118, 198, 336, 434
Marx, Louis, 320
Marx-Lenin dogma, 42
Masaryk, Jan, 91
Masaryk, Thomas Garrigue, 29, 88-91, 157, 242
Massawa, Eritrea, 375

Massu, General Jacques, 470
Matin, 117
Matteotti affair, 24-25
Maudling, Reginald, 490
Maximilian, Emperor of Mexico, 21
Mayo, Katherine, 181
McCarthy, Joseph, 323
McCormick, Kenneth, 316
McCormick, Colonel Robert S., 255
McEvoy, Dennis, 301
McKellar, Kenneth M., 284
McKenzie, John, 279
McMahon, Sir Henry, 209
Mecca, Arabia, 205, 206, 207, 210, 346
Medina, Arabia, 205, 206
Meeker, Oden and Olivia, 393 n., 405 n.
Meeman, Edward J., 285, 286
Meet Soviet Russia (Gunther), 475
Meiji (Mutsuhito), Emperor of Japan, 143, 146, 149
Meiji Restoration (1868), 142-43, 151
Meiji shrine, Tokyo, 145
Mein Kampf (Hitler), 3, 9, 10, 12, 16, 29
Memphis, Tennessee, 283-87
Memphis *Press-Scimitar,* 285
Mende, Erich, 457, 458, 461
Méndes-France, Pierre, 472
Menelik I, Emperor of Ethiopia, 378
Menelik II, Emperor of Ethiopia, 378, 383, 384
Menjinsky, 82
Menon, K. P. S., 481
Menorah Journal, 115
Menshevism, 45
Menzhinsky (head of G.P.U.), 50
Mesopotamia, 206
Mestrović, Ivan, 90
Mexican Revolution (1913), 222-23
Mexico, 87, 221-26
Mexico City, Mexico, 225
Michael, King of Rumania, 65, 67
Michelangelo, 78
Middle Way, The (Macmillan), 444
Mikhailovic, Draja, 332
Milan, Italy, 36, 64
Mills, William W., 280
Minnesota University, 265
Minobe, Dr., 141
Missouri, U.S.S., 289
Mohammed the Prophet, 204, 205, 356
Mokri, Hadj Mohammed El, 348, 354, 360
Molotov, Vyacheslav M., 52, 337, 478, 479
Moncef Bey, Mohammed El, 355
Mongols, 149
Monroe, James, 403, 408
Monrovia, Liberia, 403-05, 406, 409, 411, 414-15, 416
Montagu-Chelmsford reforms, 173-74
Monte Carlo ballet, 116
Montemezzi, Italo, 275
Montespan, Mme. de, 65

Montez, Lola, 64
Montgomery, Field Marshal Lord Bernard, 229-33, 234, 235, 236, 313, 314, 323
Morgenthau, Henry, 251
Morocco, 296, 345-54, 357
Morris, Newbold, 275
Morrison, Herbert, 394
Morse, Mildred Downie, 265
Morse, Samuel F. B., 264
Morse, Wayne Lyman, 263-67
Moscow, Russia, 53, 57, 59-60, 83, 89, 134, 195, 470, 475, 477, 478, 482
Moscow Industrial Academy, 477
Moscow *New Times,* 397
Moses, Robert, 273
Moslem Brotherhood, 363, 370-71
Moslem League, 189
Moslems and Moslemism, 167, 174, 176, 184, 198, 205, 346, 356, 357, 358, 359, 363, 378, 393, 413
Mother India (Mayo), 181
Mount Etna, 231
Mowrer, Edgar Ansel, 16
Mukden, Japan, 141
Munich, Germany, 8
Munich Agreement, 121, 181, 444, 472, 499
Munich "Beer Hall Putsch," 3, 5, 14
Murfreesboro, Tennessee, 303
Murray, "Alfalfa Bill," 255
Murrow, Edward R., 315, 441
Mussolini, Alessandro, 21
Mussolini, Anna Maria, 26
Mussolini, Arnaldo, 26, 28
Mussolini, Benito Juárez, 5, 6, 10, 13, 14, 20-36, 39, 41, 43, 50, 71, 73, 93, 99, 113, 114, 115, 129-30, 197, 216, 287, 359, 377, 383, 384
Mussolini, Bruno, 26
Mussolini, Rachele Guidi, 26
Mussolini, Romano, 26
Mussolini, Rosa Maltoni, 21
Mussolini, Vittorio, 26
Mussolini's Italy (Finer), 23
Mussoorie, India, 190
Mysticism, 140, 157, 168, 198

Nabha, India, 191
Nagako Kuni, Princess (Empress of Japan), 141, 148, 151-52, 153, 154
Nagoya, Japan, 144
Naguib, General Mohammed, 361, 365, 366, 367, 369, 371
Nahas Pasha, 370
Naidu, Mrs. Sarojini, 173
Nanking, China, 163, 165
Napier expedition (1868), 377
Napoleon Bonaparte, 19, 26
Nashville *Tennessean,* 286
Nasser, Colonel Gamal Abdal, 34, 210, 361-73, 398 n., 487
Nation, 139
National Assembly, French, 467

National Council of Corporations, 32
Nationalism, 72, 376, 389, 397
National Socialists, *see* Fascists
National University of Ireland, 100
National War Labor Board, 265-66
Nazis and Nazism, 3, 7, 9, 12, 68, 69, 70, 71, 72, 73, 113, 456, 463, 464
Needham, Massachusetts, 267
Nehru, Indira, 196, 199
Nehru, Jawaharlal, 179, 181, 183, 187-203, 215, 216, 341, 449, 487
Nehru, Kamala, 196, 197, 199
Nehru, Motilal, 179, 189, 193-95, 196, 197, 198, 199
"Nehru of India" (Gunther), 187
"Nehru Report," 199
Neuilly, France, 64
New Deal, 239, 241, 243, 244, 269, 294, 296, 392
New Delhi, India, 202
New Economic Policy (N.E.P.), 46
Newfoundland, 250
New Republic, 47
New Statesman, 443
New York, New York, 98, 103, 203, 272-82, 303, 319, 349, 381, 482, 483-84, 486-87
New York *Herald Tribune*, 327
New York Times, The, 80, 124, 333, 397
New Zealand, 58, 495
Niagara Falls, 135
Nicholas, Prince of Rumania, 63
Nicolson, Harold, 61
Nigeria, 389, 392, 401, 414
Nimitz, Admiral Chester William, 295
Nin, Andreas, 84-85
Nkroful, Ghana, 395
Nkrumah, Dr. Kwame, 388-402, 409
Nogi, General Maresuke, 149
Nonviolence, doctrine of, 167, 171, 173, 174, 184
Norman, Montague, 450
Normandy landings, 135, 313
North Africa, 233, 235, 296, 345-60, 361-73
North Atlantic Treaty Organization (NATO), 97, 457, 470, 485, 493, 497, 498
Northern Nigeria, 403
Northern Rhodesia, 401
Norway, 19, 87, 135, 462
Nover, Barnet, 256
Number of People, A (Marsh), 130
Nurmi, Paavo, 177
Nyasaland, 401
Nypels, George, 29

Obdorsk, Siberia, 86
Obregón, General Álvaro, 223
O'Connell, Kathleen, 101
October Revolution (Stalin), 46
Oguri, Admiral, 149
Ohrdruf concentration camp, 321
Oliver, Vic, 132, 333

Omaha Beach, 313
Omdurman, Battle of, 126
Oregon University, 265
Organization of African Unity (OAU), 386
Ormsby-Gore, David, 443
Outer Mongolia, 479
Oxford University, England, 126, 442, 451, 452, 492, 497, 499

Painlevé, Paul, 110, 119
Pakistan, 186, 356
Palestine, 204, 209, 210, 211, 212, 214-15, 216, 217, 232
Palestinian War, 365, 370
Panama, 243, 405
Pandit, Lakshmi Nehru, 196
Pandit, Ranjit S., 196
Papen, Franz von, 71
Paris, France, 112, 116, 118, 204, 253, 308, 309, 315, 317, 323, 332, 349, 381, 421, 422, 470, 471
Paris Missionary Society, 422, 423
Paris Summit Conference (1960), 324, 450, 453, 459, 468, 487
Parliament, British, 127, 128
Passive resistance, 167, 171, 173, 174, 184, 290
Patton, General George S., 91, 236
Patzcuaro, Mexico, 222
Paul, King of Greece, 492
Peake Pasha, 210
Pearl Harbor, Japanese attack on, 139, 165, 249, 300
Pearse, Patrick Henry, 102
Peiping, China, 165
Pendergast, Tom, 283
Pendleton, Oregon, 264
Permanent revolution, doctrine of, 79
Perry, Jennings, 286
Persia, 206
Peru, 226
Pétain, Marshal Henri Philippe, 114, 469, 471
Peter the Great, 93
Petrograd, Russia, 79
Philby, H. St. J. B., 208
Philip, Prince (Duke of Edinburgh), 492
Philippine Islands, 295, 299, 300, 303
Philosophy of Civilization (Schweitzer), 421 n.
"Philosophy of the Egyptian Revolution, The" (Nasser), 363-64
Pilsudski, Józef, 21, 60, 96, 98
Pinsk, Russia, 211, 212, 213, 215
Pittsburgh, Pennsylvania, 89
Pius XII, Pope, 341
Places in the Sun (Eden), 58
Plekhanov, Georgi V., 85
Poincaré, Raymond, 110, 120
Point Four Program, 411
Poland, 18, 54, 60, 83, 133, 460
Polaris missiles, 492
Politburo, 42, 44, 53, 477

Political Development of Japan (Uyehara), 150
Pompidou, Georges Jean Raymond, 474
Popolo d'Italia, 23
Popper, Arthur, 280
Populaire, Le, 118
Popular Front, 110, 116, 120, 121
Porbander, India, 168
Port Arthur, Siberia, 149
Port Gentil, Fr. Eq. Africa, 434
Portsmouth (N.H.) Treaty, 243
Portugal, 67, 390
Potsdam Conference, 260-61
Prague, Czechoslovakia, 57, 60, 90, 91, 132, 337
Pravda, 39, 44, 475
Prester, John, 377
Pretoria, South Africa, 127
Prinkipo, Turkey, 77, 79, 82, 84, 85, 87
Prittie, Terence, 455 n.
Profumo, John, 493-94
Profumo-Keeler scandal, 493-94
Proust, Marcel, 116
Puerto Rico, 221

Quebec Conferences, 244, 249, 250, 251
Quest of the Historical Jesus (Schweitzer), 421

Rabat, Morocco, 345
Radek, Karl, 50, 85
Radical Socialists, French, 470-73
Radioactive cobalt, 307
Rajagopalacharia, Chakravarti, 180
Rangoon, Burma, 235
Reader's Digest, 122, 139, 166, 255, 283, 301, 374, 417, 436, 455, 465
Reading, Lord, 12
Red Army, 40, 53, 479
Rehovoth, Palestine, 214-15
Reichswehr, 4, 18
Renard, Jules, 116, 117, 120
Resnick, Miss, 278, 281
Reuter, Ernst, 462
Reuther, Walter, 255
Revue Blanche, 117
Reynolds, Quentin, 254, 315
Rhineland, 18
Rhodes, Cecil, 298
Rhoendorf, Germany, 454, 456
Ribbentrop, Joachim von, 8, 18
Richard Carvel (W. Churchill), 130
Rida, Crown Prince of Libya, 358
Riddle of MacArthur, The (Gunther), 153, 272, 273
Riga, Latvia, 234, 235
Riva, Italy, 98
River War, The (Churchill), 126
Riviera, France, 64
Roberts Field, Liberia, 404
Robeson, Paul, 396
Robinson, Theodore Douglas, 243 n.
Rochat, M., 109
Rockefeller Foundation, 368

Roehm, Ernst, 4, 5, 8, 14, 30
Rogers, Ginger, 366
Rome, Italy, 29, 71, 113
Rome-Berlin Axis, 36
Rommel, Field Marshal Erwin, 231, 233, 235
Roosevelt, Eleanor, 239, 245, 250
Roosevelt, Elliott, 250
Roosevelt, Franklin Delano, 28, 53, 113, 135, 225, 239-54, 256, 257, 262, 263, 265-66, 269, 294-96, 300, 305, 321, 392, 446
Roosevelt, Franklin Delano, Jr., 245
Roosevelt, Henry L., 243 n.
Roosevelt, James, 254, 261
Roosevelt, John, 245
Roosevelt, Theodore, 99, 243-45, 246, 270
Roosevelt, Theodore, Jr., 243 n.
Roosevelt in Retrospect (Gunther), 239
Rosenberg, Alfred, 112
Rosenberg, Anna, 275
Rosenman, Judge Sam, 253
Round Table Conferences, 177, 181, 183, 184
Rovere, Richard H., 485 n.
Roving Commission, A (Churchill), 123-124, 131
Rowlatt bills, 174, 189
Roy, Dr., 179, 180
Royal Air Force, 209
Roye, Edward J., 409 n.
Rumania, 63-67
Russell, Bertrand, 21, 198
Russia, 19; *see also* Soviet Union
Russia (Gunther), 475
Russian Civil War, 80, 81
Russian Revolution, 45, 53, 54, 77, 78, 80, 331, 477
Russian Terror, 40-41
Russia's Iron Age (Chamberlin), 39
Russo-German Pact (1934), 19, 134
Russo-Japanese War, 149
Rykov, Aleksei Ivanovich, 39

Saad el Ali (High Dam) scheme, 367
Saar, 17, 59
Sadako, Empress Dowager of Japan, 151
Sadek, Si, 348-49, 350
Saint-Cyr military academy, 469
St. Petersburg, Russia, 482
St. Petersburg Soviet, 78
Salazar, Antonio de Oliveira, 467
Salem, Dr. Ben, 356
Salem, Massachusetts, 268
Salisbury, Lord, 445, 450, 499
Salmon, Edwin A., 279
Salonika, Turkey, 92, 94, 95, 98
"Salt march," Gandhi's, 176-77, 183
Saltonstall, Endicott Peabody, 268
Saltonstall, Leverett, 267-70
Saltonstall, Sir Richard, 268
Samuel, Sir Herbert, 209
Sandys, Duncan, 132
San Francisco Conference (1945), 247

Sansom, Sir George, 146
Saragat, Giuseppe, 462
Saturday Evening Post, 139, 187
Saturday Review, 324, 403
Satyagraha hermitage, 173, 174, 175, 184, 190
Saudi Arabia, 204-08, 372
Savrola (Churchill), 125
Scandinavia, 82
Schacht, Hjalmar H. G., 8
Schleicher, General Kurt von, 4, 84
Schorr, Daniel, 480
Schroeder, Gerhard, 464
Schuschnigg, Kurt von, 98, 105
Schutzbund, 70
Schweitzer, Dr. Albert, 417-36
Schweitzer, Helene Bresslau, 422, 424
Schweitzer, Rhena, 422
Scott, C. P., 214
Second International, 82-83
Seed, William H., 382 n.
"See It Now" TV show, 441
Segaon, India, 177, 178
Senussis, 358
Seoul, Korea, 293
Serrault, M., 121
Shanghai, China, 163, 165
Shaw, George Bernard, 36, 443
Sheba, Queen of, 378, 386
Sheean, Vincent, 306
Shepilov, Dimitri T., 475, 479
Sherifians, 204, 205, 356
Sherman, General William T., 318
Shertok, Moshe, 215
Sherwood, Robert E., 247, 250
Shidehara, Baron Kijuro, 291
Shinto, 145-46
Sian kidnaping of Chiang Kai-shek, 156-157, 158, 161, 162
Siberia, 86, 88
Sicilian campaign, 229, 236
Sicily, 316, 323
Sieff Research Laboratory, Daniel, 215
Sierra Leone, 408
Simon, Sir John, 57, 58, 61, 83
Simon and Schuster Publishing Company, 85
Simon Commission, 176
Simpson, Mrs. Wallis Warfield (Duchess of Windsor), 452
Sinaia, Rumania, 64, 65, 66
Singapore, Malaya, 494
Sinn Fein, 103, 104
Sivas, Congress of, 95
Skybolt missiles, 492-93
Slocombe, George, 29
Social Democrats, 72, 73, 86, 195, 457, 459, 462
Socialism and the National Question (Stalin), 44
Socialists and Socialism, 68, 70, 73, 79, 109-10, 118, 119, 121, 131, 179, 188, 190, 193, 200, 369, 372, 388, 440, 457, 471-73, 484, 485

Social security system, French, 473
Sokolnikov, Grigori Y., 44
Solomon, King, 377, 378, 386
Soong family, 158, 163
South Africa, 171, 172, 181, 189, 450
Soviet Union, 21, 37-54, 60, 77-87, 96, 128, 131, 132, 134, 135, 202, 248, 250, 251, 260, 309, 324, 331, 336, 337-39, 340, 372, 373, 449, 450, 458-59, 460, 463, 468, 475-88, 496, 498
Spain, 82, 84-86, 129
Spanish-American War, 126
Spanish Civil War, 36, 332
Sparta, Georgia, 408
Speaking Frankly (Byrnes), 251
Spectator, 450
Stalin, Josef, 13, 22, 27, 34, 37-54, 57, 60, 62, 77, 78, 81, 84, 86, 87, 98, 250, 260, 337, 349, 467, 478, 480, 483, 485
Stalin, Nadyezhda Alliluiev, 51
Stalin, Svetlana, 51
Stalin, Vassily, 51
Stalingrad, Russia, 53, 477
Stamp, Sir Josiah, 451
Stangaciu, General, 66
Stassen, Harold, 255
Stebbins, Ernest L., 276
Step by Step (Churchill), 128
Stettinius, Edward R., 251
Stevens, Edmund, 487
Stevenson, Adlai Ewing, 216, 271
Stimson, Henry L., 248
Stockholm, Sweden, 110
Stokes, Thomas L., 284 n.
Stone, Chief Justice Harlan, 254
Storm troops (SA and SS), 3, 8, 13, 18
Stotesbury, Edward T., 303
Story of My Experiments with Truth, The (Gandhi), 169, 182
Strachey, Lytton, 449
Strand Magazine, 98, 115
Strassburg University, 421, 422, 424
Strasser, Gregor, 5, 14
Strasser, Otto, 9
Strong, Anna Louise, 47
Struggle for the Liberation of Yugoslavia (Tito), 330
Subašic, Ivan, 332
Sudan, 361, 362, 494
Sudetenland, 18
Suez Canal crisis (1956), 61, 361, 372, 439, 440, 445, 452, 481
Sukarno, President of Indonesia, 341, 487
Sulzberger, Cyrus L., 333
Sun Yat-sen, Dr., 155, 156, 164
Survey Graphic, 28
Suslov, Mikhail A., 485
Sweden, 110, 375, 376, 380
Switzerland, 22, 134, 196, 385
Syria, 94, 204, 209, 372

Taft, Robert A., 255, 265
Taierchwang, Battle of, 159
Tanganyika, 389, 401

Tangier, Morocco, 345
Tardieu, André, 110, 116
Tasquillo, Mexico, 225
Tedder, Air Marshal Arthur William, 314
Teheran Conference, 135, 244, 249, 250
Tel Aviv, Palestine, 214
Teller, Judd L., 358 n.
Teru, Princess, 151
Third International (Comintern), 82, 83, 84
"This Peace Is a Cheat" (Gunther), 187
Thompson, Dorothy, 11, 15, 112, 254
Time magazine, 140, 149
Times of India, 184
Tirah Expeditionary Force, 126
Tito, Marshal (Josip Broz), 327-41, 376 n., 480, 487
Titulescu, Nicolas, 66-67
Tlemçen, Algeria, 358
Tobruk, Libya, 359
Togo, Admiral Heihachiro, 149
Togoland, 401
Tokyo, Japan, 140, 141, 145, 146, 151, 153, 261, 289, 290, 292, 293, 294, 300, 301, 304, 313
Tokyo Imperial University, 141
Tomsky, Mikhail P., 39
Tong, Hollington K., 161
Torlonia, Prince, 26
Totota, Liberia, 405, 411
Tours, France, 110
Toynbee, Arnold, 95
Transjordan, 128, 204, 206, 208-10, 232
Transjordan Frontier Force, 210
Tree, Ronald and Marietta, 62
Trinidad, 221
Tripoli, 358
Trotsky, Leon, 21, 30, 31, 39, 41, 44, 45-47, 77-87
Truman, Elizabeth ("Bess") Wallace, 258
Truman, Harry S., 256-61, 262, 265, 288, 297, 307, 309
Truman, Mary Margaret, 258, 309
Truman Committee, 259
Tsugu, Crown Prince, 152
Tubman, Harriet, 408
Tubman, William V. S., 403-16
Tunis, Tunisia, 345, 354-56
Tunisia, 230, 345, 354-56, 360
Turkestan, 82
Turkey and the Turks, 72, 77, 82, 84, 87, 92-97, 98, 204, 248, 384
Twe, Dihdwo, 415-16
Tyrrell, Lord, 450

Uganda, 211, 212, 389, 401, 403
Ulster County, Ireland, 107
Union of West African Socialist Republics, 398
United Arab Republic, 341, 372
United Front, Chinese, 157, 165
United Gold Coast Convention (UGCC), 397, 398

United Nations, 61, 107, 217, 247, 289, 298, 358, 415, 468, 487, 495
United States and the Americans, 61, 81, 111, 132-33, 165, 202, 203, 239-54, 255-71, 272-82, 283-87, 288-307, 308-324, 331, 336, 357, 360, 366, 367, 372-73, 376, 379-80, 382, 388, 395-96, 455, 456, 459, 461, 470, 474, 480, 481, 483, 485, 487, 493, 495, 497, 498
University College, Dublin, 100
University College, Geneva, 212-13
Untouchables, 167, 173, 177, 178, 183
Uyehara (Japanese cabinet minister), 150

Vahydud-Din, Crown Prince (Sultan Mehmed VI), 93-94
Valera, Eamon de, see De Valera, Eamon
Valéry, Paul, 117
Vandenberg, Arthur, 255
Van Doren, Mark, 254
Vanity Fair, 57, 63, 68, 140
Vargas, Getulio, 226
Vaterlaendische Front, 72
Versailles Treaty (1919), 5, 14
Vichy regime, 114, 121, 348, 469, 470
Victoria, Queen of England, 453
Vienna, Austria, 69, 71, 72, 73, 90, 332
Voroshilov, Kliment V., 52, 81
Vremia, 44

Wahab, Adb-el, 206
Wahabis, 205, 206, 207, 358
Wakil, Zeinab el, 370
Wallace, Henry A., 257, 265
Walsh, Patrick, 278
Wardha, India, 177, 196
Warm Springs, Georgia, 239
Warren, Earl, 261-63
Warsaw, Poland, 57, 60
Warwick, Countess of, 58
Washington, D. C., 89, 249, 254, 255, 264
Washington Post, 256
Watertown, Massachusetts, 268
Wauchope, Sir Arthur, 215
Waugh, Evelyn, 333
Wavell, General Archibald Percival, 233
Waziristan, 235
Weil, Truda T., 275, 277, 278
Weimar Republic, 455
Weizmann, Chaim, 211-17
Weizmann, Rachel Tchemetinsky, 212, 217
Welles, Orson, 254
Wells, H. G., 40, 443
West, John, 411
West, Rebecca, 443
West Berlin, 461-64
West Germany, 453-64, 485
West Point Military Academy, 288, 300, 303, 317, 320
Weygand, General Maxime, 471
Weyl, Nathaniel and Sylvia, 223 n.
Whalen, Grover, 281

Whampoa Academy, 160
Wheeler, Burton K., 255
Wheelus Field, Tripoli, 360
Whiteley, General, 316
Whitney, General Courtney, 289, 290, 291
Wilhelm II, Kaiser, 60
Williams, Aubrey, 265
Williams, Lieut. Colonel "Bill," 231
Willkie, Wendell, 230, 231, 461-62
Wilson, Charles M., 405 n.
Wilson, (James) Harold, 489, 490, 495-497, 500
Wilson, William, 279
Wilson, Woodrow, 89, 90, 99, 243, 244, 245-48, 317
Winchester School, 498
Windsor, Duke of (Edward VIII), 301, 452
Winterton, Lord, 135
Wisconsin University, 265
Wold, Ato Tafarra Worq Kidane, 376
World Crisis, The (Churchill), 124, 127, 135
World War I, 23, 58, 69, 92, 127-28, 134, 167, 173, 204, 213-14, 232, 235, 247, 249, 258, 288, 299, 347, 420, 421, 442, 456
World War II, 36, 53, 61-62, 107, 114, 122, 128, 133-34, 135, 154, 165, 217, 229-36, 239, 249, 300, 313, 316, 332, 348, 358, 383, 385, 455, 456, 457, 477, 500

World Zionist Organization, 213

Yalta Conference, 53, 135, 244, 249, 251
Yamagata, Prince, 152
Yamashita, Tomoyuki, 294
Yasu, Lij, Emperor of Ethiopia, 384
Yasukuni shrine, Japan, 147
Yeats, William Butler, 443
Yokohama, Japan, 290
Yokosuka, Japan, 294
Yorkshire Post, 58
Yoshi, Prince, 151
Yoshida, Shigeru, 291
Yoshihito ("Taisho"), Emperor of Japan, 142, 151
Young Turks, 95, 96
Yudenitch, Nikolai N., 44
Yugoslavia, 134, 327-41, 376 n., 482

Zagorije, Yugoslavia, 331
Zagreb, Yugoslavia, 330, 331, 332, 334
Zakia, Princess, 356
Zamorra y Torres, Niceto Alcalá, 85
Zanzibar, 401
Zauditu, Empress of Ethiopia, 384
Zhdanov, Andrei Aleksandrovich, 42
Zhukov, Marshal Georgi K., 479
Zimmerwald, Switzerland, 83
Zinoviev, Grigori, Evseevich, 39, 44, 45, 83, 85
Zionists and Zionism, 209, 211, 212, 213, 214, 215
Zuckerkandl, Dr., 94
Zulu rebellion, 171